Rick Steves'
BEST OF
EASTERN
EUROPE
2004

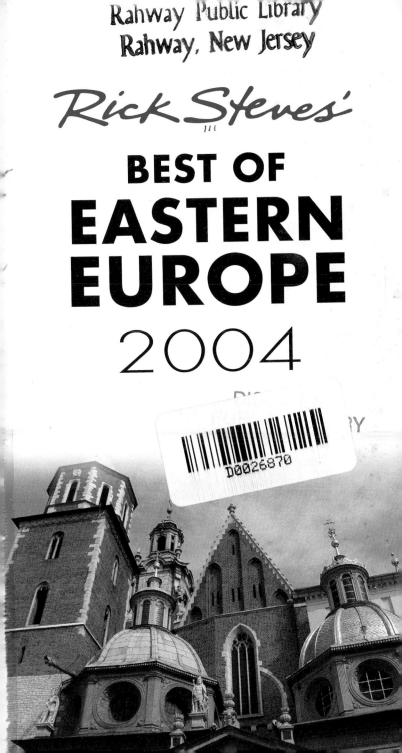

914.904
STE

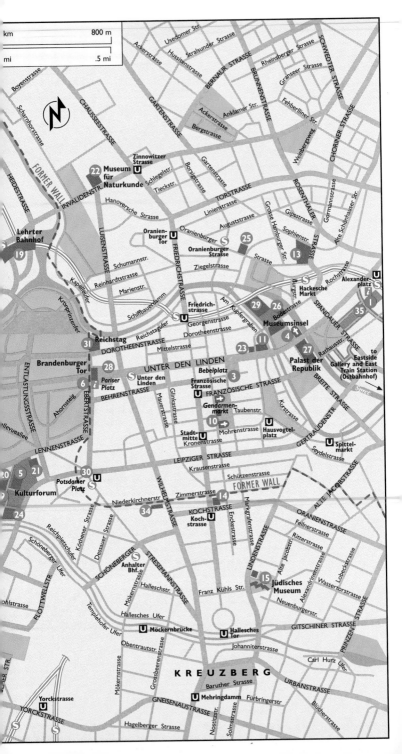

km .... 800 m

mi .... .5 mi

Boyenstrasse

Scharnhorststrasse

CHAUSSEESTRASSE

FORMER WALL

INVALIDENSTR.

HEIDESTRASSE

GARTENSTRASSE

Ackerstrasse

Hussitenstrasse

Usedomer Str.

Stralsunder Strasse

BERNAUER STRASSE

BRUNNENSTRASSE

Rheinsberger Strasse

Granseer Strasse

Anklamer Str.

Ackerstrasse

Bergstrasse

Fehrbelliner Str.

Weinbergsweg

SCHWEDTER STRASSE

CHORINER STRASSE

22 Museum für Naturkunde

Zinnowitzer Strasse

Schlegelstr.

Tieckstr.

Borsigstrasse

Gartenstrasse

TORSTRASSE

Linienstrasse

Augustrasse

Grosse Hamburger Str.

Gipsstrasse

Sophienstr.

ROSENTHALER STRASSE

Gormannstrasse

Alte Schönhauser Str.

Hanoversche Strasse

LUISENSTRASSE

Lehrter Bahnhof **19**

FRIEDRICHSTRASSE

Schumannstr.

Reinhardtstrasse

Kapelleufer

Kronprinzenufer

Marienstr.

Schiffbauerdamm

Reichstagufer

Oranien- burger Tor U

Oranienburger S Strasse

Ziegelstrasse

Oranienburger Strasse

25

Strasse

13

An Kupfergraben

Hackesche Markt S

Rochstrasse

Alexander- platz U i S

U **35**

Reichstag **31**

Brandenburger Tor **6**

Pariser Platz S i

ENTLASTUNGSSTRASSE

Ahornsteig

bellevueallee

Reichstagufer

DOROTHEENSTRASSE

Mittelstrasse

Dorotheenstrasse

Georgenstrasse

Friedrich- strasse U

UNTER DEN LINDEN

28

Unter den Linden S

BEHRENSTRASSE

Glinkastrasse

Mauerstrasse

Bebelplatz

Französische Strasse U

Gendarmen- markt

3

FRANZÖSISCHE STRASSE

Taubenstr.

29 **26**

Museumsinsel

23 **11**

4

27

Palast der Republik

SPANDAUER STRASSE

Rathausstr.

Bodestrasse

Burgstr.

BREITE STRASSE

GERTRAUDENSTR.

to Eastside Gallery and East Train Station (Ostbahnhof)

Spree

EBERTSTRASSE

LENNENSTRASSE

20 **5** **21**

Kulturforum

24

30 U

Potsdamer Platz S

Stadt- mitte U

Kronenstrasse

Mohrenstrasse

10

Hausvogtel- platz U

Kirchstrasse

Spittel- markt U

Sydelstrasse

LEIPZIGER STRASSE

Krausenstrasse

Schützenstrasse

FORMER WALL

ALTE JACOBSTRASSE

Niederkirchnerstr.

Zimmerstrasse

14

Markgrafenstrasse

ORANIENSTRASSE

Feilnerstrasse

WILHELMSTRASSE

34

KOCHSTRASSE

Koch- strasse U

Enckestrasse

Ritterstrasse

LINDENSTRASSE

Alte Jacobstr.

Alexandrinenstrasse

Wassertorstrasse

Lobeckstrasse

Reichpietschufer

Schöneberger Schleuse

Kötherner Strasse

Dessauer Strasse

SCHÖNEBERGER STRASSE

STRESEMANNSTRASSE

Anhalter Bhf.

Mökernstrasse

Halleschstr.

Franz Kühls Str.

15

Jüdisches Museum

Neuenburgerstr.

PRINZENSTRASSE

Schöneberger Ufer

FLOTTWELLSTR.

Mökernstrasse

Templehofer Ufer

Halleschestrasse

Halleschestrasse

Halleschestrasse

Halleschestrasse

Halleschestrasse

Halleschestrasse

Hallesches Ufer

Obentrautstr.

Möckernbrücke U

Hallesches Tor U

Johanniterstrasse

GITSCHINER STRASSE

Carl Hurz Ufer

URBANSTRASSE

K R E U Z B E R G

Yorckstrasse U

TORCKSTRASSE

S

LINER STR

Grossbeerenstrasse

GNEISENAUSTRASSE

Baruther Strasse

Mehringdamm U

Fürbringerstr.

Nostizstr.

Solmstr.

Hagelberger Strasse

Blücherstrasse

BERLIN

1. Alexanderplatz
2. Bahnhof Zoo Station & EurAide
3. Bebelplatz
4. Berlin Cathedral
5. Berlin Philharmonic
6. Brandenburg Gate
7. Erotic Art Museum
8. Europa Center
9. Gemäldegalerie (Painting Gallery)
10. Gendarmenmarkt
11. German History Museum
12. German Resistance Memorial
13. Hackesche Höfe (Courtyard Shops)
14. Haus am Checkpoint Charlie Museum
15. Jewish Museum Berlin
16. KaDeWe Department Store
17. Kaiser Wilhelm Memorial Church
18. Käthe Kollwitz Museum
19. Lehrter Train Station
20. Museum of Arts and Crafts
21. Music Instruments Museum
22. Natural History Museum
23. Neue Wache Memorial
24. New National Gallery (Modern Art)
25. New Synagogue
26. Old National Galler
27. Palace of the Repub
28. Pariser Platz
29. Pergamon Museum
30. Potsdamer Platz
31. Reichstag
32. Savignyplatz (Hotels)
33. Siegessäule Column
34. Topography of Terro
35. TV Tower
36. Zoo

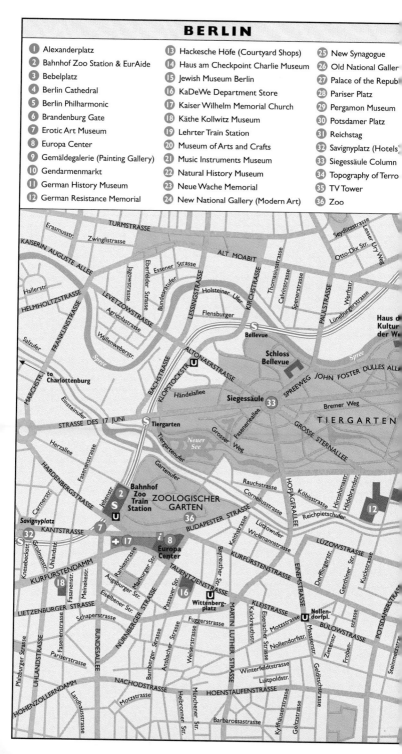

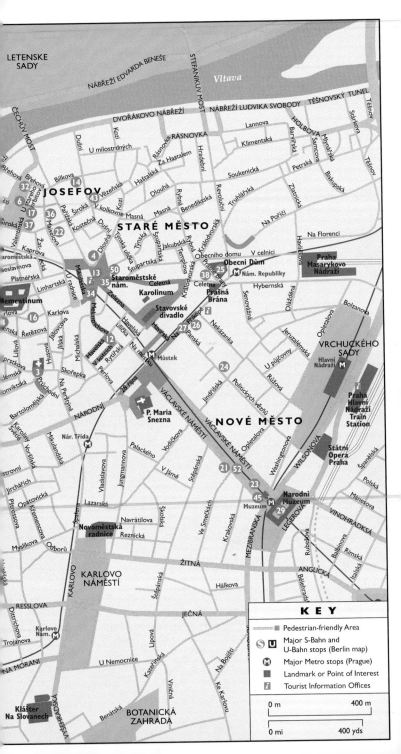

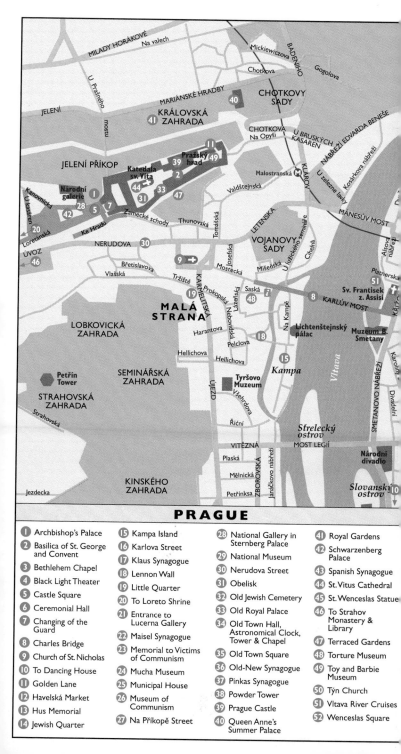

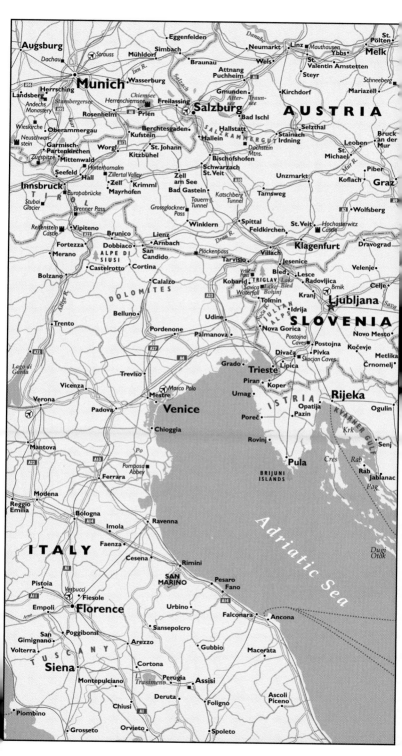

EASTERN EUROPE OVERVIEW

See following pages for detail areas shown below.

0 km   100   200 km
0 miles   50   100 m

WIELKOPOLSKA

★ **Warsaw**

• Poznań

Berlin ★

• Łódź

MAZOVIA

GERMANY

POLAND

Dresden •

• Wrocław

MAŁOPOLSKA

SILESIA

• Częstochowa

Wisła

Auschwitz ■

• **Kraków**

BOHEMIA

Ostrava •

Zakopane •

★ **Prague**

• Olomouc

CZECH

MORAVIA

CARPATHIAN MTNS.

Plzeň •

REPUBLIC

Brno •

Poprad •

• Nürnberg

Český Krumlov

SLOVAKIA

Danube

Bratislava ★

Eger •

Vienna ★

Danube

DANUBE BEND

• Munich

AUSTRIA

Budapest ★

• Salzburg

• Sopron

• Szombathely

Graz •

Lake Balaton

HUNGARY

• Innsbruck

TIROL

JULIAN ALPS

• Pécs

SERBIA

Bohinj

• **Bled**

Bled

Ljubljana ★

★ **Zagreb**

SLAVONIA

Trieste •

SLOVENIA

CROATIA

• Venice

• Rijeka

PLITVICE LAKES NATIONAL PARK

Po

• Pula

BOSNIA &

HERZEGOVINA

ITALY

• Zadar

Sarajevo ★

Adriatic Sea

• Florence

DALMATIAN COAST

• Split

• Siena

Korčula

MONTE-NEGRO

• Assisi

Dubrovnik

Rick Steves'
BEST OF
EASTERN
EUROPE
2004

by Rick Steves & Cameron Hewitt

AVALON
TRAVEL

For a complete listing of Rick Steves' books, see page 18.

Avalon Travel Publishing
1400 65th Street, Suite 250
Emeryville, CA 94608
Avalon Travel Publishing is a division of Avalon Publishing Group.

Text © 2004 by Rick Steves
Cover © 2004 by Avalon Travel Publishing, Inc. All rights reserved.
Maps © 2004 by Europe Through the Back Door

Printed in the United States of America by Worzalla.
First printing February 2004

Special thanks to Ian Watson for his innumerable contributions, from sharing his linguistic and mapmaking skills to writing about Polish and Hungarian cuisine. Many thanks also to Honza Vihan for his help with all things Czech (including writing the Czech food section).

Portions of this book were originally published in *Rick Steves' Germany, Austria & Switzerland* © 2004, 2003, 2002, 2001, 2000, 1999, by Rick Steves.

For the latest on Rick Steves' lectures, guidebooks, tours, and public television series, contact Europe Through the Back Door, Box 2009, Edmonds, WA 98020, tel. 425/771-8303, fax 425/771-0833, www.ricksteves.com, or rick@ricksteves.com.

ISBN: 1-56691-738-7 • ISSN: 1547-8505

Europe Through the Back Door Managing Editor: Risa Laib
Europe Through the Back Door Editors: Cameron Hewitt, Jill Hodges
Avalon Travel Publishing Editor and Series Manager: Laura Mazer
Avalon Travel Publishing Project Editor: Patrick Collins
Copy Editor: Matthew Reed Baker
Production & Typesetting: Patrick David Barber Design
Cover Design: Kari Gim, Laura Mazer
Interior Design: Laura Mazer, Jane Musser, Amber Pirker
Maps & Graphics: David C. Hoerlein, Rhonda Pelikan, Zoey Platt, Lauren Mills, Mike Morgenfeld
Photography: Cameron Hewitt, Rick Steves
Front Matter Color Photos: page i, Wawel Cathedral, Krakow, Poland; page xii, City Wall, Dubrovnik, Croatia, both images Cameron Hewitt
Cover Photo: Front Image, Prague: © Brian McGilloway/Robert Holmes; Back Image, Prague: © Getty Images/Photodisc.

Distributed to the book trade by Publishers Group West, Berkeley, California

CONTENTS

Top Destinations in Eastern Europe

INTRODUCTION

Until 1989, Eastern Europe was a foreboding place—a gloomy corner of the "Evil Empire." Now the obligatory grays and preachy reds of communism live only in history books, museums, and even theme restaurants. Today's Eastern Europe is a traveler's delight, with low prices, friendly locals, lively squares, breathtaking sights, fascinating history, and a sense of pioneer excitement. For the experienced traveler, the East feels like the West once did: unpredictable, challenging, and rewarding.

This book breaks Eastern Europe into its top big-city, small-town, and back-to-nature destinations. It then gives you all the information and opinions necessary to wring the maximum value out of your limited time and money. If you plan a month or less in this region, this book is all you need.

Experiencing Europe's culture, people, and natural wonders economically and hassle-free has been my goal for 25 years of traveling, tour guiding, and travel writing. With this book, I pass on to you the lessons I've learned, researched (in mid-2003) for 2004.

Rick Steves' Best of Eastern Europe is a personal tour guide in your pocket. Better yet, it's actually two tour guides in your pocket: My co-writer/researcher for this guidebook is Cameron Hewitt, who leads Eastern Europe tours at Rick Steves' Europe Through the Back Door. Inspired by his Polish roots, Cameron has a powerful passion for Eastern Europe. Together, we will keep this book up-to-date and accurate (though for simplicity, from this point "we" will shed our respective egos and become "I").

Americans approach Eastern Europe expecting grouchy, monolingual service, crumbling communist-era infrastructure, and grimy, depressing landscapes dotted with rusting factories. Many Westerners seem to think that independent travel in the East is reckless—or even dangerous. But those who visit are pleasantly surprised at the beauty, friendliness, safety, and ease of travel in these countries. You'll be amazed at how quickly Eastern European countries have Westernized. Travel in Eastern Europe is nearly as easy as travel in the West. Any remaining rough edges simply add to the charm and carbonate the experience. The language barrier is tiny—English is even more widely spoken here than in much of Western Europe. And more important, the delightful villages, cosmopolitan cities, and exciting museums are welcoming, unique, and world-class.

To today's Eastern Europeans, the Soviet regime is old news, Cold War espionage is the stuff of movies, and oppressive Stalin sculptures are a distant memory. A decade and a half after the Iron Curtain fell, Eastern Europeans think about communism only when tourists bring it up. Freedom is a generation old, and—for better or for worse—McDonald's, MTV, and mobile phones are every bit as entrenched as in the West. The Czech Republic, Poland, Hungary, and Slovenia join the European Union in 2004—and they'll be starting off with perky and fast-growing economies. They don't have the economic muscle of Germany, but things are clicking, several countries fully expect to have the euro within a few years, they're bulking up their infrastructures, and the future is promising.

You'll wander among Prague's dreamy fairy-tale spires, bask in the energy of Kraków's market square, and soak with chess players in a Budapest bath. Ponder Europe's most moving Holocaust memorial at Auschwitz. Enjoy nature as you stroll on boardwalks through the Plitvice Lakes' waterfall wonderland or glide across Lake Bled to a church-topped island in the shadow of the Julian Alps. Taste a proud Hungarian vintner's wine in an Eger cave and say, *"Egészségedre!"* (or stick with "Cheers!").

I've been selective, including only the top destinations and sights. For example, Croatia has dozens of island getaways. I take you to the quaintest: Korčula. Poland has lots of big cities—but Kraków and Warsaw are clearly the most worthwhile and interesting.

The best is, of course, only my opinion. But after more than two busy decades of researching Europe, I've developed a sixth sense for what stokes the traveler's wanderlust. Just thinking about the places featured in this book makes me want to polka.

This Information Is Accurate and Up-to-Date

This book is completely up-to-date for 2004. And, like all our city and country guidebooks, it will be updated every year. Most publishers of guidebooks that cover a region from top to bottom can afford an update only every two or three years (and even then, it's often by fax or e-mail). Since this book is selective, covering only the places I think make the top month of sightseeing in Eastern Europe, I can update it each summer.

If you're traveling with this book in 2004, I guarantee you're using the freshest information available in print. For the latest, visit www .ricksteves.com/update. Also at our Web site, check our Graffiti Wall

WHAT IS "EASTERN EUROPE"?

"Eastern Europe" means different things to different people. To most Americans, Eastern Europe includes any place that was once behind the Iron Curtain, from the former East Germany to Moscow. People in many of those countries consider themselves Central Europeans and think of Eastern Europe as nations farther east: Russia, Ukraine, Belarus, Romania, and the Baltics.

In this book, I'm using the term Eastern Europe to describe the **Czech Republic, Poland, Hungary, Slovenia,** and **Croatia.** I've also annexed a trio worth-a-visit gateway cities in Germany and Austria, each of which has important cultural and historic ties to these nations: **Vienna** was the imperial capital of Eastern Europe for centuries, and **Berlin** and **Dresden** share a more recent communist history with the region.

So what do the five Eastern European countries have in common? All of these destinations fell under communist control during the last half of the 20th century. More importantly, for hundreds of years leading up to World War I, they were all part of the Austrian Hapsburg Empire. Before the Hapsburgs, the kings and emperors of these countries also frequently governed their neighbors. And most importantly, all of these countries (except Hungary) are populated by people of Slavic heritage.

I hope that natives, sticklers, and historians will understand the liberties I've taken with the title of this book—after all, would you buy a book called *Rick Steves' Best of the Former Hapsburg Empire?*

(select "Rick Steves' Guidebooks," then "Eastern Europe") for a list of reports and experiences—good and bad—from fellow travelers.

This book will help you have a smooth, affordable trip. Your trip costs at least $10 per waking hour. Your time is valuable. This guidebook saves lots of time.

Planning Your Trip

This book is organized by destination. Each destination is covered as a mini-vacation on its own, filled with exciting sights and homey, affordable places to stay. In each chapter, you'll find:

Planning Your Time, a suggested schedule with thoughts on how to best use your limited time.

Orientation, including tourist information, city transportation, and an easy-to-read map designed to make the text clear and your arrival smooth.

Sights with ratings: ▲▲▲—Worth getting up early and skipping breakfast for; **▲▲**—Worth getting up early for; **▲**—Worth seeing if it's convenient; No rating—Worth knowing about.

Sleeping and Eating, with addresses and phone numbers of my favorite budget hotels and restaurants.

Transportation Connections, covering the most common train routes to help you lace together your trip.

Country Introductions give you an overview of each country's culture, customs, history, food, language, and other useful practicalities.

The chapter on **Understanding Yugoslavia,** which sorts out the various countries and conflicts, gives you a good picture of why Yugoslavia was formed and why it broke up.

The **appendix** contains a telephone calling chart, list of U.S. embassies, summary of national holidays, and climate chart.

Browse through this book, choose your favorite destinations, and link them together. Then have a great trip! You'll travel like a temporary local, getting the absolute most out of every mile, minute, and dollar. You won't waste time on mediocre sights because, unlike other guidebook authors, I cover only the best. Since lousy, expensive hotels are a major financial pitfall, I've worked hard to assemble the best accommodations values for each stop. As you travel the route I know and love, I'm happy you'll be meeting some of my favorite Europeans.

Trip Costs

Traveling in Eastern Europe is cheap. Generally speaking, things that natives buy—such as food, transportation, and museum tickets—are affordable (in line with the local economy). Hotels, on the other hand, are expensive, often even surpassing Western prices for comparable comfort. Still, if you avoid restaurants with inflated prices on the main tourist drag, and if you use my listings to stay only at the best-value hotels, a trip to the East is substantially less expensive than a trip to the West.

Five components make up your trip cost: airfare, surface transportation, room and board, sightseeing/entertainment, and shopping/miscellany. The prices I've listed below are more or less average for all of the destinations in this book. In general, things are cheaper in Hungary and Poland, and costlier in Croatia and Slovenia. Big cities (like Prague and Warsaw) are more expensive than smaller destinations (like Kraków and Eger).

Airfare: Don't try to sort through the mess. Get and use a good travel agent. A basic round-trip flight from the United States to Prague should cost $600 to $1,000 (even cheaper in winter), depending on where you fly from and when. Always consider saving time and money in Europe by flying "open jaw" (flying into one city and out of another). The additional cost of flying into Prague and out of Dubrovnik could be cheaper than the added expense and trouble of a two-day overland return trip to Prague.

Surface Transportation: For a three-week whirlwind trip of all my recommended destinations, allow $250 per person for public transportation (train, bus, and boat tickets) or $600 per person (based on 2 people sharing the car) for a three-week car rental, parking, gas, and insurance. Car rental is cheapest when reserved from the United States. Train travelers will probably save money by simply buying tickets along the way rather than purchasing a railpass (see "Transportation," page 20).

Room and Board: You can thrive in Eastern Europe for an average of $70 a day per person for room and board. A $70-a-day budget per person allows $10 for lunch, $15 for dinner, and $45 for lodging (based on 2 people splitting the cost of a $90 double room that includes breakfast). That's doable. Students and tightwads do it on $40 a day ($20 per bed, $20 for meals and snacks). Budget sleeping and eating require the skills and information covered later in this chapter (and in much more depth in my book *Rick Steves' Europe Through the Back Door*).

Sightseeing and Entertainment: Sightseeing is cheap here. Major sights generally cost around $2 to $4 (and can be as little as $1 and rarely more than $8). Figure $8 to $20 for splurge experiences (e.g., going to concerts, taking Danube cruises, watching Slovenia's Lipizzaner stallions, or soaking in a Budapest bath). You can hire a private guide for about $50 for four hours. An overall average of $15 a day works for most. Don't skimp here. After all, this category directly powers most of the experiences all the other expenses are designed to make possible.

Shopping and Miscellany: Figure $1 per postcard, coffee, beer, and ice-cream cone. Shopping can vary in cost from nearly nothing to a small fortune. Good budget travelers find that this category has little to do with assembling a trip full of lifelong and wonderful memories.

Exchange Rates

Whenever possible, I've priced things throughout this book in local currencies. Some vendors—especially hotels—prefer to set their prices in euros, and only in these cases, I've followed suit. Even if they list prices in euros, these places happily accept the local currency.

Germany and Austria use the euro currency. Although the Czech Republic, Poland, Hungary, and Slovenia join the European Union in 2004, it'll be another few years before they officially adopt the euro. These countries, along with Croatia, still use their traditional currencies.

EASTERN EUROPE: BEST WHIRLWIND THREE-WEEK TRIP BY TRAIN

Day	Plan	Sleep in
1	Arrive in Prague	Prague
2	Prague	Prague
3	Prague, maybe day trip to Kutná Hora or Český Krumlov; night train to Kraków	Night train
4	Kraków	Kraków
5	Kraków, day trip to Auschwitz	Kraków
6	Kraków, maybe day trip to Wieliczka Salt Mine or Warsaw; night train to Eger	Night train
7	Eger	Eger
8	Early to Budapest	Budapest
9	Budapest	Budapest
10	Budapest, maybe day trip to Danube Bend	Budapest
11	To Ljubljana (catch early, direct 8.5-hr train; no handy night-train option)	Ljubljana
12	Ljubljana	Ljubljana
13	To Bled	Bled
14	Day trips around Julian Alps	Bled
15	To Zagreb, sightseeing, then early evening bus to Plitvice Lakes National Park	Plitvice
16	Plitvice hike in morning, then afternoon bus to Split	Split
17	Split	Split
18	Boat to Korčula	Korčula
19	Korčula	Korčula
20	Boat to Dubrovnik	Dubrovnik
21	Dubrovnik	Dubrovnik
22	Dubrovnik and fly home	

This speedy, far-reaching itinerary works best by public transportation. Most of the time, you'll take the train. Exceptions: Bled and Ljubljana are better connected by bus. To get from Bled to Plitvice, take the bus to Ljubljana, train to Zagreb, then bus to Plitvice. To get from Plitvice to the coast, take an afternoon bus to Split or take the bus back to Zagreb to catch a cheap flight; if you want more time at Plitvice, you can sleep on a night bus to either Split or Dubrovnik. The Dalmatian Coast destinations are best connected to each other by boat or bus (no trains). A cheap one- or two-day car rental makes sense in countries such as Slovenia that offer inviting day-trip destinations difficult to reach by public transit.

By **car**, this is a tiring itinerary, with lots of long road days. It makes more sense to connect long-distance destinations by night train (e.g., Prague to Kraków, Kraków to Eger/Budapest), then strategically rent cars for a day or two in areas that merit having wheels (e.g., the Czech or Slovenian countryside).

Germanic Addendum: If you want to add the German gateway cities to this tour, begin with two days in Berlin, and spend a few hours in Dresden on the way to Prague. Vienna (which is well worth two days) is out-of-the-way for the above itinerary (fitting best between Budapest and Ljubljana; it also makes sense if you're going directly between Budapest and Prague).

Exchange Rates

1 Czech crown (*koruna*, kč) = about 3 cents, and 30 kč = about $1.
1 Polish złoty (zł, or PLN) = about 25 cents, and 4 zł = about $1.
230 Hungarian forints (Ft, or HUF) = about $1.
220 Slovenian tolars (SIT) = about $1.
1 Croatian kuna (HRK) = about 14 cents, and 7 kuna = about $1.
1 euro (€) = about $1.10.

To roughly convert Czech crowns into dollars, drop the last digit and divide by three (e.g., 750 kč = $25). To roughly go from Hungarian forints or Slovenian tolars into dollars, multiply by four and drop the last three digits (e.g., 10,000 Ft or SIT = around $40). To convert Polish prices into dollars, divide by four (e.g., 80 zł = $20). To convert Croatian kuna into dollars, divide by seven (e.g., 100 kuna = about $14).

So, that 20-zł Polish woodcarving is about $5, the 5,000-Ft Hungarian dinner is around $20, and the 2,000-kč taxi ride through Prague is...uh-oh.

Prices, Times, and Discounts

The prices in this book, as well as the hours and telephone numbers, are accurate as of mid-2003. But Eastern Europe is always changing, and I know you'll understand that this, like any other guidebook, starts to yellow even before it's printed.

In Europe—and throughout this book—you'll be using the 24-hour clock. After 12:00 noon, keep going—13:00, 14:00, and so on. For anything over 12, subtract 12 and add p.m. (14:00 is 2:00 p.m.)

While discounts for sightseeing and transportation are not listed in this book, youths (under 18) and students (only with International Student Identity Cards) often get discounts—but only by asking.

Sightseeing Priorities

Depending on the length of your trip, here are my recommended priorities. Assuming you're traveling by train, I've taken geographical proximity into account.

3 days:	Prague
5 days, add:	Budapest
7 days, add:	Kraków and Auschwitz
9 days, add:	Český Krumlov
12 days, add:	Ljubljana and Bled
16 days, add:	Dubrovnik and Split
22 days, add:	Korčula, Plitvice Lakes, Warsaw, Zagreb, Eger

(The map on page 7 and the 3-week itinerary on page 6 include all of these stops.)

Berlin, Dresden, and Vienna: These three gateway cities make for great destinations. But since the focus of this book is Eastern Europe,

I've included them mostly for the convenience of readers who will pass through them on their way to or from Eastern Europe. On a tour of Germany and Austria, they rate higher on the list of priorities (see *Rick Steves' Germany, Austria & Switzerland* guidebook for more information). But if your focus is Eastern Europe, there's plenty to keep you busy in the Czech Republic, Poland, Hungary, Slovenia, and Croatia.

When to Go

The "tourist season" runs roughly from May through September.

Summer has its advantages: best weather, very long days (light until after 21:00), and the busiest schedule of tourist fun.

In spring and fall—May, June, September, and early October—travelers enjoy fewer crowds, milder weather, and the ability to grab a room almost whenever and wherever they like.

Winter travelers find concert seasons in full swing, with absolutely no tourist crowds, but some accommodations and sights are either closed or run on a limited schedule. Confirm your sightseeing plans locally, especially when traveling off-season. The weather can be cold and dreary, and night will draw the shades on your sightseeing before dinnertime. Use the climate chart in the appendix as a guide.

Red Tape

Visas: Currently, Americans need only a passport, but no visa or shots, to travel in the countries covered in this book. Canadians, however, do need visas to enter the Czech Republic (www.czechembassy.org) and Poland (www.polishembassy.ca).

Borders: Americans get unnecessarily edgy at Eastern European borders, their imaginations fueled by years of Cold War espionage flicks. A Czech friend of mine remembers crossing borders in the early 1980s and having long needles poked into his back seat (to reveal any unwelcome cargo). Scary legends—about greedy, bribe-hungry border guards and passports held hostage—run rampant among travelers.

Relax! Even if any of these stories were once true, they've long since gone the way of the hammer and sickle. Borders, whether by car or by train, are generally a non-event—flash your passport, maybe wait a few minutes, and move on. You'll be quickly checked as many as four times—by the customs and immigration officers of the country you're leaving and, sometimes after continuing ahead a few feet, the one you're entering. On international night trains, you'll probably be woken up at each border for a check (though sometimes your conductor will take your passport overnight to handle the red tape for you).

The procedure at every border is different. Usually it's just a quick glance at the passport, the clunk of a stamp, and you're on your way. If there is a delay, don't panic. There may be a red-tape back-up, or the guards might just be particularly thorough (or grouchy) that day. While

EU MEMBERSHIP AND THE "NEW EUROPE"

On May 1, 2004, the Czech Republic, Poland, Hungary, Slovenia, Slovakia, and five other countries join the European Union. Each of these countries had a referendum, allowing residents to vote on whether to join the EU. In every case, the referendum passed, but sometimes by a narrow margin. EU membership—and investment— is certain to benefit these countries' economies (as it has in Ireland). But Eastern Europeans still have their doubts.

Take Poland as an example. Poles have a strong agricultural heritage. During the communist era, the Soviets collectivized small family farms in most of its satellite states—but Poland managed to preserve its traditional plots. After a half-century of successfully fighting for the rights of independent small farmers, EU-member Poland will...have to collectivize small farms.

Another prickly issue is keeping the Czech Republic Czech. After World War II, many German families living in the so-called "Sudetenland"—on the fringes of today's Czech Republic—were forced into Germany. Since then, Germans have not been able to return. But now that the Czech Republic and Germany will belong to the same European Union, Germans will be able to buy back their family homesteads in the Czech countryside...and they are likely to win any bidding war against the poorer Czechs.

Traditional Czech cuisine is also in jeopardy. EU hygiene standards dictate that cooked food can't be served more than two hours old. My Czech friend complained, "This will make many of our best dishes illegal." Czech specialties, often simmered, taste better the next day.

A wise Czech grandmother put it best. In her lifetime, she had lived in a country ruled from Vienna (Hapsburgs), Berlin (Nazis),

I have occasionally seen the offer of a cold beer help speed things along, bribery is generally not necessary—and I've never been asked outright for a bribe (even when I've got a tour bus full of 24 antsy Americans).

The worst thing you can do is get impatient or pushy. The angrier you get, the longer it'll take. A polite smile will speed things along just as fast as a cold beer.

Note that the countries in this book (except Croatia) join the European Union on May 1, 2004. Technically these borders should open up soon, and eventually you won't have to stop at all...but it remains unclear how quickly this transition will take place.

Even as borders fade, when you change countries, you must still and Moscow (communists). She said, "Now that we're finally ruled from Prague, why would we want to turn our power over to Brussels?"

Current EU members are also skeptical about adding on more countries. Wealthy nations have already seen funds taken from them to improve the floundering economies of poorer countries (like Portugal, Greece, and Ireland). This issue is especially dicey in Germany, where people living in the former West already loudly complain about the financial burden of pulling up the East.

All of this controversy was only exacerbated in February 2003, when, at the peak of the international debate about going to war in Iraq, U.S. Secretary of Defense Donald Rumsfeld called these Eastern countries the "New Europe." Rumsfeld intended the remark as a dig against France and Germany ("Old Europe," in Rumsfeld's estimation), who refused to support U.S. attacks on Iraq—compared to the Eastern European governments that did support the U.S. (even if the people in these countries didn't).

But the term—like Reagan's equally loaded "Evil Empire" line of a generation ago—has caught on, and it does capture the complicated circumstances of today's Europe. The East looks to the future, eager to distance itself from its painful recent history, while the West is more comfortable living in the past, when its power was at its peak (and French, not English, was the world's language). As Eastern Europe joins the EU, and the geographical center of Europe shifts from Brussels to Prague, the power of existing EU members—especially Germany and France—is diluted. In this "New Europe," the Czech Republic or Poland might emerge with a leading role.

change telephone cards and postage stamps.

Watt's up? If you're bringing electrical gear, you'll need a two-prong adapter plug (sold cheap at travel stores like ours, www.ricksteves.com) and a converter. Travel appliances often have convenient, built-in converters; look for a voltage switch marked 120V (U.S.) and 240V (Europe) or a label indicating that the appliance works on a voltage range (roughly 120–240).

Banking

Bring your ATM, credit, or debit card, along with cash or traveler's checks in dollars as a backup. The best and easiest way to get the local currency is to use the omnipresent bank machines (always open, low fees, quick processing); you'll need a PIN code (numbers only, no letters) to use with your Visa or MasterCard. Some ATM bank cards will work only at certain banks, though Visa and MasterCard are usually quite reliable. Before you go, verify with your bank that your card will work overseas—and let them know you'll be using the card on your trip so they won't question sudden international activity on your account. Bring two cards in case one is lost, stolen or demagnetized. The word for cash machine in all of these countries is *Bankomat*.

Traveler's checks are expensive and time-consuming, but if you bring them, you'll find that regular banks have the best rates for cashing them (except in Poland, where *kantors,* or money-changing kiosks, generally offer good rates—compare several to find the best). Many banks charge a fee per check cashed, so rather than cashing five $100 checks, cash one $500 check. For a large exchange, it pays to compare rates and fees. Post offices (business hours) and train stations (long hours) usually change money if you can't get to a bank.

Note that although the Czech Republic, Poland, Hungary, Slovenia, and Croatia haven't officially adopted the euro, many hotels, restaurants, and shops in these countries (especially in touristy areas) accept smaller euro bills (€50 or less). Most businesses will not take euro coins or larger bills, and you'll usually get bad rates (and your change in the local currency). If you're just passing through the country, your euros will probably get you by—and can actually be helpful in an emergency in any of these countries. But if you're staying awhile, get the local currency.

Just like at home, credit (or debit) cards work easily at larger hotels, restaurants, and shops, but smaller businesses prefer payment in local cash.

If Your Credit Cards are Lost or Stolen: If you lose your credit, debit, or ATM card, you can stop people from using your card by reporting the loss immediately to the respective global customer assistance centers. Call these 24-hour U.S. numbers collect: VISA (410/581-9994), MasterCard (636/722-7111), and American Express (336/393-1111).

Providing the following information will help expedite the process: the name of the financial institution that issued you the card, full card number, the cardholder's name as printed on the card, billing address, home phone number, circumstances of the loss or theft, and identification verification—Social Security number or birthdate and your mother's maiden name. (Packing along a photocopy of the front and back of your cards helps you answer the harder questions.) You can generally receive a temporary card within two business days in Europe.

If you promptly report your card lost or stolen, you typically won't be responsible for any unauthorized transactions on your account, although many banks charge a liability fee of about $50.

As you can see...it's smart to wear a money belt. Keep your cards safe inside, not in a wallet or backpack.

VAT Refunds and Customs Regulations

VAT Refunds for Shoppers: Wrapped into the purchase price of your souvenirs is a Value Added Tax (VAT) that varies per country. If you make a purchase of a minimum amount—which also differs per country—at a store that participates in the VAT refund scheme, you're entitled to get most of that tax back (see chart for VAT rates and minimum amounts). Personally, I've never felt that VAT refunds are worth the hassle, but if you do, here's the scoop.

If you're lucky, the merchant will subtract the tax when you make your purchase (this is more likely to occur if the store ships the goods to your home). Otherwise, you'll need to:

Get the paperwork. Have the merchant completely fill out the necessary refund document, called a "cheque." You'll have to present your passport at the store.

Have your cheque(s) stamped at the border when you leave the country by the customs agent who deals with VAT refunds. If you're flying home, it's best to keep your purchases in your carry-on for viewing, but if they're too large or dangerous (such as knives) to carry on, then track down the proper customs agent to inspect them before you check your bag. You're not supposed to use your purchased goods before you leave. If you show up at customs wearing a chic Czech shirt, officials

VAT RATES
AND MINIMUM PURCHASES REQUIRED TO QUALIFY FOR REFUNDS

Country of Purchase	VAT rate*	Minimum in Local Currency	Minimum in U.S. dollars**
Austria	16.7%	€75	$87
Croatia	18%	500 kn	$80
Czech Rep.	5–22%	1,000.10 kč	$36
Germany	13.8%	€25	$29
Hungary	20%	50,000 Ft	$228
Poland	18%	200 zł	$50
Slovenia	16%	15,000 SIT	$76

VAT Rate indicates the percentage of the total purchase price that is VAT.

** *Exchange rate as of 10/29/03*

Source: Global Refund Tax Free Shopping

Please note: Figures are subject to change. For more information, visit www.traveltax.msu.edu or www.globalrefund.com.

might look the other way—or deny you a refund.

To collect your refund, you'll need to return your stamped documents to the retailer or its representative. Many merchants work with a service, such as Global Refund or Cashback, which have offices at major airports, ports, or border crossings. These services, which extract a 4 percent fee, can refund your money immediately in your currency of choice or credit your card (within 2 billing cycles). If you have to deal directly with the retailer, mail the store your stamped documents and then wait. It could take months.

Customs Regulations: You can take home $800 in souvenirs per person duty-free. The next $1,000 is taxed at a flat 3 percent. After that, you pay the individual item's duty rate. You can also bring in duty-free a liter of alcohol (slightly more than a standard-sized bottle of wine), a carton of cigarettes, and up to 100 cigars. To check customs rules and duty rates, visit www.customs.gov.

Hurdling the Language Barrier

The language barrier in Eastern Europe is no bigger than in the West. In fact, I find that it's even easier to communicate in Hungary or Croatia than in Italy or Spain. Immediately after the Iron Curtain fell in 1989, English speakers were rare. But today, you'll find that most people in the tourist industry—and virtually all young people—speak excellent English.

Of course, not everyone speaks English. You'll run into the most substantial language barriers in situations when you need to deal with a lesser-educated clerk or service person (train stations and post office counters, maids, museum guard, baker, and so on). Be reasonable in your expectations. Hungarian post-office clerks and museum ticket-sellers are every bit as friendly and multilingual as they are in the United States. Luckily, it's relatively easy to get your point across in these places. I've often bought a train ticket simply by writing out the name of my destination (preferably with the local spelling—for example, "Oświęcim" instead of "Auschwitz"); the time I want to travel (using the 24-hr clock); and if necessary, the date I want to leave (day first, then month as a Roman numeral, then year). Here's an example of what I'd show a ticket-seller at a train station: "Warszawa–17:30–15.VII.03."

Most of the destinations in this book—the Czech Republic, Poland, Slovenia, and Croatia—speak Slavic languages. Czech, Polish, Slovene, and Croatian are closely related to each other and to Russian, and are, to varying degrees, mutually intelligible (though many spellings change—for example, Czech *hrad,* or castle, becomes Croatian *grad*). Slavic languages have a simple vocabulary but are highly inflected—that is, the meaning of a sentence depends on complicated endings that are tacked on to the ends of the words (as in Latin).

Slavic words are notorious for their seemingly unpronounceable, long strings of consonants. Slavic pronunciation can be tricky. In fact,

EUROPE'S BEST LINGUISTS

Why do Eastern Europeans speak English so well—especially since it wasn't commonly taught in schools before the last 15 years?

Residents of big, powerful Western countries, like Germany or France, might think that foreigners should learn their language. But Eastern Europeans are as practical as Westerners are stubborn. They realize that it's unreasonable to expect an American to learn Hungarian (with only 12 million speakers worldwide), Croatian (5 million), or Slovene (2 million). When only a few million people on the planet speak your language, it's essential to find a common language with the rest of the world—so they learn English early and well. In Croatia, for example, all schoolchildren start learning English in the third grade. (I've had surprisingly eloquent conversations with Croatian grade-schoolers.)

Many times I've heard a German and a Hungarian conversing in English—a reminder that as Americans, we're lucky to speak the world's new lingua franca.

when the first Christian missionaries, Cyril and Method, came to Eastern Europe a millennium ago, they invented a whole new alphabet to represent these strange Slavic sounds. The Cyrillic alphabet is still used today in the eastern Slavic countries (like Serbia and Russia). Fortunately, the destinations covered in this book all use the same Roman alphabet we do, but they add lots of different diacritics—little markings below and above letters—to represent a wide range of sounds (for example, č, ą, ó, đ, ł). I explain each of these diacritics in this book's various country introductions.

Hungarian is another story altogether—it's completely unrelated to Slavic languages, German, or English. For more on the challenging Magyar tongue, see page 194.

German is the language in the gateway countries of Germany and Austria. As part of the same language family as English (other members include Dutch, Swedish, and Norwegian), German will sound noticeably more familiar to American ears than the Slavic languages.

Throughout Eastern Europe, German can be a handy second language (especially in Croatia, which attracts hordes of German tourists). And a few words of Italian can come in handy in Slovenia and Croatia. Aside from the English pleasantries, there's one word that people throughout Eastern Europe will understand: *Servus* (SEHR-voos)—the old-fashioned international greeting from the days of the Austro-Hungarian Empire. If you draw a blank on how to say hello in the local language, just offer a cheery, *"Servus!"*

Learn the key phrases and travel with a phrase book—consider *Rick Steves' German Phrase Book* for Germany and Austria, and Lonely Planet's good *Eastern Europe Phrasebook,* which covers the rest of the destinations in this book.

Don't be afraid to interact with locals. Eastern Europeans can seem brusque at first—a holdover from the closed communist society—but often a simple smile is the only icebreaker you need to make a new friend. You'll find that doors open a little more quickly when you know a few words of the language. Give it your best shot. The locals will appreciate your efforts.

Travel Smart

Your trip is like a complex play—easier to follow and really appreciate on a second viewing. While no one does the same trip twice to gain that advantage, reading this book in its entirety before your trip accomplishes much the same thing. As a practical matter (to avoid redundancy), many cultural or historic details are explained for one sight and not repeated for another—even if they would pump up your understanding and appreciation of that second sight.

Reread entire chapters as you travel, and visit local tourist information offices. Upon arrival in a new town, lay the groundwork for a smooth departure. Buy a phone card and use it for reservations and confirmations. Enjoy the hospitality of Eastern Europeans. Ask questions. Most locals are eager to point you in their idea of the right direction. Wear your money belt, pack along a pocket-size notebook to organize your thoughts, and practice the virtue of simplicity. Plan ahead for banking, laundry, postal chores, and picnics. Those who expect to travel smart, do.

To maximize rootedness, minimize one-night stands. Mix intense and relaxed periods. Every trip (and every traveler) needs at least a few slack days. Pace yourself. Assume you will return.

As you read through this book, note days when sights are closed and plan your itinerary accordingly. Saturday morning feels like any bustling weekday morning, but at lunchtime, many shops close down through Sunday. Sundays have pros and cons, as they do for travelers in the United States (special events, limited hours, shops and banks closed, limited public transportation, no rush hours). Popular places are even more popular on weekends.

Tourist Information

The tourist information office is your best first stop in any new city. Try to arrive, or at least telephone, before it closes. In this book, I'll refer to a tourist information office as a TI. Throughout Eastern Europe, you'll find TIs are usually well-organized and have an English-speaking staff. Most local tourist offices in Eastern Europe are run by the government, which means their information isn't colored by a drive for profit.

Unlike in Western Europe, TIs often don't have a room-booking service—though they can almost always give you a list of local hotels, and if they're not too busy, can call around for you to check on availability. Every town has at least one travel agency that has a room-booking service. Even if there's no "fee," you'll pay more for the room than if you book direct, using the listings in this book.

Tourist Offices, U.S. Addresses

Each country's national tourist office in the United States is a wealth of information. Before your trip, get the free general information packet and request any specifics you may want (such as regional and city maps and festival schedules).

Czech Tourist Authority: 1109 Madison Avenue, New York, NY 10028, tel. 212/288-0830, fax 212/288-0971, www.czechcenter.com, travelczech@pop.net. To get a weighty information package (1–2 lbs, no advertising), send a check for $4 to cover postage and specify places of interest. Basic information and map are free.

Polish National Tourist Office: 5 Marine View Plaza #208, Hoboken, NJ 07030-5722, tel. 201/420-9910, fax 201/584-9153, www.polandtour.org, pntonyc@polandtour.org. Warsaw and Kraków information, regional brochures, and maps.

Hungarian National Tourist Office: 150 East 58th Street, 33rd floor, New York, NY 10155, tel. 212/355-0240, fax 212/207-4103, www.gotohungary.com, hnto@gotohungary.com. "Routes to your Roots" booklet for those of Hungarian descent, Budapest Guide, and horseback riding info.

Slovenian Tourist Office: 345 East 12th Street #27, New York, NY 10003, tel. 212/358-9686, fax 212/358-9025, www.slovenia-tourism.si, slotouristboard@sloveniatravel.com. "Welcome to Slovenia" brochure, map, special information on various regions, hiking, biking, winter travel, and farm stays.

Croatian National Tourist Office: 350 Fifth Avenue #4003, New York, NY 10118, tel. 800/829-4416 or 212/279-8672, fax 212/279-8683, www.croatia.hr, cntony@earthlink.net. Free brochures and maps.

German National Tourist Office: 122 East 42nd Street, 52nd floor, New York, NY 10168, tel. 212/661-7200, fax 212/661-7174, www.visits-to-germany.com, gntony@aol.com. Maps, Rhine schedules, castles, biking, and city and regional information.

Austrian Tourist Office: Box 1142, New York, NY 10108-1142, tel. 212/944-6880, fax 212/730-4568, www.austria-tourism.com, info@oewnyc.com. Ask for their "Vacation Kit" with map. Fine hikes and city information.

Rick Steves' Books, Videos, and DVDs

Rick Steves' Europe Through the Back Door 2004 gives you budget-travel skills, such as minimizing jet lag, packing light, planning your itinerary, traveling by car or train, finding rooms, changing money, avoiding rip-offs, using mobile phones, hurdling the language barrier, staying healthy, taking great photographs, and much more. The book also includes chapters on 38 of Rick's favorite Back Doors.

Rick Steves' Country Guides, annually updated and covering Europe, provide you with all you need to know for your trip, with specifics on the best places to stay, eat, relax...and marvel.

My **City and Regional Guides,** practical and annually updated, offer in-depth coverage of the sights, hotels, restaurants, and nightlife in Europe's grand cities and regions, along with illustrated tours of the great museums.

New for 2004, *Rick Steves' Easy Access Europe,* written for travelers with limited mobility, covers London, Paris, Bruges, Amsterdam, and the Rhine River.

RICK STEVES' GUIDEBOOKS

Country Guides
Rick Steves' Best of Europe
Rick Steves' Best of Eastern Europe
Rick Steves' France
Rick Steves' Germany, Austria & Switzerland
Rick Steves' Great Britain
Rick Steves' Ireland
Rick Steves' Italy
Rick Steves' Scandinavia
Rick Steves' Spain & Portugal

City and Regional Guides
Rick Steves' Amsterdam, Bruges & Brussels
Rick Steves' Florence & Tuscany
Rick Steves' London
Rick Steves' Paris
Rick Steves' Provence & the French Riviera
Rick Steves' Rome
Rick Steves' Venice
Rick Steves' Easy Access Europe
    (with a focus on London, Paris, Bruges, Amsterdam, and the Rhine)

(Avalon Travel Publishing)

Rick Steves' Europe 101: History and Art for the Traveler (co-written with Gene Openshaw) gives you the story of Europe's people, history, and art. Written for smart people who were sleeping in their history and art classes before they knew they were going to Europe, *101* helps Europe's sights come alive. However, this book focuses on Western Europe.

Rick Steves' Mona Winks (co-written with Gene Openshaw), provides fun, easy-to-follow, self-guided tours of Europe's top 25 museums and cultural sites in London, Paris, Amsterdam, Madrid, Rome, Venice, and Florence.

My new public TV series, *Rick Steves' Europe,* keeps churning out shows. Of 82 episodes (the new series plus *Travels in Europe with Rick Steves*), four shows cover Eastern Europe, and three others cover the gateway cities of Berlin and Vienna. A new series, to debut in September of 2004, will include episodes on Hungary and Poland. These shows air nationally on public television. They're also available as information-packed home videos and DVDs (order online at www.ricksteves.com or call 425/771-8303 for our free newsletter/catalog).

Rick Steves' Postcards from Europe, my autobiographical book, packs more than 25 years of travel anecdotes and insights into the ultimate 2,000-mile European adventure. Through my guidebooks, I share my favorite European discoveries with you. *Postcards* introduces you to my favorite European friends.

All Rick Steves guidebooks are published by Avalon Travel Publishing (www.travelmatters.com).

Other Guidebooks

You may want some supplemental information if you'll be traveling beyond my recommended destinations. When you consider the improvements they'll make in your $3,000 vacation, $25 or $35 for extra maps and books is money well spent. Especially for several people traveling by car, the weight and expense are negligible.

The Rough Guides (covering individually the countries in this book, except Slovenia) are packed with historical and cultural insight, but not updated annually. Lonely Planet guides are well-researched and mature (also not updated annually); their far-ranging *Eastern Europe* overview book gives you little to go on, but their country- and city-specific guides are more thorough (especially their very good *Slovenia,* the only book by a major company focusing on that country). Students, backpackers, and nightlife-seekers should consider the Let's Go guides (by Harvard students, the best hostel listings, updated annually). Dorling Kindersley publishes snazzy Eyewitness Guides covering Prague, Budapest, Kraków, Warsaw, Poland, Croatia, Berlin, and Vienna. While pretty to look at, these books weigh a ton and are skimpy on actual content.

In Your Pocket publishes regularly updated magazines on major Eastern European cities (including Prague, Budapest, Kraków, Warsaw, and Zagreb). These handy guides are especially good for their up-to-date hotel and restaurant recommendations (available locally, usually for a few dollars, but often free; condensed versions available free online at www.inyourpocket.com).

If your exploration of Germanic countries takes you beyond Vienna, Berlin, and Dresden, consider *Rick Steves' Germany, Austria & Switzerland.*

Maps

The black-and-white maps in this book, drawn by Dave Hoerlein, are concise and simple. Dave, who is well-traveled in Eastern Europe, has designed the maps to help you locate recommended places and get to the tourist offices, where you can pick up a more in-depth map of the city or region (usually free).

European bookstores, especially in touristy areas, have good selections of maps. For drivers, I'd recommend a 1:200,000- or 1:300,000-scale map for each country. Train travelers usually manage fine with the freebies they get with their train pass and from the local tourist offices.

Tours of Eastern Europe

Travel agents will tell you about all the mainstream tours, but they won't tell you about ours. At Europe Through the Back Door, we offer 18-day Best of Eastern Europe tours that feature almost every destination covered in this book, a roomy bus, and a great guide (departures May–Oct, maximum 26–28 people), and one-week Prague getaways. For more information, call 425/771-8303, ext. 217, or visit www.ricksteves.com, tour@ricksteves.com.

Transportation
By Car or Train?

The train (with buses or short-term car rentals to fill in the gaps) is best for single travelers, those who'll be spending more time in big cities, those with an ambitious multi-country itinerary, and those who don't want to drive in Europe. While a car gives you more freedom, enables you to search for hotels more easily, and carries your bags for you, the train zips you effortlessly from city to city, usually dropping you in the center and near the tourist office. Cars are great in the Czech or Slovenian countryside, but a worthless headache in places like Prague, Budapest, and Dubrovnik. If you're lacing the big cities together, the last thing you want is a car. Save lots of stress and money by taking the train (and even hiring guides with cars for your side-trips).

Public Transportation in Eastern Europe

Trains

Trains are punctual and cover cities well, but frustrating schedules make a few out-of-the-way recommendations not worth the time and trouble for the less determined (such as Croatia's Plitvice Lakes National Park, accessible only by bus). For timetables, visit Germany's excellent all-Europe timetable at http://bahn.hafas.de/english.html (expanded Czech train and bus schedules at www.vlak-bus.cz). You'll rarely need a reservation, except for night trains.

Night Trains: To cover the long distances between the major destinations in this book, use night trains as often as possible (remember, each night on the train saves a day for sightseeing). Fortunately, most of Eastern Europe's big cities are connected by night trains, even if the timing sometimes isn't ideal (e.g., arrival very early in the morning). The biggest problem night-trainers encounter is being woken up each time they cross a border to show their passports (unless the conductor offers to take your passport to deal with the red tape while you sleep).

No matter how many times you hear "totally true" stories of train cars being "gassed" with a sleep-inducing drug by thieves, it's a legend, most likely invented by travelers who felt foolish for sleeping through a theft. But as on Western European night trains, thefts do occur, so lock the door and secure your belongings (to make it difficult—or at least noisy—for thieves to rip you off). When sleeping on a night train, I wear my money belt.

Railpasses: While railpasses can be a good deal in Western Europe, they usually aren't the best option in the East for two reasons: Point-to-point tickets are cheap and simple here, and most railpasses don't conveniently combine Eastern European countries. For example, with the Eurail Selectpass, you can buy unlimited travel for up to 10 travel days (within a 2-month period) in three adjacent countries; but of the countries in this book, only Hungary, Germany, and Austria are eligible. The European East Pass covers the Czech Republic, Hungary, Poland, Slovakia, and Austria, but not Slovenia, Croatia, or Germany—and, again, since point-to-point tickets in these countries are so cheap, it isn't worthwhile for most trips. For all of the options, see the chart on the next page.

The Czech Republic, Hungary, Germany, and Austria have their own individual railpasses—valid for trips limited to their country—but the only pass offering exciting savings is Germany's; a German Flexipass can save you money in just a couple of long trips (find our free Railpass Guide online at www.ricksteves.com/rail).

Language Barrier: For tips on buying train tickets from monolingual staff in Eastern European stations, see "Hurdling the Language Barrier" on page 14.

Eastern Europe Railpasses

Prices listed are for 2004. My free *Rick Steves' Guide to Railpasses* has the latest details. To get the railpass guide, visit www.ricksteves.com/rail.

Eastern Europe:
The map shows approximate point-to-point one-way 2nd class rail fares in $US. Add up fares for your itinerary to see if a railpass will save you money. First class costs 50% more.

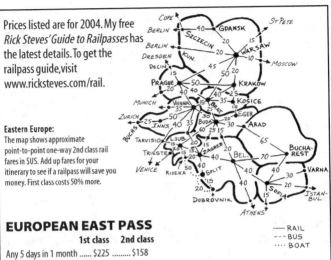

— RAIL
--- BUS
···· BOAT

EUROPEAN EAST PASS

	1st class	2nd class
Any 5 days in 1 month	$225	$158
Extra rail days (max 5)	25	18

Covers Austria, Czech Republic, Slovakia, Hungary, and Poland. Kids 4-11 half fare.

CZECH FLEXIPASS

	1st class	2nd class
Any 3 days in 15	$68	$48
Extra rail days (max 5)	9	6

Kids 4-11 half fare.

HUNGARIAN FLEXIPASS

Any 5 days out of 15 (first class)	$76
Any 10 days in a month (first class)	95

Kids 6-14 half fare, Attila goes free.

PRAGUE EXCURSION PASS

	1st class	2nd class
Adult	$55	$40
Youth (12-25)	45	35
Child (4 - 11)	28	20

Good for two train rides within a 7 day period: from any Czech border into Prague, and then from Prague to any border crossing (stops on the way are allowed). This pass is also available at EurAide offices in Berlin and Munich. Some trains may offer only 1st or only 2nd class. We recommend matching class of service to your adjoining pass.

EURAIL SELECTPASSES

This pass covers travel in three adjacent "Western European" countries such as Germany, Austria & Hungary. Please visit www.ricksteves.com/rail or see the railpass guide for four- and five-country options.

	1st class Selectpass	1st class Saverpass	2nd class Youthpass
5 days in 2 months	$356	$304	$249
6 days in 2 months	394	336	276
8 days in 2 months	470	400	329
10 days in 2 months	542	460	379

Saverpass: Price is per person for 2 or more adults traveling together at all times.
Youthpasses: Under age 26 only. Kids 4-11 pay half adult fare; under 4: free.

Car Rental

It's cheaper to arrange your car rental in advance in the United States than to wait until you get to Europe. You'll want a weekly rate with unlimited mileage. For three weeks or longer, leasing is cheaper because it saves you money on taxes and insurance. Comparison-shop through your agent. DER, a German company, often has the best rates (tel. 800/782-2424, www.dertravel.com).

Allow about $600 per person (based on 2 people sharing the car) to rent a small economy car for three weeks with unlimited mileage, including gas, parking, and insurance. I normally rent a small, inexpensive model like a Ford Fiesta. For a bigger, roomier, more powerful but inexpensive car, move up to a Ford Escort or Volkswagen Polo. If you drop your car off early or keep it longer, you'll be credited or charged at a fair, prorated price.

For peace of mind, I splurge for the CDW insurance (about $10–15 a day), which covers virtually the full value of the car (minus a small deductible) in case of an accident. A few "gold" credit cards include CDW if you rent the car using that card; quiz your credit-card company on the worst-case scenario. Travel Guard sells CDW insurance for $7 a day (800/826-1300, www.travelguard.com). With the luxury of CDW, you'll enjoy the autobahn knowing you can bring back the car in a shambles and just say, "S-s-s-sorry."

For driving in Eastern Europe, it's wise to get an international driver's license ahead of time at your local AAA office ($10 plus 2 passport-type photos).

Crossing borders with a rental car into, out of, and within Eastern Europe can be tricky. Though these countries are safe to travel in, some popular destinations (like Prague) are notorious for sky-high car-theft rates (especially of rentals). And, since American companies still think of the former Eastern Bloc as a single unit, the car thieves of Prague make it hard to drive a Western rental even into super-safe Slovenia.

Generally speaking, if you rent the car in Eastern Europe, you can cross borders within the East. But you might get hassled if you're going between Eastern and Western Europe. No matter where you're going, state your travel plans up front to the rental company. Some won't allow any of their rental cars to enter Eastern Europe, and some restrict certain types of cars: BMWs, Mercedes, and convertibles. Ask about extra fees—some companies automatically tack on theft and collision coverage for an Eastern European excursion. To avoid hassles at the borders, ask the rental agent to mark your contract with the company's permission to cross. For more on borders, see "Red Tape," above.

Driving

During the communist era, Eastern Europe's infrastructure lagged far behind the West's. Now that the Iron Curtain is long gone, superhighways

Driving: Distance and Time

are going up like crazy all over Eastern Europe. The Czech Republic, Hungary, Slovenia, Croatia, and eastern Germany all have some new freeways, but it's not unusual to find that a still-under-construction freeway ends, requiring a transfer to an older, slower road. Likewise, you'll sometimes discover that a much faster freeway option has been built between major destinations since your three-year-old map was published (a good reason to travel with the most up-to-date maps available and study them before each drive, noting which exits you'll need and which major cities you'll be traveling toward). New superhighways are already underway

between Dresden and Prague (the A17), and from Zagreb to Budapest (to the north) and Zagreb to Split (to the south). As soon as a long-enough section is completed, the roads are opened to the public. Only rarely are backcountry roads the only option (as with part of the trip between Prague and Kraków). These can be bumpy and slow, but they're almost always paved (or, at least, they once were).

Learn the universal road signs (see sidebar). Seat belts are required, and two beers under those belts are enough to land you in jail.

Tolls: Many countries charge drivers who use their roads. If you're driving on highways in the Czech Republic, buy a toll sticker *(dálniční známka)* at the border, a post office, or a gas station (100 kč/10 days, 200 kč/1 month). To drive on Hungary's three autobahns (M1, M3, and M7), you'll need a toll sticker *(autópálya matrica,* 1,900 Ft/10 days, 3,200 Ft/1 month, available at post offices and gas stations). In Slovenia and Croatia, you'll get a ticket as you enter the freeway, then pay when you get off, based on how far you've traveled. In Austria, you'll need a sticker for your rental car *(Vignette)*—€8 for one week or €22 for two months, sold at border crossings, big gas stations near borders, and rental car agencies. (Dipping into the country on regular roads requires no special payment.) No such tolls are charged in Poland or Germany.

Metric: Get used to metric. A liter is about a quart, four to a gallon. A kilometer is six-tenths of a mile. I figure kilometers to miles by cutting them in half and adding back 10 percent of the original (120 km: 60 + 12 = 72 miles, 300 km: 150 + 30 = 180 miles).

Parking: Parking is a costly headache in big cities. You'll pay about $10–15 a day to park safely. Rental-car theft can be a big problem in cities, especially Prague. Ask at your hotel for advice. I keep a pile of coins in my ashtray for parking meters, public phones, launderettes, and wishing wells.

Telephones, Mail, and E-mail

Smart travelers learn the phone system and use it daily to reserve or reconfirm rooms, get tourist information, or phone home. Many European phone booths take cards, but not coins.

Phone Cards: There are two kinds of phone cards: official phone cards that you insert into the phone (which can only be used from phone booths), and cards with scratch-off PIN codes that can be used from virtually any phone (you dial a toll-free number and enter your PIN code). Both kinds of cards can be used for making local and long-distance calls, but work only in the country where you bought them (for example, a Czech phone card is worthless in Poland).

You can buy insertable phone cards from post offices, newsstands, or tobacco shops. Insert the card into the phone, make your call, and the value is deducted from your card. These are a good deal for calling within Europe, but can make calling home to the United States expensive (at least 50 cents per minute).

PIN cards allow you to call home at the rate of about a dime a minute. To use a PIN card, dial the toll-free access number listed on the card; then, at the prompt, enter your Personal Identification Number (also listed on card) and dial the number you want to call. While you can't find these cards everywhere, their availability is growing fast and you should be able to get them in most of Eastern Europe. (Ask at newsstands, exchange bureaus, souvenir shops, and mini-marts; look for shop-window fliers that advertise long-distance rates.) Make sure you get a card that allows you to make international calls (some types permit only local calls). Buy a lower denomination in case the card is a dud.

If you use **coins** to make your calls, have a bunch handy. Avoid using hotel-room phones for anything other than local calls and PIN card calls.

Dialing Direct: You'll save money by dialing direct rather than going through an operator. You just need to learn the codes. For a listing of **international access codes and country codes,** see the appendix. The international access code for all European countries, including Eastern Europe, is 00. European time is six/nine hours ahead of the East/West Coast of the United States.

Generally, when calling long distance within Poland, Slovenia, Croatia, Germany, or Austria, first dial the area code (starting with zero), then dial the local number. For example, Kraków's area code is 012, and the number of one of my recommended Kraków hotels is 431-0010. To call the hotel within Kraków, dial 431-0010. To call it from Warsaw, dial 012/431-0010. When dialing internationally, dial the international access code (of the country you're calling from), the country code (of the country you're calling to), the area code (without the initial zero), and the local number. To call the Kraków hotel from home, dial 011 (the international access code for the U.S. and Canada), 48 (Poland's country code), 12 (Kraków's area code *without* the initial zero), and 431-0010. Note that when you make an international call to any of the countries listed above, you must drop the initial zero of the area code.

Hungary also uses area codes. You follow the above procedure when making international calls to the country (dropping the initial zero of the area code), but things change when calling long-distance within Hungary: You first dial 06, then the area code and number (see page 190 for details).

The Czech Republic has dropped area codes in favor of a direct-dial phone system—so you'll always dial the entire number, whether you're calling across the street or across the country. For example, to call a recommended Czech hotel in Prague, you'd dial the same number (tel. 257-311-150) whether you're calling from the Prague train station or from Český Krumlov. If dialing the Czech hotel from outside the country, start with the international access code (011 from U.S. or Canada;

00 from Europe), the Czech Republic's country code (420), and then the local number (257-311-150).

To call my office from anywhere in Eastern Europe, I dial 00 (Europe's international access code), 1 (U.S. country code), 425 (Edmonds' area code), and 771-8303.

Don't be surprised that in some countries, local phone numbers have different numbers of digits within the same city or even the same hotel (e.g., a hotel can have a 6-digit phone number and an 8-digit fax number).

Mobile Phones: Many travelers now buy cheap mobile phones in Europe to make both local and international calls. (Typical American mobile phones don't work in Europe, and those that do work have horrendous per-minute costs.) For about $75, you can get a phone with $20 worth of calls that will work only in the country where you purchased it. (You can buy more time at newsstands or mobile phone shops.) For about $100, you can get an "unlocked" phone that will work in most countries once you pick up the necessary chip per country (about $20). If you're interested, stop by any European shop that sells mobile phones; you'll see prominent store window displays. Depending on your trip, ask for a phone that works only in that country or one that can be used throughout Europe. If you're on a budget, skip mobile phones and buy phone cards instead.

Calling Card Services: Since direct-dialing rates have dropped, calling cards (offered by AT&T, MCI, and Sprint) are no longer the good value they used to be. In fact, they are a rip-off. You'll likely pay $3 for the first minute with a $4 connection fee; if you get an answering machine, it'll cost you $7 to say, "Sorry I missed you." Simply dialing direct (even from your hotel room) is generally a much better deal.

Mail: Get stamps at the neighborhood post office, newsstands within fancy hotels, and some mini-marts and card shops. To arrange for mail delivery, reserve a few hotels along your route in advance and give their addresses to friends, or use American Express mail services (free to AmEx cardholders and for a minimal fee to anyone else). Allow 10 days for a letter to arrive. Phoning is so easy that I've dispensed with mail stops altogether.

E-mail: You'll find Internet cafés and connection points at nearly every street corner and at many hotels throughout this region. Most hotels have e-mail addresses and Web sites (listed in this book) and prefer online bookings to fax or telephone reservations.

Sleeping

Eastern Europe simply doesn't have the quaint little family-run pensions and B&Bs that I like to list for other destinations. In this book, I've focused my listings on small hotels, and prefer options that are friendly, comfortable, professional-feeling, centrally-located, English-speaking, and family-run. Obviously, a place meeting every criterion is

SLEEP CODE

I've divided the rooms into three categories, based on the price for a standard double room with bath:

$$$ **Higher Priced**
$$ **Moderately Priced**
$ **Lower Priced**

To save space while giving more specific information for people with special concerns, I've described my recommended hotels with a standard code. Prices listed are per room, not per person. When a range of prices is listed for a room, the price fluctuates with room size or season.

S = Single room (or price for 1 person in a double).
D = Double or twin. Double beds are usually big enough for non-romantic couples.
T = Triple (often a double bed with a single bed moved in).
Q = Quad (an extra child's bed is usually cheaper).
b = Private bathroom with toilet and shower or tub.
s = Private shower or tub only (the toilet is down the hall).
No CC = Does not accept credit cards; pay in local cash.
NSE = Does not speak English. Used only when it's unlikely you'll encounter English-speaking staff.

Unless otherwise noted, you can assume that the staff speaks English and the hotel accepts credit cards or cash in payment.

According to this code, a couple staying at a "Db-2,700 kč" hotel in Prague would pay a total of 2,700 Czech crowns (about $100) for a double room with a private bathroom. English is spoken and credit cards are accepted.

rare, and all of my recommendations fall short of perfection—sometimes miserably. But I've listed the best values for each price category, given the above criteria. I've also thrown in a few hostels, private rooms, and other cheap options for budget travelers.

Prices in Eastern Europe are generally low compared to the West—except for beds. You can find some bargains, but when traveling in the sometimes-more-challenging East, it's worth paying a little more for comfort and a central location. (In some places, especially the Dalmatian Coast, good values are virtually nonexistent, so I've listed the best of the worst.) Plan on spending $70 to $120 per hotel double in big cities, and $40 to $70 in smaller towns.

While most hotels listed in this book cluster around $70 to $100 per double, they range from $10 bunks to $200-plus (maximum plumbing and more) per double. The cost is higher in big cities and heavily touristed areas and lower off the beaten track. Three or four people can save money by requesting one big room. Traveling alone can be expensive: A single room is often only 20 percent cheaper than a double.

I usually list hotel prices in the local currency. But some hotels prefer to list prices in euros or, occasionally, even dollars. In these cases, I've listed the prices they gave me. (Usually their rates will be converted to the local currency that day that you check out, so you'll actually be charged in koruna, złoty, forints, or whatever—not that you'll even notice, if you use a credit card.) Unless I note otherwise, the cost of a room includes a decent buffet breakfast.

For environmental reasons, towels are often replaced in hotels only when you leave them on the floor. In cheaper places, they aren't replaced at all, so hang them up to dry and reuse.

If asked whether they have non-smoking rooms, most hotels in Eastern Europe will say yes. When pressed, they'll sheepishly admit, "Well, *all* of our rooms are non-smoking"...meaning they air them out after a smoker has stayed there. I've described hotels as "non-smoking" only if they have specially designated rooms for this purpose. Be specific and assertive if you need a strictly non-smoking room.

Before accepting a room, confirm your understanding of the complete price. The only tip my recommended hotels would like is a friendly, easygoing guest. And, as always, I appreciate feedback on your hotel experiences.

Private Rooms

A cheap option in Eastern Europe (especially in expensive Croatia) is a room in a private home (*sobe* in Slovenia and Croatia; the German word *Zimmer* works there, too, and throughout Eastern Europe). These places are inexpensive, at least as comfortable as a cheap hotel, and a good way to get some local insight. The boss changes the sheets, so people staying several nights are most desirable—and stays of less than three nights are often charged a lot more (up to 30 percent). For more on Croatian *sobe*, see page 360.

Hostels

For $10 to $20 a night, you can stay at a youth hostel. While most hostels admit nonmembers for an extra fee, it's best to join the club and buy a youth hostel card before you go (call Hostelling International at 202/783-6161 or order online at www.hiayh.org). Travelers of any age are welcome as long as they don't mind dorm-style accommodations and lots of traveling friends. Cheap meals are sometimes available, and kitchen facilities are usually provided for do-it-yourself-ers. Expect crowds in the summer, snoring, and lots of youth groups giggling and making rude noises while you try to sleep. Family rooms and doubles are often available on request, but it's basically boys' dorms and girls' dorms. Many hostels are locked up from about 10:00 until 17:00, and a 23:00 curfew is often enforced. Hostelling is ideal for those traveling single: Prices are per bed, not per room, and you'll have an instant circle of friends. More and more hostels are getting their business acts together, taking credit-card reservations over the phone and leaving sign-in forms on the door for each available room. If you're serious about traveling cheaply, get a card, carry your own sheets, and cook in the members' kitchens.

Making Reservations

It's possible to travel at any time of year without reservations (especially if you arrive early in the day), but given the high stakes, erratic accommodations values, and the quality of the places I've found for this book, I'd trade off the flexibility that comes with a loose no-reservations itinerary and book rooms in advance. You can do this by e-mail long in advance from home or by calling a day or two in advance as you travel. (Your receptionist, fluent in the local language, will likely help you call your next hotel if you pay for the call.) Even if a hotel clerk says the hotel is fully booked, you can try calling between 9:00 and 10:00 on the day you plan to arrive. That's when the hotel clerk knows exactly who's checking out and which rooms will be available. I've listed long-distance instructions in hopes that you'll use the phone as a tool this way (see "Telephones," above and in the appendix). Most hotels listed are accustomed to English-only speakers. A hotel receptionist will trust you and hold a room until 16:00 (4:00 p.m.) without a deposit, though some will ask for a credit-card number. Honor (or cancel by phone) your reservations. Long distance is cheap and easy from public phone booths.

If you know exactly which dates you need and really want a particular place, reserve a room well in advance before you leave home. To reserve from home, e-mail, call, or fax the hotel. E-mail is a steal, phone and fax costs are reasonable, and simple English is usually fine. To fax, use the form in the appendix (or find it online at www.ricksteves .com/reservation). A two-night stay in August would be "2 nights, 16/8/04 to 18/8/04" (Europeans write the date in this order—day/month/year—and hotel jargon counts your stay from your day of arrival through your day of departure).

If you e-mail or fax a reservation request and receive a response with rates stating that rooms are available, this is not a confirmation. You must confirm that the rates are fine and that indeed you want the room. You'll often receive a response requesting one night's deposit. A credit-card number and expiration date will usually work. If you use your credit card for the deposit, you can pay with your card or cash when you arrive; if you don't show up, you'll be billed for one night. Ask about the cancellation policy when you reserve; sometimes you may have to cancel as much as two weeks ahead to avoid paying a penalty. Reconfirm your reservations several days in advance for safety.

Eating

You'll find that the local cafés, cuisine, beer, and wine are highlights of your adventure. This is affordable sightseeing for your palate. Eastern Europe offers good food for very little—especially if you venture off the main tourist trail.

Slavic cuisine is heavy, hearty, and tasty. Expect lots of meat, potatoes, and cabbage. Still, there's more variety to be had in the East than you might expect. Tune into the regional and national specialties and customs (see each country's introduction for details).

Ethnic restaurants provide a welcome break from Slavic fare. Seek out a vegetarian, Italian, Chinese, or other ethnic place, especially good in big cities like Budapest or Kraków (I've listed tasty options). Hungarian cuisine enjoys some spicy Turkish influence (think paprika), Slovenia and Croatia are as much Italian as they are Slavic (tasty pasta and pizzas), and Croatia also has excellent seafood.

When restaurant hunting, choose a spot filled with locals, not the place with the big neon signs boasting "We Speak English and Accept Credit Cards." Incredible deals abound in Eastern Europe, where locals can't afford more than $5 for a fine dinner. Venturing even a block or two off the main drag leads to local, higher-quality food for less than half the price of the tourist-oriented places. Most restaurants tack a menu onto their door for browsers and have an English menu inside. Only a rude waiter will rush you. Good service is relaxed (slow to an American).

When you're in the mood for something halfway between a restaurant and a picnic meal, look for take-out food stands, bakeries (with sandwiches and small pizzas to go), delis with stools or a table, department-store cafeterias, salad bars, or simple little eateries for fast and easy sit-down restaurant food.

Beer country is the Czech Republic, with Europe's best and cheapest brew. Poland also has fine beer, but the national drink is *wódka*. Hungary, Slovenia, and Croatia are known for their wines. Each country has its own distinctive liqueur, most of them a variation on *slivovice* (SLEE-voh-veet-seh)—a plum brandy so highly valued that it's the de-facto currency of the Carpathian Mountains (often used for bartering with farmers and other mountain folk). Menus list drink size by the tenth of a liter, or deciliter (dl).

TIPS ON TIPPING

Tipping in Eastern Europe isn't as automatic and generous as it is in the United States—but for special service, tips are appreciated, if not expected. As in the United States, the proper amount depends on your resources, tipping philosophy, and the circumstance, but some general guidelines apply.

Restaurants: Tipping is an issue only at restaurants that have waiters and waitresses. If you order your food at a counter, don't tip. At Eastern European restaurants that have a wait staff, service is generally included, although it's common to round up the bill after a good meal (usually 5–10 percent, e.g., for a 380-kč meal, pay 400 kč). All too often, American travelers, feeling guilty for paying so little for such a fine meal, are tempted to over-tip. But please believe me—it's not necessary. A tip of 10 percent is already overly generous, and 15 percent verges on extravagant.

Taxis: To tip the cabbie, round up about five percent. If the cabbie hauls your bags and zips you to the airport to help you catch your flight, you might want to toss in a little more. But if you feel like you're being driven in circles or otherwise ripped off, skip the tip.

Special services: Tour guides at public sites sometimes hold out their hands for tips after they give their spiels. If I've already paid for the tour, I don't tip extra. I don't tip at hotels, but if you do, give the porter the local equivalent of $0.50 for carrying bags and, at the end of your stay, leave a dollar's worth of local cash for the maid if the room was kept clean. In general, if someone in the service industry does a super job for you, a small tip (the equivalent of a dollar) is appropriate...but not required.

When in doubt, ask. If you're not sure whether (or how much) to tip for a service, ask your hotelier or the TI; they'll fill you in on how it's done on their turf.

Back Door Manners

While researching my guidebooks, I hear over and over again that my readers are considerate and fun to have as guests. Thank you for traveling as temporary locals who are sensitive to the culture. It's fun to follow you in my travels.

Send Me a Postcard, Drop Me a Line

If you enjoy a successful trip with the help of this book and would like to share your discoveries, please fill out and send the survey at the end of this book to Europe Through the Back Door, Box 2009, Edmonds, Washington 98020. I personally read and value all feedback. Thanks in advance—it helps a lot.

For our latest information, visit our Web site: www.ricksteves.com. To check for any updates for this book, look into www.ricksteves.com/update. My e-mail address is rick@ricksteves.com. Anyone can request a free issue of our Back Door quarterly newsletter.

Judging from the happy postcards I receive from travelers, it's safe to assume you'll enjoy a great, affordable vacation—with the finesse of an independent, experienced traveler.

Thanks, and happy travels!

BACK DOOR TRAVEL PHILOSOPHY
by Rick Steves, author of *Europe Through the Back Door*

Travel is intensified living—maximum thrills per minute and one of the last great sources of legal adventure. Travel is freedom. It's recess, and we need it.

Experiencing the real Europe requires catching it by surprise, going casual..."through the Back Door."

Affording travel is a matter of priorities. (Make do with the old car.) You can travel—simply, safely, and comfortably—anywhere in Europe for $80 a day plus transportation costs. In many ways, spending more money only builds a thicker wall between you and what you came to see. Europe is a cultural carnival, and, time after time, you'll find that its best acts are free and the best seats are the cheap ones.

A tight budget forces you to travel close to the ground, meeting and communicating with the people, not relying on service with a purchased smile. Never sacrifice sleep, nutrition, safety, or cleanliness in the name of budget. Simply enjoy the local-style alternatives to expensive hotels and restaurants.

Extroverts have more fun. If your trip is low on magic moments, kick yourself and make things happen. If you don't enjoy a place, maybe you don't know enough about it. Seek the truth. Recognize tourist traps. Give a culture the benefit of your open mind. See things as different but not better or worse. Any culture has much to share.

Of course, travel, like the world, is a series of hills and valleys. Be fanatically positive and militantly optimistic. If something's not to your liking, change your liking. Travel is addictive. It can make you a happier American, as well as a citizen of the world. Our Earth is home to six billion equally important people. It's humbling to travel and find that people don't envy Americans. They like us, but with all due respect, they wouldn't trade passports.

Globe-trotting destroys ethnocentricity. It helps you understand and appreciate different cultures. Travel changes people. It broadens perspectives and teaches new ways to measure quality of life. Many travelers toss aside their hometown blinders. Their prized souvenirs are the strands of different cultures they decide to knit into their own characters. The world is a cultural yarn shop. And Back Door travelers are weaving the ultimate tapestry. Come on, join in!

CZECH REPUBLIC

(Česká Republika)

- The Czech Republic is 30,500 square miles (the size of Maine).
- Population is 10 million (about 330 per square mile).
- 1 Czech koruna (kč) = about 3 cents, and 30 kč = about $1.
- Country code: 420.

Wedged between Germany and Austria, the Czech Republic is one of the most comfortable and easy-to-explore countries of the former Warsaw Pact.

The Czech Republic is made up of two regions, Bohemia and Moravia. Bohemia—which has nothing to do with our understanding of the beatnik bohemian—has long been the home of the Czechs. It's circled by a naturally fortifying ring of mountains and cut down the middle by the Vltava River, with Prague as its capital. The wine-growing region of Moravia (to the east) is more Slavic and more colorful.

Ninety-five percent of the Czech Republic's 10 million people are ethnic Czechs. While nearly half of the people are nominally Catholic, church attendance is very low.

Since 1989, when the Czechs won their independence from Soviet control, more Czechs have been traveling. People are working harder—but the average monthly wage is still only about $400. Facades have gotten face-lifts, roads have been patched up, and shops have been renovated. Supermarkets outnumber pubs. With seven million mobile phones, Czechs lead Europe in more than just beer per capita.

Many Czechs are caught up in the new freedom and prosperity. In fact, you'll notice a scarcity of children. Young adults are marrying later and staying kidless longer. The safe harbor of a family seems less necessary and material priorities are more pressing. Young and upwardly mobile Czechs are more interested in accumulating houses and cars and going on vacations to the West than in trading all that for the expensive task of raising a family.

Yet, even faced with such a bright future, some locals maintain a healthy dose of pessimism and are reluctant to dive headlong into the Western rat race. Things still go a little slower here.

Children, adults, and grandparents delight in telling stories. In Czech fairy tales, there are no dwarfs and monsters. To experience the full absurdity and hilarity of Czech culture, you need a child's imagination and the understanding that the best fun comes from being able to laugh at yourself. Czech writers invented the robot, the pistol, and Black Light Theater (an absurd show of illusion, puppetry, mime, and modern dance).

The most-beloved Czech literary figure is the title character of Jaroslav Hašek's *Good Soldier Švejk*, who frustrates the WWI Austro-Hungarian army he serves in by cleverly playing dumb. Other well-known Czech writers include Václav Havel (playwright who went on to become Czechoslovakia's first post-communist president; authored many essays and plays, including *The Garden Party*); Jan Neruda (whose turn-of-the-20th-century *Prague Tales* inspired the more-famous Chilean poet Pablo Neruda to take his name); Milan Kundera (author of *The Unbearable Lightness of Being*, set during the Prague Spring uprising); Karel Čapek (novelist and playwright who created the robot in the play *R.U.R.*); and Jára Cimrman (playwright, teacher, and inventor considered by some locals to be the greatest Czech). Most famous of all is the existentialist great, Franz Kafka—a Prague Jew who wrote in German about people turning into giant cockroaches *(The Metamorphosis)* and urbanites being pursued and persecuted for crimes they know nothing about *(The Trial)*.

Ninety percent of the tourists who visit the Czech Republic see only Prague. But if you venture outside the capital, you'll enjoy traditional towns and villages, great prices, a friendly and gentle countryside dotted by nettles and wild poppies, but few tourists. Since the time of the Hapsburgs, plum and cherry trees have lined the country roads for everyone to share. Take your pick.

Practicalities

Telephones: Dial 112 for emergencies, 158 for police. If an 0800 number doesn't work, replace the 0800 with 822. The basic Český Telecom card (150 kč, 200 kč, or 300 kč) works well, but remember that PIN cards often have lower per-minute charges (see page 27 for details).

To make phone calls anywhere within the Czech Republic, dial the entire nine-digit number. To call the Czech Republic from another country, first dial the international access code (00 if calling from Europe or 011 from America or Canada), then 420 (the Czech Republic's country code), then the nine-digit number. To call out of the Czech Republic, dial 00, the country code of the country you're calling (see chart in appendix), the area code if the country's phone system uses area codes (note that sometimes the initial zero is dropped depending on the country), and the local number.

Money: ATMs are the best way to get Czech cash. Don't exchange too much; Czech money is tough to change in the West. There is no black market. Assume anyone trying to sell money on the streets is peddling obsolete (or Bulgarian) currency. Buy and sell easily at train stations (5 percent fees), banks, or hotels. Change bureaus advertise no commission and decent but deceptive rates. These rates are for selling dollars. Their rates for buying your dollars are worse. Hidden fees abound; ask exactly how many crowns you'll walk away with before you agree to the transaction.

Lost Credit Cards: American Express tel. 222-800-222, Visa and MasterCard tel. 272-771-111 (also see page 12).

Red Tape: Americans don't need visas to visit the Czech Republic, but Canadians do (see www.czechembassy.org). Anyone planning to bring a rental car into the Czech Republic should check with their car-rental company first (see page 24). To drive on Czech highways, you'll need a toll sticker *(dálniční známka)*, sold at borders, post offices, and gas stations (100 kč/10 days, 200 kč/1 month).

Transportation: If you have a Eurailpass, note that it doesn't cover the Czech Republic; you'll need to buy train tickets or a Prague Excursion pass for your travels to and from Prague (see page 22).

Czech History

The Czechs have always been at a crossroads of Europe—between the Slavic and Germanic worlds, between Catholicism and Protestantism, and between the Cold War East and West. Despite these strong external influences, they have retained their distinct Czech culture...and a dark, ironic sense of humor to keep them laughing through it all.

Middle Ages

Prague's castle put Bohemia on the map in the ninth century. In the 10th century, the region was incorporated into the German Holy Roman

Empire. The 14th century was Prague's golden age, when Holy Roman Emperor Charles IV ruled from here, and Prague was one of Europe's largest and most highly cultured cities. During this period, Prague built St. Vitus Cathedral and the Charles Bridge and established the first university in Central Europe.

Emperor Charles IV

The greatest Czech ruler (14th century) was actually the Holy Roman Emperor, back when Prague was bigger and more important than Vienna. Born to a German nobleman and a Czech princess, he was a dynamic man on the cusp of the Renaissance. He spoke five languages, counted Petrarch as a friend, imported French architects to make Prague a grand capital, founded the first university north of the Alps, and invigorated the Czech national spirit. (He popularized the legend of the good king Wenceslas to give his people a near mythical, King Arthur–type cultural standard-bearer.) Much of Prague's history and architecture (including the famous Charles Bridge) can be traced to this man's rule. Under Charles IV, the Czech people gained esteem among Europeans.

Bucking the Pope and Germany

Jan Hus was a local preacher and professor who got in trouble with the Vatican a hundred years before Martin Luther. Like Luther, he preached in the people's language rather than Latin. To add insult to injury, he complained about Church corruption. Tried for heresy and burned in 1415, Hus became both a religious and a national hero. While each age has defined Hus to its liking, the way he challenged authority while staying true to himself has always inspired and rallied the Czech people.

Religious Wars

The reformist times of Jan Hus (around 1400, when Czechs rebelled against both German and Roman Catholic control) led to a period of religious wars, and ultimately the loss of autonomy under Vienna. Prague stagnated under the Hapsburgs of Austria, with the brief exception of Rudolf II's reign.

Under the late-16th-century rule of the Hapsburg King Rudolf II, Prague emerged again as a cultural and intellectual center. Astronomers Johannes Kepler, Tycho Brahe, and other scientists worked here. Much of Prague's great art can be attributed to this Hapsburg king who lived not in Vienna, but in Prague.

The Thirty Years' War (1618–1648) began in Prague when locals (Czech nobles wanting religious and political autonomy) tossed two

Catholic/Hapsburg officials out the window of the Prague Castle. Often called "the first world war" because it engulfed so many nations, this 30-year conflict was particularly tough on Prague. During this period, its population dropped from 60,000 to 25,000. The result of this war was 300 years of Hapsburg rule. Prague became a backwater of Vienna.

Czech Nationalist Revival

The 19th century was a time of nationalism for people throughout Europe, including the Czechs, as the age of divine kings and ruling families came to a fitful end. The Czech spirit was stirred by the completion of Prague's St. Vitus Cathedral, the symphonies of Anton Dvořák, and the operas of Bedřich Smetana (known as the father of Czech opera) performed in the new National Theater. With the end of World War I, the Hapsburgs were history, and in 1918, the independent country of Czechoslovakia was proclaimed, with Prague as its capital.

Troubled 20th Century

Independence lasted only until 1939, when the Nazis swept in. Prague escaped the bombs of World War II, but went directly from the Nazi frying pan into the communist fire. A local uprising freed the city from the Nazis on May 8, 1945, but the Russians "liberated" them on May 9.

For centuries, the Czechs were mostly rural folks, with German merchants running the cities. Prague's cultural make-up comes from a rich mix of Czech, German, and Jewish people—historically about evenly divided. But after World War II, only 5 percent of the Jewish population remained, and virtually all the Germans were deported.

The communist chapter (1948–1989) was grim. The "Prague Spring" uprising—initiated by a young generation of reform-minded communists in 1968—was crushed. The charismatic leader Alexander Dubček was exiled (and made a forest ranger in the backwoods), and the years following the unsuccessful revolt were particularly disheartening. In the late 1980s, the communists began constructing Prague's huge TV tower (now the city's tallest structure), not only to broadcast Czech TV transmissions, but also to jam Western signals. The Metro, built around the same time, was intended for mass transit—but first and foremost, it was designed to be a giant fallout shelter for protection against capitalist bombs.

But the Soviet empire crumbled. Czechoslovakia regained its freedom in the student- and artist-powered 1989 "Velvet Revolution" (so-called because there were no casualties). In 1993, the Czech and Slovak republics agreed on the "Velvet Divorce" and became two separate countries.

Today, while not without its problems, the Czech Republic is enjoying a growing economy and a strong democracy, and Prague has emerged as one of the most popular tourist destinations in Europe. In 2004, the Czech Republic joins the European Union.

Czech Food

Czech food is heavy on pork and kraut, but more modern bars are serving up pasta and salads. The dark yeast bread is unique. Locals drink muddy Turkish coffee—or espresso, a recent vice.

Czechs live on beer, or *pivo*. The pub is a place to have fun, complain, discuss art and politics, talk hockey, and chat with locals and visitors alike. The *pivo* that was drunk in the country before the Industrial Revolution was much thicker, providing the main source of nourishment for the peasant folk. As a result, even today it doesn't matter whether you are in a *restaurace* (restaurant), a *hostinec* (pub), or a *hospoda* (bar)—a beer will land on your table upon the slightest hint to the waiter, and a new pint will automatically appear when the old glass is almost empty. (You must tell the waiter *not* to bring more.) Each establishment has only one kind of beer on tap; to try a particular brand, look for its sign outside. Men should never order a *malé pivo* (small beer, i.e., half-pint)—it's better to leave a pint unfinished.

After a sip of beer, ask for the *jídelní lístek* (menu). *Polévka* (soup) is the most essential part of a meal. The saying goes: "The soup fills you up, the dish plugs it up." Some of the thick soups for a cold day are *zelná* or *zelňačka* (cabbage), *čočková* (lentil), *fazolová* (bean), and *dršťková* (tripe—delicious if fresh, but at worst, as chewy as gum). The lighter soups are *hovězí* or *slepičí vývar s nudlemi* (beef or chicken broth with noodles), *pórková* (leek), and *květáková* (cauliflower). *Pečivo* (bread) is either delivered with the soup, or you need to ask for it; it is always charged separately depending on how many *rohlíky* (rolls) or slices of *chleba* (yeast bread) you eat.

Main dishes are divided into *hotová jídla* (quick, ready-to-serve standard dishes, in some places available only during lunch hours, 11:30–14:30) and the more specialized *jídla na objednávku* or *minutky* (plates prepared when you order). Even the supposedly quick *hotová jídla* will take longer than what you are used to back home.

A Czech restaurant is a social place where people come to relax. Tables are not private. You can ask to join someone and will most likely make some new friends. Instead of worrying about how much sightseeing you are missing during your two-hour lunch, appreciate the opportunity to learn more about Czech culture.

Hotová jídla (ready-to-serve dishes) come with set garnishes. The standard menu across the country includes *smažený řízek s bramborem* (fried pork fillet with potatoes), *svíčková na smetaně s knedlíkem* (beef tenderloin in cream sauce with dumplings), *vepřová s knedlíkem a se zelím* (pork with dumplings and cabbage), *pečená kachna s knedlíkem a se zelím* (roasted duck with dumplings and cabbage), *maďarský guláš s knedlíkem* (the Czech version of Hungarian goulash), and *pečené kuře s bramborem* (roasted chicken with potatoes). In this landlocked country, fish options are limited to *kapr* (carp) and *pstruh* (trout), prepared in a variety of ways and served with potatoes or fries. Vegetarians can go for the delicious *smažený sýr s bramborem* (fried cheese with potatoes) or default for *čočka s vejci* (lentils with fried egg). If you are spending the night out with friends and beer, feast on the huge *vepřové koleno s hořčicí a křenem* (pork knuckle with mustard and horseradish sauce) with *chleba* (yeast bread).

The range of the *jídla na objednávku* (meals prepared on order) depends on the chef. You choose your garnishes, which are charged separately.

Šopský salát, like a Greek salad, is usually the best salad option (a mix of tomatoes, cucumbers, peppers, onion, and feta cheese with vinegar and olive oil). The waiter will bring it with the main dish, unless you specify that you want it before.

For *moučník* (dessert), there is *palačinka* (crêpes served with fruit or jam), *lívance* (small pancakes with jam and curd), or *zmrzlinový pohár* (ice-cream sundae). Many restaurants will offer different sorts of *koláče* (pastries) and *štrůdl* (apple strudel), but it's much better to get these directly from a bakery.

No Czech meal is complete without a cup of strong *turecká káva* (Turkish coffee—finely ground coffee that only partly dissolves, leaving "mud" on the bottom, drunk without milk). Although espressos and instant coffees have made headway in the past few years, many Czechs regard them as a threat to their culture.

A good alternative to a beer is *minerálka* (mineral water). These healthy waters have a high mineral content and are naturally carbonated because they come from the springs in the many Czech spas (Mattoni, the most common brand, is from Carlsbad). If you want plain water, ask for *voda bez bublinek* (water without bubbles).

You can stay in a pub as long as you want—no one will bring you an *účet* (bill) until you ask for it: *"Pane vrchní, zaplatím!"* ("Mr. Waiter, now I pay!").

Czech Language

Czech, a Slavic language closely related to its neighbors Polish and Slovak, has little resemblance to Western European languages. These days, English is "modern," and you'll find the language barrier minimal. Among older people, German is a common second language.

An acute accent *(á, é, í, ó, ú, ý)* means you linger on that vowel. The letter c always sounds like "ts" (as in "cats"). The little accent *(háček)* above the č, š, or ž makes it sound like "ch," "sh," or "zh" (as in "leisure"), respectively. A *háček* above ň makes it sound like "ny" (as in "canyon"), and over ě makes it sound like "ye." Czech has one sound that occurs in no other language: ř (as in "Dvořák"), which sounds like a cross between a rolled "r" and "zh."

KEY CZECH PHRASES

English	Czech	Pronounced
Hello (formal)	Dobrý den	DOH-bree dehn
Hi / Bye (informal)	Ahoj	AH-hoy
Do you speak English?	Mluvíte anglicky?	MLOO-vee-teh ANG-lits-kee
Yes / No	Ano / Ne	AH-no / neh
Please / You're welcome / Can I help you?	Prosím	PROH-zeem
Thank you	Děkuji	DYACK-quee
I'm sorry / Excuse me	Promiňte	PROH-meen-teh
Good	Dobře	DOHB-zhay
Goodbye	Na shledanou	nah SKLEH-dah-now
one / two	jeden / dva	YAY-dehn / dvah
three / four	tři / čtyři	tree / chuh-TEE-ree
five / six	pět / šest	pyeht / shehst
seven / eight	sedm / osm	SEH-dum / OH-sum
nine / ten	devět / deset	DEHV-yeht / DEH-seht
hundred	sto	stoh
thousand	tisíc	TYEE-seets
How much?	Kolik?	KOH-leek
local currency	koruna (kč)	koh-ROO-nah
Where is...?	Kde je...?	gday yeh
...the toilet	...vécé	vayt-SAY
men	muži	MOO-zhee
women	ženy	ZHAY-nee
water / coffee	voda / káva	VOH-dah / KAH-vah
beer / wine	pivo / víno	PEE-voh / VEE-noh
Cheers!	Na zdraví!	nah zdrah-VEE
the bill	účet	OO-cheht

PRAGUE

(Praha)

It's amazing what 15 years of freedom can do. Prague has always been historic. Now it's fun, too. No place in Europe has become so popular so quickly. And for good reason: Prague—the only Eastern European capital to escape the bombs of the last century's wars—is one of Europe's best-preserved cities. It's filled with sumptuous Art Nouveau facades, offers tons of cheap Mozart and Vivaldi, and brews the best beer in Europe. But even beyond its architecture and traditional culture, it's an explosion of pent-up entrepreneurial energy jumping for joy after 40 years of communist rule. Its low prices can cause you to jump for joy, too. Travel in Prague is like travel in Western Europe—15 years ago and for half the price.

Planning Your Time

Two days (with 3 nights, or 2 nights and a night train) make the long train ride in and out worthwhile, and you'll have time to get beyond the sightseeing and enjoy Prague's fun-loving ambience. Many wish they'd scheduled three days for Prague. From Munich, Berlin, and Vienna, it's about a six-hour train ride (you can also take a longer night train from Munich). From Budapest, Warsaw, or Kraków, it's a handy night-train.

　　With two days in Prague, I'd spend a morning seeing the castle and a morning in the Jewish Quarter—the only two chunks of sightseeing that demand any brainpower. Spend your afternoons loitering around the Old Town, Charles Bridge, and the Little Quarter and your nights split between beer halls and live music. Keep in mind that Jewish sites close on Saturday.

　　For a summary of quick day trips, see the end of this chapter. Český Krumlov (covered in the next chapter), 2.5 hours from Prague by train or bus and the perfect big-city antidote, could be a day trip, but I'd spend the night there (consider visiting Český Krumlov on your way to or from Prague).

Prague

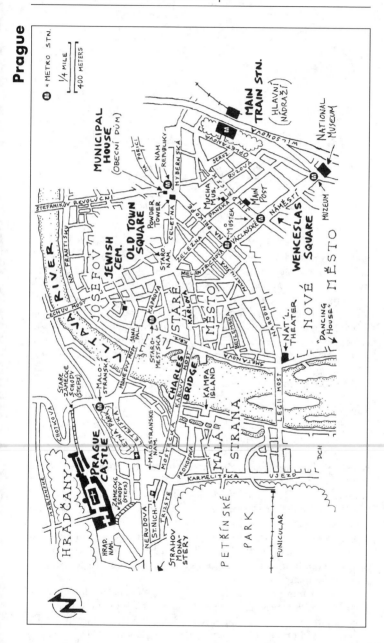

ORIENTATION

Locals call their town "Praha." It's big, with 1.2 million people, but focus on its small old center during a quick visit. As you wander, take advantage of brown street signs directing you to tourist landmarks.

The Vltava River divides the west side (castle and Little Quarter) from the east side (train station, Old Town, New Town, and most of the recommended hotels). Prague addresses come with references to a general zone. Praha 1 is in the old center on either side of the river. Praha 2 is in the new city southeast of Wenceslas Square. Praha 3 and higher indicate a location farther from the center.

Tourist Information

TIs are at four key locations: **main train station** (roughly Easter–Oct Mon–Fri 9:00–19:00, Sat–Sun 9:00–16:00, but often closed; Nov–Easter Mon–Fri 9:00–18:00, Sat 9:00–15:00, closed Sun), **Old Town Square** (Easter–Oct Mon–Fri 9:00–19:00, Sat–Sun 9:00–18:00; Nov–Easter Mon–Fri 9:00–18:00, Sat–Sun 9:00–17:00, tel. 224-482-018), **below Wenceslas Square** at Na Příkopě 20 (Easter–Oct Mon–Fri 9:00–19:00, Sat–Sun 9:00–17:00; Nov–Easter Mon–Fri 9:00–18:00, Sat 9:00–15:00, closed Sun, tel. 224-226-087), and the castle side of

PRAGUE LANDMARKS

English	Czech	Pronounced
Main Train Station	Hlavní Nádraží	HLAV-nee NAH-drah-zhee
Old Town	Staré Město	STAH-reh MYEHS-toh
Old Town Square	Staroměstské Náměstí	star-roh- MYEHST-skeh NAH-myehs-tee
New Town	Nové Město	NOH-vay MYEHS-toh
Little Quarter	Malá Strana	MAH-lah STRAH-nah
Jewish Quarter	Josefov	yoo-ZEHF-fohf
Castle Area	Hradčany	HRAD-chah-nee
Charles Bridge	Karlův Most	KAR-loov most
Wenceslas Square	Václavské Náměstí	vaht-SLAHF-skeh NAH-myehs-tee
The River	Vltava	vul-TAH-vah

Charles Bridge (Easter–Oct daily 10:00–18:00, closed Nov–Easter). For general tourist information in English, dial 12444 (Mon–Fri 8:00–19:00).

The TIs offer maps, phone cards, information on guided walks and bus tours, and bookings for concerts, hotel rooms, and rooms in private homes. There are several monthly events guides—all of them packed with ads—including *Prague Guide* (29 kč), *Prague This Month* (free), and *Heart of Europe* (free, summer only).

The English-language *Prague Post* newspaper is handy for entertainment listings and current events (sold cheap at newsstands).

Helpful Hints

Rip-offs: Prague's new freedom comes with new scams. There's no particular risk of violent crime—but green, rich tourists do get taken by con artists. Simply be on guard, particularly at these times: traveling on trains (thieves thrive on overnight trains), changing money (tellers with bad arithmetic and inexplicable pauses while counting back your change), dealing with taxis (see "Getting around Prague," page 52), paying in restaurants (see "Eating," page 87), and in seedy neighborhoods (see below).

Anytime you pay for something, make a careful note of how much it costs, how much you're handing over, and how much you expect back. Count your change. Someone selling you a phone card marked 190 kč might first tell you it's 790 kč, hoping to pocket the difference. Call the bluff and they'll pretend it never happened.

Plainclothes policemen "looking for counterfeit money" are con artists. Don't show them any cash or your wallet. If you're threatened with an inexplicable fine by a "policeman," conductor, or other official, you can walk away, scare him away by saying you'll need a receipt (which real officials are legally required to provide), or ask a passerby if the fine is legit.

Pickpockets can be little children, or adults dressed as professionals or even as tourists. They target Western tourists. Many thieves drape jackets over their arms to disguise busy fingers. Thieves work the crowded and touristy places (like train stations) in teams. They use mobile phones to coordinate their bumps and grinds. Be careful if anyone creates a commotion at the door of a Metro or tram car (especially the made-for-tourists trams #22 and #23)—it's a smokescreen for theft. Car theft is also a big problem in Prague (many Western European car-rental companies don't allow their rentals to cross the Czech border). Never leave anything valuable in your car—not even in broad daylight on a busy street.

The sex clubs on Skořepka Steet, just south of Havelská Market, routinely rip off naive tourists and can be dangerous.

They're filled mostly with Russian girls and German and Asian guys. Lately this district is the rage for British stag parties (happy to take cheap off-season flights to get to cheap beer and cheap girls). Be warned: Even on the street, aggressive girls can be all over gawkers.

Internet Access: Internet cafés—which beg for business all along Karlova Street on the city side of the Charles Bridge—are commonplace. Consider Bohemia Bagel (see "Eating," page 90).

Laundry: A full-service laundry nearest most of the recommended hotels is at Karolíny Světlé 10 (200 kč/8-pound load, wash and dry in 2 hrs, Mon–Fri 7:30–19:00, closed Sat–Sun, 200 yards from Charles Bridge on Old Town side).

American Express: It's at Václavské Náměstí 56, Praha 1 (foreign exchange daily 9:00–19:00, travel service Mon–Fri 9:00–18:00, Sat 9:00–12:00, closed Sun, tel. 222-211-136). AmEx also has offices on Celetná Street in the Old Town and on the Old Town Square.

Medical Help: For English-speaking help, contact the American Medical Center (open 24 hrs, Janovského 48, Praha 7, tel. 220-807-756). A Canadian medical care center is at Veleslavínská 30 in Praha 6 (tel. 235-360-133). A 24-hour pharmacy is at Palackého 5 (Praha 1, tel. 224-946-982).

Local Help: Athos Travel books rooms (see "Sleeping," page 81), rents cars, has guides for hire (1–5 people-700 kč/hr, see "Tours of Prague," below), and provides stress-free taxi transfers between your hotel and the airport (1–4 people-550 kč) or either train station (1–4 people-400 kč, tel. 241-440-571, fax 241-441-697). Readers of this book get a discount for booking online (2 percent discount on rooms or car rental, 10 percent discount on local guide or airport and train station transfers); to get the discount, log on to Athos Club at www.athos.cz with username: rick, password: steves.

Magic Praha is a tiny travel service run by hardworking, English-speaking Lida Šteflová. A charming Jill-of-all-trades who takes her clients' needs seriously, she's particularly helpful with accommodations, private tours, side trips to historic towns, and airport or train station transfers anywhere in the Czech Republic (Národní 17, Praha 1, 5th floor, tel. & fax 224-230-914, tel. 224-232-755, mobile 604-207-225, magicpraha@magicpraha.cz).

Best Views: Enjoy "the golden city of a hundred spires" during the early evening, when the light is warm and the colors are rich. Good viewpoints include the terrace at the Strahov Monastery (above the castle), the top of St. Vitus Cathedral (at the castle), the top of either tower on Charles Bridge, the Old Town Square clock tower (elevator), Restaurant u Prince terrace (see "Eating," page 87), and the steps of the National Museum overlooking Wenceslas Square.

PRAGUE'S FOUR TOWNS

Until about 1800, the city was actually four distinct towns with four town squares separated by fortified walls.

Castle Quarter (Hradčany): Built regally on the hill, this was the home of the cathedral, monastery, castle, royal palace, and high nobility. Even today, you feel like clip-clopping through it in a fancy carriage. It has the high art and grand buildings, yet feels a bit sterile.

Little Quarter (Malá Strana): This Baroque town of fine homes and gardens was built by the aristocracy and merchant elite at the foot of the castle. The quarter burned in the 1500s and was rebuilt with the mansions of the generally domesticated European nobility who moved in to be near the king. The tradition remains, as the successors of this power-brokering class—today's Parliament—now call this home.

Old Town (Staré Město): Charles Bridge connects the Little Quarter with the Old Town. A boom town in the 14th century, this has long been the busy commercial quarter filled with merchants, guilds, and natural supporters of Jan Hus (folks who wanted a Czech stamp on their religion). Trace the walls of this town in the modern road plan (with the Powder Tower being a remnant of a wall system that completed a fortified ring, half provided by the river). The marshy area closest to the bend—least inhabitable and therefore allotted to the Jewish community—became the ghetto.

New Town (Nové Město): Nové Město rings the Old Town, cutting a swath from riverbank to riverbank, and is fortified with Prague's outer wall. In the 14th century, the king initiated the creation of this town, tripling the size of what would become Prague. Wenceslas Square was once the horse market of this busy working-class district. When you cross the moat (Na Příkopě) that separates the Old and New Towns, you leave the tourists behind and enter the real everyday town.

Arrival in Prague

Prague unnerves many travelers—it's behind the former Iron Curtain, and you've heard stories of rip-offs and sky-high hotel prices. But in reality, Prague is charming, safe, and ready to show you a good time. The language barrier is tiny. It seems every well-educated young person speaks English.

Upon arrival, be sure to buy a city map, with trams and Metro lines marked and tiny sketches of the sights for ease in navigating (30–70 kč, many different brands, sold at kiosks, exchange windows, or tobacco stands). It's a mistake to try doing Prague without a good map—you'll refer to it constantly.

By Train: Most travelers coming from and going to bigger, international destinations use the main station (Hlavní Nádraží) or the secondary station (Nádraží Holešovice). Trains from smaller points within the country use the Masarykovo or Smíchov stations. Trains to/from Český Krumlov usually use Prague's main station, sometimes the Smíchov station. (For information on getting to Prague, see "Transportation Connections," page 93.)

Upon arrival, change money. The stations have ATMs (at the main station, a cash machine is near the subway entrance). Exchange bureau rates vary—compare by asking at two windows what you'll get for $100 (but keep in mind that rates are generally bad and many of the windows are run by the same company). Count carefully. Then buy your map, confirm your departure plans at the train-information window, and consider arranging a room or tour at the TI or AVE travel agency (AVE has branches in both stations). The left-luggage counter is reportedly safer than the lockers.

At Prague's train stations, anyone arriving on an international train will be met at the tracks by room hustlers, trying to snare tourists for cheap rooms.

At Prague's main station, **Hlavní Nádraží,** the low-ceilinged hall contains a fascinating mix of travelers, kiosks, gamblers, loitering teenagers, and older riffraff. The creepy station ambience is the work of communist architects, who expanded a classy building to make it just big, painting it the compulsory dreary gray with reddish trim. If you're killing time here (or for a wistful glimpse of a more genteel age), go upstairs into the Art Nouveau hall. The station was originally named for Emperor Franz Josef. Later it was named for President Woodrow Wilson, because his promotion of self-determination led to the creation of the free state of Czechoslovakia in 1918. Under the communists (who weren't big fans of Wilson), it was called simply the Main Station. Here, under an elegant dome, you can sip coffee, enjoy music from the 1920s, watch boy prostitutes looking for work, and see new arrivals spilling into the city.

From the main station, it's a 10-minute walk to Wenceslas Square (turn left out of the station and follow Washingtonova to the huge Národní Museum and you're there). You could instead catch tram #9 or, at night, tram #55 or #58; to find the stop, walk into the park in front of the station (nicknamed Sherwood Forest, filled with thieves and homeless people at night), take a right and walk two minutes. Or take the Metro (inside station, look for the red M with 2 directions: Háje or Florenc; catch a train to Muzeum, then transfer to the green line—

direction Dejvická—and get off at either Můstek or Staroměstská; these stops straddle the Old Town).

The train station cabbies are a gang of no-neck mafia thugs who will wait all day to charge an arriving tourist five times the regular rate. To get an honest cabbie, I'd walk a few blocks (or ride the Metro one stop) and hail one off the street. A taxi should get you to your hotel for no more than 150 kč (see "Getting around Prague," below); to avoid the train station taxi stand, call AAA Taxi (tel. 233-113-311) or arrange your transfer in advance through Athos Travel (see page 49).

The **Nádraží Holešovice** station is suburban mellow. The main hall has all the services of the main station in a compact area. Outside the first glass doors, the ATM is on the left, the Metro is straight ahead (follow *Vstup*, which means "entrance," take it 3 stops to the main station, 4 stops to the city center Muzeum stop), and taxis and trams are outside to the right (allow 200 kč for a cab to the center).

By Plane: Prague's new, tidy, low-key **Ruzyně Airport**—a delightful contrast to the old, hulking main train station—is 12 miles (about 30 min) west of the city center. The airport has ATM machines (avoid the change desks); desks promoting their transportation service (such as shuttle buses); kiosks selling city maps and phone cards; and a tourist service that has little printed material available. Airport info: tel. 220-113-314, operator tel. 220-111-111.

Getting to and from the airport is easy. You have several options:

• Dirt-cheap: Catch the bus from the terminal to Metro station Zličín, then take the Metro underground to the center (12 kč, info desk in airport arrival hall).

• Cheap: Take the Cedaz minibus shuttle to Náměstí Republiky—a.k.a. Republic Square—across from Kotva Department store (2/hr, pay 90 kč directly to driver, info desk in arrival hall).

• Moderate: Take a Cedaz minibus directly to your hotel with a couple of stops likely en route (360 kč for a group of up to 4, tel. 220-114-296).

• Expensive: Catch a taxi. Cabbies wait at the curb directly in front of the arrival hall. Carefully confirm the complete price before getting in. It's a fixed rate of 600–700 kč with no meter. You can also arrange a pick-up through your hotel or with a private car service (such as Athos Travel; see page 49).

Getting around Prague

You can walk nearly everywhere. But the Metro is slick, the trams fun, and the taxis quick and easy once you're initiated. For details, pick up the handy transit guide at the TI.

Public Transportation: Affordable and excellent public transit is perhaps the best legacy of the communist era (locals ride all month for about $10, or 275 kč). The trams and Metro work on the same cheap tickets. Buy from machines (select ticket price, then insert coins), at

Prague Metro

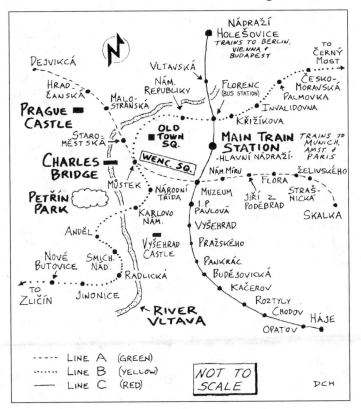

kiosks, or at hotels. For convenience, buy all the tickets you think you'll need: 15-minute ticket with no transfer—8 kč, 60-minute ticket with unlimited transfers—12 kč, 24-hour ticket—70 kč, three-day pass—200 kč. Estimate conservatively. Remember, Prague is a great walking town, so unless you're commuting from a hotel far outside the center, you will likely find that individual tickets work best. The 8-kč tickets are not good on night trams or night buses. The Metro closes at midnight, but some trams keep running all night (identified with white numbers on blue backgrounds at tram stops). Metro tips: Navigate by signs listing end stations, and when you come to your stop, push the yellow button if the doors don't automatically open.

City maps show the tram, bus, and Metro lines. The three-line Metro system is handy and simple. Although it seems that all Metro doors lead to the neighborhood of Výstup, that's simply the Czech word for "exit." Trams are also easy to use; track your route with your city map. They run every five to 10 minutes in the daytime (a schedule is posted at each stop). Be sure to validate your ticket on the tram, bus, or Metro by sticking it in the machine (which stamps a time on it). There's a complete route planner in English at www.dp-praha.cz/en/index.htm. Police routinely ambush ticketless riders (including tourists) and fine them 400 kč on the spot.

Taxis: Prague's taxis—notorious for hyperactive meters—are being tamed. Still, many cabbies are crooks who consider one sucker a good day's work. While most hotel receptionists and guidebooks advise avoiding taxis, I find Prague is a great taxi town and use them routinely. With the local rate, they're cheap (read the rates on the door: drop charge—30 kč; per-kilometer charge—22 kč; and wait-time per-min charge—5 kč). The key is to be sure the cabbie turns on the meter at the #1 tariff (look for the word *sazba,* meaning tariff, on the meter). Avoid cabs waiting at tourist attractions and train stations. Cabs labeled "AAA Taxi" and "City Taxi" are generally honest. I hail a passing taxi.

If a cabbie surprises you at the end with an astronomical fare, simply pay 200 kč, which should cover you for a long ride anywhere in

PRAGUE AT A GLANCE

▲▲▲**Old Town Square** Colorful, magical main square of Old World Prague, with fanciful, medieval clock tower (listed below). **Hours:** Always open.

▲▲▲**Jewish Quarter** The best Jewish sight in Europe, featuring various synagogues and an evocative cemetery. **Hours:** Sun–Fri 9:00–18:00, closed Sat.

▲▲▲**Charles Bridge** Atmospheric statue-lined bridge connecting the Old Town to the castle. **Hours:** Always open.

▲▲**Prague Castle** Traditional seat of Czech rulers, with St. Vitus Cathedral (see below), Old Royal Palace, Basilica of St. George, shop-lined Golden Lane, and fun toy museum. **Hours:** April–Oct daily 9:00–17:00, Nov–March 9:00–16:00. Castle grounds: Daily 6:00–24:00.

▲▲**Mucha Museum** Likeable collection of Art Nouveau works by Czech artist Alfons Mucha. **Hours:** Daily 10:00–18:00.

▲▲**Wenceslas Square** Lively boulevard at the heart of modern Prague. **Hours:** Always open.

the center. Then go into your hotel. On the miniscule chance he follows you, the receptionist will take your side.

You're likely to get a fair meter rate—which starts only when you take off—if you have a cab called from a hotel or restaurant (try AAA Taxi, tel. 233-113-311, or City Taxi, tel. 257-257-257; they're the most likely to have an English-speaking staff).

TOURS

Prague and Beyond
Walking Tours—Prague Walks offers walking tours of the Old Town, the castle, the Jewish Quarter, and more (all 300 kč, 90 min-3 hrs, tel. 261-214-603, www.praguewalks.com, pwalks@comp.cz). Consider their clever Good Morning Walk that starts at 8:00 (April–Aug only), before the crowds hit. Several other companies give good guided walks. For the latest, pick up the walking tour fliers at the TI.
Private Guides—Hiring your own personal guide can be a great value in Prague, especially if you're traveling in a group. Guides meet you where you like and tailor the tour to your interests.

▲**Old Town Hall Astronomical Clock** Intricate landmark clock attracting throngs of gawking tourists. **Hours:** Always open.

▲**St. Vitus Cathedral** The Czech Republic's most important church, featuring a climbable tower and a striking stained-glass window by Art Nouveau artist Alfons Mucha. **Hours:** April–Oct daily except Sunday morning, 9:00–17:00.

▲**Strahov Monastery and Library** Baroque center of learning with ornate reading rooms and old-fashioned science exhibits. **Hours:** Daily 9:00–12:00 & 13:00–17:00.

▲**Havelská Market** Bustling open-air market, perfect for gathering a picnic. **Hours:** Daily 9:00–18:00.

▲**Toy and Barbie Museum** Teddy bears through the centuries, plus a whole floor of Barbies. **Hours:** Daily 9:30–17:30.

▲**Museum of Communism** The rise and fall of the regime from start to Velvet finish. **Hours:** Daily 9:00–21:00.

Sara Pelantova, a wonderful young philosophy grad from a nearby town, runs "Cordial Guide Service," which is basically her showing visitors around Prague (and nearby locations). She expertly gets beyond the dates and famous buildings to provide insight into her culture and is eager to build a walk around your interests (€13/hr, mobile 777-225-205, www.prague-guide.info, saraguide@volny.cz).

Kateřina Svobodová—a licensed guide who knows her stuff and speaks excellent English—is a hardworking young woman who shows individuals and small groups around (400 kč per hour or about €13/hour, minimum 3 hrs, tel. 224-818-267, mobile 603-181-300, www.praguewalker.com, katerina@praguewalker.com).

Athos Travel's licensed guides can lead you on a general sightseeing tour or fit the walk to your interests: music, Art Nouveau, Jewish life, architecture, Franz Kafka, and more (1–5 people-700 kč/hr, more than 5 people-800 kč/hr, arrange tour at least 24 hrs in advance, tel. 241-440-571, info@athos.cz).

To get beyond Prague, call Thomas Zahn, who runs Pathways Guided Travel. Thomas, an American who married into the Czech Republic, organizes and leads creative, affordable (mostly 1-day and 2-day) excursions from Prague. Hiking, biking, horseback riding, or canoeing, you'll explore the unknown charms of the region with a small group and a committed guide. Explore Thomas' Web site for ways to connect with the rural Czech countryside and experience more than Prague on your visit (tel. 257-940-113, mobile 603-758-983, www.pathfinders.cz).

The TI also has plenty of private guides (for 3 hours: 1 person-1,200 kč, 2 people-1,400 kč, 3 people-1,600 kč, 4 people-2,000 kč, desk at Old Town Square TI, arrange and pay in person at least 2 hrs in advance, tel. 224-482-562, guides@pis.cz). For a listing of private guides, see www.guide-prague.cz.

Tram Joyride—Trams #22 and #23 (following the same route) both make a fine joyride through town. Consider it a scenic lead-up to touring the castle. Catch it at Metro stop Náměstí Míru; roll through a bit of New Town, the Old Town, and across the river, and hop out just above the castle (at Hotel Savoy, stop: Pohořelec); then hike down the hill into the castle area.

Bus Tours—Cheap big-bus orientation tours provide an efficient once-over-lightly look at Prague and a convenient way to see the castle. But in a city as walkable as Prague, bus tours should be used only in case of rain, laziness, or both. Several companies have kiosks on Na Příkopě. Premiant City Tours offers 20 different tours, including several overview tours of the city (1 hr-250 kč, 2 hrs-380 kč, 3.5 hrs-750 kč), the Jewish Quarter (700 kč, 2 hrs), Prague by night, Bohemian glass, Terezín Concentration Camp memorial, Karlštejn Castle, Český Krumlov (1,750 kč, 10 hrs), and a river cruise. The tours feature live guides and depart from near the bottom of Wenceslas Square at Na Příkopě 23. Get tickets at an AVE travel agency, hotel, on the bus, or at Na Příkopě 23 (tel. 224-946-922, mobile 606-600-123, www.premiant.cz). Tour salespeople are notorious for telling you anything to sell a ticket. Some tours, especially those heading into the countryside, can be in as many as four different languages. Hiring a private guide can be a much better value.

SIGHTS

The King's Walk (Královská cesta)

The King's Walk, the ancient way of coronation processions, is touristy but great. Follow this self-guided walk—pedestrian-friendly and full of playful diversions—to connect nearly all of the essential Prague sites (except the Jewish Quarter).

The king would be crowned in St. Vitus Cathedral in the Prague Castle, walk through the Little Quarter to the Church of St. Nicholas, cross Charles Bridge, and finish at the Old Town Square. If he hurried, he'd be done in 20 minutes. Like the main drag in Venice between St. Mark's and the Rialto Bridge, this walk mesmerizes tourists. Use it as a spine, but venture off it.

While you could cover this route in the same direction as the king, he's long gone and it's a new morning in Prague. Here are Prague's essential sights in walking order, starting at Wenceslas Square, where modern independence was proclaimed, proceeding through the Old Town and across the bridge, and finishing at the castle.

▲▲Wenceslas Square (Václavské Náměstí)—More a broad boulevard than a square (until recently, trams rattled up and down its park-like median strip), this significant spot is named for the equestrian statue of King Wenceslas that stands at the top of the boulevard. The area originated as a horse market by order of Charles IV. (Being a smart guy, he had it stretch east-west, taking advantage of the prevailing breeze to blow away the odor of horse dung.)

The square functions as a stage for modern Czech history: The Czechoslovak state was proclaimed here in 1918; in 1968, the Soviets put down huge popular demonstrations here; and in 1989, more than 300,000 converged here to claim their freedom. Starting at the top (Metro: Muzeum), stroll down the square:

The **National Museum** (Národní Muzeum) stands grandly at the top. While the museum is dull, it enjoys a powerful view, and the interior is richly decorated in the Czech Revival neo-Renaissance style that heralded the 19th-century rebirth of Czech nationalism (80 kč, May–Sept daily 10:00–18:00, winter daily 9:00–17:00, halls of Czech fossils and animals). A major renovation of the entire building is in the works.

The nearby Metro stop (Muzeum) is the crossing point of two Metro lines. From here, you could roll a ball straight down the boulevard through the heart of Prague to Charles Bridge.

Central Prague

1 TI, Old Town Hall
& Astronomical Clock

2 Hus Memorial

3 Church of St. Nicholas

4 Lucerna Gallery

5 Havelská Market

6 "Czech Sex" District

7 To Lennon Wall

8 Black Light Theater

9 Concert Box Office

10 City Bus Tours
(at #23)

Stand behind the statue facing the museum (uphill). The light-colored patches in the columns show where Russian bullets hit during the crackdown in 1968. Lowly masons—defying their communist bosses who wanted the damage to be forgotten—showed their Czech spirit by intentionally mismatching their patches.

Look left (about 10:00 on an imaginary clock) at the ugly communist-era building—it housed the rubber-stamp Parliament back when they voted with Moscow. A Social Realist statue showing workers triumphing still stands at its base. It's now home to Radio Free Europe. After communism fell, RFE lost its funding and could no longer afford its Munich headquarters. As gratitude for its broadcasts, which kept its people in touch with real news, the current Czech government now rents the building to RFE for one crown a year. (As RFE energetically beams its American message deep into Islam from here, it has been threatened recently by Al-Qaeda, and a move is underway to relocate it to an easier-to-defend locale.)

The grand square is a gallery of modern architectural styles. As you wander downhill, notice the fun mix, all post-1850: Romantic neo-Gothic, neo-Renaissance, neo-Baroque from the 19th century, Art Nouveau from 1900, ugly functionalism from the mid-20th century (the "form follows function" and "ornamentation is a crime" answer to Art Nouveau), Stalin Gothic from the 1950s "communist epoch" (a good example is the Jalta building—halfway downhill on the right), and glass-and-steel buildings of the 1970s.

St. Wenceslas (Václav), commemorated by the statue, is the "good king" of Christmas-carol fame. He was never really a king, but the wise and benevolent 10th-century duke of Bohemia. A rare example of a

well-educated and literate ruler, he was credited by his people for Christianizing his nation and lifting up the culture. Wenceslas astutely allied the Czechs with Saxony rather than Bavaria, giving the Czechs a vote when the Holy Roman Emperor was selected (and therefore more political clout). After being murdered in 929, Wenceslas became a symbol of Czech nationalism and statehood. Study the statue. Wenceslas—always sporting the Czech flag—is surrounded by the four other Czech patron saints. Notice the focus on books. A small nation without great military power, the Czech Republic chose national heroes who enriched the culture by thinking, rather than fighting. This statue is a popular meeting point. Locals say, "I'll see you under the horse's tail."

Thirty yards below the big horse is a small garden with a low-key **memorial** "to the victims of communism"—such as Jan Palach. In 1969, a group of patriots decided that an act of self-immolation would stoke the fires of independence. Jan Palach, a philosophy student who loved life but wanted it with freedom, set himself on fire for the cause of Czech independence and died a few yards from this memorial (on the steps of the National Museum). Czechs are keen on anniversaries. Huge demonstrations swept the city on the 20th anniversary of Palach's death. These led, 10 months later, to the overthrow of the Czech communist government.

Walk a couple blocks downhill through the real people of Prague (not tourists) to **Grand Hotel Europa,** with its hard-to-miss, dazzling, Art Nouveau exterior and plush café interior.

In November 1989, this huge square was filled with more than 300,000 ecstatic Czechs believing freedom was at hand. Assembled on the balcony of the Melantrich building (opposite Grand Hotel Europa; look for *KNIHY BOOKS* sign) was a priest, a rock star (famous for his kick-ass-for-freedom lyrics), Alexander Dubček (hero of the 1968 revolt), and Václav Havel (the charismatic playwright, newly released from prison, and every freedom-loving Czech's Mandela). Through a sound system provided by the rock star, Havel's voice boomed over the gathered masses, announcing the resignation of the Czech politburo and saying the Republic of Czechoslovakia's freedom was imminent. Picture the cold November evening with thousands of Czechs jingling their key chains for solidarity, chanting at the government, "It's time to go now!" (To quell this revolt, government tanks could have given it the Tiananmen Square treatment—which spilled lots of patriotic blood in China just six months earlier. Locals believe Gorbachev must have made a phone call recommending that blood not be shed over this.)

Havel ended his second (and, constitutionally, last) five-year term early in 2003. While he's still admired by Czechs, his popularity took a hit when he got married for the second time—to an actress 17 years his junior. Some say his brain dropped about three feet.

Immediately opposite Grand Hotel Europa is the **Lucerna Gallery** (use entry marked Divadlo Rokoko and walk straight in). This is a classic mall from the 1920s and 1930s with shops, theaters, a ballroom in the basement, and the fine Lucerna café upstairs. You'll see a sculpture—called *Wenceslas Riding an Upsidedown Horse*—hanging like a swing from a glass dome. Created in 1992, three years after freedom, it captured the topsy-turvy first days of free enterprise, and the scandal-ridden transition to privatization in a land with a weak legal system. Interestingly, the place was built and is owned by the Havel family. Inside you'll find a Ticketpro box office (with all available tickets, daily 9:30–18:00) and the popular Lucerna Music Bar in the basement (nightly disco themes from the '70s, '80s, and '90s, 100 kč, Tue–Sat from 21:00—see "Entertainment," page 79).

If you're in the mood for a mellow hippie teahouse, consider a break at Dobrá Čajovna (the Good Tea House) near the bottom of the square (#14, see "Eating," page 87). Or, if you'd like an old-time wine bar, pop into the plain **Senk Vrbovec** (nearby at #10); it comes with a whiff of the communist days, embracing the faintest bits of genteel culture in that age when refinement was sacrificed for the good of the working class. They serve traditional drinks, Czech keg wine, Moravian wines (listed on blackboard outside), *becherovka* (the 13-herb liqueur), and—only in autumn—*burčak* (grape juice halfway to wine).

The bottom of Wenceslas Square is called Můstek, which means bridge; a bridge used to cross a moat here, allowing entrance into the Old Town. Continuing straight, crossing that imaginary old bridge and moat, you enter the charm of Prague's Old Town. (Or, if you turn right at the bridge, you can stroll along the former moat on Na Příkopě, now a spacious pedestrian mall lined with stylish shops; for more on Na Příkopě and the nearby Municipal House, see "More Old Town Sights," below.)

Heading straight from Můstek toward the Old Town Square, you'll find the...

▲Havelská Market—Central Prague's best open-air flower and produce market scene (daily 9:00–18:00) is a couple blocks toward the Old Town Square from the bottom of Wenceslas Square. Laid out in the 13th century for the German trading community, it still keeps hungry locals and vagabonds fed cheaply. Since only those who produce their goods personally are allowed to have a stall, you'll be dealing with the actual farmer or craftsperson. This is ideal for a healthy snack; merchants are happy to sell single pieces of fruit or vegetables, and you'll find a washing fountain and plenty of inviting benches midway down the street.

▲▲▲Old Town Square (Staroměstské Náměstí)—The focal point for most visits, this has been a market square since the 11th century. It became the nucleus of a town (Staré Město) in the 13th century when its Town Hall was built. Today, the old-time market stalls have been replaced by cafés, touristy horse buggies, and souvenir hawkers.

The **Hus Memorial,** erected in 1915 (500 years after the Czech reformer's martyrdom by fire), marks the center of the square and symbolizes the long struggle for Czech freedom. Walk around the memorial.

Jan Hus stands tall between two groups of people: victorious Hussite patriots and Protestants defeated by the Hapsburgs. One of the patriots holds a cup—in the medieval Church, only priests could drink the wine at Communion. Since the Hussites fought for the right to take both the wine and the bread, the cup is their symbol. Behind Hus, a mother with her children represents the ultimate rebirth of the Czech nation. Hus was excommunicated and burned in Germany a century before the age of Martin Luther.

Do a **spin tour** in the center of the square to get a look at architectural styles: Gothic, Renaissance, Baroque, rococo, and Art Nouveau.

Spin clockwise, starting with the green domes of the Baroque Church of St. Nicholas. A Hussite church, it's a popular venue for concerts. (There's another green-domed Church of St. Nicholas—also popular for concerts—by the same architect across the Charles Bridge in Malá Strana.) The Jewish Quarter (Josefov) is a few blocks behind the church, down the uniquely tree-lined Paris Street (Pařížská), an eclectic cancan of mostly Art Nouveau facades. Paris Street leads to a bluff that

HUS AND LUTHER

The word *catholic* means "universal." The Roman Catholic Church—in many ways the administrative ghost of the Roman Empire—is the only organization to survive from ancient times. For more than a thousand years, it enforced its notion that the Vatican was the sole interpreter of God's word on earth, and the only legitimate way to be a Christian was as a Roman Catholic. Jan Hus (c. 1369–1415) lived and preached 100 years before Martin Luther. Both were college professors, as well as priests. Both drew huge public crowds as they preached in their university chapels. Both promoted a local religious autonomy. And both helped establish their national languages. (Hus gave the Czechs their unique accents to enable the letters to fit the sounds.) Both got in big trouble. While Hus was burned, Luther survived. Living after Gutenberg, Luther was able to spread his message more cheaply and effectively, thanks to the new printing press. Since Luther was high-profile and German, killing him would have caused major political complications. While Hus may have loosened Rome's grip on Christianity, Luther orchestrated the Reformation that finally broke it. Today, both are revered as national heroes as well as religious reformers.

once sported a 100-foot-tall stone Stalin, demolished in 1962 after Khrushchev exposed Stalin's crimes; it was recently replaced by a giant ticking metronome.

Spin to the right past the Hus Memorial and the fine Baroque facade (with its Art Nouveau mosaic) of the Ministry of Internal Affairs. Notice the Gothic Týn Church (described below), with its fanciful spires flanking a solid gold effigy of the Virgin Mary. Lining the uphill side of the square is an interesting row of pastel houses with Gothic, Renaissance, and Baroque facades. The pointed 250-foot-tall spire marks the 14th-century Old Town Hall, famous for its astronomical clock (described below). In front of the Town Hall, 27 white inlaid crosses mark the spot where 27 Protestant nobles, merchants, and intellectuals were beheaded in 1621 after rebelling against the Catholic Hapsburgs.

Týn Church—The towering Týn (pronounced "teen") Church facing the Old Town Square was rebuilt fancier than the original—but enjoy it. For 200 years after Hus' death, this was Prague's leading Hussite church. The lane leading to the church from the Old Town Square has a public WC and the most convenient box office in town (see "Entertainment," below).

▲**Old Town Hall Astronomical Clock**—Ignore the ridiculous human sales racks, and join the gang for the striking of the hour (daily 8:00–21:00, until 20:00 in winter) on the 15th-century Town Hall clock. As you wait, see if you can figure out how the clock works.

With revolving disks, celestial symbols, and sweeping hands, this clock keeps several versions of time. Two outer rings show the hour: Bohemian time (Gothic numbers, counts from sunset—find the zero, next to 23...supposedly the time of tonight's sunset) and modern time (24 Roman numerals, XII at the top being noon, XII at the bottom being midnight). Five hundred years ago, everything revolved around the earth (the fixed middle background).

To indicate the times of sunrise and sunset, arcing lines and moving spheres combine with the big hand (a sweeping golden sun) and the little hand (the moon showing various stages). Look for the orbits of the sun and moon as they rise through day (the blue zone) and night (the black zone).

If this seems complex today, it must have been a marvel 500 years ago. The circle below (added in the 19th century) shows the zodiac, scenes from the seasons of a rural peasant's life, and a ring of saints' names—one for each day of the year, with a marker showing today's special saint.

Four statues flanking the clock represent 15th-century Prague's four biggest worries: invasion (a Turkish conqueror, his hedonism symbolized by a mandolin), death (a skeleton), greed (a miserly moneylender, which used to have "Jewish" features until after World War II), and vanity (enjoying the mirror). Another interpretation: Earthly pleasures brought on by vanity, greed, and hedonism are fleeting because we are all mortal.

At the top of the hour (don't blink—the show is pretty quick): First, Death tips his hourglass and pulls the cord, ringing the bell; then the windows open and the Twelve Apostles parade by, acknowledging the gang of onlookers; then the rooster crows; and then the hour is rung.

The hour is often off because of daylight saving time (completely senseless to 15th-century clock makers). At the top of the next hour, stand under the tower—protected by a line of banner-wielding, powdered-wigged concert salespeople—and watch the tourists.

Old Town Hall Tower, Hall, and Chapel—The main TI, left of the astronomical clock, contains a guides' desk and these two options: zipping up the only tower in town that has an elevator (40 kč, fine views) or taking a 45-minute tour of the Gothic chapel and Town Hall, which includes a close-up of the Twelve Apostles and clock mechanism (50 kč, 2/hr).

Karlova Street—This street winds through medieval Prague from the Town Hall Square to the Charles Bridge (it zigzags...just follow the crowds). This is a commercial gauntlet, and it's here that the touristy feeding-frenzy of Prague is most ugly. Street signs keep you on track, and *Karlův Most* signs point to the bridge. Obviously, you'll find great people-watching on this drag, but no good values.

▲▲▲**Charles Bridge (Karlův Most)**—This much-loved bridge, commissioned by the Holy Roman Emperor Charles IV in 1357, offers one of the most pleasant and entertaining 500-yard strolls in Europe. Until 1850, it was Prague's only bridge crossing the river.

Before crossing the bridge, step into the little square on the right with the statue of the Holy Roman Emperor Charles IV (Karlo Quatro). Charles ruled his vast empire from Prague in the 14th century. He's holding a contract establishing Prague's university, the first in Central Europe. The women around his pedestal symbolize the university's four faculties: medicine, law, theology, and the arts. The statue was erected in 1848 to celebrate the university's 500th birthday. Enjoy the view across the river. The bridge tower—once a tollbooth—is considered one of the finest Gothic gates anywhere. Climb it for a fine view but nothing else (40 kč, daily 10:00–19:00, as late as 22:00 in summer).

Be on the Charles Bridge when the sun is low for the best light, people-watching, and photo opportunities. Before the tacky commercialism and the camera-toting mobs get you down, remember the vacant gloom of this place before 1989. Think of the crowds of Charles Bridge as a celebration of freedom.

The bridge is famous for its statues, but most of those you see today are replicas—the originals are in city museums and out of the polluted air. Two statues on the bridge are worth a comment. First, the crucifix (facing the castle, near the start on the right) is the spot where convicts would pause to pray on their way to execution on the Old Town Square. Farther on (midstream, on right), the statue of John of Nepomuk—a saint of the Czech people—draws a crowd (look for the guy with the five golden stars and the shiny dog). Back in the 14th century, he was the priest to whom the queen confessed all her sins. The king wanted to know her secrets, but Father John dutifully refused to tell. He was tortured, eventually killed, and tossed off the bridge. When he hit the water, five stars appeared. The shiny plaque at the base of the statue depicts the heave-ho. Locals touch it to help wishes come true. The shiny dog killed the queen...but that's another story. From the end of the bridge (TI in tower on castle side), the street leads two blocks to the Little Quarter Square at the base of the huge Church of St. Nicholas.

Kampa Island and Lennon Wall—One hundred yards before the castle end of the Charles Bridge, stairs lead down to the main square of Kampa Island with its relaxing pubs, breezy park, new art gallery, and river access.

From the square, Hroznová Lane on the right leads to a bridge (the water mill is one of many that once lined the canal here; notice the high-water marks from the flood of August 2002). Fifty yards beyond the bridge is the Lennon Wall (Lennonova zeď, on the right, enlivening the otherwise dull wall of the Maltese Embassy).

While the ideas of Lenin hung like a water-soaked trenchcoat upon the Czech people, the ideas of John Lennon gave many locals hope and a vision. When Lennon was killed in 1980, a memorial wall filled with graffiti spontaneously appeared. Night after night, the police would paint over the "All You Need Is Love" and "Imagine" graffiti. And day after day, it would reappear. Until independence came in 1989, travelers, freedom-lovers, and local hippies gathered here. Silly as it might seem, it's remembered as a place that gave hope to locals craving freedom. Even today, while the tension and danger associated with this wall is gone, the message stays fresh.

▲▲**Little Quarter (Malá Strana)**—This is the most characteristic, fun-to-wander old section of town. It's one of four medieval towns (along with Hradčany, Staré Město, and Nové Město) that united in the late 1700s to make modern Prague. It centers on the Little Quarter Square (Malostranské Náměstí) with the huge Church of St. Nicholas standing in the middle. The column facing the church entry (uphill side) was built by grateful townspeople after surviving a plague.

Church of St. Nicholas (Kostel Sv. Mikuláše)—When the Jesuits came, they found the perfect piece of real estate for their church and its associated school—the Little Quarter Square. The Church of St. Nicholas (built 1703–1760 in the middle of the square) is the best example of High Baroque in town. It's a Jesuit church, giddy with curves and illusions. The altar features a lavish gold-plated Nicholas flanked by the two top Jesuits: St. Ignatius Loyola and St. Francis Xavier. For a good look at the city and the church's 250-foot dome, climb the tower for

30 kč; the entrance is outside the right transept (church entry-50 kč, but free for prayer daily 8:30–9:00, open daily 9:00–17:00; tower open daily April–Oct 10:00–18:00, closed off-season). The church is a concert venue in evenings; 400-kč tickets are generally on sale at the door.

From here, you can hike 10 minutes uphill to the castle (and 5 min more to the Strahov Monastery). Or for a short, vivid detour near the church, see the...

Torture Museum—This gimmicky moneymaker is similar to other European torture museums, but is nevertheless interesting, showing models of 60 gruesome medieval tortures with well-written English descriptions (120 kč, daily 10:00–22:00, just below Church of St. Nicholas at Mostecká 21, tel. 224-215-581).

Prague's Castle Area

▲**Strahov Monastery and Library (Strahovský Kláster a Knihovna)**— Twin Baroque domes high above the castle mark the Strahov Monastery (a 15-min hike uphill from Little Quarter or 5-min walk from castle). If coming by tram, take tram #22 or #23 (from the National Theater or Malostranská) to the Pohořelec stop, visit the monastery (go uphill 200 yards and through the gate into the monastery grounds), and then hike down to the castle.

The monastery had a booming economy of its own in its heyday (with vineyards and the biggest beerhall in town—still open). It's a Romanesque structure decorated in textbook Baroque (usually closed, but look through the window inside the front door to see its interior). The adjacent library (60 kč, daily 9:00–12:00 & 13:00–17:00) offers a peek at how enlightened thinkers in the 18th century influenced learning.

Cases in the library gift shop show off illuminated manuscripts, some in old Czech. Two rooms are filled with 17th-century books under elaborately-painted ceilings. Because the Czechs were a rural people with almost no high culture at this time, there were few books in the Czech language. The theme of the first and bigger hall is philosophy, with the history of man's pursuit of knowledge painted on its ceiling. The other hall focuses on theology. Notice the gilded locked case containing the *"libri prohibiti"* (prohibited books) at the end of the room. Only the abbot had the key, and you had to have his blessing to read these books—by Nicolaus Copernicus and Jan Hus, even including the French encyclopedia. As the Age of Enlightenment took hold in Europe in the 18th century, monasteries still controlled the books. With the Enlightenment, the hallway connecting these two library rooms was filled with cases illustrating the new practical approach to natural sciences. Find the baby dodo bird (which became extinct in the 17th century).

Just downhill from the monastery and through the gate, the views from the monastery garden are among the best in Prague. From the Panorama restaurant or the public perch below the tables, you can see

Prague's Castle Area

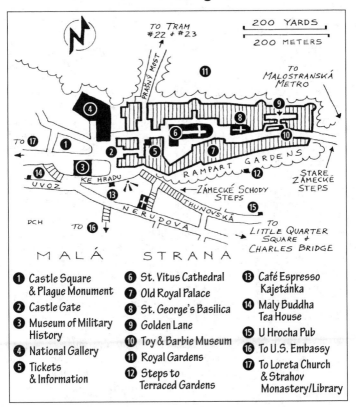

1 Castle Square
& Plague Monument

2 Castle Gate

3 Museum of Military
History

4 National Gallery

5 Tickets
& Information

6 St. Vitus Cathedral

7 Old Royal Palace

8 St. George's Basilica

9 Golden Lane

10 Toy & Barbie Museum

11 Royal Gardens

12 Steps to
Terraced Gardens

13 Café Espresso
Kajetánka

14 Maly Buddha
Tea House

15 U Hrocha Pub

16 To U.S. Embassy

17 To Loreta Church
& Strahov
Monastery/Library

the St. Vitus Cathedral (the centerpiece of the castle complex), the green dome of the Church of St. Nicholas (marking the center of the Little Quarter, or Malá Strana), the two dark towers fortifying the Charles Bridge, and the fanciful black spires of the Týn Church (marking the Old Town Square). On the horizon is the TV tower, built in 1973 and nicknamed "The Rocket."

Loreta Church (a.k.a. Loreta Shrine)—This church (between the castle and the Strahov Monastery) has been a hit with pilgrims for centuries, thanks to its dazzling bell tower, peaceful yet plush cloister, sparkling treasury, and much-venerated "holy house." The central Santa Casa (holy house) is considered by some pilgrims to be part of Mary's home in Nazareth. Because many pilgrims returning from the Holy Land docked at the Italian port of Loreto, it's called the Loreta Shrine. While all the fuss makes it seem important, you'll see only a few 15th-century frescoes and an old statue of Mary inside. The highlight is a room full of jeweled worship aids upstairs in the treasury (well-described in English). Behind vault doors you'll squint at a monstrance (relic holder) from 1699 with over 6,000 diamonds. Enjoy the short carillon concert at the top of the hour; from the lawn in front of the main entrance, you can see the racks of bells being clanged (80 kč, Tue–Sun 9:00–12:15 & 13:00–16:30, closed Mon).

▲▲**Prague Castle (Pražský Hrad)**—For more than a thousand years, Czech rulers have ruled from the Prague Castle. It's huge (by some measures, the biggest castle on earth) and confusing—with plenty of sights not worth seeing. Keep things simple, rather than worry about rumors that you should spend all day here with long lists of museums to see. Six stops matter and are explained here: Castle Square, St. Vitus Cathedral, Old Royal Palace, Basilica of St. George, the Golden Lane, and the toy museum.

You can choose from three ticket routes: Route A includes the cathedral, Old Royal Palace, Basilica, Powder Tower, Golden Lane, and sometimes also temporary exhibitions for 220 kč. Route B includes the cathedral, Old Royal Palace, and the Golden Lane for 180 kč. Route C covers only the Golden Lane for 40 kč (castle hours: April–Oct daily 9:00–17:00, Nov–March 9:00–16:00, last entry 15 min before closing, grounds are open daily 6:00–24:00, tel. 224-373-368 or 224-372-434). For most people (and for the purposes of this tour), Route B is best. If you rent the worthwhile audioguide (200 kč/2 hrs or 250 kč/3 hrs), you won't be able to exit the castle area from the bottom since you need to backtrack uphill to return the audioguide where you got it.

Hour-long **tours** in English depart from the main ticket office about three times a day, but cover only the cathedral and Old Royal Palace (80 kč, reserve a week in advance if you want a private guide-400 kč for up to 5 people, then 80 kč per additional person, tel. 224-373-368).

Getting to the Castle: You can ride a taxi, catch a tram, or hike. The easiest plan is to take a tram above the castle (see below), then wander down through the complex and on to Malá Strana and the Charles Bridge.

Trams #22 and #23 go from the National Theater (Národní Divadlo) or Malostranská to the castle. You have two options: Get off at the stop Královský Letohrádek for the castle, or stay on farther to Pohořelec to visit the Strahov Monastery (go uphill and through the gate toward the twin spires) and then hike down to the castle.

If you get off the tram at Královský Letohrádek, you'll see the Royal Summer Palace (Belvedér) across the street. This love gift—a Czech Taj Mahal—from Emperor Ferdinand I, who really did love his Queen Anne, is the finest Renaissance building in town. Notice the reliefs featuring classical rather than Christian stories. From here, walk through the park with fine views of the cathedral to the gate, which leads you over the moat and into the castle grounds. Once the private grounds and residence (you'll see the building) of the communist president, these Royal Gardens were opened to the public with the coming of freedom under Václav Havel.

Hikers can follow the main cobbled road from Charles Bridge through Malá Strana, the Little Quarter (the nearest subway stop is Malostranská). From the big church, hike uphill along Nerudova Street (described below). After about 10 minutes, a steep lane on the right leads to the castle. (If you continue straight, Nerudova becomes Úvoz and climbs to the Strahov Monastery and Library.)

Castle Square (Hradčanské Náměstí)—The big square facing the castle feels like the castle's entry, but it's actually the central square of the Castle Quarter. Enjoy the awesome city view and the two entertaining string quartets that play regularly at the gate. (If the Prague Castle Orchestra is playing, say hello to friendly, mustachioed Josef and consider getting the group's terrific CD.) A tranquil café called Espresso Kajetánka (see "Eating," page 87) hides a few steps down immediately to the right as you face the castle. From here, stairs lead into the Little Quarter.

The Castle Square was a kind of Czech Pennsylvania Avenue. Look uphill from the gate. The Renaissance Schwarzenberg Palace (Svarcenberský palác, on the left, with the fake big stones scratched on the wall) is now a museum of military history. The statue marked *TGM* honors Tomáš Masaryk, Czechoslovakia's George Washington. At the end of World War I, this pal of Woodrow Wilson united the Czechs and the Slovaks into one nation, and became its first president. A plague monument stands in the center (built by the city in thanks for surviving the Black Plague). On the right, find the archbishop's rococo yellow palace. Through the portal on the left-hand side of the palace, a lane leads to the Sternberg Palace (Šternberský palác), filled with the National Gallery's skippable collection of European paintings—mostly minor works by Albrecht Dürer, Peter Paul Rubens, Rembrandt, and El Greco (100 kč, Tue–Sun 10:00–18:00, closed Mon).

Survey the castle from this square—the tip of a 1,500-foot-long series of courtyards, churches, and palaces. Huge throngs of tourists turn the castle grounds into a sea of people during peak times; late afternoon is least crowded. The guard changes on the hour (5:00–23:00), with the most ceremony at noon. Walk under the fighting giants, under an arch, and into the second courtyard. The mod green awning with the golden winged cat (just past the ticket office) marks the offices of the Czech president. You can walk through the castle and enter the cathedral without a ticket, but you'll need a ticket to see the castle properly (see ticket options above). Continue through the next passageway to a ticket office (on the right) and the...

▲**St. Vitus Cathedral (Katedrála Sv. Vita)**—This Roman Catholic cathedral symbolizes the Czech spirit—it contains the tombs and relics of the most important local saints and kings, including the first three Hapsburg kings. What's up with the guys in suits carved into the facade below the big round window? They're the architects and builders who finished the church. Started in 1344, construction was stalled by wars and plagues. But, fueled by the 19th-century rise of Czech nationalism, Prague's top church was finished in 1929 for the 1,000th anniversary of the death of St. Wenceslas. While it looks all Gothic, it's two distinct halves: modern neo-Gothic and the original 14th-century Gothic. For 400 years, a temporary wall sealed off the unfinished cathedral.

Go inside (pickpocket alert) and find the third stained-glass window on the left. This masterful 1931 Art Nouveau window is by Czech artist Alfons Mucha (if you like this, you'll love the Mucha Museum downtown—described below under "More Old Town Sights"). Notice Mucha's stirring nationalism: Methodious and Cyril are top and center (leaders in Slavic-style Christianity). Cyril is baptizing the mythic, lanky, long-haired Czech man. Lower, you'll see two Czech flappers and the classic Czech patriarch (on right). Notice also Mucha's novel use of color: Your eyes are drawn from blue (symbolizing the past) to the golden center (where the boy and the seer look into the future).

Show your ticket and circulate around the **apse** past a carved wood relief of Prague in 1630 (before Charles Bridge had any statues), lots of faded Gothic paintings, and tombs of local saints. A fancy roped-off chapel (right transept) houses the **tomb of Prince Wenceslas,** surrounded by precious 14th-century murals showing scenes of his life, and a locked door leading to the crown jewels. More kings are buried in the royal mausoleum in front of the high altar and in the crypt underneath. You can climb 287 steps up the **spire** for a fine view (included in Route A or B ticket, or pay 20 kč at the cathedral ticket window, April–Oct daily except Sunday morning, 9:00–17:00, last entry 16:15, closes at 16:00 in winter).

Leaving the cathedral, turn left (past the public WC). The **obelisk**

was erected in 1928—a single piece of granite celebrating the 10th anniversary of the establishment of Czechoslovakia. (It was originally much taller but broke in transit—an inauspicious start for a nation destined to last only 70 years.) Find the 14th-century mosaic of the *Last Judgment* outside on the right transept. It was built Italian-style by King Charles IV, who was modern, cosmopolitan, and ahead of his time. Jesus oversees the action, as some go to heaven and some go to hell. The Czech king and queen kneel directly below Jesus and the six patron saints. On coronation day, they would walk under this arch, which would remind them (and their subjects) that even those holding great power are not above God's judgment. The royal crown and national jewels are kept in a chamber (see the grilled windows) above this entryway, which was the cathedral's main entry for centuries when the church was incomplete. Across the square and 20 yards to the right, a door leads to the...

Old Royal Palace (Starý Královský Palác)—This was the seat of the Bohemian princes in the 12th century. While extensively rebuilt, the large hall is late Gothic. It was a multipurpose hall for the old nobility. It's big enough for jousts—even the staircase was designed to let a mounted soldier gallop in. It was filled with market stalls, giving nobles a chance to shop without actually going into town. In the 1400s, the nobility met here to elect their king. This tradition survives today, as the parliament crowds into this room every five years to elect the Czech president. Look up at the impressive vaulted ceiling, look down on the chapel from the end, and go out on the balcony for a fine Prague view. Is that Paris' Eiffel Tower in the distance? No, it's Petřín Tower, built for an exhibition in 1891 (200 feet tall, a quarter of the height of the Parisian big brother built in 1889). The spiral stairs on the left lead up to several rooms with painted coats of arms and no English explanations. The downstairs of the palace sometimes houses special exhibitions. Across from the palace exit is the...

Basilica of St. George and Convent (Bazilika Sv. Jiří)—Step into the beautifully lit Basilica of St. George to see Prague's best-preserved Romanesque church. St. Wenceslas' mother, St. Ludmila, was buried here in 973. The first Bohemian convent was established here near the palace. To visit the basilica in addition to the other castle sights described here, you'll pay an extra 40 kč for the Route A ticket—worth it if you're interested in Romanesque architecture.

Today, the **convent** next door houses the National Gallery's Collection of Old Masters (best Czech paintings from Mannerism and Baroque periods, 100 kč, Tue–Sun 10:00–18:00, closed Mon). Continue walking downhill through the castle grounds. Turn left on the first street, which leads into the...

Golden Lane (Zlatá Ulička)—This street of old buildings, which originally housed goldsmiths, is now jammed with tourists and lined with expensive gift shops, boutiques, galleries, and cafés. The Czech writer Franz Kafka lived at #22. There's a deli/bistro at the top and a convenient public WC at the bottom (Golden Lane-40 kč for Route C ticket, also included in Routes A and B). Beyond that, at the end of the castle, are fortifications beefed up in anticipation of the Turkish attack—the cause for most medieval arms buildups in Eastern and Central Europe—and steps funneling the mobs of tourists back into town.

▲**Toy and Barbie Museum (Muzeum Hraček)**—At the bottom of the castle complex, just after leaving the Golden Lane, a long wooden staircase leads to two entertaining floors of old toys and dolls thought-fully described in English. You'll see a century of teddy bears, 19th-century model train sets, and an incredible Barbie collection (the entire top floor). Find the buxom 1959 first edition and you'll understand why these capitalistic sirens of material discontent weren't allowed here until 1989 (50 kč, daily 9:30–17:30, not included in any castle tickets).

After your castle visit: Tourists squirt slowly through a fortified door at the bottom end of the castle. From there, you can follow the steep lane directly back to the riverbank (Malostranská Metro station). Or, you can take a hard right and stroll through the long, delightful park to the top of the castle, where you'll find two more options: a staircase leading down into the Little Quarter, or a cobbled street taking you to the historic Nerudova Street—described below. (Halfway through that long park is a viewpoint overlooking the terraced gardens; you can zigzag down through the gardens into the Little Quarter—100 kč, April–Oct daily 10:00–18:00.)

Nerudova Street—The steep cobbled street leading to the castle is named for Jan Neruda, a 19th-century Romantic novelist. It's lined with old buildings still sporting the characteristic doorway signs that served as street addresses. In 1777, in order to more effectively collect taxes, Hapsburg Empress Maria Theresa decreed that numbers be used instead of these quaint house names. The surviving signs are carefully restored and protected by law. Signs (e.g., the lion, three violinists, house of the golden suns) represent the family name, the occupation, or the various passions of the people who once inhabited the houses. This neighborhood is filled with old noble palaces, now generally used as foreign embassies.

Prague's Jewish Quarter (Josefov)

Prague's Jewish Quarter neighborhood and its well-presented, profoundly moving museum tell the story of the Jews of this region. For me, this is the most interesting Jewish sight in Europe (and worth ▲▲▲).

The Jewish people were dispersed by the Romans 2,000 years ago. Over the centuries, their culture survived in enclaves throughout the Western world: "The Torah was their sanctuary which no army could destroy." Jews first came to Prague in the 10th century. The main intersection of Josefov (Maiselova and Široká streets) was the meeting point of two medieval trade routes.

When the pope declared that Jews and Christians should not live together, Jews had to wear yellow badges, and their quarter was walled in. It became a ghetto. In the 16th and 17th centuries, Prague had one of the biggest ghettos in Europe, with 11,000 inhabitants. Within its six gates, Prague's Jewish Quarter was a gaggle of 200 wooden buildings. Someone wrote: "Jews nested rather than dwelled."

The "outcasts" of Christianity relied mainly on profits from money lending (forbidden to Christians) and community solidarity to survive.

Prague's Jewish Quarter

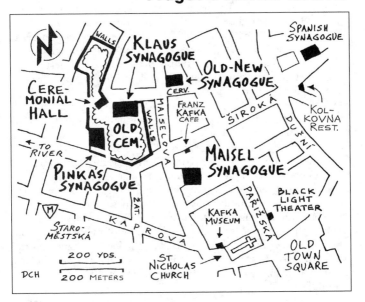

While their money protected them, it was often also a curse. Throughout Europe, when times got tough and Christian debts to the Jewish community mounted, entire Jewish communities were evicted or killed.

In the 1780s, Emperor Joseph II eased much of the discrimination against Jews. In 1848, the walls were torn down and the neighborhood, named Josefov in honor of the emperor who was less anti-Semitic than the norm, was incorporated as a district of Prague.

In 1897, ramshackle Josefov was razed and replaced with a new modern town—the original 31 streets and 220 buildings became 10 streets and 83 buildings. This is what you'll see today: an attractive neighborhood of fine, mostly Art Nouveau buildings, with a few surviving historic Jewish buildings. In the 1930s, some 50,000 Jews lived in Prague. Today, only a couple of thousand remain.

As the Nazis decimated Jewish communities in the region, Prague's Jews were allowed to collect and archive their treasures in this "museum." While the archivists ultimately died in concentration camps, their work survives. Seven sights scattered over a three-block area make up the tourists' Jewish Quarter. Six of the sights, called "the Museum," are treated as one admission. Your ticket comes with a map locating the sights and listing admission appointments—the times you'll be let in if it's very crowded. (Without crowds, ignore the times.) You'll notice plenty of security (stepped up since 9/11).

To visit all seven sights, you'll pay 500 kč (300 kč for "the Museum" and 200 kč for the Old-New Synagogue; all sights open Sun–Fri 9:00–18:00, closed Sat—the Jewish Sabbath). There are occasional guided walks in English (40 kč, 2.5 hrs, start at Maisel Synagogue, tel. 222-317-191). Most stops are described in English. The ticket lines at the cemetery and Pinkas Synagogue are longest. You'll likely save time if you buy your ticket at the Maisel Synagogue (the best place to start your visit anyway).

Maisel Synagogue (Maiselova Synagóga)—This synagogue was built as a private place of worship for the Maisel family during the 16th-century golden age of Prague's Jews. Maisel was the financier of the Hapsburg king—and had lots of money. The interior is decorated neo-Gothic. In World War II, it served as a warehouse for the accumulated treasures of decimated Jewish communities that Hitler planned to use for his "Museum of the Non-Existing Nation." The one-room exhibit (the upstairs "women's gallery" is closed for renovation) shows a thousand years of Jewish history in Bohemia and Moravia. Well-explained in English, the topics covered include the origin of the Star of David, Jewish mysticism, discrimination, and the creation of Prague's ghetto. Notice the eastern wall with the "holy ark" containing the scroll of the Torah. The central case shows the silver ornamental Torah crowns that capped the scroll.

Spanish Synagogue (Španělská Synagóga)—This 19th-century, ornate, Moorish-style synagogue continues the history of the Maisel Synagogue, covering the 18th, 19th, and tumultuous 20th centuries. The upstairs is particularly intriguing (with c. 1900 photos of Josefov). The Spanish Synagogue is now used for classical concerts, often featuring the music of Jewish composers such as Felix Mendelssohn and Gustav Mahler (ticket desk just outside at the door).

Pinkas Synagogue (Pinkasova Synagóga)—A site of Jewish worship for 400 years, today this is a poignant memorial to the victims of the Nazis. Of the 120,000 Jews living in the area in 1939, only 10,000 lived to see liberation in 1945. The walls are covered with the handwritten names of 77,297 Czech Jews who were sent from here to the gas chambers of Auschwitz and other camps. (You'll hear the somber reading of the names as you ponder this sad sight.) Hometowns are in gold, family names are in red, followed in black by the individual's first name, birthday, and last date known to be alive. Notice that families generally perished together. Extermination camps are listed on the east wall. Climb six steps into the women's gallery. The names in poor condition near the ceiling are from 1953. When the communists moved in, they closed the synagogue and erased everything. With freedom, in 1989, the Pinkas Synagogue was reopened and all the names rewritten. The Synagogue closed briefly in 2003, as flood damage meant the names needed to be rewritten once again.

Upstairs is the **Terezín Children's Art Exhibit,** displaying art drawn by Jewish children who were imprisoned at Terezín Concentration Camp and later perished. Terezín is a powerful day trip from Prague, easily accessible by local bus (see page 94) or tour bus (see "Tours," page 56).

Old Jewish Cemetery (Starý Židovský Hřbitov)—As you wander among 12,000 evocative tombstones, remember that from 1439 until 1787, this was the only burial ground allowed for the Jews of Prague. With limited space, the Jewish belief that the body should not be moved once buried, and about 12,000 graves, tombs were piled atop each other. With its many layers, the cemetery became a small plateau. And as things settled over time, the tombstones got crooked. The Jewish word for cemetery means "House of Life." Like Christians, Jews believe that death is the gateway into the next world. Pebbles on the tombstones are "flowers of the desert," reminiscent of the old days when a rock was placed upon the sand gravesite to keep the body covered. You'll likely see pebbles atop scrap of papers containing prayers.

Ceremonial Hall (Obřadní Síň)—Leaving the cemetery, you'll find a neo-Romanesque mortuary house built in 1911 for the purification of the dead (on left). It's filled with a worthwhile exhibition, described in English, on Jewish burial traditions. A series of crude but instructive paintings show how the "burial brotherhood" took care of the ill and buried the dead. As all are equal before God, the rich and poor alike were buried in embroidered linen shrouds similar to the one you'll see on display.

Klaus Synagogue (Klauzová Synagóga)—This 17th-century synagogue (also at the exit of the cemetery) is the final wing of this museum, devoted to Jewish religious practices. On the ground floor, exhibits explain the festive Jewish calendar. The central case displays a Torah (the first five books of the Bible) and solid silver pointers—necessary since the Torah is not to be touched. Upstairs features the rituals of Jewish life (circumcision, bar and bas mitzvah, weddings, kosher eating, and so on).

Old-New Synagogue (Staronová Synagóga)—For more than 700 years, this has been the most important synagogue and central building in Josefov. Standing like a bomb-hardened bunker, it feels like it has survived plenty of hard times. Stairs take you down to the street level of the 13th century and into the Gothic interior. Built in 1270, it's the oldest synagogue in Central Europe.

The lobby (where you show your ticket) has two fortified old lockers—where the most heavily taxed community in medieval Prague stored its money in anticipation of the taxman's arrival. As 13th-century Jews were not allowed to build, this was constructed by Christians. The builders were good at four-ribbed vaulting, but since that resulted in a cross, it wouldn't work for a synagogue. Instead, they made the ceiling using clumsy five-ribbed vaulting.

The interior is pure 1300s. The Shrine of the Ark in front is the focus of worship. The holiest place in the synagogue, it holds the sacred scrolls of the Torah. The old rabbi's chair to the right remains empty out of respect. The red banner is a copy of the one the Jewish community carried through town during medieval parades. Notice the yellow pointed hat, which the pope in 1215 ordered all Jewish men to wear. Twelve is a popular number (e.g., windows) because it symbolizes the 12 tribes of Israel. The horizontal slit-like windows are an 18th-century addition allowing women to view the men-only services (separate 200-kč admission includes worthwhile 10-minute tour—ask about it, Sun–Thu 9:30–18:00, Fri 9:30–17:00, closed Sat).

Before leaving the neighborhood, step out into Paris Street (Pařížská ulica, behind the Old-New Synagogue), look left and see the giant metronome slowly ticking away. This marks the spot of a 100-foot-tall sculpture of Stalin destroyed in 1962 after Khrushchev revealed Stalin's crimes.

More Old Town Sights

▲Na Příkopě—Na Příkopě (meaning "the moat") follows the line of the Old Town wall, leading from Wenceslas Square right to a former gate in that wall, the Powder Tower (Prašná Brána, not worth touring). City tour buses leave from along this street, which offers plenty of shopping temptations (see "Shopping," page 81).

▲Museum of Communism—The museum traces the story of communism in Prague: the origins, dream, reality, and nightmare; the cult of personality; and finally, the Velvet Revolution. Along the way, it gives a fascinating review of the Czech Republic's 40-year stint with Soviet economics. You'll find propaganda posters, busts of communist All-Stars (Marx, Lenin, Stalin), a photograph of the massive stone Stalin that overlooked Prague until 1962, and re-created slices of communist life—from a bland store counter to a typical classroom (with a poem on the chalkboard extolling the virtues of the tractor). Don't miss the 20-minute video showing how the Czech people chafed under the big red yoke from the 1950s through 1989—it plays continuously (180 kč, daily 9:00–21:00, Na Příkopě 10, above a McDonald's and next to a casino—Lenin would turn over in his grave, tel. 224-212-966, www.museumofcommunism.com).

▲Municipal House (Obecní Dům)—The Municipal House is the "pearl of Czech Art Nouveau" (built 1905–1911, next to Powder Tower). It features Prague's largest concert hall, a great Art Nouveau café, and two other restaurants. Pop in and wander around the lobby of the concert hall. Then choose your place for a meal or drink (see

PRAGUE: PRE-1989

It's hard to imagine the gray and bleak Prague of the communist era. Before 1989, the city was a wistful jumble of possibility. Cobbled lanes were shadowed by sooty, crusty buildings. Timbers—strung across the lanes like laundry lines—held crumbling buildings apart. Consumer goods were plain and uniform, stacked like Legos on the thin shelves in shops where customers waited in line for a tin of ham or a bottle of ersatz Coke. The Charles Bridge was as black as its statues, with no commerce except for a few shady characters trying to change money. Hotels had two price schedules: one for people of the Warsaw Pact nations and another (6 to 8 times as expensive) for capitalists. This made the rundown Soviet-style hotels as expensive as a fine Western one. At the train station, frightened but desperate characters would meet arriving foreigners to rent them a room in their flat, in order to get enough hard Western cash to buy batteries or Levis at one of the hard-currency stores.

"Eating," page 87).

Standing in front of the Municipal House, you can survey four different styles of architecture. First, enjoy the pure Art Nouveau of the Municipal House. Featuring a goddess-like Praha presiding over a land of peace and high culture, the *Homage to Prague* mosaic on the building's striking facade stoked cultural pride and nationalist sentiment. Across the street, the classical fixer-upper from 1815 was the customs house (soon to be renovated as a music hall). The stark national bank building (Česká Národní Banka) is textbook "functionalism" from the 1930s. And the big black Powder Tower was the Gothic gate of the town wall, built to house the city's gunpowder. Crossing under it, you join the beaten path as Celetná Street leads to the Old Town Square.

▲▲**Mucha Museum (Muchovo Muzeum)**—This is one of Europe's most enjoyable little museums. I find the art of Alfons Mucha (MOO-kah, 1860–1939) insistently likeable. See the crucifixion scene he painted as an eight-year-old boy. Read how this popular Czech artist's posters, filled with Czech symbols and expressing his people's ideals and aspirations, were patriotic banners arousing the national spirit. And check out the photographs of his models. With the help of this abundant supply of slinky models, Mucha was a founding father of the Art Nouveau movement. Prague isn't much on museums, but, if you're into Art Nouveau, this one is great. Run by Mucha's grandson, it's two blocks off

ART NOUVEAU

Prague is the best Art Nouveau town in Europe, with fun-loving facades gracing streets all over town. Art Nouveau, born in Paris, is "nouveau" because it wasn't inspired by Rome. It's neo-nothing...a fresh answer to all the revival styles of the later 19th century and an organic response to the Eiffel Tower art of the Industrial Age. The streets of Josefov, the Mucha window in the St. Vitus Cathedral, and Hotel Europa on Wenceslas Square are just a few highlights. The top two places for Art Nouveau fans are the Mucha Museum and the Municipal House. Prague's three top Art Nouveau architects are Jan Koula, Josef Fanta, and a guy (Osvald Polivka) whose last name means "soup" in Czech (Cola, Fanta, and Soup—easy to remember and impress your local friends).

Wenceslas Square and wonderfully displayed on one comfortable floor. Give it a once-over-lightly, just looking at the probing and haunting eyes of Mucha's models (120 kč, daily 10:00–18:00, Panská 7, tel. 224-233-355, www.mucha.cz). While the exhibit is well-described in English, the 30-kč English brochure on the art is a good supplement. The video is also worthwhile (30 min, English and Czech showings alternate, ask upon entry).

Bethlehem Chapel (Betlémská Kaple)—Emperor Charles IV founded the first university in Central Europe, and this was its chapel. The room is plain, with a focus on the pulpit and the message of the sermon. Around 1400, priest and professor Jan Hus preached his reformist ideas from this pulpit. While meant primarily for students and faculty, the Mass was open to the public. Soon, huge crowds were drawn by Hus' empowering Luther-like ideas. He proposed that the congregation should be more involved in worship (e.g., actually drink the wine at Communion) and have better access to the word of God through services and scriptures written in the people's language instead of Latin. Standing-room-only crowds of more than 3,000 were the norm when Hus preached. The stimulating and controversial ideas debated at the university spread throughout the city (tiny upstairs exhibit and big chapel with English-info sheets available, 35 kč, April–Oct daily 10:00–18:30; Nov–March Tue–Sun 10:00–17:30, closed Mon; on Bethlehem Square—Betlémská Náměstí, tel. 224-248-595).

Klub Architektu, across from the entry, has an intriguing atmosphere and good food (see "Eating," page 87).

The Dancing House (Tančící Dům)—
Prague has some delightful modern architecture. If ever a building could get your
toes tapping, it would be this one, nicknamed "Fred and Ginger." This metallic
samba is the work of Frank Gehry (who
designed the equally striking Guggenheim
Museum in Bilbao, Spain, and Seattle's
Experience Music Project). Eight-legged
Ginger's wispy dress and Fred's metal mesh
head are easy to spot (2 bridges down from
Charles Bridge where Jiráskův bridge hits
Nové Město, tram #17).

A pleasant 15-minute riverside walk from Charles Bridge to the
Dancing House takes you by a famous riverside ballroom and the grand
National Theater (Národní Divadlo). Across the street from the the-
ater is the venerable haunt of Prague's intelligentsia, **Grand Café
Slavia,** a Vienna-style coffeehouse fine for a meal or drink with a view
of the river.

ENTERTAINMENT

Prague booms with live (and inexpensive) theater, classical, jazz, and
pop entertainment. Everything's listed in several monthly cultural events
programs (free at TI) and in the *Prague News* newspaper.

You'll be tempted to gather fliers as you wander through the town.
Don't. To really understand all your options (the street Mozarts are
pushing only their concert), drop by the **Týnská Galerie** box office at
Týn Church on the Old Town Square. The event schedule posted on
their wall clearly shows what's playing today and tomorrow, including
concerts, Black Light Theater, and marionette shows, with photos of
each venue and a map locating everything (daily 10:00–19:00, tel. 224-
826-969).

Black Light Theater—A kind of mime/modern dance variety show, it
has no language barrier and is, for many, more entertaining than a classical concert. Unique to Prague, this originated in the 1960s as a playful
and almost mystifying theater of the absurd. The two main venues are
Fantastika (more puppets, traditional, sometimes a little artistic nudity,
near Charles Bridge at Karlova 8, tel. 222-221-366) and Image Theatre
(more mime and absurd—"it's precisely the fact that we are all so different that unites us," just off Old Town Square at Pařížská 4, tel. 222-
314-448). Shows last about 80 minutes and cost around 400 kč.

Concerts—Six or eight classical "tourist" concerts daily fill delightful
Old Town halls and churches with music of the crowd-pleasing sort:
Vivaldi, Best of Mozart, Most Famous Arias, and works by local boy

Anton Dvořák. People handing out leaflets are everywhere announcing the evening's events. Concerts typically cost 400–1,000 kč, start anywhere from 13:00 to 21:00, and last one hour. Common venues are in the Little Quarter Square—Malostranské Náměstí (at the Church of St. Nicholas and the Prague Academy of Music in Liechtenstein Palace), at the city end of Charles Bridge (St. Francis Church), and on the Old Town Square (another Church of St. Nicholas).

Music Clubs—Young locals keep Prague's many music clubs in business. The **Lucerna Music Bar** is popular for disco nights (at the bottom of Wenceslas Square, in the basement of Lucerna Gallery, Vodičkova 36, tel. 224-217-108, music nightly from 21:00, around 100 kč cover).

Friday and Saturdays are the "1980s Party," featuring the silly pop songs of the last years under communism when people were in the mood for revolt but didn't have the freedom to say anything directly in their lyrics. The scene is a big noisy dance hall with a giant video screen. While young and trendy, prices are cheap and the ambience is friendly and welcoming...even to older tourists (who don't mind lots of noise and smoke). Another favorite with a handy locale, **Malostranská Beseda Music Club,** offers live music nightly (on the downhill side of the Little Quarter's main square). Many of the best local rock and jazz groups perform here (nightly from 20:30, generally about 100-kč cover). For more late-night music, stroll Michalska Street in the Old Town, where you'll find several popular discos (like Meloun Club at #12).

Cruises—Prague isn't great for a boat tour. Still, the hour-long Vltava River cruises, which leave from near the Malá Strana end of Charles Bridge about hourly (100 kč), are scenic and relaxing, though not informative.

Sports—Prague's top sports are soccer (that's "football" here) and hockey (amazingly, they are a world power, routinely beating even Canada). Think about it: There are more than a hundred Czech players in America's NHL. Tickets are normally easy to get (soccer—usually late Sat or Sun afternoon Feb–May and Aug–Nov; hockey—weeknights Sept–April; see *Prague Post* newspaper). The two big Czech hockey rivals are Sparta and Slavia. Near the top of Castle Hill is the enormous 200,000-seat Strahov Stadium, used during communist times as a venue for *Spartakiade,* sort of a synchronized calisthenics encouraged by the regime. Now it's used for soccer and other sports.

SHOPPING

Prague's entire Old Town seems designed to bring out the shopper in visitors. Shop your way from the Old Town Square up Celetná to the Powder Tower, then along Na Příkopě to the bottom of Wenceslas Square (Václavské Náměstí).

Celetná is lined with big stores selling all the traditional Czech goodies. Na Příkopě has a couple of good modern malls. The best is Slovansky Dům (Na Příkopě 22), where you wander deep past a 10-theater cineplex into a world of classy restaurants and designer shops surrounding a peaceful park-like inner courtyard. Another modern mall is Černá Růže (Na Příkopě 12). Next door is Mosers, where you can climb upstairs to peruse its museum-like crystal showroom. More affordable crystal can be purchased "factory direct" at the Bohemian Crystal shop immediately across the street. Big factory shops offer more selection, are more reliable, and often have the best prices.

SLEEPING

Room-Booking Services

Prague is awash with fancy rooms on the push list; private, small-time operators with rooms to rent in their apartments; and roving agents eager to book you a bed and earn a commission. You can save about 30 percent by showing up in Prague without a reservation and finding accommodations upon arrival. If you're driving, you'll see booking agencies as you enter town. Generally, book here and your host can come and lead you to their place.

Athos Travel, run by Filip Antoš, will find the right room for you from among 140 properties (from hostels to five-star hotels), 90 percent of which are in the historical center. Or use its handy Web site, which allows you to search for a room based on various criteria (best to arrange in advance during peak season, can also help with last-minute booking off-season, tel. 241-440-571, fax 241-441-697, www.athos.cz, info @athos.cz); to get a 2 percent discount for online booking, see "Helpful Hints" on page 48.

AVE, at the main train station (Hlavní Nádraží), is a less personable but helpful booking service (daily 6:00–23:00, tel. 251-551-011, fax 251-555-156, www.avetravel.cz, ave@avetravel.cz). With the tracks at your back, walk down to the orange ceiling and past the "meeting point" (don't go downstairs)—their office is in the left corner by the exit to the rip-off taxis. AVE has several other offices—at Holešovice station, the airport, Wenceslas Square, and Old Town Square. Their display board shows discounted hotels. They have a slew of hotels and small pensions available ($70/1,900 kč pension doubles in old center, $35/960 kč doubles a Metro ride away). You can reserve by e-mail (using your credit

SLEEP CODE

(30 kč = about $1, €1 = $1.10, country code: 420)

Sleep Code: **S** = Single, **D** = Double/Twin, **T** = Triple, **Q** = Quad, **b** = bathroom, **s** = shower only, **no CC** = Credit Cards not accepted. Unless otherwise noted, credit cards are accepted. Some hotels quote prices in euros.

To help you sort easily through these listings, I've divided the rooms into three categories based on the price for a standard double room with bath:

$$$ **Higher Priced**—Most rooms 4,000 kč (€125) or more.
  $$ **Moderately Priced**—Most rooms between 3,000–4,000 kč (€95–125).
    $ **Lower Priced**—Most rooms 3,000 kč (€95) or less.

Peak time is May, June, September, October, Christmas, and Easter. July and August are not too bad. Expect crowds on weekends. I've listed peak-time prices. If you're traveling in July or August, you'll find slightly lower rates. Prices tend to go up even more on holidays. English is spoken everywhere. Reserve by phone or e-mail. Generally, you give your credit-card number to guarantee a room reservation.

card as a deposit) or just show up at the office and request a room. Many of AVE's rooms are not very convenient to the center; be clear on the location before you make your choice. They sell taxi vouchers for those who want the convenience of a ride from the station's taxi stand, though they cost double the fair rate.

For a more personal touch, contact Lida at **Magic Praha** for help with accommodations (tel. 224-230-914 or 224-232-755, magicpraha @magicpraha.cz, see "Helpful Hints," page 49).

Old Town

You'll pay higher prices to stay in the Old Town, but for many travelers, the convenience is worth the expense. These places are all within a 10-minute walk of the Old Town Square.

$$$ Hotel Central is a sentimental favorite—I stayed there in the communist days. Like the rest of Prague, it's now changing with the times: Its 69 rooms have recently been renovated, leaving it fresh and bright. The place is well-run and the location, three blocks east of the Old Town Square, is excellent (Sb-3,800 kč, Db-4,400 kč, deluxe Db-

Prague Hotels

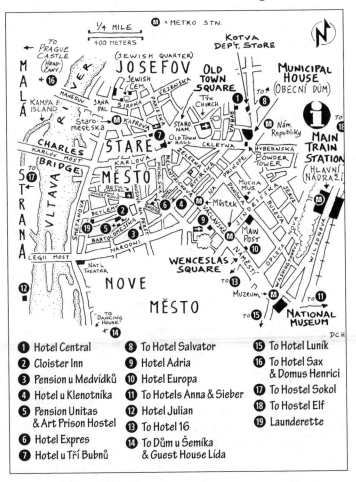

1/4 MILE
400 METERS

Ⓜ = METRO STN.

KOTVA
DEPT. STORE

TO
PRAGUE
CASTLE
(HRAD-
ČANY)

JEWISH QUARTER
JOSEFOV

OLD
TOWN
SQUARE

MUNICIPAL
HOUSE
(OBECNÍ DŮM)

JEWISH
CEM.

MANESUV

KAMPA
ISLAND

JANA
PAL.

SIROKA

VEZENSKA

TÝN
CHURCH

Staro-
městská Ⓜ KAPROVA

STARO.
NÁM.

NÁM.
Republiky Ⓜ

TO

MAIN
TRAIN
STATION
(HLAVNÍ
NÁDRAŽÍ)

STARE

OldTown
HALL

CELETNA

CHARLES
KARLUV MOST

KARLOVA

BRIDGE

MĚSTO

MICHALSKA

HYBERNSKA
POWDER
TOWER

PRIKOPE

MUCHA
MUS.

BETH.
CHAPEL

BETLEM

NA PRIKOPE

NA

PANSKA

MŮstek

JINDRISSKA

JERUZ

VLTAVA
STRANA

NAPRST KOL.

HUSOVA

NA PERST

NA MŮSTEK

Městek

RYTIRSKA

SKORE

NAPRSTKOVA

Václavské

MAIN
POST

OPLETA

WASHINGTONOVA

WILSONOVA

LEGII MOST

BARTOLOMEJSKA

NARODNI

WENCESLAS
SQUARE

NÁMĚSTÍ

NAT'L
THEATER

NOVE

MĚSTO

Muzeum

NATIONAL
MUSEUM

TO
DANCING
HOUSE

DCH

❶ Hotel Central

❷ Cloister Inn

❸ Pension u Medvídků

❹ Hotel u Klenotníka

❺ Pension Unitas
& Art Prison Hostel

❻ Hotel Expres

❼ Hotel u Tří Bubnů

❽ To Hotel Salvator

❾ Hotel Adria

❿ Hotel Europa

⓫ To Hotels Anna & Sieber

⓬ Hotel Julian

⓭ To Hotel 16

⓮ To Dům u Šemíka
& Guest House Lída

⓯ To Hotel Luník

⓰ To Hotel Sax
& Domus Henrici

⓱ To Hostel Sokol

⓲ To Hostel Elf

⓳ Launderette

4,600 kč, Tb-4,900 kč, Nov–Feb 30–40 percent less, 5 percent discount
for cash, ask for a "Rick Steves discount" with your e-mail request, elevator, Rybná 8, Praha 1, Metro: Náměstí Republiky, tel. 224-812-041,
fax 222-328-404, central@orfea.cz).

$$$ **Cloister Inn** is well-located, with 75 modern rooms. The exte-
rior is more concrete than charm—the building used to be shared by a
convent and a secret-police prison—but inside, it's newly redone and
plenty comfortable (Sb-4,000 kč, Db-4,200 kč, Tb-5,000 kč, elevator,
free Internet access and coffee, Konviktská 14, Praha 1, tel. 224-211-

020, fax 224-210-800, www.cloister-inn.com, cloister@cloister-inn.com).

$$ Pension u Medvídků has 31 comfortably renovated rooms in a big, rustic, medieval shell with dark wood furniture. Upstairs, you'll find lots of beams to smack into (Sb-2,300 kč, Db-3,500 kč, Tb-4,500 kč, extra bed-500 kč, "historical" rooms 10 percent more, apartment 20 percent more, prices flex with season, Internet access-70 kč/hr, Na Perštýně 7, Praha 1, tel. 224-211-916, fax 224-220-930, www.umedvidku.cz, info@umedvidku.cz). The pension runs a popular beer-hall restaurant that has live music most Fridays and Saturdays until 23:00.

$$ Hotel u Klenotníka, with 11 modern and comfortable rooms in a plain building, is three blocks off the Old Town Square (Sb-2,500 kč, Db-3,800 kč, Tb-4,500 kč, 10 percent off when booking direct with this book, Rytířská 3, Praha 1, tel. 224-211-699, fax 224-221-025, www.uklenotnika.cz, info@uklenotnika.cz).

$$ Hotel u Tří Bubnů is new, filling one of the oldest buildings in town 50 yards toward the river from the Old Town Square. Its 18 rooms are spacious, with high ceilings and wooden beams (Db-3,900 kč, extra bed-1,000 kč, U Radnice 8, tel. 224-214-855, fax 224-236-100, www.utribubnu.cz, utribubnu@volny.cz).

$ Pension Unitas rents 35 small, tidy, youth hostel-type rooms with plain, minimalist furnishings and no sinks (S-1,100 kč, D-1,400 kč, T-1,750 kč, Q-2,000 kč, T and Q are cramped with bunks in D-sized rooms, easy reservations without a deposit, non-smoking, quiet hours 22:00–7:00, Bartolomějská 9, Praha 1, tel. 224-221-802, fax 224-217-555, www.unitas.cz, unitas@unitas.cz). They run a fine little youth hostel in the former prison downstairs (see "Youth Hostels" page 87).

$ Hotel Expres rents 29 simple rooms and brings a decent continental breakfast to your room (S-1,000 kč, Sb-2,600 kč, D-1,400 kč, Db-2,800 kč, Tb-3,400 kč, 5 percent discount for cash, elevator, Skořepka 5, Praha 1, tel. 224-211-801, fax 224-223-309, www.pragueexpreshotel.cz, expres@zero.cz). While a good value, this place is in a red light zone and comes with late-night music from nearby clubs on weekends.

$ Hotel Salvator rents 30 comfortable rooms on a quiet street above a fun South American restaurant (D-1,850 kč, Db-2,850 kč, Qb-3,850 kč, extra bed-500 kč, elevator, Truhlářská 10, 3 minutes from Republic Square, Metro: Náměstí Republiky, tel. 222-312-234, fax 222-316-355, www.salvator.cz).

Wenceslas Square

$$$ Hotel Adria, with a prime Wenceslas Square location, cool Art Nouveau facade, and 88 completely modern and business-class rooms, is your big-time, four-star central splurge (Db-€220 but often discounted, air-con, elevator, minibars...the works, Václavské Náměstí 26, tel. 221-081-111, fax 221-081-300, www.adria.cz, accom@adria.cz).

$$ Hotel Europa is in a class by itself. This landmark place, famous for its wonderful 1903 Art Nouveau facade, is the centerpiece of Wenceslas Square. But someone pulled the plug on the hotel about 50 years ago, and it's a mess. It offers haunting beauty in all the public spaces, 92 dreary and ramshackle rooms, and a weary staff. They're waiting for a billion-crown investor to come along and rescue the place, but for now they offer some of the cheapest rooms on Wenceslas Square (S-1,600 kč, Sb-3,000 kč, D-2,600 kč, Db-4,000 kč, T-3,100 kč, Tb-5,000 kč, some rooms have been very slightly refurbished, some remain in unrefurbished old style, they cost the same either way, every room is different, elevator, Václavské Náměstí 25, Praha 1, tel. 224-228-117, fax 224-224-544, www.europahotel.cz).

East of Center in Vinohrady

$$$ **Hotel Sieber,** with 20 rooms, is in an upscale residential neighborhood (near former royal vineyards, or Vinohrady). It's a classy four-star business-class hotel that does a good job of being homey and welcoming (Sb-4,480 kč, Db-4,800 kč, extra bed-1,000 kč, 20 percent discount on Fri, Sat, and Sun, elevator, air-con, 3-min walk to Metro: Jiřího z Poděbrad, or tram #11, Slezská 55, Praha 3, tel. 224-250-025, fax 224-250-027, www.sieber.cz, reservations@sieber.cz).

$$ **Hotel Anna,** with 24 bright, pastel, and classically charming rooms, is a bit closer in—10 minutes by foot east of Wenceslas Square (Sb-2,300 kč, Db-3,100 kč, Tb-3,900 kč, 20 percent cheaper off-season, non-smoking rooms, elevator, Budečská 17, Praha 2, Metro: Náměstí Míru, tel. 222-513-111, fax 222-515-158, www.hotelanna.cz). The hotel runs a cheaper but similarly pleasant annex, the **Dependence,** two blocks away (Sb-1,860 kč, Db-2,560 kč, cheaper off-season, no elevator but all rooms on first floor, reception and breakfast at main hotel).

Away from the Center

Moving just outside the Old Town saves you money—and gets you away from the tourists and into some more workaday residential neighborhoods. These listings (great values compared to Old Town hotels) are all within a five- to 15-minute tram or Metro ride from the center.

$$ **Hotel Julian,** an oasis of professional, predictable decency in a quiet, untouristy neighborhood, is a five-minute taxi or tram ride from the action on the castle side of the river. Its 32 spacious, fresh, well-furnished rooms and big, homey public spaces hide behind a noble neo-classical facade. The staff is friendly and helpful (Sb-3,500 kč, Db-3,800 kč, suite Db-4,500 kč, extra bed-900 kč, family room, July–Aug 13 percent less, 5 percent discount off best quoted rate with this book, elevator, free "pay" TV, free tea and coffee in room, Internet access, parking lot, Elišky Peškové 11, Praha 5, tel. 257-311-150, reception tel. 257-311-145, fax 257-311-149, www.julian.cz, casjul@vol.cz). Free lockers and a shower are available for those needing to check out early but stay until

late (e.g., for an overnight train). Mike's Chauffeur Service, based here, is reliable and affordable (see "Transportation Connections," page 93).

$$ Hotel 16, a stately little place with an intriguing Art Nouveau facade, high ceilings, and a clean, sleek interior, rents 14 fine rooms (Sb-2,500 kč, Db-3,400 kč, Db suite-3,900 kč, Tb-4,600 kč, 10 percent lower off-season, back/quiet rooms face the garden, front/noisier rooms face the street, air-con, elevator, a 10-min walk south of Wenceslas Square, Metro: I. P. Pavlova, Kateřinská 16, Praha 2, tel. 224-920-636, fax 224-920-626, www.hotel16.cz, hotel16@hotel16.cz).

$ Dům u Šemíka, a friendly hotel named for a heroic mythical horse, is in a residential neighborhood just below Vyšehrad Castle, a 10-minute tram ride from the center (25 rooms, Sb-1,700 kč, Db-2,100–2,650 kč, apartment-2,800–4,850 kč depending on size, extra bed-700 kč, from the center take tram #18 to Albertov then walk 2 blocks uphill, or take tram #7 to Výtoň, go under rail bridge, and walk 3 blocks uphill to Vratislavova 36, Praha 2, tel. 224-920-736, fax 224-911-602, www.usemika.cz).

$ Hotel Luník, with 35 rooms, is a dignified but friendly, no-nonsense place out of the medieval faux-rustic world in a normal, pleasant business district. It's two Metro stops from the main station (Metro: I. P. Pavlova) or a 10-minute walk from Wenceslas Square (Sb-2,050 kč, Db-2,900 kč, Tb-3,350 kč, prices 20 percent lower Nov–March, 10 percent discount with this book if claimed with reservation, elevator, some street noise, Londýnská 50, Praha 2, tel. 224-253-974, fax 224-253-986, www.hotel-lunik.cz, recepce@hotel-lunik.cz).

$ Guest House Lída, with 12 homey and spacious rooms, fills a big house in a quiet residential area a 30-minute walk or 15-minute tram ride from the center. Jan and Jiří Prouza, who run the place, are a wealth of information and know how to make people feel at home (small Db-1,440 kč, Db-1,760 kč, Tb-2,110 kč, 10 percent off Nov–March, no CC, family rooms, top-floor family suite with kitchenette, parking in garage-200 kč/day, Metro: Pražského Povstání, exit Metro and turn left on Lomnicka between the Metro station and big blue glass ČSOB building, follow Lomnicka for 500 yards, then turn left on Lopatecka, go uphill and ring bell at Lopatecka #26, no sign outside, Praha 4, tel. & fax 261-214-766, lida@login.cz). The Prouza brothers also rent four apartments across the river, equally far away (Db-1,500 kč, Tb-1,920 kč, Qb-2,100 kč).

Across the River, near the Castle

$$$ Hotel Sax, on a quiet corner a block below the Malá Strana action, will delight the artsy yuppie with its 22 rooms, fruity atrium, and modern, stylish decor (Sb-3,700 kč, Db-4,400 kč, Db suite-5,100 kč, extra bed-1,000 kč, cheaper off-season, elevator, near Church of St. Nicholas, 1 block below Nerudova at Jánský Vršek 3, Praha 1, reserve long in advance, tel. 257-531-268, fax 257-534-101, www.sax.cz, hotelsax@bon.cz).

$$$ **Residence Domus Henrici,** just above Castle Square, is a quiet retreat that charges—and gets—top prices for its eight smartly appointed rooms, some of which include good views (Ds-5,100 kč, Db-5,600–6,200 kč depending on size, extra bed-900 kč, less off-season, pleasant terrace, Loretánská 11, Praha 1, tel. 220-511-369, fax 220-511-502, www.domus-henrici.cz, henrici@hidden-places.com). This is a five-minute walk above the castle gate in a quiet, elegant area.

Youth Hostels

$ **Hostel Sokol,** plain and institutional, with 100 beds, is peacefully located just off the park-like Kampa Island in the Tryš House buildings (the seat of the Czech Sokol Organization). Big WWI-style hospital rooms are lined with single beds and lockers (8–14 per room). From the main station, ride tram #9 to Újezd. From the Holešovice station, take tram #12 to Újezd (350 kč per bed with no breakfast, D-900 kč, no CC, easy to reserve by phone or e-mail without deposit, open 24/7, members' kitchen, Nosticova 2, Praha 1, tel. 257-007-397, fax 257-007-340, www.sokol-cos.cz, hostel@sokol-cos.cz).

$ **Art Prison Hostel** fills a former prison in the basement of Pension Unitas (see above). Rooms are stark with tiny high windows and no plumbing—but not as stark as when Václav Havel did time here (64 beds, S-1,000 kč, D-1,100 kč, dorm beds in 4–5 bed cells for 370 kč, includes sheets and breakfast, easy reservations without deposit if arriving by 17:00, no curfew, no smoking, shared modern facilities, lockers, Bartolomějská 9, tel. 224-221-802, www.unitas.cz, unitas@unitas.cz).

$ **Hostel Elf,** a fun-loving ramshackle place covered with noisy self-inflicted graffiti, has cheap basic beds, a helpful staff, and lots of creative services—kitchen, free luggage room, laundry, no lockout, free tea, cheap beer, a terrace, and lockers (dorm beds-260–340 kč, D-820 kč, includes sheets and breakfast, on a train line a 10-min walk from main train station and Florenc bus station, Husitská 11, Praha 3, tel. 222-540-963, www.hostelelf.com, info@hostelelf.com).

EATING

The beauty of Prague is wandering aimlessly through the winding old quarters, marveling at the architecture, watching the people, and sniffing out fun restaurants. You can eat well for very little money. What you'd pay for a basic meal in Vienna or Munich will get you an elegant meal in Prague. Choose between traditional, dark Czech beer-hall-type ambience; elegant *Jugendstil* early-20th-century atmosphere; ethnic; or hip and modern.

Watch out for scams. Many restaurants put more care into ripping off green tourists (and even locals) than in their cooking. Tourists are routinely served cheaper meals than what they ordered, given a menu with a "personalized" price list, charged extra for things they didn't get, or shortchanged. Avoid any menu without clear and explicit prices. Carefully examine your itemized bill and understand each line (a 10-percent service charge is sometimes added—in that case, there's no need to tip extra). Be careful of waiters padding the tab: Tax is always included in the price, so it shouldn't be tacked on later. Part with very large bills only if necessary, and deliberately count your change. Never let your credit card out of your sight and check the numbers carefully. Make it a habit to get cash from an ATM to pay for your meals. Remember, there are two parallel worlds in Prague: the tourist town and the real city. Generally, if you walk two minutes away from the tourist flow, you'll find better value, ambience, and service.

In the Old Town
Art Nouveau Restaurants

The sumptuous Art Nouveau concert hall—**Municipal House**—has three special restaurants: a café, a French restaurant, and a beer cellar (Náměstí Republiky 5). The dressy café, **Kavarna Obecní Dům,** is drenched in chandeliered Art Nouveau elegance (light pricey meals and drinks with great atmosphere and bad service, 1 hot meal special daily—250 kč, daily 7:30–23:00, live piano or jazz trio 16:00–20:00, tel. 222-002-763). **Francouzska Restaurace,** the fine and formal French restaurant, is in the next wing (700–1,000 kč meals, daily 12:00–16:00 & 18:00–23:00, tel. 222-002-777). **Plzeňská Restaurace,** downstairs, brags it's the most beautiful Art Nouveau pub in Europe (cheap meals, great atmosphere, daily 11:30–23:00, tel. 222-002-780).

Restaurant Mucha is touristy, with decent Czech food in a formal Art Nouveau dining room (300-kč meals, daily 12:00–24:00, Melantrichova 5, tel. 224-225-045).

Cheap and Uniquely Czech Places near Old Town Square

Prices go way down when you get away from the tourist areas. At least once, eat in a restaurant with no English menu.

Pivnice u Zeleneho Stromu (Pub of the Green Tree) is a new beer garden/cellar in an old building serving great beer and inexpensive traditional cuisine from a fun, imaginative menu. The courtyard is quiet and the cellar is bright and fresh (daily 11:00–23:00, good fresh veggies, next to Bethlehem Chapel at Betlémská Náměstí 6, tel. 222-220-228).

Klub Architektu is a mod student hangout with a medieval cellar serving cheap vegetarian meals, hearty salads, and a few "gourmet entrées" next to Bethlehem Chapel (Betlémská Náměstí 169, tel. 224-401-214).

U Medvídků, which started out as a brewery in 1466, has been a huge and popular beer hall since the 19th century. The food, beer, and service are fine and the ambience is bright, noisy, and not too smoky

Prague Restaurants

- ❶ Municipal House (3 restaurants)
- ❷ Restaurant Mucha
- ❸ Pivnice u Zeleneho Stromu Pub & Klub Architektu
- ❹ Beerhall u Medvídků
- ❺ Plzeňská Restaurace u Dvou Koček
- ❻ Restaurace Mlejnice
- ❼ Country Life Vegetarian Restaurant
- ❽ Czech Kitchen
- ❾ Bohemia Bagel (2 locations)
- ❿ Havelská Market
- ⓫ Ethnic eateries
- ⓬ Restaurant Zofin
- ⓭ To Rest. La Perle de Prague
- ⓮ Grand Café Slavia
- ⓯ Restaurant u Prince Terrace
- ⓰ Pub u Zlateho Tygra
- ⓱ Dobrá Čajovna Teahouse

(daily 11:30–23:00, a block toward Wenceslas Square from Bethlehem Square at Na Perštýně 7, tel. 224-211-916).

Plzeňská Restaurace u Dvou Koček is a typical Czech pub with cheap, no-nonsense, hearty Czech food and beer, and—once upon a time—a local crowd (200 kč for 3 courses and beer, serving original Pilsner Urquell with accordion music nightly until 23:00, under an arcade, facing tiny square between Perlová and Skořepka Streets).

Restaurace Mlejnice is a fun little pub strewn with farm implements and happy eaters, tucked away just out of the tourist crush two blocks from the Old Town Square (order carefully and understand your itemized bill, daily 11:00–24:00, between Melantrichova and Železná at Kožná 14, reservations smart in evening, tel. 224-228-635).

Country Life Vegetarian Restaurant is a bright, easy, and smoke-free cafeteria that has a well-displayed buffet of salads and veggie hot dishes. It's midway between the Old Town Square and the bottom of Wenceslas Square. They are serious about their vegetarianism, serving only plant-based, unprocessed, and unrefined food (Mon–Thu 8:30–19:00, Fri 8:30–18:00, Sun 11:00–18:00, closed Sat, through courtyard at Melantrichova 15/Michalská 18, tel. 224-213-366).

Česká Kuchyně (Czech Kitchen) is a blue-collar cafeteria serving steamy old Czech cuisine to a local clientele. There's no English inside, so—if you want apple charlotte but not tripe soup—be sure to review the small English menu in the window outside before entering. Note the numbers of the dishes you'd like that correspond to the Czech menu you'll see inside. Pick up your tally sheet as you enter, grab a tray, point liberally to whatever you'd like, and keep the paper to pay as you exit. It's extremely cheap...unless you lose your paper (daily 9:00–20:00, across from Havelská Market at Havelská 23, tel. 224-235-574).

Bohemia Bagel is hardly authentic Czech—exasperated locals insist that bagels have nothing to do with Bohemia. Owned by an American, this trendy place caters mostly to youthful tourists, with good sandwiches (100–125 kč), a little garden out back, and Internet access (1.50 kč/min) close to the Old Town Square (daily 7:00–24:00, locations at Újezd 16, tel. 257-310-529, and Masná 2, tel. 224-812-560, www.bohemiabagel.cz).

Havelská Market, surrounded by colorful little eateries, offers piles of picnic fixings.

Ethnic Restaurants for Local Yuppies near Old Town Square

With the recent economic boom, young professional Czechs have money to eat out and trendy little ethnic eateries are popping up everywhere. Within the space of a couple of blocks, you can eat your way around the world. Two blocks north of Old Town Square (up Dlouhá Street), wander along Rámová Street to Haštalská Square. You'll pass the **Ariana** (Afghan), **Orange Moon** (Thai/Indian), **Chez Marcel** (French), and **Dahab** (fancy or cheap Moroccan buffet, daily 12:00–24:00, Dlouhá 33, tel. 224-827-375).

Dining with an Old Town Square View

Restaurant u Prince Terrace, in the five-star U Prince Hotel, facing the astronomical clock, is designed for foreign tourists. A sleek elevator takes you to its rooftop, where every possible inch is used to serve good food (fish, Czech, and international) to its guests. The view is arguably the best in town—especially at sunset, when a reservation is smart. The menu is a fun and impressively affordable mix with photos to make ordering easy (daily until 24:00, Staroměstské Náměstí 29, tel. 224-213-807).

Above the Castle

To locate the following restaurants, see the Prague Castle map on page 67.

Maly Buddha ("Little Buddha") serves delightful food—especially vegetarian—and takes its theme seriously. You'll step into a mellow, low-lit escape of bamboo and peace to be served by people with perfect complexions and almost no pulse. Ethnic eateries like this are trendy with young Czechs (Tue–Sun 13:00–22:30, closed Mon, smoke-free, from the castle hike up the hill nearly to the monastery, Úvoz 46, tel. 220-513-894).

U Hrocha ("By the Hippo"), a very local little pub packed with beer drinkers and smoke, serves simple traditional meals—basically meat dishes with bread. Just below the castle near Malá Strana's main square, it's actually the haunt of many members of Parliament—located just around the corner (daily 12:00–23:00, chalkboard lists daily meals in English, Thunovská 10).

Café Espresso Kajetánka, just off Castle Square, is a pricey café worth considering for the view and convenience (daily 10:00–20:00, on Ke Hradu, tel. 257-533-735).

The Jewish Quarter

Kolkovna is a big, new, woody yet modern place catering to locals and serving a fun mix of Czech and international cuisine (ribs, salads, cheese plates, good beer, daily 11:00–24:00, across from Spanish Synagogue at V Kolkovně 8, tel. 224-819-701).

The **Franz Kafka Café** is pleasant for a snack or drink (daily 10:00–21:00, a block from the cemetery, Široká 12).

Dining Fine near the River in Nové Město

Restaurant Zofin is a Prague institution, taking you back to the era of waltzing elegance. Nicknamed for Franz Josef's mother Sofia, it shares a circa-1880 palace with a famous ballroom on a small island south of Charles Bridge (mostly traditional 3-course menus range from simple/310 kč to gourmet/990 kč, huge and reasonable wine list, plain garden tables or sumptuous reserve-in-advance indoor tables, Slovanský Island, reach island by bridge south of National Theater, tel. 224-934-548).

La Perle de Prague fills the seventh and eighth floors of Frank Gehry's wild and modern Dancing House building with Prague's high society and top-end visitors enjoying a fine river view and gourmet French cuisine. It's white-tablecloth dressy and offers terrace seating in good weather. While few tables are actually by the window, be sure to enjoy a pre-dinner drink or sip your last glass of wine upstairs, next to Fred Astaire's wire-mesh head on the roof terrace (business lunch-500 kč, dinner menu-900 kč, daily 12:00–14:00 & 19:00–22:30, reservations required to even get in the elevator, 15-min walk south of Charles Bridge, Tančící Dům, Rašínovo nábřeží 80, tel. 221-984-160, www.laperle.cz).

Grand Café Slavia, across from the National Theater (facing the Legií Bridge on Národní Street), is a fixture in Prague, famous as a hangout for its literary elite. Today, it's a bit tired, with its Art Deco interior, lousy piano entertainment, and celebrity photos on the wall. But its cheap and fun menu, filled with interesting traditional dishes (meals, sweets, coffees, liqueurs—including absinthe for 55 kč), make it a fun stop (daily 8:00–23:00, sit nearest the river). Notice the *Drinker of Absinthe* painting on the wall (and on the menu)—with the iconic Czech writer struggling with reality.

Drinks
Czech Beer

For many, *pivo* (beer) is the top Czech tourist attraction. After all, the Czechs invented lager in nearby Plzeň (Pilsen in German). This is the famous Pilsner Urquell, a great lager on tap everywhere. A classic place to enjoy a Pilsner Urquell is **U Zlateho Tygra** ("The Golden Tiger"), just south of Karlova on Husova (daily 15:00–23:00—often jam-packed).

Be sure to venture beyond Pilsner Urquell. There are plenty of other good Czech beers. Budvar is the local Budweiser, but it's not related to the American brew.

Czechs are among the world's biggest beer drinkers—adults drink about 80 gallons a year. The big degree symbol on bottles and menus marks the beer's heaviness, not its alcohol content (12 degrees is darker, 10 degrees lighter). The smaller figure shows alcohol content. Order beer from the tap (*tocene* means "draft," *sudove pivo* means "keg beer"). A *pivo* is large (0.5 liter, or 17 oz); a *malé pivo* is small (0.3 liter, or 10 oz). Men invariably order the large size.

In many restaurants, a beer hits your table like a glass of water in the United States. *Pivo* for lunch has me sightseeing for the rest of the day on Czech knees. *Na Zdraví* is "cheers" in Czech. Later they say *Nádraží* (which means "train station").

Liqueurs

In bars and restaurants, you can go wild with memorable liqueurs, most of which cost about a dollar a shot. Experiment. *Fernet,* a bitter drink made from many herbs, is the leading Czech apéritif. Absinthe, made from wormwood and herbs, is a watered-down version of the hallucinogenic drink that's illegal in the United States and much of Europe. It's famous as the muse of so many artists, like Henri de Toulouse-Lautrec in Paris a century ago. *Becherovka*, made of 13 herbs and 38 percent alcohol, was used to settle upset medieval tummies and promote sexual arousal. This velvety drink remains popular today. *Becherovka* and tonic mixed together is nicknamed *bedon* ("concrete"). Drink three and you'll find out why. *Medovina*, literally honey wine, is mead, and you'll find it all over the Czech Republic.

Tea

Many Czech people are bohemian philosophers at heart and prefer the mellow, smoke-free environs of a teahouse to the smoky, traditional beer hall. While there are teahouses all over town, one fine example in a handy locale is **Dobrá Čajovna** (The Good Tea House, Mon–Sat 10:00–21:30, Sun 14:00–21:30, near the base of Wenceslas Square, opposite McDonald's at Václavské Náměstí 14). This teahouse, just a few steps off the bustle of the main square, takes you into a very peaceful world that elevates tea to an almost religious ritual. At the desk you'll be given an English menu and a bell. Grab a seat, study the menu—which lovingly describes each tea. Then ring your bell to beckon a tea monk— likely a member of the "lovers of tea society." This is Prague's original teahouse, established in 1991. The menu lists a world of tea (very fresh, prices by the small pot), "accompaniments" (such as Exotic Miscellany), and light meals "for hungry tea drinkers" (www.cajovna.com).

TRANSPORTATION CONNECTIONS

Getting to Prague: Centrally-located Prague is a logical gateway between Western and Eastern Europe. If you're coming from the West and using a Eurailpass, you must purchase tickets to cover the portion of the journey from the Czech border into Prague (buy at station before you board train for Prague). Or supplement your pass with a Prague Excursion pass, giving you passage from any Czech border station into Prague and back to any border station within seven days (first-class-€50, second class-€40, youth second class-€35). EurAide, a travel agency with offices in Berlin (see page 457) and Munich, also sells these passes for a bit less from their American office (U.S. tel. 941/480-1555, fax 941/480-1522). From the East, prague has convenient night-train connections with Budapest, Kraków, and Warsaw (see below).

For Czech train and bus schedules, see www.vlak-bus.cz. Train info tel. 221-111-122 (little English).

By train to: Benešov (10-min walk from **Konopiště Castle**; hrly, 45 min), **Karlštejn** (hrly, 40 min, then a 20-min walk to castle), **Kutná Hora** (7/day, 60 min, more with change in Kolín), **Český Krumlov**

(8/day, 1/day direct, 4 hrs, verify departing station), **Berlin** (5/day, 5 hrs), **Munich** (3/day with changes, 6 hrs, 1 direct overnight departure), **Frankfurt** (4 direct/day, 6 hrs), **Vienna** (3/day, 5 hrs), **Budapest** (5 direct/day, 7 hrs), **Kraków** (1 direct night train/day, 8.5 hrs; otherwise transfer in Katowice, Wrocław, or Ostrava-Svinov, 8–11 hrs), **Warsaw** (2/day direct, including 1 night train, 9–12 hrs; or 1/day, 9 hrs, with transfer in Ostrava-Svinov).

By bus to: Český Krumlov (7/day, 3.5 hrs, from Florenc station; an easy direct 3-hr bus leaves at about 9:00), **Terezín Concentration Camp** (hrly, 60 min, from Florenc station).

By car, with a driver: Mike's Chauffeur Service is a reliable little company with fair and fixed rates around town and beyond. Friendly Mike's motto is, "We go the extra mile for you" (round-trip fares with waiting time included, guaranteed through 2004 with this book: Český Krumlov-3,500 kč, Terezín-1,700 kč, Karlštejn-1,500 kč, up to 4 people, minibus also available, tel. 241-768-231, mobile 602-224-893, www.mike-chauffeur.cz, mike.chauffeur@cmail.cz). On the way to Krumlov, Mike will stop at no extra charge at Hluboká Castle or České Budějovice, where the original Bud beer is made. Mike offers a "Panoramic Transfer to Vienna" for 7,000 kč (depart Prague at 8:00, arrive Český Krumlov at 10:00, stay up to 6 hrs, 1-hr scenic Czech riverside-and-village drive, then 2-hr Autobahn to your Vienna hotel, maximum 4 people).

DAY TRIPS

These four intriguing destinations, in different directions, take an hour to reach from Prague. Terezín, a walled town, served as a containment camp for Jews during World War II. The two historic castles—Konopiště (better interior) and Karlštejn (better exterior)—give you a good look at the Czech version of this European medieval architectural form. Kutná Hora attracts visitors to its monk-designed chapel of bones.

Terezín

Terezín, an hour by bus from Prague, was a fortified town named after Maria Theresa (Theresienstadt). It was built in the 1780s with state-of-the-art walls designed to keep out the Prussians. In 1941, the Nazis moved its 7,000 inhabitants out and moved in 60,000 Jews, creating Terezín Concentration Camp. The town's medieval walls, originally meant to keep Germans out, were now used by German conquerors to keep the Jews in. This was their model "Jewish town," a concentration camp dolled up for propaganda purposes. Here in this "self-governed Jewish settlement area," Jewish culture seemed to thrive, as "citizens" put on plays and concerts, published a magazine, and raised their families in ways impressive to Red Cross inspectors. But virtually all of

Terezín's Jews ultimately ended up dying either here or at concentration camps farther east. (The art of the children of Terezín survives as a striking testimony to the horror of the Holocaust—well-displayed and described in English in Prague's Pinkas Synagogue.) Terezín is an unforgettable day trip from Prague for those interested in touring the concentration camp memorial/museum and the adjacent SS prison.

Getting There: Buses leave from Florenc station in Prague and arrive in Terezín at the public bus stop, which is on the marketplace in the town center, facing the museum (hrly, 60-min journey). Note bus departure times when you arrive.

Self-Guided Tour: Start with the museum (where you buy your Terezín ticket). You'll find two floors of exhibits on the camp and an excellent cinema showing two 10-minute films (a slice-of-camp-life video and a propaganda video produced by the Nazis and used to fool the Red Cross about conditions here for the Jewish inmates). Note the show times as you enter. The same movies also play in the small fortress.

Then walk through the walled town following the numbered map that explains the various sights (pick up map at museum).

Leave the fortified city and cross the river. Walk about 300 yards around the vast cemetery to the small fortress (you'll see its black-and-white striped gate). Inside the gate, at the ticket checkpoint, wait for the obligatory guided tour (English tours leave twice hourly; try asking at the museum when the next one leaves). This Gestapo police prison—opened in 1942—was filled not with Jews but with other enemies of the Reich (who now fill the graveyard you passed to get here). The powerful 45-minute tour shows the demonic *modus operandi* used by the SS: torture followed by execution.

Konopiště Castle

Konopiště, more interesting to tour than Karlštejn Castle (below), is 30 miles south of Prague, on the way to Český Krumlov (see next chapter).

This 14th-century castle houses the extravagant 17th-century hunting lodge of the Hapsburgs. It's bursting with skins, antlers, stuffed birds, weapons, Meissen porcelain, and fancy furniture. The grounds are also entertaining, with bears in the moat and a chorus of pheasants and peacocks welcoming you into the formal gardens (castle open daily May–Oct 9:00–12:00 & 13:00–17:00, less off-season, castle grounds always open).

Hourly trains from Prague's Hlavní Nádraží station drop you at Benešov, a 10-minute walk from the castle (trip takes 45 min).

Karlštejn Castle

One of the Czech Republic's top attractions, Karlštejn Castle was built by Charles IV in about 1350 to house the crown jewels of the Holy Roman Empire. While a striking fairy-tale castle from a distance, it's not much inside. The castle interior's highlight, the much-venerated and sumptuous Chapel of the Holy Cross (built to house the crown jewels), can be seen only with an advance reservation (May–Sept Tue–Sun 9:00–12:00 & 13:00–18:00, closed Mon; Oct–April Tue–Sun 9:00–12:00 & 13:00–15:00, closed Mon, tel. 274-008-154, www.hradkarlstejn.cz). The castle, 20 miles southwest of Prague, is accessible by train (departures from Smíchov Station, hrly, 40 min, then a 20-min walk) or by car (30 min, direction Plzeň).

Kutná Hora

This delightful town of 20,000 sits on what was Europe's largest silver mine. The mine was so productive that, in its day, Kutná Hora was the second most important Czech town (after Prague). The standard coinage of much of Europe was minted right here. By about 1700, the mining and minting petered out and the city slumbered...once rich, then ignored. Today tourists are charmed by its wonderful state of preservation and interesting sights: the fine St. Barbara's Cathedral, fascinating silver mine, and eerie bone chapel.

Tourist Information: The TI is on Palackého Náměstí (generally Mon–Fri 9:00–18:00, Sat–Sun 10:00–16:00, tel. 0327-512-378, www.kutnahora.cz).

Sights

St. Barbara's Cathedral (Chram sv. Barbory)—The cathedral, dating from about 1400, has a dazzling interior, celebrating the town's sources of wealth with frescoes featuring mining and minting (daily 9:00–18:00 in season, shorter hours off-season).

District Museum of Mining (Okresni Muzeum)—At the museum, located in Kutná Hora's 15th-century castle, visitors see an exhibit on mining and an intriguing horse-powered winch that hoisted 2,000 pounds of rock at a time out of the mine. Then they don miner's coats and helmets and climb deep into the mine for a wet, dark, and claustrophobic 45-minute tour of the medieval shafts that honeycomb the land under the town (Tue–Sun 10:00–18:00, closed Mon).

Bone Church (Kostnice)—The church is a mile from town in Sedlec (walk, taxi, or catch a city bus on Masarykova Street—buy a ticket at a Tobak shop). Inside this little church, which looks so normal on the outside, the bones of 40,000 people decorate the walls and ceilings. Fourteenth-century plagues and 15th-century wars provided all the raw material necessary for monks to vent their creative spirit. The monks who first stacked these bones 400 years ago wanted viewers to remember that the earthly church is a community of both the living and the dead, a countless multitude that will one day stand before God. Later bone-stackers were more into design than theology—a chandelier includes every bone in the human body (July–Aug daily 8:00–18:00, off-season 9:00–16:00 and closed Mon).

Transportation Connections

Kutná Hora is 40 miles east of Prague. Trains from Prague's Hlavní Nádraží station (7/day, 60 min) get you near Kutná Hora, two miles from the town center. From there, local trains run to the central Kutná Hora Město station.

ČESKÝ KRUMLOV

Lassoed by its river and dominated by its castle, this enchanting town feels lost in a time warp. Český Krumlov is the Czech Republic's answer to Germany's Rothenburg—but has yet to be turned into a medieval theme park. With its awe-inspiring castle, delightful old town of shops and cobbled lanes, characteristic little restaurants, and easy canoeing options, having fun is a slam-dunk here.

Český Krumlov (CHESS-key KROOM-loff) means roughly "Czech bend in the river." Calling it Český for short sounds silly to Czech-speakers (since dozens of Czech town names begin with "Český"). Krumlov for short is okay.

The second-most visited town (1.5 million visits annually) and castle in the Czech Republic (after Prague), there's enough tourism to make things colorful and easy—but not so much that it feels fake. The town of 15,000 attracts a young, bohemian crowd, drawn here for its simple beauty and cheap living.

Planning Your Time

As the castle and theater can be visited only with a guide (and English tours are offered just a few times a day), serious sightseers should call the castle to reserve these tours first thing and then build their day around these times. A paddle around the town is a highlight (easy in an hour or two). Other sights are quick visits and worthwhile only if you have a particular interest (Egon Schiele, puppets, torture, and so on). The town itself is a joy. Evenings are for atmospheric dining and drinking. Those interested in music can ask at the TI and plan for it. Sights are generally open 10:00 to 17:00 and closed on Monday.

Český Krumlov

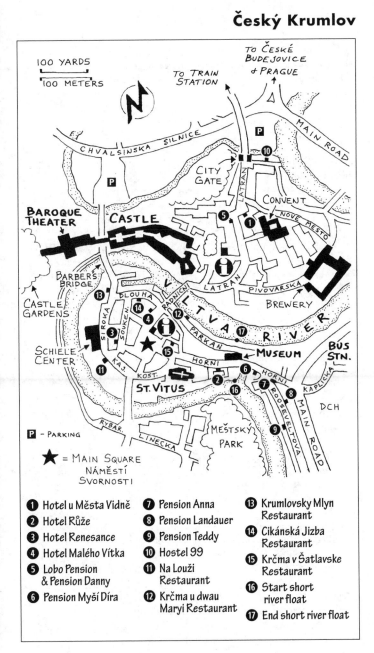

100 YARDS

100 METERS

TO TRAIN STATION

TO ČESKÉ BUDEJOVICE & PRAGUE

CHVALSINSKA SILNICE

MAIN ROAD

P

CITY GATE

LATRAN

CONVENT

NOVE MESTO

BAROQUE THEATER

CASTLE

P

BARBER'S BRIDGE

LATRAN

PIVOVARSKA

BREWERY

CASTLE GARDENS

DLOUHA

RADNICNI

VLTAVA RIVER

SOUKEN.

SIROKA

PARKAN

BUS STN.

SCHIELE CENTER

KAJ.

HORNI

MUSEUM

KOST.

ST. VITUS

HORNI

KAPLICKA

ROOSEVELTOVA

MAIN ROAD

DCH

P – PARKING

RYBAR.

LINECKA

MĚSTSKÝ PARK

★ = MAIN SQUARE NÁMĚSTÍ SVORNOSTI

1 Hotel u Města Vídně
2 Hotel Růže
3 Hotel Renesance
4 Hotel Malého Vítka
5 Lobo Pension & Pension Danny
6 Pension Myší Díra

7 Pension Anna
8 Pension Landauer
9 Pension Teddy
10 Hostel 99
11 Na Louži Restaurant
12 Krčma u dwau Maryi Restaurant

13 Krumlovsky Mlyn Restaurant
14 Cikánská Jizba Restaurant
15 Krčma v Šatlavske Restaurant
16 Start short river float
17 End short river float

ORIENTATION

Český Krumlov is extremely easy to navigate. The snaking Vltava River, which makes a perfect S through the town, ropes the old town into a tight peninsula. (It's the same river that flows through Prague.) One main street also winds through town, from the isthmus, through the peninsula, across the bridge, up through the "castle town" and through the castle complex (a long series of courtyards) to the castle gardens high above the town.

The main square, Náměstí Svornosti—with the TI, ATMs, banks (close at 17:00), and taxis—marks the center of the peninsula and dominates the old town. All recommended restaurants and hotels are within a few minutes' walk of the square. No sight in town is more than a five-minute stroll away.

Tourist Information: The eager-to-please TI on the main square recently won the best TI in the Czech Republic award (July–Aug daily 9:00–20:00, June and Sept daily 9:00–19:00, March–May and Oct daily 9:00–18:00, Nov–Feb daily 9:00–17:00, tel. 380-704-622, www.ckrumlov.cz). Pick up the free city map. The 129-kč *City Guide* book explains everything in town and includes a fine town and castle map in the back. The TI can check train, bus, and flight schedules, and change traveler's checks (fair rate). Ask about concerts, city walking tours in English, car rentals, and canoe trips on the river. The TI can reserve a room, but it'll take a 10 percent deposit that will be deducted from your hotel bill. Save your host money and go direct.

Historic Town Walking Tour: The TI offers worthwhile 90-minute guided town walks in English (July–Sept daily at 10:00 and noon, just show up, meet in front of TI on main square, buy 150-kč ticket from guide, minimum 2 people). The TI also rents a self-guided audioguide for 60 kč per hour.

Arrival in Český Krumlov

Taxis are cheap; don't hesitate to take one from the train station (about 100 kč) or bus station (around 60 kč).

By Train: The train station is a 15-minute walk from town (turn right out of the station, then walk downhill onto a steep cobbled path leading to an overpass into the town center).

By Bus: The bus station is just three blocks away from the old town (from the bus station lot, drop down to main road and turn left, then turn right at Potraviny grocery store to reach the center).

Helpful Hints

Internet Access: Fine Internet cafés and points are all over town and in many of the accommodations. The TI on the main square has several fast, cheap stand-up stations for a quick visit.

Laundry: Pension Lobo runs a self-service launderette under the castle (daily, Latrán 73).

Private Guides: Jiří (George) Václavíček is a local teacher who enjoys showing visitors around on his off-hours (afternoons, evenings, and weekends). Jiří —a gentle and caring man who seems to fit mellow Český Krumlov perfectly—is a joy to share this town with. He's happy to work for as little as an hour (350 kč/hr, tel. 380-726-813, mobile 603-927-995, vaclavicek@cmail.cz).

Another guide service provides private tours for 250 kč per hour (you name the place and time, mobile 723-069-561).

SIGHTS

Old Town

Main Square (Náměstí Svornosti)—Lined by Renaissance and Baroque homes of burghers, the main square has a grand charm. There's continuity here. Lekarna, with the fine, red Baroque facade on the lower corner of square, is still a pharmacy, as it has been since 1620. McDonald's tried three times to get a spot here but was turned away. The Town Hall flies the Czech flag and the town flag, which shows the rose symbol of the Rosenberg family who ruled the town for 300 years.

Imagine the history this square has seen: In the 1620s, the rising tide of Lutheran Protestantism was threatening Catholic Europe. As Krumlov was a seat of Jesuit power and learning, the intellectuals of the Roman church burned 5,000 books on this square. Later, when there was a bad harvest, locals blamed witches—and burned them. Every so often, terrible plagues rolled through the countryside. In a village nearby, all but two residents were killed by a plague. But the plague stopped before devastating the people of Český Krumlov, and in 1715—as a thanks to God—they built the plague monument that marks the center of the square today. Much later, in 1938, Hitler stood right here before a backdrop of long Nazi banners to celebrate the annexation of the Sudetenland. And, in 1968, Russian tanks spun their angry treads on these same cobblestones to intimidate locals who were demanding freedom. Today, thankfully, this square is part of an unprecedented peace and prosperity for the Czech people.

Torture Museum—This is just a lame haunted house: dark, with sound effects, cheap modern models, and prints showing off the cruel and unusual punishments of medieval times (80 kč, daily 9:00–20:00, English descriptions, facing the main square).

Barber's Bridge (Lazebnicky most)—This wooden bridge, decorated with 19th-century statues, separates the Castle Town and Old Town. On the center stands a statue of St. John of Nepomuk. Among other responsibilities, he is the protector against floods. In the great floods of

ČESKÝ KRUMLOV HISTORY

With the natural moat provided by the sharp bend in the Vltava, it's no wonder this has been a choice spot for eons. Celtic tribes first settled here a century before Christ. Then came German tribes. The Slavic tribes arrived in the ninth century. The Rosenbergs—Bohemia's top noble family—ran the city from 1302 to 1602. In many ways, the 16th century was the town's golden age, when Český Krumlov hosted an important Jesuit college. The Hapsburgs bought the region in 1602, ushering in a more Germanic period.

The rich mix of Gothic, Renaissance, and Baroque buildings is easy to under-appreciate. As you wander, look up...notice the details in the stonework that survive. Step into shops, snoop into back lanes and tiny squares. Gothic buildings curve with the winding streets. Many precious Gothic and Renaissance frescoes were whitewashed in Baroque times (when things Gothic and Renaissance were way out of style). Today these precious frescoes are being rediscovered and restored.

With its rich German heritage, it was easy for Hitler to claim that this region—the Sudetenland—was rightfully part of Germany. So, in 1938, in one of the bold and arrogant moves that led to World War II, he just took it. After the war, in a kind of Potsdam Treaty-approved ethnic cleansing, three million Germans in Czech lands were sent west to Germany. Český Krumlov turned into a ghost town inhabited mostly by robbers and Gypsies. Picture Gypsy squatters with their fires in the stately noble homes that line the town's main square.

In 1945, Americans liberated the town. But, in the post-WWII world as planned by Stalin and FDR, the border of the Soviet and American spheres of influence fell about here. As the town was essentially Slavic, it remained with the East. While the communist government established order, the period from 1945 to 1989 was a smelly time capsule. The town was infamously polluted—its now-pristine river was foamy from the paper mill just up stream. The bleak years of communism here paradoxically provided a cocoon to preserve the town. There was no money, so little changed, apart from a build-up of grime. Today, with its new prosperity, it's emerging as a fairy-tale town. In fact, movie producers consider it ideal for fairy-tale films. (*The Adventures of Pinocchio*, starring Jonathan Taylor Thomas, was filmed right here.)

August 2002, the angry river submerged the bridge and swept away the banisters…but the bridge survived.

Church of St. Vitus—Český Krumlov's main church was built as a bastion of Catholicism in the 15th century, when the Roman Catholic Church was fighting the Hussites. The Baroque 17th-century high altar, showing St. Vitus and the Virgin Mary, is capped with Duke Wenceslas. He was the patron saint of the Czech people—long considered their ambassador in heaven. The canopy now in the back—featuring a Rosenberg atop a horse—was once at the high altar. Too egotistical for Jesuits, it was moved to the rear of the nave.

Museum of Regional History—Located in the center, this small museum gives you a quick look at regional costumes, tools, and traditions; ask for the simple English translation that also includes a lengthy history of Krumlov. Start on the second floor, where you'll see old paintings, a glimpse of noble life in Krumlov, and a ceramic model of town as it was in 1800. The first floor comes with fine folk costumes and domestic art and a Bronze Age exhibit. The postcards in the hallway offer a fun look at Český Krumlov in the old days (50 kč, daily 10:00–17:00, across from Hotel Růže at Horní 152).

Egon Schiele Art Center—This classy contemporary-art gallery has top-notch temporary exhibits generally featuring 20th-century Czech artists and a top-floor permanent collection celebrating the hometown boy, Egon Schiele (pron: Sheila, like the girl's name). A friend of Gustav Klimt and important figure in the Secessionist movement in Vienna, Schiele lived a short life, from 1890 to 1918. Alas, his cutting-edge lifestyle and harsh and graphic nudes didn't fit the conservative small-town style of Český Krumlov (180 kč, daily 10:00–18:00, Široká 70, tel. 380-704-011).

Krumlov Castle (Krumlovský Zámek)

The castle complex, worth ▲▲, includes bear pits, the castle itself, a rare Baroque theater, and groomed gardens.

Round Tower (Zámecká Věž)—The strikingly colorful round tower marks the place of the first castle, built here to guard the ford. With its 16th-century Renaissance paint job colorfully restored, it looks exotic, featuring a fancy astrological decor, terra-cotta symbols of the zodiac, and a fine arcade (you can climb its 162 steps for a great view, 30 kč).

Bear Pit—At the site of the castle drawbridge, the bear pit holds a family of brown European bears, as it has since the Rosenbergs started this tradition in the 16th century. Bears implied a long and noble family lineage.

Castle—The immense castle is a series of courtyards with shops, contemporary art galleries, and tourist services. To tour the inside, choose between Tour #1 (of most general interest) and Tour #2 (19th-century castle life, Baroque art, and tapestries). After getting your ticket and tour time (request English), wait in the richly-decorated Renaissance court-yard (the third courtyard). You'll get a glimpse of the places where the Rosenbergs, Eggenbergs, and Schwarzenbergs dined, studied, worked, prayed, entertained, and slept.

Imagine being an aristocratic guest here riding the dukes' assembly line of fine living: You would promenade through a long series of elegant spaces and dine in the sumptuous dining hall before enjoying a concert in the Hall of Mirrors, which leads directly to the theater. After the play, you'd go out into the château garden for a fireworks finale (Tour #1-150 kč, Tour #2-140 kč, each tour 1 hr, 8–45 per group, June–Aug Tue–Sun 9:00–12:00 & 13:00–18:00, spring and fall until 17:00, closed Mon and Nov–March).

▲▲Baroque Theater (Zámecké Divadlo)—Europe once had several hundred fine Baroque theaters. Using candles for light and fireworks for special effects, most burned down. Today only two survive in good shape and are open to tourists: one at Stockholm's Drottningholm Palace and one here at this castle. Along with a look at the precious theater itself and a video of it in action, you'll see lots of surviving theater gear: a dozen or so painted sets, hundreds of costumes, and original special effects and sound-making machinery. Scenes could be changed in 10 seconds. (Fireworks blinded the audience and, when the smoke cleared, it was a new scene.) Unfortunately, the number of visitors is strictly reg-ulated and there are only three English tours a day—often sold out in advance (170 kč, 45-min tours daily May–Oct only, departures at 10:00, 11:00, 13:00, 14:00, 15:00 and 16:00, call 380-704-721 to establish English-language tour times and reserve a space). It's generally a frus-trating experience.

Castle Gardens—This 2,300-foot-long garden crowns the castle com-plex. It was laid out in the 17th century, when the noble family would light it with 22,000 oil lamps, torches, and candles for special occasions. The lower part is geometrical and symmetrical—French style. The upper is rougher—English style (free, daily 8:00–19:00, April and Oct until 17:00, closed in winter).

ACTIVITIES

▲▲Canoeing and Rafting the Vltava—Český Krumlov lies in the middle of the most popular boating river valley in the Czech Republic. Make time to paddle around the town or through Bohemian forests and villages of the nearby countryside.

The easy half-hour experience is to float around the city's penin-sula, starting and ending at opposite sides of the tiny isthmus. (Heck, you can do it twice.) Longer trips involve a minibus transfer. If you're starting upriver from Krumlov (Rozmberk direction), you'll go faster with more whitewater—but the river parallels a road, so it's a little less idyllic. Going downstream from Krumlov (direction České Budějovice), you'll have more pastoral scenery and less excitement. You can choose among destinations involving one to eight hours of floating and paddling (there is lots of work involved, even though you're going downstream). At a set time and place, the minibus will meet you. You'll encounter plenty of inviting pubs and cafés for breaks along the way. Plan on getting wet. There's a little whitewater, but the river is so shallow that if you tip, you simply stand up and climb back in.

Choose from a kayak, canoe (fastest, less work, more likely to tip), or inflatable raft (harder rowing, slower but very stable). Rates vary from 300 kč for the 30-minute canoe or raft trip around the town; to 700 kč for a three-hour, 15-km (9-mile) float; to 1,000 kč for a 35-km (22-mile), all-day trip. Prices are per boat (2–6 people) and include a map and transportation to or from the start and end points. Several companies offer this lively activity. Perhaps the handiest is Půjčovna Lodí Maleček Boat Rental (daily April–Oct, long hours, they also run the recommended Pension Myší Díra—see "Sleeping," below, Rooseveltova 28, tel. 337-712-508, lode@malecek.cz).

Slupenec Horseback Riding Club—Head about a mile out of town for horseback rides and lessons at this local riding club (Tue–Sun 9:00–18:00, 1 hr outdoors or in the ring-250 kč, all-day ride-1,800 kč, helmets provided, Renéa Srncová, Slupenec 1, tel. 380-711-052, www .jk-slupenec.cz).

SLEEPING

$$$ **Hotel u Města Vídně** (Vienna Hotel) is a new three-star business-class hotel with a no-nonsense German-style classiness and efficiency in a well-designed concrete shell on a quiet street below the castle. They rent 50 fine rooms and offer all the comforts and services—sauna, exercise room, and so on—you'd expect in a big business hotel (Sb-2,700 kč, Db-3,300 kč, suite-5,000 kč, Latrán 77, tel. 380-720-111, fax 380-720-119, www.hmv.cz, info@hmv.cz).

$$$ **Hotel Růže**, Krumlov's four-star splurge, fills a beautifully renovated Jesuit seminary. While it boasts grand public spaces, a brilliant backyard terrace overlooking the river, and red-carpeted halls, its rooms are about what you'd expect for half the price. The place, though vast and historic, feels a little forlorn (Sb-4,200 kč, Db-5,200 kč, deluxe Db-5,900 kč, apartment-6,600 kč, extra bed-1,060 kč, 30 percent less in winter, 10 percent more on holidays, Horní 154, tel. 380-772-100, fax 380-713-146, www.hotelruze.cz, info@hotelruze.cz).

$$ **Hotel Renesance**—just opened in 2003—is a plush place a block off the main square offering the best Old World elegant rooms in town. Their eight doubles and three suites are tastefully decorated with open beams, chandeliers, and old photos (Sb-1,400 kč, Db-1,800 kč,

SLEEP CODE

(30 kč = about \$1, country code: 420)
Sleep Code: **S** = Single, **D** = Double/Twin, **T** = Triple, **Q** = Quad, **b** = bathroom, **s** = shower only, **no CC** = Credit Cards not accepted. Unless otherwise noted, credit cards are accepted and prices include breakfast.

To help you sort easily through these listings, I've divided the rooms into three categories based on the price for a standard double room with bath:

\$\$\$ **Higher Priced**—Most rooms 3,000 kč or more.
  \$\$ **Moderately Priced**—Most rooms between 1,500–3,000 kč.
   \$ **Lower Priced**—Most rooms 1,500 kč or less.

Krumlov is filled with small, good, family-run pensions offering doubles with baths from 1,000–1,500 kč and hostel beds for 300 kč. Summer weekends and festivals are busiest and most expensive; reserve ahead when possible. Hotels speak some English and accept credit cards; pensions rarely do either.

Db suite-2,200 kč, extra bed-500 kč, Soukenická 33, tel. 380-725-911, fax 380-725-910, www.hotelrenesance.cz, hotel@hotelrenesance.cz).

\$\$ Hotel Malého Vítka is right in the old center and consists of a tangle of Gothic vaults and staircases connecting comfy woodsy rooms. As some standard doubles are much bigger than others and all are the same price, it's worth requesting a larger standard room. The deluxe rooms—unless you're dying for a Jacuzzi—aren't worth the higher cost (standard Db-1,450 kč, bigger deluxe Db-2,400 kč, Radniční 27, tel. & fax 380-711-925, www.vitekhotel.cz, vitekhotel@email.cz).

Cheap Pensions Under the Castle

A quiet cobbled pedestrian street (Latrán) below the castle just over the bridge from the Old Town and a 10-minute walk downhill from the train station is lined with characteristic shops and a couple of fine little family-run eight-room pensions.

\$ Lobo Pension fills a modern, efficient concrete building with fresh and spacious rooms (Sb-700 kč, Db-1,000 kč, Tb-1,400 kč, Latrán 73, tel. & fax 380-713-153, www.pensionlobo.cz, pensionlobo@cmail.cz).

\$ Pension Danny is a little funkier, with homier rooms and a tangled floor plan above a restaurant (Db-850 kč, apartment Db-1,000 kč, breakfast in room, Latrán 72, tel. 380-712-710, www.pensiondanny.cz, pensiondanny@tiscali.cz).

Cheap, Comfy Rooms between the Bus Station and Old Town

$ **Pension Myší Díra** (the Mouse Hole) hides eight sleek, spacious, bright, and wooden Bohemian contemporary rooms overlooking the Vltava River just outside the Old Town. The reception, which closes at 20:00, runs a tourist service and rents river boats (standard Db-1,000–1,700 kč depending on season, deluxe Db-1,200–2,000, Fri–Sat most expensive, choose rooms from Web photos, breakfast in your room, 28 Rooseveltova Street, tel. 337-712-853, fax 380-711-900, www.ceskykrumlov-info.cz, pension@ceskykrumlov-info.cz). The deluxe rooms are bigger, with river views, and cost 300 kč extra.

$ **Rooseveltova Street,** midway between the bus station and the Old Town (a 4-minute walk from either), is lined with fine little eight-room places, each with easy free parking. **Pension Anna** is well-run with comfortable rooms and a restful little garden (Db-1,200 kč, apartment Db at 1,500 kč is a great deal, Tb-1,800 kč, apartment Qb-2,100 kč, Rooseveltova 41, tel. & fax 380-711-692, pension.anna@quick.cz). **Pension Landauer**, with small and simple but comfortable rooms, is a fair value (Sb-500 kč, Db-1,000 kč, no CC, Rooseveltova 32, tel. & fax 380-711-790). **Little Pension Teddy** has several riverview rooms sharing a common balcony (Db-1,200 kč, Tb-1,700 kč, no CC, Rooseveltova 38, tel. 380-711-595, info@teddy.cz).

$ **Hostel 99,** one of several hostels in the Old Town, is closest to the train and bus stations and has a pleasant, mellow feel. Its fine picnic table terrace looks out on the Old Town and the gentle sound of the river gurgles outside your window. It caters to its guests, offering free inner tubes for river floats, rental bikes, and a free keg of beer each Wednesday. The adjacent Hospoda 99 restaurant serves good, cheap soups, salads, and local meals (55 beds in 6- to 10-bed rooms—300 kč, D-700 kč, T-900 kč, use the lockers, no curfew or lockout, a 10-min downhill walk from train station or two bus stops to Spicak, Vezni 99, tel. & fax 380-712-812, www.hostel99.com, hostel99@hotmail.com).

EATING

Na Louži seems to be everyone's favorite little Czech bistro, with 40-seats in one 1930s-style room surrounded by funky old advertisements. They serve inexpensive, tasty Czech cuisine and the hometown Eggenberg beer. If you've always wanted to play the piano for an appreciative Czech crowd in a colorful little tavern...do it here (Kájovská 66, tel. 337-711280).

Krčma u Dwau Maryi (the Tavern of the Two Marys) is a characteristic old place with idyllic riverside picnic tables serving traditional
Czech cuisine and drinks (daily from 11:00, Parkán 104, tel. 337-717-
228). The fascinating menu explains the history of the house and makes
a good case that the food of the poor medieval Bohemians was tasty and
varied. The menu offers many dishes from those old times, featuring
buckwheat, millet, and unusual herbs and spices.

Krumlovsky Mlyn (the Krumlov Mill) is a big rollicking farm-
fresh place with an open fire and strewn with dried onions. It offered
the best riverside dining I found—especially fun on hot days when giddy
canoers and kayakers tackle the fiercest waters around the town's weir,
right in front of the restaurant (daily 10:00–22:00, Široká 80, tel. 380-
712-838).

Cikánská Jizba is a Gypsy tavern filling one den-like barrel-vaulted
room. Krumlov has a big Gypsy history, and even today 1,000 live on
the edge of town. While this little 40-seat restaurant won't win any cuisine awards, the characteristic Gypsy food is served under a mystic-feel-
ing Gothic vault, and you never know what festive and musical activities
will erupt (2 blocks toward castle from main square at Dlouhá 31, tel.
380-717-585).

Krčma v Šatlavske is an old prison gone cozy with an open fire,
big wooden tables under a rustic old medieval vault, and tables outdoors
on the pedestrian lane. It's great for game cooked on an open spit or a
late drink. *Medovina* is the hot honey wine (on Šatlavská, a lane leading
uphill from TI on main square, tel. 380-713-344).

TRANSPORTATION CONNECTIONS

Check both train and bus schedules at the TI or www.vlak-bus.cz.

By train to: Prague (7/day, change usually required, 4 hrs), **Vienna**
(4/day, 6 hrs), **Budapest** (4/day with at least one change, 11 hrs).
Virtually all train rides to/from Český Krumlov require a transfer in
České Budějovice.

By bus to: Prague (the best way—faster, cheaper, and easier than
by train, 140 kč, 7/day, 3.5 hrs, 2 departures a day—11:35 and 16:45—
can be reserved and paid for at TI, or buy tickets from driver), **Vienna**
(the Travellers' Hostel offers a direct bus service to Vienna three times
weekly in summer: 14:00 Mon, Wed, and Fri; 900 kč, 4 hrs, tel. 380-
711-345, www.travellers.cz). A five-minute walk out of town, the Český
Krumlov bus station is just a big parking lot with numbered stalls for
various buses.

By private car: If money is no object, hiring a private car can be
efficient, especially to Budapest (the TI has referrals).

POLAND

(Polska)

- Poland is 120,700 square miles (about the size of New Mexico).
- The population is 39 million people (about 320 people per square mile); 95 percent are Catholic, 75 percent are practicing.
- 1 złoty (zł, or PLN) = 100 groszy (gr) = about 25 cents, and 4 zł = about $1.
- Country code: 48.

Americans who think of Poland as run-down—full of rusting factories, smoggy cities, and gloomy natives—are speechless when they step into Kraków's vibrant main square or Warsaw's colorful Old Town. While parts of the country are still cleaning up the industrial mess left by the Soviets, Poland also has some breathtaking medieval cities that show off its warm and welcoming people, dynamic history, and striding-into-the-future optimism.

The Poles are a proud people—as moved by their spectacular failures as by their successes. They place a lot of importance on honor, and you'll find fewer scams and con artists here than in other countries.

Despite the many "Polack jokes" you've heard (and maybe repeated), Poles are smart. You know many famous Polish intellectuals—you just don't know they're Polish. The "Dumb Polack" Hall of Fame includes Karol Wojtyła (Pope John Paul II), Mikołaj Kopernik (Nicolas Copernicus), composer Fryderyk Chopin, scientist Marie Curie (née Skłodowska), writer Teodor Józef Korzeniowski (better known as Joseph Conrad, author of *Heart of Darkness*), filmmaker Roman Polański *(The Pianist)*…and one of this book's co-authors.

Poland is one of Europe's most devoutly Catholic countries. Catholicism defines these people, holding them together through times when they've had little else. Squeezed between Protestant Germany (originally Prussia) and Orthodox Russia, Poland wasn't even a country for generations (1795–1918). Its Catholicism helped keep it alive. In the last century, while "under communism" (as that age is referred to), Poles found their religion a source of strength as well as rebellion—they could express dissent by going to church. Some of Poland's best sights are churches, usually filled with locals praying silently. While these church interiors are worth a visit, be especially careful to show the proper respect (maintain silence and keep a low profile—snap pictures only discreetly).

Visitors are surprised at how "Jewish" the story of Poland is. Before World War II, 80 percent of the world's Jews lived in Poland. Warsaw was the world's largest Jewish city, with 380,000 Jews (out of a population of 1.2 million). Poland was a magnet for Jews because of its relatively welcoming policies. Still, Jews were forbidden to own land; that's why they settled mostly in the cities. Before the war, along with its huge Jewish minority, the country had an exhilarating ethnic mix—including Germans, Russians, Ukrainians, and Lithuanians. A third of Poland spoke no Polish. But World War II (and a later Soviet policy of sending troublemaking Jews to Israel) ended that. Today 97 percent of the country speaks Polish, and only a couple thousand Polish Jews remain.

Poland is historically extremely pro-American. Of course, their big neighbors (Russia and Germany) have been their historic enemies. When Hitler invaded in 1939, their supposed European friends (France and Britain) let them down. America has always been regarded as the big ally from across the ocean. In 1989, when Poland finally won its freedom, many Poles only half-joked that they should apply to become the 51st state of the United States. Not surprisingly, when President George W. Bush took America to war in Iraq, Poland supported him.

On my first visit to Poland, I had a poor impression of Poles, who seemed brusque and often elbowed ahead of me in line. I've since learned that all it takes is a smile and a cheerful greeting—preferably in Polish—to break through the thick skin that helped these kind people survive the difficult communist times. With a friendly hello *(Dzień dobry!)*, you'll turn any grouch into a new friend.

Practicalities

Red Tape: Although Americans do not need a visa to enter Poland, Canadians do (www.polishembassy.ca).

Restrooms: To confuse tourists, the Poles have devised a secret way of marking their WCs. You'll see doors marked with *męska* (men) and *damska* (women)—but even more often, you'll simply see a triangle (for men) or a circle (for women). Likewise, a sign with a triangle, a circle, and an arrow is directing you to the closest WCs.

Telephones: Chip cards, sold at newsstands and kiosks everywhere, get you access to the modern public phones. Cheap international phone cards (with a scratch-off PIN code) are the key to calling the United States inexpensively—if you can find them (see page 27 for details).

In an emergency, dial 112; to summon the police, call 997. Remember these prefixes: 0800 is toll-free, and 0700 is expensive (like phone sex). Many Poles use mobile phones (which come with 060 and 050 prefixes).

When calling locally, simply dial the seven-digit number. To call long distance within the country, start with the area code (which begins with 0). To call Poland from another country, dial the international access number (00 if you're calling from Europe, or 011 from America or Canada) followed by 48 (Poland's country code), then the area code (without the initial 0), and the seven-digit number. To call out of Poland, dial 00, the country code of the country you're calling (see chart in appendix), the area code if applicable (may need to drop initial zero), and the local number (see page 525 for details).

Polish History

Poland is flat. Take a look at a topographical map of Europe, and it's clear—the path of least resistance from northern Europe to Russia is right through Poland. Over the years, many invaders—from Napoleon to Hitler—have taken advantage of Poland's strategic location. The country is nicknamed the "gods' playground" for the many wars that have rumbled through its territory. Poland has been invaded by Soviets, Germans, French, Austrians, Russians, Prussians, Swedes, Teutonic Knights, Tartars, Bohemians, Magyars—and, about 1,300 years ago, Poles.

Medieval Greatness

The first Poles were a tribe called the Polonians ("people of the plains"), a Slavic band that showed up in these parts in the eighth century. In 966, Mieszko I, Duke of the Polonian tribe, adopted Christianity and founded the Piast dynasty (which would last for over 400 years). Poland was born.

The last Piast was also the greatest: Kazimierz the Great, who famously "found a Poland made of wood and left one made of brick and stone"—bringing Poland (and its capital, Kraków) to international prominence (see page 129). The progressive Kazimierz also invited Europe's much-persecuted Jews to settle here, establishing Poland as a haven for the Jewish people—which it would remain until the Nazis arrived.

Kazimierz the Great died at the end of the 14th century without a male heir. His grand-niece Jadwiga became queen and married Lithuanian Prince Władysław Jagiełło, uniting their countries against a common enemy, the Teutonic Knights. Their marriage marked the beginning of the Jagiellonian dynasty and set the stage for Poland's golden age. With territory spanning from the Baltic Sea to the Black Sea, Poland flourished.

Foreign Kings and Partitions

When the Jagiellonians died out in 1572, political power shifted to the nobles. Poland became a nation governed by its wealthiest 10 percent—the *szlachta*, or nobility, who elected a series of foreign kings. Many of these kings made bad diplomatic decisions and squandered the country's resources. By the late 18th century, Poland was floundering—and surrounded by three land-hungry empires (Russia, Prussia, and Austria). Over the course of less than 25 years, these countries divided Poland's territory among themselves in a series of three partitions. In 1795, "Poland" (nicknamed "the cake of kings"—to be sliced and eaten at will) disappeared from Europe's maps, not to return until 1918.

Even though Poland was gone, the Poles wouldn't go quietly. As the partitions were taking place, Polish soldier Tadeusz Kościuszko (a hero of the American Revolution) returned home to lead an unsuccessful military resistance against the Russians. After another failed uprising against Russia in 1830, many of Poland's top artists and writers fled to Paris—including pianist Fryderyk Chopin and Romantic poet Adam Mickiewicz (whose statue adorns Kraków's main square and Warsaw's Royal Way). These Polish artists tried to preserve the nation's spirit with music and words; those who remained in Poland continued to fight with swords and fists. By the end of the 19th century, the image of the Pole as a tireless, romantic insurgent emerged.

At the end of World War I, Poland finally regained its independence—but the peace didn't last long.

THE HERITAGE OF COMMUNISM

While Poland has been free, democratic, and capitalist since 1989, even young adults carry lots of psychological baggage from living under communism. Although the young generally embrace the fast new affluence with enthusiasm, many older people tend to be nostalgic about that slower-paced time that came with more security. And even young professionals, with so much energy and hope now, don't condemn everything about living "under communism." A friend who was 13 in 1989 recalled those days this way:

"My childhood is filled with happy memories. I remember we had a special way to make red stars. I spent much time coloring the red star of communism. Of course, we had real chocolate only for Christmas. The rest of the year, for treats we got something called 'chocolate-like product'—it was sweet, dark, and smelled vaguely of chocolate. And we had oranges from Cuba for Christmas, too. Everybody was excited when the newspapers announced, 'The boat with the oranges from Cuba is just five days from Poland.' We waited with excitement all year for chocolate and those oranges. The smell of Christmas was so special. Now we have that smell every day. My best Christmases were under communism."

She continued, wistfully, "Under communism, life was family-oriented. There was no way to get rich so we had time. People always had time. I remember my mother and father had to 'organize' for special events…somehow find a good sausage and some Coca-Cola. My uncle would bring a string of toilet paper rolls—absolutely the best gift anyone could give. So many things were 'in deficit.' And during the period of martial law—that was 1981 to 1983—the government said it had to crack down on the dissenters and Solidarity in order to 'forestall Soviet intervention.' During martial law the churches were packed…you couldn't get inside."

World War II, Communism, and Beyond

On September 1, 1939, Hitler began World War II by attacking the Polish Baltic port city of Gdańsk. With six million deaths in the next six years, Poland suffered the worst per-capita WWII losses of any nation. At the war's end, Poland's borders were shifted significantly westward—forcing the resettlement of millions of Germans, Poles, and

Ukrainians, resulting in Poland becoming one of Eastern Europe's most ethnically homogenous countries (97 percent Polish).

During the communist era, the Poles were characteristically resistant to Soviet rule—staging major protests and uprisings in 1956, 1968, 1970, and 1976. (Stalin famously noted that introducing communism to the Poles was like putting a saddle on a cow.) In the early 1980s, Lech Wałęsa, an electrician at the shipyards in Gdańsk, became the leader of the Solidarity movement, the first worker's union in communist Eastern Europe. Poland's head of state, General Wojciech Jaruzelski, declared martial law to stop Solidarity's strikes and save the regime. But Polish workers struggled on, and Solidarity went underground and became a united movement of all demographics, 10 million members strong (a quarter of the population).

In July of 1989, the ruling Communist Party agreed to hold open elections. Their goal was to appease Solidarity, but the plan backfired: communists didn't win a single seat. These elections helped spark the chain reaction across Eastern Europe that eventually brought down the Iron Curtain. Lech Wałęsa, a shipyard electrician from Gdańsk, became Poland's first postcommunist president.

Polish Food

Hearty and tasty, Polish food has a lot in common with Czech, German, and Hungarian cuisine—but here on the north slope of the Carpathian Mountains, the weather is colder, the fruits and vegetables more northern, and the cuisine slightly more similar to that in Russia or Scandinavia. This means more dill, sour cream, vodka, berries, and bread. Much of what Americans think of as Jewish food turns up on Polish menus (gefilte fish, potato pancakes, chicken soup, and so forth)—not because either group influenced the other, but because they lived in the same area for centuries under the same climatic and culinary influences.

The two most typical Polish soups are *żurek* and *barszcz*. *Żurek* is a white or light-colored soup made from a sourdough base, usually with a hard-boiled egg and pieces of *kiełbasa* (sausage) in it. *Barszcz* (borscht) generally means *barszcz czerwony* (red borscht), made with beets. *Barszcz ukraiński* (Ukrainian borscht) starts with beets and adds cabbage, beans, carrots, and other vegetables. (Confusingly, there is also *biały barszcz*, or white borscht—with no beets at all.) In summer, you can try *chłodnik*, a cold beet soup (think gazpacho).

Main-dish specialties include *bigos* (a tasty sauerkraut stew cooked with meat, mushrooms, and whatever's in the pantry), usually inexpensive *pierogi* (ravoli-like dumplings with various fillings—minced meat, sauerkraut and mushroom, cheese, or fruit), and *kotlet schabowy* (fried pork chop). You can also try *gołąbki*—cabbage leaves stuffed with minced meat and rice in a tomato sauce. Like Hungarians, Poles consume more *kaczka* (duck) than Americans do. Fish is common: Look for *pstrąg* (trout), *karp* (carp, beware of bones), and *węgorz* (eel). Poles eat lots of potatoes, which are served with nearly every meal.

You'll enjoy an array of excellent pastries, such as *szarlotka* (apple cake), *sernik* (cheesecake), and *makowiec* (poppy-seed cake). You should also try *pączki*, which are glazed Polish donuts (try to find the traditional ones filled with a wild-rose jam). The bagel-like rings you'll see on the street, *obwarzanki,* are fresh, tasty, and cheap. *Lody* (ice cream) is popular. The most beloved traditional candy is *ptasie mleczko* (birds' milk), which is like a semi-sour marshmallow covered with chocolate.

Thirsty? *Woda* is water, *woda mineralna* is bottled water (*gazowana* is with gas, *niegazowana* is without), *kawa* is coffee, *herbata* is tea, *sok* is juice, and *mleko* is milk. Żywiec and Okocim are the best-known brands of *piwo* (beer). *Wódka* (vodka) is a Polish staple—the name is actually derived from the Polish word for "water." *Wódka* comes in many varieties, the most famous being Żubrówka, flavored with grass from the bison reserves in eastern Poland (often mixed with apple juice). Look for the bottle with the bison. Cheers is *Na zdrowie!* (think "nice driving").

Unusual drinks to try if you have the chance are *kwas* (a cold, fizzy, Ukrainian-style non-alcoholic beverage made from day-old rye bread) and *kompot* (a hot drink made from stewed berries). Poles are unusually fond of carrot juice (often cut with fruit juice); Kubuś is the most popular brand.

"Bon appétit" *is* "*Smacznego.*" To pay, ask for the *rachunek* (rah-KHOO-neck) or say, "*Płacę*" (PWOTS-eh, "I'll pay").

Polish Language

Polish is closely related to its neighboring Slavic languages (Slovak and Czech), with the biggest difference being that Polish has lots of fricatives (hissing sounds—"sh" and "ch"—often in close proximity). Consider the opening line of Poland's most famous tongue-twisting nursery rhyme: *W Szczebrzeszynie chrzaszcz brzmi w trzcinie* ("In Szczebrzeszyn, a beetle is heard in the reeds"—pronounced vuh shih-chehb-zhehsh-ee-nyeh khzhahshch bzh-mee vuh tzhuh-cheen-yeh...or something like that).

Polish intimidates Americans with long, difficult-to-pronounce words. But if you take your time and sound things out, you'll quickly develop an ear for it. First of all, the stress is always on the next-to-last syllable. The letter *c* always sounds like "ts" (as in "cats"). The letter combinations *ć, ci,* and *cz* all sound like "ch"; *ś, si,* and *sz* all sound like "sh"; and *ź, ż, zi,* and *rz* all sound like "zh" (as in "leisure"). The letter *ń* and the combination *ni* sound like "ny" (as in "canyon").

Some Polish vowels have a nasalized sound, like in French. If you see *ę* or *ą,* pronounce them as "en" or "an."

One of the trickiest changes to get used to: *w* sounds like "v," and *ł* sounds like "w." So "Lech Wałęsa" isn't pronounced "lehk wah-LEH-sah,"

KEY POLISH PHRASES

English	Polish	Pronounced
Hello (formal)	Dzień dobry	jehn DOH-bree
Hi / Bye (informal)	Cześć	cheshch
Do you speak English? (asked of a man)	Czy Pan mówi po angielsku?	chee pahn MOO-vee poh ahn-GYEHL-skoo
Do you speak English? (asked of a woman)	Czy Pani mówi po angielsku?	chee PAH-nee MOO-vee poh ahn-GYEHL-skoo
Yes / No	Tak / Nie	tahk / nyeh
Please / You're welcome / Can I help you?	Proszę	PROH-sheh
Thank you	Dziękuję	jehn-KOO-yeh
I'm sorry / Excuse me	Przepraszam	pzheh-PRAH-shahm
Good	Dobrze	DOHB-zheh
Goodbye	Do widzenia	doh veed-ZAY-nyah
one / two	jeden / dwa	YEH-dehn / dvah
three / four	trzy / cztery	trzhee / chuh-TEH-ree
five / six	pięć / sześć	pyench / sheshch
seven / eight	siedem / osiem	SYEH-dehm / OH-syehm
nine / ten	dziewięć / dziesięć	JEH-vyench / JEH-shench
hundred	sto	stoh
thousand	tysiąc	TEE-shants
How much?	Ile?	EE-leh
local currency	złoty (zł)	ZWOH-tee
Where is...?	Gdzie jest...?	gdzeh yehst
...the toilet	...toaleta	toh-ah-LEH-tah
men	męska	MEHN-skah
women	damska	DAHM-skah
water / coffee	woda / kawa	VOH-dah / KAH-vah
beer / wine	piwo / wino	PEE-voh / VEE-noh
Cheers!	Na zdrowie!	nah ZDROH-vyeh
the bill	rachunek	rah-KHOO-nehk

as Dan Rather used to say—but "lehk vah-WEHN-sah."

As you're tracking down addresses, these words may help: *miasto* (town), *plac* (square), *rynek* (big market square), *ulica* (road), *aleja* (avenue), and *most* (bridge).

KRAKÓW

Kraków is the Boston of Poland: a beautiful old-fashioned city buzzing with history, enjoyable sights, tourists, and college students. Even though the country's political capital moved from here to Warsaw 400 years ago, Kraków remains Poland's cultural and intellectual center.

Kraków grew wealthy from trade in the 12th century. Traders who passed through were required to stop here for a few days and sell their wares at a reduced cost. Local merchants turned around and sold those goods with big price hikes...and Kraków thrived. In 1038, it became Poland's capital.

Tartars invaded in 1241, leaving the city in ruins. Krakovians took this opportunity to rebuild their streets in a near-perfect grid, a striking contrast to the narrow, mazelike lanes of most medieval towns. The destruction also paved the way for the spectacular Main Market Square—still Kraków's best attraction.

King Kazimierz the Great sparked Kraków's golden age in the 14th century (see page 129). In 1364, he established the university that still defines the city (and counts Copernicus and Pope John Paul II among its alumni).

But Kraków's power waned as Poland's political center shifted to Warsaw. In 1596, the capital officially moved north. Two centuries later, a series of partitions divided Poland among three neighboring powers. Warsaw ended up as a satellite of oppressive Moscow, and Kraków became a poor provincial backwater of Vienna. But despite Kraków's reduced prominence, Austria's comparatively liberal climate helped turn the city into a haven for intellectuals and progressives (including a young revolutionary thinker from Russia named Vladimir Lenin).

Kraków emerged from World War II virtually unscathed. But when the communists took over, they decided to give intellectual (and potentially dissident) Kraków an injection of good Soviet values—in the form of heavy industry. They built Nowa Huta, an enormous steelworks

Kraków

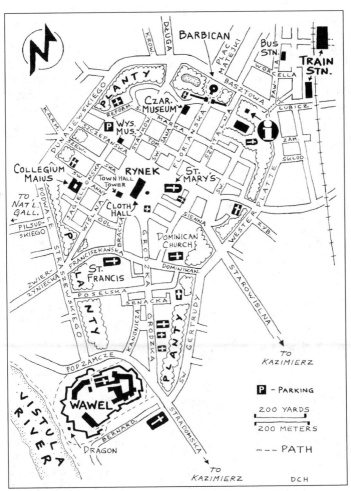

on the city's outskirts, which doomed the city to decades of smog. Thankfully, Kraków is now much cleaner than it was 15 years ago.

Pope John Paul II was born (as Karol Wojtyła) in nearby Wadowice, and served as archbishop of Kraków before being called to Rome. Poland is devoutly Catholic; make sure to visit a few of Kraków's many impressive churches. University life, small but thoughtful museums, great restaurants, sprawling parks, and Jewish history round out the city's attractions.

Planning Your Time

Kraków—with its important side-trips—deserves at least two full days on the busiest itinerary. The city's sights are quickly exhausted, but more than any town in Europe, Kraków is made for aimless strolling.

Auschwitz, a worthwhile side-trip, requires the better part of a day.

Ideally, spend two full days in Kraków itself, plus a visit to Auschwitz (either as a side-trip on the third day, or en route to or from Kraków). In a pinch, spend one day sightseeing in Kraków, another at Auschwitz, and two evenings on the Main Market Square. The square is pure magic.

With more time, nearby Wieliczka Salt Mine makes another good day trip. And even Warsaw, 2.5 hours away by train, is possible to do in a day (see Warsaw chapter).

With two full days in and around Kraków, this is the maximum you could do:

Day 1: Take the Self-Guided Royal Way Walk to cover the city's core. Visit any Old Town museums that interest you (Wyspiański Museum, Gallery of 19th-Century Polish Art, Czartoryski Museum, University), and have lunch on or near the Main Market Square. Spend the afternoon at the castle (note that many sights close at 15:00). Savor the town square over dinner or a drink, or enjoy traditional Jewish music and food in Kazimierz.

Day 2: Get an early start to see the concentration camp at Auschwitz. With a local driver or a good public transit connection, you could get back in time to visit the Wieliczka Salt Mine or Kazimierz.

ORIENTATION

(area code: 012)

Kraków (KROCK-oof, sometimes spelled "Cracow" in English), unlike Prague or Budapest, is mercifully flat and easy to navigate. While it's big (with about 800,000 people), it feels small. You could easily do your entire visit on foot. A greenbelt called the Planty rings the Old Town (Stare Miasto) where the walls and moat once stood (a great place for a stroll or jog). Most sights, except for the castle and the Jewish quarter (Kazimierz), and almost all recommended hotels and restaurants are in the Old Town (inside the Planty). In the center of the Old Town lies the Main Market Square (Rynek Główny), with the Cloth Hall in the middle and St. Mary's Church in the corner.

From the Main Market Square, 10 minutes' walk to the south, you'll find the Wawel sights (castle and cathedral) and just beyond, the Vistula River; five minutes to the north are some remnants of the city walls, and five minutes beyond that (veering northeast), the train station. Kazimierz, the old Jewish quarter, is 20 minutes by foot to the southeast.

KRAKÓW LANDMARKS

English	Polish	Pronounced
Main Train Station	Kraków Główny	KROCK-oof GWOHV-nee
Park around the Old Town	Planty	PLAHN-tee
Old Town	Stare Miasto	STAH-reh mee-AH-stoh
Main Market Square	Rynek Główny	REE-nehk GWOHV-nee
Cloth Hall	Sukiennice	soo-kyeh-NEET-seh
Castle Hill	Wawel	VAH-vehl
Jewish Quarter	Kazimierz	kah-ZHEE-meerzh
Vistula River	Wisła	VEES-wah

Tourist Information

Reliable tourist information is hard to find in Kraków. The city has one state-run **TI** (Mon–Fri 8:00–16:00, Sat–Sun 9:00–15:00, in round green-roofed kiosk between train station and square in the Planty park at ulica Szpitalna 25, tel. 012/432-0110, www.krakow.pl). This is your best chance to pick up a pile of free information: Grab the one-page map, the thick Kraków Tourist Information booklet, the "Karnet" cultural events booklet, and a copy of *Kraków in Your Pocket* (see below). Because it's government-funded, this office is not legally allowed to actually sell anything, so all resources are free. This is both good (to get things free that cost money elsewhere) and bad (they can tell you about the Kraków Tourist Card...but they can't sell it to you).

More central, in the Cloth Hall on the Square, is the privately-run, decidedly for-profit **MCIT** (Małopolskie Centrum Informacji Turystycznej, fluid hours based on demand, but generally summer Mon–Fri 9:00–18:00, Sat–Sun 9:00–14:00, winter Mon–Fri 9:00–17:00, Sat 9:00–14:00, closed Sun, in middle of Cloth Hall facing St. Mary's Church at Rynek Główny 1–3, tel. 012/421-3051, www.mcit.pl). They offer minimal tourist information, sell maps and Kraków Tourist Cards, book local tours, arrange local transportation and car rentals, and have a room-booking service.

Kraków in Your Pocket: With no good TI in town, this excellent bimonthly magazine fills the void. It's packed with up-to-date, comprehensive hotel and restaurant reviews, as well as good sightseeing coverage.

The cover price is 10 zł, but you can usually find it for free in hotel lobbies or at the government-run TI.

Kraków Tourist Card: This card covers public transportation in Kraków, admission to several city museums (Czartoryski, Cloth Hall Gallery), and moderate discounts to outlying sights (30 percent off Cracow Tours to Wieliczka Salt Mine or Auschwitz). Since public transportation is mostly unnecessary and museums are so cheap, this card doesn't make sense for most visitors (45 zł/2 days, 65 zł/3 days; buy at MCIT office in Cloth Hall, travel agencies, and many hotels).

Arrival in Kraków

By Train: The Kraków Główny ("main") station is a 10-minute walk northeast of the Square. The station has two parts, connected by a covered walkway: Stairs lead from the tracks down to the long, skinny, low-ceilinged arrival hall, which is stark and functional, with only a handful of ticket windows and luggage lockers (4 zł). A parallel tunnel under the tracks is a second-hand book market. The big old-fashioned main terminal is more comfortable, with more ticket windows, lockers, WCs, and other amenities. From the long skinny arrival hall, follow signs to the center *(wyjście do centrum).* At street level, turn left into a jumble of market stalls and a chaotic bus station scene. The bus station is across the street on the right. A small market square is 100 yards directly ahead. And the main train terminal is ahead on the left. Foreigners will encounter people hustling rides to Auschwitz and cheap rooms.

Getting downtown: **Taxis** park in front of the main terminal; the fair metered rate to downtown is 10–15 zł. To make the 10-minute **walk** to the center and most recommended hotels, exit from the front of the main terminal and walk through the small market square. (Because this area is slated to be developed into a Nowy Miasto, or "New Town," construction may impede your progress.) At the far end of the market, a pedestrian underpass leads beneath the busy ring road. When you emerge in the Planty park, you'll see the round TI kiosk on your left; the Main Market Square is a few blocks straight ahead.

By Car: Check with your hotel. The most central parking lot is on ulica Szczepańska, a block west of the Square (during 10:00–20:00, it's 7 zł/hr; from 20:00–10:00, it's 4 zł/hr; 90 zł/24 hr).

By Plane: Kraków's small, modern **Balice Airport** is 10 miles west of the center. Buses #152 and #208 take you to the train station and the edge of the Old Town (3 zł, 40 min), or you can catch a cab (around 50 zł). Airport info: tel. 012/285-5120, www.lotnisko-balice.pl.

Getting around Kraków

Kraków's top sights and best hotels are easily accessible by foot. You'll only need wheels if you're going to the Kazimierz Jewish quarter or the Nowa Huta suburbs.

By Public Transit: Trams and buses zip around Kraków's urban sprawl. The same tickets are used for both, and can be purchased at kiosks (cheaper) or on board (for 0.50 zł more). There are three kinds of tickets: A *bilet jednorazowy* (single ticket, no transfers) costs 2.20 zł (from a kiosk). A *bilet czasowy* is good for an hour and allows transfers (2.80 zł). Always validate your ticket when you board the bus or tram. A *bilet dzienny* (day ticket)—which must be validated the first time you use it—costs 9 zł, and can be purchased only at special MPK ticket booths. You technically have to buy a ticket for your bag, too, or pay a 44-zł fine if you're caught. The only trams you'll likely use are #4 to Nowa Huta, #4 and #13 connecting the train station and the town center, and #8 and #13 to get to Kazimierz, the Jewish quarter.

By Taxi: Just as in other big Eastern European cities, only take cabs that are clearly marked (company logo and telephone number). Kraków taxis start at 5 zł and charge around 2 zł per kilometer. Rides are very short and generally run less than 10 zł. You're more likely to get the fair metered rate by hailing a cab rather than taking one waiting at tourist spots. To call a cab, try **Radio Taxi** (tel. 012/919, or toll-free 0800-500-919).

By Buggy: Romantic horse-drawn buggies trot around Kraków from the Main Market Square. The going rate is 70 zł for a 30-minute tour.

By Golf Cart: OK, it's not quite so romantic. But several golf-cart companies based on the Square offer both taxi and tour service. You can pay by the car (e.g., 20 zł taxi service to Kazimierz, 50 zł for half-hour tour of Old Town, 80 zł for full-hour tour) or join a tour (15 zł per person for half-hour tour, 25 zł for full-hour tour). The tours can be live or tape-recorded (just dial English). These guys are pretty competitive; it pays to shop around.

By Bicycle: Wypozyczalnja Rowerow Rent-a-Bike, half a block off the Square, is easygoing with fine bikes. Biking the Planty park and along the riverside promenades gives your trip a great extra dimension and gets you out of the touristy old town zone to see a slice of untouristy Kraków (4 zł/hr, 30 zł/day, ulica Św. Anny 4, mobile 0501-745-986).

Helpful Hints

Sightseeing Schedules: Note that Kraków sights have short hours (most close around 15:00, last entry 30 min before). Confirm sight hours carefully when you plan your day.

Changing Money: As this is not yet a euro zone, you'll be changing currency when you arrive. ATMs are plentiful and work fine. If you have hard currency, you'll find lots of exchange desks. Analyze the rates. The buying and selling rates should be within about 7 percent (e.g., 17 Hungarian forints buy one złoty, one złoty sells for 18 forints). At the train station a forint buys only 12 złoty. If you need cash upon arrival, just change a little at the station (no commission...just lousy rates). Save any big exchange of hard cash for better rates at exchange offices *(kantor)* in the center.

Internet Access: Kraków's many Internet cafés—it seems there's one on every corner—charge around 1 zł for 15 min. **Internet Klub Garinet** is convenient (daily until 24:00, on the Royal Way just a block north of the Square at ulica Floriańska 10).

Post Office: In peak season, a small postal wagon sells stamps in the middle of the Square (opposite what was Poland's first post office— back when a Pony Express-type system delivered mail to Vienna within 40 hours). The main post office (Poczta Główna) is at the intersection of Starowiślna and the Westerplatte ring road (a few blocks east of the Square).

Travel Agency: Orbis, on the Square, books local guides and bus tours, changes money, and sells train tickets (Mon–Fri 9:00–19:00, Sat 9:00–15:00, closed Sun, Rynek Główny 41, www.orbis.krakow.pl). Since they speak English, the 1-zł booking fee for getting train tickets here is worth it to save the frustration of dealing with the surly monolingual grannies at the station. The agency posts a handy complete train schedule in their window.

Tours: Cracow Tours runs several bus-plus-walking itineraries, including a general city overview (105 zł, daily, 3 hrs), Auschwitz (115 zł, daily, 6 hrs), Wieliczka Salt Mine (115 zł, daily, 4 hrs), and other regional side-trips (30 percent discount with Kraków Tourist Card, book tours at Orbis travel agency—see "Travel Agency," above).

Local Guide: Marta Chmielowska is good and has a car (half-day-200 zł, 250 zł with her car, full day just a little more, tel. 012/411-9912, mobile 0603-668-008, martamu@free.polbox.pl). **Anna Gega** also does a fine job (4 hrs-200 zł, all day-350 zł, tel. 012/411-2523, mobile 0604-151-293, leadertour@wp.pl). Local guides have a passion for all the legends and stories. If Marta and Anne are booked, the Orbis travel agency (see above) can find a guide for you.

Laundry: There are no self-serve launderettes. Your hotel can do your wash, but it's expensive (washing a pair of socks costs more than buying a new pair). Stick with washing in the sink for now. If you must have something laundered, a central option is **Betty Clean** (about 9 zł per shirt, 12 zł for pants, takes 24 hrs, pay more for express service, Mon–Fri 7:30–19:30, Sat 8:00–15:30, closed Sun, ulica Zwierzyniecka 6, tel. 012/423-0848). Unfortunately, they don't do socks or underwear—so get back to that sink.

SELF-GUIDED ROYAL WAY WALK

Most of Kraków's major sights are conveniently connected by this self-guided walking tour. This route is known as the "Royal Way," because the king used to follow this same path when he returned to Kraków after a journey. After the capital moved to Warsaw, most kings were still both coronated and buried in Wawel Cathedral at the far end of town—and they followed this same route for both occasions. You could sprint through this walk in an hour (less than a mile altogether), but it's much more fun if you take it slow.

Part 1: Barbican to Main Market Square

Begin the walk at the north end of the Old Town, at the Barbican.

▲▲**Barbican (Barbakan), Florian Gate (Brama Floriańska), and City Walls**—Tartars invaded Kraków three times in the 13th century. After the first attack destroyed the city in 1241, Krakovians built this wall. The original rampart had 47 watchtowers and eight gates. The big, round defensive fort standing outside the wall is the Barbican. These provided extra fortification to weak sections. Imagine in 1500, when this structure stood outside the town moat with a long bridge leading to the Florian Gate—the city's main entryway.

Before you step through the gate yourself, look to the left and right of the Barbican to see the...

▲▲**Planty**—By the 19th century, Kraków's no-longer-necessary city wall had fallen into disrepair. Krakovians decided to tear down what remained, fill in the moat, and plant trees. Today, the Planty is a beautiful park that stretches for 2.5 miles around the entire perimeter of Kraków's Old Town.

Go through the gate into the Old Town.

▲▲**Floriańska Street (ulica Floriańska)**—You're standing at the head of Kraków's historic (and now touristic) gamut. On the inside of the city wall, you'll see a makeshift **art gallery** (left and right) where starving students hawk the works they've painted at the Academy of Fine Arts (across the busy street from the Barbican). Portraits, still lifes, landscapes, local scenes, nudes...this might just be Kraków's best collection of art. If you were to detour along the gallery (to the left as you face the gate), in a block you'd arrive at another fine collection—the eclectic Czartoryski Museum, home to a rare Leonardo da Vinci oil painting (see "Museums," below).

Walking down Floriańska Street, you can't miss the **McDonald's.** When renovating this building, they discovered a Gothic cellar—so they excavated it and added seating. Today you can super-size your ambience by dining on a Big Mac and fries under a medieval McVault.

Cukiarnia Jama Michalika (farther down on left at #45), a dark, atmospheric café popular with locals for its coffee and pastries, began in 1895 as a simple bakery in a claustrophobic back room. Poke around inside. A brothel upstairs scared off respectable types, so the owner attracted students by creating a cabaret act called "The Green Balloon" (see how many you can spot inside). To this day, the cabaret—political satire set to music—still runs (Polish only). Around the turn of the 20th

KRAKÓW AT A GLANCE

▲▲▲**Main Market Square** Stunning heart of Kraków and a people-magnet any time of day. **Hours:** Always open.

▲▲**Barbican and City Walls** Formidable 13th-century fort and walls. **Hours:** Always viewable.

▲▲**Planty** Once a moat, now a scenic park encircling the city. **Hours:** Always open.

▲▲**Floriańska Street** Kraków's main shop-lined touristic artery. **Hours:** Always open.

▲▲**St. Mary's Church** Extraordinary wood-carved Gothic altarpiece. **Hours:** Mon–Sat 11:30–18:00, Sun 14:00–18:00.

▲▲**Cloth Hall** Fourteenth-century market hall with 21st-century souvenirs. **Hours:** Daily 8:00–21:30, less off-season.

▲▲**St. Francis' Basilica** Lovely Gothic church with some of Poland's best Art Nouveau. **Hours:** Open long hours daily.

▲▲**Czartoryski Museum** Varied collection, with European painting (Leonardo da Vinci and Rembrandt) and Polish armor, handicrafts, and decorative arts. **Hours:** Tue–Sun 10:00–15:30, Fri until 18:00, closed Mon.

▲▲**Jewish Cemeteries** Two touching burial sites—the New (post-1800) and Old (1552–1800)—in Kazimierz. **Hours:** New Cemetery

century, this was a hangout of the Młoda Polska (Young Poland) movement—the Polish answer to Art Nouveau. The walls are papered with sketches from poor artists who couldn't pay their tab.

A block ahead on the left (at #19), step into the *bar mleczny,* or "milk bar." In the communist era, the government subsidized the food at these restaurants to provide Poles with a cheap meal out. The tradition continues, and today Poland still foots the bill for most of your milk-bar meal. Prices are astoundingly low—soup for less than a złoty—and, while communist-era fare was gross, today's milk-bar cuisine is usually quite tasty. Just head to the counter in the back, point to what you want, and get a quick and hearty meal for a half the cost of McDonald's (see "Eating," below).

Sun–Fri 9:00–18:00, until 16:00 in winter, closed Sat; Old Cemetery Mon–Fri 9:00–16:00, closed Sat–Sun.

▲▲**Wawel Castle Grounds** Historic hilltop with views, castle, cathedral, courtyard with chakra, and a passel of museums. **Hours:** Grounds always open.

▲**Wawel Cathedral** Poland's splendid national church, with tons of tombs, a crypt, and climbable tower. **Hours:** Ticket sales for crypt and tower May–Sept Mon–Sat 9:00–17:15, Sun 12:15–17:15; Oct–April Mon–Sat 9:00–15:00, Sun 12:15–15:00.

▲**Gallery of 19th-Century Polish Art** Work by Poland's finest painters, little known outside of the country. **Hours:** Tue 11:00–18:00, Wed and Fri 9:00–15:30, Thu 11:00–18:00, Sat–Sun 10:00–15:30, closed Mon.

▲**Wyspiański Museum** Art by the talented leader of the Young Poland Art Nouveau movement. **Hours:** Tue–Sun 10:00–15:30, Thu until 18:00, closed Mon.

▲**Kazimierz Market Square (Plac Nowy)** The people's market, good for lunching with locals. **Hours:** Stalls open Tue–Sat 6:00–14:00, a few also open later and Sun 7:00–14:00.

▲**Polish Folk Museum** Traditional rural Polish life on display—an open-air museum moved inside. **Hours:** Mon and Wed–Fri 10:00–17:00, Sat–Sun 10:00–14:00, closed Tue.

Farther ahead on the left (at #3, 50 yards before the big church), you'll see **Jazz Club U Muniaka.** In the 1950s, Janusz Muniak was one of the first Polish jazzmen. Now he owns this place, and jams regularly here in a cool cellar surrounded by jazzy art (live jazz nightly at 21:00, 20-zł cover, cheap drinks after that, best bands Thu–Sat).

Continue on into the Main Market Square to...

▲▲**St. Mary's Church (Kościół Mariacki)**—A church has stood on this spot for 800 years. The original church was destroyed by the first Tartar invasion in 1241, but all subsequent versions—including the current one—have been built on the same foundation. You can look down the sides to see how the square has risen about 6.5 feet over the centuries.

How many church towers does St. Mary's have? Technically, the answer is one. The shorter tower belongs to the church; the taller one is a municipal watchtower, from which you'll hear a bugler playing the hourly *hejnał*. During that first Tartar invasion, so the story goes, a watchman in the tower saw the enemy approaching and sounded the alarm. Before he could finish the tune, an arrow pierced his throat—which is why even today, the *hejnał* stops *subito* partway through.

Today's buglers are firemen first—technically serving as fire lookouts—and musicians second. Two at a time, they work a 48-hour shift, sharing a tiny apartment and taking turns playing the *hejnał* on the hour, every hour (broadcast on national Polish radio at noon). In July and August, you can climb up and meet them (Wed and Sat).

The church's front door is open 14 hours a day and free to those who come to pray. Tourists use the door around the right side (4 zł, Mon–Sat 11:30–18:00, Sun 14:00–18:00). The rusty neck-stock (behind the tourists' left door) was used for public humiliation until the 1700s. Inside, you're drawn to one of the most impressive medieval woodcarvings in existence—the exquisite three-part Gothic **altarpiece** by German Veit Stoss (Wit Stwosz in Polish). Carved in 12 years and completed in 1489, it's packed with emotion rare in Gothic art. Stoss used oak for the structural parts and 500-year-old linden trunks for the figures. When the altar doors are closed, you see scenes from the lives of Mary and Jesus. The open altar depicts the Dormition (death) of the Virgin. The artist catches the apostles (11, without Judas) around Mary reacting in the seconds after she collapses.

Mary is depicted in three scenes: dying, being escorted to heaven by Jesus, and (at the very top) being crowned in heaven (flanked by two Polish saints—Adalbert and Stanisław). The six scenes on the sides are: the Annunciation, birth of Jesus, visit by the Three Magi, Jesus' Resurrection, his Ascension, and Mary becoming the mother of the apostles.

The altar is open daily between noon and 18:00. Try to be there by 11:45 for the ceremonial opening or at 18:00 for the closing. While you're admiring this church's art, notice the fine and flowery neo-Gothic painting covering the choir walls.

▲▲▲**Main Market Square (Rynek Główny)**—Kraków's marvelous Main Market Square is one of Europe's most gasp-worthy public spaces. The Square bustles with street musicians, colorful flower stalls, cotton-candy vendors, loitering teenagers, businesspeople commuting by foot, gawking tourists, and the lusty coos of pigeons. This square is where

THE GREATEST KAZIMIERZ:
KAZIMIERZ THE GREAT
(1333–1370)

Poland has had many kings named Kazimierz. But only one is considered "great": Kazimierz the Great.

K. the G., who ruled Poland from Kraków in the 14th century, was one of those larger-than-life medieval kings who left his mark on all fronts—from war to diplomacy, art patronage to womanizing. His scribes bragged that Kazimierz found a Poland made of wood, and left one made of brick and stone. He put Kraków on the map as a major European capital. He founded many villages (some of which still bear his name) and replaced wooden structures with stone ones (such as Kraków's Cloth Hall). He also established the Kraków Academy (today's Jagiellonian University), the second-oldest university in Central Europe (after Prague's).

Most of all, Kazimierz is remembered as a progressive, tolerant king. In the 14th century, other nations were deporting—or even interning—their Jewish subjects, who were commonly scapegoated for anything that went wrong. But the enlightened and kindly Kazimierz actively encouraged Jews to come to Poland by granting them special privileges, such as in banking and trade, establishing the country as a safe haven for Jews in Europe.

Kazimierz the Great was the last of Poland's long-lived Piast dynasty. Although he left no male heir—at least, no legitimate ones—Kazimierz's advances set the stage for Poland's golden age. After his death, Poland united with Lithuania (against the common threat of the Teutonic Knights), the Jagiellonian dynasty was born, and Poland became one of Europe's mightiest medieval powers.

Kraków lives. On my last visit, local teens practiced break dancing moves at one end of the square while activist types protested Poland's EU membership at the other.

This square was established in the 13th century, when the city had to be rebuilt after the Tartars destroyed it. At that time, the square was the biggest in medieval Europe. It was illegal to sell anything on the street, so everything had to be sold here on the market square. It was divided into smaller markets: the butcher stalls, the ironworkers' tents, and the Cloth Hall (see below).

The statue in the middle of the Square is Romantic poet **Adam Mickiewicz** (1789–1855). His epic masterpiece, *Pan Tadeusz,* is still regarded as one of the greatest works in Polish, and Mickiewicz as the Polish Shakespeare. A wistful, nostalgic tale of Polish-Lithuanian nobility, *Pan Tadeusz* stirred patriotism in a Poland that had been dismantled by surrounding empires.

Near the end of the square, you'll see the tiny **Church of St. Adalbert,** the oldest church in Kraków (10th century). This Romanesque structure predates the Square. Like St. Mary's (described above), it seems to be at an angle because it's aligned east-west, as was the custom when it was built. (The churches aren't crooked—the Square is.)

As the square buzzes around you, imagine this place before 1989. There were no outdoor cafés, no touristy souvenir stands, no salesmen hawking cotton candy. The communist government shut down all but a handful of the businesses (keeping open, for instance, the Cloth Hall, which was a tourist arcade with its shops much like today). They didn't want people to congregate here—they should be at home, resting, because "a rested worker is a productive worker." The buildings were covered with soot from the nearby Nowa Huta steelworks. (The communists denied the pollution, and when the student "Green Brigades" staged a demonstration in this square to raise awareness in the 1970s, they were immediately arrested.)

Drinks are cheap here (6 zł); find a place where you like the view and the chairs, and then sit and sip. Enjoy the folk band. Tip them and you can photograph their traditional Kraków garb up close. (A big tip gets you "The Star-Spangled Banner.")

The huge yellow building right in the middle of the Square is the...

▲▲**Cloth Hall (Sukiennice)**—In the Middle Ages, this was where the cloth sellers had their market stalls. In the 14th century, Kazimierz the Great made the Cloth Hall a permanent structure. In 1555, it burned down, and was replaced by the current structure. The letter "S" (above the entryway) stands for King Sigismund the Old, who commissioned this version of the hall. As Sigismund fancied things Italian (he imported Italian architects and married an Italian princess), this structure (and parts of Wawel Castle) are in the Italianate Renaissance style.

The Cloth Hall is still a functioning market—mostly souvenirs, including wood carvings, chess sets, jewelry, painted boxes, and trinkets (daily 8:00–21:30, less off-season). Cloth Hall prices are slightly inflated, but you're paying for the convenience and the atmosphere... and locals insist they buy gifts here, too. Upstairs in the Cloth Hall is the good Gallery of 19th-Century

Polish Art (see "Museums," below). WCs are at each end.

Browse through the Cloth Hall passageway. As you emerge into the other half of the Square, the big tower on your left is the...

Town Hall Tower—This tower is all that remains of a Town Hall building from the 14th century—when Kraków was the powerful capital of Poland. After the 18th-century partitions of Poland, Kraków's prominence was on the decline. By the 19th century, Kraków was Nowheresville. As the town's importance crumbled, so did its Town Hall. Krakovians tore down everything but this tower, nearly 200 feet tall. It's climbable, with 117 steps, a museum on Kraków history, and good views down on the Square at the top (4 zł, daily May–Oct 10:00–17:00, closed off-season).

There are plenty of diversions to keep you busy here on the Square (including some good restaurants; see "Eating," below). When you're ready to continue down the Royal Way, follow Part 2 of the walk (below).

Part 2 of Royal Way Walk: Main Market Square to Wawel Castle

After the king passed through the grand Main Market Square, he'd continue on to his castle. We'll take a one-block detour from his route to introduce you to one of Kraków's best churches. Leave on the street in the middle of the bottom of the Square. Ulica Bracka leads one long block (and across the busy Franciszkańska Street) directly to the side door of a big red brick church. Go ye.

▲▲**St. Francis' Basilica (Bazylika Św. Franciszka)**—This beautiful Gothic church features some of Poland's best Art Nouveau *in situ* (in the setting for which it was intended). After an 1850 fire, it was re-decorated by members of the turn-of-the-century Młoda Polska (Young Poland) movement—Poland's answer to Art Nouveau.

Highlights include:

1. Paintings and stained glass by Młoda Polska poster boy **Stanisław Wyspiański.** The stained glass windows over the high altar represent St. Francis (the church's namesake) and the Bessed Salomea (the church's foundress, buried in a side chapel). The one in the rear of the nave is *God the Father in the Act of Creation.* Wyspiański also painted the delightful floral designs decorating the walls of the nave. (For more on the artist, see page 139.)

2. The chapel on the left side of the nave (as you face the altar) features the 12 Stations of the Cross painted by **Józef Mehoffer.** Wyspiański and Mehoffer—who both studied under Jan Matejko, Poland's greatest Romantic painter—were fiercely competitive. The glorious decorations of this church are the results of this great rivalry. (For more Wyspiański or Mehoffer, visit their museums—see "Museums," below.)

3. The modern painting (with an orange background, midway up the nave on the right as you face the altar) depicts **Saint Maksymilian**

Kolbe, the Catholic priest who traded his own life to save a fellow inmate at Auschwitz (see his story on page 160).

Stepping outside (through the door you entered), look left. The light-yellow building (100 yards away) is the archbishop's palace, Pope John Paul II's home-away-from-Rome for visits to his hometown. From the window (above the ornate stone entryway), he's addressed thousands of Krakovians filling the square and this street.

Once outside the church, turn right, cross the little square, and turn right again on Grodzka at the light-purple building. You're back on the Royal Way proper. Grodzka street leads to a square on your right...

Mary Magdalene Square (Plac Św. Marii Magdaleny)—In the Middle Ages, Kraków was known as "Small Rome" for its many churches. Today, there are 142 churches and monasteries within the city limits (32 in the Old Town alone), more per square mile than anywhere outside Rome. You can see several of them from this spot: the nearest, with the white facade and red dome, is the **Church of Saints Peter and Paul** (Kraków's first Baroque church). The next one down, with the twin towers, is the Romanesque **St. Andrew's,** with a spring inside; during Tartar invasions in the 13th century, citizens holed up here and lived off the water. If you look farther down the street, you can see three more churches. And the courtyard you're standing next to used to be a church, too. It burned in 1855 and only its footprint survives.

Go through the square (admiring the sculpture on the column that won Kraków's distinguished "ugliest statue" award in 2002), and turn left down...

Kanonicza Street (ulica Kanonicza)—With so many churches around here, the clergy had to live somewhere. Many lived on this well-preserved street. Continue left down Kanonicza. As you walk, look for the three Cardinal hats over doorways. Find the yellow house (#19) on the right near the end of the street. The top window over the doorway is where a priest named **Karol Wojtyła** lived for 10 years after World War II. Wojtyła was born in nearby Wadowice in 1920. His mother died when he was a teenager, and he moved with his dad to Kraków to study drama at Jagiellonian University, just a few blocks from here. The Nazis shut down the school during World War II, and Wojtyła had to work in a quarry. When the war ended, he resumed his studies—this time at the theology faculty. Wojtyła graduated in 1947, and by 1964, he had become Archbishop of Kraków. In 1967, he became the youngest Cardinal ever in the Roman Catholic Church. Eleven years after that, he was elected pope.

Your Majesty's journey is almost finished. At the end of Kanonicza street, a ramp leads up to...

▲▲Wawel Hill—Wawel (VAH-vehl), a symbol of Polish royalty and independence, is sacred ground to every Polish person. A castle has stood here since the beginning of recorded history. Today Wawel—

awash in tourists—is the most-visited sight in the country. Crowds and a ridiculously complex admissions system for the hill's many historic sights can be exasperating. Thankfully, for most non-Polish visitors, a stroll through the cathedral and around the castle grounds requires no tickets and—with the help of the following self-guided commentary—is enough. The many museums on Wawel (described below) are mildly interesting but can be skipped.

Walk up the long ramp to the castle entry. When Kraków was part of the Hapsburg Empire in the 19th century, the Austrians turned this castle complex into a fortress—destroying much of its delicate beauty. When Poland regained its independence after World War I, the castle was returned to its former glory. The bricks you see on your left as you climb the ramp bear the names of Poles from around the world who donated to the cause.

The jaunty equestrian statue ahead is **Tadeusz Kościuszko** (1746–1817)—whom you might remember from your American History classes. Kościuszko was a hero of the American Revolution and helped design West Point before returning to Poland to fight against the Russians (during the partitions that would divide Poland's territory among three neighboring powers).

Hiking through the gate next to Kościuszko, you pass the ticket office (see "Castle Tickets," below) and, as you crest the hill, you'll see to your left...

▲**Wawel Cathedral**—Poland's national church is its Westminster Abbey. While the history buried here is pretty murky to most Americans, to Poles, this church is *the* national mausoleum. It holds the tombs of nearly all of Poland's most important rulers and greatest historical figures. There has been a cathedral on this spot for a millennium, and the current incarnation (the third) is a jumble of architectural styles.

Exterior View: Go around to the far side of the cathedral to take in its impressive profile. The white base of the nearest tower is from the 12th-century Romanesque church. Kazimierz the Great and his predecessors gradually surrounded the cathedral with some 20 Gothic chapels. To the right of the tall tower, two domed chapels survive. The gold one is the Renaissance Sigismund's Chapel, housing memorials to the Jagiellonian kings. The green one (which looks the same—but is a copy, built 150 years later) is home to the Swedish Waza dynasty.

Go back around and face the front entry. You see Gothic chapels flanking the door, a Renaissance ceiling, lavish Baroque decoration over the door, and big bones (thought to come from extinct animals). Years ago, these were taken for the bones of giants, and put here for protection. It's said that as long as they hang here, the cathedral will stand. The door is the original from the 14th century, with fine wrought-iron work. The K with the crown stands for Kazimierz the Great. The black marble frame is made of Kraków stone from nearby quarries.

Interior: The cathedral interior is slathered in Baroque memorials and tombs. Find the few Polish kings you know. (Kazimierz the Great is on the right—look for "Kazimierz Wielki.") The silver tomb under a canopy in the center is that of St. Stanisław (dating from the 15th century and inspired by the one in St. Peter's at the Vatican). Circling around to the left (behind the main altar), you'll find a black crucifix marking the relics of St. Jadwiga, the 14th-century "Queen of Poland," who helped Christianize Lithuania and was sainted by Pope John Paul II in 1997. All the candles flickering here indicate she's popular with Poles today. The 16th-century Sigismund Chapel (midway up the nave on the right)—with its silver altar—is considered by Poles to be the finest Renaissance chapel north of the Alps. Check out the high altar. For 200 years, the colorful chair on the right has been the seat of Kraków's archbishops, including Karol Wojtyła, who served here for 14 years before becoming pope. As you leave, peek into the Gothic chapel (left of door on your way out) with its Russian Orthodox-style 15th-century frescoes.

Other Interior Sights: Claustrophobic wooden stairs lead up to the 11-ton **Sigismund Bell.** Then, descend into the **crypt** and the royal tombs, where the war heroes Kościuszko and Piłsudzki and several Polish royals are buried. Marshal Józef Piłsudzki, the WWI hero who ruled Poland from 1926 to 1935, has the last grave on the right. His tomb was moved here so the soldiers who came to party on his grave wouldn't disturb the others. (It's interesting to note that Piłsudzki encouraged Britain and France to preemptively attack Hitler in 1933. He was ignored and Poland was devastated a decade later. Perhaps that is why Poles were predisposed to support America's preemptive war against Iraq.) Save the tombs for last, since you'll exit back out into the courtyard.

Cost and Hours: While most of the cathedral is free, you'll need a ticket to climb into the crypt or up the tower to see the bell (tickets sold across from entrance, 8 zł, May–Sept Mon–Sat 9:00–17:15, Sun 12:15–17:15; Oct–April Mon–Sat 9:00–15:00, Sun 12:15–15:00).

Cathedral Museum—This small museum, with various holy robes and replicas of what's buried with the kings, plus the Sigismund Bell's original clapper, is nearby (5 zł, Tue–Sun 10:00–15:00, closed Mon).

When you're finished in the cathedral, stroll around the...

▲▲**Wawel Castle Grounds**—This hill has seen lots of changes over the years. Kazimierz the Great turned a small fortress into a mighty

Gothic castle in the 14th century. Today you'll see the cathedral and a castle complex, but little remains of Kazimierz's grand castle. In the grassy field across from the cathedral, you'll see the foundations of two Gothic churches that were destroyed when the Austrians took over Wawel in the 19th century and needed a parade ground for their troops.

Behind the cathedral, a grand green entryway leads into the palace **courtyard.** When Kazimierz's castle burned down in 1499, this court-yard was rebuilt in the Italian Renaissance style. The dark ivy-covered side later served as the headquarters of the notorious Hans Frank, Nazi governor of German-occupied Poland. (He was tried and executed in Nürnberg after the war.) The entrances to most Wawel museums are here (see "Wawel Castle Museums," next page), and some believe that you'll find something even more special: chakra.

Adherents of the Hindu doctrine of **chakra** believe that a powerful energy field connects all living things. There are seven points on the sur-face of the earth where this chakra energy is most concentrated: Delhi, Delphi, Jerusalem, Mecca, Rome, Velehrad...and Wawel Hill—specifi-cally over there in the corner (immediately to your left as you enter the courtyard). Look for peaceful people (here or elsewhere on the castle grounds) with their eyes closed. One thing's for sure: They're not think-ing of Kazimierz the Great. The smudge marks on the wall are from people pressing up against this corner, trying to absorb some of the chakra's power. The Wawel administration seems creeped out by all this. They've done what they can to discourage this ritual, but believers still gravitate from far and wide to hug the wall. (Just for fun, ask a Wawel tour guide about chakra and watch him squirm—they're forbidden to talk about it.) Give it a try...and let the Force be with you.

If you plan to visit some of the castle museums, now's the time (see "Castle Museums," next page). But if you're looking for a scenic wrap-up to this royal ramble...

Leave the courtyard the way you came in and keep going straight toward the opening in the wall. You'll be rewarded with a beautiful view over the Vistula River and Kraków's outskirts. Directly below you, along the riverbank, is a fire-breathing monument to the **dragon** that was instrumental in the founding of Kraków...

Once upon a time, a prince named Krak founded a town on Wawel Hill. It was the perfect location—except for the fire-breathing dragon who lived in the caves under the hill and terrorized the town. Prince Krak had to feed the dragon all of the town's livestock to keep the fire-breather from going after the townspeople. But clever Krak had a plan. He stuffed a sheep's skin with sulfur and left it outside the dragon's cave. The dragon swallowed it down, and before long, he developed a terrible case of heartburn. To put the fire out, the dragon started drinking water from the Vistula. He kept drinking and drinking until he finally exploded. The town was saved and Kraków thrived.

Your Self-Guided Royal Way Walk is finished. If you want to head down to see the Vistula and the dragon close-up, take a shortcut through the nearby **Dragon's Den.** It's just a 135-step spiral staircase and a few underground caverns—worthwhile only as a quick way to get from the top of Wawel down to the banks of the Vistula (3 zł, enter around corner from bookstore on courtyard overlooking the river, May–Oct daily 10:00–17:00, closed off-season).

Wawel Castle Museums—There are five museums and exhibits in Wawel Castle (not including the cathedral and Cathedral Museum). Each has its own admission ranging from 6–15 zł (complex hours for all museums, unless otherwise noted: April–Oct Sun 10:00–15:00, Mon 9:30–12:00, Tue and Fri 9:30–16:00, Wed–Thu and Sat 9:30–15:00, Nov–March Sun 10:00–15:00, Tue–Sat 9:30–15:00, closed Mon, tel. 012/422-5155, www.wawel.krakow.pl).

The **Royal State Rooms,** while precious to Poles, are mediocre by European standards (enter through courtyard). The top-floor rooms are best, with original wooden ceilings, "leather tooled" walls, and precious 16th-century Brussels tapestries (140 of the original series of 300 survive). Wandering these halls (with their period furnishings), you get a feeling for the 16th- and 17th-century glory days of Poland, when it was a leading power in Central Europe. The Senate Room, with its throne and fine tapestries, is the climax.

The **Royal Private Apartments** are more of the same, and the only part of the complex that must be visited with a guided tour (enter through courtyard, April–Oct English-language tours Tue–Sun at 10:50, 12:00, and 13:10; Nov–March English-language tour Tue–Sun at 12:00; always closed Mon).

The **Crown Treasury and Armory** is a decent collection of swords, saddles, and shields; ornately decorated muskets and crossbows; and cannons in the basement (closed Sun–Mon off-season).

The small **Oriental Art** exhibit displays swords, carpets, vases, and remarkable Turkish tents (upstairs, next to the Senate Room) used by the Ottomans during the 1683 Battle of Vienna. These are trophies of Jan Sobieski, the Polish king who led a pan-European army to victory in that battle (tickets sold at the door, enter through courtyard, don't miss entry on your way back downstairs from Royal State Rooms; closed Mon in season, closed Sun–Mon off-season)).

The **Lost Wawel** exhibit traces the history of this hill and its various churches and castles. The one-way route leads through excavations of a 10th-century church, and exhibits include a model of the cathedral in its original Gothic form, a replica of the entire castle complex in the 18th century (pre-Austrian razing), fascinating decorative tiles from 16th-century stoves that once heated the place, and some medieval artifacts (enter near snack bar across from side of cathedral; open Mon but closed Tue off-season).

Tickets and Reservations: Tickets are sold at several points around the Wawel grounds (most convenient at top of long entry ramp, shorter lines inside bookstore around corner from Dragon's Den). Tickets are limited for the Royal State Rooms, Crown Treasury and Armory, and Royal Private Apartments (which can be visited only with a tour). Boards show how many tickets for each of these are still available today. Tickets come with an assigned entry time (though you can usually sneak in before your scheduled time). In the summer, ticket lines can be long, and sights can sell out by midday. You can reserve tickets ahead for the tour of the Royal Private Apartments (no fee) and the Royal State Rooms and the Crown Armory and Treasury (15-zł reservation fee; tel. 012/422-1697). Frankly, the sights aren't worth all the fuss—if it's sold out, you're not missing much.

MUSEUMS

Kraków's **National Museum (Muzeum Narodowe)** is made up of a series of small but interesting museums scattered throughout the city. Oddly enough, the main branch is the least worth visiting, with 20th-century Polish art and temporary exhibits (5 zł, Tue–Sun 10:00–15:30, Wed until 18:00, closed Mon, aleja 3 Maja 1). I've listed the best of the National Museum's branches below, followed by the Jagiellonian University Museum.

▲▲**Czartoryski Museum (Muzeum Czartoryskich)**—The best of the museums is this eclectic collection, the life's work of Romantic-era princess Izabela Czartoryska. Inspired by Poland's 1791 constitution (Europe's first), she began collecting bits of Polish history and culture. She fled with the collection to Paris after the 1830 insurrection, and 45 years later her grandson returned it to its present Kraków location. When he ran out of room, he bought part of the monastery across the street, joining the buildings. The Nazis took the collection to Germany, and although most of it has been returned, some pieces are still missing.

The museum features armor, handicrafts, decorative arts, and paintings. The first floor is dedicated mostly to artifacts of Polish history and decorative arts; the top floor is European art. There are only three surviving portraits of women by Leonardo da Vinci in the world; *Mona Lisa* in the Louvre is the most famous, but one is in this very museum—*Lady with an Ermine.* In the painting, the mistress of Leonardo's patron sensually strokes an ermine (like a ferret). The patron's nickname was "Ermelino"—meaning, um, "ermine." Hmm...

You'll also see Rembrandt's *Landscape with the Good Samaritan.* The Nazis swiped a famous Rembrandt self-portrait, which was never recovered (7 zł, Tue–Sun 10:00–15:30, Fri until 18:00, closed Mon, 2 blocks north of the Square at ulica Św. Jana 19, tel. 012/422-5566).

▲**Gallery of 19th-Century Polish Art (Galeria Sztuki Polskiej XIX Wieku)**—This place is surprisingly classy for a museum above a market hall. The enjoyable collection features some significant painters, such as Jan Matejko (see his impressive painting of Tadeusz Kościuszko doffing his hat after his unlikely victory over the Russians at the battle at Racławice). But other paintings are clearly just plain good, even if you haven't heard of the artists—such as Józef Chełmoński's energy-charged *Four-in-Hand* and misty *Cranes*. Don't miss Władysław Podkowiński's gripping *Frenzy*, with a pale, sensuous woman clutching an all-fired-up black stallion. The painting caused a frenzy at its 1894 unveiling—leading the unbalanced artist to attack his creation with a knife (7 zł, free on Sun, good English guidebook-35 zł, all paintings labeled in English, Tue and Thu 11:00–18:00, Wed and Fri 9:00–15:30, Sat–Sun 10:00–15:30, closed Mon; above the Cloth Hall on Main Market Square—enter on east side, facing St. Mary's; tel. 012/422-1166).

▲**Wyspiański Museum (Muzeum Wyspiańskiego)**—If you enjoyed Stanisław Wyspiański's paintings and stained glass in St. Francis' Basilica, visit the museum that collects his work. You'll get a good sense of the artist's life and his art, though his best work is still in the basilica (5 zł, Tue–Sun 10:00–15:30, Thu until 18:00, closed Mon, 1 block west of the Square at ulica Szczepańska 11, tel. 012/422-7021).

More National Museums—You can also check out the museum of Wyspiański's rival, the **Józef Mehoffer House** (Dom Józefa Mehoffera, 5 zł, free on Sun, Tue–Sun 10:00–15:30, Wed until 18:00, closed Mon, ulica Krupnicza 26, tel. 012/421-1143), and the former residence of their mentor, the **Jan Matejko House** (Dom Jana Matejki, 4 zł, free on Sun, Tue–Sun 10:00–15:30, Fri until 18:00, closed Mon, ulica Floriańska 41, tel. 012/422-5926).

Jagiellonian University Museum: Collegium Maius—Kraków had the second university in Central Europe (after Prague). Its alumni include Copernicus and Pope John Paul II. This city is still very much a university town, and Jagiellonian University proudly leads tours of its historic oldest building, the 15th-century Collegium Maius. Tour groups routinely duck into the building's Gothic courtyard for free. To visit the interior, you have two choices. The shorter route includes the library, refectory, treasury, assembly hall, and an exhibit of Copernicus' original instruments (10 zł, free on Sat, 30 min, leaves every 20 min Mon–Sat 10:00–14:20, only some in English, none Sun). The deluxe version adds some medieval sculptures, a Rubens, a Rembrandt, some old scientific instruments, and Chopin's piano (usually in English, 15 zł, 1 hr, Mon–Fri at 13:00, none Sat–Sun). It's always smart to call ahead to find out when the shorter tour is scheduled in English, and to reserve for either tour; the shorter tour is especially popular and books up long in advance, particularly on Saturdays, when it's free (tel. 012/422-0549, extension 1307, 1 block west of the Square at ulica Jagiellońska 15, www.uj.edu.pl).

POLISH ARTISTS

Though Poland has produced world-class scientists, musicians, and writers, the country isn't known for its artists. Polish museums greet foreign visitors with fine artwork by unfamiliar names. If you're planning to take in any museums in Poland, there are three artists worth remembering:

Jan Matejko (mah-TAY-koh, 1838–1893) is Poland's best Romantic painter and likely Poland's greatest painter, period. He's known for his many dramatic grand-scale paintings of important moments in Polish history. These paintings—of great successes and failures—stir the patriot in any Pole. You'll see Matejko's works in Warsaw's National Museum and Royal Castle, as well as in Kraków's Gallery of 19th-Century Polish Art (above the Cloth Hall). You can also visit his former residence in Kraków.

Stanisław Wyspiański (vees-PAYN-skee, 1869–1907) was a student of Matejko's. He was the leading figure of the turn-of-the-century Kraków-based Młoda Polska (Young Poland) movement, the Polish version of Art Nouveau. He produced beautiful artwork, from simple drawings to the stirring stained-glass images in Kraków's St. Francis' Basilica. The versatile Wyspiański was also an accomplished stage designer and writer. His patriotic play *The Wedding* is regarded as one of Poland's finest dramas. The largest collection of Wyspiański's art is in the museum devoted to him in Kraków, but you'll also see examples in Warsaw's National Gallery.

Józef Mehoffer (MAY-hoh-fehr), Wyspiański's good friend and rival, was another great Młoda Polska artist. See his work in Kraków's St. Francis' Basilica and at the artist's former residence.

Aside from the courtyard, the only part of the Colleguim Maius you can see without a tour is an interactive exhibit that allows you to tinker with replicas of old scientific tools (6 zł, Mon–Sat 10:00–14:00, closed Sun).

SIGHTS

Kazimierz (Jewish Quarter)

The neighborhood of Kazimierz (kah-ZHEE-merzh), 20 minutes by foot southeast of Kraków's Old Town, is the historic heart of Kraków's once-thriving Jewish community. After years of neglect, the district is

Kazimierz

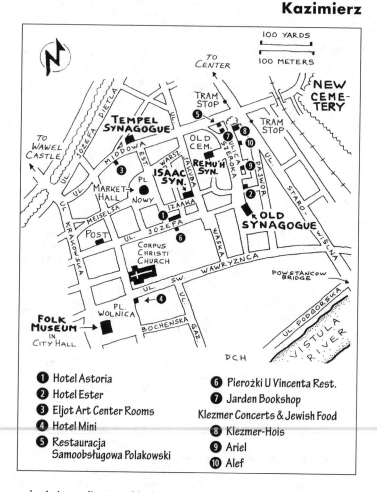

100 YARDS
100 METERS

1 Hotel Astoria
2 Hotel Ester
3 Eljot Art Center Rooms
4 Hotel Mini
5 Restauracja Samoobsługowa Polakowski
6 Pierożki U Vincenta Rest.
7 Jarden Bookshop Klezmer Concerts & Jewish Food
8 Klezmer-Hois
9 Ariel
10 Alef

today being rediscovered by locals and tourists alike. With a smattering of new restaurants and hotels, it's accessible to travelers but still retains its local flavor.

Orientation: Start your visit to Kazimierz on **ulica Szeroka,** which is more of a long, parking-lot square than a street, surrounded by Jewish restaurants, hotels, and synagogues. Check in at the **Jarden Bookshop** at the top of the square (daily 10:00–18:00, ulica Szeroka 2, tel. 012/429-1374, www.jarden.pl, jarden@jarden.pl). They sell a wide variety of books on Kazimierz and Jewish culture in the region, including a good 4.50-zł Kazimierz map and the popular *Retracing "Schindler's List"* guidebook (5 zł). They also run several tours: Jewish Kazimierz overview (35 zł, 2 hrs, walking), Kazimierz and the WWII ghetto (45 zł, 3 hrs, walking, the best overview), *Schindler's List* sights (65 zł, 2 hrs, by car), and Auschwitz-Birkenau (95 zł, 6 hrs, by car). Call to reserve ahead, as tours are by appointment only. Tours will run if a minimum of three people sign up (4 for Auschwitz tour), but pairs or singles can join an already-scheduled tour.

If you visit on Saturday, you'll find only the Old Synagogue museum open. For hotel and restaurant suggestions, see "Sleeping—Kazimierz" and "Eating—Kazimierz" (some restaurants offer live traditional Jewish music nightly in summer), below.

Getting to Kazimierz: It's about a 20-minute **walk** from the Old Town. From the square, walk down ulica Sienna (near St. Mary's Church). At the fork, bear right through the Planty park. At the intersection with the busy Westerplatte ring road, you'll continue straight ahead (bear right at fork) down busy Starowiślna for 15 more minutes. To hop the **tram,** go to the stop on the left-hand side of ulica Sienna (at the intersection with Westerplatte, across the street from the Poczta Główna, or main post office). Catch tram #3, #13, or #24 and go two stops to Miodowa. Walking or by tram, at the intersection of Starowiślna and Miodowa, you'll see a small park across the street and to the right. To reach the heart of Kazimierz—ulica Szeroka—cut through this park. To get back into the Old Town, catch tram #3, #13, or #24 from the intersection of Starowiślna and Miodowa and go two stops back to the Poczta Główna stop. Go uphill five minutes, and you're in the Square.

▲▲**Jewish Cemeteries**—Kazimierz has two Jewish cemeteries, both far more undiscovered and powerful than the famous one in Prague. The more evocative of the two is the **New Cemetery** (Nowy Cmentarz), with graves of those who died after 1800 (free, Sun–Fri 9:00–18:00, until 16:00 in winter, closed Sat, tricky to find—go under railway bridge at east end of ulica Miodowa, jog left as you emerge, cemetery is to your right, enter through gate or door at #55). Nazis vandalized this cemetery, but many of the gravestones have since been returned to their original positions (look for white chalk numbering, used to catalog and replace the stones). Other headstones could not be replaced, and were used to create the moving mosaic wall and Holocaust monument (to the right as you enter).

The **Old Cemetery** (Stary Cmentarz), nearly as moving, was used from 1552–1800. It's smaller, and has been renovated—so it actually feels newer (5 zł, Mon–Fri 9:00–16:00, closed Sat–Sun, enter through the Remu'h Synagogue at ulica Szeroka 40).

JEWS IN KRAKÓW

After King Kazimierz the Great encouraged Jews to come to Poland in the 14th century (see page 129), a large Jewish community settled in and around Kraków. According to legend, Kazimierz (the king) established Kazimierz (the village) for his favorite girlfriend—a Jewish woman named Ester—just southeast of the city walls. (If you have a 50-zł note, take a look at it: that's Kazimierz the Great on the front, and on the back is his capital, Cracovia, and the most important town he founded, Casmirus.)

By the end of the 15th century, there were large Jewish populations in both Kazimierz and in Kraków. Kraków's Jewish community and the university students clashed, and when a destructive fire broke out in 1495, the Jews were blamed. The king forced all of Kraków's Jews to move to Kazimierz.

Kazimierz was an autonomous community, with its own Town Hall, market square, and city walls (though many Jews still commuted into Kraków's square to do business). The Christian (west) and Jewish (east) neighborhoods were also separated by a wall. But by 1800, the walls came down, Kazimierz became part of Kraków, and the Jewish community flourished.

By the start of World War II, 65,000 Jews lived in Kraków (mostly in Kazimierz)—making up more than a quarter of the city's population. Soon after the Nazis arrived, they forced Kraków's Jews into a walled ghetto at Podgórze, across the river. The Jews' cemeteries were defiled and their buildings ransacked and destroyed. In 1942, the Nazis began transporting Kraków's Jews to death camps. Many others were worked to death in the Podgórze ghetto. Only 6,000 Kraków Jews survived the war.

Today's Kraków has only about a hundred Jewish residents. Kazimierz still has an empty feeling, but the neighborhood has enjoyed a renaissance of Jewish culture, following the popularity of *Schindler's List* (which was filmed partly in Kazimierz—look for handwritten letters from Steven Spielberg and the cast in local restaurants—like Ariel—and hotels). While few Jews live here now, the spirit of the Jewish tradition lives on in the many synagogues, as well as in the soulful cemeteries.

Synagogues—Two synagogues sit right on Kazimierz's main square, ulica Szeroka. The **Old Synagogue** (Stara Synagoga), the oldest surviving Jewish building in Poland, is now a three-room museum on local Jewish culture, with English descriptions (6 zł, mid-April–mid-Oct Mon 10:00–14:00, Tue–Sun 10:00–17:00; mid-Oct–mid-April Mon 10:00–14:00, Wed–Thu and Sat–Sun 9:00–15:30, Fri 10:00–17:00, closed Tue, ulica Szeroka 24). **Remu'h Synagogue,** from 1553, is tiny and attached to the Old Cemetery (included in cemetery 5-zł entry fee, Mon–Fri 9:00–16:00, closed Sat, ulica Szeroka 40).

Isaac Synagogue (Synagoga Isaaka), a block west of ulica Szeroka, is the most accessible place to learn more about the Kazimierz Jewish community. The synagogue, the biggest in Kraków, was built in the 17th century. During a recent renovation, they discovered giant wall paintings of the most important prayers (for people who couldn't afford to buy books). In a side room, the synagogue continually runs a 98-minute loop of six films (mostly silent, others in Hebrew, Polish, Yiddish, and English) showing the town before the Nazis came and then the forced transition to a ghetto. Two of the most important films (lasting a total of 7 min) run continuously in the main hall (7 zł, Sun–Fri 9:00–19:00, closed Sat, ulica Kupa 18, tel. 012/430-5577).

Tempel Synagogue (Synagoga Templu), three blocks northwest of ulica Szeroka, has the most impressive interior—big and dark, with elaborately-decorated, gilded ceilings and walls—and most lived-in feel of the bunch (5 zł, unpredictable hours, corner of ulica Miodowa and ulica Podbrzezie).

▲**Kazimierz Market Square (Plac Nowy)**—Locals shop at plac Nowy's market stalls, a gritty factory-workers-on-lunch-break contrast to Kraków's touristy main square (stalls open Tue–Sat 6:00–14:00, a few also open later and Sun 7:00–14:00). Consider dropping by here for some shopping (sorry, no souvenirs), people-watching, or a quick, cheap, and local lunch (see "Eating," page 149).

▲**Polish Folk Museum (Muzeum Etnograficzne)**—This clever and refreshingly good museum hides a few blocks west of the Jewish area of Kazimierz, in the former town hall. The square it's on, plac Wolnica, was Kazimierz's main market square, once almost as big as Kraków's. Inside the museum you'll find models of traditional rural Polish homes, as well as musty replicas of the interiors (like an open-air folk museum—but inside). On the second floor are traditional Polish folk costumes, Christmas decorations, and even bagpipes. The top floor has some imaginatively carved beehives (6 zł, Mon and Wed–Fri 10:00–17:00, Sat–Sun 10:00–14:00, closed Tue, ulica Krakówska 46, tel. 012/430-6023).

Schindler's List **Sights**—Fans of Spielberg's Holocaust movie—and the compassionate Kraków businessman who did his creative best to save the lives of his Jewish workers—can see Oskar Schindler's actual factory, currently the Telpod electronics manufacturing plant (beyond

Kazimierz, southeast of the Old Town, near Kraków-Zabłocie train station at ulica Lipowa 4). Closer to the center, Schindler's apartment is a block from Wawel Castle at ulica Straszewskiego 7 (unmarked and not available for tours). For more information, look for *Retracing "Schindler's List,"* available at the Jarden bookshop (see above).

Near Kraków

▲▲Wieliczka Salt Mine (Kopalnia Soli Wieliczka)—This remarkable mine, 10 miles southeast of Kraków, has been producing salt since 1250. Under Kazimierz the Great, one-third of Poland's income came from these precious deposits. Wieliczka miners spent much of their lives underground, rarely emerging into daylight. To pass the time, 19th-century miners began to carve figures, chandeliers, and eventually even a chapel out of the salt.

From the lobby, your guide escorts you 210 feet down to a spot where you begin a 1.5-mile generally downhill stroll past 20 of the mine's 200 chambers (with signs saying when they were dug), finishing 443 feet below the surface. When you're done, a lift beams you back up.

The tour shows how the miners lived and worked (using horses who lived their whole lives without ever seeing the light of day), takes you through some impressive underground caverns past subterranean lakes, and introduces you to some of the mine's many sculptures (including an army of salt elves and this region's favorite son, Pope John Paul II). Your jaw will drop as you enter the enormous **Chapel of the Blessed Kinga,** carved over three decades in the early 20th century. Look for the salt-relief carving of the *Last Supper.*

While advertised as two hours, your tour finishes in a deep-down shopping zone 90 minutes after you started (and they hope you'll hang out and shop). Note when the next elevator departs (just 3/hr) and you can be out-a-there on the next lift. Zip through the shopping zone in two minutes or step over the rope and be immediately at the line for the great escape (you'll be escorted 300 yards to the skinny industrial elevator, into which you'll be packed like mine workers).

Cost and Hours: Visits are by tour only (40 zł for a guided tour, 9 zł more to use your camera). English tours are generally daily at 10:00 and 12:30 all year; June and Sept–Oct also at 15:00; July–Aug also at 11:30, 13:45, 15:00, and 17:00. If you miss the English-language tour (or decide to just show up and take whatever's going next), follow the fine 3-zł guidebook, which narrates the exact route the tours do and actually gives you more info than the tour guide (April–Oct daily 7:30–19:30, Nov–March daily 8:00–16:00, ulica Daniłowicza 10, tel. 012/278-7302, www.kopalnia.pl). Dress warmly—the mine is a constant 57 degrees Fahrenheit. When buying a ticket, you'll be asked if you want the mine museum. It adds an hour to the mine tour (and is discouraged by local guides: "1.5 miles more walking, colder, more of the same").

Getting to Wieliczka: The salt mine, 10 miles from Kraków, is best reached by minibus (2 zł, 4/hr or with demand). Buses leave from Kraków's train/bus station (look for *Wieliczka Soli* sign in window—confirm that it's actually going to the salt mine) and from the mine exit. Taking a taxi is fastest and taking the train makes no sense.

▲**Nowa Huta**—Literally "new steel works," this factory originally was called Nowa Huta Lenin. When the communists took over Poland, they were nervous about Kraków's long tradition of progressives and intellectuals. To put the city in its place, they built a massive steelworks six miles east of the center (supposedly using plans stolen from a Pittsburgh plant). A walk through this planned worker town is a step back in time to the communist era. From its main square, Nowa Huta radiates numbered streets and trolleys zip workers directly to the immense factory, which still produces steel.

For the best quick visit, take tram #4 from Kraków's old center (from Main Market Square, follow Szczepańska to the ring road outside the Planty park) or from Kraków's train station to Nowa Huta's main square, plac Centralny (about 30 min), and just wander. Gape at the Stalinist architecture and reflect on what it would be like to be one of the 200,000 Poles who live in Nowa Huta. (Actually, it may not be as bad as you imagine—these buildings look stark and gloomy outside, but they're packed with happy little apartments filled with color, light, and warmth.) Tram #4 continues a few minutes further to the main gate of the factory (little to see other than the big sign, stern office headquarters, and smokestacks in the distance), and then it returns to Kraków.

The factory remains, but Krakovians had the last laugh: Nowa Huta, along with Lech Wałęsa's factory in Gdańsk, was one of the home bases of the Solidarity strikes that eventually brought down Poland's communist regime.

SLEEPING

Old Town

$$$ Hotel Maltański is in the beautifully renovated former royal stables, just outside the Planty and only two blocks from Wawel Castle. This fine hotel has an excellent location, friendly and helpful staff, and 17 rooms with classy amenities (like a fluffy bathrobe for every guest). It's a great-value splurge for its location and luxurious touches (Sb-350 zł, "business class" Sb-450 zł, Db-510 zł, 15 percent discount for readers of

SLEEP CODE

(4 zł = about $1, €1 = about $1.10, country code: 48, area code: 012)
Sleep Code: **S** = Single, **D** = Double/Twin, **T** = Triple, **Q** = Quad, **b** = bathroom, **s** = shower only, **no CC** = Credit Cards not accepted. Breakfast is included, credit cards are accepted, and English is spoken at each place (unless otherwise noted).

To help you easily sort through these listings, I've divided the rooms into three categories, based on the price for a standard double room with bath:

$$$ **Higher Priced**—Most rooms 400 zł (€85) or more.
 $$ **Moderately Priced**—Most rooms between 300–400 zł (€65–85).
  $ **Lower Priced**—Most rooms 300 zł (€65) or less.

Kraków's Old Town is filled with affordable hotels with similar prices and interchangeable rooms. This healthy competition has kept prices reasonable, even just a few steps off the Square. Rates are soft—hoteliers don't need much of an excuse to offer you 10 to 20 percent off, especially on weekends or in the off-season. Some hotels quote prices in euros.

While you could stay away from the center, hotel values here are so good that there's not much need to sleep beyond the Planty. Most of my listings are inside (or within a block or two of) the old city walls.

To save a little more money and experience a more local alternative, consider the Kazimierz neighborhood—once Kraków's sister town, later the Jewish quarter, and now part of the city.

this book, off-season try to negotiate even better deal—up to 25 percent off, parking-30 zł/day, ulica Straszewskiego 14, tel. 012/431-0010, fax 012/431-0615, www.maltanski.com, hotel@maltanski.com).

$$$ Hotel Senacki is a business-class place renting 20 elegant rooms between Wawel Castle and the Main Market Square (Sb-€105, Db-€116, deluxe Db-€168, €25 for extra bed, 10 percent cheaper Fri–Sun, 15 percent cheaper Nov–March, parking-80 zł/day, non-smoking rooms, elevator, ulica Grodzka 51, tel. 012/421-1161, fax 012/422-7934, www.senacki.krakow.pl, recepcja@senacki.krakow.pl).

$$ Hotel Saski, renting 60 frou-frou, high-ceilinged rooms a few steps from the Square, is an excellent value for the location (S-190 zł,

Kraków Restaurants and Hotels

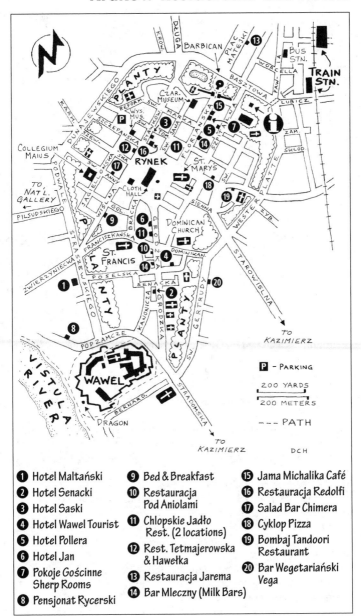

P – PARKING

200 YARDS

200 METERS

- - - PATH

DCH

1. Hotel Maltański
2. Hotel Senacki
3. Hotel Saski
4. Hotel Wawel Tourist
5. Hotel Pollera
6. Hotel Jan
7. Pokoje Gościnne Sherp Rooms
8. Pensjonat Rycerski
9. Bed & Breakfast
10. Restauracja Pod Aniolami
11. Chlopskie Jadło Rest. (2 locations)
12. Rest. Tetmajerowska & Hawełka
13. Restauracja Jarema
14. Bar Mleczny (Milk Bars)
15. Jama Michalika Café
16. Restauracja Redolfi
17. Salad Bar Chimera
18. Cyklop Pizza
19. Bombaj Tandoori Restaurant
20. Bar Wegetariański Vega

Sb-240 zł, D-210 zł, Db-310 zł, "superior" Db-380–410 zł, T-250 zł, Ts-280 zł, Tb-360 zł, antique elevator, ulica Sławkowska 3, tel. 012/421-4222, fax 012/421-4830, www.hotelsaski.com.pl, info@hotelsaski.com.pl).

$$ Hotel Wawel Tourist's classy marble lobby seems too fancy for its prices, but its rooms live up to the fuss—making this place another great value with a good location. Most of its 49 rooms have been recently renovated and cost a bit more; the older, cheaper rooms are a bit worn (Sb-170–195 zł, D-170–180 zł, Db-250–280 zł, big "retro" Db-330 zł, Tb-300–330 zł, Qb-340–380 zł, apartment-310–330 zł, elevator, ulica Poselska 22, tel. 012/424-1300, fax 012/424-1333, www.wawel-tourist.pl, hotel@wawel-tourist.pl).

$$ Hotel Pollera rents 42 fine rooms in a grand, once-plush, old building that are an especially good value off-season (Sb-295 zł, Db-345 zł, Tb-420 zł, apartment-495 zł, extra bed-80 zł, 35 percent cheaper Nov–March, between station and Square, just inside Planty park at ulica Szpitalna 30, tel. 012/422-1044, fax 012/422-1389, www.pollera.com.pl, rezerwac@pollera.com.pl).

$$ Hotel Jan rents 25 slightly worn rooms a few feet from the Square. While a little overpriced, it's central (Sb-250 zł, Db-330 zł, Tb-440 zł, Qb-500 zł, apartment-520 zł, a few rooms on ground floor with a skylight and no window are 10 percent cheaper, elevator, ulica Grodzka 11, tel. 012/430-1969, fax 012/430-1992, www.hotel-jan.com.pl, recepcja@hotel-jan.com.pl).

$ Pokoje Gościnne Sherp rents six simple but delightful little rooms (none with a sink or bathroom facilities) on the fourth floor of a beautifully-located building. It's a long but actually enjoyable climb up a fine old wooden staircase (S-165 zł, D-240 zł, 10 percent cheaper without breakfast and off-season, ulica Floriańska 39, tel. 012/292-0266, tel. & fax 012/429-1778, www.sherp.com.pl, info@sherp.com.pl).

$ Pensjonat Rycerski has 17 tired, outmoded, but cheap rooms above a restaurant, just down the street from Wawel Castle and across the street from a riverside park. The place is a little dark, but hotelesque and a fine budget option (D-120 zł, Db-230 zł, Db apartment-300 zł, extra bed-33 zł, breakfast-18 zł, 15 percent cheaper mid-Oct–March, nearby parking-44 zł/day, plac Na Groblach 22, tel. 012/422-6082, fax 012/422-3399, recepcion@rycerski.com).

$ Bed & Breakfast offers 14 cheap, ramshackle rooms with a tree-house floor plan in a great location (S-60–70 zł, D-110 zł, Db-130 zł, T-170 zł, extra bed-40 zł, breakfast-8 zł, can pay with plastic only on weekdays, ulica Wiślna 10, tel. 012/421-9871, mobile 0604-199-902, wislna@wp.pl).

Very cheap private apartments: You'll be met at the station by people renting cheap apartments, generally in the old center. From my experience, these folks are legit and offer great values for vagabonds who want a memorable local experience with comfort on a super-tight budget.

Kazimierz

Kazimierz has become a mecca for Jewish visitors to Eastern Europe. A decade ago, Kazimierz was crumbling, but today, the neighborhood is undergoing a wave of renovation. Sleep here to be close to Kraków's Jewish heart—or simply to experience a cheaper, less touristy, more local-feeling neighborhood outside the Old Town. The downside: You are a long walk from the fairy-tale medieval ambience of Kraków's old center. For locations, see map on page 140.

$$ **Hotel Astoria,** a new place renting 33 comfy rooms, is popular with Israeli tour groups (Sb-280 zł, Db-350 zł, Db suite-400 zł, extra bed-65 zł, less on weekends and with an Internet reservation, underground parking-30 zł/day, air-con, non-smoking floor, elevator, ulica Józefa 24, tel. 012/432-5010, fax 012/432-5020, www.astoriahotel.pl, biuro@astoriahotel.pl).

$ **Hotel Ester,** fresh and modern, is a good value with friendly staff, perfectly located in the middle of the Kazimierz action (Sb-250 zł, Db-280 zł, Tb-320 zł, Qb-360 zł, air-con, non-smoking rooms, elevator, ulica Szeroka 20, tel. 012/429-1188, fax 012/429-1233, www.hotel -ester.krakow.pl, biuro@hotel-ester.krakow.pl).

$ **Eljot Art Center** rents 15 rooms in addition to running a theater and an art gallery. It's a classy mix of old and new, with huge discounts (up to 25 percent) for booking rooms online or via e-mail (Sb-239 zł, Db-299 zł, Tb-379 zł, 2-room apartment-429 zł, prices 15 percent lower on weekends, ulica Miodowa 15, tel. & fax 012/430-6506, www .eljotcenter.pl, centrum@eljotcenter.pl).

$ **Hotel Mini,** with four simple fourth-floor rooms and no elevator, sits on a pretty, laid-back Kazimierz square a few blocks from the Jewish sights (Sb-110 zł, Db-200 zł, Tb-250 zł, Qb-300 zł, all separate beds, no CC, free parking nearby, plac Wolnica 7, tel. 012/430-6100, tel. & fax 012/430-5988, friendly Weronika Ostrowska speaks just enough English).

EATING

Kraków is one of Eastern Europe's best dining towns, with surprising diversity, high quality, and low prices. Prices are reasonable even on the Square. And a half-block away, they get even better. The city offers plenty of good Polish and Jewish cuisine, of course (see Poland introduction). But if you're tired of starchy Eastern European fare, this is also a great place to sample some international restaurants.

Polish Food in the Old Town

Restauracja Pod Aniolami (Under Angels) offers a dressy jazz-and-candles atmosphere outside on a covered patio or inside in a romantic cellar with rough wood and medieval vaults. The cuisine is traditional

Polish with an emphasis on grilled foods and trout, and the service is top-notch (main dishes 30–40 zł, daily 13:00–24:00, reservations smart, ulica Grodzka 35, tel. 012/421-3999). If you want a fast, cheap, and tasty lunch, drop by their tiny sandwich bar for delightful open-faced sandwiches to take away or enjoy on their sidewalk tables.

Chlopskie Jadło—literally "Peasant Food"—is part of a successful chain serving inexpensive, authentic Polish food. The peasant theme begins with your rustic bread that comes with farmer cheese and lard. It's kitschy—touristy and fun, with "bed board" chairs—but the food is good. Their two central locations are just off the Square: a smaller one north at ulica Św. Jana 3, and one with a farmyard patio and a sprawling labyrinthine series of cellars south at ulica Grodzka 9.

Tetmajerowska, with a plush dining room, serves up some of the finest cooking in town—game, Polish, and European—in an elegant Modernist (c. 1911) interior. The presentation is classy, the service formal, and the ambience as romantic as the piano is live. It's on the Square but upstairs with no view (main dishes 30–60 zł, daily 13:30-23:00, reservations recommended, near the corner of Szczepańska at Rynek Główny 34, tel. 012/422-0631).

Restauracja Jarema offers a tasty reminder that Kraków used to rule a large swath of Ukraine and Lithuania. They serve eastern Polish/Ukranian cuisine, with savory borscht in a 19th-century aristo-cratic elegance. You'll feel like you're dining in an old mansion (main dishes 20–35 zł, daily from 12:00, generally live music from 19:00, reser-vations wise, across the street from Barbican at plac Matejki 5, tel. 012/429-3669).

Bar Mleczny (Milk Bars) are the locals' choice for a quick, cheap, filling, lowbrow lunch in the center. Milk bars date back to communist times when the government subsidized the food, allowing lowly workers to enjoy a meal out. The government still subsidizes the food (note that the soup costs less than a złoty) and the service is aimed at locals—no English menu and a confusing ordering system. (Tips: *Nalesniki* is pan-cakes, *pierogi* are various Polish ravolis, and *kotlet* is a meat cutlet...good luck.) The bar at ulica Floriańska 19 is most characteristic. The one at Grodzka 45 is just as cheap but lacks that communist feeling.

Cukiarnia Jama Michalika café is legendary for its great home-made ice cream, *szarlotka* (apple cake), *kawa* (coffee), and unique turn-of-the-century atmosphere (Sun–Thu 9:00–22:00, Fri–Sat until 23:00, a rare smoke-free interior, ulica Floriańska 45, tel. 012/422-1561). While most think of it as a café, this place is a restaurant with a full menu, too.

Dining on the Square

You'll find plenty of traditional, relatively expensive, tourist-oriented Polish food on the Square. While tourists go for the ye olde places, the most popular spots serve pizza to locals. Poles generally afford this zone on their meager incomes by just having a drink on the Square after eating at home.

Restauracja Redolfi comes with my favorite Square view, friendly service, great salads, international cuisine, and an impressive selection of desserts. This place is fine for a just a drink or a full meal, and despite its prime location, it's not expensive (20-zł salads, main dishes around 30 zł, daily 9:00–24:00, Rynek Główny 38).

Restauracja Hawełka serves proudly traditional Polish cuisine with good seats overlooking the Square's action (main dishes 20–40 zł, daily 11:00–23:00, near the corner of Szczepańska at Rynek Główny 34).

Non-Polish Food

Salad Bar: Bar Chimera, just off the square, is a cafeteria serving fast traditional meals to locals, either outside on their quiet courtyard or inside in what seems like a fake Old World stage set (great salad buffet: small plate-7 zł, big plate-10 zł, 15 zł meals, fine for vegetarians, daily 9:00–23:00, near University at ulica Św. Anny 3). I'd skip their attached full-service restaurant.

Pizza: Cyklop, with 10 tables wrapped around the cook and his busy oven, has excellent wood-fired pizzas (one-person pizzas for about 15 zł, daily 11:30–22:00, near St. Mary's Church at Mikołajska 16, tel. 012/421-6603). But pizza places on the main Square (like Sphinx, kitty-corner from the big church) come with much better views and are popular with locals.

Indian: If you need a tandoori-and-naan fix, **Bombaj Tandoori** offers decent Indian fare two blocks off the Square (most main dishes around 20 zł, daily 12:00–23:00, ulica Mikołajska 11).

Vegetarian: For a healthy, cheap, fast meal, nothing beats **Bar Wegetariański Vega,** pleasantly mellow and packed with sophisticated university students (soups for 3 zł, main dishes 4–7 zł, salads about 2 zł per scoop, order at counter then take food to table, daily 9:00–21:00, ulica Św. Gertrudy 7, tel. 012/422-3494).

Kazimierz

The entire district is bursting with lively cafés and bars—it's a happening night scene. See map on page 140.

If you want fancy dining with a Jewish folk-music serenade, this is the place. Several restaurants on ulica Szeroka (Kazimierz's main square) offer **Klezmer concerts**—traditional Jewish music from 19th-century Poland, generally with violin, string bass, clarinet, and accordion—nightly in the summer at 20:00. Each place has a similar menu with main dishes for around 20 zł. While it'd be nice to pop in each place to compare the music, it's customary to reserve ahead at a single place to dine. **Klezmer-Hois,** filling a venerable former Jewish ritual bathhouse, feels like you're dining in a rich grandparent's home (#6, tel. 012/411-1245). **Ariel** is an elegant restaurant with a good reputation both for its food and music (request to sit upstairs in the larger dining hall for the best music experience, #18, tel. 012/421-7920). Or consider **Alef** (#17, tel. 012/421-3870).

Restauracja Samoobsługowa Polakowski is a homey little self-service cafeteria with a Polish-village interior, serving fast, inexpensive, and tasty traditional meals (main dishes about 6 zł, point to what you want, daily 8:00–22:00, 100 yards from Szeroka at ulica Miodowa 39, tel. 012/421-2117).

Pierożki u Vincenta is a tiny, modern eatery a couple blocks from plac Nowy serving great *pierogi*—Polish-style ravioli—with both traditional fillings and creative newfangled versions (7 zł, daily 11:00–20:00, ulica Józefa 11, tel. 012/430-6834).

The **plac Nowy market** offers a fully authentic blue-collar Polish experience. Join the workers on their lunch break at the little food windows on Kazimierz's market square.

TRANSPORTATION CONNECTIONS

By train to: Warsaw (hrly, 2.5 hrs), **Gdańsk** (2/day direct, 7 hrs; plus 1 direct night train, 10.75 hrs; more with transfer in Warsaw), **Prague** (1 direct night train/day, 8.5 hrs; otherwise transfer in Katowice, Wrocław, or Ostrava-Svinov, 8–11 hrs), **Berlin** (2/day direct, including 1 night train, 9.5–10.5 hrs; otherwise transfer in Warsaw, 9–11 hrs, 350 zł gets you a second-class ticket and a bunk in a 3-bed *couchette* on the 21:37 to 8:21 night train), **Budapest** (1 direct night train/day, 11 hrs; otherwise transfer in Katowice, Poland, or Břeclav, Czech Republic, 9–10 hrs), and **Vienna** (2/day direct, including 1 night train, 6.5–8.25 hrs).

Auschwitz-Birkenau

The unassuming regional capital of Oświęcim (ohsh-VEENCH-im) was the site of one of humanity's most unspeakably horrifying tragedies: the systematic murder of at least 1.1 million innocent people. From 1941 until 1945, Oświęcim was the site of Auschwitz, the biggest, most notorious concentration camp in the Nazi system. Today, Auschwitz is the most poignant memorial anywhere to the victims of the Holocaust.

A visit here is obligatory for Polish 14-year-olds; students usually come again during their last year of school as well. You'll often see Israeli high school groups walking through the grounds waving their Star of David flags. Many people, including Germans, leave flowers and messages. One of the messages reads: "Nations who forget their own history are sentenced to live it again."

WHY VISIT AUSCHWITZ?

Why visit a notorious concentration camp on your vacation? Auschwitz-Birkenau is one of the most moving sights in Europe, and certainly the most important of all the Holocaust memorials. Seeing the camp can be difficult: many visitors are overwhelmed with some combination of sadness and anger over the tragedy, as well as inspiration at the remarkable stories of survival. But Auschwitz survivors and victims' families want tourists to come here and experience the scale and the monstrosity of the place to be sure that the Holocaust is always remembered—so it never happens again.

Auschwitz isn't for everyone. But I've never met anyone who toured Auschwitz and regretted it. For many, it's a profoundly life-altering experience—and at the very least, it will affect forever the way you think about the Holocaust.

ORIENTATION

"Auschwitz" actually refers to a series of several camps in Poland, most importantly Auschwitz I, in the village of Oświęcim (50 miles west of Kraków, a 75-minute drive), and Auschwitz II (a.k.a. Birkenau, about 2 miles west of Oświęcim). Those visiting Auschwitz generally see both Auschwitz I and Birkenau.

Begin at Auschwitz I. The museum's main building has ticket booths, bookstores (consider the good 3-zł "Guide-Book"), exchange offices, WCs, eateries, and the Oświęcim TI (desperate for interest in anything in town besides the camp, lots of free materials about Oświęcim, tel. 033/843-0091). You'll also find maps of the camp (posted on the walls), a tour office (tours described below), and a theater that shows a powerful movie (see below).

Cost, Hours, and Information: Entrance to the camp is free, but donations are gladly accepted. The museum opens every day at 8:00, and closes in June–Aug at 19:00, May and Sept 18:00, April and Oct 17:00, March and Nov–mid-Dec 16:00, and mid-Dec–Feb 15:00. Information: tel. 033/844-8107, www.auschwitz.org.pl.

Movie: The 17-minute movie (too graphic for children) was shot by Ukrainian troops days after the Soviets liberated the camp. Upon your arrival, note the times the English-language version will run (2/day, always in English at 11:00, usually at 13:00, and often at other times—schedule above cashier at the end of the hall of main building, buy your 3-zł ticket and come back for the showing).

Tours of Auschwitz: To join a scheduled English tour of the camp, find the tour office (on right-hand side in main building about halfway down hallway). The Auschwitz Museum has a network of excellent guides who are serious, frank, and feel a strong sense of responsibility about sharing the story of the camp. There is a daily **English-language tour** of Auschwitz and Birkenau at 11:00 (lasts 3.5 hrs), which includes the film at the main museum and the bus between the two camps. There is usually another tour at 13:00, and during busy times, there are often a lot more, depending on demand and the availability of an English-speaking guide (25 zł, includes Birkenau shuttle bus mid-April–Oct). Scheduled tours can sell out—so it's smart to call ahead to reserve a space (no extra charge, tel. 033/844-8102).

ON THE WAY TO AUSCHWITZ: THE POLISH COUNTRYSIDE

You'll spend about an hour gazing out the window as you drive or ride the bus to Auschwitz. This may be your only real look at the Polish countryside. Ponder these thoughts about what you're passing: The small houses you see are traditionally inhabited by three generations at the same time. Nineteenth-century houses (the few that survive) often sport blue stripes. Back then, parents announced that their daughters were now eligible by getting out the blue paint. Once they saw these blue lines, village boys were welcome to come a-courtin'.

Big churches mark small villages. Tiny roadside memorials and crosses mark places where fatal accidents occurred.

The farmers have small lots and are notorious for not being very productive. They dread the coming entry to the European Union, when a new economic toughness will sweep the land. But, for now, they remain Poland's sacred cows: producing little, paying almost no tax, and draining government resources.

As most people don't own cars, bikes are common and public transit is excellent (lots of bus stops, minibuses that stop anywhere if you wave for a 2-zł ride). The bad roads are a legacy of communist construction, exacerbated by heavy truck use and brutal winters.

Poland has well over 2,000 counties or districts, each with its own coat of arms (you'll pass several along the way). The forests are state-owned and locals enjoy the right to pick berries in the summer and mushrooms in the autumn (which are dried and then boiled to make tasty soups in the winter).

You can also hire your own **private guide** for the basic 3.5-hour tour of the camp (200 zł per group), or for a longer six-hour "study tour" (250 zł). This guide service is a great value and worthwhile if you have special interest in the camp. To hire a private guide, go to the cashiers at the end of the hall. Remember, you can also hire your own private guide in Kraków with a car (about 500 zł, 300 zł without a car), and several companies sell package tours from Kraków (see "Helpful Hints," above).

Visiting without a guide (given the abundance of English descriptions, English-language tours to freeload on, and the self-guided tour of both camps described below) works just fine.

Getting to Auschwitz: Round-trip tours from Kraków to Auschwitz take care of your transportation for you. But with a tour, you pay triple and have to adhere to a strict schedule. The most rewarding visit is to go on your own, take one of the camp's organized tours, and then be free to explore the grounds on your own.

Two different **bus** companies connect Kraków and Oświęcim (10 zł, 1.5 hours): PKS Kraków (4/day, 3/day Sat-Sun, leave from stalls behind bus station, buy ticket in bus station or on board) and PKS Oświęcim (more frequent but less convenient location; 14/day, 13/day Sat–Sun, leave from Jordan kiosk on ulica Bosacka at far side of train station; take stairs near station entry down to pedestrian underpass and go left when you emerge on the other side, tel. 012/430-4035).

Try to take a bus that will drop you off right at the museum (asking for "Auschwitz Museum" improves your odds). Some buses take you instead to the Oświęcim **train station.** If you wind up here, it's about a 25-minute walk to the camp (turn right out of station, go straight, then turn left at roundabout, camp is several blocks ahead on left). Or, from the Oświęcim station, you can reach the camp by catching a bus (#24, #25, #26, #27, #28, or #29, 1.90 zł, buy *bilet* at kiosk or buy from driver for 0.30 zł more, 1–4/hr, 1–2/hr Sat–Sun) or taking a taxi (around 10 zł). You could ride the **train** to Oświęcim, but it's less comfortable than the bus (14/day, 1.25–1.75 hrs).

Returning to Kraków: Buses may depart from a different spot than where you arrived (closest stop to the camp: leave Auschwitz I building through main entry and walk straight along parking lot, turn right on road near end of lot, at dead end go to bus stop across the street). As this can be confusing and frustrating, figure out your return with the help of the information desk upon arrival in Auschwitz. Note that there's no public transportation back to Kraków from Birkenau, where most people end their tours; you'll have to take the shuttle bus back to Auschwitz I first.

Shuttle Bus from Auschwitz I to Birkenau: Buses shuttle visitors two miles between the camps nearly hourly (leaving Auschwitz I at the bottom of the hour and Birkenau at the top of the hour, confirm times posted at the bus stop outside the main building of each site, buy the 2-zł ticket on the bus). Taxis are also standing by.

Eating: There's a café and decent cafeteria at the main Auschwitz building (daily 8:00–18:00) and two places across the street (Art Burger is fast, Art Deco restaurant is slower but good).

AUSCHWITZ I

Before World War II, this camp was a base for the Polish army. When Hitler occupied Poland, he took over these barracks and turned it into a concentration camp for his Polish political enemies. The location was ideal, with a nearby rail junction and rivers providing natural protective boundaries. In 1942, Auschwitz became a death camp for the extermination of European Jewry. By the time the camp was liberated in 1945, at least 1.1 million people had been murdered here—960,000 of them Jewish.

As you exit the entry building's back door and go towards the camp, you see the notorious gate with the cruel message, *"Arbeit Macht Frei"* ("Work sets you free"). Note that the B was welded on upside down by belligerent inmates. On their arrival, new prisoners were told the truth: The only way out of the camp was through the crematorium chimneys.

Just inside the gate and to the right, the camp orchestra (made up of prisoners) used to play marches; having the prisoners march made them easier to count.

The main road leads past the barracks. An average of 14,000 prisoners were kept at this camp at one time. (Birkenau could hold up to 100,000.) The first row of barracks contains the **National Memorials,** created by the home countries of the camps' victims. The most interesting are the **Suffering and Struggle of the Jews** exhibit (block 27) and the nearby **Gypsy** exhibit. Most of the other national memorials were created during the communist era, so they have a decidedly socialist spin; some have been updated (including Hungary, block 18, and the Czech and Slovak republics, block 16).

The most interesting part of the camp is the second row of barracks, which hold the museum exhibitions. Blocks 4 and 5 focus on how Auschwitz prisoners were killed. Blocks 6, 7, and 11 explore the conditions for prisoners who survived here a little longer than most.

Auschwitz I

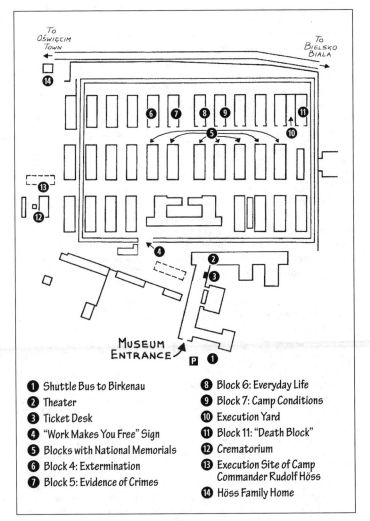

To Oświęcim Town ←
To Bielsko Biala →

1 Shuttle Bus to Birkenau
2 Theater
3 Ticket Desk
4 "Work Makes You Free" Sign
5 Blocks with National Memorials
6 Block 4: Extermination
7 Block 5: Evidence of Crimes
8 Block 6: Everyday Life
9 Block 7: Camp Conditions
10 Execution Yard
11 Block 11: "Death Block"
12 Crematorium
13 Execution Site of Camp Commander Rudolf Höss
14 Höss Family Home

MUSEUM ENTRANCE
P

Block 4 focuses on extermination. In the first room is a map showing all of the countries Auschwitz prisoners were brought from—as far away as Norway and Greece. You'll also find an urn filled with ashes, a symbolic memorial to all of the camp's victims. In Room 2, a map shows that victims were transported here from all over Europe. To prevent a riot, the Nazis claimed that this was only a transition camp for resettlement in Eastern Europe. Room 3 displays the only photos that exist of victims inside the camp—taken by proud SS men.

Upstairs in Room 4 is a chilling model of a Birkenau crematorium. People entered on the left, then got undressed in the underground rooms (hanging their belongings on numbered hooks and encouraged to remember their numbers to retrieve their clothes later). They then moved into the "showers" and were killed by Cyclon-B gas. This efficient factory of murder took about 20 minutes to kill 20,000 people in four gas chambers. Elevators brought the bodies up to the crematorium. Members of the *Sonderkommand*—Jewish inmates who were kept isolated and forced by the Nazis to work here—removed the corpses' gold teeth and shaved off hair (to be sold) before putting the bodies in the ovens. It wasn't unusual for a *Sonderkommand* worker to discover a wife, child, or parent among the dead. A few committed suicide by throwing themselves at electric fences; those who didn't were systematically executed by the Nazis after a two-month shift. Across from the model of the crematorium are canisters of Cyclon-B (hydrogen cyanide), the German-produced cleaning agent that is lethal in high doses. Across the hall in Room 5 is a wall of victims' hair—4,400 pounds of it—another source of camp income. Also displayed is cloth made with the hair, used to make Nazi uniforms.

Back downstairs in Room 6 is an exhibit on the plunder of victims' personal belongings. People being transported here were encouraged to bring luggage—and some victims had even paid in advance for houses in their new homeland. After they were killed, everything of value was sorted and stored in warehouses that prisoners named "Canada" (a country they associated with great wealth). Although the Canada warehouses were destroyed, you can see a few of these items in the next building.

Block 5 focuses on material evidence of the crimes that took place here. It consists mostly of piles of the victims' goods, a tiny fraction of everything the Nazis stole. As you wander through the rooms, you'll see eyeglasses; fine Jewish prayer shawls; crutches and prosthetic limbs (the first people the Nazis ever exterminated were mentally and physically ill German citizens); a seemingly endless mountain of shoes; and suitcases with names of victims—many marked *Kind*, or "child." Visitors often wonder if the suitcase with the name "Frank" belonged to Anne, one of the Holocaust's most famous victims. After being discovered by the Nazis, the Frank family was transported here and split up, though it's unlikely the suitcase was theirs. Anne Frank and her sister Margot were sent to the Bergen-Belsen camp in northern Germany, where they died of typhus shortly before the war ended. Their father, Otto Frank, survived Auschwitz and was found barely alive by the Russians who liberated the camp in January 1945.

CHILLING STATISTICS: THE HOLOCAUST IN POLAND

The majority of people murdered by the Nazis during the Holocaust were killed right here in Poland. For centuries, Poland was known for its tolerance of Jews, and right up until the beginning of World War II, Poland had Europe's largest concentration of Jews: 3,500,000. Throughout the Holocaust, the Nazis murdered 4,500,000 Jews in Poland (many of them brought in from other countries) at camps including Auschwitz and ghettos such as Warsaw's.

By the end of the war, only 300,000 Polish Jews had survived—less than one in 10 of the original population. Many of these survivors were granted "one-way passports" (read: deported) to Israel by the communist government in 1968 (following a big student demonstration with a strong Jewish presence). Today, only about 2,000 Jews live in all of Poland.

As horrific as these statistics are, mere numbers on paper don't do justice to the scale of the atrocities committed here. A visit to Auschwitz-Birkenau hits you at a gut level, giving you a greater sense of the appalling inhumanity, suffering, and irreplaceable loss.

Although the purpose of Auschwitz was to murder its inmates, not all of them were killed immediately. After an initial evaluation, some prisoners were registered and forced to work. (This did not mean they were chosen to live—but rather to die later.) In **Block 6,** you see elements of the everyday life of the prisoner. The halls are lined with photographs of victims. Notice the dates of arrival *(przybył)* and death *(zmarł)*—those who were registered survived here an average of two to three months. (Flowers are poignant reminders that these victims still have loved ones.) Room 1 displays drawings of the arrival process—sketched by survivors of the camp. After the initial selection, those chosen to work were showered, shaved, and photographed. After a while, photographing each prisoner got to be too expensive, so prisoners were tattooed instead (see photographs)—on the chest, on the arm, or—for children—on the leg. A display shows the symbols that prisoners had to wear to show their reason for internment—Jew, Gypsy, homosexual, political prisoner, and so on.

Room 4 shows the starvation that took place here. The prisoners here when the camp was liberated were living skeletons (the healthier

ST. MAKSYMILIAN KOLBE

Among the many inspirational stories of Auschwitz is that of Maksymilian Kolbe, a priest interned here in 1941.

When a prisoner escaped, the Nazis punished remaining inmates by selecting 10 of them to put in the Starvation Cell until they died (based on the Nazi "doctrine of collective responsibility").

After the selection had been made, Kolbe offered to replace one of the men. The Nazis agreed. (The man Kolbe saved is said to have survived and raised a family after the war.)

All 10 of the men—including Kolbe—were put into Starvation Cell 18. Two weeks later, when the door was opened, only Kolbe had survived. The story had spread throughout the camp, and Kolbe had become a hero. To squelch the hope he had given the other inmates, Kolbe was executed by lethal injection. In 1982, Kolbe was canonized by the Catholic Church.

ones had been forced to march to Germany). Of the 7,500 prisoners who were liberated by the Soviets, 20 percent died soon after of disease and starvation. Look for the prisoners' daily ration (in the glass case): a pan of tea or coffee in the morning; thin vegetable soup in the afternoon; and a piece of bread (often made with sawdust or chestnuts) for dinner. This makes it clear that Auschwitz was never intended to be a "work camp," where people were kept alive, healthy, and efficient to do work. Rather, people were meant to die here—if not in the gas chambers, then through malnutrition and overwork (as Hitler put it, "extermination through work").

You can see scenes of the prisoner's workday (sketched by survivors after liberation) in Room 5. Prisoners worked as long as the sun shined—eight hours in winter, up to 12 hours in summer—mostly on farms or in factories. Room 6 is about Auschwitz's child inmates, 20 percent of the camp's victims. Blond, blue-eyed children—like the girl in the bottom row on the right—were either "Germanized" in special schools or, if younger, adopted by German families. Dr. Josef Mengele conducted experiments on children, especially twins and triplets, to try to figure out ways to increase fertility for German mothers.

Block 7 shows living and sanitary conditions at the camp—which you'll see in more detail later at Birkenau. Blocks 8–10 are vacant, but step into the **courtyard** between Blocks 10 and 11. The wall at the far end is where the Nazis shot several thousand political prisoners, leaders of camp resistance, and religious leaders. Notice that the windows are covered, so that nobody could witness the executions. Also take a close look at the memorial—the back of it is made of the same material designed by Nazis to catch the bullets without a ricochet. Inmates were shot at short range—about three feet. The pebbles represent prayers from Jewish visitors.

The most feared place among prisoners was the **"Death Block" (#11),** from which nobody ever left alive. In Room 5, you can see how prisoners lived in these barracks—three-level bunks, with three prisoners sleeping in each bed (they had to sleep on their sides so they could fit). Death here required a trial (the room in which sham trials were held—lasting about two minutes each—is on display). In Room 6, people undressed before they were executed. In the basement, you'll see several different types of cells. The Starvation Cell (#18) held prisoners selected to starve to death when a fellow prisoner escaped; Maksymilian Kolbe voluntarily spent two weeks here to save a man's life (see sidebar). In the Dark Cell (#20), which held up to 30, people had only a small window for ventilation—and if it became covered with snow, the prisoners suffocated. At the end of the hall in Cell 21, you can see where a prisoner scratched a crucifix (left) and Jesus (right) on the wall. In the Standing Cells (#22), four people would be forced to stand together for hours at time (of course, the bricks went all the way to the ceiling then). Upstairs is an exhibit on resistance within the camp.

Before you leave Auschwitz, visit the **crematorium** (from Block 11, exit straight ahead and go past first row of barracks, then turn right and go straight on the road between the two rows of barracks; pass through the gap in the fence and look for the chimney on your left). People undressed outside, or just inside the door. Up to 700 people at a time could be gassed here. Inside the door, go into the big room on the right. Look for the vents in the ceiling—this is where the SS men dropped the Cyclon-B. Through the door is a replica of the furnace. This facility could burn 340 bodies a day—so it took two days to burn all of the bodies from one round of executions. The Nazis didn't like this inefficiency, so they built four more huge crematoria at Birkenau.

Shortly after the war, camp commander Rudolf Höss was tried, convicted, and sentenced to death for his work here. Survivors requested that he be executed at Auschwitz. In 1947, he was hung. The site is preserved behind the crematorium (about a hundred yards from his home where his wife—who loved her years here—read stories to their children, very likely by the light of a human-skin lampshade).

Take your time with Auschwitz I. When you're ready, catch the shuttle bus (or a taxi) two miles to the second stage of the camp—Birkenau.

BIRKENAU (BRZEZINKA)

When the original Auschwitz camp got to be too small for the capacity the Nazis envisioned, they built a second camp in some nearby farm fields. The original plan was for a camp that could hold 200,000 people, but at its peak, Birkenau held only 100,000. They were still adding on to it when the camp was liberated in 1945.

Train tracks lead past the main building and into the camp. The first sight that greeted prisoners was the guard tower (familiar to Americans from the stirring scenes in *Schindler's List*). Climb to the top

of the entry building (also houses WCs and bookstore) for an overview of the massive camp. As you look over the camp, you'll see a vast field of chimneys and a few intact wooden and brick barracks. The train tracks lead straight back to the dividing platform, and then dead-end at the ruins of the crematorium and camp monument at the far side.

Some of the barracks were destroyed by Germans. Most were dismantled to be used for fuel and building materials shortly after the war. But the first row has been reconstructed (using components from the original structures). Visit the barracks on the right. The first building was the **latrine:** The front half of the building was washrooms, and the back was a row of toilets. There was no running water; prisoners were in charge of keeping these clean. Because of the unsanitary conditions, the Nazis were afraid to come in here—so it was the heart of the black market and the inmates' resistance movement.

The fourth building was a **bunk** building. Each inmate had a personal number, a barrack number, and a bed number. Inside, you can see the beds (angled so that more could fit). An average of 400 prisoners—but up to 1,000—would be housed in each of these buildings. These wooden structures, designed as stables by a German company, came in prefab pieces that made them cheap and convenient (look for the horse-tying rings on the wall). Two chimneys connected by a brick duct provided a little heat. The bricks were smoothed by inmates who sat here to catch a bit of warmth.

Follow the train tracks toward the monument about a half-mile away at the back end of Birkenau. At the intersection of these tracks and the perpendicular gravel road (halfway to the monument) was the gravel **dividing platform.** A Nazi doctor would stand facing the guard tower and evaluate each prisoner. If he pointed the right, the prisoner sentenced to death, and trudged—unknowingly—to the gas chamber. If he

Auschwitz II–Birkenau

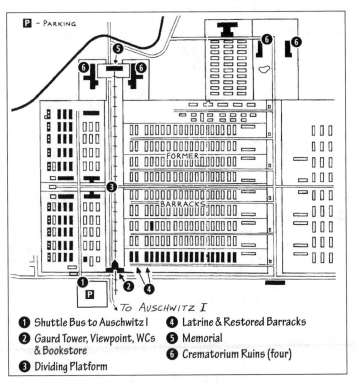

P – PARKING

① Shuttle Bus to Auschwitz I
② Gaurd Tower, Viewpoint, WCs & Bookstore
③ Dividing Platform
④ Latrine & Restored Barracks
⑤ Memorial
⑥ Crematorium Ruins (four)

pointed to the left, the person would be registered and live a little longer. It was here that families from all over Europe were torn apart forever.

On the left-hand side of the tracks are some **brick barracks.** Either now or on your way back, look inside one of them. The supervisors lived in the two smaller rooms near the door. Further in, most barracks still have the wooden bunks that held about 700 people per building. Four or five people slept on each bunk, including the floor—reserved for new arrivals. There were chamber pots at either end of the building. After a Nazi doctor died of typhus, sanitation improved, and these barracks got running water.

As you walk along the camp's only road, which leads along the tracks to the crematorium, imagine the horror of this place—no grass, only mud, all the barracks packed with people, with smoke blowing in from the busy crematoria. This was an even worse place to die than Auschwitz I.

The train tracks lead to the camp **memorial** and **crematorium.** Finish with the memorial. At the end of the tracks, go 50 yards to the left and climb the three concrete steps to view the ruin. This is number two of four crematoria here at Birkenau, with a capacity to cremate 4,000 people per day. At the far-right end of the ruins, see the stairs where people entered the rooms to undress. People were given numbered lockers, conning them into thinking they were coming back. (Nazis didn't want a panic.) Then they piled into the "shower room"—the underground passage branching away from the memorial—and were killed. Their bodies were burned in the crematorium (on the left), giving off a scent of sweet almonds (the Cyclon-B). Beyond the remains of the crematorium is a hole—once a gray lake where tons of ashes were dumped. This efficient factory of death was destroyed by the Nazis as the Soviet army approached, leaving today's evocative ruins.

The Soviets arrived on January 27, 1945 and the nightmare of Auschwitz was over. The Polish parliament voted to turn these grounds into a museum, so that the world would understand, and never forget, the horror of what happened here. The **monument** at the back of the camp, built in 1967 (by the communist government in its heavy "Social Realist" style), represents gravestones and the chimney of a crematorium. The plaques, written in each of the languages spoken by camp victims (including English, far right), explain that the memorial is "a cry of despair and a warning to humanity."

WARSAW

(Warszawa)

Warsaw is Poland's capital and biggest city. It's huge, famous, and important...but not particularly pretty. Warsaw's outskirts look basically the way Americans expect: an endless sea of communist apartment blocks. The most appealing part of the city, the reconstructed Old Town, has lanes and squares as charming as any in Europe—an odd contrast to the concrete sprawl around it. But even though it's not quaint or cute, Warsaw is fascinating. It's an open-air display of 20th-century history. As one proud Varsovian told me, "Warsaw is ugly because its history is so beautiful."

While Warsaw (vah-SHAH-vah in Polish) was the capital of a once-mighty Polish empire, the city saw more than its share of hardships in the last century. In the waning days of World War II, the Germans systematically destroyed the city to avenge an uprising—literally working from block to block to demolish every building. At the war's end, Warsaw was devastated. An estimated 800,000 Varsovians were dead—a staggering two-thirds of the city's prewar population. The city itself was more than 85 percent destroyed, and the Poles seriously considered building a brand-new capital from scratch elsewhere, rather than rebuild from the rubble.

But ultimately a painstaking reconstruction did take place. Different sectors were rebuilt in different styles, creating today's Warsaw, a city of contrasts. Visitors encounter crumbling communist apartment blocks (*bloki* in Polish); cobbled medieval squares rebuilt in quaint fashion; and a new wave of postcommunist, super-modern glass-and-steel skyscrapers. Between the buildings, you'll find fragments of a complex and often tragic history. Parts of the city have an undeniable appeal (like the Old Town and Łazienki Park), but even Warsaw's "ugly" parts become beautiful when you understand the history.

Planning Your Time

Most American travelers see only idyllic Kraków, but a visit to bustling and very urban Warsaw is helpful for understanding modern Poland. Still, on the Richter scale of sightseeing thrills, Warsaw doesn't compare to Kraków, Budapest, or Prague. It doesn't merit a long visit or a time-consuming detour—but it is well worth spending a few hours or a day here if you're passing through. If you're coming from Germany, consider connecting to Warsaw via a night train from Berlin before moving on to Kraków later that same day (hrly trains, 2.5 hrs).

With a few hours, gape at Stalin's towering Palace of Culture and Science, then wander through the Old Town. With a little more time, enjoy the city's beautiful Łazienki Park or seek out some museums and sights that interest you—whether it's Holocaust history, art galleries, or Chopin.

ORIENTATION

(area code: 022)

Warsaw sprawls, with nearly two million residents. But virtually everything of interest to travelers is on the "Left Bank" (west) of the Vistula River. The city's main train station (Warszawa Centralna) is in the shadow of its biggest landmark: the can't-miss-it skyscraping Palace of Culture and Science (Pałac Kultury i Nauki, a.k.a. Stalin's Penis). Between there and the river runs the "Royal Way" street, connecting the sights in the north (Old Town and New Town) with the sights in the south (Łazienki Park, and farther out, Wilanów Palace, just outside the city). Most major sights and recommended hotels and restaurants are along this spine.

Tourist Information

Warsaw's helpful, youthful, well-run TI has four offices: **Castle Square** in the Old Town (May–Sept daily 9:00–20:00, Oct–April daily 9:00–18:00, ulica Krakowskie Przedmieście 89), the **central train station** (May–Sept daily 8:00–20:00, Oct–April daily 8:00–18:00), the **western coach station** (May–Sept daily 9:00–18:00, Oct–April daily 8:00–17:00, aleja Jerozolimskie 144), and the **airport** (May–Sept daily 8:00–20:00, Oct–April daily 8:00–18:00). The general information number for all TIs is 022/9431 (www.warsawtour.pl). All four branches offer several free, useful materials: a city map (with important phone numbers and a schedule for the made-for-tourists bus #100 on the back), a booklet called *Warsaw: In Short*, a museum guide, and a series of brochures on sights and neighborhoods (Old Town, Royal Way, Jewish sights). The TI also has a free room-booking service.

Tours of Warsaw: Mazurkas offers a pricey bus-plus-walking tour (120 zł, 4.5 hrs, includes Old Town, Wilanów Palace, and other sights,

Warsaw

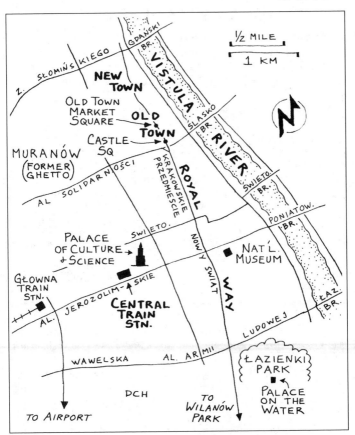

picks up at various hotels daily around 9:00, tel. 022/629-1878, www
.mazurkas.com.pl).

Arrival in Warsaw

By Train: Most trains arrive at the big, dreary Warszawa Centralna station, a monstrosity (resembling the Flying Nun's habit) next to the
Palace of Culture and Science. As there's little to see around the station,
most travelers head directly for the Royal Way and the Old Town.

The station has several platforms *(peron)*, each of which has two
tracks *(tor)*. Departures are listed by the *peron*, so keep your eye on both
tracks for your train. Arrivals are *przyjazdy*, and departures are *odjazdy*.

WARSAW LANDMARKS

English	Polish	Pronounced
Warsaw	**Warszawa**	vah-SHAH-vah
Main Train Station	**Warszawa Centralna**	vah-SHAH-vah tsehn-TRAHL-nah
Palace of Culture and Science	**Pałac Kultury i Nauki** (or simply *Pałac*)	PAH-wahts kool-TOO-ree ee nah-OO-kee
New Town	**Nowe Miasto**	NOH-vay mee-AH-stoh
Old Town	**Stare Miasto**	STAH-reh mee-AH-stoh
Old Town Market Square	**Rynek Starego Miasta**	REE-nehk stah-RAY-goh mee-AH-stah
Castle Square	**Plac Zamkowy**	plahts zahm-KOH-vee
Vistula River	**Wisła**	VEES-wah

You'll emerge from your *peron* into a confusing labyrinth of passageways. At this underground level, you'll find **lockers** downstairs near *peron* 4—look for *przechowalnia bagażu* (4 zł/1 hr, 5 zł/up to 6 hrs, 6 zł for longer). It's best to emerge quickly into the **main arrival hall** (follow signs to *Hala Główna*) to get your bearings (and take your first gawk at the nearby Palace of Culture and Science). For **international tickets,** look for the *Kasy Międzynarodowe* office in the corner of the main hall (under the big orange *Apteka Non Stop* sign). In front of the station, **bus #175** takes you right to the Royal Way and Old Town (about 10 min). Train info: tel. 022/9436.

By Car: Warsaw is a stressful city to drive and park in. Arrange parking with your hotel and get around by foot or public transit. You must pay to park in the city Mon–Fri 8:00–18:00 and Sat 8:00–15:00. Park your car, find the meter, and insert coins until the proper amount of time appears in the left-hand window (about 2.60 zł/hr). Press the green button, wait for your ticket, and put it on your dashboard.

By Plane: Warsaw's **Fryderyk Chopin International Airport** is about six miles southwest of the center. The airport is small and user-friendly (with signs in English). You'll find a branch of the TI, plus lots of ATMs and exchange offices *(kantor)*. Bus #175 runs into the center (train station, Royal Way, and Old Town) from the bus stop just in

WARSAW AT A GLANCE

▲▲**Old Town Market Square** Recreation of Warsaw's glory days, with lots of colorful architecture. **Hours:** Always open.

▲▲**Royal Way Stroll** Self-guided walk through the most interesting part of the Royal Way, starring statues, churches, and historic squares, with a tower finale. **Hours:** Royal Way always open; tower open daily 10:00–18:00, until 20:00 in summer.

▲▲**Palace of Culture and Science** Huge Art Deco skyscraper with a more impressive exterior than interior, housing theaters, multiplex cinema, observation deck, and more. **Hours:** Observation deck—daily 9:00–20:00.

▲**Castle Square** Colorful spot with whiffs of old Warsaw—Royal Castle (below), monuments, and a chunk of the city wall, with cafés just off the square. **Hours:** Always open.

▲**Royal Castle** Warsaw's most interesting palace, rebuilt after World War II but stocked with original furnishings (hidden during war). **Hours:** Mid-April–Sept Tue–Sat 10:00–18:00, Sun 11:00–18:00, Oct–mid-April until 16:00 and closed Mon.

▲**Historical Museum of Warsaw** Interesting glimpse of the city before and after World War II. **Hours:** Mid-March–mid-Sept Tue and Thu 12:00–19:00, Wed and Fri–Sun 11:00–16:30; off-season Tue and Thu 11:00–18:00, Wed and Fri–Sun 10:00–15:30; always closed Mon.

▲**Piłsudski Square** Tomb of the Unknown Soldier, Saxon Garden, National Theater, and historic monuments. **Hours:** Always open.

▲**Łazienki Park** Lovely, sprawling green space with peacocks and neoclassical buildings. **Hours:** Always open.

▲**Ghetto Walking Tour** Pilgrimage from Ghetto Heroes Square along the Path of Remembrance to the infamous Nazi "transfer spot" where Jews were sent to death camps. **Hours:** Always open.

front of the terminal (2.40 zł, 4–6/hr, less Sat–Sun, 30 min). A 20-minute taxi ride to the center shouldn't cost you more than 35 zł (though hucksters who approach you offering a ride may try to charge you more than twice that much—to get a fair deal, find a taxi marked with a company name and telephone number). The trip into town can take much longer during rush hour (because only one main thoroughfare connects the airport to the center). Airport info: tel. 022/650-4100.

Getting around Warsaw

By Public Transit: You can use the same tickets on any of Warsaw's trams, city buses, or the Metro. A single ticket costs 2.40 zł (*bilet jedno-razowy,* good for one trip, no transfers); a one-day ticket costs 7.20 zł (*bilet dobowy,* good until 24:00 on the day purchased); and a three-day ticket is 12 zł *(bilet trzydniowy).* Buy your ticket at a post office or kiosk (with a RUCH sign), and be sure to validate it as you board. You can also buy the basic one-ride tickets from your bus or tram driver for an extra 0.60 zł. Bus #100 runs a handy circular route to virtually all of the sights and neighborhoods of interest to tourists (get map and schedule from TI). Bus #175 goes from the Old Town down the Royal Way to the train station and the airport.

By Taxi: As in most big Eastern European cities, it's wise to use only cabs that are clearly marked with a company logo and telephone number (or call your own: locals like MPT Taxi, tel. 022/919). All official taxis have similar rates: a drop fee of 6 zł, then a rate of 2 zł per km (more after 22:00 or in the suburbs).

SIGHTS

Warsaw's Old Town (Stare Miasto)

In 1945, not a building remained standing in Warsaw's "Old" Town. Everything you see is rebuilt, mostly finished by 1956. This is the city's only must-see sight. Some find it artificial and phony in a Disney World kind of way. For others, the painstaking postwar reconstruction just feels right, with charming-enough Old World squares and lanes to give Kraków a run for its money. Before 1989, stifled by communist repression and choking on smog, the Old Town felt like an empty husk of its historic self. But now the market stalls have returned and the locals are out strolling.

These sights are listed in order from south to north, beginning at Castle Square and ending at the entrance to the New Town. For an interesting route from the train station to the Old Town, see "Royal Way Stroll," page 177.

▲**Castle Square (Plac Zamkowy)**—This lively square is dominated by the big, pink Royal Castle, the historic heart of Warsaw's political power. After the second great Polish dynasty, the Jagiellonians, came to

THE WARSAW UPRISING

By the summer of 1944, it was becoming clear that the Nazis' days in Warsaw were numbered. The Red Army drew near, and by late July, Soviet tanks were beginning to gather just across the Vistula River from downtown Warsaw.

The Varsovians could have simply waited for the Soviets to cross the river and force the Nazis out. But they knew that Soviet "liberation" would also mean an end to Polish independence. The Polish Home Army (which numbered 50,000 and was the biggest underground army in military history) decided to take matters into their own hands. On August 1, thousands of Polish resistance fighters launched a surprise attack on their Nazi oppressors. They poured out of the sewers and caught the Nazis off-guard, initially having great success.

But the Nazis regrouped quickly, and within a few days, they had retaken several areas of the city—murdering tens of thousands of innocent civilians as they went. By September 2, the Home Army was surrounded, and 2,000 soldiers fled through the sewers. Most drowned or were killed by Nazi bullets and bombs.

Just two months after it had started, the Warsaw Uprising ended with the surrender of the Home Army. Twenty thousand Polish soldiers were killed, along with a staggering 225,000 innocent civilians. An infuriated Hitler ordered that the city be destroyed—which it was, systematically, block-by-block, until virtually nothing remained.

Through all of this, the Soviets sat across the river, watched, and waited. When the smoke cleared and the Nazis left, the Red Army marched in and claimed the pile of rubble that was once called Warsaw. After the war, General Dwight D. Eisenhower said that the scale of destruction here was the worst he'd ever seen.

Depending on whom you talk to, the desperate uprising of Warsaw was incredibly brave, stupid, or both. As for the Poles, they remain fiercely proud of their struggle for freedom.

an end in 1572, the Republic of Nobles (about 10 percent of the population) elected various foreign kings to their throne. The guy on the 72-foot-tall **pillar** is Sigismund III, the first Polish king from the Swedish Waza family. In 1596, he moved the capital from Kraków to Warsaw. This made sense because Warsaw was closer to the center of

16th-century Poland (which had expanded to the east) and because the city had been gaining political importance as the meeting point of the *Sejm*, or parliament of nobles, over the past 30 years. Along the right side of the castle, notice the two previous versions of this pillar lying on a lawn. The first one, from 1644, was falling apart and was replaced in 1887 by a new one made of granite. In 1944, a Nazi tank broke this second pillar—a symbolic piece of Poland's heritage—into the four

pieces that you see here today. As Poland rebuilt, it put Sigismund III back on his pillar.

Across the square from the castle, you'll see the partially rebuilt defensive wall. This rampart once enclosed the entire Old Town. Situated at the crossroads of Central Europe, Warsaw—like all of Poland—has seen invasion from all sides.

Explore the café-lined lanes that branch downhill off of the Castle Square. Street signs (from the early '50s) indicate the year that each street was originally built.

The first street leading off the square is **ulica Piwna** (literally "Beer Street"), where you'll find **St. Martin's Church** (Kościół Św. Martina, on the left). Run by Franciscan nuns, this church has a simple, modern interior (free entry). Notice the partly destroyed crucifix—all that survived World War II. Farther down ulica Piwna (on right at #6), admire the carefully carved doorway of Restauracja Pod Gołębiami ("Under Doves")—dedicated to the memory of an old woman who fed birds amid the ruins after the Old Town was destroyed in World War II.

Back on Castle Square, find the white **plaque** with the red stripes in the middle of the second block (by plac Zamkowy 15/19). It explains that 50 Poles were executed by Nazis on this spot on September 2, 1944. You'll see plaques like this all over the Old Town, each one commemorating victims or opponents of the Nazis. Notice the brick planter under the plaque; it's often filled with fresh flowers to remember the victims.

▲**Royal Castle (Zamek Królewski)**—After Warsaw became the capital in 1596, this massive building was used both as the king's residence and as the meeting place of the parliament *(Sejm)*. There has been a castle here since the Mazovian dukes (this region is called Mazovia) built a wooden version in the 14th century. It has shifted shape with the tenor of the times, being rebuilt and remodeled by many different kings. Destroyed in World War II, it was rebuilt in the 1950s and not completed until the 1970s.

This is the most interesting to tour of Warsaw's many palaces—which isn't saying much. While the exterior is entirely reconstructed, many of the furnishings are original, having been hidden away before the city was destroyed. Each room is well-described in English.

Wander through the throne room. Note the crowned eagle, the symbol of Poland, decorating the banner behind the throne. The Soviets didn't allow anything royal or aristocratic, so postwar restorations came with crown-less eagles. Only after 1989 were the crowns replaced (in the case of this banner, sewn on).

Canvases of late 18th-century Warsaw painted in exquisite detail by Bernardo Canaletto fill a nearby room. These paintings actually came in handy when the city needed to be rebuilt. (This Canaletto, also known for his panoramas of Dresden, was the nephew of the artist with the same nickname who was famous for painting Venice's canals.)

The grand senators' chamber with the king's throne is surrounded by coats of arms of the diverse kingdom's regions that existed back when Poland stretched from the Baltic to the Black Sea. In this room, the constitution of 1791 was adopted. It was the first in Europe (just after America's and just months before France's). And, like the United States', it was very progressive, based on the ideals of the Enlightenment. But the partitions followed in 1793 and 1795, Poland was divided between neighboring powers and disappeared from the map until 1918, and the constitution was never really put into action. The next room features paintings by Jan Matejko that capture the excitement surrounding the adoption of this ill-fated constitution.

The castle makes a great Polish history textbook. In fact, you'll likely see grade school classes sitting cross-legged on the floors. Watching the teachers drilling eager young history buffs, you can only imagine what it's like to be a young Pole with such a tumultuous recent history. It puts America's Great Depression and our 9/11 tragedy in a different perspective.

The castle admission comes with two self-guided options: Route Two (15 zł, 39 rooms) is open all year; Route One (10 zł, 22 rooms) is off-season only (private guide-70 zł, otherwise no good English info except free floor plan, mid-April–Sept Tue–Sat 10:00–18:00, Sun 11:00–18:00, Oct–mid-April until 16:00 and closed Mon, last entry 1 hr before closing, plac Zamkowy 4, tel. 022/657-2170, www.zamek -krolewski.art.pl). A public WC is on the courtyard just around the corner of the castle.

When you're ready to continue exploring the Old Town, turn left at the end of the square onto **Świętojańska** (St. John's Street). On the plaque under the street name sign, you can guess what the dates mean even if you don't speak Polish: This building was constructed 1433–1478, destroyed in 1944, and rebuilt 1950–1953. Partway down the street on the right, you'll come to the big brick...

Cathedral of St. John the Baptist (Katedra Św. Jana Chrzciciela)— This cathedral-basilica is the oldest (1339) and most important church in Warsaw. Poland's constitution was consecrated here on May 3, 1791. This church became the final battleground of the 1944 Warsaw Uprising—when a Nazi tank literally drove into the church to massacre the rebels. Despite its importance, the interior is pretty dull (closed 13:00–15:00). If you visit, look for the crucifix ornamented with real human hair (chapel left of high altar). The high altar holds a copy of the Black Madonna—proclaimed "everlasting queen of Poland" after a victory over the Swedes in 17th century. The original Black Madonna is in Częstochowa (125 miles south of Warsaw), which is nearly a mecca to Slavic Catholics who visit in droves in hopes of a miracle.

Continue up the street and enter Warsaw's grand...

▲▲Old Town Market Square (Rynek Starego Miasta)—Seventy years ago, this was one of the most happening spots in Central Europe. Sixty years ago, it was rubble. And today, like a phoenix from the ashes, it reminds locals and tourists alike of the prewar glory of the Polish capital. Enjoy the colorful architecture.

Go to the **mermaid fountain** in the middle of the square. The mermaid is an important symbol in Warsaw—you'll see her everywhere. Legend has it that a mermaid lived in the Vistula River and protected the townspeople. While this siren supposedly serenaded the town, Varsovians like her more for her strength (notice she's brandishing a sword). Each of the square's four sides is named for an important 18th-century Varsovian: Kołłątaj, Dekert, Barss, and Zakrzewski. These men served as "Presidents" of Warsaw (more or less the mayor), and Kołłątaj was also a framer of Poland's 1791 constitution. Take some time to explore the square. Find the jovial chap hanging out above a doorway (hint: using an imaginary clock as a directional compass, he's at the mermaid's 4-o'clock and changes his clothes with the seasons). Notice that many of the buildings intentionally lean out into the square—to simulate the old-age wear-and-tear of the original buildings.

On the west side of the Old Town Market Square, the pricey **Gessler** restaurant runs a tasty, inexpensive bakery (Cukiernia Gessler at #21, see "Eating," below, for this and even better values nearby).

On the Dekert (north) side of the square is the...

▲Historical Museum of Warsaw (Muzeum Historyczne Warszawy)— The labyrinthine museum rambles through several buildings. With limited descriptions in English (and only a paltry 2-zł or slightly-less-paltry 5-zł English brochure available), the museum is difficult to appreciate. The exhibits near the end—photos of the Old Town before and immediately after its WWII destruction—are most interesting. The museum shows an excellent 15-minute film in English about wartime Warsaw that's worth the price of admission alone; unfortunately, it runs only Tuesday through Saturday at 12:00. The movie finishes: "They say that there are no miracles. Then what is this city on the Vistula?" Emotionally drained, you can only respond, "Amen." (5 zł, mid-March–mid-Sept Tue and Thu 12:00–19:00, Wed and Fri–Sun 11:00–16:30, closed Mon; off-season Tue and Thu 11:00–18:00, Wed and Fri–Sun 10:00–15:30, closed Mon; Rynek Starego Miasta 28/42, tel. 022/635-1625.)

Leave the square on Nowomiejska (at the mermaid's 2-o'clock, by the second-story niche sculpture of St. Anne). After a block, you'll reach the defensive gate of the **Barbican** (Barbakan). Cross through the gate and enter Warsaw's...

New Town (Nowe Miasto)—This 15th-century neighborhood is "new" in name only: It was the first part of Warsaw to spring up outside of the city walls (and therefore newer than the Old Town). The New Town is only slightly less charming than the Old Town, and full of affordable restaurants (see "Eating," below). Its centerpiece is the **New Town Square** (Rynek Nowego Miasta), watched over by the distinctive green dome of St. Kazimierz Church.

Scientists will want to pay homage at the museum dedicated to Warsaw native **Marie Skłodowska-Curie** (at her birthplace, ulica Freta 16). This Nobel Prize-winner was the world's first radiologist—discovering both radium and polonium (named for her native land) with her husband, Pierre Curie. Since she lived at a time when Warsaw was controlled by oppressive Russia, she conducted her studies in France.

From New Town to Castle Square—You can backtrack the way you came, or, to get a look at Warsaw's back streets, consider this route from the Barbican gate (where the New Town meets the Old): Go back through the Barbican gate and turn right, walking along the inside of the wall. You'll pass a courtyard on the left—a reminder that people actually live here inside the Old Town walls. Just beyond the garden on the right, look for the carpet-beating rack, used to clean area rugs (these are common fixtures in people's backyards). Go left into the square called Szeroki Dunaj ("Wide Danube") and look for another mermaid (hint: it's over the Thai restaurant). Continue through the square and turn right at Wąski Dunaj ("Narrow Danube"). After about 100 yards, you pass the city wall. Just to the right (outside the wall) you'll see the monument to the **Little Upriser** of 1944, an imp wearing a grown-up's helmet and too-big boots, and carrying a machine gun. Children—and especially Scouts *(Harcerze)*—played a key role in the resistance against the Nazis. Their job was mainly carrying messages and propaganda, marking walls with the symbol of the resistance: an anchor made up of a P atop a W (which stands for the Polish phrase for "Poland Fighting").

Old Town and Royal Way Stroll

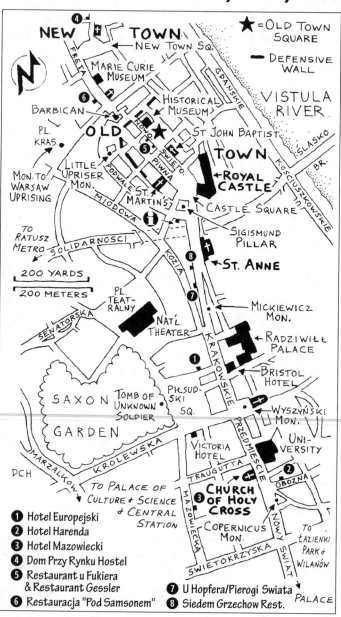

★ = OLD TOWN SQUARE
━ = DEFENSIVE WALL

NEW TOWN

NEW TOWN SQ.

MARIE CURIE MUSEUM

BARBICAN

HISTORICAL MUSEUM

VISTULA RIVER

OLD

PL. KRAS.

St JOHN BAPTIST

LITTLE UPRISER MON.

TOWN

ROYAL CASTLE

MON. TO WARSAW UPRISING

ST. MARTIN'S

CASTLE SQUARE

SIGISMUND PILLAR

TO RATUSZ METRO

MIODOWA

SOLIDARNOSCI

St. ANNE

200 YARDS
200 METERS

PL. TEAT-RALNY

NAT'L. THEATER

KOZLA

MICKIEWICZ MON.

RADZIWIŁŁ PALACE

SENATORSKA

KRAKOWSKIE

BRISTOL HOTEL

SAXON

TOMB OF UNKNOWN SOLDIER

PIŁSUD-SKI SQ.

WYSZYŃSKI MON.

GARDEN

UNI-VERSITY

MARZAŁKOW

KROLEWSKA

VICTORIA HOTEL

PRZEDMIESCIE

TRAUGUTTA

OBOZNA

DCH

TO PALACE OF CULTURE & SCIENCE & CENTRAL STATION

CHURCH OF HOLY CROSS

COPERNICUS MON.

MAZOWIECKA

NOWY SWIAT

TO ŁAZIENKI PARK & WILANÓW

SWIETOKRZYSKA

PALACE

1 Hotel Europejski
2 Hotel Harenda
3 Hotel Mazowiecki
4 Dom Przy Rynku Hostel
5 Restaurant u Fukiera & Restaurant Gessler
6 Restauracja "Pod Samsonem"
7 U Hopfera/Pierogi Swiata
8 Siedem Grzechow Rest.

Warsaw's Royal Way (Szlak Królewski)

The "Royal Way" is the six-mile route that kings of Poland used to take from their main residence (at Castle Square in the Old Town) to their summer residence (Wilanów Palace, south of the center). In the heart of the city, the Royal Way is made up of two busy boulevards: vibrant **Nowy Świat** (south, literally "New World"), which offers a good look of urban Warsaw, and **Krakowskie Przedmieście** (north, ending at the Old Town), which is lined with historic landmarks and better for sightseeing.

Royal Way Stroll

This self-guided walk, rated ▲▲, takes 30 minutes and follows a perfectly straight line (with a small side-trip) down the last stretch of the Royal Way: from the Church of the Holy Cross (where the street becomes Krakowskie Przedmieście) to the Castle Square at the start of the Old Town. If you're walking from the train station to the Old Town, you could easily incorporate this stroll. Bus #175 from the train station to the Old Town also takes this route (get off at the Swietokrzyska stop to start the walk).

The tour begins at the big statue of **Copernicus** in the middle of the street, in front of the Polish Academy of Science. Mikołaj Kopernik was born in Poland and went to college in Kraków. The Nazis stole this statue and took it to Germany (which, like Poland, claims Copernicus as its own). Now it's back where it belongs.

You'll pass many churches along this route, but the **Church of the Holy Cross** is unique (Kościół Św. Krzyża, across from Copernicus). Stepping inside, you feel it's more alive than other churches in Europe. Locals often drop in. Check out the bright gold chapel on the left. It's dedicated to a saint who Polish Catholics believe helps them with "desperate and hopeless cases." People praying here are likely dealing with some tough issues. The beads draped from the altarpieces help power their prayers and the many little brass plaques are messages of thanks for prayers answered. The church's claim to fame? Composer Fryderyk Chopin's heart is in one of the pillars of the main nave. Chopin's final wish was to have his heart brought back to his native Poland.

Just up and across the street from the Church of the Holy Cross are the gates to the main campus of **Warsaw University,** founded in 1816. This area is a lively student district with plenty of bookstores and cafés. (Also across the street, at #20, is a milk bar—a subsidized government cafeteria filled with students and others in need of a bargain. Soup costs less than a złoty at this remnant of communist times.)

The 18th century was a time of great decline for Poland, with a series of incompetent foreign kings mishandling crises and squandering funds. But ironically, it was also Warsaw's biggest boom time. This boulevard is lined with **mansions** built during this period by aristocratic families—destroyed during World War II and rebuilt since, some with curious flourishes. Just past the university on the right, look for the doorway supported by four bearded brutes admiring their overly defined abs. Over time, many of these families donated their mansions to the university.

The yellow church a block up from the university is the Church of the Nuns of the Visitation (Kościół Sióstr Wizytek). The monument in front of the church commemorates **Cardinal Stefan Wyszyński,** who was the Polish primate (not a monkey, but the head of the Polish Catholic Church) from 1948 to 1981. He took this post soon after the arrival of the communists, who opposed the Church, but also realized it would be dangerous to shut down the churches in such an ardently religious country. The Communist Party and the Catholic Church coexisted tensely in Poland, and when Wyszyński protested a Stalinist crackdown in 1953, he was arrested and imprisoned. Three years later, in a major victory for the Church, Wyszyński was released. He went on to become a great hero of the Polish people in their struggle against the regime.

Farther up you'll see elegant **Hotel Bristol,** Warsaw's classiest. Detour here to Piłsudski Square (a block away on the left, up the street opposite Hotel Bristol).

▲**Piłsudski Square (Plac Marszałka Józefa Piłsudskiego)**—The historic square has been important Warsaw real estate for years, constantly changing with the times. An Orthodox cathedral here was torn down in the 1920s, when anti-Russian passions were running high in newly-independent Poland. During the Nazi occupation, it took the name "Adolf-Hitler-Platz." Under the communists, it was Zwycięstwa, meaning "Victory" (of the Soviets over Hitler's fascism). When martial law was imposed in 1981, the people of Warsaw silently protested by filling the square with a giant cross made of flowers.

Find the sewer lid at the very center and stand on it for this quick spin-tour orientation: Ahead is the Tomb of the Unknown Soldier and Saxon Garden, to the right is the old National Theater eclipsed by a beautiful new shopping mall/parking garage, further to the right is a statue of Piłsudski (which you passed to get here—see below), and to the right of that—past the big gray Polish Ministry of Defense building—is the Victoria Hotel (the ultimate plush, top-of-the-top hotel where all communist-era VIPs stayed).

Walk to the fragment of colonnade by the park that marks the **Tomb of the Unknown Soldier** (Grób Nieznanego Żołnierza). The colonnade was once part of a much larger palace built by the Saxon prince electors (Dresden's Augustus the Strong and his son), who became kings of Poland in the 18th century. After the palace was destroyed in World War II, this fragment was kept to memorialize Polish soldiers. The names of important battles are etched into the columns, urns contain dirt from major Polish battlefields, and the two guards are pretty stiff.

Just behind the Tomb is **Saxon Garden** (Ogród Saski), a pleasant park to stroll, also built by the Saxon kings of Poland. Like most foreign kings, Augustus the Strong and his son cared little for their Polish territory, building gardens like these instead of investing in more pressing needs. Poles say that foreign kings like Augustus did nothing but "eat, drink, and loosen their belts" (it rhymes in Polish). According to Poles, these selfish absentee kings are the culprits for Poland's eventual decline.

Walk to the statue (on the side of the square where you first entered). In 1995, the square was again re-named—this time for **Józef Piłsudski**, the guy with the big walrus moustache. Piłsudski forced out the Russian Bolsheviks from Poland in 1920 in the so-called "Miracle on the Vistula." Piłsudski is credited with creating a once-again-independent Poland after over a century of foreign oppression, and he essentially ran Poland after World War I. Of course, under the communists, Piłsudski was swept under the rug, but today he's enjoying a renaissance as Poland's favorite prototype anti-communist hero (his name adorns streets, squares, and bushy-mustachioed monuments all over the country).

Return to Hotel Bristol, turn left, and continue your Royal Way walk. Next door to the hotel, you'll see the huge **Radziwiłł Palace**—the Polish White House, which houses the offices of Poland's president. The Warsaw Pact was signed here in 1955, officially uniting the Soviet satellite states in a military alliance against NATO. The newest flag in the courtyard is Europe's (celebrating the May 1, 2004, entry of Poland into the EU).

Beyond Radziwiłł Palace, you'll reach a statue (on a pillar) of **Adam Mickiewicz**, Poland's national poet. Polish high school students have a big ball (like the prom) 100 days before graduation. After the ball, if students come here and hop around the statue on one leg, it's supposed to bring them good luck on their finals. Mickiewicz, for his part, looks like he's suffering from a heart attack—perhaps in response to the impressively ugly National Theater and Opera a block in front of him.

For a scenic finale to your Royal Way stroll, climb the 150 steps of the view tower by **St. Anne's Church** (daily 10:00–18:00, until 20:00 in summer). You'll be rewarded with a great view of the old town, river, and Warsaw's skyline, complete with Stalin's Penis (see "More Sights in Warsaw," page 184).

From St. Anne's Church, it's just another few blocks—past inviting art galleries and restaurants (see "Eating," page 187)—to the Castle Square, the TI, and the start of the Old Town (to continue your walk all the way to the New Town, see "Warsaw's Old Town," page 170).

The Rest of the Royal Way

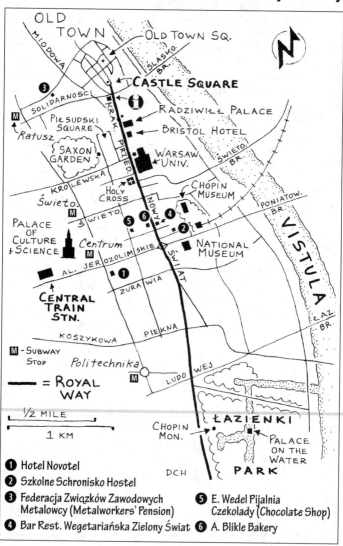

❶ Hotel Novotel
❷ Szkolne Schronisko Hostel
❸ Federacja Związków Zawodowych Metalowcy (Metalworkers' Pension)
❹ Bar Rest. Wegetariańska Zielony Świat
❺ E. Wedel Pijalnia Czekolady (Chocolate Shop)
❻ A. Blikle Bakery

The Rest of the Royal Way

Nowy Świat—This segment of the Royal Way stretches in the opposite direction, running south from the Copernicus monument all the way to Łazienki Park (triple the distance you just walked from the Copernicus monument north to the Old Town).

Nowy Świat, meaning "the new world," is a fine, nearly traffic-free shopping boulevard—nicknamed by locals the "Champs-Élysées of Warsaw." Ulica Chmielna (near the end, on the right) is an appealing pedestrian boutique street that leads to Wedel's chocolate heaven (see below). Bus #503 runs along this route from the Old Town to the Chopin statue at Łazienki Park.

On or near Nowy Świat, you'll find two venerable spots for memorable taste treats (both just a few blocks in front of the train station). Poland's most famous bakery is **A. Blikle**, serving *pączki*—doughnuts filled with a wild-rose jam (2.40 zł per fancy glazed doughnut—to go or at a table, Mon–Fri 9:00–19:00, Sat 9:00–18:00, Sun 10:30–17:00, Nowy Świat 35).

Chocoholics will venture (down ulica Chmielna and then a block to the right) to **E. Wedel Pijalnia Czekolady**. Emil Wedel made Poland's favorite chocolate, and today his former residence houses this chocolate shop (Mon 10:00–17:00, Tue–Fri 9:00–20:00, Sat 9:00–16:00, closed Sun) and café (Mon–Sat 10:00–22:00, Sun 12:00–17:00, tel. 022/827-2916). This is the spot for a *real* hot chocolate (that means a cup of melted chocolate, not just hot chocolate milk) and delicious pastries. Cadbury bought the company when Poland privatized after communism, but they kept the E. Wedel name, which is close to all Poles' hearts...and taste buds (between Palace of Culture and Science and Nowy Świat at ulica Szepitalna 1). *Czekolada do picia* is the basic drink (8 zł). The menu describes it as "chocolate to drink, true Wedel ecstasy for your mouth that will take you to a world of dreams and desires." Or, if you fancy pudding, try *pokusa*. Wedel's was *the* Christmas treat for locals under communism.

▲**Łazienki Park (Park Łazienkowski)**—This huge, idyllic park is where Varsovians go to play. The park is sprinkled with fun neoclassical buildings, peacocks, and young Poles in love. It was built by Poland's very last king (before the final partition), Stanisław August Poniatowski, who wanted it to serve as his summer residence and to provide a place for his citizens to relax.

On the edge of the park (along Belwederska) is a **monument to Fryderyk Chopin**, Poland's greatest composer. The monument, in a beautiful rose garden, is flanked by platforms where free summer piano concerts are given weekly (generally Sun at 12:00 and 16:00). The statue (from 1926) shows Chopin sitting under a wind-blown willow tree. While he spent his last 20 years and wrote most of his greatest music in France, his inspiration came from wind blowing through the willow trees of his native land, Poland. The Nazis melted the statue down for

WARSAW'S JEWS AND THE GHETTO UPRISING

From the Middle Ages until World War II, Poland was a safe haven for Europe's Jews. When other kings were imprisoning and deporting Jews in the 14th century, the progressive king Kazimierz the Great welcomed Jews into Poland, even granting them special privileges (see page 129).

By the 1930s, there were more than 380,000 Jews in Warsaw—nearly a third of the population (and the largest concentration of Jews in the world). The Nazis arrived in 1939. Within a year, they had pushed all of Warsaw's Jews into one neighborhood and surrounded it with a wall, creating a miserably overcrowded ghetto (crammed full of a half-million people, including many from nearby towns). Over the next year, the Nazis brought in more Jews from throughout Poland, and the number had grown by a million.

By the summer of 1942, more than half of the Jews in the ghetto had already died of disease, murder, or suicide. The Nazis started moving Warsaw's Jews (at the rate of 5,000 a day) into what they claimed were "resettlement camps." Most of these people were actually murdered at Treblinka or Auschwitz. After hundreds of thousands of Jews had been taken to concentration camps, the waning population—now about 60,000—began to get word from

its metal. Today's copy was recast after World War II. Savor this spot; it's great in summer, with roses wildly in bloom, and in autumn, when the trees provide a golden backdrop for the black, romantic statue.

Venture to the center of the park, where (after a 10-min hike) you'll find King Poniatowski's striking **Palace on the Water** (Pałac na Wodzie)—literally built in the middle of a river. Nearby you'll spot a clever amphitheater with seating on the riverbank and the stage on an island. Poniatowski was a real man of the Enlightenment, hosting weekly dinners here for artists and intellectuals (free entry to park, just south of the city center on the Royal Way, take buses #100, #116, #119, #180, #195, #318, #503, or #513 south from the center and get off at stop Bagatela by Belweder Palace). Maps at park entrances locate the Chopin monument, Palace on the Water, and other park attractions.

concentration camp escapees escapees about what was actually going on there. Spurred by this knowledge, Warsaw's surviving Jews staged a dramatic uprising.

On April 19, 1943, the Jews attacked Nazi strongholds and had some initial success—but within a month, the Nazis crushed the Ghetto Uprising. The ghetto's residents and structures were "liquidated." About 300 of Warsaw's Jews survived, thanks in part to a sort of "underground railroad" of courageous Varsovians.

The sights of Warsaw's Jewry are moving, but even more so if you know some of their stories. Many Americans have heard of **Władysław Szpilman,** a Jewish concert pianist who survived the war with the help of Jews, Poles, and even a Nazi officer. Szpilman's life story was turned into the highly-acclaimed, Oscar-winning 2002 film *The Pianist,* which powerfully depicts events in Warsaw during World War II.

Less familiar to Americans—but equally affecting—is the story of Henryk Goldszmit, better known by his pen name, **Janusz Korczak.** Korczak wrote imaginative children's books that are still enormously popular among Poles. He also worked at an orphanage in the Warsaw ghetto. When his orphans were sent off to concentration camps, the Nazis offered the famous author a chance at freedom. Korczak turned them down and chose to die at Treblinka with his children.

Jewish Sights

After centuries of living peacefully in Poland, Warsaw's Jews suffered terribly at the hands of the Nazis (see "Warsaw's Jews and the Ghetto Uprising" sidebar). You can visit several sights in Warsaw that commemorate those who were murdered—and those who fought back. Because of the ferocity of Nazi hatred, there is literally nothing left of the ghetto except the street plan and the heroic spirit of its former residents.

▲**Ghetto Walking Tour**—For a quick walking tour of the former ghetto site, begin at **Ghetto Heroes Square** (plac Bohaterow Getta). To get here from the Old Town, either hop a taxi (10 zł) or walk (go through Barbican gate 2 blocks into New Town, turn left on Świętojerska, and walk straight 10 min—passing new green-glass Supreme Court building—until you reach grassy park on Zamenhofa Street). The square is in the heart of what was the Jewish ghetto—now surrounded by bland Soviet-style apartment blocks. After the Uprising, the entire ghetto was reduced to dust by the Nazis—leaving the communists to rebuild to their own specifications. The district is called Muranów (literally "Rebuilt") today.

The **monument** in the middle of the square commemorates those who fought and died "for the dignity and freedom of the Jewish Nation, for a free Poland, and for the liberation of humankind." The big park across the street is the future site of the Museum for the History of Polish Jews. It's been in the works for years, with its progress slowed by controversy over exactly what form the museum will take (for the latest, see www.jewishmuseum.org.pl).

Facing the monument, head left (with the park on your left) up Zamenhofa—which, like many streets in this neighborhood, is named for a hero of the Ghetto Uprising. From the monument, you'll follow a series of three-foot-tall black stone monuments to Uprising heroes—the **Path of Remembrance.** Like Stations of the Cross, each recounts an event of the uprising. On April 19th (the day the Uprising began), huge crowds follow this path. In a block, at the corner of Miła, you'll find a **bunker** where organizers of the Uprising hid out (and where they committed suicide when the Nazis discovered them on May 8, 1943).

Continue following the black stone monuments up Zamenhofa, then turn left around the corner and cross the busy Stawki. A long block up Stawki and on the right, you'll see the **Umschlagplatz** monument—shaped like a cattle car. That's German for "transfer spot," and it marks the spot where the Nazis brought Jewish families to prepare them to be loaded onto trains bound for Treblinka or Auschwitz (a harrowing scene vividly depicted in *The Pianist*). In the walls of the monument are inscribed the first names of some of the victims.

Jewish Historical Institute of Poland—For more in-depth information about Warsaw's Jewish community, including the Ghetto Uprising, visit this museum housed in the former Jewish Library building. The main floor displays well-described old photos. The 37-minute movie about life and death in the ghetto—played in English upon request—is graphic and powerful. Upstairs you'll find more on Jewish art, culture, and temporary exhibits (10 zł, Mon–Wed and Fri 9:00–16:00, Thu 11:00–18:00, closed Sat–Sun, ulica Tłomackie 3/5, 022/827-9221).

The Peugeot building next door—appropriately dubbed by locals simply "the blue skyscraper"—is on the former site of Warsaw's biggest synagogue, destroyed by the Nazis as a victorious final kick.

More Sights in Warsaw

▲▲**Palace of Culture and Science (Pałac Kultury i Nauki, or PKiN)**—This massive Art Deco skyscraper, dating from the early 1950s, is Poland's tallest building (760 feet). It was a "gift" from Stalin that the people of Warsaw couldn't refuse. Varsovians call it "Stalin's Penis," using cruder terminology than that. There were five such "Stalin Gothic" erections in Moscow. Because it was to be "Soviet in substance, Polish in style," Soviet architects toured Poland to absorb the local culture before starting the project. Since the end of communism, the

younger generation doesn't mind the structure so much—and some even admit to liking it. The clock was added in 1999 as part of the millennium celebrations.

Everything about the *Pałac* is big. It's designed to impress, to show off the strong, grand-scale Soviet aesthetic and architectural skill. The *Pałac* contains various theaters (the culture), a museum of evolution (the science), a congress hall, a multiplex (showing current movies), an observation deck (see below), and lots of office space (including UNICEF's Polish headquarters). With all of this culture and science under one roof, it's a shame that none of it makes for worthwhile sightseeing—viewing the building from the outside is a quintessential Warsaw experience, but the interior is eminently skippable.

If you're killing time between trains, you could zip up to the observation deck (15 zł, daily 9:00–20:00, enter through main door on side of *Pałac* opposite from train station, tel. 022/656-6000, www.pkin.pl). Better yet, snap a photo from down below and save your money—the view's a letdown. You can hardly see the Old Town, and Warsaw's most prominent big building—the *Pałac* itself—is missing.

Warsaw Uprising Monument—The most important sight relating to the 1944 Warsaw Uprising is the monument at plac Krasińskich (intersection of ulica Długa and Miodowa, a few blocks northwest of the New Town). Larger-than-life soldiers and civilians race for the sewers in a desperate attempt to flee the Nazis. Just behind the monument is the brand new rusting-copper facade of Poland's Supreme Court.

Chopin Museum (Muzeum Fryderyka Chopina)—Composer Fryderyk Chopin's surname (and father) was French and he lived most of his adult life in exile in France. But the composer was born in Poland, to a Polish mother, and his music was decidedly influenced by Polish culture. This modest museum to Poland's most famous musician features artifacts from Chopin's life, including his last piano (5 zł, Wed–Mon 10:00–14:00, closed Tue, 3 blocks east of Nowy Świat on ulica Ordynacka).

National Museum (Muzeum Narodowe)—This museum, while short on big-name pieces, will interest art-lovers. You'll see examples of ancient art (from Egyptian and Greek to works by early Polish tribes), along with lots of Polish artists—including Romantic painter Jan Matejko (most notably, his huge *Battle of Grünwald*) and Art Nouveau headliner Stanisław Wyspiański (11 zł, more for temporary exhibits, free on Sat, Tue–Wed and Fri 10:00–16:00, Thu 12:00–17:00, Sat–Sun 10:00–16:00, closed Mon, 1 block east of Nowy Świat at aleja Jerozolimskie 3, tel. 022/621-1031, www.mnw.art.pl). For more on Polish artists, see page 139.

SLEEP CODE

(4 zł = about $1, €1 = about $1.10, country code: 48, area code: 022)

Sleep Code: **S** = Single, **D** = Double/Twin, **T** = Triple, **Q** = Quad, **b** = bathroom, **s** = shower only, **no CC** = Credit Cards not accepted. Unless otherwise noted, English is spoken, breakfast is included, and credit cards are accepted.

To help you easily sort through these listings, I've divided the rooms into three categories, based on the price for a standard double room with bath:

$$$ **Higher Priced**—Most rooms €85 (400 zł) or more.
  $$ **Moderately Priced**—Most rooms between €65–85 (300–400 zł).
    $ **Lower Priced**—Most rooms €65 (300 zł) or less.

The hotel scene in central Warsaw is pretty grim. Most hotels are poorly located and overpriced, with well-worn rooms. Only Hotel Harenda and Hotel Mazowiecki are actually desirable and good values. Since this is a convention town, prices can go up during convention times and way down on weekends. Some hotels quote prices in euros.

SLEEPING

$$$ **Novotel,** with 740 rooms, is at Poland's busiest intersection, across the street from the Palace of Culture and Science. It's worth considering, especially on weekends, when prices plummet. Its newly renovated rooms are the freshest in Warsaw; the non-renovated rooms, though dated, aren't bad (Mon–Fri: Sb-€142, Db-€160; Sat–Sun: Sb/Db-both €78; try asking for discount on non-renovated rooms when paying weekday prices; elevator, ulica Nowogrodzka 24/26, tel. 022/621-0271, fax 022/625-0476, www.orbis.pl, nov.warszawa@orbis.pl).

$$$ **Hotel Europejski** is a last resort—with overpriced, outdated rooms—acceptable only because of its excellent location, on the Royal Way at Piłsudski Square (standard Sb-€120–130, Db-€140, "superior" rooms €20 more, non-smoking rooms, elevator, Krakowskie Przedmieście 13, tel. 022/826-3104, fax 022/826-3247, europejski@orbis.pl).

$$ **Hotel Harenda,** which is well-located, well-maintained, and the best value in town, rents out 43 rooms on the third floor of an office building in the charming neighborhood where Nowy Świat becomes

Krakowskie Przedmieście and the Royal Way really gets interesting (March–mid-June and Sept–Oct: Sb-320 zł, Db-360 zł, price drops if you stay more than one night to 250 zł; rest of year: Sb-290 zł, Db-320 zł; on Fri–Sun second night is free; some street noise so request quiet room, Krakowskie Przedmieście 4/6, tel. 022/826-0071 fax 022/826-2625, www.hotelharenda.com.pl, hh@hotelharenda.com.pl).

$ **Hotel Mazowiecki** is a family-run jewel on a drab urban street between the Palace of Culture and Science and Nowy Świat. Its 53 fresh rooms boast new furnishings and TLC (S-150 zł, Sb-210 zł, D-200 zł, Db-270 zł, prices include tax, non-smoking rooms, elevator, ulica Mazowiecka 10, tel. 022/827-2365 or 022/687-9117, fax 022/827-2365, www.mazowiecki.com.pl, rezerwacja@mazowiecki.com.pl).

$ The IYHF **Szkolne Schronisko** hostel is well-run, bright, and very clean. If you reserve ahead, this is the best deal on single and twin rooms in Warsaw. The downside: It's on the fifth floor, with no elevator (non-members welcome, all prices per person: dorm beds-33 zł, 30 zł with hostel membership, S-60 zł, twin D-55 zł, T-50 zł, Q-40 zł, plus 5 zł per person for sheets and 2 zł for towels, no CC, no breakfast but members' kitchen, closed 10:00–16:00, curfew at 23:00, e-mail or fax ahead to reserve S, D, and T rooms—there are only two of each, good location across street from National Museum at ulica Smolna 30, tel. & fax 022/827-8952, ssmsmolna@poczta.onet.pl).

$ **Dom Przy Rynku Hostel** is a small, friendly, charming 40-bed place with two goals: housing kids from dysfunctional families and raising money for its work by renting out beds to tourists (when it's not housing children). Located in the peaceful New Town, the cozy rooms are decorated for grade-schoolers. Beds are rented in July and August and on Friday and Saturday nights all year (35 zł per bed in 3- to 5-bed rooms, rooms segregated for boys and girls, bus #175 from station or airport to Franciszkańska stop, corner of Kościelna and Przyrynek streets at Rynek Nowego Miasta 4, tel. & fax 022/831-5033, www.cityhostel .net, info@cityhostel.net).

$ **Federacja Związków Zawodowych Metalowcy,** meaning "Federation of Trade Union Metalworkers," is a cheap, old, but reasonably well-maintained trade-union subsidized place with piles of stairs in a neighborhood packed with communist apartment blocks a 10-minute walk from the Old Town (S-75 zł, D-114 zł, Db-161 zł, all doubles are twins, some with beds in different rooms, no CC, no breakfast, ulica Długa 29, tel. 022/831-4021, fax 022/635-3138, NSE).

EATING

In or near Warsaw's Old Town

The most atmospheric—and most expensive—eating in Warsaw is on the Old Town Market Square. Locals agree that the best are **U Fukiera** (daily from 12:00, #27, tel. 022/831-1013) and **Gessler** (#21, tel. 022/831-4427). In Gessler's lobby hang photos of famous patrons. It's the only place you'll see Hillary Rodham Clinton, George H. W. Bush, and Henry Kissinger side-by-side—and smiling.

If you want good food nearby without dropping a bundle, head into the New Town, where you'll find several fine places with much lower prices. Dine on affordable Polish-Jewish fare with well-dressed locals at **Restauracja "Pod Samsonem"** ("Under Samson," daily 10:00–23:00, ulica Freta 3/5, tel. 022/831-1788). You'll get a fun menu, surly service, and great prices. *Bigos*, the traditional sauerkraut stew, is a good choice here.

Warsaw's Royal Way

U Hopfera/Pierogi Świata ("Pierogi of the World") offers reasonably-priced *pierogi*—Polish ravioli—in a local-feeling restaurant on the Royal Way (a few blocks before castle at Krakowskie Przedmieście 53, tel. 022/828-7352). This is the Heinz of *pierogi*, with 36 varieties.

Siedem Grzechow ("Seven Sins") is an old-style Warsaw restaurant serving top-notch Polish and international cuisine in a 1930s lace, velvet, and burgundy ambience. The place fills a dressy cellar with locals and jazz (main courses 30–60 zł, daily 11:00–23:00, Krakowskie Przedmieście 45, tel. 022/826-4770).

For a quick, tasty, inexpensive Asian-style vegetarian meal just off Nowy Świat, try **Bar Restauracja Wegetariańska Zielony Świat** (daily 10:30–21:30, enter through passageway at Nowy Świat 42 to reach ulica Gałczyńskiego 5/9, tel. 022/826-4677).

TRANSPORTATION CONNECTIONS

Virtually all trains into and out of Warsaw go through the hideous, hulking Warszawa Centralna station (see "Arrival in Warsaw: By Train," page 167.)

By train to: Kraków (hrly, 2.5 hrs), **Gdańsk** (hrly, 3.75 hrs), **Prague** (2/day direct, including 1 night train, 9–10 hrs; or 2/day, 9 hrs, with transfer in Ostrava–Svinov), **Berlin** (3/day direct, 5.75 hrs; plus 1 direct night train, 7.75 hrs), **Budapest** (2/day direct, including 1 night train, 10.5–11.5 hrs; or 1 each per day with transfer in Győr, Hungary, or Břeclav, Czech Republic, both 10 hrs), and **Vienna** (2/day direct, including 1 night train, 7.75 or 9.5 hrs; or 1/day with transfer in Břeclav, Czech Republic, 7.75 hrs).

HUNGARY

(Magyarország)

- Hungary is 35,653 square miles (the size of Indiana).
- Population is 10 million (about 280 people per square mile, 90 percent Hungarian).
- 230 forints (Ft, or HUF) = about $1.
- Country code: 36.

Hungary is an island of Asian-descended Magyars in a sea of Slavs. It's noticeably different from the rest of Eastern Europe in terms of history, language, culture, and food. Even though the Hungarians have integrated with their Slavic and German neighbors, there's still something about the place that's distinctly Magyar (MUD-jar).

Hungarians are formal and old-fashioned, clinging to former greatness as a multinational capital. When a waiter comes to your table in a restaurant, he'll say, *"Tessék parancsolni"*—literally "Please command, sir."

As evidenced by the many grandiose structures built in Budapest in the late 1800s, Hungarians are also romantic and prone to exaggeration. There's a glimmer of the marauding Magyar in every Hungarian's eye, as the Hapsburgs and the communists can attest—both empires had to put down major uprisings here.

Hungarians, like their Austrian neighbors, enjoy the good life. Favorite activities include splashing and soaking in their many thermal baths. Hungarians are also reviving an elegant Vienna-style café culture that was dismantled by the communists.

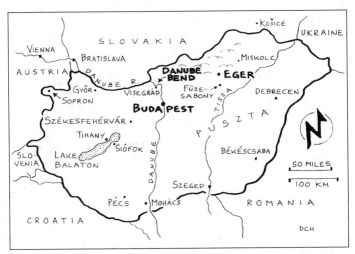

In Hungary, a person's family name is listed first, and their given name is last—just as in many other Eastern cultures (think of Kim Jong Il). The composer known as Franz Liszt in German is Liszt Ferenc in his native land. To help reduce confusion, many Hungarian business cards list the last name first, in capital letters.

Hungarians have an endearing habit of using the English word "Hello" like the Italian *ciao* for both "hi" and "bye." You'll often overhear a Hungarian end a telephone conversation with a cheery "Hello!" While the language is overwhelming for tourists, one easy word is "Szia" (SEE-yah), which actually does mean hello or goodbye.

Somehow, Hungary (particularly Budapest) has managed to become cosmopolitan while remaining perfectly Hungarian. In the

countryside, where less mixing has occurred, Magyar culture and Asian facial features are more evident. But in the cities, the "Hungarians"—like Hungary itself—are a cross-section of Central European cultures: Magyars, Germans, Czechs, Poles, Serbs, Jews, Turks, Romanians, Gypsies, and many others.

Practicalities

Telephones: Hungary has different codes to dial whether you're calling locally or long distance within the country. To dial a number in the same city, simply dial direct, with no area code. To dial long-distance within Hungary, you have to add the prefix 06 followed by the area code (e.g., Budapest is 1).

To dial internationally to Hungary, start with the international access code (00 if calling from Europe, 011 from the United States or Canada), then Hungary's country code (36), then the area code (but not the 06) and number. To make international calls from Hungary, dial 00, the country code of the country you're calling (see chart in appendix), the area code if applicable (may need to drop initial zero), and the local number.

Hungarian phone numbers beginning with 0680 are toll-free; those beginning with 0620, 0630, or 0670 are mobile phones; and 0681 or 0690 are expensive toll lines.

Phone cards, sold locally at tobacco and newsstands, make it easy to call from phone booths. If you want the option of dialing the United States from your hotel room and the savings of cheaper-per-minute calls, buy an international calling card that has a scratch-off PIN code (see page 27 for details).

Hungarian History

Hungary has a colorful and illustrious history. In terms of political influence in Eastern Europe's past, the Hungarians rank with the Germans and the Russians. So, in a way, Hungarian history is Czech, Polish, Croatian, and Slovenian history, too.

Welcome to Europe

The Magyars, led by the mighty Árpád, thundered into the Carpathian Basin from the steppes of Russia in A.D. 896. They were a rough-and-tumble nomadic people from Central Asia who didn't like to settle down in one place. They'd camp out in today's Hungary in the winters, and in the summers they'd go on raids throughout Europe—terrorizing the Continent from Constantinople (modern-day Istanbul) to the Spanish Pyrenees. For half a century, they ranked with the Vikings as the most feared people in Europe. But the Hungarians were finally defeated by a German and Czech army at the battle of Augsburg in 955. If they were to survive, the nomadic Magyars had to settle down. King Géza baptized his son, István (who was Árpád's great-great-grandson), and married him to a Bavarian princess at an early age.

Magyars Tamed

On Christmas Day in the year 1000, King István (Stephen) was crowned by the pope, and Hungary became a legitimate Christian nation. The domestication of the nomadic Magyars was difficult—but Hungary eventually emerged as a major Central European power. The kingdom reached its peak in the late 15th century, when the enlightened King Mátyás Corvinus fostered the arts and sparked a mini-Renaissance.

Turkish Invasion

Soon after the reign of good king Mátyás, the Turks came slicing their way through the Balkan Peninsula towards Central Europe. In 1526, they entered Hungary. By 1541, they took Buda. During the Turkish occupation, the Magyars moved the capital of what little remained of their land—called "rump" Hungary—to Bratislava (which they called Pozsony). During this era, the Ottomans built the many baths that you'll still find throughout Hungary—and spiced up the food with paprika.

Crippled by the Turks and with few other options, Hungary came under control of the Austrian Hapsburg Empire, which finally wrested Buda from the Turks in 1686. The Hapsburgs repopulated Buda and Pest with Germans, while Magyars reclaimed the countryside.

The Hapsburgs

The Hungarians resisted Hapsburg rule, and three Magyars in particular are still noted for their rebellion against Vienna: Ferenc Rákóczi, who led Hungarians in the War of Independence (1703–1711); Lajos Kossuth, who was at the forefront of the 1848 Revolution; and Kossuth's contemporary, Count István Széchenyi, who fought the Hapsburgs with money—building structures like the iconic Chain Bridge (the first permanent link between Buda and Pest). Countless streets, squares, and buildings throughout the country are named for these three Hungarian patriots.

But centuries of alliance with the Hapsburgs eventually paid off. After the 1848 Revolution in Hungary and an important military loss to the Prussians, Austria realized that it couldn't control its rebellious Slavic holdings all by itself. With the Compromise of 1867, Austria granted Budapest the authority over the eastern half of their lands, creating the so-called "Dual Monarchy" of the Austro-Hungarian Empire (at the expense of the Slavs).

Hungary enjoyed a golden age and Budapest boomed, governing large parts of today's Slovakia, Croatia, and Transylvania (northwest Romania). Composers Franz Liszt (more German than Magyar) and Béla Bartók incorporated the folk and Gypsy songs of the Hungarian and Transylvanian countryside into their music.

The Crisis of Trianon

After Hungary came up on the losing end of World War I, the Treaty of Trianon reassigned two-thirds of its former territory and half of its population to Romania, Czechoslovakia, Slovenia, Croatia, and Serbia. Even today, this is regarded as one of the greatest tragedies of Hungarian history. Many Hungarians claim that these lands still belong to the Magyars, and more than two million ethnic Hungarians live outside Hungary (mostly in Romania). The sizeable Magyar minorities in these countries have often been mistreated—particularly since World War II in Romania (under Ceauçescu), Yugoslavia (under Milošević), and Slovakia (under Mečiar).

Communism...with a Pinch of Paprika

After World War II, the Soviets moved into Hungary, installing Mátyás Rákosi as head of state. In 1956, Hungary staged an uprising, led by Communist Party reformer Imre Nagy. Moscow sent in troops, 25,000 Hungarians were killed, and 250,000 fled to Austria. János Kádár was installed, and though he cooperated with Moscow, he eventually allowed the Hungarians more freedom than citizens of neighboring countries had.

Life here was better and more colorful than elsewhere in the Soviet bloc—a system dubbed "goulash communism." With little fanfare, the Hungarian parliament—always skeptical of the Soviets—peacefully voted to end the communist regime in February of 1989. Later that year, Hungary was the first Eastern Bloc nation to open its borders to the West, a major advance in the fall of communist regimes across Eastern Europe.

Hungarian Food

You'll notice a big change in the cuisine, here in the land of the Magyars. Hungarian food is known in Central Europe for its spiciness—one of the many elements introduced by the Ottoman invaders.

Hungarians dine at a *vendéglő* (restaurant), *kávéház* (café, literally coffee house), or *cukrászda* (pastry shop—*cukr* means "sugar").

Hungary is known for its delicious soups *(levesek)*. Try *bableves* (bean soup), *zöldségleves* (vegetable soup—*zöldség,* literally "greenery," means vegetables), *gombaleves* (mushroom soup—*gomba* means "mushroom"), *halászlé* (fish broth with paprika), or *gulyás leves* (shepherd's soup—clear spicy broth with meat and potatoes). *Gulyás leves* is the origin of the German term "Gulasch," from which English gets the word "goulash." (To Americans, "goulash" means a thick stew—but here in Hungary, it'll get you a thin broth with chunks of meat and vegetables.) An unusual Hungarian soup, almost like a dessert, is *hideg gyümölcs leves* (cold fruit soup), made with *meggy* (sour cherries), *alma* (apples), or *körte* (pears) in a cream base.

Hungarians love meat *(hús)* of all kinds. *Csirke* is chicken, *borjú* is veal, *kacsa* is duck, *liba* is goose, *libamáj* is goose liver, *sertés* is pork, *sonka* is ham, *kolbász* is sausage, *szelet* is schnitzel *(Bécsi szelet* means Wiener schnitzel)—and the list goes on. Meat goes well with *káposzta* (cabbage), which may be *töltött* (stuffed) with the meat. Anything cooked *paprikás* (with paprika) will be a little spicy. Vegetarians have a tricky time here, with many restaurants able to offer only a plate of deep-fried vegetables.

In Hungary, you sometimes pay for *köretek* (starches) separately from the meat course, which can be confusing for foreigners. You'll be asked to choose between *galuska* (noodles, traditional and recommended), *burgonya* (potatoes), *krumpli* (French fries), *krokett* (like Tater Tots), or *rizs* (rice). *Kenyér* (bread) often comes with the meal.

For dessert, look for *palacsinta* (pancakes), usually served *diós* (with walnut), *mákos* (with poppy seeds), or *gündel* (with nuts, chocolate, cream, and raisins). Hungary has a great pastry-making tradition. Try the *Dobos torta* (a layered chocolate and caramel cream cake), *somlói galuska* (a dumpling with vanilla, nuts, and chocolate), anything with *gesztenye* (chestnuts), and *rétes* (strudel, with various fillings, including *túrós,* curds). There's always *fagylalt* (ice cream, *fagyi* for short), sold by the *gomboc* (ball).

To drink: *Sör* means beer, and *bor* means wine (*vörös* is red and *fehér* is white). *Kávé* and *tea* (pronounced TEY-ah) are coffee and tea, and *víz* (water) comes as *szódavíz* (soda water, sometimes just carbonated tap water) or *ásványvíz* (spring water, more expensive, which you can order by name). If you're drinking with some new Magyar friends, impress them with the standard toast: *Egészségedre* (literally "to your health"). Be warned: Saying this correctly can take years of practice.

When your waiter brings your food, he'll likely say, *"Jó étvágyat!"* (Bon appétit!). When you're ready for the bill, you can simply say, *"Fizetek"* (I'll pay).

Hungarian Language

Even though Hungary is surrounded by Slavs, Hungarian is not at all related to Slavic languages. In fact, Hungarian isn't related to any European language (except for very distant relatives Finnish and Estonian). It isn't even an Indo-European language—which means that English is more closely related to Hindi, Russian, and French than it is to Hungarian. Not only do Americans struggle with Hungarian—but the Magyars' German- and Slavic-speaking neighbors do, too.

Hungarian is agglutinative, which means that you start with a simple root word and then start tacking on suffixes to create meaning—sometimes resulting in a pileup of extra sounds at the end of a very long word. The emphasis always goes on the first syllable, and the following syllables are droned downhill in a kind of a monotone—giving the language a distinctive sound that Hungary's Slavic neighbors love to tease about.

But to be fair, Hungarian is easier to pronounce than some Slavic tongues. It's pretty straightforward, once you remember a few key rules. The trickiest: *s* alone is pronounced "sh," while *sz* is pronounced simply "s." This explains why you'll hear in-the-know travelers pronouncing Budapest as "BOO-dah-pesht." You might even catch the *busz* up to Castle Hill—pronounced just like we say "bus." And "Franz Liszt" is easier to pronounce than it looks: it sounds just like "list."

The letter *c* and the combination *cz* are both pronounced "ts" (as in "cats"). The combination *zs* is pronounced "zh" (like "measure"). The letters *j* and *ly* are interchangeable, and both are pronounced as "y."

Hungarian has a set of unusual palatal sounds that don't quite have a counterpart in English. To make these sounds, gently press the thick part of your tongue to the roof or your mouth (instead of using the tip of your tongue behind your teeth, as we do in English): *gy* sounds more or less like "dg" in "ledger"; *ny* sounds kind of like the "ny" in "canyon"; and *cs* sounds like "ch."

As for vowels: The letter *a* almost sounds like o ("aw"), but with an accent (á), it brightens up to the more standard "ah." As with Czech, an accent *(á, é, í, ó, ú)* indicates that you linger on that vowel (but not necessarily that you stress that syllable). Like German, Hungarian has umlauts *(ö, ü),* meaning you purse your lips when you say that vowel. A long umlaut *(ő, ű)* is the same sound, but you hold it a little longer.

Okay, maybe it's not *so* simple. But you'll get the hang of it.

As you're tracking down addresses, these definitions will help: *tér* (square), *utca* (road), *út* (boulevard), *fürdő* (bath), and *híd* (bridge). Words ending in *k* are often plural.

KEY HUNGARIAN PHRASES

English	Hungarian	Pronounced
Hello (formal)	Jó napot kívánok	yoh NAH-pot KEE-vah-nohk
Hi / Bye (informal)	Szia	SEE-yah
Do you speak English?	Beszél angolul?	BEH-sehl AHN-goh-lool
Yes / No	Igen / Nem	EE-gehn / nehm
Please	Kérem	KAY-rehm
You're welcome	Szívesen	SEE-veh-shehn
Can I help you?	Tessék	TEHSH-shehk
Thank you	Köszönöm	KUR-sur-nurm
I'm sorry / Excuse me	Bocsánat	BOH-chah-nawt
Good	Jól	yohl
Goodbye	Viszontlátásra	VEE-sohnt-lah-tahsh-rah
one / two	egy / kett...	edj / KEH-tur
three / four	három / négy	HAH-rohm / nedj
five / six	öt / hat	urt / hawt
seven / eight	hét / nyolc	heht / NEE-ohlts
nine / ten	kilenc / tíz	KEE-lehnts / teez
hundred	száz	sahz
thousand	ezer	EH-zehr
How much?	Mennyi?	MEHN-yee
local currency	forint	FOH-reent
Where is...?	Hol van...?	hohl vawn
..the toilet	...a toalet	aw TOH-ah-leht
men	férfi	FEHR-fee
women	női	NUR-ee
water / coffee	víz / kávé	veez / KAH-veh
beer / wine	sör / bor	shewr / bohr
Cheers!	Egészségedre!	EH-gehs-sheh-geh-dreh
the bill	fizetek	FEE-zeh-tehk

BUDAPEST

Budapest is *the* capital of Eastern Europe. It's a city of nuance and paradox—cosmopolitan, complicated, and challenging for the first-timer to get a handle on. Seasoned travelers like Budapest more with each return visit. Though Prague and Kraków have more romance (and crowds), many find Budapest to be Eastern Europe's most fascinating and rewarding destination.

Budapest is hot—literally. The city sits on a thin crust above thermal springs, which power its many baths. Even the word *pest* comes from a Slavic word for "oven." Two thousand years ago, the Romans had a settlement, Aquincum, on the north edge of today's Budapest. Several centuries later, in A.D. 896, the Magyars arrived from the steppes of Russia and took over the Carpathian Basin (roughly today's Hungary). In the 16th century, the Ottoman Turks invaded—occupying the region for 145 years. When the Turks were forced out, Buda and Pest were in ruins—so the Hapsburgs repopulated them with Germans, giving the cities a more Austrian style.

The Great Compromise of 1867 granted Hungary an equal stake in the Austro-Hungarian Empire. Six years later, the cities of Buda, Pest, and Óbuda united to form the capital city of Budapest, which governed a huge chunk of Eastern Europe. For the next few decades, Hungarian culture enjoyed a golden age, and Budapest was a boomtown. The boom reached its peak with a flurry of construction surrounding the year 1896—Hungary's 1,000th birthday (see page 233).

During the Soviet era, Hungary's milder "goulash" communism meant that Budapest, though still oppressive, was a place where other Eastern Europeans felt they could let loose. Twenty years ago, a stroll down Váci utca was the closest Czechs and Poles could get to a day pass to the West—including a chance to taste a Big Mac at the first McDonald's behind the Iron Curtain.

Budapest was built as the head of a much larger empire than it currently governs. Like Vienna, the city today feels a bit too grandiose for the capital of a relatively small country. But Budapest remains the cultural capital of Eastern Europe. It's a rich cultural stew made up of Hungarians, Germans, Slavs, and Jews, with a dash of Turkish paprika—simmered for centuries in a thermal bath. Each group has left its mark, but through it all, something has remained that is distinctly...Budapest.

Planning Your Time

Budapest demands at least three nights and two full days.

Day 1: Begin at Vörösmarty tér (stop by TI and decide on today's and tomorrow evening's entertainment), consider coffee at Gerbeaud, and stroll down Váci utca (following this chapter's self-guided tour). At the end of the street, explore the Great Market Hall, a fine place for a characteristic lunch. Take tram #2 to the Chain Bridge, cross it, and ride the funicular (or taxi) to Castle Hill. Following this chapter's self-guided walk, visit Matthias Church, Fisherman's Bastion, and the museums of your choice (the Commerce and Catering Museum is best). Speedy sightseers can zip out to Statue Park. After dinner, take a twilight sightseeing cruise, go to a concert (folk music nightly at 20:00) or opera, or stroll the Danube embankments and bridges.

Day 2: Start at the Great Synagogue (opens at 10:00). Then walk past the square called Deák square to reach St. Stephen's Basilica at the base of the Andrássy út (boulevard). From there, work your way up Andrássy út. Depending on your interests, you can stop at (in this order) the Postal Museum, the Opera House (duck in to see the lobby, or do a full-blown tour at 15:00 or 16:00), Franz Liszt Square (lots of lunch options), the lively Oktogon square, and the House of Terror Museum (allow 90 min). To skip ahead (or backtrack quickly), hop on the M1 Metro line, which runs beneath the boulevard from start to finish. At the end of Andrássy út, explore Heroes' Square and the City Park. Reward yourself with a nice long soak in the Széchenyi Baths (secure lockers, rentable suits, open until 19:00, last entry 18:00, get there by 17:00). The ritzy Gundel Restaurant is across from the baths. Same evening options as for Day 1. To fit in Statue Park on Day 2, start with the park in the morning, then do the Andrássy ramble (skipping the Synagogue and Opera tour to make it all fit).

With a third day, you can slow down and take more tours.

Eger is the most enjoyable day trip (takes a full day, and well worth an overnight—see Eger chapter); Szentendre is closer but very touristy (doable in a half day or even just in the late afternoon/evening). With a car (or a driver—quite reasonable), spend a day seeing the entire Danube Bend—Szentendre, Visegrád, and Esztergom—ideally on the way to Vienna or Bratislava (see Danube Bend chapter).

ORIENTATION

Budapest is big—with more than 2 million people, it's twice the size of Prague. The city is split down the center by the Danube River. On the west side of the Danube is hilly **Buda,** dominated by Castle Hill (packed with tourists by day, dead at night); the pleasant Víziváros ("Water Town"; VEE-zee-vah-rohsh) neighborhood is between the castle and the river.

On the east is flat **Pest** (pesht), the commercial heart of the city, which bustles day and night. The red-domed, riverside Parliament, visible from any point along the Danube, marks the northern edge of the tourists' Pest. A few blocks to the south, the Váci utca pedestrian drag runs parallel to the Danube, ending in the south at the steps of the Great Market Hall. From downtown, Andrássy út (and the M1 line beneath

Budapest

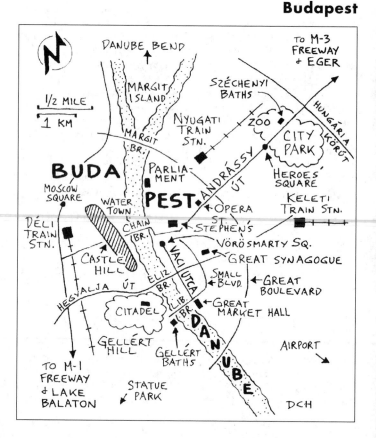

it) runs from the center of Pest (Deák Square) out past the Opera House to the Oktogon, Heroes' Square, City Park, and Széchenyi Baths.

Buda and Pest are connected by a series of very different **bridges.** From north to south, there's the Margaret Bridge (Margit híd, crosses Margaret Island), the famous Chain Bridge (Széchenyi lánchíd), the white and modern Elizabeth Bridge (Erzsébet híd), and the green Liberty Bridge (Szabadság híd). The bridges are fun to cross by foot, but it's faster to go under the river (on the M2 line) or on a bus (#16 over the Chain Bridge and #8 across the Elizabeth Bridge are both handy).

Pest is surrounded by a series of **ring roads** *(körút).* The innermost ring road—called the *Kiskörút,* or "Small Boulevard"—surrounds central Pest. The outer ring road—*Nagykörút,* or "Great Boulevard"—is about halfway between the river and City Park. The ring roads change names every few blocks, but they are always called *körút.* Arterial **boulevards** called *út* (such as Andrássy út) stretch from central Pest into the suburbs, like spokes on a wheel. Almost everything a tourist wants to see in Pest is either inside the innermost ring (**Belváros,** or "Inner City") or along one of these main boulevards (and therefore well-covered by public transit). Buda is also surrounded by a ring road, and the busy Hegyalja út rumbles through the middle of the tourists' Buda (between Castle and Gellért Hills).

Budapest uses a **district** system (like Paris and Vienna), and addresses often start with the district number (as a Roman numeral). Districts are called *kerület.* Castle Hill is district I. Notice that the district number does not necessarily indicate how central a location is: Districts II and III are to the north of Buda, where few tourists go, while the very heart of Pest is district V.

Tourist Information

Tourist information points are scattered around Budapest. Two are run by the Hungarian National Tourist Office (called TourInform), and also provide information about other Hungarian destinations: just off **Vörösmarty Square** (open daily 24 hrs a day, ominously sharing a storefront with the police information office, Vigadó utca 6) and just off **Deák tér** (daily 8:00–20:00, Sütő utca 2). The central telephone number for TourInform offices is 1/438-8080 (www.hungarytourism.hu).

The other TIs are run by the City of Budapest (www.budapestinfo .hu), and focus only on the capital. There are four: across from the Matthias Church on **Castle Hill** (daily 8:00–20:00, Szentháromság tér, tel. 1/488-0453); **Franz Liszt Square,** a block south of the Oktogon (May–Sept daily 9:00–19:00, Oct–April daily 10:00–18:00, Liszt Ferenc tér 11, tel. 1/322-4098); **Nyugati Rail Station** (daily 9:00–18:00, March–Sept until 19:00, tel. 1/302-8580); and at the **airport.**

At all of the TIs, you can collect a pile of free brochures (on sights, bus tours, and more). The most important: the free, good city map and

BUDAPEST LANDMARKS

English	Hungarian	Pronounced
square	tér	tehr (said pulling cheeks back)
street	utca	OO-tzah
bath	fürdő	FEWR-dur
(Buda) Castle	(Budai) vár	BOO-die vahr
Castle Hill	Várhegy	VAHR-hayj
Chain Bridge	Széchenyi lánchíd	SAY-chehn-yee LAHNTS-heed
Liberty Bridge (green, a.k.a. Franz Josef Bridge)	Szabadság híd	SAW-bawd-shahg heed
Elizabeth Bridge (white, modern)	Erzsébet híd	EHRZ-sheh-bayt heed
Margaret Bridge (crosses Margaret Island)	Margit híd	MAWR-geet heed
Danube River	Duna	DOO-naw
Eastern Rail Station	Keleti pályaudvar	KEH-leh-tee PAH-yuh-uhd-vahr
Western Rail Station	Nyugati pályaudvar	NYOO-gaw-tee PAH-yuh-uhd-vahr
Southern Rail Station	Déli pályaudvar	DAY-lee PAH-yuh-uhd-vahr
Suburban Train System	HÉV	hayv
City Park	Városliget	VAH-rohsh-lee-geht
Pest's main pedestrian street	Váci utca	VAH-tsee OO-tzah
Main square in Pest	Vörösmarty tér	VOO-roosh-mar-tee tehr
Grand boulevard	Andrássy út	AHN-drah-shee oot

Budapest Panorama events guide. You can also pick up the *Budapest Guide* booklet (cover price 500 Ft, but you can often get it free). TIs are handy places to buy your Budapest Card (see below).

Budapest Card: The Budapest Card is a great tool for efficient sightseeing. Costing the equivalent of about $10 a day, it includes public transportation and entry to virtually all of Budapest's museums, plus discounts to other attractions, including baths and tours. With the Budapest Card, you have the freedom to hop the Metro for one stop to save 10 minutes of walking, or drop into that semi-interesting sight for a quick visit. The card costs 3,950 Ft for 48 hours, or 4,950 Ft for 72 hours (includes handy 100-page booklet with maps, updated hours, and brief museum descriptions). You can buy the card all over Budapest—at the TI, travel agencies, major Metro stations, sights, and many hotels. Be sure to sign and date your card before you use it.

Arrival in Budapest

Budapest has three major train stations *(pályaudvar,* abbreviated *pu.);* the two most important are in Pest. Most international trains (and some domestic trains, such as those that connect to Eger) use the **Keleti (Eastern) Station** (Keleti pu., east of central Pest). Some international trains—especially those heading to the east—use the **Nyugati (Western) Station** (Nyugati pu., actually northeast of central Pest). The **Déli (Southern) Station** (Déli pu., which is west of central Buda) has mostly domestic trains, including those to Lake Balaton. The taxi stands in front of each train station are suspect—unless you want to get ripped off, it's better to call for one (see "Getting around Budapest—By Taxi," page 204).

By Train at the Keleti (Eastern) Station: The Keleti Station is just south of City Park, east of central Pest. On arrival, go to the front of the long tracks 6-9. Near the head of the tracks cluster several travel agencies with "Tourist Information" signs; none are official, but all have a few helpful flyers and most can sell you a Budapest Card. The **international information and ticket windows** and **lockers** are hiding down a hallway halfway down track 6 (look for *nemzetközi pénztár*). A baggage-check desk is nearby (250 Ft/day). An **ATM** is across the tracks near the head of track 9 (at the K&H Bank).

If you go out the front door, you'll stumble over a cluster of suspicious-looking taxis (call instead). The big staircase at the front of the tracks leads down to domestic ticket windows and WCs. To reach the **Metro,** go straight at the bottom of the stairs, then proceed straight through the open-air courtyard to the big "M" sign.

By Train at the Nyugati (Western) Station: This is the most central of Budapest's stations, on the northeast edge of downtown Pest. Most international arrivals use tracks 1-5, which are set back from the main entrance. With these tracks at your back, exit straight ahead into a parking lot with taxis, or use the stairs just inside the doors to reach an underpass and the Metro. If you're homesick, leave through the door that leads to the taxis and go immediately to the right to discover the huge, American-style **Westend Citycenter** mall (complete with a T.G.I. Friday's, shops open Mon–Sat 10:00–21:00, Sun 10:00–20:00). The mall has a tethered balloon ride that affords a grand city view.

SIGHTSEEING MODULES

Budapest is a sprawling city, with sights scattered over a huge area. But if you organize your sightseeing efficiently and dive into the easy-to-master public transportation system, Budapest gets small. Break the city into manageable chunks, and digest them one at a time:

Buda
1. **Castle Hill** (Royal Palace, Matthias Church, various museums)
2. **Gellért Hill** (Gellért Baths, Citadella, Cave Church)

Pest
1. **Central Pest, a.k.a. Belváros** (north to south: Parliament and Kossuth Square, Vörösmarty Square, Váci utca, Danube embankment and cruises, Great Synagogue, Great Market Hall)
2. **Andrássy út** (from center to outskirts: St. Stephen's Basilica, Opera, Oktogon, House of Terror, Heroes' Square, City Park, Széchenyi Baths)

Near Budapest
1. **Statue Park**
2. **Óbuda** (Vasarely Museum, Imre Varga Collection, Aquincum Roman ruins)
3. **Danube Bend** (begins just north of Óbuda: Szentendre, Visegrád, Esztergom; see Danube Bend chapter)

To reach an official **TI** and **ticket windows,** follow tracks 10-13 to the station's main entrance. The TI is by the head of track 10 (daily 9:00–18:00, March–Sept until 19:00); ticket windows are through an easy-to-miss door across the tracks, by platform 13 (marked *cassa* and *információ*; once you enter the ticket hall, international windows are in a second room at the far end—look for *nemzetközi*).

From the front of tracks 10-13, exit straight ahead and you'll be on Teréz körút, the very busy Great Boulevard ring road. (Váci utca, at the center of Pest, is dead ahead, about 20 minutes away by foot). In front of the building is another taxi stand and access to handy trams #4 and #6 (zipping all the way around Pest's great ring); to the right you'll find stairs leading to an underpass (use it to avoid crossing this busy intersection, or to reach the Metro); and to the left you'll see the classiest Art

Nouveau McDonald's on the planet. (Seriously. Take a look inside.)

By Car: A car is unnecessary at best and a headache at worst. Unless you're heading to an out-of-town sight (like Statue Park), park the car at your hotel and take public transportation. Public parking costs 120-400 Ft per hour (pay in advance at machine and put ticket in windshield—watch locals and imitate; free parking Mon–Fri after 18:00, Sat after 12:00, and all day Sun).

By Plane: Ferihegy Airport is 15 miles east of Budapest. Hungarian Airlines uses Terminal A, and others use Terminal B. The general airport info line is tel. 1/296-9696 (departure info tel. 1/296-7000). The best inexpensive way downtown from the airport is by **minibus** (about 2,100 Ft to any hotel in the city center, desk at arrival lobby, call 1/296-8555 to arrange a pick-up). You can also take the BKV Plusz Reptér **bus** to the Kőbánya-Kispest M3 Metro station; allow 40 minutes total for the trip to the center. A **taxi** between the center and the airport runs about 5,000 Ft, but it's cheaper if you call Főtaxi (guaranteed no-meter rate of 3,500 Ft to Pest or 4,000 Ft to Buda, tel. 1/222-2222, toll-free 0680-222-222).

Getting around Budapest

Budapest is huge. Connecting your sightseeing by foot is tedious and unnecessary; use the excellent public-transportation system instead. The same tickets work for Metro, trams, and buses (buy them at kiosks, Metro ticket windows, or automated orange machines: put in the appropriate amount of money—see below—then press button).

Your options are:

• Single ticket (*vonaljegy,* for a ride of up to an hour with no transfers) for 130 Ft.

• Short single Metro ride (*metroszakaszjegy,* 3 stops or fewer on the Metro) for 90 Ft.

• Transfer ticket (*átszállójegy*—allowing up to 90 minutes, including one transfer) for 220 Ft.

• Unlimited travelcards (1-day for 975 Ft, 3-day for 1,950 Ft, 7-day for 2,250 Ft)—but if you're here more than a day and plan to sightsee, you might as well get a Budapest Card instead (see "Tourist Information," above).

Always validate your ticket as you enter the bus, tram, or Metro station (stick it in the little elbow-high box). A transfer ticket must be validated a second time (at the other end of the ticket) when you transfer. The serious-looking guys with red armbands waiting as you exit the Metro want to see your validated ticket or Budapest Card. Cheaters get fined 1,600 Ft. All public transit runs until 23:00. A useful route-planning Web site is www.bkv.hu.

By Metro: Budapest's Metro is every bit as convenient and efficient as Paris' or Berlin's. There are three lines:

• **M1 (yellow)**—The first on the Continent, this runs under Andrássy út from the center to City Park.

• **M2 (red)**—Built during the communist days, it's 115 feet deep, doubles as a bomb shelter, and comes with a tornado ventilation system—notice the gale. The only line going under the Danube to Buda, M2 connects the Déli station, Moszkva tér (where you catch the *vár* bus to the castle), Batthyány tér (where you catch the HÉV train to Óbuda or Szentendre), and the Keleti station.

• **M3 (blue)**—This line makes a broad boomerang-shaped swoop north to south.

The three lines cross only once: at the **Deák Square** stop in the heart of Pest, where Andrássy út begins. Most Metro stations are at intersections of ring roads and other major arterials. You'll usually exit the Metro into a confusing underpass. These are packed with kiosks, fast-food stands, and makeshift markets—but orange directional signs help you find the right exit.

The Metro stops themselves are usually very well marked, with a list of upcoming stops on the wall behind the tracks. The red digital clocks tell you how long it's been since the last train left; you'll rarely wait more than five or six minutes for the next.

By Tram: Budapest's trams are convenient and frequent, taking you virtually anywhere the Metro doesn't. Here are some trams likely to come in handy:

Trams #2 and #2A: Run along Pest's Danube embankment.

Tram #19: Runs along Buda's Danube embankment, from the Gellért Hotel to the bottom of the funicular (Adam Clark tér) to Batthyány tér (HÉV and M2 Metro station).

Trams #4 and #6: Zip along Pest's Grand Boulevard ring road *(Nagykörút),* connecting the West Station and Oktogon with Buda's Moszkva tér (M2 metro station).

By Bus: The tram and Metro network can get you nearly anywhere, so you're less likely to take a bus. One exception is getting to the top of Castle Hill—accessible only by the *várbusz* ("castle bus," from Moszkva tér—see "Sights—Buda Castle Hill," page 209). Bus #16 is handy (Deák tér, Roosevelt tér, crossing the Chain Bridge, Adam Clark tér, and up to Dísz tér atop Castle Hill near the Royal Palace).

By Taxi: Budapest's public transportation is good enough that you probably won't need to take many taxis. If you do, you may run into a dishonest driver. Locals always call a cab from a reputable company (Főtaxi, tel. 1/222-2222, toll-free 0680-222-222; City Taxi, tel. 1/211-1111; or Taxi 2000, tel. 1/2000-000).

To protect you, taxis are not allowed to charge more than a drop rate of 300 Ft and 240 Ft per kilometer (more 22:00–6:00)—though the more reputable companies charge less. Prices are per ride, not per passenger. A 10 percent tip is expected.

Many cabs you'd hail on the streets are there only to prey on rich, green tourists. Avoid hotel taxis, unmarked taxis, and cabs waiting at tourist spots and train stations. If you do wave down a cab on the street, choose one that's marked with a company logo and telephone number. Ask for a rough estimate before you get in—if it doesn't sound reasonable, walk away. If you wind up being dramatically overcharged for a ride, simply pay what you think is fair and go inside. If the driver follows you (unlikely), your hotel receptionist will defend you.

Helpful Hints

Theft Alert: Budapest feels—and is—safe, especially for a city of its size. There are fewer con artists than in Prague, but in any big city it's especially important to beware of pickpockets—in crowded and touristed places, particularly on the Metro and in trams. Wear a money belt and keep a close eye on your valuables.

Scams: Budapest's biggest crooks are unscrupulous cabbies (see "Getting around—By Taxi," above).

If you're a male in a touristy area and a gorgeous local girl (*Konzumlany* means "consumption girl") takes a liking to you, avoid her. The only foreplay going on here will climax in your grand rip-off.

A common scam involves a man stopping you on the street to "change money." A policeman arrests him—and you—and needs to see your wallet to find out if he's a con artist. They are a team and you are being robbed. And, as in many big cities, the famous shell games on the streets have everybody winning...until you give it a try.

Internet Access: You'll find the easiest access (and highest prices) along the touristy north end of the Váci utca pedestrian drag in Pest. They all seem to charge about 700 Ft per hour. In Buda's Víziváros neighborhood, try the Soho Coffee Company (on Fő utca).

Post Offices: These are marked with a smart green *posta* logo (Mon–Fri 8:00–18:00, Sat 8:00–12:00, closed Sun).

Banking: Banks are generally open Mon–Thu 8:00–15:00, Fri 8:00–13:00, closed Sat–Sun.

English Newspaper: For an English-speaking expatriate take on the city, including listings of movies in English, pick up a copy of the weekly *Budapest Sun* (349 Ft, sold at newsstands).

Local Guidebook: András Török's *Budapest: A Critical Guide* is the best book by a local writer (available in English at most souvenir stands).

Travel Agencies: Carlson Wagonlit Travel is 40 yards north of Pest's Vörösmarty tér and handy for rail and air needs (Mon–Fri 9:00–17:00, closed Sat–Sun and for lunch 12:30–13:30, Dorottya utca 3, tel. 1/483-3383, www.carlsonwagonlit.hu). Vista Travel Center, at the base of Andrássy út, is a sprawling, user-friendly

BUDAPEST AT A GLANCE

▲▲▲**House of Terror** Harrowing remembrance of Nazis and communist secret police in former headquarters/torture site in Pest. **Hours:** Tue–Sun 10:00–18:00, closed Mon.

▲▲▲**Baths** Budapest's steamy soaking scene. **Hours:** Széchenyi Baths in Pest, popular with locals, daily 6:00–19:00, until 16:00 in winter; touristy Gellért Baths in Buda, May–Sept daily 6:00–19:00, Oct–April Mon–Fri 6:00–19:00, Sat–Sun 6:00–17:00.

▲▲**Váci utca** Hopping pedestrian boulevard and tourist magnet in Pest with the East's first McDonald's. **Hours:** Always open.

▲▲**Great Market Hall** Colorful Old World mall in Pest with produce, cheap eateries, souvenirs, and great people-watching. **Hours:** Mon 6:00–17:00, Tue–Fri 6:00–18:00, Sat 6:00–14:00, closed Sun.

▲▲**Heroes' Square** Mammoth tribute in Pest to Hungary's historic figures, fringed by a couple art museums and Countryrama 3-D movie screening room. **Hours:** Square always open, sights closed Mon.

▲▲**City Park** Pest's backyard, with Art Nouveau zoo, Transylvanian castle, amusement park, and Széchenyi Baths. **Hours:** Park always open.

▲▲**Statue Park** Bigger-than-life communist big-shots all collected in one park, on the outskirts of town. **Hours:** Daily 10:00–sunset.

▲▲**Matthias Church** Landmark neo-Gothic church in Buda with revered 16th-century statue of Mary and Jesus. **Hours:** Mon–Fri 9:00–17:00, Sat 9:00–13:00, Sun 13:00–17:00.

▲**Fishermen's Bastion** Neo-Romanesque rampart in Buda with fabulous Parliament views across the Danube. **Hours:** Rampart always open; bastion climb daily 9:00–23:00.

travel service with cheap flights, all the train-ticket and reservation services, guidebooks, hotels, tours, and so on. Step in and grab a number from the receptionist (Mon–Fri 9:00–18:30, Sat 9:00–14:30, closed Sun, Andrássy út 1, tel. 1/429-9999). The central "MAV" train office, a block past the opera house at the corner of Andrássy and Nagymező, is useful for any train ticket business you may have (Mon–Fri 9:00–18:00, closed Sat–Sun).

▲**Hungarian Commerce and Catering Museum** Intriguing time-tunnel look at 19th-century businesses. **Hours:** Wed–Fri 10:00–17:00, Sat–Sun 10:00–18:00, closed Mon–Tue.

▲**Vörösmarty tér** Lively people-watching square in Pest with venerable Gerbeaud café. **Hours:** Always open.

▲**Hungarian Parliament** Vast, riverside neo-Gothic government center in Pest. **Hours:** Tours usually daily at 10:00, 12:00, and 14:00.

▲**Great Synagogue** The world's second-largest after New York's, with museum and garden memorial in Pest. **Hours:** Mid-April–Oct Mon–Thu 10:00–17:00, Fri and Sun 10:00–14:00, Nov–mid-April Mon–Thu 10:00–15:00, Fri and Sun 10:00–14:00, always closed Sat and Jewish holidays, often closed mid-Dec–mid-Jan.

▲**Danube Embankment** Pest's best stretch for a riverside stroll. **Hours:** Always open.

▲**Chain Bridge** Lion-gated beauty connecting Pest and Buda. **Hours:** Always open.

▲**Postal Museum** Funky tribute to old, postal service objects in elegant old Pest mansion. **Hours:** Tue–Sun 10:00–18:00, closed Mon.

▲**Hungarian State Opera House** Neo-Renaissance splendor and affordable opera in Pest. **Hours:** Lobby/box office Mon–Sat 11:00–19:00, Sun 16:00–19:00; performances nearly nightly.

▲**Imre Varga Collection** Evocative sculpture collection capturing communist times, in Óbuda. **Hours:** Tue-Sun 10:00–18:00, closed Mon; artist visits at 10:00 Sat.

Driver: Kiraly József runs a 10-car company with good, generally English-speaking drivers (3,000 Ft/hr, mobile 0630-949-1253, artoli@axelero.hu).

    Friendly, English-speaking Gábor Balázs can drive you around the city or into the surrounding countryside (3,000 Ft/hr, 3-hr minimum in city, 4-hr minimum in countryside—good for a Danube Bend excursion, mobile 209-364-317, balazs.gabor@chello.hu).

Best Views: Budapest is a city of marvelous vistas. Some of the best are from the Citadella (high on Gellért Hill), the promenade in front of Buda Castle, the embankments or many bridges spanning the Danube (especially the Chain Bridge), the balloon ride from the mall at the Nyugati station, and tour boats on the Danube—especially at night.

Laundry: Laundry options in Budapest are scarce. The most central is **Patyolat** at the corner of Vármegye utca and Városház utca (just up from Váci utca). The laundry ladies will monitor your use of the "self-service" facilities (allow 2,500 Ft to wash and dry a load, Mon–Fri 7:00–19:00, Sat 8:00–13:00, closed Sun). For full service, try your hotel, or go to **Laundry Házimosoda,** centrally located in Pest between the Danube and Váci utca (figure 600 Ft per shirt, 950 Ft for pants, pick-up after 17:00 the following day, Mon–Fri 8:00–19:30, Sat 9:00–13:00, closed Sun, Galamb utca 9).

TOURS

Bus Tours—Several companies run bus tours that glide past all the big sights (not hop-on, hop-off). A basic three-hour bus tour will run you about 6,000 Ft per person, and the different companies are essentially the same; pick up flyers at the TI or in your hotel lobby. These companies also run a wide variety of other tours—including boat cruises and dinners and trips to the Danube Bend. Perhaps the best quickie is **City Tour**'s two-hour tape-recorded swing through town with one photo stop off the bus (5,000 Ft or €20, departing from Andrássy út 3, near M1: Bajcsy-Zsilinszky, covered bus leaves at 10:30 and 13:30 year-round, open-top bus in summer at 11:30 and 14:30, peak season hrly 9:30–17:30).

Walking Tours—The youthful Absolute Walking Tours—run by an American, Ben Friday, and a Hungarian, András Oros—have an overview tour (4,000 Ft, June–Aug daily at 9:30 and 13:30, off-season daily at 10:30, 3–4 hrs). They also offer an inventive "Hammer and Sickle" tour (including a visit to a communist flat, 5,000 Ft, depart 10:30, 4/week, 4 hrs) and a pub crawl (5,000 Ft, 4/week, at least 3 hrs, sometimes continuing late into the night). All tours depart from Deák tér (tel. 1/266-8777, www.absolutetours.com). Travelers with this book get a 500 Ft discount, as does anyone under 26.

Private Guide—Budapest has plenty of enthusiastic, hardworking young guides who speak fine English and enjoy showing off their exciting city. Considering the reasonable fees and efficient use of your time, hiring your own personal expert is an excellent value. I have two favorites: **Peter Polczman** charges 14,000 Ft (€70) for a four- or five-hour half day and 20,000 Ft (€100) for a full day (tel. 20/926-0557, polczman@freestart.hu). **Andrea Makkay** charges 4,000 Ft per hour on foot or 5,000 Ft per hour in her car (tel. 1/351-9298, mobile 0620-9629-363, amakkay@axelero.hu, arrange details by e-mail). Both Peter and Andrea are good in-town and for side-tripping up the Danube Bend.

Danube Boat Tours—Cruising the Danube, while touristy, is fun and convenient. The most established company, Legenda, runs boats day and night. By day, the one-hour cruise costs 3,600 Ft (2,750 Ft with Budapest Card) and includes an optional one-hour walking tour around Margaret Island, Budapest's playground (6/day July–Aug, 4/day May–June and Sept, 2/day mid-March–April, 1/day Oct, 1/day Fri–Sat only Nov–mid-Dec, no cruises mid-Dec–Feb).

By night, the one-hour cruise (with no Margaret Island option) costs 4,200 Ft (3,250 Ft with Budapest Card; 3/day May–Sept, 1/day mid-March–April and Oct–mid-Dec, no cruises mid-Dec–Feb).

Both cruises include two drinks and headphone commentary. TV monitors actually show the interior of the great buildings as you float by. The Legenda dock is on the Pest embankment (in front of the Marriott; find pedestrian access under tram tracks just downriver from Vigadó tér, tel. 1/317-2203, www.legenda.hu).

SIGHTS

Buda

Castle Hill (Várhegy)

Buda's main sights are all on Castle Hill. While many visitors expect this high-profile district to be time-consuming, for most it's enough to simply stroll through in an hour or two. The major landmarks are the huge, green-domed Royal Palace at the south end of the hill (not much to see inside) and the frilly-spired Matthias Church near the north end. In between are tourist-filled pedestrian streets and historic buildings. Several interesting but inessential museums are also scattered around the hill. I've listed the sights in order from south to north, and linked them together on a self-guided tour.

Getting to Castle Hill: The Metro and trams won't take you to the top of Castle Hill. You can hike, taxi, ride the funicular, or catch bus #16 from either side of the Chain Bridge (departs from Deák, Roosevelt, and Adam Clark squares). A special **castle bus** *(várbusz)* does a loop from Moszkva tér (Moscow Square) just north of the castle (M2: Moszkva tér, bus stop just uphill from Metro stop, look for bus with the word *vár* and a little picture of a castle). Castle Hill buses are specially designed to be light, as the hill is honeycombed with limestone caves. You'll notice the hill is a gated community with carefully regulated traffic.

The **Buda Funicular** *(sikló),* lifting visitors from the Chain Bridge to the top of Castle Hill, is a Budapest landmark. Built in 1870 to provide cheap transportation to Castle Hill workers, today it is a pricey little

Buda Center Sights

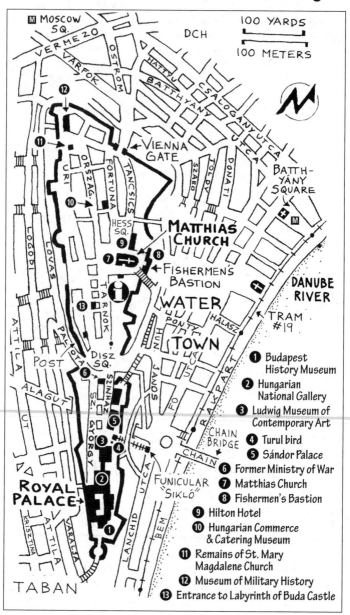

100 YARDS

100 METERS

1 Budapest History Museum
2 Hungarian National Gallery
3 Ludwig Museum of Contemporary Art
4 Turul bird
5 Sándor Palace
6 Former Ministry of War
7 Matthias Church
8 Fishermen's Bastion
9 Hilton Hotel
10 Hungarian Commerce & Catering Museum
11 Remains of St. Mary Magdalene Church
12 Museum of Military History
13 Entrance to Labyrinth of Buda Castle

tourist trip. Read the fun first-person history you'll see in glass cases at the top station (500 Ft up, 400 Ft down, not covered by Budapest Card, daily 7:30–22:00, departs every 5 min, closed every other Mon).

From the funicular, enjoy the views of the Danube and go a few yards to the big bird at the top of the stairs overlooking the immense palace. You can survey the scene from here or wander to the equestrian statue and circle through and around the huge building.

The *Turul*—This mythical bird of Magyar folk tales watches over the palace. The *turul* led the Hungarian migrations in the ninth century. He dropped his sword in the Carpathian Basin, indicating that this was to be the permanent home of the Magyar people. During a period of strong nationalism in the 1920s, a movement named for this bird worked to revive traditional Hungarian culture.

Royal Palace (Királyi Palota)—The imposing palace on Castle Hill is a dull contemporary construction that barely hints at the colorful story that stretches from the day that the legendary *turul* dropped his sword until the time this modern palace was built.

Originally, the capital of Hungary wasn't Buda or Pest, but Esztergom (just up the river; see Danube Bend chapter). In the 13th century, Tartars swept through Eastern Europe, destroying much of Hungary. King Béla IV decided to move the capital here, a more protected location in the interior of the country. He rebuilt a walled Buda on top of this hill, and the city has dominated the region ever since. Béla IV was smart enough to divide his new town of Buda in half between two feuding factions: the native Hungarians and the Germans who came here to trade. Each had their own turf and church (we'll see both farther along the hill).

The first Hungarian dynasty (the Árpáds) died out in 1301, and the new French line—the Anjous (or Angevins)—took over Buda and the rest of Hungary. They replaced Béla IV's modest castle with a luxurious palace that expanded over the years until the early 15th century, when it was one of Europe's biggest. The 15th-century King Mátyás Corvinus made the palace even more extravagant, putting Buda—and Hungary—on the map.

Just a few decades later, the invading Ottoman Turks occupied Buda and turned the elegant palace into a garrison. When the Hapsburgs laid siege to the hill in 1686, gunpowder stored in the cellar exploded, destroying the palace. The Hapsburgs took the hill, but Buda was deserted and in ruins. The town was resettled by Austrians, who built a new Baroque palace, hoping that the Hapsburg monarch would move in—but none ever did (preferring to live up the river in Vienna, or occasionally in Prague). The useless palace became a garrison, a university, and the viceroy's residence. It was damaged again during the 1848 Revolution, but was repaired and continued to grow right along with Budapest's prominence.

As World War II drew to a close, Buda became the front line between the Nazis and the approaching Soviets, who laid siege to the hill for six months. The palace was again destroyed.

Most Budapesters (and historians) don't much care for the current tame post-WWII reconstruction of the palace. It's a loose rebuilding of previous versions, lacking the style and sense of history that this important site deserves.

Today's palace is devoted to several museums. Visit one now (listed below), or head to the Matthias Church from here (Castle Hill self-guided tour continues below).

Castle Museums—The palace houses three worthwhile (but not must-see) museums. The first two are off of the big enclosed courtyard (make your way to the other side of the dome; once you're in the courtyard, face the dome—the Budapest History Museum is behind you, and the National Gallery is at 2 o'clock). The third is just north of the courtyard, across from the fancy fountain monument to Mátyás Corvinus.

The **Budapest History Museum** (Budapesti Történeti Múzeum), celebrating the earlier grandeur of Castle Hill, is most interesting for history buffs. Inside you'll find the remains of an original Gothic chapel, a knights' hall, and marble remnants (reliefs and fountains) of Mátyás Corvinus' lavish Renaissance palace. There's also a good collection of 14th-century sculptures, many of them with strong Magyar features—that is, Central Asian (600 Ft, covered by Budapest Card, mid-May–mid-Sept daily 10:00–18:00, March–mid-May and mid-Sept–Oct Wed–Mon 10:00–18:00, closed Tue, Nov–Feb Wed–Mon 10:00-16:00, closed Tue, tel. 1/225-7815).

The **Hungarian National Gallery** (Magyar Nemzeti Galéria), with an excellent collection of 15th-century winged altars, is the best place to see Hungarian artwork (700 Ft, covered by Budapest Card, March–Nov Tue–Sun 10:00–18:00, closed Mon, Dec–Feb Tue–Sun 10:00–16:00, closed Mon, tel. 1/375-8584).

The **Ludwig Museum of Contemporary Art** (Kortárs Művészeti Múzeum) features mostly Hungarian artists, with a few Picassos and American Pop Artists such as Warhol and Lichtenstein (500 Ft, covered by Budapest Card, Tue–Sun 10:00–18:00, Thu until 20:00, closed Mon, tel. 1/375-9175, www.ludwigmuseum.hu).

From the Funicular and Royal Palace to Matthias Church—To connect the palace to Matthias Church, the closest major sight, follow this self-guided walk:

From the *turul* bird and the top of the funicular (with back to Royal Palace), walk along the non-river side of the big white building, the **Sándor Palace.** This mansion underwent a very costly renovation under the previous Hungarian prime minister, who hoped to make it his residence. But in 2002, the same year it was finished, he lost his bid for reelection. The spunky new PM refused to move in. By way of compromise, now the president lives here.

As you continue along the side of the Sándor Palace, you'll notice the remains of a medieval monastery and church in the field to your left. Beyond that, past the flagpoles, is the ongoing excavation of the medieval Jewish quarter—more reminders that most of what you see on today's Castle Hill has been destroyed and rebuilt many times over.

After the Sándor Palace, you'll pass the yellow National Dance Theater—where Beethoven once performed. Beyond that on the left, you'll see the still-damaged building that used to house the **Ministry of War.** Most of the bullet holes you see are from World War II; others are from the guns of the Soviets who occupied this hill in response to the 1956 Uprising. The building is a political hot potato—prime real estate, but nobody can decide what to do with it. (Note that 50 yards beyond the Ministry of War is a bus stop for bus #16, offering a quick return to the Pest side of the Chain Bridge.)

Cross the street and continue uphill through "Parade Square" (Dísz tér) and up **Tárnok utca.** This area often disappoints visitors. After being destroyed by Turks, it was rebuilt in sensible Baroque, lacking the romantic twisty-alley charm of a medieval old town. But if you poke your head into some courtyards, you'll almost always see some original Gothic arches and other elements.

Continue along the street; after two blocks, past the TI (on your right), you'll see a warty plague column marking the main square of old Buda. It faces...

▲▲**Matthias Church (Mátyás Templom)**—One of Budapest's landmarks, Matthias Church has been destroyed and rebuilt several times in the 800 years since it was founded by King Béla IV.

The prominent church has an elaborate gilded interior with a Gothic nucleus. The frilly, flamboyant steeple and other fanciful elements were added for the 1896 celebrations. Inside it's wallpapered with motifs reminiscent of various stages in local history since 896: Turkish rule, Magyar folk designs, and the Renaissance era—all under Gothic arches. Notice the 500-year-old Hungarian battalion banners, left here after the Mass that celebrated János Hunyadi's 1456 victory over the Turks. The stained glass is 160 years old; during World War II, it was removed and hidden to avoid destruction.

The **Loreto Chapel** (rear of nave, left of stairs) holds the church's prize possession. Peer through the black iron grill to see the 1515 statue of Mary and Jesus. Anticipating Turkish plundering, locals walled over this precious statue. The occupying Turks used the church as their primary

MÁTYÁS CORVINUS:
THE LAST HUNGARIAN KING
(r. 1458–1490)

The Árpád dynasty—descendants of the original Magyar tribes—died out in 1301. For more than 600 years, Hungary would be ruled by foreigners...with one exception.

In the middle of the 15th century, Hungary had bad luck hanging on to its foreign kings: Two of them died unexpectedly within seven years. Meanwhile, military general János Hunyadi was enjoying great success on the battlefield against the Turks. When the five-year-old Ladislas V was elected king, Hunyadi was appointed regent and essentially ruled the country. Hunyadi defeated the Turks in the 1456 Battle of Belgrade—temporarily preventing them from entering Hungary—but he died of the plague soon after.

When Ladislas died in 1458 at the tender age of 16, Hunyadi's son, Mátyás (Matthias), rode his father's coattails to victory among the Hungarian nobility—becoming the first Hungarian-descended king in more than 150 years. Mátyás Hunyadi took the nickname Corvinus (after the raven on his coat of arms). Progressive and well-educated, Mátyás Corvinus was the quintessential Renaissance king—a benefactor of the poor and a true humanist. He patronized the arts and built palaces legendary for their beauty. He dressed up as

mosque—oblivious to the statue plastered over in the niche. Then, 150 years later, during the siege of Buda in 1686, gunpowder stored in the castle up the street detonated, and the wall crumbled. Mary's triumphant face showed through, freaking out the Muslim Turks. According to legend, this was the only part of town taken from the Turks without a fight. Ever since, the church has officially been the Church of Our Lady. But it's more commonly referred to as Matthias Church, for the popular Renaissance king who got married here...twice (500 Ft, covered by Budapest Card, 12-stop audioguide-200 Ft, Mon–Fri 9:00–17:00, Sat 9:00–13:00, Sun 13:00–17:00, Szentháromság tér 2, 1/355-5657, www.matyas-templom.hu). The crypt holds the Museum of Ecclesiastical Art (Egyházművészeti Gyűjteménye, same hours as church).

Toward the Danube from Matthias Church is the...

▲**Fishermen's Bastion (Halászbástya)**—This neo-Romanesque fantasy rampart offers beautiful views over the Danube to Pest. In the Middle Ages, the fish market was just below here (in today's Víziváros, or "Water Town"), so this part of the rampart actually *was* guarded by fishermen. The current structure, though, is completely artificial—one a commoner and ventured into the streets to see firsthand how the nobles of his realm treated his people.

Mátyás was a strong, savvy leader. He created Central Europe's first standing army—30,000 mercenaries known as the "Black Army." No longer reliant on the nobility for military support, Good King Mátyás was able to drain power from the nobles and make taxation of his subjects more equitable—earning him the nickname the "people's king."

King Mátyás was a shrewd military tactician. Realizing that squabbling with the Turks would squander his resources, he made peace with the Ottoman sultan to stabilize Hungary's southern border. Then he swept north, invading Moravia, Bohemia, and even Austria. By 1485, Mátyás moved into his new palace in Vienna, and Hungary was enjoying a golden age.

Five years later, Mátyás died mysteriously at the age of 47, and his empire disintegrated. It is said that when Mátyás died, justice died with him. To this day, Hungarians consider him the greatest of all kings, and they sing of his siege of Vienna in their national anthem. They're proud that for a few decades in the middle of half a millennium of foreign oppression, they had a truly Hungarian king—and a great one, at that.

more example of Budapest sprucing itself up for 1896 (see page 233). Its seven towers represent the seven Magyar tribes. The cone-headed arcades are reminiscent of tents the nomadic Magyars called home before they moved west to Europe.

Survey Pest across the Danube from this viewpoint. The two domes are Parliament and St. Stephen's Basilica—both 96 meters high, built in...you guessed it...1896. The Chain Bridge cuts Pest in two halves: The left is administrative, with government ministries, embassies, banks, and so on; the right (stretching to the modern, white Elizabeth Bridge) is the commercial center of Pest, with the best riverside promenade (do this tonight).

Paying to climb up the bastion makes little sense (300 Ft, not covered by Budapest Card, daily 9:00–23:00, free Oct–mid-March and after 22:00). Enjoy virtually the same view through the windows (left of café) for free. The café offers a scenic break if you don't mind the tour groups.

Statue of St. István (Stephen)—Hungary's first Christian king sits atop his horse in the courtyard between the church and the bastion. He tamed the nomadic and pagan Magyars, established strict laws and the concept of private property, and made his people Christian. The reliefs show the pope crowning St. István (EESHT-vahn) in the year 1000, bringing Hungary into Christendom. This meant the rest of Europe was now inclined to help Hungary against the Turks and to bully Slavs. Without this pivotal event, locals believe that the Magyar nation would have been lost. A passionate evangelist—more for the survival of his Magyar nation than for the salvation of his people—István beheaded those who wouldn't convert. To make his point perfectly clear, he quartered his reluctant uncle and sent him on four separate, simultaneous tours of the country to show Hungarians that Christianity was a smart choice. Gruesome as he was, István was sainted within 30 years of his death.

To continue your exploration of Buda, take a self-guided walk along...

North Castle Hill—The following 30-minute stroll takes you through Buda north of Matthias Church. As this was the site of the Nazi military headquarters, it was heavily bombed towards the end of World War II. (During a six-week siege, 30 percent of the city was destroyed.)

Leave the courtyard beside the church and turn right—passing the 1713 Holy Trinity plague column on your left—so that you're walking along the front of the glassy modern **Hilton Hotel.** To minimize the controversy of building upon so much history, architects thoughtfully incorporated the medieval ruins into its modern design. Built in 1976, the Hilton was the first plush Western hotel in town. Before 1989, it was a gleaming center of capitalism, offering a cushy refuge for Western travelers and a stark contrast to what was at the time a very gloomy city. Halfway down the hotel's facade, you'll see fragments of a 13th-century wall with a monument to the Renaissance King Mátyás Corvinus.

After the wall, continue along the second half of the Hilton Hotel facade. Turn right into the gift-shop entry, and then go right again inside the second glass door. Stairs on the left lead down to the Faust Wine Cellar (below a reconstructed 13th-century Dominican cloister), a friendly place with fine wine by the glass. For an even better look at what was here back then, go back up the stairs and turn left. As you enter the lounge, look out the back windows to see fragments of the 13th-century Dominican church incorporated into the structure of the hotel. If you stood here eight centuries ago, you'd be looking straight down the church's nave. You can even see crypt markers in the ground.

Back out on the street, cross the little park and duck into the entryway of the **Fortuna Passage.** Along the passageway to the courtyard, you can see the original Gothic arches of the house that once stood here. In the Middle Ages, every homeowner had the right to sell wine without paying taxes—but only in the passage of his own home. He'd set up a table here, and his neighbors would come by to taste the latest vintage. These passageways evolved into very social places, like the corner pub.

Leaving the Fortuna, turn left down Fortuna utca, where after a block you'll find the excellent little...

▲**Hungarian Commerce and Catering Museum (Magyar Keres-kedelmi És Vendéglátóipari Múzeum)**—Far more interesting than it sounds, this museum—filling two ground-floor wings of an old building—gives a look at workaday 19th-century Pest commerce. With the help of good English descriptions, you'll enjoy a peek into the fancy hotels, restaurants, and coffeehouses of the day. There's even a section on the 1896 festivities. The attendants are enthusiastic grannies who seem old enough to remember all this history firsthand. The second half (across the driveway, opposite the entrance) is the "Made in Hungary 1900–1950" exhibit with fun ads, toys, and fashions (200 Ft, covered by Budapest Card, Wed–Fri 10:00–17:00, Sat–Sun 10:00–18:00, closed Mon–Tue, Fortuna utca 4, Budapest I, tel. 1/375-6249).

At the end of Fortuna utca, you'll come to the...

Remains of St. Mary Magdalene Church—Remember that medieval Buda consisted of two segregated towns. Matthias Church was for Germans. But this half of the town was Hungarian, and these are the remains of the Hungarian church. Later, it became known as the Kapisztrán Templom, named after a hero of the Battle of Belgrade in 1456, an early success in the struggle to keep the Turks out of Europe. (King Mátyás' father, János Hunyadi, was another hero of that battle.) The pope was so tickled by the victory that he decreed that all church bells should toll at noon in memory of the battle—and, technically, they still do. Californians will recognize the Kapisztrán's Spanish name—San Juan de Capistrano. This church was destroyed by bombs in World War II, though no worse than the Matthias Church. But, since this part of town was depopulated after the war, there was no longer a need for a second church. The remains of the church were torn down, the steeple was rebuilt as a memorial, and a carillon was added—so that every day at noon, the bells can still toll.

Across the square from the church is a monument to San Juan de Capistrano. Walking around the big building, you come to a viewpoint overlooking modern Buda, and on the green hill beyond that, you find the Beverly Hills of Budapest—where the local rich and famous live. To the right, near the flagpole, is the entry to the...

Museum of Military History (Hadtörténeti Múzeum)—Exhibits cover Hungary's 1848 Revolution against the Hapsburgs and feature interesting photos of the revolts of 1956 and 1989. The 1848 revolt ended with the Hapsburg execution of 13 great Hungarian leaders. The Hapsburgs clinked their beer mugs to the victory. To this very day, many Hungarians don't clink their mugs; it's just bad style (400 Ft, covered by Budapest Card, April–Sept Tue–Sun 10:00–18:00, closed Mon, Oct–March Tue–Sun 10:00–16:00, closed Mon, closed first half of Jan, Tóth Árpád sétány 40, Budapest I, tel. 1/356-9522).

HUNGARIAN REVOLUTIONS

Foreign powers that have oppressed the Hungarians have found them tough to keep under control. Two revolutions in particular stand out. In each case, the Hungarians initially encountered bloodshed and more oppression, but ultimately brought about positive change. The dates these revolutions began remain national holidays.

Lajos Kossuth and the 1848 Revolution
Of the many Hungarian uprisings against Hapsburg rule (1526-1918), the 1848 Revolution was the most dramatic. In 1848, a wave of nationalism spread across Europe. The spirit of change caught on in Hungary, where lawyer and parliamentarian Lajos Kossuth led an uprising sparked on March 15th. Though the Austrians were initially overwhelmed by the revolt, they eventually brought in Russian troops to regain control. For a few years, the Hapsburgs cracked down on their Hungarian subjects—but within 20 years, they ceded half the authority of their empire to Budapest, creating the "Dual Monarchy."

Imre Nagy and the 1956 Uprising
The Hungarian politician Imre Nagy (EEM-ray nawzh, 1896–1958) was a lifelong communist. In the 1930s, he allegedly worked for the

Our guided stroll is finished. Under your feet lies one more sight-seeing attraction:

Labyrinth of Buda Castle—Between the Royal Palace and Matthias Church is the Labyrinth of Buda Castle (Budavári Labirintus). There are miles of caves burrowed under Castle Hill, carved out by water, expanded by the Turks, and used by locals during the siege of Buda at the end of World War II. If you've done everything else in town, you can explore these caverns and see a conceptual exhibit that traces human history (1,000 Ft, 25 percent discount with Budapest Card, daily 9:30–19:30, Úri utca 9, Budapest I, tel. 1/212-0207). After 18:00, they turn the lights out and give everyone gas lanterns. The exhibit loses something in the dark, but it's nicely spooky and a fun chance to startle amorous Hungarian teens—or be startled by mischievous ones.

Gellért Hill (Gellérthegy)
The hill rising from the Danube banks just downriver from the castle is Gellért Hill. When King István converted Hungary to Christianity in the year 1000, some of his relatives had other ideas. Bishop Gellért, a monk from Venice, came here to tutor István's son. But rebellious

Soviet secret police. In the late 1940s, he quickly moved up the hierarchy of Hungary's communist government, becoming prime minister in 1953. But in the Moscow shuffle following Stalin's death, Nagy was quickly demoted.

When violence broke out in Budapest on October 23, 1956, Nagy re-emerged as the leader of the reform movement. For a few short days, it seemed as though Hungary's communism would moderate—until Soviet tanks rumbled into Budapest, brutally put down the uprising, and occupied the city. By the time the Red Army left, 25,000 protesters were dead, and 250,000 Hungarians had fled to Austria. Nagy was arrested, given a sham trail, and executed in 1958. He was buried disgracefully, face-down in an unmarked grave, and his name was taboo in Hungary for 30 years.

Though the Uprising met a tragic end, within a few years Hungary's harshness did soften, and the milder, so-called "goulash communism" emerged. As the Eastern Bloc thawed in 1989, Nagy became a hero. His body was discovered and given a proper reburial in July of that exciting year—heralding the quickly approaching end of the communist era.

Magyars put the bishop in a barrel, drove long nails in from the outside, and rolled him down this hill, tenderizing him to death. Gellért became the patron saint of Budapest and gave his name to the hill that killed him.

Gellért Hill's only real attraction is the **baths** at the Gellért Hotel (see "Budapest's Baths," page 237). The hill is a fine place to commune with nature through a hike or jog.

Monument Hike—The north slope of Gellért Hill is good for a low-impact hike. You'll see many interesting monuments, most notably the memorial to Bishop Gellért himself (can't miss it as you cross the Elizabeth Bridge on Hegyalja út). A bit farther up, seek out a newer monument to the world's great philosophers—Eastern, Western, and in between, from Gandhi to Plato to Jesus. Nearby is a scenic overlook with a king and a queen holding hands on either side of the Danube.

Citadella—This strategic hill-capping fortress was built by the Hapsburgs after the 1848 Revolution to keep an eye on their Hungarian subjects. There's not much to do up here (no museum or exhibits, just a hotel), but it's a good destination for an uphill hike, and provides excellent views over all of Budapest.

The hill is crowned by the **Liberation Monument,** featuring a woman holding aloft a palm branch. The locals call it "the lady with the big fish" or "the great bottle opener." She originally held a plane propeller, since the monument was designed to commemorate Admiral Horthy's son, who had died in a plane crash. But when the communists moved in, they decided to make it a monument to their own "liberation" of Hungary instead. The heroic Soviet soldier—who once inspired the workers with a huge red star from the base of the monument—is now in Statue Park (see below).

Cave Church (Sziklatemplom)—Hidden in the hillside on the south end of the hill (across the street from Gellért Hotel) is Budapest's atmospheric cave church—literally burrowed into the rock face. The communists bricked up this church when they came to power, but now it's open for visitors once again (free entry, but closed to sightseers during services).

Pest

Central Pest (Belváros), Along Váci utca

▲**Vörösmarty tér**—This prominent square (VOO-roosh-mar-tee tehr) at the north end of the Váci utca pedestrian boulevard is named for a 19th-century Romantic poet (see his statue in the center) who stirred nationalistic spirit with his writing. It's a good place to get oriented to Pest. Find the landmark **Gerbeaud** pastry shop at the north end of the square. Between the World Wars, the well-to-do ladies of Budapest would meet here after shopping their way up Váci utca. Today it's still *the* meeting point in Budapest (described under "Cafés and Pastry Shops," below).

As you face Gerbeaud, the street to your left leads to the Danube embankment (ideal for a scenic stroll), and the street to your right leads past Erzsébet tér (once Pest's market square) to Andrássy út, lined with sights, restaurants, and hotels (see "Andrássy út" sights, below). If you were to jog left around Gerbeaud and then go straight, you'd reach the Parliament in about 10 minutes (see "More Sights in Central Pest," below).

The yellow Metro stop in the middle of the square is the entrance to the shallow *Földalatti,* or "underground"—the first subway on the Continent (built for the millennial celebration in 1896). Today, it still carries passengers to Andrássy út sights (it runs under that street all the way to City Park).

Three hundred years ago, Vörösmarty tér was a rough-and-tumble, often-flooded quarter just outside the Pest city walls. People came here to enjoy brutal, staged fights between bloodhounds and bears (like cockfights, only bigger and angrier, with more fur and teeth). The Turkish invaders had finally been forced out of Pest, and the city was nearly deserted. After a series of battles for Hungarian independence, the

Pest Center Sights

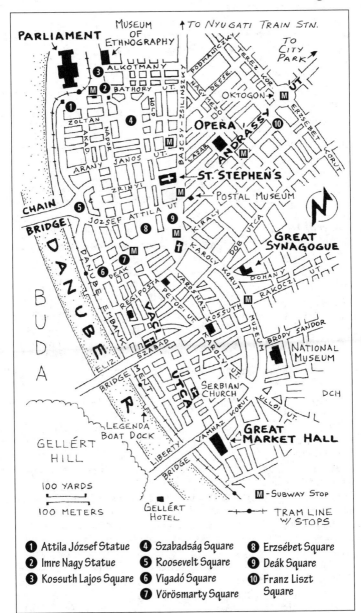

1 Attila József Statue
2 Imre Nagy Statue
3 Kossuth Lajos Square
4 Szabadság Square
5 Roosevelt Square
6 Vigadó Square
7 Vörösmarty Square
8 Erzsébet Square
9 Deák Square
10 Franz Liszt Square

Austrian Hapsburgs moved into ruined Pest in the 1710s. They populated the city with Germans. (While there was a small Hungarian minority, most Magyars lived in the country.) The Germans of Pest began rebuilding the city, virtually from scratch—so most of the buildings you'll see are no older than 300 years.

For more of the story, stroll down the street across the square from Gerbeaud: Váci utca.

▲▲Váci utca—This pedestrian boulevard—Budapest's shopping and tourism artery—was dreamland for Eastern Europeans back in the 1980s. It was here that they fantasized about what it might be like to be free, while drooling over Nikes, Reeboks, and Big Macs before any of these Western evils were introduced elsewhere in the Warsaw Pact region.

Many tourists are mesmerized by this people-friendly stretch of souvenir stands, Internet cafés, and upscale boutiques—thinking wrongly that this is the "real" Budapest. But a ramble along Váci utca (VAH-tsee OO-tzah) does have stories to tell, and you're sure to stroll here at some point during your visit. The following self-guided walk will help you uncover artifacts of authentic Pest between the postcard racks.

"Váci utca" literally means "street to Vác"—a town 25 miles to the north. This has long been the street where the elite of Pest would go shopping, then strut their stuff for their neighbors on an evening promenade (*korzó* in Hungarian). Today, the tourists do the strutting here—and the Hungarians go to suburban shopping malls.

As you walk, be sure to look up. Along this street and throughout Pest, spectacular facades begin on the second floor, above a plain entryway (in the 1970s, ground-floor shop windows were made uniformly dull by the communist government). Pan up to see some of Pest's best architecture. These were the townhouses of the aristocracy whose mansions dotted the countryside.

At the end of the first block, next to the Tatuum store on the right, a **plaque** notes that Pest's medieval town wall was torn down in 1789. The no-longer-needed wall had been gradually crumbling for centuries, and as residents rebuilt from the Turkish occupation, it was just getting in the way.

On the next block find the quirky **Modernist facade** at #8 on the left (over the Clinique shop). Compare this one to the building marked *Douglas* (#11a, across the street a few doors up). The first is more traditional Modernism, but the second is a great example of the **Secession** style. Modernist architecture was rebellious: It rejected what came before—which is why it still looks "weird" to us today. But the Secession did one better and rejected Modernism.

At the end of the block, the unassuming **McDonald's** (on the right, down Régiposta utca) was a landmark in Eastern Europe—the first McDonald's behind the Iron Curtain. Budapest has always been a little more rebellious, independent, and cosmopolitan than its Eastern

European neighbors, who flocked here during the communist era. Long lines for a burger famously went down the street—but it wasn't "fast food," it was "West food." Today McDonald's actually feels sophisticated and cutting-edge—definitely not a cheap place for locals, but popular nevertheless.

Continuing your stroll, you'll notice that some of the **facades** are plain (like the one above the tobacco shop on the right, just after the street leading to McDonald's). Many of these used to be more ornate, like the others, but they were destroyed by WWII bombs and rebuilt boring.

At the halfway point on your Váci utca stroll (midway between the square and the big market hall), an underpass takes you under busy Szabad street (Szabad sajtó út). While you're down there, enjoy photos of Budapest (with English descriptions) from the turn of the 20th century, when the city was booming.

The last stretch of Váci utca dead-ends at the huge market hall. This used to be a strongly Serbian neighborhood. (Around the next corner to the left, there's still a **Serbian Orthodox church**—heavy with incense and packed with icons.) Traditionally, Hungary's territory included most of Slovakia and large parts of Romania, Croatia, and Serbia—and people from all of those places (along with Jews and Gypsies) flocked to Buda and Pest. And yet, most of the locals in this cosmopolitan city still speak Hungarian. Through centuries of foreign invasions and visitors, Budapest remains Magyar. (Remember that after the Turks left, Budapest was mostly German. The Germans didn't go anywhere...they "became" Hungarian, assimilated into the local culture.)

At the end of Váci utca, you'll come to the...

▲▲**Great Market Hall (Nagyvásárcsarnok)**—This market hall (along with 4 others) was built—you know it—around the year 1896. The cavernous interior features three levels.

The ground floor has produce stands, bakeries, butcher stalls, heaps of paprika, goose liver, and sausages. Upstairs are fun, super-cheap stand-up Hungarian-style fast-food joints and six-stool pubs, along with a great selection of traditional souvenirs (you're welcome to haggle). Downstairs it's pungent with tanks of still-healthy carp, catfish, and perch, and piles of pickles.

The market was kept open during communism. Margaret Thatcher came to visit in 1989 (find the photo midway down the main aisle on right). She expected atrocious conditions compared to English markets, but was pleasantly surprised to find this place up to snuff. This was, after all, "goulash communism" (Hungary's pragmatic mix that allowed a little private enterprise to keep people going). On the steps of this building, she delivered a historic speech about open society, heralding the impending arrival of the market economy.

The market hall is ideal for lunch, picnic shopping, and people-watching (Mon 6:00–17:00, Tue–Fri 6:00–18:00, Sat 6:00–14:00, closed Sun, Fővám körút 1-3, Budapest IX, M3: Kálvin tér). See "Eating," below, for ideas.

From the market, walk to the river. You'll pass (on the left) the University of Economics, which was called Karl Marx University 15 years ago. The bridge leads straight to the Gellért Hotel with its famous hot-springs bath at the foot of Gellért Hill (see "Budapest's Baths," page 237). Trams #2 and #2A run from here directly back to central Pest and the Chain Bridge.

More Sights in Central Pest

▲Hungarian Parliament (Országház)—The Parliament building, like so much of Budapest, was built around the city's millennial celebration in

1896. Its elegant neo-Gothic design and riverside location were inspired by its counterpart in London. This enormous building—with 12 miles of stairs—was appropriate for a time when Budapest ruled much of Eastern Europe. But today it's just plain too big—the legislature only occupies an eighth of the building. Architecture snobs shake their heads and wonder why this frilly Gothic monstrosity is topped with a Renaissance dome. (To make matters worse, there used to be a huge red communist star on top of the tallest spire.)

The best views of the building are from across the Danube—especially in the late-afternoon sunlight. Tours of the Parliament's opulent interior include the elegant main entryway, a legislative chamber, and the Hungarian crown, under the ornate dome (2,000 Ft, English tours often daily at 10:00, 12:00, and 14:00, but can change so confirm in advance; follow signs around to entry "X," find the line for individual tickets, join the disorganized queue and make it clear to the guard that you want an *individual* ticket; eventually you'll be allowed to enter the door marked *X*, pay cashier and return to the mob to wait for your tour; Kossuth tér 1-3, Budapest V, M2: Kossuth tér, tel. 1/441-4904, www.mkogy.hu).

Kossuth tér—The square behind the Parliament building has several interesting monuments. Close to the water, on the end of the Parliament facing the Chain Bridge, look for a statue of **Attila József,** a popular modern poet who committed suicide at age 32. Straight back from the river, on Vértanúk tere, a statue of the pensive **Imre Nagy,** hero of the 1956 Uprising, stands on a bridge (see page 218). Also on Kossuth tér is the...

Museum of Ethnography (Néprajzi Múzeum)—This museum has exhibits on both Hungarian and international culture (500 Ft, covered by Budapest Card, March–Oct Tue–Sun 10:00–18:00, closed Mon,

Nov–Feb Tue–Sun 10:00–17:00, closed Mon, Kossuth tér 12, Budapest V, M2: Kossuth tér, tel. 1/473-2400).

Hungarian National Museum (Magyar Nemzeti Múzeum)—One of Budapest's biggest museums features all manner of Hungarian historic bric-a-brac, from pre-Magyar Roman artifacts to communist kitsch. Twenty rooms (with English descriptions) take you up to the 1989 revolution. The 1848 Revolution against Hapsburg rule was declared from the steps of this building (600 Ft, covered by Budapest Card, Tue–Sun 10:00–18:00, closed Mon, near Great Market Hall at Múzeum körút 14-16, Budapest VIII, tel. 1/338-2122).

▲**Great Synagogue (Zsinagóga)**—The impressively restored synagogue is the second-biggest in the world, after New York City's. As the former co-capital of an empire that included millions of Jews, Budapest itself always had a large concentration of Jewish residents. Before World War II, 5 percent of Hungary's population and 25 percent of Budapest's was Jewish. Today, only half of one percent of Hungarians are Jewish—and most of them are in Budapest.

While several traditional synagogues are nearby (this is Pest's Jewish quarter), the Great Synagogue is reformed and—with its nave, pulpit, and pipe organ flanking the high altar—it looks like a church with the symbols switched. It was built in the 1860s, when Jews wanted to feel more integrated into the community. The balconies were originally for women, but today men and women sit anywhere and together. The Moorish-flavored decor is a reminder of how Jewish culture flourished in Iberia.

Your synagogue ticket includes, in the same building, the **Jewish Museum** (Zsidó Múzeum, 600 Ft, covered by Budapest Card, mid-April–Oct Mon–Thu 10:00–17:00, Fri and Sun 10:00–14:00, Nov–mid-April Mon–Thu 10:00–15:00, Fri and Sun 10:00–14:00, always closed Sat and Jewish holidays, often closed mid-Dec–mid-Jan, last entry 30 min before closing, Dohány utca 2, Budapest VII, M1, M2, or M3: Deák tér, tel. 01/342-8949).

Behind the synagogue, the **"Tree of Life"** sculpture was built on the site of mass graves of those killed by the Nazis. (Hungary lost 600,000 Jews to the Holocaust.) The willow makes an upside-down menorah, each individual leaf lists the name of a victim, and pebbles represent prayers. You can visit the Tree even if you don't buy a ticket for the synagogue (enter through synagogue security gate and go straight ahead through doors and under arcade to the park behind the synagogue; if synagogue is closed, go around left side to view monument through a fence).

Aviv Travel leads **tours** of the synagogue and the Jewish quarter (basic 1-hr English tour covers synagogue, museum, and Tree of Life, 1,900 Ft or 1,700 Ft with Budapest Card, includes admission, Mon–Thu hrly on the half-hour 10:30–15:30, Fri and Sun 10:30, 11:30, and 12:30 only, kiosk by synagogue entry, tel. 1/462-0477).

▲**Danube Embankment (Dunakorzó)**—Pest's breezy riverfront promenade (from Elizabeth Bridge to the Chain Bridge) is a fine place for a stroll. Start on Vigadó tér, two blocks towards the river from Vörösmarty tér, and head southward. Along the way, keep an eye out for the Little Princess statue leaning on the railing—one of Budapest's symbols, even though it's just over a decade old. When Prince Charles visited Budapest, he liked this statue so much that he had a replica made for himself. You'll pass a few souvenir stalls and big, fancy hotels (including Hyatt and InterContinental), and enjoy sweeping views of Buda, some of the international river-cruise ships, and the city's many bridges.

Roosevelt Square—If you walk to the Chain Bridge, you'll hit Roosevelt Square, fringed by impressive architecture. The blocky "Spinach House"—an ugly green communist office block—is infamous for its terrible design and craftsmanship, a loud reminder of how wretched those times were for most. The fine Art Nouveau Grasham Palace faces the bridge. Originally the local headquarters of an English insurance company, it's now a new Four Seasons Hotel. (From here, the riverside tram #2 or #2A, which stops near the modern InterContinental hotel, zips you three stops to the Great Market Hall, or bus #16 will take you up Castle Hill.)

▲**Chain Bridge (Széchenyi Lánchíd)**—One of the world's great bridges

connects Pest's Roosevelt tér and Buda's Adam Clark tér. This historic, iconic bridge, guarded by lions (symbolizing power), is Budapest's most enjoyable and convenient bridge to cross on foot. (This is especially handy for commuting to the top of Castle Hill, since both bus #16 and the funicular to the top begin from the Buda end of the bridge.)

Until the mid-19th century, only pontoon barges spanned the Danube between Buda and Pest. In the winter, the pontoons had to be pulled in, leaving locals to rely on ferries (in good weather) or a frozen river. People often walked across the frozen Danube only to get stuck on the other side during a thaw, with nothing to do but wait for another cold snap.

Count István Széchenyi was stranded for a week trying to get to his father's funeral. After missing it, Széchenyi decided to commission Budapest's first permanent bridge. The Chain Bridge was built by

MILLENNIUM UNDERGROUND OF 1896

Built to get the masses of visitors conveniently out to Heroes' Square, this fun and extremely handy little Metro line follows Andrássy út from Vörösmarty Square (Pest's main square) to City Park. Just 20 steps below street level, it's so shallow you must follow the signs on the street (listing end points) to gauge the right direction, because there's no underpass for switching platforms. The first underground on the Continent (London's is older), it originally had horse-drawn trains. Trains depart every couple of minutes. Recently renovated, the M1 line retains its 1896 atmosphere along with fun B&W photos of the age.

Scotsman Adam Clark between 1842 and 1849, and it immediately became an important symbol of Budapest. Like all of the city's bridges, the Chain Bridge was destroyed by Nazis at the end of World War II, but was quickly rebuilt.

Margaret Island (Margitsziget)—Budapesters come to play in this huge leafy park, a wonderful spot for strolling and people-watching (accessible from Margaret Bridge—trams #4 and #6 stop at the gateway to the island). The island is also home to some of Budapest's many baths.

Andrássy út

Connecting central Pest to City Park, Andrássy út is Budapest's main boulevard, lined with shops, theaters, cafés, and locals living well. Budapesters claim it's like the Champs-Élysées and Broadway rolled into one. While that's a stretch, it is a good place to stroll and get a feel for today's urban Pest. The best part to wander is between the boulevard's beginning at Deák tér and the Oktogon.

The following sights are listed in order, from Deák tér (in central Pest) to City Park. The M1 line runs every couple minutes just under the street—so if you get tired of walking, it's a snap to skip several blocks ahead (stops marked by yellow *Földalatti* signs, see above).

St. Stephen's Basilica (Szent István Bazilika)—Step into Budapest's largest Catholic church and you'll see not Jesus but St. István (Stephen), Hungary's first Christian king, glowing above the high altar in the otherwise vast and gloomy interior. (See Statue of Saint St. István listing, above, for more on St. István.) The church is only about 100 years old—like most Budapest landmarks, it was built around 1896. Its primary claim to fame is that it's the resting place of the "holy right hand" of St.

István. The sacred fist is in a jeweled box in the chapel to left of main altar (follow signs for *Szent Jobb Kápolna,* chapel is free). Pop in a 100-Ft coin for two minutes of light. Although it looks like a major and important landmark and it's packed with tour groups, the rest of the church isn't that compelling (free, Mon–Fri 9:00–17:00, Sat 9:00–13:00, Sun 13:00–17:00, Szent István tér, Budapest V, M1: Bajcsy-Zsilinszky út or M3: Arany János utca).

The church also has a measly treasury and panoramic **observation deck,** with a decent view that gives a sense of the sprawl of Pest (600 Ft, 20 percent discount with Budapest Card, elevator to mid-level then 137 stairs or smaller elevator plus a few stairs to top of tower, April–May daily 10:00–16:30, June–Aug daily 9:30–18:00, Sept–Oct daily 10:00–17:30, closed Nov–March).

▲**Postal Museum (Postamúzeum)**—This quirky museum has a delightful collection of old post boxes, telephones, and paraphernalia that was cutting-edge a century ago. The elegant old merchant's mansion—with big glass chandeliers and creaky parquet floors, lived in until 1938—is as interesting as the museum's collection (100 Ft, covered by Budapest Card, Tue–Sun 10:00–18:00, closed Mon, take advantage of the loaner English-language sheets, just up the street from St. Stephen's at Andrássy út 3, Budapest VI, M1: Bajcsy-Zsilinszky út, look for easy-to-miss sign and ring bell to get upstairs, tel. 1/269-6838).

▲**Hungarian State Opera House (Magyar Állami Operaház)**—The neo-Renaissance home of the Hungarian State Opera features performances at bargain prices almost daily (see "Budapest Music Scene," page 239). Even if you don't see an opera here, you can slip in the front door and check out the ornate entryway when the box office is open (Mon–Sat 11:00-19:00, Sun 16:00-19:00, Andrássy út 22, Budapest VI, M1: Opera).

For a more in-depth visit, take one of the excellent **tours** in English (nearly daily at 15:00 and 16:00, reservations not necessary, 2,000 Ft, 20 percent discount with Budapest Card, buy in opera shop—around to the right as you face main entrance, shop open Mon–Fri 10:30–13:00 & 13:30–17:00, Sat–Sun 13:30–17:00, tel. 1/332-8197, ext. 275).

Franz Liszt Square (Liszt Ferenc tér)—The leafy, trendy square on the right (south) side of Andrássy út is surrounded by hip, overpriced cafés and restaurants. This is *the* scene for Budapest's yuppies. At the far end of the square is the Music Academy also named for Liszt—a German composer with a Hungarian name who loved his family's Magyar heritage (though he didn't speak Hungarian) and spent his last five years in Budapest.

Oktogon—During the communist era, this square—at the intersection of Andrássy út and the Great Ring Road *(Nagykörút)*—was called

Sights, Hotels and Restaurants

1 K+K Hotel Opera
2 Cotton House
3 Hotel Ambra
4 Hotel Medosz
5 Hotel Délibáb
6 Radio Inn
7 Best Hostel
8 Liszt Sq. eateries
9 Articsóka Rest.
10 Restaurant Művészinas & Duran Szendvics Sandwich Shop
11 Gundel Restaurant
12 Művész Kávéház Café

COUNT ANDRÁSSY AND SISSY

You'll see the names Andrássy and Sissy (or Elizabeth) a lot in Budapest. A key player in the 1848 Revolution, **Count Julius Andrássy** ultimately helped forge the "Dual Monarchy" of the Austro-Hungarian Empire. He served as the Hungarian prime minister and Austro-Hungarian foreign minister (1871-1879), eventually being forced to step down after his unpopular campaign to appropriate Bosnia and Herzegovina (and consequently boost the Slav population).

Sissy was **Empress Elizabeth,** the Princess Diana of the early 20th-century Hapsburgs (see page 427). While she was married to Emperor Franz Josef, she spent seven years in Budapest—enjoying horseback riding, the local cuisine, and the company of the charming and good-looking Count Andrássy. Her third daughter—believed to be the count's—was known as the Little Hungarian Princess.

November 7 tér in honor of the Bolshevik Revolution (and Andrássy út was renamed Stalin út, and later People's Republic boulevard). Today kids nickname the square "American tér" for the fast-food joints littering the square and streets nearby. From this square, Andrássy út gradually becomes the dull diplomatic quarter—less colorful, with tame, embassy-lined streets and stately mansions. From the center of Andrássy út, you can see the column of Heroes' Square at the end of the boulevard.

▲▲▲**House of Terror (Terror Háza)**—The former headquarters for the darkest sides of two different regimes, the Arrowcross (Nazi-occupied Hungary's version of the Gestapo) and the ÁVO/ÁVH (communist Hungary's secret police) is now, fittingly, an excellent museum of that time of terror. An overhang casts the shadow of the word "TERROR" onto the building.

Hungary initially allied with Hitler to retain a degree of self-determination, to try to regain their huge territorial losses after World War I, and to avoid having to ship Jews to concentration camps. But in the waning days of World War II, the country eventually was overtaken by the Nazi-affiliated Arrowcross, whose members did their best to exterminate Budapest's Jews. They killed Jews one by one in the streets, and were known to tie several victims together, shoot one of them, and throw him into the freezing Danube—dragging the others in with him. They executed hundreds in the basement of this building. When the communists moved into Hungary, they took over the same building as headquarters for their secret police (the ÁVO, later renamed ÁVH). To keep dissent to a minimum, the secret police terrorized, tried, deported, or executed anyone suspected of being an enemy of the state.

The museum's atrium features a Soviet tank and a huge wall covered with portraits of the victims of this building. The modern, stylish, high-tech exhibit (starting on the top floor and spiraling down) is designed for Hungarians, but the included English audioguide gives tourists the same powerful experience. Each room is stocked with free English fliers.

The museum has many memorable exhibits—including rooms featuring gulag life, social realist art and propaganda, a labyrinth of pork-fat bricks reminding old-timers of the harsh conditions of the 1950s (lard on bread for dinner), and religion (joining the Church was a way to express rebellion). For elderly Hungarian visitors, this is a powerful experience—they know many of the victims and the perpetrators, and have personal memories of the terrors that came with Hungary's "double occupation."

The last section begins with a three-minute video of a guard explaining the execution process, which plays as you descend by elevator into the prison basement. In the early 1950s, this basement was the scene of torture; in 1956, it became a clubhouse of sorts for the local communist youth club. It's renovated today circa 1955. During the 1956 Uprising, 250,000 fled to Austria and the West during the two weeks of chaos before the USSR pulled a Tiananmen Square-style crackdown (see page 218). The Hall of Tears remembers 25,000 who died in '56. The last two rooms—with the only color video clips—show the festive and exhilarating days in 1989 when the Soviets departed, making way for freedom. Scenes include the reburial of local hero, Imre Nagy; the Pope's visit; and walls of "victimizers"—local members and supporters of the Arrowcross and ÁVO, many of whom are still living, and who were never brought to justice (3,000 Ft—yes, it's the most expensive admission in Hungary, locals pay only 1,000 Ft, no CC, café, bookshop, Tue–Sun 10:00–18:00, closed Mon, Andrássy út 60, Budapest VI, M1:Vörösmarty utca, tel. 1/374-2600, www.terrorhaza.hu).

▲▲Heroes' Square (Hősök tere)—Like much of Budapest, this "Who's Who in Hungarian History" at the end of Andrássy út was built to celebrate the city's thousandth birthday in 1896 (M1: Hősök tere). More than just the hottest place in town for skateboarding, this is the site of several museums and the gateway to City Park (filled with diversions for sightseers).

Step right up to the **Millennium Monument** to meet the world's most historic Hungarians (who look to me like their language sounds). The granddaddy of all Magyars, Árpád, stands proudly at the bottom of the pillar, looking down Andrássy út. The 118-foot-tall pillar supports the archangel Gabriel as he offers the crown to St. István (he accepted it and Christianized the Magyars). In front of the pillar is the Hungarian War Memorial (fenced in now to keep skateboarders from enjoying its perfect slope). Behind the pillar, colonnades feature Hungarian VIPs. Look for names you recognize: István, Béla IV, Mátyás Corvinus. But hey...where are the Hapsburgs? At the time of the monument's construction, Budapest was part of the Austrian Empire, and Hapsburgs stood in the right-hand colonnade. When Hungary regained its independence in World War I, the people tore down the sculpture of the unpopular Franz Josef. (The less-hated Maria Theresa was left alone...but was ultimately destroyed by a WWII bomb.) After World War II, the Hapsburgs were replaced with Hungarians. In fact, the last two heroes—Ferenc Rákóczi and Lajos Kossuth—were revolutionaries who fought against Austria. The sculptures on the top corners of the two colonnades represent, in order from left to right, Work & Welfare, War, Peace, and the Importance of Packing Light.

As you face Árpád, the **Museum of Fine Arts** (Szépművészeti Múzeum), which has an especially good Spanish collection, is to your left (800 Ft, covered by Budapest Card, Tue–Sun 10:00–17:30, closed Mon, tel. 1/469-7100). The **Palace of Art** (Műcsarnok), used for temporary contemporary-art exhibits, is to your right (600 Ft, covered by Budapest Card, Tue–Sun 10:00–18:00, Thu until 20:00, closed Mon, tel. 1/363-2671). In the basement of the Palace of Art, you'll find a fun but over-priced 25-minute **Countryrama 3-D movie** about Hungary (1,000 Ft, 50 percent discount with Budapest Card, shown every 30 min on the half hour, mid-March–Sept Tue–Sun 10:30–17:30, closed Mon, Oct–mid-March Fri–Sun 10:30–14:30, closed Mon–Thu, tel. 1/460-7033, www.countryrama.hu). While the 3-D is fuzzy, this tired video overview of the countryside is relaxing and affords a quick swing through Hungary in a Travel Channel kind of way. Since majority rules for language, the movie is generally in English (and everyone else gets headphones).

If you leave Heroes' Square between the two colonnades behind the main pillar, you'll cross a bridge into the...

▲▲**City Park (Városliget)**—This is the city's not-so-central Central Park. The park was the site of the overblown 1896 Millennium Exhibition, celebrating Hungary's 1,000th birthday...and it's still packed with huge party decorations: a zoo with quirky Art Nouveau buildings, a replica of a Transylvanian castle, a massive bath/swimming complex, walking paths, and an amusement park. The park is filled with unwind-

TONIGHT WE'RE GONNA PARTY LIKE IT'S 1896

Visitors to Budapest need only remember one date: 1896. For the millennial celebration of their ancestors' arrival in Europe, Hungarians threw a huge blowout party. In a thousand years, the Magyars had gone from being a nomadic Central Asian tribe that terrorized the Continent to sharing the throne of one of the most successful empires Europe had ever seen.

Much as the year 2000 saw a fit of new construction worldwide, Budapest used their millennial celebration as an excuse to build monuments and buildings appropriate for the capital of a huge empire, including:

- **Heroes' Square Millennium Monument**
- **Vajdahunyad Castle** (in City Park)
- The riverside **Parliament** building (96 meters tall, with 96 steps at the main entry)
- **St. István's Basilica** (also 96 meters tall)
- The M1 (yellow) Metro line, a.k.a. *Földalatti* ("Underground")—the first subway on the Continent
- The **Great Market Hall** (and four other market halls)
- **Andrássy út** and most of the fine buildings lining it
- The **State Opera House**
- A complete rebuilding of the **Matthias Church** (on Castle Hill)
- The **Fishermen's Bastion** decorative terrace (by Matthias Church)

Ninety-six is the key number in Hungary—even the national anthem (when sung in the proper tempo) takes 96 seconds. But after all this fuss, it's too bad that the date was wrong: A commission—convened to establish the exact year of the Magyars' debut—determined it happened in 895. But city leaders knew they'd never make an 1895 deadline, and requested the finding be changed to 896.

ing locals. If the sightseeing grind's got you down, spend the afternoon taking a mini-vacation from your busy vacation, the way Budapesters do—stroll in the park and soak in the baths.

Orient yourself from the bridge behind Heroes' Square: The huge Vajdahunyad Castle is on your right (go straight and look for bridge to enter complex). Straight into the park and on the left are the big green domes of the fun, relaxing Széchenyi Baths (see "Budapest's Baths," below). And the zoo is past the lake on the left. The fancy Gundel restaurant (see "Eating," page 237) is near the zoo.

Vajdahunyad Castle (Vajdahunyad vára)—The huge complex is a replica of a famous castle in Transylvania (part of Hungary for centuries), surrounded by other styles of traditionally Hungarian architecture (textbook Romanesque, Gothic, Renaissance, and Baroque). Some find it artificial in a Walt Disney World sort of way; others think it's pretty cool. You can enter the "castle" complex for free to poke around the grounds. (After crossing the bridge behind Heroes' Square, turn right and walk for 3 minutes.)

As you enter the complex through the castle facade, you'll see a replica of a 13th-century **Benedictine chapel** on the left—Budapest's most popular spot for weekend weddings in the summer. Farther ahead on the right, you'll see an ornate Baroque mansion—which houses, of all things, the **Museum of Hungarian Agriculture** (Magyar Mezőgazdasági Múzeum, 500 Ft, covered by Budapest Card, March–Oct Tue–Fri and Sun 10:00–17:00, Sat 10:00–18:00, closed Mon, Nov–Feb Tue–Fri 10:00–16:00, Sat–Sun 10:00–17:00, closed Mon, last entry 30 min before closing). The museum brags that it's Europe's biggest agriculture museum...but the sumptuous interior is more interesting than the exhibits.

Across the street from the museum entry, you'll see a monument to **Anonymous,** specifically the Anonymous who penned the first Hungarian history in the Middle Ages.

Zoo (Állatkert)—Aside from animals, the zoo also has redeeming sightseeing value: Many of its structures—including the entry gate and the elephant house—are playful bits of turn-of-the-century Art Nouveau. Just inside the gate, look for the *Információ* kiosk to the left to grab the handy "A Walk in the Zoo" brochure. To reach the Art Nouveau elephant house, turn right inside the entry, then right again at the fork, and look for the white-and-turquoise tower. The zoo is a perfect example of a sight that's not really worth the price of entry, but makes for a fun 15-minute walk-through with the Budapest Card (1,800 Ft, covered by Budapest Card, May–Aug daily 9:00–19:00, April and Sept until 18:00, March and Oct until 17:00, Nov–Feb until 16:00, Állatkerti út 6-12, Budapest XIV, tel. 1/364-0109).

Óbuda

Budapest was originally three cities: Buda, Pest, and Óbuda. Óbuda (or "old Buda") is the oldest of the three—the first known residents of the region (Celts) settled here, and today it's still littered with ruins from the next occupants (Romans). Despite all the history, the district is disappointing, worth a look only for those interested in Roman ruins or

20th-century Hungarian painting and sculpture. To reach Óbuda, go to Batthyány tér in Buda (M2 Metro line) and catch the HÉV suburban train north to the Árpád híd stop. The Vasarely Museum is 50 yards from the station. The town square is 100 yards beyond that, and 200 yards later (turn left at the ladies with the umbrellas), you'll find the Imre Varga Collection.

Vasarely Museum—This museum features two floors of eye-popping, colorful paintings by the founder of Op Art, Victor Vasarely. The exhibition follows his artistic evolution from his youth as a graphic designer to the playful optical illusions he was most famous for. If this art gets you pondering Rubik's cube, it may come as no surprise that Ernő Rubik was a professor of mathematics right here in Budapest. Vasarely, and the movement he pioneered (heavy on optical illusions), helped inspire the trippy styles of the 1960s (400 Ft, covered by Budapest Card, Tue–Sun 10:00v17:30, closed Mon, Szentlélek tér 6, Budapest III, HÉV north to Árpád híd stop, tel. 1/388-7551). This museum is immediately on the right as you leave the Árpád híd HÉV station.

Óbuda Town Square—If you keep going past the Vasarely Museum and turn right, you enter Óbuda's cute Town Square (Fő tér). The big, yellow building was the Óbuda Town Hall when this was its own city. Today it's still the office of the district mayor. To the right of the Town Hall, you'll see a whimsical, much-photographed statue of women with umbrellas. Replicas of this sculpture, by local artist Imre Varga, decorate the gardens of wealthy summer homes on Lake Balaton. Varga created many of Budapest's distinctive monuments. His museum is just down the street (at the umbrella ladies, turn left).

▲**Imre Varga Collection (Varga Imre Kiállítóház)**—Imre Varga worked from the 1950s through the 1990s. His statues, while occasionally religious, were mostly comments on life during communist times, when there were three types of artists: banned, tolerated, and supported. Varga was tolerated. Themes include forced marches and mass graves. One headless statue comes with medallions nailed into his chest. (These medallions were Varga's own, from his pre-communist military service; anyone with such medallions was persecuted by communists in the 1950s...so Varga disposed of his this way.) Varga actually drops by each Saturday morning at 10:00 to chat with visitors. He speaks English, and, while now in his 80s, he enjoys explaining his art. Don't miss the garden, where you'll see three prostitutes illustrating "the passing of time" (250 Ft, covered by Budapest Card, Tue–Sun 10:00–18:00, closed Mon, Laktanya utca 7, Budapest III, tel. 1/250-0274).

Aquincum Museum—Long before Magyars laid eyes on the Danube, Óbuda was the Roman city of Aquincum. Here you can explore the remains of the 2,000-year-old Roman town and amphitheater. The museum is proud of its centerpiece, a water organ (700 Ft, covered by Budapest Card, May–Sept Tue–Sun 9:00–18:00, closed Mon; Oct and latter half of April Tue–Sun 9:00–17:00, closed Mon; closed Nov–mid-April, Szentendrei út 139, Budapest III, HÉV north to Aquincum stop, tel. 1/250-1650). From the HÉV stop, cross the busy road and turn to the right. Go through the railway underpass, and you'll see the ruins ahead and on the left as you emerge.

Southwest of Buda

▲▲Statue Park (Szoborpark)—When regimes fall, so do their monuments. Just think of all those statues of Stalin and Lenin—or Saddam Hussein—crashing to the ground. Throughout Eastern Europe, people couldn't wait to get rid of these reminders of their oppressors. But some clever entrepreneur hoarded Budapest's and now has collected them in a park just outside of the city—where tourists flock to get a taste of the communist era.

Under the communists, creativity was discouraged. Art was acceptable only if it furthered the goals of the state. The only sanctioned art in communist Europe was **social realism.** Aside from a few important figureheads, individuals didn't matter. Everyone was a cog in the machine—strong, stoic, doing their job well and proudly for the good of the people. Individual characteristics and distinguishing features were unimportant; people are represented as machines serving their nation.

At Statue Park, you'll see the Communist All-Stars (Marx, Engels, and Lenin—in his favorite "hailing a cab" pose), along with other Socialist symbols (the stoic soldier, the faceless worker, and the tireless and heroic mother). The gift shop is a fun parade of communist kitsch; consider picking up the good English guidebook, the CD of "Communism's Greatest Hits," and maybe a model of a Trabant (600 Ft, covered by Budapest Card, daily 10:00–sunset, 6 miles southwest of center at the corner of Balatoni út and Szabadkai út, Budapest XXII, tel. 1/424-7500, www.szoborpark.hu).

Getting to Statue Park: The Park runs a direct bus from Deák tér in downtown Budapest (where all three Metro lines converge, bus stop well-marked with Statue Park logo, year-round daily at 11:00, March–Oct also at 15:00, July–Aug also at 10:00 and 16:00; round-trip takes 105 min total including a 40-min visit to the park, 1,950 Ft round-trip, 1,350 Ft with Budapest Card, price includes park entry). The trip by public transportation is too complicated: Take M3 line to Ferenciek tere, then red #7 bus to its end at Etele tér, then yellow Volán Bus from stall 2-3 in the direction Diosd-Erd (let the driver know your destination when you board); Statue Park is about 15 minutes into the trip—look for the red-brick entry and the statues on your right, and then signal for a stop.

Budapest's Baths

Hungary's Carpathian Basin is a thin crust on top of a lot of hot water. The Romans named their settlement here Aquincum—meaning "abundant waters"—and took advantage of those waters by building many baths. Centuries later, the occupying Turks revived the custom. Today, locals brag that if you poke a hole in the ground anywhere in Hungary, you'll find a hot-water spring. Judging from Budapest, they may be right: The city has 123 natural springs and 27 thermal baths *(fürdő)*. While these spas have traditionally served a medicinal purpose for the elderly, today Hungary is trying a new angle on its hot water: fun. Adventure water parks are springing up all over the country. (The preventative-health component is the icing on the cake.)

Budapest's baths were taken over by the communist government, and they're all still owned by the city. The two baths listed here are the best known, most representative, and most convenient for first-timers—one for locals, the other elegant and touristy. Both are equally good and should be a high priority for your visit. The uninitiated need not fear the baths—it's basically a series of warm swimming pools. While Budapest has some mostly-nude, segregated Turkish baths, the following two baths are generally mixed, with men and women clothed and together most of the time.

▲▲▲**Széchenyi Baths (Széchenyi fürdő)**—To soak with the locals, head for this bath complex—the big, green-domed building in the middle of City Park. Széchenyi Baths (SAY-chehn-yee) is the most accessible, local, and fun of Budapest's many bath experiences (daily 6:00–19:00, until 16:00 in winter, last entry 1 hr before closing, Állatkerti körút 11, Budapest XIV, M1: Széchenyi fürdő).

The sliding entry-fee scale covers thermal baths, the swimming pool, sauna, and a locker (2,000 Ft if you arrive before 15:00, 1,700 Ft if you arrive by 16:00, 1,400 Ft if you arrive by 17:00, 1,100 Ft if you arrive after 17:00; you also get money back later if your stay is short—explained below). A massage costs extra. You can rent a swimsuit, towel, or robe (500 Ft each with deposit).

Here's the procedure: Enter through the main door (under the middle dome) and pay the cashier. You'll be given a receipt and an electronic chit. Men are *férfi* and women are *nôi*—but you'll be ushered into the same dressing room, where everyone gets a private cabin to change.

As you enter the locker room, pass your electronic chit over the turnstile, and an attendant will show you to a changing cabin and give you a key. (This is where you can rent a swimsuit or towel if you need one.) After you change, lock your belongings in your cabin and hang on to your key—an attendant will double-lock it with her own key. Many locals bring plastic shopping bags with the essentials: towels, leisure reading, and sunscreen.

Follow the crowds to a series of indoor pools (quite hot—most around 40 degrees Celsius, or 104 Fahrenheit, and some with quite green water—supposedly because of some very healthy minerals). Beyond the pools you'll find your way outside, where the action is.

There are three outdoor pools. Orient yourself with your back to the main building: The pool to the right is for fun (cooler water—30 degrees Celsius, or 86 Fahrenheit, warmer in winter, lots of jets and bubbles, lively and often-crowded current pool); the pool on to the left is for relaxation (warmer water—38 degrees Celsius, or 100 Fahrenheit, mellow atmosphere, chess); and the main pool in the center is all business (the coolest water, doing laps, swimming cap required). Stairs to saunas are below the doors to the inside pools.

Relax and enjoy some Hungarian good living. Magyars of all shapes and sizes stuff themselves into tiny swimsuits and strut their stuff. Housewives float blissfully in the warm water. Intellectuals and Speedo-clad elder statesmen stand in chest-high water around chessboards and ponder their next moves. This is Budapest at its best.

On your way out, drop your electronic chit in the slot. A receipt will print out, indicating how much of a refund you get *(Visszatérités: Jár ___ Ft)*. Present this and your original receipt at the cashier on your way out to claim your "time-proportional repayment." Then continue your sightseeing...soggy but relaxed.

▲▲▲**Gellért Baths (Gellért fürdő)**—Budapest's classic bath experience is at the Gellért Hotel. You'll pay more, won't have as much fun, and won't run into nearly as many locals—this is definitely a more upscale-touristy scene. But if you want a soothing, luxurious bath experience in an elegant setting, this is the place (2,700 Ft includes changing cabin, 2,200 Ft includes locker, cheaper after 15:00, 10 percent discount with Budapest Card, 500 Ft for "visitor ticket" to see—but not use—the baths, towel rental-500 Ft with a 3,000-Ft deposit, swimsuit rental also available; open May–Sept daily 6:00–19:00, Oct–April Mon–Fri 6:00–19:00, Sat–Sun 6:00–17:00, last entry 1 hr before closing, on the Buda side of the green Liberty Bridge, baths' entrance under the white dome opposite bridge, Kelenhegyi út 4-6, Budapest XI, tel. 1/466-6166).

Choose from the dizzying array of options at the ticket window (from mud baths to foot massages—2,000–3,000 Ft), pay, and glide through the swanky lobby. Look for the swimming pool on your right about halfway down the main hall, and you'll find the stairs leading down to a maze of corridors that take you to the changing rooms (left for *férfi*—men—and right for *nõi*, or women). If you paid to rent a towel or swimsuit, get it from the attendant on your way.

Once you've changed, you have three options: Outside is a big **wave-pool** and several smaller pools (closed off-season). Inside is a cool-water **swimming pool** (swimming cap required—free loaners available) and a crowded hot-water pool. Off of that pool are doors to the gender-segregated, clothing-optional massage rooms and **thermal baths,** with pools at 36 and 38 degrees Celsius (97 and 100 Fahrenheit), as well as cold plunge pools and eucalyptus-scented steam rooms.

When you're finished, return your towel and swimsuit to get the slip to reclaim your deposit money (at cashier as you leave). If you were at the bath for less than four hours, you'll also get money back when you leave (take little paper slip to cashier).

Budapest Music Scene

Budapest is a great place to catch a good—and inexpensive—concert. In fact, Viennese music lovers often make the 2.5-hour trip here just to take in some fine, cheap opera in a luxurious setting. Options range from world-class opera in one of the world's great opera houses to light, touristy "Gypsy" folk concerts (with musicians and routines suspiciously similar to tomorrow's "Hungarian folk music" concerts). The tourist concerts are the simplest option—you'll see the flyers everywhere—but you owe it to yourself to do a little homework and find something more authentic. The monthly *Budapest Panorama* brochure makes it easier (free, available at the TI)—listing performances with dates, venues, performers, and contact information for getting tickets. The Megnyitotta Uj Irodajat box office lists everything on its walls and is a good clearinghouse for tickets and info (across from opera at Andrássy út 15, Mon–Fri 10:00–18:00, closed Sat–Sun, tel. 1/267-1267).

A Night at the Opera—Consider taking in an opera by one of the best companies in Europe, in one of Europe's loveliest opera houses, for bargain prices. The Hungarian State Opera performs almost nightly, both at the main Opera House (Andrássy út 22, Budapest VI, M1: Opera; see "Sights—Andrássy út," above) and in the Erkel Színház (not nearly as impressive, near the Keleti Train Station at Köztársaság tér 30, Budapest VIII, tel. 1/333-0540). Be careful to get a performance in the Opera House—not the Erkel Színház. Ticket prices range from 800–6,300 Ft, but the best music deal in Europe may be the 300-Ft standing-room tickets (easy to get, as they rarely run out). If you chose to buy one of these opera-tickets-for-a-buck, you'll have the option of sitting (can't see the stage) or standing (see the stage). If a full evening of opera is too much for you, you can leave early or come late (but buy ticket ahead of time, as box office closes when performance starts). To get tickets, call, fax, or visit the box office at the main Opera House, or order online (box office open and phone answered Mon–Sat 11:00-19:00, Sun 16:00–19:00, box office tel. 1/353-0170 or 1/472-0447, fax 1/311-9017, www.opera.hu, in English at http://online.jegymester .hu/index_eng.html). If you reserve by phone, fax, or online, pick up tickets at the Opera House two days before the performance (Andrássy út 22, Budapest VI, M1: Opera). You can only pick up tickets 30 minutes before performance by request. There are generally some tickets available at the door.

Tourist Concerts—The biggest promoter is **Duna Palota** (main office Zrínyi utca 5, call or visit for tickets Mon–Fri 8:00–21:00, Sat–Sun 9:00–21:00, tel. 1/317-2754, http://ticket.info.hu). Concerts include Gypsy folk music and Hungarian folk music and dancing (4,600–5,600 Ft, May–Oct daily at 20:00), classical "greatest hits" by the impressively-named Danube Symphony Orchestra (the best group, 6,400–8,100 Ft, 15 percent discount with Budapest Card for this concert only, May–Oct Sat at 20:00), and organ concerts in a Baroque church (3,600 Ft, June–Sept Fri and Sun at 20:00, May only Fri at 20:00). While high-brow classical music buffs will want a more serious concert, these shows are real crowd-pleasers.

American-Style Musicals—If you've ever wanted to hear "Music of the Night" in the Magyar tongue—as it was meant to be performed—here's your chance. Two pieces of American-style musical theater run permanently in Budapest, both in Hungarian with English subtitles: *Phantom of the Opera* (the only company in Central Europe, www.azoperahazfantomja .hu) and *Mozart!* (www.mozartbudapest.hu). Pick up details at the TI.

SLEEPING

Pest

Staying in Pest is more convenient, but a little less romantic, than sleeping in Buda. Most sights worth seeing are in Pest, and this half of the city also has a much higher concentration of Metro and tram stops, making getting around a snap. Pest also feels more lively and local than touristy Buda. I've arranged my listings by neighborhood, clustered around the most important sightseeing sectors.

Near Váci utca

Sleeping on the very central and convenient Váci utca comes with unnecessarily high prices. But these three gems—just a block or two off Váci utca—offer some of the best values in Budapest.

$$ Peregrinus Elte Hotel, a well-located, new-feeling place with 25 rooms and thoughtful touches, is run by a nearby law faculty (Sb-17,500 Ft, Db-23,000 Ft, extra bed-8,000 Ft, 25 percent cheaper Nov–March, no CC, elevator, just off Váci utca at Szerb utca 3, Budapest V, 5-min walk to M3: Kálvin tér, or tram #47 or #49 to Fövám tér, tel. 1/266-4911, fax 1/266-4913).

$$ Leo Panzió is a peaceful oasis with 14 modern rooms in a hulking building that's seen better days. The location is central, and the double-paned windows keep out most of the noise from the busy street below (Sb-€66, Db-€82, extra bed-€26, 15 percent cheaper Nov–March,

SLEEP CODE

(€1 = $1.10, 230 Ft = about $1, country code: 36, area code: 1)
Sleep Code: **S** = Single, **D** = Double/Twin, **T** = Triple, **Q** =
Quad, **b** = bathroom, **s** = shower only, **no CC** = Credit Cards
not accepted. Unless otherwise noted, breakfast is included and
credit cards are accepted. Everyone speaks English and most
prices are quoted in euros.

To help you easily sort through these listings, I've divided
the rooms into three categories, based on the price for a standard double room with bath:

$$$ **Higher Priced**—Most rooms €100 (25,750 Ft) or more.
$$ **Moderately Priced**—Most rooms between €70–100
(18,000–25,750 Ft).
$ **Lower Priced**—Most rooms €70 (18,000 Ft) or less.

Budapest has lots of good hotel values—it's cheaper to sleep
centrally here than in most European capitals. Stick with my
listings and you'll get a good value. Most rates drop 10-25 percent in the off-season (usually Nov–March).

old elevator, air-con, Kossuth Lajos utca 2A, Budapest V, M3:
Ferenciek tere, tel. 1/266-9041, tel. & fax 1/266-9042, panzioleo@mail
.datanet.hu).

$$ Kálvin-Ház, a long block up from the Great Market Hall, is a
little farther from the action. It offers 24 big, well-maintained rooms
with old-fashioned furnishings and squeaky parquet floors (Sb-€62, Db-
€82, apartment-€102, extra bed-€20, 20 percent cheaper Nov-March,
non-smoking rooms, Gönczy Pál utca 6, Budapest IX, M3: Kálvin tér,
tel. 1/216-4365, fax 1/216-4161, www.kalvinhouse.hu, kalvin.house
@axelero.hu).

Near Andrássy út
Andrássy boulevard is handy, local-feeling, and endlessly entertaining.
It's lined with appealing cafés, restaurants, theaters, and bars—and the
living is good. The frequent Metro stations make getting around the city
easy from here. None of these hotels is on Andrássy út, but they're all
within a three-block walk away. For locations, see page 229.

$$$ K+K Hotel Opera is a wonderfully located splurge, beside the
opera in the fun "Broadway Quarter." True to its name, it's a regal place,
where wicker seems classy. With 205 rooms it needs an enticing price,

Pest Hotels and Restaurants

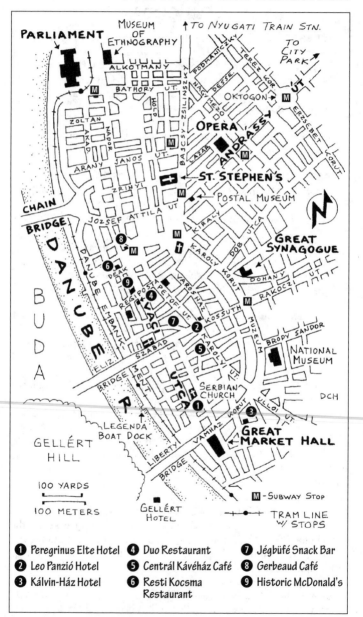

① Peregrinus Elte Hotel ④ Duo Restaurant ⑦ Jégbüfé Snack Bar
② Leo Panzió Hotel ⑤ Centrál Kávéház Café ⑧ Gerbeaud Café
③ Kálvin-Ház Hotel ⑥ Resti Kocsma Restaurant ⑨ Historic McDonald's

and it's generally a great value—unless you hit it on a rack-rate day (Sb-
€110, Db-€130, but prices go way up for conventions or holidays,
Sb/Db-€100 in winter, non-smoking floors, elevator, air-con, free
Internet access, parking garage-€10/day, Révay utca 24, Budapest VI,
M1: Opera, tel. 1/269-0222, fax 1/269-0230, www.kkhotels.com,
kk.hotel.opera@kkhotel.hu).

$$ Cotton House is a bit farther from Andrássy út than the other
listings, but still has a good location, close to the Nyugati Station. Its
13 retro rooms are fresh and comfy, with 1930s themes; each room is
devoted to a different mobster (Al Capone) or old-time performer (Ella
Fitzgerald). Some rooms are very plush—you can select from their Web
site. There's a jazz club in the basement, deep enough not to be a noise
problem (Sb or Db-€80 with shower, €90 with bath, €100 for Jacuzzi, air-
con, guests get discounts at club, Jókai utca 26, M3: Nyugati pu., tel.
1/354-0886, fax 1/354-1341, www.cottonhouse.hu, cottoncl@axelero.hu).

$$ Hotel Ambra—centrally located two blocks from the Opera—
is bright and mod, with 16 spacious, well-decorated apartments and five
rooms. Apartments give you double the size and a kitchenette for €10
more. It's a good value, but there's a catch: It's on a grimy, smelly, but
safe street (rooms: Sb-€65, Db-€85; apartments: Sb-€75, Db-€95, Tb-
€105, Qb-€115; 10 percent cheaper Oct–March, 10 percent cash discount, non-smoking rooms, elevator, garage-€9/day, Kisdiófa utca 13,
Budapest VII, M1: Opera, tel. & fax 1/321-1533 or 1/321-1538,
www.hotelambra.hu, ambrahotel@axelero.hu).

$ Hotel Medosz is cheap and dumpy but beautifully located,
around the corner from the Oktogon and the trendy Franz Liszt Square.
Beyond the chilling concrete communist facade and gloomy lobby are
67 rooms—old and uninspired but perfectly adequate, comrade (Sb-
10,000 Ft, Db-13,000 Ft, 15 percent cheaper Nov–March, elevator,
Jókai tér 9, Budapest VI, M1: Oktogon, tel. 1/374-3000, fax 1/332-
4316, www.medoszhotel.hu, info@medoszhotel.hu).

Sleeping Cheap near City Park

Andrássy út cruises through the diplomatic quarter before ending at
Heroes' Square. These two places are at the end of Andrássy út, near
City Park. See page 229.

$$ Hotel Délibáb is spartan but a great value across the street from
Heroes' Square. The 34 rooms are a little old and worn, but clean and
comfy enough (Sb-€66, Db-€76, prices 15 percent cheaper Nov–March,
parking-€10/day, Délibáb utca 35, M1: Hősök tere, tel. 1/342-9301, fax
1/342-8153, www.hoteldelibab.hu, info@hoteldelibab.hu).

$ Radio Inn has 37 big, cheap, but musty rooms facing a dingy
courtyard a few blocks from City Park (Sb-€48, Db-€65, 2-bedroom
apartment-€84 for up to 4, extra bed-€13, 25 percent cheaper Nov-
March, breakfast-€5 per person, non-smoking rooms, kitchens in each

room, elevator, Benczúr utca 19, Budapest VI, M1: Bajza utca, tel. 1/342-8347, fax 1/322-8284, www.radioinn.hu, radioinn@mail.elender.hu).

Budget Options Elsewhere in Pest

$ **Maria and István,** your chatty Hungarian aunt and uncle, are saving a room for you in their Old World apartment. For warmth and hospitality at youth-hostel prices, consider bunking in one of their two rooms, which share a bathroom (S-€20, D-€30-35, T-€39, extra bed-€6, no CC, elevator, Ferenc körút 39, Budapest IX, M3: Ferenc körút, tel. & fax 1/216-0768, mariaistvan@axelero.hu). Maria and István also rent two apartments farther from the center (Db-€44, Tb-€57, Qb-€64, family apartment, 50 yards from Metro: Nagyvarad tér).

$ **Youth Hostel:** The scruffy "Best Hostel" is not modest. Their brochure reads, "Staying at Best Hostel is a little bit like crashing at a friend's house on short notice." This super-casual little place is a run-down, ramshackle, transformed apartment. While it comes with lots of street noise, it's well-run and handy (some dorms mixed, some only girls, bed in 6- to 9-bed rooms-2,800 Ft; 3- to 4-bed rooms-3,400 Ft; D-8,000 Ft; discount with hostel membership, open to all, no curfew, 29 beds, lockers, not a party hostel, a block from Nyugati Station on the corner of Teréz körút and Podmaniczky utca, at Podmaniczky utca 27, doorbell #33, tel. 1/332-4934, www.besthostel.hu, bestyh@mail.satanet.hu). From the Keleti station take tram #73 to the eighth stop, Teréz körút.

Buda
Víziváros ("Water Town")

The Víziváros neighborhood—literally "Water Town"—is the lively part of Buda, squeezed between Castle Hill and the Danube, where fishermen and tanners used to live. Directly across the river from the Parliament building, it comes with fine views. Today, it's the most pleasant, central area to stay on the Buda side of the Danube. It's expensive and a little less convenient than Pest, but also more charming. For a good hangout near the recommended Víziváros hotels, try **Soho Coffee Company.** It's a taste of Seattle with a Hungarian accent, combining good American-style lattes, cozy stay-a-while atmosphere, Internet access, and a classic jazz soundtrack (daily 7:30–21:00, Főutca 25).

The following places are between the Chain Bridge and Buda's busy Margit körút ring road. Batthyány tér—a few minutes' walk away—is a handy center with a Metro stop.

$$$ **Art'otel** impresses New York City sophisticates. Every detail of the 164-room art'otel—from the breakfast dishes to the carpets—was designed by American artist Donald Sultan. This big, stylish hotel (part of a German chain of upscale theme hotels) is a fun, classy splurge. The location on the Danube embankment, close to the Batthyány tér Metro stop, is another big plus (rack rates: Sb-€198, Db-€218, bigger "executive"

Buda Hotels and Restaurants

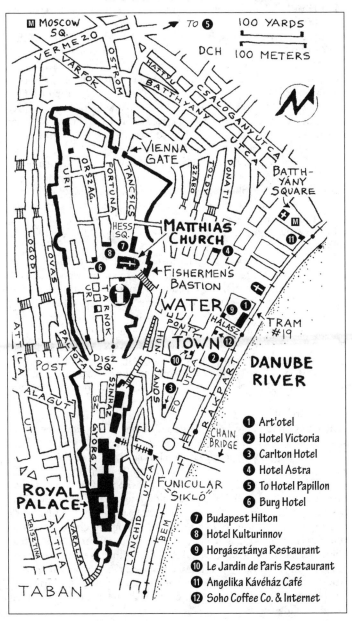

100 YARDS

100 METERS

1 Art'otel
2 Hotel Victoria
3 Carlton Hotel
4 Hotel Astra
5 To Hotel Papillon
6 Burg Hotel
7 Budapest Hilton
8 Hotel Kulturinnov
9 Horgásztánya Restaurant
10 Le Jardin de Paris Restaurant
11 Angelika Kávéház Café
12 Soho Coffee Co. & Internet

rooms-€20 more, deluxe "art suites"-€100 more, rates drop as low as Sb-€114/Db-€134 during slow times which are often Aug–Sept; you'll save lots—often Db-€120—by booking on the Web; non-smoking rooms, elevator, free Internet access, Bem rakpart 16-19, Budapest I, tel. 1/487-9487, fax 1/487-9488, www.artotel.hu, budapest@artotel.hu).

$$$ **Hotel Victoria,** with 27 business-class rooms—each with a grand river view—is a great value. This tall, narrow place (9 floors, 3 rooms on each) is run with pride (Sb-€97, Db-€102, extra bed-€41, prices 30 percent lower Nov–March, non-smoking rooms, elevator, free sauna, Internet access, parking garage-€9/day or park free on street, Bem rakpart 11, Budapest I, tel. 1/457-8080, fax 1/457-8088, www.victoria .hu, victoria@victoria.hu).

$$$ **Carlton Hotel,** located where the Castle Hill funicular meets the Chain Bridge, has 95 small rooms in a great location for getting to either Buda or Pest (Sb-€90, Db-€105, extra bed-€21, prices 20 percent lower Nov–March, ask about lower prices on weekends, parking garage-€12/day, non-smoking rooms, elevator, Apor Péter utca 3, Budapest I, tel. 1/224-0999, fax 1/224-0990, www.carltonhotel.hu, carltonhotel @axelero.hu).

$$$ **Hotel Astra** is a quiet, old-fashioned, but well-maintained place surrounding a peaceful courtyard. Its 12 rooms are woody, elegant, and spacious (Sb-€90, Db-€105, Sb or Db suite-€135, 10 percent less Nov–March, extra bed-€20, no CC, Vám utca 6, Budapest I, tel. 1/214-1906, fax 1/214-1907, www.hotelastra.hu, hotelastra@euroweb.hu).

$ **Hotel Papillon** is farther north—a 10-minute walk past Moszkva tér—in a forgettable residential area. It's a cheery little place with 20 pastel and homey rooms, a garden with a tiny pool, and great prices (Sb-€38, Db-€48, Tb-€61, tram #4 or #6 to Mechwart station, Rózsahegy utca 3B, tel. 1/212-4750, www.hotelpapillon.hu, papillon2@axelero.hu).

Castle Hill

Romantics often like calling Castle Hill home. The next three places share Holy Trinity Square (Szentháromság tér) with Matthias Church. They couldn't be closer to the Castle Hill sights, but they're in a tourist zone—dead at night—and less convenient to Pest than other listings.

$$$ **Burg Hotel** is *the* place for those who want to stay on Castle Hill with a little more class than the Kulturinnov offers (see below). This 26-room place is simply efficient: concrete, spacious, and comfy. You'll find more conveniently located hotels for less money elsewhere, but if you simply *must* stay in a modern hotel across the street from Matthias Church, this is it (Sb-€99, Db-€109, Db apartment-€129, extra bed-€39, 30 percent cheaper for three-night stays, prices 15 percent cheaper Nov-March, non-smoking rooms, Szentháromság tér 7-8, Budapest I, tel. 1/212-0269, fax 1/212-3970, www.burghotelbudapest.com, hotel .burg@mail.datanet.hu).

$$$ Budapest Hilton is a landmark—the first big Western hotel in town, back in the gloomy days of communism. Today it remains the top of the top, offering a complete escape from Hungary and a chance to be surrounded by rich tourists from mostly Japan, Germany, and the United States. Rates can be surprisingly reasonable if you land on a slow day (Sb or Db ranges from €120–500 depending on day and room, deals on the Web, Hess András tér 1 on Castle Hill next to Matthias Church, tel. 1/889-6000, fax 1/889-6644, www.budapest.hilton.com, res_budapest @hilton.com).

$$ Hotel Kulturinnov, run by the Hungarian Culture Foundation, is in a big building that feels more like a museum than a hotel. The 16 rooms are basic, with old, frumpy furnishings, but it's still a great value for the location—or for anywhere in central Budapest (Db-€80, Tb-€92, 25 percent less Nov–March, elevator, Szentháromság tér 6, Budapest I, tel. 1/355-0122, fax 1/375-1886, mka3hotel@dbassoc.hu).

EATING

Good Hungarian restaurants abound in Budapest (see "Hungarian Food," page 193), but you'll also find some good international options. I've listed both types, in neighborhoods convenient to hotels and sightseeing. Don't leave town without sampling a *lángos,* a savory deep-fried doughnut, spread with cheese, garlic, and sour cream (around 250 Ft).

Pest
Near Váci utca
For locations, see page 242.
Great Market Hall: At the far south end of Váci utca, you can eat a quick and cheap lunch on the upper floor of the Great Market Hall (Nagyvásárcsarnok). The **Fakanál Étterem** (Wooden Spoon Cafeteria)—a glassed-in sit-down cafeteria above the entrance—is good, with real tables and English on the blackboard (Mon 6:00–17:00, Tue–Fri 6:00–18:00, Sat 6:00–14:00, closed Sun, Fővám körút 1-3, Budapest IX, M3: Kálvin tér). But the stalls along the side of the building offer better prices with more choice and adventure. Grab a bar stool or you'll stand while you munch.

Duo Restaurant, along the touristy (expensive) Váci utca, has acceptable Hungarian cuisine and good service in a classy setting with nightly live Gypsy music (daily 12:00–23:00, music nightly 19:00–23:00, most main dishes 2,500–3,000 Ft, pricey wine list, the bottom-end Matraaljai Kékfrankos is fine, Váci utca 15-17, Budapest V, tel. 1/318-3814).

Centrál Kávéház, while famous as a traditional café, is great for a characteristic meal in an elegant turn-of-the-century atmosphere. The enticing menu offers traditional specials (especially the "Solo" plates), serious vegetarian plates, traditional desserts, and some fun history you should read (main plates 1,000-2,000 Ft, daily 8:00–24:00, Károlyi Mihály utca 9, Budapest V, tel. 1/266-4572).

Resti Kocsma, with a communist-kitsch theme, offers a taste of the Red old days. Live Gypsy music stirs the ambience, and even though the sign above the door eggs workers on with a "Let's cheer the First of May," the place is often quiet and glum (Mon–Sat 12:00–23:00, closed Sun, Deák Ferenc utca 2, Budapest V, tel. 1/226-6210).

Danube Promenade, the riverbank facing the castle, is lined with hotel restaurants and permanently moored restaurant boats. You'll find bad service, mediocre food, mostly tourists, and high prices. But the atmosphere and people-watching is marvelous.

On or near Andrássy út
For locations, see page 229.

Franz Liszt Square (Liszt Ferenc tér) has attracted a trendy cluster of yuppie restaurants, many with outdoor seating. Take the Metro to Oktogon and follow your nose. The high prices (most main dishes hover around 2,000 Ft) keep many Budapesters away, but—especially on a balmy summer evening—the scene is lively.

Articsóka, a few blocks behind the Opera, is hip, classy, and mellow, with its own theater in the back. This is where young Budapesters go to splurge for special occasions, enjoying modern Hungarian and Mediterranean cuisine (most dishes around 2,000 Ft, splurges up to 4,000 Ft, daily 12:00–24:00, Zichy J. utca 17, Budapest VI, tel. 1/302-7757).

Restaurant Művészinas is a fancy, central splurge, serving traditional Hungarian and Mediterranean cuisine. Its 1920s and 1930s atmosphere is plush yet homey—like the candle-lit living room of an artist who happens to be playing his favorite jazz on the phonograph (big-ticket main dishes 3,000-4,000 Ft, always several good vegetarian options, daily 12:00–24:00, 100 yards from Deák tér Metro stop near base of Andrássy út, Bajcsy-Zsilinszky út 9, Budapest VI, tel. 1/268-1439).

Duran Szendvics, a cheery little eatery, is reminiscent of Scandinavian open-faced sandwich shops, where a dozen or so tempting little treats are displayed. Two sandwiches and a drink make a quick and healthy meal for about $2. Look at the window outside before ordering. This is your chance to try caviar cheaply (100 Ft per sandwich, they'll box things to go for classy picnic, Mon–Fri 8:00–18:00, Sat 8:00–13:00, closed Sun; near Basilica, Postal Museum, and Deák tér Metro stop at the start of Andrássy út, Bajcsy-Zsilinszky utca 7, tel. 1/267-9624).

Splurge in the Park
Gundel Restaurant, on the fringe of City Park, has been *the* dining spot for VIPs and celebrities since 1894. The place is an institution—

President Bill Clinton ate here. The Pope didn't, but when his people called out for dinner, they called Gundel. The elegant main room is decorated with fine 19th-century Hungarian paintings. The furnishings come with an Art Deco flair. And the musicians are fast-fingered (on the violin) Gypsies. Reservations are wise—request near or far from the music. The food is traditional Hungarian (main courses €15-25, fancy €25 menu, music daily 18:30–24:00, in the park behind Heroes' Square at Állatkerti út 2, tel. 1/468-4040, www.gundel.hu). The dress code is formal. (While jackets are required, free loaners are available at the door if you travel like me. Ties and dresses are not required.)

Buda

The following restaurants are in or near the Víziváros ("Water Town") neighborhood between Castle Hill and the river. You'll find plenty of touristy places in the castle complex itself, but these less-touristy restaurants are just a quick downhill hike (or funicular ride) away. For locations, see page 245.

Horgásztánya ("Fishermen's Pub") is a local spot for reliable, traditional Hungarian food—and a fisherman suspended from the ceiling (daily 12:00–23:00, lots of fish, most main dishes around 1,500 Ft, a block from Danube at corner of Halász utca and Fő utca, Budapest I).

Le Jardin de Paris is a small, peaceful place with an upscale clientele and live jazz nightly from 19:00–23:00. Depending on the weather, the music is either in the leafy garden (May–Sept) or in the charming dining room (Oct–April). Most main dishes run 2,500–3,000 Ft (daily 12:00–23:00, reservations smart, Fő utca 20, Budapest I, tel. 1/201-0047).

Cafés and Pastry Shops
(Kávéház and Cukrászda)

Budapest once had a thriving café culture, like Vienna's. But realizing that these neighborhood living rooms were breeding grounds for dissidents, the communists closed the cafés or converted them into *esszpresszós* (with uncomfortable stools instead of easy chairs) or *bisztros* (stand-up fast food joints with no chairs at all). Today Budapest's café scene is slowly coming back to life.

In Buda

In Víziváros: Angelika Kávéház, in the heart of Víziváros, has coffee, pastries, and light food inside—or outside, with a riverside Parliament view. While the terrace is simply riverfront, the charmingly stale 1960s interior was a famous spot during communist days. It's changed little, and while it's hard to imagine this being posh...it was (daily 9:00–24:00, Batthyány tér 7, tel. 1/212-3784).

In Pest

On Vörösmarty Square: Gerbeaud (zher-BOW) isn't just a café—it's a landmark, the most famous restaurant in Budapest. Aside from coffee and pastries, you can also get a sandwich, salad, or other light meals. It's touristy but central, historic, and great for people-watching (daily 9:00–21:00, on Vörösmarty tér).

Halfway down Váci utca: Centrál Kávéház is the Budapest café that best recaptures the turn-of-the-century ambience, with elegant cakes and coffees, loaner newspapers, and a management that encourages loitering (daily 8:00–24:00, Károlyi Mihály utca 9, Budapest V, tel. 1/266-4572). This is also a great place for a meal (see "Eating," above).

Jégbüfé is where Pest urbanites get their quick, cheap, stand-at-a-counter fix of coffee and cakes. And for those feeling nostalgic for the good old days, little has changed here: First choose what you want at the counter, try to explain that to the cashier where you pay, then take your receipt back to the appropriate part of the counter (look up at the 4 signs: coffee, soft drinks, ice cream, cakes). Finally, trade your receipt for your goodie, go to the bar, and enjoy it standing up (daily 7:00–21:30, Ferenciek tere 10). Now...back to work.

Near the Opera: Müvész Kávéház is a classic coffeehouse with 19th-century elegance, conveniently located just across from the Opera House (daily 9:00–23:45, Andrássy út 29).

TRANSPORTATION CONNECTIONS

Budapest has three main stations (*pályaudvar,* or *pu.* for short): **Keleti** (Eastern, most international trains), **Nyugati** (Western, domestic and some international—especially eastbound), and **Déli** (Southern, mostly domestic trains and some international—especially southbound). Expect exceptions, and always confirm carefully which station your train leaves from. For general rail information in Hungary, call 1/461-5400; for information about international trains, call 1/461-5500.

By train to: Vienna (that's *Bécs* in Hungarian, 7/day direct, 3 hrs, from Keleti/Eastern; or hrly with a transfer in Bruck an der Leitha, Austria, from Keleti/Eastern, 3 hrs), **Bratislava** (that's *Pozsony* in Hungarian, hrly, direct, 2.5–3 hrs from either Keleti/Eastern or Nyugati/Western), **Prague** (5/day direct, including 1 night train, 7–9.5 hrs; most from Keleti/Eastern, some from Nyugati/Western), **Kraków** (1 direct night train/day from Keleti/Eastern with early arrival in Kraków, 11 hrs; otherwise transfer in Katowice, Poland, or Břeclav, Czech Republic, 9–10 hrs), **Ljubljana** (2/day direct, 8.5 hrs from Deli/Southern; no direct night train), **Munich** (1/day direct from Deli/Southern, 7.5 hrs; plus 1 direct night train/day from Keleti/Eastern, 10 hrs; otherwise transfer in Regensburg, Germany, or Vienna), **Berlin** (1/day direct, 12 hrs from Nyugati/Western; plus 1 direct night train/day, 14 hrs from

Keleti/Eastern), **Eger** (5/day direct, 2 hrs from Keleti/Eastern; or more from same station with transfer in Füzesabony), **Szentendre** (4–7/hr, 40 min on suburban HÉV train, leaves from Batthyány tér), **Visegrád** (trains arrive at Nagymaros, across the river—take shuttle boat to Visegrád; hrly, 1 hr from Nyugati/Western), and **Esztergom** (hrly, 1.5 hrs from Nyugati/Western). Note that Nagymaros (the Visegrád station) and Esztergom are on opposite sides of the river—and on different train lines.

By Boat: In the summer, Mahart runs daily high-speed hydrofoils up the Danube to Vienna. The boat leaves Budapest in April and Sept–Oct at 9:00 and arrives in Vienna at 15:20 (Vienna to Budapest: 9:00–14:30); May through August, the boat leaves Budapest at 8:00 and arrives in Vienna at 14:20 (Vienna to Budapest: 8:00–13:30). In August, a second boat does the same trip, leaving Budapest at 13:00 and arriving Vienna at 19:20 (Vienna to Budapest 13:00–18:30). The trip costs €75 one-way. On any of these boats, you can also stop in the Slovak capital, Bratislava. To confirm times and prices, and to buy tickets, contact Mahart (Budapest tel. 1/484-4000, www.mahartpassnave.hu).

THE DANUBE BEND

(Dunakanyar)

The Danube, which begins as a trickle in Germany's Black Forest, becomes the Mississippi River of Central Europe as it flows east through Vienna, then makes a sweeping right turn—called the Danube Bend—south to Budapest, Belgrade, and the Black Sea. Three river towns, north of Budapest on the Danube Bend, offer a convenient day-trip getaway for urbanites who want to commune with nature.

Hungarians sunbathe and swim along the banks of the Danube Bend, or hike in the rugged hills that rise up from the river. This is also one of Hungary's most historic stretches—for centuries, Hungarian kings ruled not from Buda or Pest, but from the Danube Bend.

Closest to Budapest is Szentendre, a colorful, storybook-cute Baroque village packed with tourists. A mighty castle high on a hill watches over the town of Visegrád. Esztergom, birthplace of Hungary's first Christian king, has the country's biggest and most important church. All of this is within a one-hour drive of the capital, with decent public transportation connections.

Planning Your Time

With so much to do in Budapest itself, the Danube Bend ranks low on the list of priorities. Szentendre is the easiest and most worthwhile Danube Bend destination—just a quick suburban-train (HÉV) ride away, it can be done in a half day.

Visegrád and Esztergom are frustrating and time-consuming to reach by public transportation, especially if you try to visit all three towns in one day. If you don't have a car, consider taking a tour or hiring a driver (see "Helpful Hints" in Budapest

Danube Bend

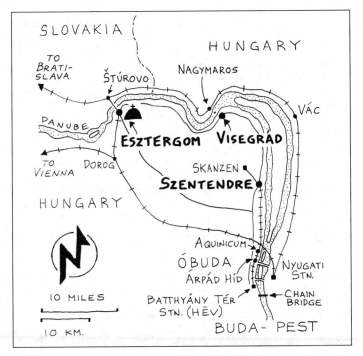

chapter). If you're driving between Budapest and Vienna (or Bratislava), the Danube Bend towns are a perfect way to break up the journey.

Ideally, if you visit all three towns by car, do it this way: 9:00–Leave Budapest, 9:30–Arrive at Szentendre and see the town, 12:00–Leave Szentendre, 12:30–Lunch in Visegrád, 13:30–Tour Visegrád Royal Palace, 14:30–Visit Visegrád Citadel above town, 15:30–Leave Visegrád, 16:00–Visit Esztergom Basilica, 17:00–Head back to Budapest or move on to Vienna or Bratislava. If you want to spend more time on the Danube Bend, add a visit to the Hungarian Open-Air Museum ("Skanzen") near Szentendre.

Getting around the Danube Bend

Going north from Budapest, the three towns line up along the same road on the west side of the Danube—Szentendre, Visegrád, Esztergom—each spaced about 15 miles apart.

By Car: It couldn't be easier. Get on road #11 going north out of Buda, and it'll take you through each of the three towns—the road bends with the Danube. As you approach Szentendre, watch for signs for Centrum Szentendre to branch to the right off the main road, and follow the Danube to the bottom of town.

Returning from Esztergom to Budapest, consider cutting the "bend": Road #10 is fastest, but can have heavy traffic on weekdays; the smaller road farther north (via Pilisszentkereszt) is slower and windier but more scenic and less crowded.

By Boat: In the summer, Budapest-based Mahart runs boats and hydrofoils up the Danube Bend, some going all the way to Vienna. Confirm 2004 times and prices and buy tickets at Mahart in Budapest (dock near Vigadó tér in Pest, tel. 1/484-4000, www.mahartpassnave .hu). For details, see "Transportation Connections" at the end of the Budapest chapter.

On summer weekends, a high-speed **hydrofoil** leaves Budapest at 9:30, arriving in Visegrád at 10:30 and Esztergom at 11:00; the return trip leaves Esztergom at 15:30 and Visegrád at 15:55, arriving back in Budapest at 16:45 (runs Sat–Sun June–Aug, one-way to Visegrád-1,990 Ft, to Esztergom-2,190 Ft; round-trip to Visegrád-3,290 Ft, to Esztergom-3,700 Ft).

There are also several slower **"pleasure boats"** that connect the Danube Bend villages in summer. Unless otherwise noted, these boats run June–Aug: **Budapest to Szentendre** (only this direct boat uses Szentendre's convenient downtown dock; leaves Budapest at 10:30 and 14:00, leaves Szentendre at 12:20 and 17:00, trip takes 1–1.5 hrs, 1,400 Ft round-trip); **Budapest to Szentendre and Visegrád** (leaves Budapest at 9:00, stops in Szentendre at 10:35, arrives Visegrád 12:15, returns from Visegrád 16:00 or 16:30, stops in Szentendre 17:15 or 17:45, arrives Budapest 18:20 or 19:00, also runs April–May); **Budapest to Visegrád and Esztergom** (leaves Budapest 7:30, arrives Visegrád 10:50 and Esztergom 12:50; leaves Esztergom 16:00, arrives Visegrád 17:30 and Budapest 19:55); and **Esztergom to Visegrád** (leaves Esztergom 9:00, arrives Visegrád 10:25; returns from Visegrád 15:30, arrives Esztergom 17:30). One-way prices: Budapest–Szentendre 950 Ft, Budapest–Visegrád 1,050 Ft, Budapest–Esztergom 1,200 Ft, and Esztergom–Visegrád 700 Ft.

By Train: Szentendre is handiest by train—Budapest's suburban HÉV zips you right there (4–7/hr, 40 min each way, Budapest Card covers all but 360 Ft round-trip, buy this supplement before boarding, sometimes requires change in Békásmegyer, last train returns from Szentendre around 23:00).

To Visegrád and Esztergom, trains run hourly from Budapest's Nyugati/Western Station (1 hr to Visegrád, 1.5 hrs to Esztergom). Visegrád's train station is across the Danube, in Nagymaros (catch a ferry to Visegrád). Visegrád and Esztergom are actually on different train lines. However, note that many Nagymaros/Visegrád trains continue on to Štúrovo, Slovakia—across the bridge from Esztergom Basilica (you'll cross the Slovak border twice—entering Slovakia on the train, exiting on foot. This actually gets you closer to the basilica than the Esztergom station, about a mile south.

By Bus: Buses connect the three towns at least hourly, but it's a slow way to go—since they stop at all of the smaller villages along the way (one-way prices: Szentendre–Visegrád 210 Ft, Szentendre–Esztergom 579 Ft, Visegrád–Esztergom 631 Ft). For the easiest connection, zip up to Szentendre on the HÉV suburban train and then take the bus from there to Visegrád or Esztergom (regional buses leave from next to the tracks).

By Tour from Budapest: If you want to see all three towns in one day, don't have a car, don't want to hassle with public transportation, and don't want to shell out for a private driver, a bus tour is the most convenient way to go. All of the companies are about the same (all three towns in 9–10 hrs, including Renaissance lunch feast in Visegrád and shopping stops, plus return on boat, for around 18,000 Ft); look for fliers at the TI or in your hotel's lobby.

Szentendre

Szentendre (SEHN-tehn-dreh; St. Andrew in English) may well be the most touristy town in Hungary, but with good reason. It rises gently from the Danube, a postcard-pretty village with a twisty Mediterranean street plan filled in with Austrian Baroque houses. This is where Budapesters bring their wives or girlfriends for a special weekend lunch. The town has a long tradition as an artists' colony, and it still has more than its share of museums and galleries. The biggest downside: streets clogged with tourists and tacky shops. But if you venture a bit off the crowded main streets, you'll soon have quiet back lanes under colorful Baroque steeples all to yourself.

Tourist Information: The **TI** is two blocks from the main square on the tourist-clogged Dumtsa Jenő utca (#22, just before the stream, tel. 26/317-965, www.szentendre.hu, tourinform@szentendre.hu). Pick up a free town map and a brochure about the Danube Bend.

Arrival in Szentendre: The **train/HÉV** and **bus stations** are on the southern edge of town, and the route to the center is poorly marked. Leave through the side of the HÉV station and cut through the bus-station lot. Cross the busy road at the stoplight, bear left, and follow Dunakorzó along the river into town (about a 10-min walk). Some **boats** arrive right in town, but most come to a pier about a 15-minute walk north of the center. After you get off the boat, take the first path to your left; stay on this, and it'll lead you straight ahead into town.

SIGHTS

Main Square (Fő tér)—Szentendre's top sight is the town itself; start at the Main Square (Fő tér). Take a close look at that cross, erected in 1763 to give thanks for surviving the plague. Notice the Cyrillic lettering? After the Turks were forced out of Hungary, this town was rebuilt primarily by Serb and Greek merchants who had fled those same Turks back home. Look at the very narrow alleyways around the square. Mediterranean towns often have walls close together to create shade in the hot sun. Even though Hungary has a milder climate, old habits die hard: The Serbs and Greeks built the town in that style anyway.

Stand at the bottom of the square and face the cross in the middle. The street to your left (Dumtsa Jenő utca) leads to the **TI**. On your way there, you'll pass a hokey but intriguing **Marzipan Museum**, filled with little figures and dioramas made from the distinctive almond-flavored candy (May–Sept daily 10:00–19:00, Oct–April until 18:00, #12, tel. 26/311-931).

Near the square is the **Margaret Kovács Museum** (Kovács Margit Múzeum), dedicated to the local artist famous for her whimsical, wide-eyed pottery sculptures based on Hungarian folktales and biblical themes (550 Ft, daily 10:00–18:00, Vastagh György utca 1). To reach the museum from the square, face the old church at the bottom of the square and follow the street to the right of it, then take the first right.

Enjoy a stroll through town. Head off to the back streets (try the hill behind the square) and you'll be surprised at how quickly you find yourself alone with Szentendre. As you explore, keep an eye out for Serbian and Greek Orthodox churches, many with impressive icon collections.

Hungarian Open-Air Folk Museum (Szabadtéri Néprajzi Múzeum, a.k.a. "Skanzen")—Three miles northwest of Szentendre is an open-air museum featuring examples of traditional Hungarian architecture from all over the country. These aren't replicas—each building was taken apart at its original location, transported piece by piece, and reassembled here. Eventually the museum will have samples from nine different regions, plus some Roman ruins. The huge museum is spread out, so a thorough visit can take hours; for help, pick up one of two decent English-language guidebooks (800 or 1,500 Ft). My favorites are the impressive thatched-roof houses (700 Ft, 100 Ft more every other weekend for special programming; July–Aug Tue–Sun 9:00–19:00, buildings close 17:00; April–June and Sept–Oct 9:00–17:00, always closed Mon, closed Nov–March, last entry 30 min before closing, Sztaravodai út, tel. 26/502-500, www.skanzen.hu).

Getting to Skanzen: Buses leave from the Szentendre train station for Skanzen hourly (2/hr mid-afternoon on weekdays, 100 Ft). To catch the **bus** from the Main Square, go down Dumtsa Jenő utca, and just after you pass the TI, follow the stream to the right. When you get to the busy road #11, wait at the bus stop for a bus marked "Skanzen." A **taxi** to the museum should cost no more than 2,000 Ft; the TI can call one for you. Plans are in the works for the museum to buy a new bus to make it easier to get there (ask at the TI).

SLEEPING

In recent years, the delightful little burg of Szentendre has become a bedroom community for nearby Budapest. I don't advise staying here—it takes too long to get into the city to make an efficient or good-value option (hotels in Budapest aren't too expensive anyway). But if you must stay here, these two places rent basic but acceptable second-story rooms along the Danube embankment just north of the center.

Corner Panzió rents five cozy, woody rooms with prices that vary with the season (Sb or Db: June–Sept 10,000 Ft with air-con, breakfast-1,000 Ft per person; Oct–May 8,000 Ft without air-con, breakfast-500 Ft per person; no CC, Dunakorzó 4, tel. & fax 26/301-524, www.radoczy.hu).

Centrum Panzió has six pleasant-enough rooms with thinning carpets (Sb-9,000 Ft, Db-9,900 Ft, includes breakfast, no CC, Bogdányi utca 15, tel. & fax 26/302-500, www.szvsz.hu/centrum, hotel.centrum@axelero.hu).

Visegrád

Visegrád (VEE-sheh-grahd, Slavic for "high castle") is a small village containing the remains of two major-league castles: a hilltop fortress and a riverside palace. At this strategic site overlooking the river, there has been—since Roman times—a fortress atop the steep hill, further fortified after Tartars swept across Hungary in the 13th century.

Soon after, Károly Róbert (Charles Robert), from the French Anjou dynasty, became Hungary's first non-Magyar king. He was so unpopular with the nobles in Buda that he had to set up court in Visegrád, where he built a new residential palace down closer to the Danube. King Mátyás Corvinus—notorious for his penchant for Renaissance excess—made Visegrád his summer home, and turned the palace into what some called a "paradise on earth." With red marble fountains that flowed with wine, Mátyás knew how to party.

In honor of this grand Renaissance palace, **Hotel Visegrád** today runs a Renaissance-themed restaurant, with Renaissance cookware, food, costumed waitstaff, and live lute music—just the spot for Danube Bend tour groups (can't miss it at north end of town).

Today, both castles are but a shadow of their former selves. The

THE VISEGRÁD CONNECTION

The Royal Palace at Visegrád has been the site of two important meetings of Eastern European leaders. In 1335, as Hapsburg Austria was rising to the west, the kings of Hungary, Poland, and Bohemia converged on the Visegrád Palace to strategize against this new threat. The meeting wasn't successful; all of the countries involved were ultimately absorbed by the Hapsburgs.

In February of 1991, the Iron Curtain had fallen and the East was looking to the future. The heads of state of these same countries—Hungary, Poland, and Czechoslovakia—once again came together in the Visegrád Palace, this time to compare notes about westernization. To this day, these countries are still often referred to as the "Visegrád Countries."

fortress was blown up by nervous Hapsburgs (to prevent the rebellious Magyars from using it for an attack), while the palace was covered by a mudslide during the Turkish occupation, and is only now being excavated. Non-drivers who don't want to make the steep hike up to the citadel should skip this town. But hardy castle fans find enough to get excited about in Visegrád.

Tourist Information: The Visegrád Tours travel agency acts as this small town's **TI,** handing out a few free leaflets (April–Oct daily 8:00–18:00, Nov–March daily 10:00–16:00, Rév utca 15, tel. 26/398-160, www.visegradtours.hu).

Arrival in Visegrád: Boats dock at the north end of town, near Hotel Visegrád. Continue straight ahead with the river on your right. After a block, when you see the monument to King Mátyás, fork left to get to his Renaissance palace. (To reach the TI, you'd continue straight for about 10 minutes, past the gas station, then go left up Rév utca near the Nagymaros ferry dock—look for Visegrád Tours on the right.) **Train** travelers arrive at Nagymaros, across the river (take the hrly 200-Ft shuttle ferry to Visegrád, arriving a block from the Visegrád Tours office).

SIGHTS

▲▲**Visegrád Citadel (Fellegvár)**—Though Visegrád's citadel was destroyed by the Hapsburgs, its remains are fun to explore. Scramble across the ramparts, try your hand with a bow and arrow, or pose with a bird of prey perched on your arm. Fun wax sculptures enjoy a medieval feast—and demonstrate the collection of torture devices. There are no English descriptions, but you can buy a small English-language book

(350 Ft) about the castle at the little kiosk inside the hunting exhibit at very top of castle—after you've already seen the whole thing (ask for it at postcard stands out front just in case). At the top, you have commanding views over the Danube Bend—which, of course, is exactly why they built it here (700 Ft, daily mid-March–mid-Nov, usually 9:30–18:00, can close earlier or later depending on the weather, open only Sat–Sun in winter, usually 9:30–15:30 depending on weather).

Getting to Visegrád Citadel: To **drive** to the citadel from the town center, turn left from road #11 at the town's main junction (Rév utca, after gas station at ferry dock) and follow signs for Fellegvár. If you continue on the same road after you leave the citadel, you'll pass a luge ride and then head back downhill to the town.

To get to the castle from the town center without a car, you have three options: 1) **hike** (figure 40 steep min; from town center, follow signs for Fellegvár); 2) **taxi** (called "city bus," minivan trip costs 2,000 Ft total no matter how many people, TI can arrange); or 3) public **bus** (200 Ft, only 3/day in summer—usually 9:28, 12:28, and 15:28, none in winter, confirm schedules with TI, catch at bus stop across from TI).

Royal Palace (Király Palota)—Under King Mátyás Corvinus, this was one of Europe's most elaborate Renaissance palaces. During the Turkish occupation, it was deserted and eventually buried by a mudslide. For generations, the existence of the palace faded into legend, so its rediscovery in 1934 was a surprise. Today the partially excavated  remains are tourable and interesting; unfortunately, there's no English-language guidebook. Keep your eye out for the red marble fountain, which spouted wine for parties (500 Ft, Tue–Sun 9:00–16:30, closed Mon, Fő utca 27-29, tel. 26/398-026, www.visegrad.hu/muzeum).

Solomon's Tower—This tower, just up from the ferry dock and Renaissance restaurant, is a reminder that the castle walls once extended all the way down to the banks of the Danube. The tower once held Vlad the Impaler (1462–1475), who inspired author Bram Stoker to create the character Dracula. Today it houses a skippable museum (500 Ft, May–Sept Tue–Sun 9:00–16:30, closed Mon and Oct–April).

Esztergom

Esztergom (EHS-tehr-gohm) is an unassuming little college town with a youthful population and a big Suzuki factory. You'd never guess it was the first capital of Hungary—until you see the enormous Esztergom Basilica, the country's biggest and most important church.

CARDINAL JÓZSEF MINDSZENTY
(1892–1975)

Mindszenty was a Catholic Church leader who spoke out aggressively against the communist government. In 1948, the communists arrested him and tortured him for 39 days. He was imprisoned in Budapest until the 1956 Uprising, when he was freed and took refuge in the U.S. Embassy. There he stayed for 15 years, unable to leave for fear of being captured. (Many Catholic Americans remember praying for Cardinal Mindszenty every day when they were kids.) In 1971, he agreed to step down from his position and fled to Austria.

On his deathbed in 1975, Mindszenty said that he did not want his body returned to Hungary as long as there was a single Russian soldier still stationed there. As the Iron Curtain was falling in 1989, Mindszenty emerged as an important hero to post-communist Hungarians, who wanted to bring his remains back to his homeland. But Mindszenty's secretary, in accordance with the Cardinal's final wishes, literally locked himself to the coffin—refusing to let the body be transported as long as any Soviet soldier remained in Hungary. In May 1991, when only a few Russians were still in Hungary, Mindszenty's remains were finally brought to the crypt in the Esztergom Basilica.

Arrival in Esztergom: No matter how you arrive, just head for the basilica that towers over Esztergom—you can't miss it, and it's the only worthwhile sight in town (train station about 1 mile south of town; walk 20 min or catch bus #1 or #5 from station). Note that there is also a handy train station across the river in Štúrovo, Slovakia (cross the border on foot as you cross the bridge).

Esztergom Basilica

There has been a church here for centuries, but the current version was completed in 1869. With a 330-foot-tall-dome, this is the biggest church in Hungary. St. István was born in Esztergom, and in A.D. 1000, he was crowned here by the Pope—an act that tamed the nomadic Magyars and established

Hungary as a legitimate European nation (for more on St. István, see page 215). The remains of his birth castle house a mediocre museum next to the basilica.

Enter the basilica (as you face it, entrance is on left side, main door reserved for special occasions, church entry free, daily 6:30–18:00).

In the foyer, you'll see a plaque translated in several languages commemorating **Cardinal József Mindszenty,** revered for standing up to the communist government. His remains are in the crypt (100 Ft, daily 9:00–16:30, last entry 15 min before closing).

Enter the cavernous nave. There are plenty of fancy tour-guide stats about this church: For example, the altarpiece is the biggest single-canvas painting in the world—but mostly the size is what impresses visitors.

As you face the altar, find the chapel on the left before the transept. This Renaissance **Bakócz Chapel** actually predates the basilica by 350 years. When the basilica was built, they broke the chapel into 1,600 pieces and rebuilt it, piece-by-piece, inside the new structure. The heads around the chapel's altar were defaced by Turks, who believed that only God can create man—not sculptors.

Consider visiting the **treasury,** to the right of the main altar (400 Ft, daily 9:00–16:30). Though the collection is pretty standard ecclesiastical stuff, there are some interesting models inside the entry: a big one showing off the original plans for the enormous basilica complex (never fully completed); smaller ones of the frames of the basilica's wooden nave and metal dome; and yet another showing what Esztergom looked like in the early 16th century (notice the more modest church that stood where this basilica is today).

When you're finished in the basilica, head around to the back for a thrilling Danube overview. That's Štúrovo, Slovakia, across the river. The bridge connecting them was destroyed in World War II and rebuilt only recently. Before it was completed, no bridges spanned the Danube between Budapest and Bratislava.

EGER

You've probably never heard of the enchanting Back Door town of Eger (EH-gehr). It's a mid-sized city (pop. 70,000) in northern Hungary, the seat of a bishop and home to a small teacher-training college. Hungarians think proudly of Eger as the town that, against all odds, successfully held off the Turkish advance into Europe in 1552. Eger is the mecca of Hungarian school field trips because of its stirring history. If the town is known internationally for anything, it's for the surrounding wine region (the best-known product is Bull's Blood, or Egri Bikavér).

But don't let its lack of popularity keep you away—in fact, that's part of Eger's charm. Rather than growing jaded from floods of American tourists, Egerites go about their daily routines amidst charming Baroque buildings, watched over by Hungary's most important castle. It all comes together to make Eger an ideal introduction to small-town Hungary.

Planning Your Time

Eger is worth a relaxing day on a trip between Kraków and Budapest (or as a side-trip from Budapest—possible in a day, but better as an overnight). The sights are few, the ambience is great, and strolling is a must.

A perfect day in Eger begins with a browse through the colorful market and a low-key ramble on the castle ramparts. Then head to the Lyceum to visit the library and astronomy museum, and to climb up to the thrillingly low-tech camera obscura. Take in the midday organ concert in the cathedral across the street from the Lyceum. In the afternoon, relax on the square or, better yet, at the spa. If you need more to do, consider an afternoon drive into the countryside (including visits to local vintners—get details from the TI). Round out your day with a visit to Eger's touristy wine caves at Sirens' Valley.

Eger

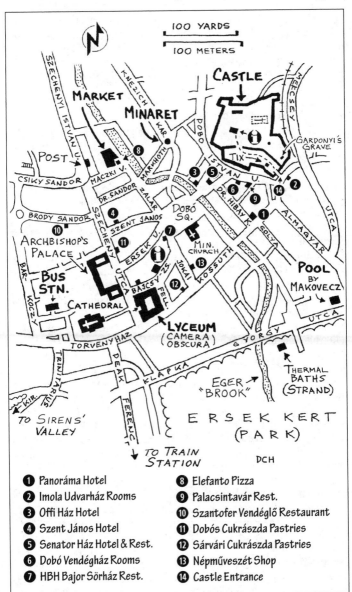

❶ Panoráma Hotel
❷ Imola Udvarház Rooms
❸ Offi Ház Hotel
❹ Szent János Hotel
❺ Senator Ház Hotel & Rest.
❻ Dobó Vendégház Rooms
❼ HBH Bajor Sörház Rest.
❽ Elefanto Pizza
❾ Palacsintavár Rest.
❿ Szantofer Vendéglő Restaurant
⓫ Dobós Cukrászda Pastries
⓬ Sárvári Cukrászda Pastries
⓭ Népműveszét Shop
⓮ Castle Entrance

ORIENTATION

Eger Castle sits at the top of the town, hovering over Dobó Square (Dobó István tér). This main square is divided in half by Eger Brook, which bisects the town. Two blocks west of Dobó Square is the main pedestrian drag, Széchenyi utca, where you'll find the Lyceum and the cathedral. A few blocks due south from the castle (follow Eger Brook) are Eger's various spas and baths.

Tourist Information

Eger's on-the-ball, eager-to-please **TI (TourInform)** is the most efficient place to get any Eger question answered. They give out a free brochure and town map, as well as piles of other brochures about the city and region. They can't book rooms, but they can help you find one—or anything else you're looking for (mid-June–mid-Sept daily 9:00–19:00, off-season Mon–Fri 9:00–17:00, Sat 9:00–13:00, closed Sun, Bajcsy-Zsilinszky utca 9, tel. 36/517-715, www.tourinform.hu/eger).

Arrival in Eger

By Train: Eger's tiny train station is a 20-minute walk south of the center. The closest **ATM** is at the Spar grocery store just up the street (turn left out of station, go straight about two blocks between seemingly abandoned warehouses, and look for red-and-white supermarket on your right). A taxi into the center will cost you an affordable 800 Ft.

To catch the **bus** towards the center, go straight out of the station, and when the road you're on veers right, cross it to get to the bus stop on the busier road above it. Bus #11, #12, or #14 cut about 10 minutes off the walk into town (120 Ft, buy ticket from driver, get off when you see the big, yellow cathedral). To **walk** all the way, leave the station straight ahead, turn right with the road, and then continue straight ahead (on Deák Ferenc utca) until you run into the cathedral. With your back to the cathedral entry, the main square is two blocks in front of you and to the left.

By Car: In this small town, most hotels will provide parking or help you find a lot. For a short visit, the most central lot is behind the department store on Dobó Square.

Getting around Eger

Everything of interest in Eger is within walking distance, except maybe the Sirens' Valley wine caves—for these, catch a cab (starts at 220 Ft, then 200 Ft/km; try City Taxi, tel. 36/555-555).

Helpful Hints

Language Barrier: Having fewer American visitors means that Egerites are not as likely to speak English as in more mainstream Eastern European destinations. (Consider it part of the fun.) Eger does get

EGER LANDMARKS

English	Hungarian	Pronounced
Main Square ("Dobó Square")	Dobó István tér	DOH-boh-EESHT-vahn tehr
(Eger) Castle	(Egri) vár	(EHG-ree) vahr
Market Hall	Csarnok	CHAWR-nohk
Bull's Blood (local blend of red wines)	Egri Bikavér	EH-gree BEE-kah-vehr

lots of German tourists, so if you speak any German, it may come in handy. Even if you don't share a language, most people from Eger are eager to find some way to communicate. The TI is happy to act as a go-between with a Hungarian-only sight or business.

Tours of Eger: A couple of hokey little **tourist trains** do a 45-minute tour of Eger, leaving the main square every hour on the hour (300 Ft, beginning at 9:00). There are no organized town walking tours, but the TI can put you in touch with a **local guide.**

Internet Access: The Egri Est Café has two terminals in the back (600 Ft/hr, Mon–Fri 10:00–23:00, Sat–Sun until 2:00, Széchenyi utca 16).

Shopping: For folk art, try the Népművészét shop (Mon–Fri 9:30–18:00, Sat–Sun until 17:00, Bajcsy-Zsilinszky utca 1).

Concerts: Daily from mid-May to mid-October, Hungary's second-biggest organ booms out a free 30-minute concert in the Eger Cathedral (400 Ft, Mon–Sat at 11:30, Sun at 12:45). Every Monday in July and August, a musical about Eger history is performed on a stage in Dobó Square (free, starts at 18:00).

SIGHTS

▲▲**Dobó Square (Dobó István tér)**—Dobó Square is at the heart of Eger. In most touristy towns, the main square is packed with postcard stalls and other tourist traps. Refreshingly, Eger's square seems mostly packed with Egerites.

The statue in the middle is **István Dobó**, the square's namesake and Eger's greatest hero. In the 16th century, Turkish invaders swept into Europe, working their way up the Balkan Peninsula and threatening to overrun the entire Continent. When Buda and Pest fell to the Turks in 1541, all of Europe looked to Eger as the last line of defense. Dobó István was put in charge of Eger's forces, so he prepared the castle (behind the statue) and waited.

On September 11, 1552, 60,000 Turks arrived in Eger. Only about 2,000 Egerites (soldiers, their wives, and their children) remained to protect their town. The siege lasted 38 days. Eger's soldiers fought valiantly, and the women of Eger also joined the fray, pouring hot tar down on the Turks...everyone pitched in. Finally, the Turks left in shame, Eger was saved, and Dobó was a national hero. (The unfortunate epilogue: The Turks came back in 1596 and, this time, succeeded in conquering an Eger Castle guarded by unmotivated mercenaries. The Turks sacked the town and controlled the region for close to a century.)

Use the square to orient yourself to the town. Behind the statue of Dobó is a bridge over the stream that bisects the city, and on the other side of the bridge is the charming "**Little Dobó Square,**" home to the town's two best hotels (see "Sleeping," page 272). If you cross the bridge towards Little Dobó Square, look to the left and you'll see the north-ernmost minaret in Europe—once part of a Turkish mosque. Hovering above Little Dobó Square is Eger Castle (described below).

Now face the opposite direction, with Dobó's statue at your back. On your right is a handy department store. On your left, dominating the square, is the beautiful pink Minorite Church. The

monument in front of you and on the left also com-memorates the 1552 defense of Eger against two Turkish soldiers, reminding us of the townspeople's bravery despite the odds. Straight ahead, two blocks beyond the end of the square, runs Széchenyi utca, Eger's main pedestrian drag. To the left on Széchenyi utca are the cathedral and Lyceum. To reach the TI, jog left at the end of the square, then right onto Bajcsy-Zsilinszky utca (TI one block ahead on right). To visit the Market Hall, leave Dobó Square to the right (on Zalár József utca, with department store on your right-hand side; you'll see Market Hall on left).

▲**Eger Castle (Egri Vár)**—This castle is Hungary's Alamo, where Dobó István defended Eger from the Turks in 1552 (see above). The great St. István—Hungary's first Christian king—built a church on this hill a thousand years ago. The church was destroyed by Tartars in the 13th century, and this fortress was built to repel another attack.

Long after the Turks were forced from Hungary, a castle archaeol-ogist named Géza Gardonyi wrote a book about Dobó István and the 1552 Siege of Eger called *Egri Csillagok* (translated into English as *Eclipse of the Crescent Moon*, available at local bookstores and souvenir stands). Today the book is required reading for all Hungarian school children, and the castle is usually crawling with school-age kids on field trips from all over the country.

The castle grounds feature several small museums (closed Mon), including a history museum, picture gallery, dungeon, underground casements (tunnels through the castle walls), "Heroes' Hall" (with the grave of Dobó István), and temporary exhibits. None of the castle museums is particularly fascinating, but most merit a quick look. The most rewarding way to visit the castle is to stroll up, wander around the grounds, enjoy the view overlooking the town (find the minaret and other landmarks), and then head back down, past a gaggle of colorful shops.

Cost and Hours: 260 Ft for grounds only, 600-Ft ticket gets you into any museum you want (but underground casements and Heroes' Hall only accessible by English tour—500 Ft extra, call ahead to get schedule for English tour: tel. 36/312-744, ext. 111). The castle grounds are open April–Aug daily 8:00–20:00, Sept until 19:00; March and Oct until 18:00; Nov–Feb until 17:00. The castle museums are open March–Oct Tue–Sun 9:00–17:00, closed Mon; Nov–Feb Tue–Sun 9:00–15:00, closed Mon. General castle info: tel. 36/312-744.

Other Castle Sights: In addition to the castle museums, there are three privately-run exhibits, each with its own hours and prices: the **Archery** exhibit (about 100 Ft per arrow to use old-fashioned bows and crossbows); the **Wax Works,** or "Panoptikum," offering a small taste of the casements (250 Ft, daily 9:00–18:00, less in winter); and the **Mint** (150 Ft, usually 9:00–15:30, unpredictable hours).

Getting to Eger Castle: To reach the castle from Dobó Square, go toward Senator Ház Hotel, then jog right around the hotel, turning right on Dobó István utca. Take this street a few blocks until it swings down to the right; the ramp up to the castle is to your left.

▲▲**Eger Cathedral**—Eger's 19th-century bishops peppered the city with beautiful Baroque buildings—including the second-biggest cathedral in Hungary (after Esztergom's; see Danube Bend chapter). With a quirky, sumptuous interior, Eger's cathedral is well worth a visit.

Eger Cathedral was built in the 1830s by an Austrian archbishop who had previously served in Venice, and he thought Eger could use a little more class. The colonnaded neoclassical facade boasts some fine Italian sculpture. As you walk up the main stairs, first you'll pass saints István and László—Hungary's first two Christian kings—and then the apostles Peter and Paul.

Enter the cathedral (free) and walk to the collection box partway down the nave. Then, facing the door, look up at the ornate **ceiling fresco:** On the left, it shows Hungarians in traditional dress, and on the right, the country's most important historical figures. At the bottom you see this cathedral, celestially connected with St. Peter's in Rome (at the top). This symbol of devotion to the Vatican was a brave statement when it was painted, in 1950. The communists were closing churches in other small Hungarian towns, but the Eger archbishop was powerful enough to keep this one open.

Continue to the **transept**. A few years ago, the windows at either end were donated to the cathedral by a rich Austrian couple to commemorate the millennial anniversary of Hungary's conversion to Christianity—notice the dates 1000 (when King István was coronated by the Pope) and 2000.

As you leave, notice the enormous **organ**—Hungary's second-largest—above the door. In the summer, try to catch one of the cathedral's daily half-hour organ concerts (400 Ft, Mon–Sat at 11:30 and Sun at 12:45, mid-May–mid-Oct only; cathedral is the big, can't-miss-it yellow building at Pyrker János tér 1, just off Széchenyi utca).

If you walk up Széchenyi utca from here, you'll see the fancy Archbishop's Palace on your left—still the archbishop's residence.

▲▲**Lyceum (Líceum)**—In the mid-18th century, Bishop Károly Eszterházy wanted a university in Eger—but Hapsburg Empress Maria Theresa refused to allow it. Instead, Eszterházy built the most impressive teacher-training college on the planet. Today, the elegant Baroque Lyceum still trains local teachers (enrollment: about 2,000). Since Eger is expensive by Hungarian standards, many families live in the surrounding countryside. The kids all come into Eger for school—and lots of teachers are needed.

Aside from training teachers, the Lyceum houses three small, offbeat, interesting museums (350 Ft for all 3, April–Sept Tue–Sun 9:30–15:00, closed Mon; Oct–March Sat–Sun only 9:30–13:00, closed Mon–Fri; Eszterházy tér 1, at south end of Széchenyi utca at intersection with Kossuth utca, enter through main door across from cathedral and buy tickets just inside and to the left).

First, visit the old-fashioned **library** (from main entry hall, head right and go up stairs partway down the hall on your right-hand side; at top of first flight of stairs, turn right into the hall and look for the library halfway down on the right; watch for easy-to-miss signs). The library houses 50,000 books (plus another 100,000 elsewhere in the building). Say hello to Dénes Szabó, who has spent the last 11 years cataloging these books—no easy task, since they're in over 100 languages (from Eskimo to Ethiopian) and are shelved according to size rather than topic. If he's not away for a choral contest, Mr. Szabó will be happy to show you a copy of the library's pride and joy, a letter from Mozart. While the Lyceum now belongs to Eger, the library is still the property of the archbishop.

A few flights above (leave library to the right, go to end of hall to reach stairs) is the **Astronomical Tower**, with some dusty old stargazing instruments, as well as a meridian line in the floor (the dot of sunlight hits the line every day exactly at noon).

HUNGARY'S ORGANIC ARCHITECTURE

In recent years, a uniquely Hungarian style of architecture has caught on: Organic, devised by Imre Makovecz. After being blackballed by the communists for his nationalistic politics, Makovecz was denied access to building materials—so he taught himself to make impressive structures with nothing more than sticks and rocks.

Now that the regime is dead and Makovecz is Hungary's premier architect, he still keeps things simple. He believes that a building should be a product of its environment, rather than a cookie-cutter copy. Organic buildings use indigenous materials (especially wood) and take on untraditional forms—often inspired by animals or plants—that blend in with the landscape. Organic buildings look like they're rising up out of the ground, rather than plopped down on top of it. You won't find this back-to-nature style in big cities like Budapest; Makovecz prefers to work in small communities like Eger, instead of working for corporations (see photo next page).

Organic architecture has caught on throughout Hungary, becoming *the* post-communist style. Even big supermarket chains are now imitating Makovecz. If you see a building with white walls and a big, overhanging roof (kind of looks like a big mushroom)...that's Organic.

A few more flights up is the Lyceum's treasured **camera obscura.** You'll enter a dark room around a big bowl-like canvas, and the guide will fly you around the streets of Eger. Fun as it is today, this camera must have seemed like a miracle when it was built in 1776—before TV or movies. It's a bit of a huff up here (9 flights of stairs all together)—but the camera obscura and the view of Eger from the outdoor terrace are worth it.

▲**Market Hall (Csarnok)**—Wandering Eger's big indoor market will give you a taste of local life—and maybe some local food, too (leave Dobó Square with castle to your back; turn right on Zalár József utca, and you'll see market on your left in 2 blocks at intersection with Dr. Sándor utca).

Minaret—Once part of a mosque, this slender 130-foot-tall minaret represents the century of Turkish rule that left its mark on Eger and on all of Hungary. Look closely—the cross at the top symbolizes the eventual Christian victory over the Turkish invaders. You can climb the minaret's 97 steps, but it's not for those scared of heights or close spaces (100 Ft, daily 10:00–18:00; if it's locked, ask for the key at nearby Hotel Minaret).

Minorite Church—The beautiful church that stands over Dobó Square is often said to be the most beautiful Baroque church in Hungary—even if it could use some touch-up work. It's exquisitely photogenic outside, but the shabby interior is less interesting—aside from the hand-carved pews, each of which is a little different.

▲**City Bath (Strand)**—For a refreshing break from the sightseeing grind, consider a splash in the spa. The city recently added an "adventure bath," making it an even better way to soak away a lazy afternoon—with cascades, jets, bubbles, and seven pools kept at different temperatures (700 Ft, adventure bath included Oct–April but 500 Ft extra May–Sept, kids get their own adventure bath-500 Ft, May–Sept Mon–Fri 6:00–19:30, Sat–Sun 8:00–19:00, Oct–April daily 9:00–18:30, Petőfi tér 2, follow stream 4 blocks south from Dobó Square, enter through park, tel. 36/412-202).

The traditional **Turkish Bath,** next door, is open to the public only on weekends (700 Ft, Sat 14:00–18:00, Sun 8:00–18:00, Fürdő utca 1–3, tel. 36/413-356).

Bitskey Aladár Pool—Swimming and water sports are as important to Egerites as good wine. They're proud that many of Hungary's Olympic

medalists in aquatic events have come from this county. Their striking new swimming pool—built at great expense to Eger taxpayers, stirring up controversy—was designed by Imre Makovecz, the father of Organic Architecture. You don't need to be an architecture student to know that the pool is something special. It's worth the five-minute walk from Dobó Square just to take a look...oh, and you can swim in it, too (550 Ft, Mon–Fri 6:00–21:00, Sat–Sun 8:00–18:00, follow Eger Brook south from Dobó Square to Frank Tivadar utca, tel. 36/511-810).

Eger Wine

Eger is at the heart of one of Hungary's best-known wine regions, internationally famous for its **Bull's Blood** (Egri Bikavér). You'll likely hear various stories as to how Bull's Blood got its name during the Turkish siege of Eger, but they're all myths—the term dates only from 1851. Egri Bikavér is a blend—everyone has their own recipe—so you generally won't find it at small producers. Cabernet Sauvignon, Merlot,

Kékfránkos, and Kékoportó are the most commonly-used grapes. Try Egri Bikavér, but then move quickly on to the more special and characteristic Hungarian wines, such as Furmint, Hárslevélű, Leányka, Kéknyelű, and Kékfránkos. You also might have heard of **Tokaji Aszú** wine (a sweet white made from a grape of Hungarian origin, also grown in the Alsace region of France—where it's known as *tokay*). Tokaj is a town (not too far from Eger), and Aszú is the method for producing the wine (involving tubes of paste made from "noble rot" grapes).

Sirens' Valley (Szépasszony-völgy)—When the Turkish invaders first occupied Eger, residents moved into the valley next door, living in caves dug into the hillside. Eventually the Turks were driven out, and the Egerites moved back to town, and the caves became wine cellars. (Most Eger families who can afford it have at least a modest vineyard in the countryside.) There are more than 300 such caves in the valley to the southwest of Eger, several of which are open for visitors.

The best selection of these caves is in the **Sirens' Valley** (sometimes also translated as "Valley of the Beautiful Women," or, on local directional signs, the less-poetic "Nice Woman Valley"). It's a fun scene—vintners showing off their latest vintage, with picnic tables and tipsy tourists spilling out into the street. Most caves offer something to eat with the wine, and you'll also see lots of non-cave, full-service restaurants. Some of the caves are fancy and finished, staffed by multilingual waiters in period costume. Others feel like a dank basement, with grandpa leaning on his moped out front. (The really local places—where the decor is cement, bottles don't have labels, and food consists of potato chips and buttered Wonder bread—are the most fun.) Hopping from cave to musky cave can make for an enjoyable evening, but be sure to wander around a bit to see the options before you dive in (cellars generally open 10:00–20:00 in summer; fewer cellars are open, with shorter hours, off-season).

Getting to the Sirens' Valley: The valley is a 25-minute walk southwest of Eger. Figure no more than 1,000 Ft for a **taxi** between your hotel and the caves. To **walk,** leave the pedestrian zone on the street next to the cathedral (Törvényház utca), with the cathedral on your right-hand side. Take the first left just after the back end of the cathedral (onto Trinitárius utca), go one long block, then take the first right (onto Király utca). At the fork, bear to the left. You'll stay straight on this road—crossing busy Koháry István utca—for several blocks, through some nondescript residential areas (on Szépasszony-völgy utca). When you crest the hill and emerge from the houses, you'll see the caves (and tour buses) below you on the left—go left (downhill) at the fork to get there. First you'll come to a stretch of touristy non-cave restaurants; keep going past these, and eventually you'll see a big loop of caves on your left.

SLEEPING

$$$ Panoráma Hotel is a good big-hotel option, still close to Dobó Square. You'll miss the quaintness of some of the other listings—its 38 rooms are all business—but you get free access to its "Unicornis Thermarium" spa facility (small Sb-12,500 Ft, large Sb-16,500 Ft, Db-19,500 Ft, Tb-23,500 Ft, 10 percent cheaper Nov–March, apartments also available, non-smoking rooms, elevator, free parking, Dr. Hibay K. utca 2, tel. 36/412-886, fax 36/410-136, www.hotels.hu/panorama _hotel, panhotel@elender.hu).

$$$ Imola Udvarház rents six spacious apartments—with kitchen, living room, bedroom, and bathroom—all decorated modern Scandinavian (read: IKEA). They're pricey, but roomy and well-maintained, with a great location near the castle entrance (prices no matter how many people: April–Oct 22,000 Ft, Nov–March 16,500 Ft, prices soft during slow times, enter through restaurant courtyard at Dózsa György tér 4, tel. & fax 36/516-180, www.imolanet.hu, udvarhaz @imolanet.hu).

SLEEP CODE

(€1 = about $1.10, 230 Ft = about $1, country code: 36, area code: 36)

S = Single, **D** = Double/Twin, **T** = Triple, **Q** = Quad, **b** = bathroom, **s** = shower only, **no CC** = Credit Cards not accepted, **NSE** = does not speak English. Unless otherwise noted, English is spoken, breakfast is included, and credit cards are accepted.

To help you easily sort through these listings, I've divided the rooms into three categories, based on the price for a standard double room with bath:

   $$$ **Higher Priced**—Most rooms 19,000 Ft (€74) or more.
   $$ **Moderately Priced**—Most rooms between 16,000–19,000 Ft (€62–74).
   $ **Lower Priced**—Most rooms 16,000 Ft (€62) or less.

Eger is a good overnight stop, and a couple of quaint, well-located hotels in particular—Senator Ház and Offi Ház—are well worth booking in advance. The TI can help you find a room; if you're stumped, the area behind the castle has a sprinkling of guesthouses *(vendégház)*. A tax of 250 Ft per person will be added to your bill (not included in the prices listed here).

$$ Offi Ház Hotel shares "Little Dobó Square" with Senator Ház (below). Its five rooms are classy, with newer decor and higher prices (Sb-15,500 Ft, Db-17,500 Ft, Db suite-20,500 Ft, Tb suite-23,500 Ft, 10 percent cheaper Jan–April, 25 percent cheaper Oct–Dec, non-smoking, Dobó István tér 5, tel. & fax 36/311-005, www.offihaz.hu, offihaz @mail.matav.hu).

$$ Szent János Hotel, less charming and more business-like than the Offi Ház, offers a slightly worse location, 10 rooms, and a better value (Sb-€48, Db-€65, extra bed-€22, 25 percent cheaper Nov–March, non-smoking rooms, McDonald's walk-up window across the street can be noisy at night—especially weekends—so request a quiet back room, a long block off Dobó Square at Szent János utca 3, tel. 36/510-350, fax 36/517-101, hotelszentjanos@hotelszentjanos.hu).

$ Senator Ház Hotel is my favorite spot in Eger. Though the 11 rooms are a bit worn, it's cozy and well-run by András Cseh, with a picture-perfect location just under the castle on "Little Dobó Square" (Sb-11,000 Ft, Db-15,500 Ft, 15–30 percent cheaper Nov–mid-May, Dobó István tér 11, tel. & fax 36/320-466).

$ Dobó Vendégház, run by friendly Mariann Kleszo, has seven simple rooms just off Dobó Square. Mariann speaks nothing but Hungarian, but gets simple reservation e-mails translated by a friend (Sb-€30, Db-€40, Tb-€45, Qb-€55, Dobó utca 19, tel. 36/421-407, www.hotels.hu/dobo_vendeghaz, csillagd@axelero.hu).

EATING

On Dobó Square, the **Bajor Sörház** (a.k.a. "HBH" for the brand of beer on tap) is favored by tourists and locals alike for its excellent Hungarian and Bavarian cuisine (most main dishes 1,000–1,500 Ft, daily 11:30–22:00, Bajcsy-Zsilinszky utca 19, tel. 36/515-516).

Senator Ház Hotel's restaurant, at the other end of Dobó Square, has picturesque seating on the square—*the* place to see and be seen in Eger (Dobó István tér 11, tel. 36/320-466).

Elefanto, above the Market Hall, offers good, inexpensive pizzas (mostly 600–800 Ft) and a pleasant ambience. In good weather, enjoy the covered terrace seating (daily 12:00–24:00, Katona István tér 2, tel. 36/412-452).

Palacsintavár (Pancake Castle), near the castle entrance, isn't your hometown IHOP. This place serves up inventive crepe-wrapped main courses, popular with local students (Dobó utca 9).

At **Szantofer Vendéglő,** enjoy local food at local prices, from a menu that is either remarkably creative or terribly translated (most main dishes under 1,000 Ft, daily 11:30–22:00, Bródy Sándor utca 3, tel. 36/517-298).

For **dessert,** there are two ways to go. For deluxe, super-decadent pastries of every kind imaginable—most for under a buck—drop by **Dobós Cukrászda** (daily 9:00–21:00, point to what you want inside and they'll bring it out to your table, Széchenyi utca 6, tel. 36/413-335). For a more local scene, find the tiny **Sárvári Cukrászda,** behind the Lyceum. Their pastries are good—but Egerites line up here after a big Sunday lunch for their locally-famous homemade gelato (90 Ft/scoop, Mon–Fri 7:00–18:00, Sat–Sun 10:00–18:00, Kossuth utca 1, between Jókai utca and Fellner utca).

TRANSPORTATION CONNECTIONS

By train: The only major destination you'll get to directly from Eger's train station is **Budapest** (5/day direct to or from Budapest's Keleti/Eastern, 2 hrs). For most other destinations, you'll connect through Budapest. For destinations to the north—like Kraków—you'll save time by transferring in **Füzesabony** (13/day, 50 min), a nearby smaller village that happens to be on the Budapest–Kraków line. The very rustic Füzesabony station does not have lockers or an ATM, but—oddly enough—does have a modest museum of local artifacts.

SLOVENIA

(Slovenija)

- Slovenia is 7,800 square miles (smaller than New Hampshire, or about the same size as Israel).
- Population is 2 million (about 255 people per square mile).
- 220 tolars (SIT) = about $1.
- Country code: 386.

Tiny, overlooked Slovenia is one of Europe's most unexpectedly charming destinations. At the intersection of the Slavic, German, and Italian worlds, Slovenia is an exciting mix of the best of each culture. Though it's just a quick trip away from the tourist throngs in Venice, Munich, Salzburg, and Vienna, Slovenia has stayed off the tourist track, a handy detour for in-the-know Back Door travelers.

Today it seems strange to think that Slovenia was ever part of Yugoslavia. Even during the Yugoslav era, it felt more like Austria. Visitors expecting minefields and rusting Yugo factories are pleasantly surprised to find Slovenia's rolling countryside dotted instead with quaint alpine villages and the spires of miniature Baroque churches, with breathtaking snow-capped peaks in the distance.

Only half as big as Switzerland, but remarkably diverse for its size, Slovenia can be easily appreciated on a brief visit. Travelers can hike on alpine trails in the morning and explore some of the world's best karstic caves in the afternoon, before relaxing with a seafood dinner on the

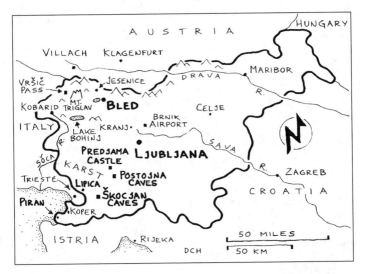

Adriatic (along the nation's 29 miles of coastline—about one inch per inhabitant).

Slovenia enjoys a powerhouse economy—the healthiest in Eastern Europe. Thanks to its long-standing ties to the West and can-do spirit, Slovenia already feels more Western than any other destination in this book.

Slovenes are a remarkably friendly bunch. The country has a funny way of making people fall in love with it. Many of today's American visitors to Slovenia are soldiers who participated in the conflict in Bosnia and have good memories of their vacations here. Now they're bringing their families back with them. They're not the only ones. One of your co-authors has decided that Slovenia is his hands-down favorite European country.

Keep your eyes open for two uniquely Slovenian bits of folk art: roofed hay-drying racks *(toplarji)* and beehives with intricately painted panels *(panjske končnice)*. The residents of this tiny country are proud of the few things that are distinctly Slovenian.

To really stretch your *tolar,* try one of Slovenia's 200 farmhouse B&Bs, called "tourist farms" *(turistične kmetije).* Use the B&B as a home base to explore the entire country—remember, the farthest reaches of Slovenia are only a day trip away. You can get a comfortable, hotelesque double with private bathroom—plus a traditional Slovenian dinner and a hearty breakfast—for as little as $40. Request a listing from the Slovenian Tourist Board (see page 17) or visit www.slovenia-tourism.si/touristfarms.

Practicalities

Telephones: Chip cards, sold at newsstands and kiosks everywhere, get you access to the modern public phones.

When calling locally, dial the seven-digit number. To make a long-distance call within the country, start with the area code (which begins with 0). To call a Slovenian number from abroad, dial the international access number (00 if calling from Europe, 011 from the United States or Canada) followed by 386 (Slovenia's country code), then the area code (without the initial 0) and the seven-digit number. To call out of Slovenia, dial 00, the country code of the country you're calling (see chart in appendix), the area code if applicable (may need to drop initial zero), and the local number.

Slovenian phone numbers beginning with 080 are toll-free; 090 and 089 denote expensive toll lines. Mobile-phone numbers, usually beginning with 031, 041, 051, 040, or 070, are likely to change in 2004.

If a mobile number doesn't work, ask at a TI or hotel for assistance tracking down the new digits.

Slovenian History

Slovenia has a long and not-very-interesting history as part of various larger empires. Charlemagne's Franks conquered the tiny land in the eighth century, and ever since, Slovenia has been a backwater of the German world—as a holding of the Germanic Holy Roman Empire and, later, the Hapsburg Empire. Slovenia often seems as much German as Slavic. But even as the capital, Ljubljana, was populated by Austrians (called "Laibach" by its German-speaking residents), the Slovenian language and cultural traditions survived in the countryside.

Ljubljana rose to international prominence for half a decade (1809–1813) when Napoleon named it the capital of his "Illyrian Provinces," stretching from Austria's Tirol to Croatia's Dalmatian Coast. During this time, the long-suppressed Slovene language was used for the first time in schools and government. Inspired by the patriotic poetry of France Prešeren, nationalism surged.

The most interesting chapter in Slovenian history has come in the last century. Some of WWI's fiercest fighting occurred at the Soča (Isonzo) Front in northwest Slovenia, witnessed by young Ernest Hemingway, who drove an ambulance. After the war, from 1918 to 1991, Slovenia was the smallest, northernmost, and most affluent republic in the former Yugoslavia. Concerned about Slobodan Milošević's politics, Slovenia seceded in 1991. Because more than 90 percent of the people here are ethnic Slovenes, the break with Yugoslavia was simple and virtually uncontested. Its war for independence lasted just 10 days and claimed only 66 lives (For more details, see "Understanding Yugoslavia," page 517).

After centuries of looking to the West, in 2004 Slovenia becomes the first of the former Yugoslav republics to join the European Union.

Slovenian Food

Slovenian cuisine has enjoyed influence from a wide variety of sources. Like Croatian food, you'll find some pan-Balkan elements; the red-bell-pepper condiment *ajvar* is popular here, and for fast food, you'll find *burek, čevapčići, pljeskavica,* and *ražnjići* (see "Croatian Food," page 338). Italian influence is notable in Slovenia, with a pizza or pasta restaurant on seemingly every corner. You'll also find Hungarian flavors in the northeast corner of the country (where many Magyars reside).

But most of all, Slovenian food has a distinctly German vibe—sausages, schnitzels, strudels, and sauerkraut are common here, as well as *repa* (turnip prepared like sauerkraut). Slovenes brag that their cuisine melds the best of Italian and German cooking.

Traditional Slovenian dishes are prepared with groats—kind of a

SLOVENIA, SLOVAKIA, AND SLAVONIA

"The only thing I know about Slovakia is what I learned firsthand from your foreign minister, who came to Texas." —George W. Bush, to a Slovak journalist. Bush had actually met with Dr. Janez Drnovšek, then Slovenia's prime minister.

Maybe it's understandable that many Americans confuse Slovenia with Slovakia. Both are small, mountainous countries that not too long ago were parts of bigger, better-known, now-defunct nations. But anyone who has visited Slovenia and Slovakia will set you straight—they feel worlds apart.

Slovenia, wedged between the Alps and the Adriatic, is a tidy, prosperous country with a strong economy that leads the pack of nations joining the European Union in 2004. Until 1991, Slovenia was one of the six republics that made up Yugoslavia. Historically, Slovenia has had very strong ties with Germanic culture—so it feels German.

Slovakia, two countries to the northeast, is slightly bigger (like New Hampshire plus Vermont). Much of its territory is covered by the Carpathian Mountains, most notably the dramatic, jagged peaks of the High Tatras. In 1993, the Czechs and Slovaks peacefully chose to go their separate ways, so the nation of Czechoslovakia dissolved into the Czech Republic and the Slovak Republic (a.k.a. Slovakia). Slovakia is at the bottom of the heap of new EU members, with a weak economy and high poverty levels. Slovakia was part of Hungary until the end of World War I, and feels Hungarian (especially the southern half of the country, where many Hungarians still live).

To make things even more confusing, there's also **Slavonia.** This is the thick, inland "panhandle" that makes up the northeast half of Croatia, along Slovenia's southeast border. Much of the warfare in Croatia's 1991–1995 war took place in Slavonia (including Vukovar; see Understanding Yugoslavia chapter).

I won't tell on you if you mix them up. But if you want to feel smarter than the president, do a little homework and get it right.

grainy mush—which can be made with buckwheat, barley, or corn. Buckwheat is often on Slovenian menus, because the country's climate is ideal for growing it. You'll also see plenty of *štruklji* (dumplings), which can be stuffed with cheese, meat, or vegetables. Among the hearty soups in Slovenia is *jota*—a staple for Karst peasants made from *repa*, beans, and vegetables.

The cuisine of Slovenia's Karst (the arid limestone plain south of Ljubljana) is notable. The small farms and wineries of this region have been inspired by Italy's "Slow Food" movement (www.slowfood.com), and believe that cuisine is meant to be gradually appreciated, not rushed, making the Karst a destination for gourmet tours. Karstic cuisine is similar to France's nouvelle cuisine—several courses in small portions, with a focus on unusual combinations and preparations—but with an Italian flair. The Karst's tasty air-dried ham *(pršut)*, available throughout the country, is worth seeking out. Istria (the peninsula just to the south of the Karst, in southern Slovenia and Croatia) produces truffles that, locals boast, are as good as Piedmont's—but much cheaper.

Slovenian food, with all of its influences—Italian, Austrian, Balkan, Hungarian, and Karst—comes together in Ljubljana. The capital city also has a cosmopolitan diversity of options, from Mexican to Chinese to Moroccan.

Voda is water and *kava* is coffee. Radenska, in the bottle with the three little hearts, is Slovenia's best-known brand of mineral water—good enough that the word *Radenska* is synonymous with bottled water all over Slovenia and throughout the former Yugoslavia. Adventurous teetotalers should forego the Coke and sample Cockta (a Slovenian soft drink like a cola, but with a slight cherry, smoky aftertaste).

To toast, say, *"Na ZDRAV-yeh!"*—if you can't remember it, think of "Nice driving!" The premier Slovenian brand of *pivo* (beer) is Union (OO-nee-ohn). Slovenia produces some fine *vino* (wine). The Celts first grew wine in Slovenia; the Romans improved the process and spread it throughout the country. Slovenia has three primary wine regions. Podravje, in the northeast, is dominated by Laški and Renski Riesling and other top-quality wines. Posavje, in the southeast, produces both white and red wines, but is famous for the light, russet-colored Cviček wine. Primorska, in the southwest, has a Mediterranean climate and produces mostly reds, including Teran, made from *refošk* grapes.

Slovenia's most popular desserts are *potica* (filled nut roll) and *prekmurska gibanica* (pastry filled with poppy seeds, walnuts, apple, and cheese). Bled is known for its *kremna rezina,* a vanilla custard and cream cake. Locals claim that Ljubljana has the finest gelato outside of Italy—which, after all, is just 90 minutes away by car.

KEY SLOVENE PHRASES

English	Slovene	Pronounced
Hello (formal)	Dober dan	DOH-behr dahn
Hi / Bye (informal)	Živjo	ZHEEV-yoh
Do you speak English?	Ali govorite angleško?	AH-lee goh-VOH-ree-teh ahng-LEHSH-koh
yes / no	ja / ne	yah / neh
Please / You're welcome	Prosim	PROH-seem
Can I help you?	Izvolite	eez-VOH-lee-teh
Thank you	Hvala	HVAH-lah
I'm sorry / Excuse me	Oprostite	oh-proh-STEE-teh
Good	Dobro	DOH-broh
Goodbye	Nasvidenje	nahs-VEE-dehn-yeh
one / two	ena / dve	EH-nah / dveh
three / four	tri / štiri	tree / SHTEE-ree
five / six	pet / šest	peht / shehst
seven / eight	sedem / osem	SEH-dehm / OH-sehm
nine / ten	devet / deset	deh-VEHT / deh-SEHT
hundred	sto	stoh
thousand	tisoč	TEE-sohch
How much?	Koliko?	KOH-lee-koh
local currency	tolar (SIT)	TOH-lar
Where is...?	Kje je...?	kyeh yeh
...the toilet	...vece	VEHT-seh
men	moški	MOHSH-kee
women	ženski	ZHEHN-skee
water / coffee	voda / kava	VOH-dah / KAH-vah
beer / wine	pivo / vino	PEE-voh / VEE-noh
Cheers!	Na zdravje!	nah ZDRAHV-yeh
the bill	račun	rah-CHOON

Slovenian Language

Slovene is surprisingly different from languages spoken in the other former Yugoslav republics. While Serbian and Croatian are virtually identical, Slovene is another story. Of all Slavic languages, Slovene has changed the least over the centuries—it's still closest to the proto-Slavonic spoken over a millennium ago in the plains of present-day Ukraine.

Most Slovenians know Serbo-Croatian because, a generation ago, everybody in Yugoslavia had to learn it, along with the Cyrillic alphabet used in Serbia. The tiny country of Slovenia borders Italy and Austria, with important historical and linguistic ties to both. For self-preservation, the Slovene population has always been forced to function in many different languages. All of these factors make Slovenes excellent linguists. Most young Slovenes speak effortless, flawless English—then admit that they've never set foot in the U.S. or Britain, but love watching American movies and TV shows.

Slovene is perhaps the easiest Eastern European language to pronounce. As with most Slavic languages, *c* is pronounced "ts" (like "cats"). The letter *j* is pronounced as "y"—making "Ljubljana" easier to say than it looks (lyoob-lyonna). In contrast to other Eastern European languages—which tend to have a wide array of confusing little doohickeys over the letters—Slovene only has one diacritical mark: the *strešica,* or "little roof." This makes *č* sound like "ch," *š* sound like "sh," and *ž* sound like "zh" (as in "measure"). The only trick: As in English, which syllable gets the emphasis is unpredictable.

As you're tracking down addresses, these definitions will help: *trg* (square), *ulica* (road), and *most* (bridge).

LJUBLJANA

Slovenia's capital, Ljubljana (lyoob-lyonna)—with a lazy old town clustered around a castle-topped mountain—is often compared to Salzburg. It's an apt comparison—but only if you inject a healthy dose of breezy Adriatic culture, add a Slavic accent, and replace Mozart with local architect Jože Plečnik.

Ljubljana feels much smaller than its population of 300,000. Festivals fill the summer, and people enjoy a Sunday stroll any day of the week. Fashion boutiques and cafés jockey for control of the old town, and the leafy riverside promenade crawls with stylishly dressed students sipping *kava* and polishing their near-perfect English. Laid-back Ljubljana is the kind of place where crumbling buildings seem elegantly atmospheric instead of shoddy.

Centuries ago, Ljubljana was on the waterway that connected the Black Sea to the Mediterranean. Legend has it that Jason and his Argonauts founded the town when they stopped here for the winter on their way home with the Golden Fleece. The city was Romanized (and called Emona) before being overrun by Huns—only to later be re-settled by Slavs. In 1335, the city fell under the jurisdiction of the Hapsburg Emperors (who called it Laibach). After six centuries of Hapsburg rule, Ljubljana feels Austrian—especially the abundant Austrian Baroque and Viennese *Jugendstil* (Art Nouveau) architecture.

Napoleon put Ljubljana on the map when he made it the capital of his Illyrian Provinces (1809–1813). A half-century later, the railway connecting Vienna to the Adriatic (Trieste) was built through town—and Ljubljana boomed.

Much of Ljubljana was destroyed by an earthquake in 1895. It was rebuilt in the Art Nouveau style so popular in Vienna, its capital at the time. A generation later, architect Jože Plečnik bathed the city in his distinctive, artsy-but-sensible, classical-meets-modern style.

Ljubljana

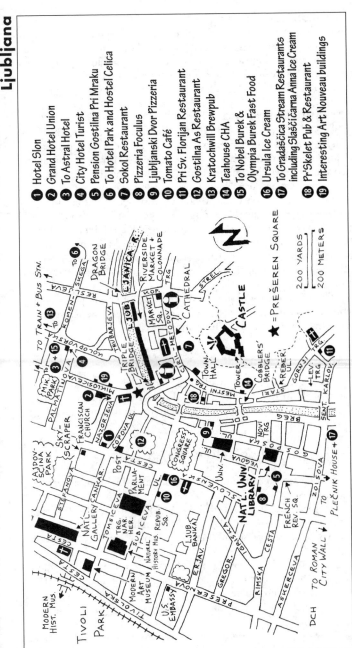

1. Hotel Slon
2. Grand Hotel Union
3. To Astral Hotel
4. City Hotel Turist
5. Pension Gostilna Pri Mraku
6. To Hotel Park and Hostel Celica
7. Sokol Restaurant
8. Pizzeria Foculus
9. Ljubljanski Dvor Pizzeria
10. Tomato Café
11. Pri Sv. Florijan Restaurant
12. Gostilna As Restaurant
13. Kratochwill Brewpub
14. Teahouse CHA
15. To Nobel Burek & Olympia Burek Fast Food
16. Ursula Ice Cream
17. To Gradaščica Stream Restaurants including Slaščičarna Anna Ice Cream
18. Pr'Skelet Pub & Restaurant
19. Interesting Art Nouveau buildings

In the Karst region south of Ljubljana, you'll find some of the most impressive cave systems on the planet, a chance to see the famous Lipizzaner stallions for a fraction of what you'd pay in Vienna, and one of Europe's most dramatically situated castles—built into the face of a mountain. Picture-perfect Piran, on Slovenia's tiny coastline, might be the best Adriatic village this side of the Dalmatian Coast.

Planning Your Time

Ljubljana deserves at least a full day. While there are few must-see sights, Ljubljana's biggest attraction is its ambience. You'll spend much of your time strolling the pleasant town center, exploring the many interesting squares and architectural gems, shopping the boutiques, and sipping coffee at outdoor tables along the river.

Begin your day on Prešeren Square, at the heart of the city. Then wander through the market across the river (best in the morning). If you're here on a Tuesday or Thursday, the Jože Plečnik House is a must. Otherwise, the next best museum in town is the Museum of Modern History (which comes with a peaceful stroll through Tivoli Park). A visit to the castle is also worthwhile (reached by a good hike or an easy ride on the tourist train).

There are plenty of good day trips close to Ljubljana. With a second day, visit a cave system and nearby sights in the Karst region south of the city (see end of this chapter).

ORIENTATION

The Ljubljanica River, lined with cafés, restaurants, and a buzzing outdoor market, divides the city in half. Most sights are either on or just a short walk from the river, which is crossed by several interesting bridges,

LJUBLJANA'S TWO BIG P'S

The two most important names you'll hear in Ljubljana are easy to confuse:

Jože Plečnik (YOH-zheh PLAYCH-neek, 1872–1957) is the architect who shaped Ljubljana, designing virtually all of the city's most important landmarks. For more information, see page 297.

France Prešeren (FRAHN-tseh preh-SHAY-rehn, 1800–1849) is Slovenia's greatest poet and the namesake of Ljubljana's main square.

Mind your P's, and your visit to Ljubljana will be smoother.

LJUBLJANA LANDMARKS

English	Slovene	Pronounced
Prešeren Square	**Prešernov trg**	preh-SHEHR-nohv trrg
Ljubljana Castle	**Ljubljanski Grad**	lyoob-lyonskee grahd
Triple Bridge	**Tromostovje**	troh-moh-STOHV-yeh
Dragon Bridge	**Zmajski Most**	ZMAY-skee mohst

the most famous being Plečnik's Triple Bridge. The center of Ljubljana is Prešeren Square, watched over by a big statue of the Slovene national poet, France Prešeren.

Tourist Information

Ljubljana's helpful TI has an office across the **Triple Bridge** from Prešeren Square (June–Sept daily 8:00–21:00, Oct–May daily 8:00–19:00, Stritarjeva ulica, tel. 01/306-1215, www.ljubljana-tourism.si); another is at the **train station** (June–Sept daily 8:00–22:00, Oct–May daily 10:00–19:00, Trg O.F. 6, tel. 01/433-9475). A third TI, at the top of the **market** at Krekov trg 10, also offers information about the rest of Slovenia, Internet access, and a ticket box office (June–Sept daily 8:00–21:00, Oct–May daily 8:00-19:00, tel. 01/306-4575).

At any TI, pick up a pile of free resources: the Tourist Guide, the *Ljubljana A to Z* directory, the monthly *Where to?* events guide, *Ljubljana Life* magazine (with restaurant reviews), the detailed one-page city map, and the bigger map with sight information. If you fall in love with this city's quirky buildings, consider the excellent but expensive 8,000-SIT *Architectural Guide to Ljubljana.* In 2004, there are plans for a new Ljubljana City Card, which includes access to public transportation and free entry or discounts at several city museums (likely 3,000 SIT/3 days).

Arrival in Ljubljana

By Train: Ljubljana's modern, user-friendly train station (Železniška Postaja) is on the north edge of the city center. In the underground passage that connects the tracks *(tiri),* you'll find a library branch with free **Internet access** (usually limited to 15 min, look for the @ sign). When you emerge from the passage, turn right (passing the Tir Bar, with the cheapest rental bikes in town—see "By Bike," below). If you cut through the yellow arrivals hall, you'll find a **TI,** an **ATM** (by the ticket windows), and helpful English signage (station open daily 5:00–22:00). Arrivals are *prihodi* and departures are *odhodi*. To get to the city center, leave the arrivals hall to the right and walk a long block along the busy Trg Osvobodilne fronte (or "Trg O.F." for short). When you reach the post office (yellow *pošta* sign), cross Trg O.F. and head straight down Miklošičeva; in 10 minutes, you'll be at Prešeren Square.

By Bus: Ljubljana's bus station (Autobusna Postaja) is a low-profile building in the middle of Trg O.F., right in front of the train station (see above).

By Car: Follow signs for *Center*. For longer visits, park in one of the many well-marked garages (about 400 SIT/hr) or lots (around 250 SIT/hr).

By Plane: Slovenia's main international airport, Aerodrom Ljubljana (airport code: LJU), is at Brnik, 14 miles north of the city—conveniently located about halfway between Ljubljana and Bled. Almost every flight is operated by Adria, Slovenia's national airline (www.adria -airways.com). Don't hurry to get there far in advance; at this tiny airport, check-in doesn't even start until 90 minutes before each flight (tel. 04/206-1000, www.lju-airport.si). An airport **bus** connects Brnik with Ljubljana's bus station (700 SIT, Mon–Fri hrly, Sat–Sun every 2 hrs, 50 min); a private **shuttle** does the same trip in half the time (1,000 SIT, every 2 hrs). Figure 6,000 SIT for a **taxi** to the airport.

Getting around Ljubljana

By Bus: Virtually all of Ljubljana's sights are easily accessible by foot, so public transportation probably isn't necessary. But just in case, here's what you need to know: One trip on an LPP bus costs 250 SIT (pay exact change on bus, or buy a 180-SIT token—*žeton*—in advance at kiosk or bus station). An all-day ticket costs 700 SIT (available only at bus station or LPP office).

By Taxi: Taxis start around 200 SIT, then charge 200 SIT per kilometer. There are some dishonest cabbies in Ljubljana, so it's smart to establish the price up front. Even better, call for a cab—it's cheaper anyway. There are 10 different companies, all essentially the same (dial any number between 01/9700 and 01/9709). Intersiti Taxi has a good reputation (tel. 01/9708). Taxi telephone numbers may change in 2004; if these don't work, ask the TI or your hotel for the new numbers.

By Bike: Ljubljana is a biker's delight, with lots of well-marked bike lanes. The cheapest rental place in town is Tir Bar at the train station (200 SIT/hr, 500 SIT/day, low prices subsidized by mobile phone company Debitel which puts ads on bikes, daily 8:00–20:00, by passageway to tracks). Closer to the center, the riverside bar Maček rents more expensive bikes (500 SIT/hr, 2,500 SIT/day, daily 8:00–24:30, Krojaška ulica 5).

Helpful Hints

Important Days: Many Ljubljana museums (except the Castle) are closed on Mondays. On Tuesdays and Thursdays, make it a priority to visit Jože Plečnik's house (open only these 2 days 10:00–14:00).

Flea Market: Every Sunday from 8:00–13:00, a colorful local flea market sprawls along the castle side of the Ljubljanica River (south of the TI)—ideal for bargain-hunting and people-watching.

Internet: Access is tricky and ever-changing in Ljubljana—get the latest scoop from the TI or your hotel. The TI at the market has several terminals (see "Tourist Information," page 285). Many hotel lobbies have Internet access for guests, and some also let non-guests pay to log on (including the City Hotel Turist, 220 SIT/20 min, see "Sleeping," below). Free terminals in the TIs allow you to check your e-mail (but only Hotmail and Yahoo!). The Müller department store just up Čopova from Prešeren Square has three free terminals on the fourth floor (Mon–Fri 8:30–20:00, Sat 8:30–14:00, closed Sun).

Post Office: The main post office (pošta) is a block up Čopova from Prešeren Square, at the intersection with the busy Slovenska cesta (Mon–Fri 7:00–20:00, Sat 7:00–13:00, closed Sun).

Banking: Most banks are open Mon–Fri 9:00–12:00 & 14:00–17:00, Sat 9:00–12:00, closed Sun.

Laundry: Self-service places, used mainly by students, are far from the center (get details at TI). Most hotels can do laundry, but it's expensive. The best option in town is the Hostel Celica, which sometimes lets non-guests use their self-service laundry facilities; call first (Metelkova 9, tel. 01/430-1890).

Car Rental: Avis is friendly and central (about €60/day includes tax and insurance, Čufarjeva 2, tel. 01/583-3572, www.avis.si).

Best Views: The best view in Ljubljana is from atop the Nebotičnik skyscraper (see below), followed by the castle tower. On sunny blue-sky days, the colorful architecture on Prešeren Square springs to life, and you'll burn through film quickly along the river promenade.

Tours of Ljubljana

Walking Tour: The TI organizes a guided town walk of Ljubljana in Slovene and English (1,200 SIT, June–Sept daily at 17:00, June and Sept also Fri–Sun at 11:00, July–Aug also daily at 11:00; Oct–May Sat–Sun only at 11:00; meets at Town Hall around corner from Triple Bridge TI).

By Boat: Consider seeing Ljubljana from the Ljubljanica River. Guided cruises leave a block from the Triple Bridge TI (away from the market) daily at 17:30 from mid-May through September (also at 11:30 Sat–Sun; 1,500 SIT, 1 hr). Sometimes the boat goes on additional unguided tours; ask the TI for details.

LJUBLJANA AT A GLANCE

▲▲▲**Jože Plečnik House** Final digs of the famed hometown architect who built so much of Ljubljana. **Hours:** Tue and Thu 10:00–14:00, other weekday times sometimes by appointment.

▲▲**Stroll through Riverside Market at Vodnikov Trg** Picturesque market area in the old town with produce, clothing, souvenirs—even bear salami. **Hours:** Best on Saturday mornings.

▲▲**Town Square** Home to the Town Hall, its clock tower and loggia, and a lavish fountain. **Hours:** Always open.

▲▲**Ljubljana Castle** Worthwhile 3-D film and tower with stunning views. **Hours:** May–Sept daily 9:00–21:00, Oct–April daily 10:00–18:00, castle grounds open until 22:00 in summer and 20:00 in winter.

▲▲**Modern History Museum** Baroque mansion in Tivoli Park with exhibit highlighting Slovenia's last 100 years. **Hours:** Tue–Sun 10:00–18:00, closed Mon.

▲▲**National and University Library** Plečnik's pièce de résistance with an intriguing facade, piles of books, and a bright reading room.

Local Guide: Ljubljana's hardworking guides lead tours on a wide variety of topics (figure 7,000 SIT/2 hrs, 25 percent more on Sun or for same-day booking, contact TI for details). **Marijan Krišković** is an excellent guide (7,000 SIT/2 hrs, mobile 031-815-509, kriskovic@yahoo.com).

SIGHTS

Prešeren Square Spin-Tour

The heart of Ljubljana is lively Prešeren Square (Prešernov trg). The city's meeting point is the large **statue of France Prešeren,** Slovenia's greatest poet (who wrote, among other things, the Slovene national anthem). Prešeren, an important catalyst of 19th-century Slovenian nationalism, is being inspired from overhead by the Muse. This statue provoked a scandal and outraged the bishop when it went up a hundred years ago—a naked woman sharing the square with a church! To

Hours: July–Aug Mon–Sat 8:00–14:00, Wed until 16:00, closed Sun, Sept–June Mon–Fri 8:00–20:00, Sat 8:00–14:00, closed Sun.

▲**Dragon Bridge** Cool-looking Secessionist bridge featuring Ljubljana's mascot. **Hours:** Always open.

▲**Square of the Republic** Eclectic mix of modern buildings, including the Slovenian Parliament and a shopping mall, plus interesting public art. **Hours:** Always open.

▲**Skyscraper** Art Deco high-rise with view café on top. **Hours:** Usually Mon–Sat 10:00–24:00, closed Sun except sometimes in summer. Café's hours are unpredictable.

▲**French Revolution Square** Site of Plečnik's columned tribute to Ljubljana's brief reign as capital of Napoleon's Illyrian Provinces. **Hours:** Always open.

▲**Architectural Museum of Ljubljana** Castle-cum-Plečnik-exhibit on the fringes of town. **Hours:** Mon–Thu 10:00–14:00, closed Fri–Sun.

ensure that nobody could be confused about the woman's intentions, she's conspicuously depicted with typical Muse accessories: a laurel branch and a cloak.

Stand at the base of the statue to get oriented. Notice the bridge crossing the Ljubljanica River. This is one of Ljubljana's most important landmarks, Jože Plečnik's **Triple Bridge** (Tromostovje). The bridge's Venetian vibe is intentional: Plečnik recognized that Ljubljana, midway between Venice and then-capital Vienna, is itself a bridge between the Italian and Germanic worlds. On the other side of the bridge is the TI, an ATM, WCs, the market and cathedral (to the left), and the Town Hall (straight ahead).

Now turn 90 degrees to the right, and look down the first street after the riverbank. Find the orange woman in the picture frame on the second floor of the yellow house. This is **Julija,** the love of Prešeren's life. Tour guides love to spin romantic tales about the couple, saying that they met at a Mass at Trnovo Church, and Prešeren immediately fell in love with her. But the truth is far less exciting: He was a teacher in her father's house when he was in his 30s and she was four. Later in life, she inspired him from afar—as she does now, from across the square—

but they probably never had a relationship. She married another man.

Ljubljana—especially the streets around this square—is an architecture-lover's paradise, starting with **Hauptmann House** to the right of Julija. This was the only building in town that survived the devastating 1895 earthquake. A few years later, the owner renovated it anyway in the then-trendy Viennese Secession style you see today. All that remains of the original is the Baroque balcony above the entrance.

Just to the right of the Hauptmann House is a small **model** of the city center—helpful for orientation. The street next to it (with the McDonald's) is Čopova—once the route of Ljubljana's Sunday promenade. A century ago, locals would put on their Sunday best and stroll from here to Tivoli Park, listening to musicians and dropping into cafés along the way. Today the busy Slovenska cesta and railroad tracks cross the route, making the promenade less inviting. But in the last decade, Ljubljana has been trying to recapture its golden age, and parts of the center are pedestrians-only on weekends once again.

Continue looking to the right, past the big, pink landmark Franciscan Church of St. Mary. The street to the right of the church, **Miklošičeva cesta,** connects Prešeren Square to the train station. When Ljubljana was rebuilding after the 1895 earthquake, they envisioned this street as a showcase of its new, Vienna-inspired Art Nouveau image. Down the street and on the left is the prominent **Grand Hotel Union,** with a stately domed spire on the corner. When these buildings were designed, Prague was the cultural capital of the Slavic world. The new look of Ljubljana paid homage to "the golden city of a hundred spires" (and co-opted Prague's romantic image). There was actually a law for several years that corner buildings had to have these spires. When the architect Plečnik designed the Ljubljanica River embankments a generation later, he kept this in mind, planting tall, pointy poplar trees and squat, rounded willows—imitating the spires and domes of Prague.

Across the street from the Grand Hotel Union (not visible from here, but worth a look later) is a classic blue-and-white Secessionist building next to the pink zig-zagged **Cooperative Bank.** The bank was designed by Ivan Vurnik, an ambitious Slovene architect who wanted to invent a distinctive "national style" after World War I, when the Hapsburg Empire broke up and Eastern Europe's nations were proudly emerging for the first time. What he came up with is unusual, to be sure, but it didn't catch on—architecture highbrows say he copied too much from other styles.

On the near corner of Miklošičeva cesta, look for the distinctive glass awning of **Centromerkur**—the first big post-quake department store, today government-protected. Step inside to admire the interior, which is exactly the same as when it was built. The old-fashioned layout isn't convenient for modern shoppers—no elevator, tight aisles—but no matter how much anyone complains, the management isn't allowed to change anything.

Prešeren Square is the perfect springboard to explore the rest of Ljubljana. Now that you're oriented, visit some of the areas listed below.

East of the River (Under the Castle)

The castle side of the river is the city's most colorful and historic quarter, packed with Old World ambience.

▲▲**Stroll through Riverside Market at Vodnikov trg**—In Ljubljana's thriving old town market, big-city Slovenians enjoy buying directly from the producer. The market is worth an amble anytime, and best on Saturday mornings, when the locals take their time wandering the stalls. In this tiny capital of a tiny country, you may even see the president searching for the perfect produce.

Begin your walk through the market at the Triple Bridge (and TI). The riverside **colonnade** was designed by (who else?) Jože Plečnik. This first stretch—nearest the Triple Bridge—is good for souvenirs. Further in, the market is almost all local, and the colonnade is populated by butchers, fishermen, and lazy cafés.

Walk along the colonnade with the river on your left. When you come to the first small market square on your right, notice the big **cone.** Architect Jože Plečnik wanted to make Ljubljana the "Athens of the North" and imagined a huge hilltop cone as the center of a national acropolis—a complex for government, museums, and culture. This ambitious plan never panned out, but part of Plečnik's Greek idea did: the marketplace, based on an ancient Greek *agora.*

At the top of this square, you'll find the 18th-century **cathedral** *(stolnica),* standing on the site of a 13th-century Romanesque church. The cathedral is dedicated to Nicholas, patron saint of the fishermen and boatmen who have long come to sell their catch at the market. Take a close look at the intricately decorated side door under the passageway. This remarkable door, created for the Pope's visit here in 1996, traces the history of Christianity and the history of Slovenia in one swoop. You'll find crusaders, Turks, Pope John Paul II (at the top), the man who will become Slovenia's first saint (below the Pope), and lots more. Around back is a similar door, carved with images of the six 20th-century bishops of Ljubljana.

The building at the end of this first market square is the seminary palace. In the basement is a **market hall** with vendors selling cheeses, meats, dried fruits, and other goodies (Mon–Sat 7:00–14:00, Thu–Fri until 16:00, closed Sun). This place is worth a graze. Most merchants are happy to give you a free sample (point to what you want and ask for a *probat*).

When you leave the market hall, continue on to the big **main market square,** packed with produce and clothing stands. (Don't miss the colorful flower market, hiding behind the seminary palace/market hall.) Over time, shoppers develop friendships with their favorite producers. On busy days, you'll see a long line at one stand, while the other merchants stand bored. Your choice is simple: get in line or eat sub-par produce. Look for the little scales in the wooden kiosks marked *Kontrola Tehtnica*—allowing buyers to immediately check whether the producer cheated them (not a common problem, but just in case).

Near the middle of the market, you'll notice a big gap along the riverfront colonnade. This was to be the site of a huge, roofed **Butchers' Bridge** designed by Jože Plečnik, but the plans never materialized. Aware of Plečnik's newfound touristic currency, some local politicians have recently dusted off the old plans and proposed building the bridge after all these years. (If you look across the river, you'll see that the cornerstone was already put in place by an overzealous politician.) It's a controversial project, and anytime a new mayor is elected, the decision is reversed.

If you want an interesting taste as you finish exploring the market, enter the colonnade near the very end and find the **Divjač'na Hubert** stand at #22, specializing in game (Mon–Fri 8:00–15:00, Sat 7:00–13:00, closed Sun). If you dare, ask for a *probat* (taste) of *medvedova salama*—bear salami. Not bad, but not grrrreat.

Just beyond the end of the market colonnade is the...

▲**Dragon Bridge (Zmajski Most)**—The dragon has been the symbol

of Ljubljana for centuries. Nobody is sure how it started, but one popular myth is that Jason (of Argonauts and Golden Fleece fame) slew a dragon in a nearby swamp. Oddly enough, the Austrian city of Klagenfurt, just over the border, had a similar story surrounding its dragon-like *Lindenwurm* mascot—centuries before Ljubljana's legend. Hmm...

Whatever its origins, the dragon is the star of this very photogenic Secessionist bridge. It was officially built to commemorate the 40th year of Hapsburg Emperor Franz Josef's rule (1848–1888). But the Franz Josef name never stuck—those dragons are just too darn memorable. (For Franz Josef's sake, maybe they should have gone with the original design: Hapsburg eagles.)

▲▲**Town Square (Mestni Trg)**—This square is home to the **Town Hall** (Rotovž), highlighted by its clock tower and pillared loggia; step inside the Renaissance courtyard to see artifacts and a map of late-17th-century Ljubljana.

In the square is the **Fountain of Three Carolinian Rivers,** inspired in style and theme by Rome's many fountains. The figures with vases represent this region's three main rivers: Sava, Ljubljanica, and Krka.

For years, Ljubljana consisted mainly of this single street running along the base of Castle Hill (plus a small "New Town" across the river).

Stretching south from here are two other "squares"—Stari trg (Old Square) and Gornji trg (Upper Square)—that have long since grown together into one big, atmospheric promenade lined with quaint shops and cafés (perfect for a stroll). Virtually every house along this street has a story to tell—a famous resident or an infamous incident. As you walk, keep your eyes open for Ljubljana's mascot dragon—it's everywhere.

▲▲**Ljubljana Castle (Ljubljanski Grad)**—The castle above town offers

marvelous views of Ljubljana and the surrounding countryside. There has probably been a settlement on this site since prehistoric times, though the first castle here was Roman. The 12th-century version was gradually added on to over the centuries, until it fell into disrepair in the 17th century. Today's castle was rebuilt in the 1940s, renovated in the 1970s, and is still technically unfinished (subject to ongoing additions). The castle houses a restaurant, a gift shop, temporary exhibition halls, and a Gothic chapel with Baroque paintings of the coat of arms of St. George (Ljubljana's patron saint, the dragon-slayer). Above the restaurant are two wedding halls—Ljubljana's most popular place to get married.

You only have to pay for two sights in the castle, and they're both worthwhile: an excellent 20-minute **3-D film** about the history of Ljubljana, and the **castle tower,** which you can climb (92 steps) for commanding views over the city (castle grounds free, tower and film-700 SIT, May–Sept daily 9:00–21:00, Oct–April daily 10:00–18:00, castle grounds open until 22:00 in summer and 20:00 in winter, tel. 01/232-9994, www.ljubljanskigrad.com).

Tours of the castle in Slovene and English leave from the entry bridge daily June–Sept at 10:00 and 16:00 (1,000 SIT, less if more than 8 people, tour lasts 60–90 min). The castle is also home to the Ljubljana Summer Festival, with **concerts** throughout the summer (tel. 01/426-4340, www.festival-lj.si).

Getting to the Castle: There are two handy **trails** to the castle. The steeper-but-faster route begins near the parking lot just up from the Dragon Bridge, on Ciril-Metodov trg. Slower but easier is to go up Reber, just off of Stari trg a few blocks south of the Town Hall (once on the trail, always bear left, then go right when you're just under the castle). A sweat-free route to the top is via the **tourist train** that leaves at the top of each hour from Prešeren Square (550 SIT, 15-min trip, daily 10:00–18:00, shorter hours and weather-dependent in winter). For years, Ljubljana politicians have been debating the construction of a funicular that would connect the market to the castle. Given the project's history, it may be years more before work begins.

West of the River (Beyond Prešeren Square)

The Prešeren Square side of the river is the heart of modern Ljubljana, and home to several interesting squares and fine museums. These sights are listed roughly in order from Prešeren Square, and can be linked to make an interesting walk.

If you leave Prešeren Square in the direction the poet is looking and bear to your left, by the picture of Julija, you'll walk a block to...

Congress Square (Kongresni trg)—The square is ringed by many of Ljubljana's most important buildings: the University headquarters, the Baroque Ursuline Church of the Holy Trinity, a classical mansion called the Kazina, and the Philharmonic Hall. At the top end of the square, by the entry to a pedestrian underpass, is a small statue of a **Roman citizen**—a replica of an artifact from 1,700 years ago, when this town was called "Emona."

Take the underpass beneath busy Slovenska cesta to the...

▲Square of the Republic (Trg Republike)—This unusual square is essentially a parking lot ringed by an odd collection of buildings. While hardly quaint, the Square of the Republic gives you a good taste of a modern corner of Ljubljana. And it's historic—this is where Slovenia declared its independence in 1991.

The twin office towers (with the world's biggest digital watch) were designed by Plečnik's protege, Edvard Ravnikar. As harrowing as these seem, imagine if they had followed the original plans—twice as tall as they are now and connected by a bridge, representing the gateway to Ljubljana. These buildings were originally designed as the Slovenian parliament—but the ambitious plans were scaled back when Tito didn't approve (since it would make Slovenia's parliament bigger than the Yugoslav parliament in Belgrade). Instead, the Slovenian Parliament is across the square, in the strangely low-profile office building with the sculpted entryway. Completing the square are a huge conference center (Cankarjev Dom, around the base of the skyscrapers); a shopping mall; and some intriguing public art.

Just a block north (on Trg Narodni Herojev, more interesting public art), you'll find the...

Slovenian Museum of Natural History—Find your mummy downstairs and lots of stuffed reptiles, fish, and birds upstairs, along with a big exhibit on human fish (500 SIT, free Sun after 13:00, Tue–Sun 10:00–18:00, Thu until 20:00, closed Mon, Muzejska 1, tel. 01/241-0940, www2.pms-lj.si).

Another block to the northwest, you'll find two decent but skippable art museums:

National Gallery (Narodna Galerija)—This museum has three parts: European artists, Slovenian artists, and temporary exhibits. Those going to Bled might enjoy Marko Pernhart's huge panorama of the Julian Alps (700 SIT, free on Sat after 14:00, open Tue–Sun 10:00–18:00, closed

Mon, enter through big glass box between two older buildings at Prešernova 24, tel. 01/2415434, www.ng-slo.si).

Museum of Modern Art (Moderna Galerija Ljubljana)—This has a ho-hum permanent collection of modern and contemporary Slovene artists, as well as temporary exhibits by both Slovenes and international artists (1,000 SIT, Tue–Sat 10:00–18:00, June–Aug until 19:00, closed Mon, Tomšičeva 14, tel. 061/214-092).

The big **Serbian Orthodox church** near the art museums was built in 1936, soon after the Slovenes joined a political union with the Serbs. Although there were very few Serbs in Ljubljana then, today's Ljubljana has a big Serbian population, and this church has an active congregation. Nearby is...

Tivoli Park (Park Tivoli)—This huge park, just west of the center, is where Slovenes relax on summer weekends. The easiest access is by underpass from Cankarjeva cesta (between the National Gallery and the Museum of Modern Art). As you emerge, the neoclassical pillars leading down the promenade clue you in that this part of the park was designed by Jože Plečnik. Aside from a leisurely stroll, the best thing to visit in the park is the...

▲▲Modern History Museum (Muzej Novejše Zgodovine)—In this Baroque mansion in Tivoli Park, a well-done exhibit called "Slovenians in the 20th Century", traces the last hundred years of Slovene history. Downstairs is a replica of a 1950s-era house, and upstairs are several rooms using models, dioramas, and light-and-sound effects to creatively tell the story of one of Europe's youngest nations. The most moving room has artifacts from the Slovenes' brave declaration of independence from a hostile Yugoslavia in 1991. (The well-organized Slovenes had only to weather a 10-day skirmish to gain their autonomy.) The free English brochure explains everything, but consider the intriguing 2,000-SIT essay collection *Over the Hill Is Just Like Here*, which all Slovenian schoolchildren study (entry-500 SIT, free on Sun, Tue–Sun 10:00–18:00, closed Mon, in Tivoli Park at Celovška cesta 23, tel. 01/232-3968). The museum is a 20-minute walk from the center, best combined with a wander through Tivoli Park (fastest approach: as you emerge from Cankarjeva cesta underpass into park, turn right and go straight ahead for 5 min, continue straight up ramp, then turn left after tennis courts and look for the big pink mansion).

On your way back to the center, consider a trip to the top of the...

▲Skyscraper (Nebotičnik)—This 1933 Art Deco building was the first skyscraper in Slovenia—and one of the earliest European buildings that was clearly influenced by American architecture. Ride the elevator up to the sporadically open 12th-story café and breezy observation deck, with Ljubljana's best view. They charge 500 SIT for the panorama, but it's free if you buy a drink, and coffee's half that much (quirky and arrogant staff, Mon–Sat 10:00–24:00, closed Sun except sometimes in summer, often closes unexpectedly, 2 blocks from Prešeren Square at Štefanova ulica 1). The observation deck had to close a few years back because it had become the most popular spot in the country for suicide attempts (Slovenia has Europe's second-highest suicide rate). Now it has been retrofitted to prevent people from diving off.

Jože Plečnik's Architecture

Like Antoni Gaudí in Barcelona, Ljubljana has a way of turning people who couldn't care less about architecture into huge Jože Plečnik fans. There's plenty to see. Aside from the "top five" below, Plečnik designed the embankments along the Ljubljanica and Gradaščica Rivers in Trnovo; the Church of St. Francis with its classicist bell-tower; St. Michael's Church on the Marsh; Orel Stadium; Žale Cemetery; and many more buildings throughout Slovenia.

▲▲▲Jože Plečnik House (Plečnikova Zbirka)—Ljubljana's favorite son lived here from 1921 until his death in 1957. Today it's decorated exactly as it was the day he died, including much of Plečnik's equipment and plans. There are no cordons or barriers, so you are in direct contact with the world of the architect. Perhaps no other museum in Europe gives such an intimate portrait of an artist; you'll feel like Plečnik invited you over for dinner. This museum is a hit even with people who know nothing about the architect. It's officially open only eight hours each week—Tuesday and Thursday from 10:00–14:00—but you can sometimes visit by appointment during regular weekday business hours (usually only for groups of 7 or more, but they'll often open for even a couple of people—call and ask; 600 SIT, from the center, it's a 15-min stroll south through the delightful Krakovo gardens to Karunova ulica 4, after the canal and behind the twin-spired church, tel. 01/280-1600, www.arhmuz.com).

▲▲National and University Library (Narodna in Univerzitetna Knjižnica, or NUK)—Just a block up from the river at Novi trg, you'll find Plečnik's masterpiece. The library, housing about 1.5 million books, is all about the transcendence of obstacles to attain knowledge. The facade has blocks of odd sizes and shapes, representing a complex numerological pattern that suggests barriers on the path to enlightenment. The sculpture on the river side is Moses—known for leading his people through 40 years of hardship to the Promised Land. On the right

side of the building, find the horse-head doorknobs—representing the winged horse Pegasus (grab hold, and he'll whisk you away to new levels of enlightenment). Step inside. The main staircase is dark and gloomy—modeled after an Egyptian tomb. But at the top is the bright, airy main reading room: the ultimate goal, a

JOŽE PLEČNIK
(1872–1957)

There is probably no single architect who has shaped one city as Jože Plečnik (YOH-zheh PLAYCH-neek) shaped Ljubljana. Everywhere you go, you can see where he left his mark.

Plečnik was born in Ljubljana and studied in Vienna under the Secessionist architect Otto Wagner. His first commissions, done around the turn of the 20th century in Vienna, were pretty standard Art Nouveau stuff. Then Tomáš Masaryk, president of the new nation of Czechoslovakia, decided that the dull Hapsburg design of Prague Castle could use a new look to go with its new independence. But he didn't want an Austrian architect; it had to be a Slav. In 1921, he chose Jože Plečnik, who sprinkled the castle grounds with his distinctive touches. By now Plečnik had perfected his simple, eye-pleasing style that mixes modern and classical influences, with lots of columns and pyramids.

By the time Plečnik finished in Prague, he had made a name for himself. He returned home to Ljubljana and set to work redesigning the city, both as an architect and as an urban planner. He lived in a simple house behind the Trnovo Church (now a tourable musuem), and on his walk to work every day, he pondered ways to make the city even more livable. Many of his ideas became reality; even more did not. (It's fun to imagine what this city would look like if Plečnik always got his way.)

After his death in 1957, Plečnik was virtually forgotten by Slovenes and scholars alike. His many works in Ljubljana were taken for granted. But in 1986, an exposition about Plečnik at Paris' Pompidou Center jump-started interest in the architect, and within a few years, Plečnik was back in vogue. Today, scholars hail him as a genius who was ahead of his time...while locals and tourists simply enjoy the beauty of his brilliant works.

place of learning (free, July–Aug Mon–Sat 8:00–14:00, Wed until 16:00, closed Sun, Sept–June Mon–Fri 8:00–20:00, Sat 8:00–14:00, closed Sun, corner of Turjaška and Gosposka ulica). You can duck into the main stairwell without a problem, but you'll need a visitor's badge to get into the reading room (ask at the reception desk inside and to the right; depending on who's on duty, you'll either get a badge or be told it's impossible—in which case, if you're determined, you can just stick close to a student going inside).

▲**French Revolution Square (Trg Francoske Revolucije)**—Many of Plečnik's finest works are on or near this square, just around the corner from NUK. Plečnik designed the column in the middle of the square to commemorate Napoleon's short-lived decision to make Ljubljana the capital of his Illyrian Provinces. The Teutonic Knights of the Cross established the nearby monastery (Križanke) in 1230, and the adaptation of these monastery buildings into the Ljubljana Summer Theatre was Plečnik's last major work (1950–1956). To reach French Revolution Square from Prešeren Square, follow the river several blocks south, then cut up two blocks at Salendrova.

Roman City Wall—Between the world wars, Plečnik arranged the rebuilding of the archaeological remains of Emona's defensive wall (along Mirje, south of the center).

▲**Architectural Museum of Ljubljana**—Plečnik fans can make a trek out to this interesting museum, located in Fužine Castle on the outskirts of Ljubljana. The permanent exhibit features parts of the 1986 Paris exhibition that made Plečnik famous all over again. Downstairs is a display of plans and photos from Plečnik's earlier works in Vienna and Prague, and upstairs you'll find an exhibit on his works in Slovenia, including some detailed plans and models for ambitious projects he never completed (like the huge cone-shaped parliament atop Castle Hill). It's worthwhile, but a bit of a hassle to get to, so that only true fans should pay a visit (300 SIT, Mon–Thu 10:00–14:00, closed Fri–Sun, Pot na Fužine 2, tel. 01/540-9798, www.arhmuz.com). Take bus #20 from Kongresni trg (direction: Fužine) to the end of the line (about 20 min).

SLEEPING

$$$ The Best Western **Hotel Slon** has 171 modern but musty rooms just a block off Prešeren Square on busy Slovenska cesta (request quieter back room). This location is legendary as the home of an elephant *(slon)* who visited Ljubljana with a circus centuries ago (Sb-€81–111, Db-€117–157, Tb-€174, prices vary with room size, non-smoking rooms, elevator, Internet-200 SIT/30 min, parking lot-1,400 SIT/day, Slovenska cesta 34, tel. 01/470-1100, fax 01/251-7164, www.hotelslon .com, sales@hotelslon.com).

$$$ Grand Hotel Union is as much a landmark as a hotel, but you'll pay for its class, friendly staff, and perfect location, right on Prešeren Square. The 193 plush "Executive" rooms are in the main building (Sb-€133–142, Db-€171, prices 20 percent higher during conventions, can be 10–20 percent cheaper during slow times, non-smoking floors, elevator, Internet-€5/30 min, parking-€10/day, Miklošičeva cesta 1, tel. 01/308-1270, fax 01/308-1015, www.gh-union.si, hotel.union @gh-union.si). The 133 "Business" rooms next door are a lesser value:

SLEEP CODE

(€1 = about $1.10, 220 SIT = about $1, country code: 386, area code: 01)

Sleep Code: **S** = Single, **D** = Double/Twin, **T** = Triple, **Q** = Quad, **b** = bathroom, **s** = shower only, **no CC** = Credit Cards not accepted. Unless otherwise noted, credit cards are accepted, breakfast is included, and the modest tourist tax (154 SIT per person, per night) is not. Hotels generally quote prices in euros rather than tolars. Everyone speaks English.

To help you sort easily through these listings, I've divided the rooms into three categories based on the price for a standard double room with bath:

$$$ **Higher Priced**—Most rooms €100 (24,000 SIT) or more.

$$ **Moderately Priced**—Most rooms between €50–100 (12,000–24,000 SIT).

$ **Lower Priced**—Most rooms €50 (12,000 SIT) or less.

Ljubljana's biggest downside is its abysmal accommodations scene. Only a handful of places are within convenient walking distance of the center, and they're all shockingly overpriced. While most Slovenes are unaccountably friendly, hotel desk clerks are the rare exception—indifferent and cranky. You'll pay dearly if you want a central location, good rooms, and friendly staff. The most expensive places raise their prices even more during conventions (often Sept–Oct and sometimes also June).

The good news is that the situation is improving. The city is aware of the problem, and is working on establishing a network of cheaper private rooms in the center (ask TI for details). And the brand-new Hostel Celica—subsidized by the local government—provides cheap beds near the station in a unique building that's more museum than hostel (see next page).

not as nice but almost as expensive (Sb-€126–137, Db-€158, prices 20 percent higher during conventions—often Oct–Nov, can be 10–20 percent cheaper during slow times, non-smoking floors, elevator, parking and Internet at main hotel, Miklošičeva cesta 3, tel. 01/308-1170, fax 01/308-1914, www.gh-union.si, hotel.business@gh-union.si).

$$$ Astral Hotel has 74 modern business-class rooms and a great location between Prešeren Square and the train station (Sb-€107,

Db-€140, extra bed-€35, during conventions: Sb-€127, Db-€170, non-smoking rooms, elevator, free Internet, parking garage-€9/day, Miklošičeva cesta 9, tel. 01/308-4300, fax 01/230-1181, www.astralhotel .net, info@astralhotel.net).

$$$ **City Hotel Turist,** recently renovated, has 123 tight, cookie-cutter rooms, an indifferent staff, and a good location just a few blocks off Prešeren Square (Sb-€57–94, Db-€98–110, Tb-€131, prices depend on room size, apartment also available, non-smoking rooms, elevator, Internet-220 SIT/20 min, Dalmatinova 15, tel. 01/234-9130, fax 01/234-9140, www.hotelturist.si, info@hotelturist.si).

$$ **Gostilna Pri Mraku** would be no great shakes in other cities—but it's Ljubljana's best value, with 30 comfortable but worn rooms and a convenient location. The downside: lots of stairs with no elevator, a lousy breakfast, and a sometimes-flaky staff (Sb-12,600–15,500 SIT, Db-19,800–23,000 SIT, Tb-24,400–25,600 SIT, price depends on room size and air-con, prices about 20 percent cheaper July–Aug, non-smoking floor, Rimska 4, tel. 01/421-9600, fax 01/421-9655, www.daj -dam.si, daj-dam@daj-dam.si).

$$ **Hotel Park** has 91 simple but fresh rooms at good prices. But it's in a poor location—in a sea of communist apartment blocks a 10-minute walk from Prešeren Square—and has an often-frustrating staff (Sb-€42–45, Db-€53–58, Tb-€79, strange old elevator, Tabor 9, tel. 01/433-1306, fax 01/433-0546, www.tabor.si, hotel.park@siol.net).

$ **Hostel Celica** is the lone bright spot on Ljubljana's dreary accommodations scene. The innovative new hostel is funded by the city and run by a non-profit student arts organization. This remarkable place took over an old military prison and converted 20 cells *(celica)* into hostel rooms—each one unique, decorated by a different designer. (Guests are asked to leave the outer door open and the inner door—with bars—locked, so that visitors can look into the rooms.) There are more typical dorm rooms on the top-floor loft (combining open beams with modern amenities). The building also houses an art gallery, tourist information point, Internet access, self-serve laundry, restaurant, and shoes-off Oriental café. The neighborhood is a bit rundown but safe, and a 10-minute walk from Prešeren Square, but these are the cheapest beds in town in an unforgettable setting (prices range from €18–20 per person in a "cell"—some for 2 people—to dorm beds for €10, non-smoking, Metelkova 9, tel. 01/430-1890, fax 01/231-9488, www.souhostel.com, info@souhostel.com).

EATING

Though plenty of heavy meat-and-starch Slovene food is available, Ljubljana also offers an abundance of pizza and other Italian fare (you're just 150 miles from Venice), as well as other international options

(Moroccan, Chinese, even Mexican).

For Slovenian food, tourists flock to **Sokol**—famous, atmospheric, and central. Since it's increasingly been deluged by guidebook-toting tourists, the quality has declined in recent years, but it's still your easiest bet for local cuisine (main dishes 1,000–2,500 SIT, Mon–Sat 6:30–23:00, Sun 12:00–22:00, on castle side of Triple Bridge at Ciril-Metodov trg 18, tel. 01/439-6855).

Ljubljana has lots of great sit-down pizza places; expect to pay 1,000–1,500 SIT for an average-sized pie (wide variety of toppings). The best is arguably at **Pizzeria Foculus** (good salad bar, Mon–Fri 10:00–24:00, Sat–Sun 12:00–24:00, hiding down alley at Gregorčičeva 3, tel. 01/251-5643), but the handiest with the most scenic setting is **Ljubljanski Dvor** (Mon–Sat 10:00–24:00, Sun 13:00–23:00, Dvorni trg 1, also take-away window in back of building on Kongresni trg, tel. 01/251-6555).

For a cheap and tasty meal, stop by colorful **Tomato,** with good sandwiches and salads, near the top of Kongresni trg (most items under 1,000 SIT, Mon–Fri 7:00–22:00, Sat 7:00–16:00, closed Sun, Šubičeva ulica 1, tel. 01/252-7555).

There are several fine restaurants around Levstikov trg and Gornji trg in the old town, just underneath the castle. Pick the one that looks best, or try the upscale **Pri Sv. Florijan** (figure €20 per person; Slovenian upstairs, Moroccan downstairs, daily 12:00–24:00, Gornji trg 20, tel. 01/251-2214).

Tucked into a courtyard just off Prešeren Square is **Gostilna As** ("Ace"), featuring a tempting gelato stand and a good restaurant with indoor or outdoor seating. This pricey, pretentious place prefers not to use menus, since everything is freshly prepared each day (pasta dishes around 1,800 SIT, main dishes around 3,000 SIT, limited options, most with an emphasis on seafood, Čopova ulica 5A or enter courtyard with *As* sign near image of Julija, tel. 01/425-8822).

The brew pub **Kratochwill** has good beer and affordable pub grub (900–1,500 SIT) near the train station (daily 9:00–24:00, Kolodvorska ulica 14, tel. 01/433-3114).

Be sure to spend some time along the Ljubljanica River embankment sipping coffee and people-watching. If coffee's not your cup of tea, go a block inland to the teahouse **CHA,** which has a wide range of exotic flavors (Mon–Fri 9:00–23:00, Sat 9:00–15:00 & 18:00–23:00, closed Sun, Stari trg 3, tel. 01/425-5213).

Burek, the typical Balkan snack (see "Croatian Food," page 338), can be picked up at street stands around town. Most are open 24 hours and charge 400 SIT for a hearty portion (try **Nobel Burek** next to Miklošičeva cesta 30 or **Olympia Burek** around the corner on Pražakova ulica).

Ljubljana is known for its **ice cream.** Good options are the courtyard garden at **As** (see above); **Ursula** (above Kongresni trg at the corner

THE STUDENT CURSE

In most European cities, it's a smart idea to seek out places where locals eat—and students are a sure sign of cheap, good grub. But in this university town, a student crowd is not necessarily a good omen. Ljubljana's university students can buy government coupons that subsidize 80 percent of their restaurant bill. When a restaurant starts accepting these coupons, locals take it as a sure sign that the place is going downhill. Even if the food is decent, the service is sure to get grouchier.

of Slovenska cesta and Šubičeva); and **Slaščičarna Anna** (experimental flavors like sage, in the back of a café on Eipprova along the Gradaščica stream near Plečnik House).

During Ljubljana's golden age a century ago, the café scene here was as lively as Vienna's or Budapest's. Most cafés have since shut their doors, but a new tradition has taken its place in recent years: Instead of sweaty discos, Ljubljana's young people spend their time in fun theme pubs. **Pr'Skelet**—just up from the river on Ključavnižorska ulica—has decent but expensive food in the upstairs restaurant (main dishes 3,000 SIT, Wed–Fri 16:00–23:00, Sat–Sun 14:00–23:00, closed Mon–Tue, tel. 040-852-363), but the real scene is in the pub downstairs—packed with skeletons that light up or grab for your hair when you leave the bathroom (daily 10:00–1:00).

TRANSPORTATION CONNECTIONS

Note that in Slovene, Vienna is "Dunaj."

By train to: Lesce-Bled (roughly hrly, 1 hr), **Postojna** (roughly hrly, 1 hr), **Zagreb** (8/day, 2.5 hrs), **Vienna/**(that's *Dunaj* in Slovene, 1/day direct, 6 hrs; otherwise 6/day, 7 hrs with transfer in Villach, Maribor, or Graz), **Munich** (3/day direct, 7 hrs, including 1 night train; otherwise transfer in Salzburg), **Salzburg** (5/day direct, 5 hrs), **Budapest** (2/day direct, 9 hrs). Train info: tel. 01/291-3332, www.slo-zeleznice.si.

By bus to: Bled (hrly, 1.25 hrs, 1,370 SIT), **Divača** (close to Škocjan caves and Lipica, every 2 hrs, 1.5–2 hrs, 1,530 SIT), **Postojna** (at least hrly, 1 hr, 1,290 SIT), **Piran** (7/day, 3 hrs, 2,610 SIT). Bus info: tel. 090-4230 (toll number—about 160 SIT/min), www.ap-ljubljana.si. If you pick up the blue phone in the bus station, you'll be connected to a free information line.

Near Ljubljana: The Karst and the Slovenian Adriatic

THE KARST

Slovenia's Karst region—about an hour by expressway south of Ljubljana—is fertile ground for a day trip, easier by car than by public transportation. The term "karst" is used worldwide to refer to an arid limestone plateau—but Slovenia's is the original. (The general word "karst" comes from the Slovenian word Kras—a specific region near the Italian border.)

Your top Karst priority is a cave visit. Since limestone is easily dissolved by water, karstic regions are punctuated with remarkable networks of caves and underground rivers. Choose between Slovenia's two best caves, Škocjan or Postojna—each with a handy side-trip nearby. Slovenes debate long and hard about which cave system is better. If you prefer a more touristy, less active experience (on a Disney World-type people mover), visit Postojna. But if you want to get in a good hike with your cave visit, plus a chance to walk through one of the world's most

Karst Region

impressive caverns—complete with a raging underground river—head for Škocjan.

In the neighborhood of Škocjan is Lipica, where the famous Lipizzaner stallions strut their stuff. Just up the road from Postojna is Predjama Castle, picturesquely burrowed into the side of a cliff.

Sleeping in the Karst: Tourist Farm Hudičevec—halfway between Škocjan and Postojna—is as comfortable and private as a hotel. A roomy, spick-and-span double with a private bathroom—including a delicious Slovenian feast for dinner and farm-fresh eggs for breakfast—costs only €40 for two people (Db without dinner-€32, €4 more for 1- or 2-night stays, Razdrto 1, tel. 05/703-0300, fax 05/703-0320, www.hudicevec .com, hudicevec@siol.net, Simčič family).

Škocjan Caves and the Lipica Stud Farm
Škocjan Caves (Škocjanske Jame)
Slovenia boasts several fine cave systems, but Škocjan (SHKOHTS-yahn) is arguably the best. After wandering through plenty of stalactites and stalagmites, you emerge into a colossal underground cavern with a mighty river crashing through it (and spanned only by a breathtaking footbridge 150 feet above the current—not quite as scary as it sounds). You'll wind up walking around two miles, going up and down over 400 steps. The hike is a bit strenuous, especially as you climb from the caves at the end—but it's worth it. Bring a sweater; it's cool.

Cost and Hours: The guided tour is mandatory and takes 90 minutes (2,000 SIT, tours almost hrly 10:00–17:00 June–Sept, fewer tours off-season with last tour at 15:00 or 15:30, call or pick up brochure to confirm schedule before making the trip, tel. 05/763-2840, www.park -skocjanske-jame.si).

Getting to Škocjan: By car, take the expressway south from Ljubljana about 90 minutes and get off at the Divača exit (also marked with brown signs for Lipica and Škocjanske jame) and follow signs for Škocjanske jame. (Before or after Škocjan, drivers can easily visit the Lipica Stud Farm, described below.)

By public transportation, it's trickier. Take the train or bus to Divača (see "Transportation Connections," above), which is about three miles from the caves. Either hike in or take a taxi from the Divača station (tel. 05/734-5428). A better but less predictable option is to take one of the buses from Ljubljana to Piran that goes along the older road (not all of them do; ask for details at bus station). This bus can drop you off closer to the caves (1 mile away, ask for Škocjanske jame).

Lipica Stud Farm (Kobilarna Lipica)
The Lipica (LEE-peet-suh) Stud Farm, a short drive from the Škocjan Caves, was founded in 1580 to provide horses for the Hapsburg court in Vienna. Horse-loving Hapsburg Archduke Charles wanted to create the

perfect animal: He imported Andalusian horses from his homeland of Spain, then mixed them with a local line to come up with an extremely intelligent and easily trainable breed. Charles' creation, the Lipizzaner stallions—known for their noble gait and Baroque shape—were made famous by Vienna's Spanish Riding School. Italian and Arabian blood-lines were later added to tweak various characteristics. These regal horses have changed shape with the tenor of the times: They were bred strong and stout during wars, frilly and slender in more cultured eras. But they're always born black, fade to gray, and turn a distinctive white in adulthood.

Until World War I, Lipica bred horses for Austria's needs. Now, Austria breeds its own line, and these horses prance for Slovenia—a treasured part of the cultural heritage. Tour the stables to visit the mag-nificent animals (labeled with purebred bloodlines). Unlike in Vienna, tickets to see the horses perform here are cheap and easy to get. Visitors thrill to the Lipizzaners' clever routine—stutter-stepping sideways to the classical beat.

This excursion—offering an up-close horse encounter—is less pol-ished (and cheaper) than the Lipizzaner experience in Vienna (see page 430). It's worth a visit only if you're a horse enthusiast or if you have a car and it fits your schedule (for example, drivers visiting the Škocjan Caves are only a few minutes away).

By the way, the hills less than a mile away are in Italy. Aside from the horses, Lipica's big draw is its casino. Italians across the border are legally forbidden from gambling in their own town's casinos—for fear of addiction—so they flock here to Slovenia to try their luck. Further north, the Slovenian border town of Nova Gorica has Europe's biggest casino, packed with gamblers from the Italian side of town.

Visiting the Stud Farm: There are three activities at Lipica: **Touring** the farm for a look at the horses (and a dull little 17th-century chapel); watching a **performance** of the prancing stallions; and, on days when there's no performance, watching a **training session.** If you're coming all the way to Lipica, you might as well time it so that you can do both the tour and a performance (or a training session). Call ahead to confirm performance and tour times before you make the trip.

Cost: Stud farm tour only-1,300 SIT, tour plus performance-2,500 SIT, tour plus training session-1,800 SIT.

Tours: April–June and Sept–Oct daily on the hour 10:00–17:00 (except 12:00; also at 9:00 Sat–Sun); July–Aug daily on the hour 9:00–18:00 (except 12:00); off-season daily at 11:00, 13:00, 14:00, and 15:00 (plus 10:00 and 15:00 Sat–Sun in March).

Performances: May–Oct Tue, Fri, and Sun at 15:00, April Fri and Sun at 15:00, none Nov–March.

Training Sessions: April–Oct Wed and Thu at 12:00. Note that on days when there's a performance, you can tour the farm before

(14:00) or after (15:40) the show; for a training, the tour is before (11:00). Tel. 05/739-1580, www.lipica.org.

Getting to Lipica: Lipica Stud Farm is in Slovenia's southwest corner (a stone's throw from Trieste, Italy). By car, exit the freeway at Divača and follow brown signs to Lipica. (As you drive into the farm, you'll go through pastures where the stallions often roam.) It's a major hassle by public transportation. You can take the train or bus from Ljubljana to Divača (see "Getting to Škocjan," above)—but that's about five miles from Lipica, with no bus connections. Take a taxi (about 3,000 SIT one-way from Divača station, tel. 05/734-5428) or try hitching a ride on a friendly tour bus.

Postojna Caves and Predjama Castle
Postojna Caves (Postojnska Jama)

Postojna (poh-STOY-nah) is the most accessible—and touristy—cave experience in the region. It's the biggest cave system in Slovenia (and, a few generations ago, it was the biggest in Italy, a fact that Italians still haven't forgotten). The stalagmites and stalactites, as tall as 100 feet, are more abundant and colorful than at Škocjan. On the tour, you'll see several translucent "curtains" of rock and skinny "spaghetti stalactites," and you'll wind up at an exhibit on the strange "human fish" *(Proteus anguinus)*—sort of a long, skinny, flesh-colored salamander with fingers and toes. The world's biggest cave-dwelling animal, the human fish can survive up to seven years without eating (the live specimens you see here are never fed during four months they're on display).

Postojna is far less strenuous to visit than Škocjan—of the three-mile route, you'll walk only about a mile (the rest of the time, you're on a people-mover). But Postojna is also much more touristy—you'll wade through tour buses and tacky souvenir stands on your way to the entrance—and it lacks Škocjan's spectacular massive cavern finale.

Cost, Hours, Location: Your visit, which is by tour only, costs 2,600 SIT and lasts 90 minutes. Tours leave May–Sept daily at the top of each hour 9:00–18:00 (off-season daily at 10:00 and 14:00, also Nov–Feb Sat–Sun at 12:00, sometimes additional tours depending on month—especially Sat–Sun in Oct; call to get schedule or pick up brochure at any TI). From mid-May through August, it's smart to show up at least 30 minutes early for the morning tours (popular with tour buses); otherwise, aim for 15 minutes ahead. The caves are just outside the town of Postojna, about an hour by expressway south of Ljubljana (Jamska cesta 30, tel. 05/700-0100, www.postojna-cave.com). The cave temperature is a steady 8 degrees Celsius (46 degrees Fahrenheit). Bring a sweater.

Getting to Postojna: By car, take the expressway south from Ljubljana and get off at the Postojna exit. Turn right after the tollbooth and follow the *jama/grotte/cave* signs through town until you see the tour buses. The train from Ljubljana to Postojna arrives at a station 20 minutes by foot from the caves. The bus drops you just five minutes from the caves.

Predjama Castle (Predjamski Grad)

Burrowed into the side of a mountain close to Postojna is dramatic Predjama Castle (prehd-YAH-mah), one of Europe's most scenic castles.

The current version of the castle was built in the 16th century, but the best legends date from a hundred years earlier. In the 15th century, a nobleman named Erasmus killed the emperor's cousin in a duel. He was imprisoned under Ljubljana Castle, and spent years nursing a grudge. When he was finally released, he used his castle—buried deep inside the cave above this current version—as a home base for a series of Robin Hood-style raids on the local nobility and merchants. (Actually, Erasmus stole from the rich and kept for himself—but that was good enough to make him a hero to the peasants, who hated the nobles.)

Soldiers from Trieste were brought in to put an end to Erasmus' raids, laying siege to the castle for over a year. Back then, the only way into the castle was through the cave in the valley below—then up, through an extensive labyrinth of caves, to the top. While the soldiers down below froze and starved, Erasmus' men sneaked out through the caves to bring in supplies. (They liked to drop their leftovers on the soldiers below to taunt them, letting them know that the siege wasn't working.)

Eventually, the soldiers came up with a plan. They waited for Erasmus to visit the latrine—which, by design, had to be on the thin-walled outer edge of the castle—and then, on seeing a signal by a secret agent, blew Erasmus off his throne (literally—with a cannonball). It worked, and today Erasmus is supposedly buried under the huge linden tree in the parking lot.

The exhibits inside the castle are sparse, with no explanations, but be sure to pick up the free, good English brochure at the entry. You'll see various scenes from medieval life, including a kitchen; notice the old-fashioned garbage disposal with a 300-foot-deep drain.

Cost, Hours, Location: 800 SIT, June–Sept daily 9:00–19:00, May daily 9:00–18:00, March–April and Oct daily 10:00–17:00, Nov–Feb Tue–Fri 10:00–16:00, Sat–Sun 10:00–17:00, closed Mon. Predjama Castle is on a twisty rural road 5.5 miles beyond Postojna Caves (tel. 05/751-6015).

Cave Tours: If you're already visiting the caves at Postojna or Škocjan, a visit to the caves under this castle is unnecessary (900 SIT, 45 min, May–Sept daily at 11:00, 13:00, 15:00, and 17:00).

Getting to Predjama: By car, just continue on the winding road past Postojna and follow signs for Predjama and Predjamski Grad (coming back, follow signs to Postojna). By public transportation, it's difficult. There is one bus per day from Postojna to Predjama, and another to Bukovje (just over a half-mile from Predjama), but you'll be stranded at Predjama, with no return bus. A taxi is easier, but pricey—expect around 5,000 SIT round-trip from Postojna, plus one hour waiting time (mobile 040-217-169). Consider hitching a ride at Postojna on a friendly Predjama-bound tour bus.

THE SLOVENIAN ADRIATIC: PIRAN

From Ljubljana, you're just a couple of hours from Croatia's Istria peninsula. Seedy, touristy, but fun Croatian resort towns like Rovinj or Poreč deserve a visit, but don't overlook Slovenia's own 29 miles of Adriatic coastline. As with other attractions in Slovenia, it's friendlier, quainter, and tidier than the alternatives in other countries.

There are only a handful of towns on the Slovenian coast: big, industrial Koper; lived-in and crumbling Izola; and swanky but soulless Portorož. But the Back Door gem of the Slovenian Adriatic is Piran. Most Adriatic towns are all tourists and concrete, but Piran has kept itself charming and in remarkably good repair while holding the tourist sprawl at bay. It's one of the most pleasant Adriatic towns from here to Dalmatia.

Piran's main square, Tartinijev trg (named for the famous violinist born here), spills into its harbor. The town has only two hotels (see below) but an abundance of ambience. Aside from its maritime museum, you can see everything in Piran in a quick 20-minute walk—then just bask in its quaintness. Enjoy a gelato or a *kava* on its sleek marbled square, surrounded by neoclassical buildings and watched over by a bell tower. Wander its piers and shoot a roll of film at sunset. Enjoy a spectacular seafood and pasta feast for a third what you'd pay in Venice (just across the sea).

Sleeping in Piran: The town has two comparable hotels, both comfortable and with some seaview rooms: **Hotel Tartini** (Sb-€51, seaview Db-€84, non-view Db-€75, more on holidays and most of July–Aug, less off-season, Tartinijev trg 15, tel. 05/671-1666, fax 05/671-1665, www.hotel-tartini-piran.com, info@hotel-tartini-piran.com), and **Hotel Piran** (Sb-€51, sea-view Db-€80, non-view Db-€64, more July–Aug and holidays, less off-season, Kidričevo nabrežje 4, tel. 05/676-2502, fax 05/676-2520, www.hoteli-piran.si, marketing@hoteli-piran.si).

Getting to Piran: The most direct option from Ljubljana is by bus (see "Transportation Connections," on page 302). You could also take a train to Koper, then take a local bus to Piran, but it takes an hour longer.

BLED AND THE JULIAN ALPS

The Alps begin in France, tumble across Central Europe, and come to an end here, along Slovenia's northern border. These are the Julian Alps—named for Julius Caesar—where mountain culture has a Slavic flavor. The Slovenian mountainsides are laced with hiking paths, blanketed in a deep forest, and speckled with ski resorts and vacation chalets. Around every ridge is a peaceful Alpine village sprawled around a quaint Baroque steeple. In the center of it all is Mount Triglav, ol' "Three Heads"—Slovenia's symbol and tallest mountain.

Spend a day or two exploring the Julian Alps and Triglav National Park—as spectacular as anything just over the border in Austria—and relaxing in the region's tourism capital, the resort town of Bled. Hike up to Bled Castle for beautiful views, make a wish and ring the bell at the island church, and wander the dreamy path around the lake. To get up into the mountains, drive the 50 hairpin turns of the breathtaking Vršič Pass, then explore the Hemingway-haunted WWI sights of the Soča River Valley.

Planning Your Time

On a three-week trip through Eastern Europe, the Julian Alps deserve two days. With one day, spend it in and around Bled. With a second day and a car, drive the circular route up and over the stunning Vršič Pass, down the scenic and historic Soča River Valley, and back to Bled (or on to Ljubljana). Without a car, skip the second day—or, to relax, spend it doing nearby day trips: bus to Radovljica to see the Bee Museum, hike to Vintgar Gorge, or (less convenient) visit the more rustic Lake Bohinj.

Getting around the Julian Alps

By public transportation, you can easily get a good taste of the Julian Alps: Bled and nearby side-trips. But to really tackle the high-mountain scenery—the Vršič Pass and Soča Valley—you'll need a car.

By Bus: Bled is a good home base, with easy and frequent bus connections to day-trip destinations (Radovljica, the Vintgar Gorge, and Bohinj; specific bus connections explained under "Sights—Near Bled" and "Transportation Connections," below).

By Car: The region is ideal by car. The good *Autokarta Slovenija* map sold by the TI and other local shops is all you need for the country (1,400 SIT), though smaller-scale maps focusing on the Bled region and the whole of Triglav National Park are also available. Even if you're doing the rest of your trip by train, consider renting a car here in tiny, easy-to-navigate Slovenia to take advantage of its many enjoyable day trips (see car rental tips under "Helpful Hints," below).

By Tour: To hit several far-flung day-trip destinations at one go, consider taking a tour from Bled (sold by various agencies, including Kompas Bled, see "Tourist Information," below). Destinations range from Ljubljana and the Karst region (both covered in Ljubljana chapter) to the Austrian or Italian Alps to Venice (yes, Venice—it's doable as a long day trip from here). An all-day Julian Alps trip to the Vršič Pass and Soča Valley runs about 6,600 SIT. This tour is handy, but two people can rent a car for the day for less (around €40; see "Helpful Hints," below) and do it at their own pace using the information in this chapter.

By "Old-Timer Train": This old-fashioned steam engine chugs from Bled past Lake Bohinj and on to Most na Soči (at the southern end of the Soča River Valley). It's essentially an expensive package tour by train instead of by bus, with a stop at a gorge and a riverboat ride on the Soča (12,500 SIT, leaves Bled Thu at 9:30 July–Sept, get details at Kompas Bled—see "Tourist Information," below).

Bled

Lake Bled—Slovenia's leading mountain resort—comes complete with a sweeping alpine panorama, a fairy-tale island, a cliff-hanging medieval castle, a lakeside promenade, and the country's most sought-after desserts. While Bled has all the modern resort-town amenities, its most endearing qualities are its stunning setting, its natural romanticism, and its fun-loving wedding parties.

The first official mention of Bled was in the year 1004—when Holy Roman Emperor Henry II turned it over to the Bishops of Brixen. Bled celebrates its millennium in 2004. You'll see the town's symbol everywhere: a peacock, or "bird of paradise," based on an artifact found under the castle.

Since the Hapsburg days, Lake Bled is the place where Slovenes have wowed visiting diplomats. Tito had one of his vacation homes here (today's Hotel Vila Bled), and more recent visitors have included Prince Charles and Madeleine Albright.

The lake's main town—also called Bled—has plenty of ways to cruise through a lazy afternoon. While the town itself is more functional than quaint, it offers handy access to the region and breathtaking views of the lake. Bled quiets down at night—no nightlife here—giving hikers and other vacationers a chance to recharge.

Planning Your Time

On a speedy visit, you can get a good-enough taste of Bled in one day. Spend the morning strolling around the lake; along the way, hire a gondolier to take you out to visit the island. In the afternoon, hike up to the castle for great views, take a side-trip to Radovljica or Bohinj, hike to Vintgar Gorge, or linger along the lakeside with some swans, the Alpine panorama, and a piece of cream cake. With more time, spread these activities over two days, relax more, or—better yet—use Bled as a springboard for a drive over the Vršič Pass to Ljubljana (or loop back to Bled).

ORIENTATION

(area code: 04)

The town of Bled is on the east end of the 1.5-mile-long Lake Bled. The lakefront is lined with cafés and resort hotels. A 3.5-mile path leads around the lake.

The tourists' "center" of Bled is a cluster of big resort hotels, dominated by the giant red Park Hotel (dubbed by locals the "red can"). The busy street **Ljubljanska cesta** leads out of Bled town towards Ljubljana and most other destinations. Just up from the lakefront, across Ljubljanska cesta from Park Hotel, the modern **commercial center** (Trgovski Center Bled) houses a travel agency, Internet café, grocery store, and ATM. Just up the road from the commercial center, you'll find the **post office** and library (with more Internet access). Bled's less-touristy old town is under the castle, surrounding the pointy spire of St. Martin's Church. There you'll find the bus station, several good restaurants, a few hotels, and more locals than tourists.

The mountains poking above the ridge at the far end of the lake (in good weather) are the Julian Alps, including Mount Triglav. The big mountain behind the town of Bled is Stol (literally "Chair"), part of the Karavanke range that makes up the Austrian border.

Tourist Information

Bled's helpful **TI** is in the long lakefront building across from the big, red Hotel Park (as you face the lake, the TI is hiding around front at the far left end, by the casino). Pick up the free information brochure (with updated prices and schedules) and consider the helpful 300-SIT guide booklet. Get advice on local hikes and day trips. If you're doing any hiking, spring for one of the many excellent regional maps. The TI

Bled Town

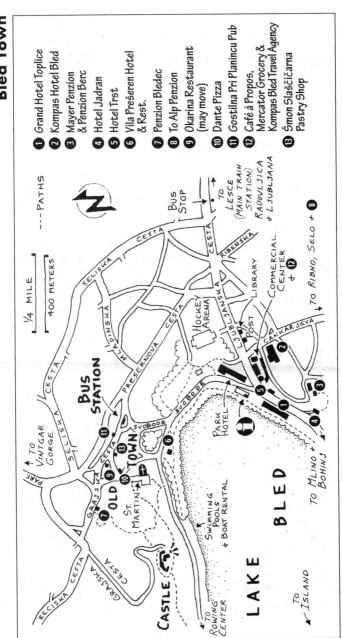

1 Grand Hotel Toplice
2 Kompas Hotel Bled
3 Mayer Penzion & Penzion Berc
4 Hotel Jadran
5 Hotel Trst
6 Vila Prešeren Hotel & Rest.
7 Penzion Bledec
8 To Alp Penzion
9 Okarina Restaurant (may move)
10 Dante Pizza
11 Gostilna Pri Planincu Pub
12 Café á Propos, Mercator Grocery & Kompas Bled Travel Agency
13 Šmon Slaščičarna Pastry Shop

LAKE BLED LANDMARKS

English	Slovene	Pronounced
Lake Bled	Blejsko Jezero	BLAY-skoh YAY-zay-roh
The Island	Otok	OH-tohk
Bled Castle	Blejski Grad	BLAY-skee grahd

can't find you a room, but can give you a list of local accommodations (unpredictable hours, but usually May–Sept Mon–Sat 8:00–19:00, Sun 11:00–17:00, July–Aug Mon–Sat until 21:00, Sun until 18:00, Oct–April Mon–Sat 9:00–18:00, Sun 12:00–16:00, cesta Svobode 10, tel. 04/574-1122, www.bled.si).

Kompas Bled travel agency, in the commercial center, picks up where the TI leaves off. They exchange money, rent bikes, offer a room-booking service (including many cheap rooms in private homes—though most are away from the lake), and sell various tours around the region (Mon–Sat 8:00–19:00, Sun 8:00–12:00 & 16:00–19:00, June–Sept until 20:00, Ljubljanska cesta 4, tel. 04/574-1515, www.kompas-bled.si, info @kompas-bled.si).

Arrival in Bled

By Train: Two train stations have the name "Bled." You will most likely use the station called "Lesce-Bled." The "Bled Jezero" station isn't on the main line, and only sees a few regional trains a day.

*Important note: If you're buying a train ticket to Bled, specify that you want to go to **Lesce** (lest-SEH)—not "Bled." If the ticket agent types in "Bled," you'll be routed to the poorly-connected **Bled Jezero** station.*

The small Lesce-Bled station is in the village of Lesce, about 2.5 miles from Bled. The nearest ATM is upstairs in the shopping center (with your back to the station, it's across the street and to the left). A taxi to Bled should run around 2,000 SIT, or you can take the bus (at least hrly, 10 min, 300 SIT).

By Bus: Bled's bus station is just up from the lake in the old town. To reach the lake, walk downhill on cesta Svobode. To get to the commercial center, jog uphill and turn right on Prešernova cesta, which runs into Ljubljanska cesta just above the commercial center.

By Car: Traffic from the freeway comes into Bled on Ljubljanska cesta, which rumbles through the middle of town before swinging left at the lake. Ask your hotel about parking.

Getting around Lake Bled (Literally)

By Bike: You can rent a mountain bike at the Kompas Bled travel agency, great for biking around the lake (700 SIT/hr, 1,500 SIT/half-day, 2,200 SIT/full day, see "Tourist Information," above).

By Buggy: Buggies called *fijakers* are easily the most expensive—and romantic—way to get around the lake (4,500 SIT; also 4,500 SIT up to the castle, or 5,500 SIT includes waiting time and trip back down, along the lakefront between Hotel Park and the castle, mobile 041-516-688).

By Tourist Trolley: A touristy little train makes a circuit around the lake every 40 minutes in summer (550 SIT, daily 11:00–18:00, tel. 04/163-7211).

By Shuttle Bus: A handy tourist bus passes through Bled once daily in summer. It leaves the bus station at 10:00, stops at a few hotels (including Grand Hotel Toplice), then goes up to the castle and on to the Vintgar Gorge entrance (350 SIT, mid-June–Sept only, confirm schedule at TI or bus station).

By Taxi: Štefan Jerebic can take you to various destinations near Bled (2,000 SIT to Lesce-Bled train station, 2,500 SIT to Radovljica, 10,000 SIT to airport, mobile 041-633-772). You'll pay more than these rates if you let your hotel or a travel agency call a taxi for you.

By Boat: For information on boat rental—and the cute, characteristic *pletna* boats—see "Getting to the Island," page 317.

Helpful Hints

Internet Access: Most of the bigger hotels have access for guests in the lobby. The public library has fast and reasonable Internet access with a one-hour minimum—so use it only if you want lots of time online (1,000 SIT/hr, daily 14:00–19:00, just beyond the post office on Ljubljanska cesta). For a shorter session or longer hours, several other spots in town—like Café á Propos in the commercial center—have access for a reasonable cost.

Post Office: Coming up from the lake, it's just beyond the commercial center at Ljubljanska cesta 4 (Mon–Fri 7:00–19:00, Sat until 12:00, closed Sun; July–Aug Mon–Fri until 20:00, Sat until 13:00, closed Sun, tel. 04/575-0200).

Banking: The handiest ATMs are SKB Banka (in upstairs of round building at commercial center) and Gorenjska Banka (at far end of Hotel Park).

Laundry: Most hotels can do laundry for you, but it's expensive. The only self-service option is at the campground at the far end of the lake (950 SIT/load, April–Oct only). The more convenient Pension Bledec youth hostel does laundry for guests (1,000 SIT/load), and may also do it for non-guests off-season if you ask nicely (call first, tel. 04/574-5250).

Car Rental: The Julian Alps are ideal by car. While several big chains rent cars in Bled (around €55–60/day), the best deal is at the only locally owned outfit, InterGlobe (€40/day includes unlimited mileage, tax, and insurance; Mon–Fri 8:00–19:00, Sat 8:00–17:00, closed Sun, less off-season; downstairs along Ljubljanska cesta in the commercial center, tel. 04/576-6310, www.interglobe.si).

SIGHTS AND ACTIVITIES

Bled

Bled doesn't have many "sights" (except the lame castle museum, see below). But there are plenty of rewarding and pleasant activities.

▲▲**The Island (Otok)**—Bled's little island—topped with a super-cute church—nudges the lake's quaintness level over the top. Since this is the

only island in Slovenia, locals call it simply "the island" *(otok)*. While it's pretty to look at from afar, it's also fun to visit (for options, see below).

The island has long been a sacred site with a romantic twist. On summer Saturdays, a steady procession of brides and grooms cheered on by their entourages head for the island. Leading up from the island's dock to the Church of the Assumption on top are 98 steps. It's tradition for the groom to carry—or try to carry—his bride up these steps. About four out of five are successful (proving themselves "fit for marriage"). The church was closed and weddings here outlawed during the communist era. But the tradition reemerged—illegally—even before the regime ended, with a clandestine ceremony in 1989.

An eighth-century Slavic pagan temple dedicated to the goddess of love and fertility once stood here; the current Baroque version (with Venetian flair—the bell tower separate from the main church) is the fifth to occupy this spot. As you enter the church, look straight ahead to the fresco of Mary on the wall. She doesn't quite look like other madonnas, because she has the face of Maria Theresa, the Hapsburg empress who controlled Slovenia when this fresco was done. This not-so-subtle propaganda was typical in those times.

During renovation in the 1970s, medieval graves were discovered around the church (you can see one through the Plexiglas under the bell rope). They also discovered Gothic frescoes on either side of the altar, including, above the door on the right, an unusual ecclesiastical theme: the bris (Jewish circumcision ritual) of Christ. Superstitious locals (and every tour guide in town) claim that ringing the church bell will make your dreams come true.

A café and tourist stands are near the church at the top of the steps.

Getting to the Island: The most romantic route to the island is on one of the distinctive *pletna* boats. There are 22 *pletnas* on Lake Bled,

and they all cost the same (1,800 SIT per person round-trip, includes 30-min wait time at the island, catch one at several spots around the lake including just below Hotel Park, generally run from dawn until around 20:00 in summer, stop earlier off-season, none in winter, mobile 031-316-575). The *pletna* gondoliers all belong to the same union. They dump all of their earnings into one fund and divide it evenly among themselves. Still, competition is fierce...and gondoliers have been known to sink each other's boats if someone doesn't report all of his earnings.

No motorized boats are allowed on the lake, but you'll find **rental rowboats** at the swimming pool under the castle (small 3-person boat: 1,800 SIT/1 hr, 3,000 SIT/2 hrs, 900 SIT/each additional hr; bigger 6-person boat: 2,300 SIT/1 hr, 4,000 SIT/2 hrs, 1,100 SIT/each additional hr), or at the campground on the far side of the lake (4-person boat-2,000 SIT/hr, closed in bad weather and off-season).

It's possible to **swim** to the island—especially from the far end of the lake (see "Take a Dip," next page). But note that you're not allowed into the church in your swimsuit.

▲▲**Walk around the Lake**—Strolling the 3.5 miles around the lake is fun, relaxing, and scenic. It takes about 1.5 hours—not counting stops to snap photos of the ever-changing view. On the way, you'll pass some great villas, mostly from the beginning of the 19th century, including the former residence of Marshal Tito—today the Hotel Vila Bled (big, white, James Bond-style villa with long staircase at southern end of lake, near village of Mlino). For the more adventurous, there are also hiking paths up into the hills surrounding the lake (ask TI for details and maps; or hike to Vintgar Gorge, described under "Sights—Near Bled," below).

▲**Bled Castle (Blejski Grad)**—Bled's cliff-hanging castle, dating in one form or another from a thousand years ago, was the seat of the Austrian Bishops of Brixen. The castle offers a range of sub-par sightseeing opportunities: a small and uninspired castle museum, a tiny frescoed chapel, a working printing press from Gutenberg's time (called Tiskarna, daily 10:00–13:00, closed Oct–March), a wine cellar (Klet, daily 10:00–13:00 & 16:00–19:00, closed Oct–March), an "herbal gallery"

(Zeliščna Galerija, gift shop of traditional-meets-modern herbal brandies, cosmetics, and perfumes, Tue–Sun 10:00–13:00 & 16:00–18:00, closed Mon and Oct–March), and a fancy restaurant (see below). None of these attractions is worth the hike up—but the spectacular views are (castle and museum entry-800 SIT, other parts free once inside castle, May–Sept daily 8:00–20:00, Oct–April daily 9:00–17:00, tel. 04/578-0525).

To save the entry price, consider eating at the scenic but moderately expensive castle **restaurant**; if you call to reserve ahead (even immediately before you head up), you'll get into the castle complex free (most main dishes 2,000–3,000 SIT, daily 10:00–22:00, tel. 04/574-1607). It's still cheaper to pay the entry fee and bring your own **picnic** to the most scenic spot in town.

Getting to the Castle: Most people **hike** up the steep hill (20 min). The handiest trails are behind the big St. Martin's Church: Walk past the church with the lake at your back and look left after the first set of houses for the *Grad* signs; or, for a longer but less steep route, continue on the street, bear uphill at the fork, and find the *Grad* sign just after the Pension Bledec hostel on the left. Once you're on this second trail, don't take the sharp-left uphill turn at the fork. Instead of hiking, you can take the **shuttle bus** up (see "Getting around Bled," above), your rental car, a taxi (around 1,500 SIT), or, if you're wealthy and romantic, a **buggy** (4,500 SIT, see "Getting around Bled," above).

Take a Dip—There are several suitable spots for a swim. The swimming pools under the castle—filled with lake water—routinely earn the "blue flag," meaning the water is top-quality (all day-1,000 SIT, afternoon only-700 SIT, closed Oct–May). Bled's two beaches are at the far end of the lake. Both are free; the one at the campground (southwest corner) has lots of tourists, but locals prefer the one at the rowing center (northwest corner). If you swim to the island, remember that you can't get in the church in your swimsuit.

Near Bled

There are several day trips from Bled that can be done easily without a car. The three listed here are the best (one village/museum experience, two hiking/back-to-nature options). They're more convenient than can't-miss, but each one is worthwhile on a longer visit, and all give a good taste of the Julian Alps.

▲**Radovljica**—The village of Radovljica (rah-DOH-vleet-suh) is larger than Bled, perched on a plateau above the Sava River. The town itself is so-so, though its old center pedestrian zone, Linhartov trg, makes for a pleasant stroll. But the town is home to an offbeat and interesting beekeeping museum—which, with only a few rooms, still ranks as one of Europe's biggest.

Radovljica's **Apicultural Museum** (Čebelarski Muzej) celebrates Slovenia's long beekeeping heritage. Since the days before Europeans had sugar, Slovenia has been a big honey producer. The Slovene farmer Anton Janša is considered the father of modern beekeeping—he was Europe's first official teacher of beekeeping (in Hapsburg Vienna).

The first two rooms of the museum trace the history of beekeeping, from the time when bees were kept in hollowed-out trees to the present day. Notice the old-fashioned tools in the first room. When a new queen bee is born, the old queen takes half the hive's bees to a new location. Experienced beekeepers used the long, skinny instrument (a beehive stethoscope) to figure out when the swarm would fly the coop. Then, once the bees had moved to a nearby tree, they'd use the big spoons to retrieve the queen—surrounded by an angry ball of her subjects—and put that gang into a manmade hive, allowing for easier, more sanitary collection of the honey. You can also see the tools beekeepers used to create smoke, which makes bees less aggressive. But even today, some of Slovenia's old-fashioned beekeepers simply light up a cigarette and blow smoke on any bees that get ornery.

The third room features the museum's highlight: whimsically painted beehive frontboards (called *panjske končnice*). Nineteenth-century farmers, believing these paintings would actually help the bees find their way home, developed a tradition of decorating their hives with religious, historical, and satirical folk themes (look for the devil sharpening a woman's tongue). The depiction of a hunter's funeral shows all the animals happy...except his dog. There's everything from portraits of Hapsburg emperors, to a "true crime" sequence of a man murdering his family as they sleep, to 18th-century erotica (one with a woman showing some leg, and another with a flip-up peekaboo panel).

The life-size wooden statues were used to "guard" the beehives—and designed to look like the Slovenes' most feared enemies (Turkish and French soldiers).

You'll also find an interactive multimedia exhibit, temporary exhibitions, and—in the summer only—an actual, functioning beehive (try to find the queen). The gift shop is a good place for souvenirs, with hand-painted replicas of frontboards, honey brandy, candles, ornaments, and other bee products (museum entry-400 SIT, English descriptions, free sheet of English info, 400-SIT English-language guidebook is a nice souvenir, May–Oct Tue–Sun 10:00–13:00 & 15:00–18:00, closed Mon; Nov–Dec and March–April Wed and Sat–Sun 10:00–12:00 & 15:00–17:00, closed Mon–Tue and Thu–Fri; closed Jan–Feb, Linhartov trg 1, tel. 04/532-0520).

Eating in Radovljica: Several Radovljica restaurants near the bee museum have view terraces overlooking the surrounding mountains and valleys. One of them, **Lectar,** offers hearty Slovenian fare in a traditional setting. Locals love it (Wed–Mon 12:00–23:00, closed Tue, Linhartov trg 2, tel. 04/537-4800). The restaurant is also known for its heart-shaped cookies, called *lect*, with messages on them.

Getting to Radovljica: Buses to Radovljica generally leave Bled every half hour (check schedules at hotel or station; trip takes about 15 min). The Radovljica TI is behind the bus station (go behind station and to the right to find small passageway next to Mercator supermarket). To reach the old town square and the Bee Museum, leave the station straight ahead, cross the bus parking lot and the next street, then turn left down the far street (following brown sign for *Staro Mesto*). In five minutes, you'll get to the pedestrianized Linhartov trg; at the end of the square, just before the church, you'll see the bee museum, which shares an old Baroque mansion with a music school (bee museum upstairs). Coming back to Bled, there are fewer buses—check the schedule when you arrive (at least 2/hr, but fewer Sat–Sun). **Drivers** leave Bled on Ljubljanska cesta, then turn right at the sign for Radovljica and go through the village of Lesce; the road dead-ends at Radovljica's pedestrian zone.

▲**Vintgar Gorge**—Just north of Bled, the river Radovna has carved this mile-long scenic gorge into the mountainside. Boardwalks and bridges put you right in the middle of the action of this "poor man's Plitvice." You'll cross over several scenic waterfalls and marvel at the clarity of the water. The easy hike is on a boardwalk trail with handrails (sometimes narrow and a bit slippery). At the end of the gorge, you'll find a restaurant, WCs, and a bridge with a nice view. Go back the way you came, or take a more scenic return to Bled (see "Scenic Hike Back to Bled," below). The gorge is easily reachable from Bled by bus or foot (see below), and is the best option for those who are itching for a hike and don't have a car (600 SIT, mid-April–late-Oct daily 8:00–19:00 or until dusk, June–Aug until 20:00, closed late-Oct–mid-April).

Getting to Vintgar Gorge: The gorge is 2.5 miles north of Bled. You can walk (1 hr) or bus (10-min ride plus 20-min walk, or 30-min ride on summer "tourist bus") to the gorge entrance. **Walkers** leave Bled on the road between the castle and St. Martin's Church and take the uphill (left) road at the fork. Soon after you pass the Pension Bledec hostel, turn right at the stop sign, then turn left at the bend in the road (following signs for Podhom and Vintgar; ignore the other *Vintgar* sign pointing the way you came). At the fork just after the little bridge, go left for Podhom, then simply follow signs for Vintgar. You can also take a **local bus** to Podhom (10 min, almost hrly). You'll be dropped at a pedestrian underpass; go through it and follow the Vintgar signs for 20 minutes. In summer, a **tourist shuttle bus** takes you right to the gorge entrance in 30 minutes (see "Getting around Bled," above). **Drivers** follow signs to Podhom, then Vintgar (see walking instructions, above).

Scenic Hike Back to Bled: If you still have energy once you reach the end of the gorge, consider a more scenic return. Behind the restaurant, find the trail marked *Katarina Bled*. You'll go uphill for 25 fairly strenuous minutes (following the red-and-white circles and arrows) before cresting the hill and enjoying beautiful views over Bled town and the region. Continue straight down the road 15 minutes to the typical, narrow old village of Zasip, then walk (about 30 min) or take the bus back to Bled.

Lake Bohinj—Pristine alpine Lake Bohinj (BOH-heen), 16 miles southwest of Bled, enjoys a quieter scene and (some locals argue) even better views of Triglav and the surrounding mountains. This is a real back-to-nature experience, with just a few campgrounds and lodges. It offers just two main activities: a waterfall hike and cable-car ride.

Hikers follow the moderate-to-strenuous uphill trail to the **Savica Slap** waterfall, cascading into a remarkably pure pool of snowmelt. Hardy hikers find it worth the 570 steps (400 SIT, daily 8:00 until dusk in summer, round-trip about 2 hrs, leave from trailhead at far end of lake—a shuttle-bus ride or 45-min walk from Bohinj Zlatorog bus stop).

If you like mountain vistas more than hiking, take the cable car up to **Vogel Mountain**, which offers panoramic views of the Julian Alps (1,600 SIT round-trip, every 30 min, daily 8:00–18:00). While you're up there, visit the Alpine hut Merjasec (Wild Boar), which has tasty strudel and brandy.

Back at the lake, walk through the campground to the little dock and catch the boat in the direction of Bohinj Jezero. There, you can visit one of the oldest churches in the area, St. John the Baptist (150 SIT, borrow key from TI near post office), and then catch a bus back to Bled.

Getting to Bohinj: From Bled, there are two different Bohinj **bus** destinations: Bohinj Zlatorog (closer to waterfall hike and cable-car ride, 7/day, 40 min, 850 SIT) and Bohinj Jezero (at the little village and church, 8/day, 30 min, 740 SIT). **Drivers** leave Bled south along the lakefront; once you reach Mlino, you'll peel off from the lake and follow signs to Bohinj.

SLEEPING

$$$ Grand Hotel Toplice is Bled's best splurge, with 87 rooms, all the amenities, and a long list of high-profile guests—from Madeleine Albright to Jordan's King Hussein. Non-lake-view rooms to the back are cheaper, but overlook a very noisy street—try to get one as high up as possible (non-view: Sb-€112, Db-€152; lake view: Sb-€144, Db-€184; suites mostly with lake views-€242, less off-season, elevator, cesta Svobode 12, tel. 04/579-1000, fax 04/574-1841, www.hotel-toplice .com, info@hotel-toplice.com). The hotel's name—*toplice*—means "spa"; guests are free to use the hotel's natural-spring-fed indoor swimming pool (a chilly 22 degrees Celsius, or 72 degrees Fahrenheit).

$$$ Kompas Hotel Bled has 105 new-feeling business-class

SLEEP CODE

(€1 = about $1.10, 220 SIT = about $1, country code: 386, area code: 04)

Sleep Code: **S** = Single, **D** = Double/Twin, **T** = Triple, **Q** = Quad, **b** = bathroom, **s** = shower only, **no CC** = Credit Cards not accepted. Unless otherwise noted, breakfast is included and credit cards are accepted. Everyone speaks English, and prices are quoted in euros.

To help you sort easily through these listings, I've divided the rooms into three categories based on the price for a standard double room with bath:

 $$$ **Higher Priced**—Most rooms €90 (21,700 SIT) or more.
  $$ **Moderately Priced**—Most rooms between €60–€90 (14,500–21,700 SIT).
   $ **Lower Priced**—Most rooms €60 (14,500 SIT) or less.

Bled is packed with gradually decaying convention hotels from the communist era. A few have been halfheartedly renovated, but most are stale, outmoded, and overpriced. It's a strange, incestuous little circle—nearly three-quarters of the town's big hotels and restaurants are owned by the Sava company (which is in turn part of the Goodyear tire company).

Only a handful of Bled accommodations are modern and a good value, and I've listed them here—along with a few older places that work in a pinch. Quaint little family-run pensions are rare, and an excellent value—so they book up fast with Germans and Brits (reserve these places as far ahead as possible). I've listed the high-season prices (May–Oct). Off-season, the big hotels lower prices 10–15 percent. Bled levies a €0.80 tourist tax per person, per night (not included in below prices unless noted).

For cheaper beds, consider one of the many *sobes* (room in a private home) scattered around the lake (around €15–20 per person in peak season, often with a hefty 30 percent surcharge for stays shorter than 3 nights). Several agencies in town can help you find a *sobe* (including Kompas Bled, listed under "Tourist Information," above)—but if you don't have a car, be sure the location is convenient before you accept.

rooms around a mod, airy atrium. It has little charm but a good location and all the comforts (non-view: Sb-€80, Db-€100, apartment-€129;
lake view: Sb-€90, Db-€110, apartment-€159; non-smoking rooms, elevator, Cankarjeva cesta 2, tel. 04/578-2100, fax 04/578-2499, www.kh
-bled.si, info@kh-bled.si).

$$ **Mayer Penzion,** perched on a bluff above Grand Hotel Toplice
(a 5-min walk from lake), is a family-run place with 16 great-value
rooms, a friendly and professional staff, and an excellent restaurant. The
summer books up fast with return clients, so reserve early—this place is
worth it (Sb-€40, Db-€60–75 depending on size and balcony, extra bed-
€20, elevator, Želeška cesta 7, tel. 04/576-5740, fax 04/576-5741, www
.mayer-sp.si, penzion@mayer-sp.si, Trseglav family). Mayer Penzion
also rents a cute little two-story Slovenian farm cottage next door.
Modernized for comfort, it's remarkably cheap (Db-€55, Tb-€78, Qb-
€85) because people who've been staying here for years would squawk
if the rates went up. If it's available, jump on it.

Grand Hotel Toplice runs two nearby annexes—Hotels Jadran and
Trst—with worn rooms and much lower prices: $$ **Hotel Jadran,** on a
hill behind the Toplice, has 45 rooms scheduled for renovation, but
better lake views than the Trst (reception tel. 04/579-1365). The $$
Hotel Trst's 31 rooms were recently spruced up a bit (reception and
breakfast at the Toplice). Both have the same prices and can be reserved
through Grand Hotel Toplice (non-view: Sb-€50, Db-€70; lake view:
Sb-€70, Db-€90, cesta Svobode 12, tel. 04/579-1000, fax 04/574-1841,
www.hotel-toplice.com, info@hotel-toplice.com).

$$ **Vila Prešeren**—named for Slovenia's national poet—is literally
a few steps from the lake. Its eight rooms are small but well-maintained,
nicely furnished, and wonderfully located (non-view: Sb-€52, Db-€72;
lake view: Sb-€68, Db-€88; cheaper off-season, lake-view apartment-
€140–154 depending on size, non-smoking rooms, Kidričeva 1, tel.
04/578-0800, fax 04/578-0810, www.vila.preseren.s5.net, vila.preseren
@siol.net).

$ **Penzion Bledec** is just below the castle in the old town. While
it's technically an IYHF hostel, each of the 13 rooms has its own bathroom, and some can be rented as doubles (separate beds can be pushed
together; reserve ahead for doubles, especially June–Oct). The friendly
staff is justifiably proud of the excellent value they provide (all prices per
person: bed in 3- to 7-bed dorm-€16, Db-€18, 2-room apartment for up
to 3 people-€19, non-members pay 10 percent more, includes sheets and
breakfast, prices lower Nov–April, no CC, non-smoking rooms, great
family rooms, Internet access-1,000 SIT/hr, full-service laundry-1,000
SIT/load, Grajska 17, tel. 04/574-5250, fax 04/574-5251, www.mlino.si,
bledec@siol.net).

$ **Penzion Berc,** next door to Mayer Penzion (listed above) and run
by a cousin, offers 11 cheaper, almost-as-nice rooms. It's an equally good

value and worth reserving ahead (Sb-€27, Db-€44–50, 10 percent more for one-night stays and off-season, includes tax, no CC, free loaner bikes, free Internet, free self-serve laundry with hang-dry, Želeška cesta 15, tel. & fax 04/574-1838, www.berc-sp.si, penzion@berc-sp.si, Berc family).

Another five minutes by foot beyond the Mayer and Berc pensions (10 min uphill from lake) is **$ Alp Penzion.** Its 11 rooms are small and faded but comfortable, and there are lots of fun activities on the premises: tennis court, summer barbecue grill, and sauna (Sb-€40, Db-€50–60, extra bed-€20, apartment-€80, 15 percent more for 1-night stays, Cankarjeva cesta 20-A, tel. 04/574-1614, fax 04/574-4590, www .alp-penzion.com, alp.penzion@siol.net, Sršen family).

EATING

Charming, well-traveled **Leo Ličof** serves excellent Slovenian cuisine with an Indian twist at his restaurant, Okarina. The location and name might change in the future, but Leo's fine food and atmosphere are worth seeking out (call ahead or ask locally for new location, Riklijeva 9, tel. 04/574-1458).

The recommended **Mayer Penzion,** just up the hill from the lakefront, has a great restaurant that's worth the short hike (Mon–Fri

BLED DESSERTS

While you're in Bled, be sure to enjoy the town's specialty, a vanilla-custard-and-cream cake called *kremna rezina* (KRAYM-nah ray-ZEE-nah). It's often referred to by its German name *kremšnita* (KRAYM-shnee-tah). This dish was first created right here in Bled, at the big, red Park Hotel. Slovenes travel from all over the country to sample this famous dessert.

Slightly less renowned—but just as tasty—is *grmuda* (gur-MOO-dah, literally "bonfire"). This dessert was developed by Hotel Jelovice as a way to get rid of their day-old dessert leftovers. Start with the remains of cakes, add rum, milk, custard, and raisins, and top it off with whipped cream and chocolate syrup.

These desserts are best enjoyed with a lake-and-mountains view—the best spots are the Panorama restaurant by Grand Hotel Toplice, the recommended Vila Prešeren restaurant, and the terrace across from the Park Hotel (figure around 800 SIT for cake and coffee at any of these places). For a more local (but non-lake-view) setting, consider the Šmon Slaščičarna (only slightly cheaper; see "Eating," next page).

17:00–24:00, Sat–Sun 12:00–24:00, above Hotel Jadran at Želeška cesta 7, tel. 04/576-5740).

Dante has good wood-fired pizzas, plus pastas and salads, in the old town (daily 12:00–23:00, marked only with low-key *pizzeria* sign at Riklijeva cesta 13, tel. 04/576-8900).

Gostilna Pri Planincu is a homey, informal bar packed with fun-loving and sometimes-rowdy locals. The big menu features good-enough Slovene pub grub (daily 9:00–23:00, Grajska cesta 8, tel. & fax 04/574-1613).

The **Vila Prešeren** serves expensive food in a classy dining room or on a scenic terrace right on the lake (main dishes 2,000–3,000 SIT, daily 11:00–23:00, Kidričeva 1, tel. 04/578-0800).

Café á Propos, in the commercial center, features light sandwiches and Internet access, plus cocktails in the evening (daily 8:00–24:00, Ljubljanska cesta 4, tel. 04/574-4044).

The **Mercator** grocery store, also in the commercial center, has the makings for a bang-up picnic. They sell pre-made sandwiches, or will make you one to order (point to what you want). This is a great option for hikers or budget travelers (Mon–Sat 7:00–19:00, Sun 8:00–12:00).

For dessert, locals go to the **Šmon Slaščičarna** (with brown bear on sign, near bus station). It's nicely non-touristy, but with less atmosphere than the lakeside spots (daily 7:30–22:00, Grajska cesta 3, tel. 04/574-1616).

TRANSPORTATION CONNECTIONS

The most convenient train connections to Bled leave from the Lesce-Bled station, about 2.5 miles away. Remember, when buying a train ticket to Lake Bled, make it clear that you want to go to the Lesce-Bled station. The Bled Jezero station is closer to Bled, but it takes longer to reach because it's served by only a handful of regional trains.

By train to: Ljubljana (11/day, 1 hr, but bus is better since it departs conveniently from Bled town, not from train station outside of town), **Salzburg** (5/day, 4 hrs), **Munich** (3/day, 6 hrs), **Vienna** (that's *Dunaj* in Slovene, 5/day, 6 hrs, transfer in Villach, Austria), **Venice** (1/day with transfer in Villach, 6 hrs), **Zagreb** (5/day, 3.5 hrs).

By bus to: Ljubljana (Mon–Fri 11/day, Sat–Sun 8/day, 80 min, 1,320 SIT), **Radovljica** (Mon–Fri at least 2/hr, Sat hrly, Sun almost hrly, 15 min, 350 SIT), **Lesce-Bled train station** (at least hrly, 10 min, 300 SIT), **Lake Bohinj-Jezero stop** (8/day, 30 min, 740 SIT), **Lake Bohinj-Zlatorog stop** (7/day, 40 min, 850 SIT), **Podhom** (20-min hike away from Vintgar Gorge, Mon–Fri 9/day, none Sat, 1/day Sun, 15 min, 290 SIT). Confirm times at the helpful Bled bus station.

By plane: Brnik airport is between Bled and Ljubljana. A taxi will cost you 8,000 SIT. You can also get there by bus (total cost: 1,100

SIT), but it's a complicated connection from Bled: First go to Kranj (Mon–Fri 12/day, Sat–Sun 8/day, 35 min), then transfer to a Brnik-bound bus (at least hrly, 20 min).

Triglav National Park
(Triglavski Narodni Park)

The countryside around Lake Bled has its own distinctive beauty: alpine rivers with great fishing, rural rest stops, and charming mountain hamlets.

The best day in the Julian Alps is spent driving up and over the Vršič Pass (vrr-SHEECH, open May–Oct) and back down via the Soča River Valley (SOH-chah). This daylong circular drive features some spectacular mountain scenery (on challenging, twisty roads), as well as some offbeat WWI sights.

This is a long trip, divided into two parts: the Vršič Pass and the Soča River Valley—plan a whole day. It makes sense to start in Bled and wind up in Ljubljana (which you'll pass by at the end anyway). Not counting stops, figure an hour from Bled to the top of the pass, a half

---

TRIGLAV

Mount Triglav (literally "three heads") stands watch over the Julian Alps and all of Slovenia. Slovenes say that its three peaks are the guardians of the water, air, and earth. This mountain defines Slovenes, even adorning the nation's flag: Look for the national seal, with three peaks. The two squiggly lines under it represent the Adriatic.

From the town of Bled, you'll see Triglav peeking up over the ridge on a clear day. (You'll get an even better view from nearby Lake Bohinj.)

It's said that you're not a true Slovene until you've climbed Triglav. One native took these words very seriously, and climbed the mountain 853 times...in one year. Climbing to the summit—at 9,396 feet—is an attainable goal for any hiker in decent shape. If you're here for a while and want to become an honorary Slovene, befriend a local and ask if he or she will accompany you to the top.

If mountain climbing isn't your style, relax at an outdoor café with a piece of cream cake and a view of Triglav. It won't make you a Slovene...but it's close enough on a quick visit.

Northwest Slovenia

hour back down to the start of the Soča Valley, and an hour on to the town of Kobarid. From Kobarid, figure another two hours back to the expressway via Idrija, then an hour to Ljubljana or 90 minutes back to Bled. If you return via Nova Gorica (see below), it takes slightly longer.

VRŠIČ PASS

This self-guided driving tour takes you up and over the highest mountain pass in Slovenia—with stunning scenery and a few quirky sights along the way. It's a challenging drive—not for stick-shift novices—but all but the most timid drivers will agree the scenery is worth the many hairpin turns.

Begin in Bled. Take the freeway north towards Jesenice. If the weather's clear, you'll enjoy views of **Mount Triglav** to the left as you drive. When you approach the industrial city of Jesenice—within yodeling distance of Austria—keep your eye out for the Hrušica exit (also marked for Jesenice, Kranjska Gora, and the Italian border; it's after the gas station, just before the tunnel to Austria). When you exit, turn left towards Kranjska Gora and the Italian border.

As you drive towards Kranjska Gora, on your left is the **Vrata Valley,** the starting point for climbing Mount Triglav. On the right, keep an eye out for the statue of **Jako Palaš,** who actually bought Triglav back when such a thing was possible (he's pointing at his purchase). When you cross the bridge, you'll have a great head-on view of **Špik Mountain.**

Entering Kranjska Gora, you'll see a turnoff to the left marked for Vršič. But winter sports fans may want to take a 15-minute detour to see the biggest ski jump in the world, a few miles ahead (stay straight through Kranjska Gora, then turn left at signs for **Planica,** the last stop before the Italian border). Every year, tens of thousands of sports fans flock here to watch the ski-jumping world championships. The competitors routinely set new world records (right now it's 758 feet—or 17 seconds in the air; www.planica.info). From the ski jump, you're a few minutes' walk from Italy or Austria. This region—spanning three nations—lobbied to host the 2006 Winter Olympics (as *senza confini*—Italian for "without borders"). The Italian city of Turin won instead.

Back in Kranjska Gora, follow the signs for Vršič. Before long, you'll officially enter **Triglav National Park** and come to the first of this road's 50 hairpin turns—each one numbered and labeled with the altitude in meters. In addition to the ever-changing alpine panorama, there are several worthwhile stops along the way, as well as frequent pull-outs for photo stops. If the drive seems intimidating, remember that 50-seat tour buses routinely conquer this pass...if they can do it, so can you.

After switchback #8, park on the right and hike up the stairs to the little **Russian chapel.** This road was built during World War I by 10,000 Russian POWs of the Austro-Hungarian Empire to supply the front lines of the Soča Front. The POWs lived and worked in terrible conditions, and several hundred died of illness and exposure. On March 8, 1916, an avalanche thundered down the mountains, killing hundreds of workers. This chapel was built where the final casualty was found. Sign the little guest book and pay your respects to the men who built the road you're enjoying today.

After #22, at the pull-off for Erjavčera Koča restaurant, you may see tour buses making a fuss about the mountain vista. They're looking for a ghostly face in the cliff wall, supposedly belonging to the mythical figure **Ajda,** a village girl who was cursed by the townspeople after correctly predicting the death of the Golden Horn, a magical goat-like animal. Her image is just above the treeline, a little to the right—try to get a local to point her out to you (you can see her best if you stand far to the left in the parking lot).

After #24, you'll reach the **summit** (5,285 feet). On the 26 hairpin turns on the way down, keep an eye out for old WWI debris. Just after the pass, the tunnel marked *1916* on the left used to be the original path of this road. At #48, you'll see a statue of **Julius Kugy,** a Slovene botanist who wrote books about alpine flora. As you near the end of the switchbacks, follow signs for Bovec. You'll cross the Soča River—which you'll now follow for the second half of this trip.

SOČA RIVER VALLEY

During World War I, the terrain between here and the Adriatic made up the Soča (Isonzo) Front. As you follow the Soča River south, the scenic mountainsides around you tell the tale of this terrible warfare. Imagine a young Ernest Hemingway driving his ambulance through these same hills.

After the last Vršič switchback (#50), you'll come to the village of Trenta. On the left, look for the **Triglav National Park Information Center.** The helpful staff has lots of brochures about the park (May–Oct daily 10:00–18:00, closed Nov–April, tel. 05/388-9330, www.tnp.si).

About five miles after Trenta, you'll reach the town of Soča. Pull over to visit the village **Church of St. Joseph** (with red onion dome, hiding behind the big tree on the right). During World War II, a local artist hiding out in the mountains filled this church with patriotic symbolism. The interior is bathed in Yugoslav red, white, and blue—a brave statement when such nationalistic sentiments were discouraged. On the ceiling is St. Michael (clad in Yugoslav colors) with Yugoslavia's three WWII enemies at his feet: the eagle (Germany), the wolf (Italy), and the serpent (Japan). The tops of the walls along the nave are lined with saints—but these are Slavic, not Catholic. Finally, look carefully at the Stations of the Cross and find the faces of hated Yugoslav enemies Hitler (fourth from altar on left) and Mussolini (first from altar on right).

Roughly five miles after the town of Soča, you'll exit the National Park and come to a fork. The main route leads to the left, through Bovec. But first consider a 10-minute detour to the right, to see the

THE SOČA FRONT

The northwest corner of Slovenia saw some of World War I's fiercest fighting. While the Western Front gets more press, this eastern border between the Central Powers and the Allies was just as significant. In a series of 13 battles involving 16 different nationalities, 300,000 soldiers died, 700,000 were wounded, and 100,000 were declared MIA. In addition, tens of thousands of civilians died. Among the injured soldiers was a young Ernest Hemingway, who drove an ambulance for the Italian army. (Later in life, he would write the novel *A Farewell to Arms* about his experiences here.)

On April 26, 1915, Italy joined the Allies. A month later, they declared war on the Austro-Hungarian Empire (which included Slovenia). Italy invaded the Soča Valley, quickly taking the tiny town of Kobarid, which they planned to use as a home base for attacks deeper into Austrian territory. For the next 29 months, Italy launched 10 more offensives, all of them unsuccessful. This was difficult warfare—Italy had to attack uphill, waging war high in the mountains, in the harshest of conditions.

In October of 1917, the Central Powers of Austria-Hungary and Germany retook Kobarid, launching a downhill attack of 600,000 soldiers. For the first time ever, the Austrian-German army used a new surprise-attack technique called *Blitzkrieg*, which was carried out by a German general named Rommel—against orders from a superior. (He was demoted for his insolence despite its success, but climbed the ranks again to become famous as Hitler's "Desert Fox" in North Africa.) The Central Powers caught the Italian forces off-guard, quickly breaking through three lines of defense. Within three days, the Italians were forced to retreat. The Austrians called it the "Miracle at Kobarid," but Italy felt differently—to this day, when an Italian finds himself in a mess, he says he had a *Caporetto* (the Italian name for Kobarid).

A year later, Italy came back—this time with the aid of British, French, and U.S. forces. The Allies were successful, and on November 4, 1918, Austria-Hungary conceded defeat. After more than a million casualties, the fighting at Soča was finally over.

WWI **Kluže Fort,** keeping a close watch over the narrowest part of a valley leading to Italy. In the 15th century, the Italians had a fort here to defend against the Turks. Half a millennium later, during World War I, it was used by Austrians to keep Italians out of their territory. Notice the ladder rungs fixed to the cliff face across the road from the fort—allowing soldiers to quickly get up to the mountaintop. Today the fort hosts a peace festival every summer, where costumed Italian and Austro-Hungarian soldiers dance and embrace each other.

Continue back through **Bovec,** which saw some of the most vicious fighting of the Soča Front. Today it's the adventure-sports capital of the Soča River Valley, famous for its whitewater activities. As you head south along the river (with water somehow both perfectly clear and spectacularly turquoise), watch for happy kayakers, and pull over to scramble onto one of the many rickety rope bridges. When you pass the intersection at Žaga, you're just over four miles from Italy.

Follow signs to the town of **Kobarid,** site of many WWI battles claiming nearly half a million lives (see "The Soča Front" sidebar, facing page). Today this small town is home to the world-class **Kobarid Museum** (Kobariški Muzej), offering a haunting look at the tragedy of the Soča Front (700 SIT, good 600-SIT museum guide, 1,900-SIT Soča Front book, April–Sept Mon–Fri 9:00–18:00, Sat–Sun 9:00–19:00, Oct–March Mon–Fri 10:00–17:00, Sat–Sun 9:00–18:00, Gregorčičeva 10, www.kobariski-muzej.si, 05/389-0000). This proud little place, described in English, was voted Europe's best museum in 1993. In the entry, you'll see stone-cross grave markers of casualties, pictures of soldiers, and flags of all of the nationalities involved in the fighting. The rotating ground-floor exhibit features one country in particular (Hungary in 2004). Upstairs are exhibits on the way these soldiers lived, the tragedies they encountered (with some horrific images of war injuries), the devastating effects of the war on local civilians, the strategies involved in the various battles (including a huge model of the successful Austrian-German *Blitzkrieg* attack), and the history of this region before and after World War I. At the museum, WWI buffs can pick up free brochures on self-guided "walks of peace" through town; call ahead if you want a private guide (2,500 SIT/hr).

In the 55 miles between here and the Adriatic, you'll still find more than a hundred cemeteries filled with casualties of the Soča Front battles.  One of the most dramatic is the **Italian Mausoleum** (Kostnica) overlooking Kobarid. Find the access road across Kobarid's main square from the church (look for gate with cross on one side, star on the other). Follow this road up Gradič Hill (passing Stations of the Cross on the way up) until you reach the mausoleum. Built in 1938 around the existing Church of St. Anthony, this fascist-style octagonal pyramid holds the remains of 7,014 Italian soldiers. Names are listed alphabetically, along with mass graves for more than 1,700 unknown soldiers *(militi ignoti)*. Inside the church, look above the door to see a brave soldier standing over the body of a fallen comrade, fending off enemies with nothing but rocks. When Mussolini came to dedicate the mausoleum, local revolutionaries plotted an assassination attempt that couldn't fail. But at the last minute, the triggerman had a change of heart, Mussolini had an uneventful trip, and fascism continued to thrive in Italy.

Continue south along the Soča to **Tolmin.** Before you reach Tolmin, decide your route back to Ljubljana or Bled. The option you'll encounter first (turnoff to the right before town) is to head southwest through Tuscan-esque landscapes towards Nova Gorica (literally divided in half by the Italian border) and eventually to the bustling Italian port of Trieste (which was Slovenian before World War II). From Nova Gorica or from Trieste, freeways lead back to Ljubljana and Bled.

I prefer the more rural second option: Continue through Tolmin, then head southeast through the hills back towards Ljubljana. Keep an eye out for the distinctive Slovenian hay-drying racks—but notice that here, unlike the northern part of the country, they don't have roofs (less rain). Along the way, stop for lunch and some sightseeing at **Idrija** (EE-dree-yah), known to all Slovenes for three things: its tourable mercury mine, fine delicate lace, and tasty *žlikrofi* (like ravioli). Back at the freeway, head north to Ljubljana or on to Bled.

CROATIA

(Hrvatska)

- Croatia is 21,800 square miles (the size of West Virginia, but with a boomerang shape).
- Population is 4.5 million (about 200 people per square mile, 90 percent Catholic, 5 percent Serbian Orthodox).
- 1 kuna (kn, or HRK, Croatian for marten or fox) = about 14 cents, and 7 kuna = about $1.
- Country code: 385.

Croatia is known for two very different reasons: as a top fun-in-the-sun tourist destination, and as the site, only a decade ago, of one of the bloodiest European wars in a generation. Today the bloodshed is in the past. Be aware of the war, but focus on Croatia's natural beauty—the dramatic Dalmatian coastline and the striking waterfalls of Plitvice Lakes National Park—and its underrated capital, Zagreb.

Croatia feels more Mediterranean than "Eastern European." It's sometimes hard, especially on the coast, to distinguish this lively, chaotic place from Italy. Be prepared to fall victim to the Croatian Shrug—a simple gesture that conveys the simple message, "Don't know, don't care."

Ten years of war, no tourists, and economic troubles mean that Croatia's service standards and infrastructure still lag behind other parts of Eastern Europe. (Notice that Croatia is the only country in this book *not* joining the European Union in 2004.) While prices are on par with Western Europe, you get less for your money, especially at coastal hotels.

But most visitors happily put up with Croatia's minor frustrations to take advantage of its spectacular scenery. Like Mexico for Americans, Croatia is known among Europeans as *the* place for a sunny holiday.

Nude beaches are a big deal in Croatia, especially with vacationing Germans and Austrians. If you want to work on an all-around tan, seek out one of the beaches marked FKK (from the German *Freikörper Kultur,* or "free body culture"). First-timers get comfortable in a hurry, finding they're not the only pink novices on the rocks. But don't get too excited—these beaches are most beloved by people you'd rather see with their clothes on.

Croatian music, the mariachi music of Europe, graces German and Italian airwaves. The crooner Oliver Dragojević—singing soulful Mediterranean ballads with his gravelly, passionate voice—is the Croatian Tony Bennett.

Even a few years ago, the newly rebuilt streets of Dubrovnik were empty. But not anymore. Croatian resorts and beaches are quickly filling back up to pre-war levels. Visit soon, before the crowds return in full force.

Practicalities

Safety: Americans worry about the potential dangers of traveling in a country that was in the headlines for its bloody war just a decade ago. But as soon as they arrive, they're surprised by how peaceful and stable Croatia feels. Croatia's primary tourist region—the coast—was barely touched by the war (except Dubrovnik, which has been painstakingly restored). The inland is sprinkled with destroyed homes, but villages are gradually being refurbished.

If there's anything visitors need to be aware of, it's that much of the Croatian interior was once full of landmines. Almost all have been removed, and fields that may be dangerous are usually clearly marked. But as a precaution, stay on roads and paths, and don't go wandering through overgrown fields and deserted villages.

The biggest impact from the war has been on the people. Throughout the country, but especially in the war-torn interior, sadness and anger hang heavy in the air. Though the country is repairing itself admirably, the Croatians' souls will take the longest to heal.

For more on Croatia during and after the war, see "Understanding Yugoslavia," page 517.

Telephones: Croatia's phone system uses area codes. To make a long-distance call within the country, start with the area code. To call Croatia from another country, first dial the international access code (00 if calling from Europe, 011 from United States or Canada), 385 (Croatia's country code), the area code (without the initial zero), and the local number. To call out of Croatia, dial 00, the country code of the country you're calling (see chart in appendix), the area code if applicable (may need to drop initial zero), and the local number.

Croatian History

Croatia's history is complicated. For nearly a millennium, bits and pieces of what we today call "Croatia" were batted back and forth between foreign powers: Hungarians, Venetians, Turks, Hapsburgs, and—of course—Yugoslavs. Only in 1991 did Croatia (violently) regain its independence.

Early History

Croatia's first inhabitants were the Illyrians (ancestors of today's Albanians). Romans began to settle the Dalmatian Coast as early as 229 B.C., and Emperor Diocletian had his retirement palace in the coastal town of Split. The Slavic Croats—ancestors of today's Croatians—arrived in the seventh century, and in A.D. 925, the Dalmatian duke Tomislav united most of present-day Croatia.

Loss of Independence

By the early 12th century, the Croatian kings had died out and neighboring powers (Hungary, Venice, and Byzantium) threatened the Croats. For the sake of self-preservation, Croatia entered into an alliance with the Hungarians in 1102—and for the next 900 years, Croatia was ruled by foreign states. The Hungarians gradually took more and more power from the Croats, exerting control over the majority of inland Croatia. Meanwhile, the Venetian Republic conquered most of the coast and peppered the Croatian Adriatic with bell towers and statues of St. Mark. Through it all, the tiny Republic of Dubrovnik flourished—paying off whomever necessary to maintain its independence and becoming one of Europe's most important shipbuilding and maritime powers.

The Ottoman Turks conquered most of inland Croatia in the 15th century, and challenged the Venetians—unsuccessfully—for control of the coastline. In the 17th century, the Turks were forced out and the Hapsburgs arrived, taking over inland Croatia. After Venice and Dubrovnik fell to Napoleon, the coast went to the Hapsburgs—beginning a long tradition of Austrians basking on Croatian beaches.

The Yugoslav Era

When the Austro-Hungarian Empire broke up at the end of World War I, Croats banded together with the Serbs and Slovenes in the union that would become Yugoslavia. But throughout the Yugoslav era, the

FRANJO TUĐMAN
(1922–1999)

Independent Croatia's first president was the complicated, contro-versial Franjo Tuđman (FRAHN-yoh TOOJ-mahn). Tuđman began his career fighting for Tito on the left, but later had a dramatic ideological swing to the far right. His anti-communist, highly nation-alistic HDZ party was the driving force for Croatian statehood, making him the young nation's first hero. But even as he fought for independence from Yugoslavia, his own ruling style grew more and more authoritarian. As president, he expressed support for the Ustaše, who had ruled Croatia under the Nazis (and whom he considered to be the original Croatian "freedom fighters"). Croatia's currency, the kuna, seems harmless enough...but since it was first used during the Ustaše era, Tuđman raised some eyebrows when he reintroduced it.

Tuđman espoused some of the same single-minded attitudes about ethnic divisions as the ruthless Serbian leader Slobodan Milošević, with whom he had secret under-the-table, Hitler-and-Stalin-esque negotiations for divvying up Bosnia. When Tuđman's successor moved into the president's office, he discovered a top-secret hotline to Milošević's desk. And even today, Croatian newspapers routinely uncover photos of secret summits between the two leaders in Vienna.

To ensure that he stayed in power, Tuđman played fast and loose with his new nation's laws. He was notorious for changing the

Croats often felt they were treated as lesser partners under Serbia. (Many Croats objected to naming the country's official language "Serbo-Croatian"—why not "Croato-Serbian?") For more details about this complicated union and its break-up, see "Understanding Yugoslavia," page 517.

Independence Regained

Croatia became its own nation in 1991 after nine centuries of foreign domination. The Croatians seized their hard-earned freedom with a nationalist fervor that bordered on fascism. This was a heady and absurd time, which today's Croatians recall with disbelief, sadness...and maybe a tinge of nostalgia.

In the Croatia of the early 1990s, even the most bizarre notion seemed possible. Croatia's first post-Yugoslav president, the extreme nationalist Franjo Tuđman, proposed ludicrous directives for the new nation—such as privatizing all of the nation's resources and handing constitution as it suited him. By the late 1990s, when his popularity was slipping, Tuđman extended Croatian citizenship to anyone who lived in Croatia, or anyone of Croatian heritage—a ploy aimed at getting votes from Croats living in Bosnia, who were sure to line up with him on the far right.

Through it all, Tuđman kept a tight grip on the media, making it illegal to report anything that would disturb the public—even if true. When Croatians turned on their TV sets and saw the flag flapping in the breeze to the strains of the national anthem, they knew something was up...and switched to CNN to get the real story. In this oppressive environment, many bright young Croatians fled the country, causing a "brain drain" that hampered the country's recovery after the war.

Tuđman died of cancer at the end of 1999. While it seems that history will judge him harshly, the opinion in today's Croatia is qualified. Most agree that Tuđman was an important and even admirable figure in the struggle for Croatian statehood, but he ultimately went too far and got too greedy. All over the country, streets, squares, and bridges have recently been named for this "hero" of Croatian nationalism (by local politicians belonging to his still-active party). But if he were still alive, Tuđman would be standing trial in The Hague next to Milošević.

them over to 200 super-elite families (that one never happened). The government began calling the language "Croatian" rather than "Serbo-Croatian," creating new words from specifically Croat roots (see "Language," below). The Croats even briefly considered replacing the Roman alphabet with the ninth-century Glagolitic script to invoke Croat culture and to further differentiate Croatian from Serbia's Cyrillic alphabet. Fortunately for tourists, this plan didn't take off.

After Tuđman's death in 1999, Croatia began the new millennium with a more truly democratic leader, Stipe Mesić. The popular Mesić, who was once aligned with Tuđman, split when Tuđman's politics grew too extreme. Tuđman spent years tampering with the constitution to give himself more and more power, but when Mesić took over, he reversed those changes and handed more authority back to the parliament. After a fitful adjustment to independence, today's Croatia is on the right track.

Croatian Food

Like its people, the food in Croatia's
different regions has been shaped by
various influences, predominantly
Italian, Turkish, and Hungarian. No
single cuisine is distinctly Croatian.
Choosing between strudel and baklava on the same menu, you're constantly reminded that this is a land
where East meets West.

To the north (Zagreb) and east (Slavonia), the food has more of a
Hungarian flavor, heavy on meat, served with cabbage, noodles, or potatoes
(see Hungarian Food, page 193). If Croatian food has one thing in
common, it's lots and lots of meat.

The Ottoman Turks left their mark on inland Croatia (around
Plitvice Lakes), where a popular fast food is *burek*, phyllo dough filled
with meat, cheese, spinach, or apples. The more familiar *baklava* is
phyllo dough layered with honey and nuts. Also look for *ćevapčići*
(minced meat in a pita wrap, like a kebab); *pljeskavica* (similar to
ćevapčići, except the meat is in the form of a hamburger-like patty
instead of cut up); and *ražnjići* (small pieces of steak on a skewer, like a
shish kebab). A popular condiment you'll enjoy throughout the Balkans
is *ajvar*, made from red bell pepper and eggplant—sort of like ketchup,
but with more kick.

On the Dalmatian Coast, seafood is a specialty, and the Italian
influence is obvious. Dalmatians say that a fish should swim three times:
once in the sea, then in olive oil, and finally in wine—when you eat it.
You can get all kinds of seafood along the coast—fish, scampi, mussels,
calamari, you name it. On menus, prices for seafood dishes are listed by
the kilogram (figure about a half-kilo, or one pound, for a large portion).
Consider *riblja juha*—fish soup.

If you're not a seafood eater, keep an eye out for pizza and pasta
(try the gnocchi). Another Dalmatian specialty is *pašticada*—braised beef
in a wine-and-herb sauce. Finally, Dalmatia is known for its mutton.
Since the lambs graze on salty seaside pastures, the meat—often served
on a spit—has a distinctive flavor.

Throughout Croatia, salad is served with the main dish unless you
request it be served beforehand.

There are many good local varieties of cheese, made with sheep's or
goat's milk. Pag, an island in the Kvarner Gulf near Rijeka, produces a
famous, very salty, fairly dry sheep's milk cheese *(paški sir)*, which is said
to carry the flavor of the sparse herbs that the sheep graze on.

For dessert, you'll find lots of good, homemade ice cream *(sladoled)*,
especially on the Dalmatian Coast. Dalmatia's typical dessert is flan
(crème caramel), which they call *rozata*.

Mineral water is *mineralna voda*. Jamnica is the main Croatian brand (its spokesperson is the similarly-named Croatian skiing sensation Janice Kostelić, who won three medals at the 2002 Winter Olympics in Salt Lake). As in most Slavic countries, *voda* gets you water, *kava* gets you coffee, *pivo* gets you beer, and *vino* gets you wine. When toasting with some new Croatian friends, raise your glass with a hearty *"Živjeli!"* (ZHEE-vyeh-lee).

Croatia has good wine, but it's comparatively expensive. The sunny mountains north of Zagreb are covered with vineyards producing white wine. In the south and along the coast, you'll find mostly reds—except in the Istrian peninsula to the far north, which corks up some whites, including *malvazija,* a very popular mid-range wine. Each Adriatic island produces its own wine. Along the coast, it is very common to drink wine mixed with mineral water.

Saying *"Meni, molim"* (Menu, please) will get you a menu. *"Konobar"* (waiter) should get the attention of your waiter. When he brings your food, he'll likely say, *"Dobar tek!" (Bon appétit!)* When you're ready for the bill, ask for the *račun*.

Croatian Language

Croatian was once known as "Serbo-Croatian," the official language of Yugoslavia. Despite what Croatians and Serbians tell you, the languages spoken in today's Croatia and Serbia are essentially the same—like the English spoken in New York versus Dallas. The biggest difference is in the writing: Croatian uses the Roman alphabet, while Serbian uses Cyrillic letters (which every young Yugoslav had to learn).

In recent years, a fit of hyper-nationalism has led Croatia to intentionally distance its vocabulary from Serbian. A decade ago, you'd catch a plane at the *Aerodrom.* Today you'll catch that same flight at the *Zračna Luka*—a new coinage that combines the old Croatian words for "air" and "port." These new words, once created, are artificially injected into the lexicon. Croatians watching their favorite TV show will suddenly hear a character use a word they've never heard before...and think, "Oh, we have another new word."

Croatian is relatively easy to pronounce (and if you're just coming from Slovenia, you'll notice definite similarities). The accent is usually on the first syllable (and never on the last). As with other Slavic tongues, *c* is pronounced "ts" (as in "cats"). The letter *j* is pronounced as "y." The letters *č* and *ć* are slightly different, but they both sound more or less like "ch"; *š* sounds like "sh" and *ž* sounds like "zh" (as in "leisure"). One Croatian letter that you won't see in other languages is *đ,* which sounds like the "dj" sound in "jeans." In fact, this letter is often replaced with "dj" in English.

As you're tracking down addresses, these definitions will help: *trg* (square), *ulica* (road), and *most* (bridge).

KEY CROATIAN PHRASES

English	Croatian	Pronounced
Hello (formal)	**Dobar dan**	DOH-bahr dahn
Ciao (both "Hi" and "Bye"—informal)	**Zdravo**	ZDRAH-voh
Do you speak English?	**Govorite li engleski?**	GOH-voh-ree-teh lee eng-LEHS-kee
yes / no	**da / ne**	dah / neh
Please / You're welcome	**Molim**	MOH-leem
Can I help you?	**Izvolite?**	EEZ-voh-lee-teh
Thank you	**Hvala**	HVAH-lah
I'm sorry / Excuse me	**Oprostite**	oh-PROH-stee-teh
Good	**Dobro**	DOH-broh
Goodbye	**Do viđenija**	doh veed-JAY-neeah
one / two	**jedan / dva**	YEH-dahn / dvah
three / four	**tri / četiri**	tree / cheh-TEE-ree
five / six	**pet / šest**	peht / shehst
seven / eight	**sedam / osam**	SEH-dahm / OH-sahm
nine / ten	**devet / deset**	DEH-veht / DEH-seht
hundred	**sto**	stoh
thousand	**tisuča**	TEE-soo-chah
How much?	**Koliko?**	KOH-lee-koh
local currency	**kuna**	KOO-nah
Where is...?	**Gdje je...?**	guh-DYEH yeh
..the toilet	**...vece**	VEHT-seh
men	**muški**	MOOSH-kee
women	**ženski**	ZHEHN-skee
water / coffee	**voda / kava**	VOH-dah / KAH-vah
beer / wine	**pivo / vino**	PEE-voh / VEE-noh
Cheers!	**Živjeli!**	ZHEE-vyeh-lee
the bill	**račun**	RAH-choon

THE
DALMATIAN
COAST

Dubrovnik, Split, and Korčula

Sunny beaches, succulent seafood, and a taste of *la dolce vita*...in Eastern Europe? Croatia's Dalmatian Coast—the southern half of the country's coastline, stretching from Zadar to Dubrovnik—is Eastern Europe's Riviera. Many tourists were scared off after the recent war with Serbia (which damaged only Dubrovnik—completely repaired since). Now Croatia's resorts are aggressively advertising their once-again-undiscovered charms. It's paying off: The tourists are most decidedly back, in droves.

Dalmatia feels like Italy. Historically, it has more in common with Venice and Rome than Vienna or Budapest. People here speak Croatian with a lively Italian rhythm—and live the easygoing lifestyle that comes with it.

Dubrovnik is Croatia's best destination. With a picture-perfect Old Town and colorful history, it's like Venice without the canals. Big, bustling Split is the capital of the coast—boasting an in-love-with-life seaside promenade and a lived-in city of twisting lanes sprouting out of a massive Roman palace. Right between them, the island town of Korčula may be the best village on the Croatian coast.

Getting around the Dalmatian Coast

There are no trains along the Dalmatian Coast (the last station is in Split, with only a few slow trains to Zagreb). You'll rely on ferries, buses, or a rental car.

By Boat: Ferries and speedy hydrofoils shuttle tourists between major cities and quiet island towns. Most of the ferries are run by Jadrolinija, which conveniently connects the three destinations in this chapter, plus a lot more. Advance reservations are not necessary for deck passengers; you can almost always find a seat on the deck or in the on-board café. To reserve a cabin or take a car, make the arrangements several weeks in advance (main office in Rijeka: tel. 051/666-128, fax 051/337-110, www.jadrolinija.hr, passdept_e@jadrolinija.hr). I've listed

The Dalmatian Coast

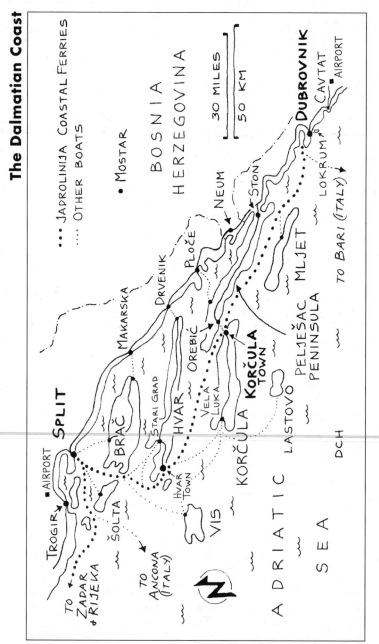

the most useful boat schedules in the "Transportation Connections" section for each destination.

By Boat to Italy: Four different companies connect Croatia to Italy, across the Adriatic, at least once daily in summer. Split is the main hub for these boats, but you can also go from other cities (usually Dubrovnik or Zadar; many international ferries also stop at smaller Dalmatian towns). Almost all boats go to Ancona, Italy. Most trips are overnight and last about 10 hours, but there is one superfast catamaran that takes only four hours (by Aliscafi SNAV, see below). On the slower boats, figure about €40 per person for one-way deck passage (about 10–20 percent more in peak season, roughly July–Aug), plus more for on-board accommodation (around €10 per person for a *couchette* in a 4-berth compartment, €45 per person in 2-bed compartment with private shower and WC).

These are your options to get to Italy: **Jadrolinija** runs boats from Split to Ancona or Zadar to Ancona, as well as from Dubrovnik to Bari (Croatian tel. 051/666-128, www.jadrolinija.hr). **Blue Line/SEM** offers sailings from Split, Zadar, or Mali Lošinj to Ancona (www.bli-ferry .com, can book at SEM Marina travel agency in Split, tel. 021/338-292). **Aliscafi SNAV** is the speedy catamaran that connects Split to Ancona in just four hours (daily mid-June–Sept, €60 one-way, or €75 in Aug; also connects Zadar with Ancona, and Split plus various smaller islands—such as Brač, Hvar, and Vela Luka on Korčula—to Italian towns Giulianova and Pescara, tel. 021/322-252, Italian tel. 0814-285-555, www.snav.it). **Adriatica Navigazione** does Split to Ancona (can book at Jadroagent in Split, tel. 021/338-335, Italian tel. 041-781-861, www.adriatica.it).

By Bus: Buses run between Dubrovnik and Split nearly hourly (5 hrs). The island town of Korčula is off the main route, and sees only one direct bus from Dubrovnik each day (but it's just as fast as the boat). Don't attempt the lengthy, complicated bus connection between Split and Korčula; take the boat instead.

By Car: Be prepared for twisty seaside roads, wonderful views, and plenty of tempting stopovers. Notice that between Split and Dubrovnik, you'll actually pass through Bosnia-Herzegovina for a few miles (the borders are a breezy formality). As you approach any town, follow the signs to *Centar*. Get parking advice from your hotel, or look for the blue-and-white *P* signs.

By Plane: The Dalmatian Coast is time-consuming to reach overland from northern Croatia (e.g., Zagreb to Split takes at least 6 hrs by bus; to Dubrovnik, 11 hrs). The best sight between Zagreb and the Dalmatian Coast is Plitvice Lakes National Park (see Inland Croatia chapter)—but if you just want to make a beeline for the sea, skip the park and catch an inexpensive flight from Zagreb. Croatia Airlines flies from Zagreb to the small airports in Zadar, Split, and Dubrovnik (Croatian tel. 062/777-777, www.croatiaairlines.hr). American-based Europe by

Air sells one-way tickets on Croatia Airlines for $99, though taxes and other fees bring the price closer to $160 (tickets can be purchased only in United States, www.europebyair.com, U.S. tel. 888/387-2479).

Helpful Hints

Siesta: Dalmatians eat their big meal at lunch, then take a traditional Mediterranean siesta. This means that many stores, museums, and churches close in the mid-afternoon. This can make for frustrating sightseeing—but you're on vacation. If you can't beat 'em, join 'em.

Seasonal Changes: Dalmatia's crowds fluctuate wildly by season. Some museums literally double their opening hours overnight when peak season hits. But here on the Adriatic, schedules are made to be broken, and opening times can change suddenly based on demand. The hours I've listed *should* be right...but if you have your heart set on a certain sight, confirm times with the TI on your arrival.

Addresses: Addresses listed with a street name, followed by "b.b.," have no street number.

Dubrovnik

Dubrovnik is a living fairy-tale that shouldn't be missed. It feels like a small town today, but 500 years ago, Dubrovnik was a major maritime power, with the third-biggest navy in the Mediterranean. Still jutting confidently into the sea and ringed by thick medieval walls, Dubrovnik deserves its nickname: the Pearl of the Adriatic. Within the ramparts, the traffic-free Old Town is a fun jumble of quiet, cobbled back lanes; tasty seafood restaurants; narrow, steep alleys; and kid-friendly squares. After all these centuries, the buildings still hint at old-time wealth, and the central promenade remains the place to see and be seen.

Dubrovnik, which feels Italian, actually began as a Roman colony. Although Croatian eventually became the official language, even today, people from Dubrovnik are teased by their Zagreb cousins for their Italian-influenced accent and vocabulary.

The city's charm is the sleepy result of its no-nonsense past. Busy merchants, the salt trade, and shipbuilding made Dubrovnik rich. But the city's most important commodity was always its freedom—even today, you'll see the proud motto *Libertas* displayed all over town (see sidebar, next page).

Dubrovnik flourished in the 15th and 16th centuries, but an earth-quake destroyed nearly everything in 1667. Most of today's buildings in the Old Town are post-quake Baroque, although a few palaces, monas-teries, and convents survive from Dubrovnik's earlier golden age.

While the war took its toll (see "The Siege of Dubrovnik"), today the only reminders are lots of new orange roof tiles...and fewer tourists.

LIBERTAS

Libertas—liberty—has always been close to the heart of every Dubrovnik citizen. Dubrovnik was an independent republic for centuries, even as most of Croatia became Venetian and Hungarian. Dubrovnik believed so strongly in *libertas* that it was the first foreign state in 1776 to officially recognize an upstart, experimental republic called the United States of America.

In the Middle Ages, the city-state of Dubrovnik (then called Ragusa) had to buy its independence from whomever was strongest—Byzantium, Venice, Hungary, the Turks—sometimes paying off more than one at a time. Dubrovnik's ships flew whichever flags were necessary to stay free, earning the nickname "Town of Seven Flags." As time went on, Europe's major powers were glad to have a second major seafaring power in the Adriatic to balance the Venetian threat. A free Dubrovnik was more valuable than a pillaged, plundered Dubrovnik.

In 1808, Napoleon conquered the Adriatic and abolished the much-loved Republic. After Napoleon was defeated, the fate of the continent was decided at the Congress of Vienna. Anyone who wanted to participate had a seat at the table...but Dubrovnik's delegate was denied entry. The more powerful nations, no longer concerned about Venice and fed up after years of being sweet-talked by Dubrovnik, were afraid that he'd play old alliances off of each other to reestablish an independent Republic of Dubrovnik. Instead, the city became a part of the Hapsburg Empire, and entered a long period of decline.

Libertas still hasn't completely died in Dubrovnik. In the surreal days of the early 1990s, when Yugoslavia was reshuffling itself, a movement for the creation of a new Republic of Dubrovnik gained some momentum (led by a judge who, in earlier times, had convicted others for the same ideas). But, for the most part, today's locals seem content to be part of an independent Republic of Croatia.

Planning Your Time

Dubrovnik's individual sights are pleasant but nothing to jump ship for: several convents, a few works by famous painters, some mediocre museums, and Europe's oldest pharmacy (1317). The attraction here is the city itself. While Dubrovnik could easily be seen in a day, a second day to unwind makes the long trip here more worthwhile.

Dubrovnik is most crowded during the Summer Festival—a month and a half of theater and musical performances (July 10–Aug 25, www.dubrovnik-festival.hr).

ORIENTATION

(area code: 020)

All of the sights worth seeing are in Dubrovnik's traffic-free, walled Old Town peninsula (Stari Grad). The main pedestrian promenade through the middle of town is Stradun (most locals don't use its official name, Placa); from this artery, the Old Town climbs uphill in both directions to the walls. The Old Town connects to the mainland through two gates (Pile Gate to the west and Ploče Gate to the east; there is also a stairway and passage to the mainland at the top of Boško Vićeva). The Old Port (Gradska Luka), with lazy leisure boats to nearby destinations, is at the east end of town.

Unfortunately, there are hardly any hotels in Dubrovnik's Old Town, so most visitors stay in big resorts a mile or two away. Most are on the lush Lapad Peninsula to the west (buses run frequently from just outside Pile Gate and take 15 min). North of Lapad Peninsula is Port Gruž, where ferries connect Dubrovnik to other Adriatic destinations.

Tourist Information

Dubrovnik has three TIs: The main branch is just beyond the bus stop in front of **Pile Gate** (mid-May–Sept Mon–Sat 8:00–20:00, Sun 9:00–13:00, Oct–mid-May Mon–Fri 8:00–12:00 & 16:00–19:00, Sat 9:00–13:00, closed Sun, Dr. Ante Starčevića 7, tel. 020/427-591, www.tzdubrovnik.hr); other branches are inside the **Old Town** (mid-May–Sept Mon–Sat 8:00–20:00, Sun 9:00–13:00, shorter hours off-season, a block off the main drag on Miha Pracata, tel. 020/323-587) and across the street from the Jadrolinija ferry dock at **Port Gruž** (Mon–Sat 8:00–14:00, Tue and Sat until 17:00, closed Sun, shorter hours off-season, Gruška obala, tel. 020/417-983). All three branches are run by the government, and legally can't sell you anything—but they can answer questions and give you a copy of the free monthly information booklet *Dubrovnik Riviera* (with helpful maps, hotel and restaurant listings, bus and ferry schedules, current museum prices and hours, and more).

Greater Dubrovnik

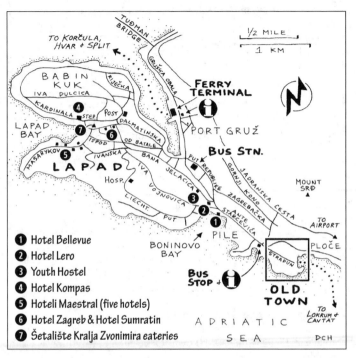

● Hotel Bellevue
❷ Hotel Lero
❸ Youth Hostel
❹ Hotel Kompas
❺ Hoteli Maestral (five hotels)
❻ Hotel Zagreb & Hotel Sumratin
❼ Šetalište Kralja Zvonimira eateries

Arrival in Dubrovnik

By Boat: The big boats arrive at Port Gruž, two miles northwest of the Old Town. On the road in front of the ferry terminal, you'll find a bus stop (#1a, #1b, and #3 to Old Town's Pile Gate) and a taxi stand (figure 75 kn to the Old Town and most hotels). Across the street is the Jadrolinija office (with an ATM out front) and a TI. You can book a private room *(sobe)* at Atlas Travel Agency (room-booking desk in boat terminal building) or at Gulliver Travel Agency (behind TI); you'll likely also be ambushed by locals wanting you to stay at their place (for more on the *sobe* option, see "Accommodations in Dalmatia" on page 360).

By Bus: Dubrovnik's bus station (Autobusni Kolodvor) is 1.5 miles northwest of the Old Town, where Lapad Peninsula connects to the mainland (Put Republike 19). Out front, you'll find city bus stops (#1a, #1b, #3, and #6 to Old Town's Pile Gate) and a taxi stand (figure 40–50 kn to the Old Town and most hotels). Bus info: tel. 020/357-088.

By Plane: Dubrovnik's small airport (Zračna Luka Čilipi) is 13 miles south of the city. A Croatia Airlines bus leaves from the main bus

DUBROVNIK LANDMARKS

English	Croatian	Pronounced
Old Town	**Stari Grad**	STAH-ree grahd
Old Port	**Stara Luka**	STAH-rah LOO-kah
Pile Gate	**Gradska Vrata Pile**	GRAHD-skah VRAH-tah PEE-leh
Ploče Gate	**Gradska Vrata Ploče**	GRAHD-skah VRAH-tah PLOH-cheh
Main Promenade	**Stradun or Placa**	STRAH-doon, PLAH-tsah
Adriatic Sea	**Jadran**	YAH-drahn

station 90 minutes before each flight, and meets each arriving flight at the airport (25 kn, 40 min). Airport info: tel. 020/773-377. Figure a hefty 250 kn for a taxi between the airport and the center.

Getting around Dubrovnik

Since most hotels are a mile or two out of town, you'll rely on the bus to connect to Dubrovnik's Old Town. Once there, everything is easily walkable.

By Bus: Libertas runs Dubrovnik's public buses, which go to all hotels west of the center from just outside the Old Town's Pile Gate (bus schedules and map in TI booklet; 10 kn if you pay on bus, 8 kn if you buy ticket from kiosk—ask for *autobusna karta*). If you're staying for a while, you can buy 20 tickets (shareable) from a kiosk for 100 kn—half the price of buying them on the bus. When you enter the bus, drop your ticket or your payment (no change given) in the little box by the driver.

By Taxi: Taxis start at 25 kn, then cost 8 kn per kilometer. You call for a taxi by neighborhood. Old Town's Pile Gate: tel. 020/424-343; Lapad (most hotels): tel. 020/435-715; bus station: tel. 020/357-044; ferry dock: tel. 020/418-112; and Ploče (just east of the Old Town): tel. 020/423-164.

Helpful Hints

Travel Agency: Of the many travel agencies in town, Atlas has the handiest locations and most helpful staff. They book rooms in private homes, sell seats on excursions, rent cars, and provide other travel-related services. Atlas has a desk at the ferry-terminal build-

THE SIEGE OF DUBROVNIK

In June of 1991, Croatia declared independence from Yugoslavia. Within weeks, the nations were at war (see "Understanding Yugoslavia," page 517). Though warfare raged in the Croatian interior, nobody expected that it would reach Dubrovnik.

At 6:00 in the morning on October 1, 1991, Dubrovnik residents were stunned to see Yugoslav warships on the horizon. The ships shelled the hillsides above Dubrovnik to clear the way for land troops—who quickly surrounded the city. For the first time in generations, the city walls were used to protect its people from an invading army. A month later, the Serb-dominated Yugoslav army began bombing the Pearl of the Adriatic. Defenseless townspeople took shelter in their cellars, and sometimes even huddled together in the city wall's 15th-century forts.

Dubrovnik resisted the siege better than anyone expected. The Serbs were hoping that residents would flee the town, allowing the Yugoslav army to move in. But the people of Dubrovnik stayed. Many brave young locals lost their lives when they slung old hunting rifles over their shoulders and, under the cover of darkness, climbed the hills above Dubrovnik to meet the Serbs face-to-face.

After eight months of bombing, Dubrovnik was liberated by the Croatian army, which attacked Serb positions from the north. Two-thirds of Dubrovnik had been damaged, but the siege was over.

Why was Dubrovnik—so far from the rest of the fighting—dragged into the conflict? The Serbs wanted to catch the city and the region off-guard, gaining a toehold on the southern Dalmatian Coast so they could push north to Split, Croatia's second city. They also hoped to ignite pro-Serb passions in the nearby Serb-dominated areas of Bosnia and Montenegro. But perhaps most of all, Yugoslavia wanted to hit Croatia where it hurt—its proudest, most historic, and most beautiful city, the tourist capital of a nation dependent on tourism.

The war initially devastated the tourist industry. Now, to the casual observer, Dubrovnik seems virtually back to normal. Aside from a few pockmarks and bright, new roof tiles, there are few reminders of what happened here just over a decade ago. But locals will tell you that people are different than before the war: still friendly, but wary...and a little less in love with life.

ing and two offices near the Old Town: by St. Blaise's Church at Lučarica 1 (June–Sept Mon–Sat 8:00–20:00, Sun 8:00–12:00, Oct–May Mon–Sat 8:00–16:00, closed Sun, tel. 020/323-609) and just outside Pile Gate at Sv. Đurđa 1 (June–Sept daily 8:00–20:00, Oct–May Mon–Sat 8:00–19:00, closed Sun, tel. 020/442-574; www.atlas-croatia.com, atlas@atlas.hr).

Tours of Dubrovnik: Several local travel agencies (including Atlas, listed above) book seats on bus-plus-walking tours of Dubrovnik, as well as guided excursions throughout the region; figure about 140 kn for a 2.5-hour tour of the city.

Internet: There are a few Internet terminals inside the main TI (Dr. Ante Starčevića 7, run by separate company). You'll also see Internet signs along the Old Town's main drag.

Best Views: Walking the wall at sunset is a treat—film disappears fast. A stroll east of the city walls offers nice views back on the Old Town (best light early in the day).

SIGHTS

These sights are listed roughly in order from Pile Gate (at the west end of town), along Dubrovnik's main promenade, to Luža Square just inside Ploče Gate (at the east end of town).

▲▲▲ **Walk the Walls (Gradske Zidine)**—Dubrovnik's single best activity is to stroll the scenic mile around the city walls. If you bring your map and pick out landmarks as you go, it's an ideal way to get your bearings. Walking the walls also offers the best illustration of the damage Dubrovnik sustained during the recent war. It's easy to see that more than 70 percent of Dubrovnik's roofs were replaced after the bombings (notice the new, bright-orange tiles).

There have been walls here almost as long as there's been a Dubrovnik. The fortifications were beefed up in the 15th century, when the Turks became a naval threat. Around the perimeter are several substantial forts, which protected residents both during the Republic of Dubrovnik's golden age and during the recent war with Serbia.

You can enter the walls at three points: just inside Pile Gate, near the Dominican Monastery north of Ploče Gate, and by the Maritime Museum south of the Old Port. The highest point is the Minčeta Tower, above the Pile Gate at the west end of town. If you huff your way up here first, then proceed clockwise, it's mostly downhill all the way around. Speed demons with no cameras can walk the walls in less than an hour; strollers

Dubrovnik's Old Town

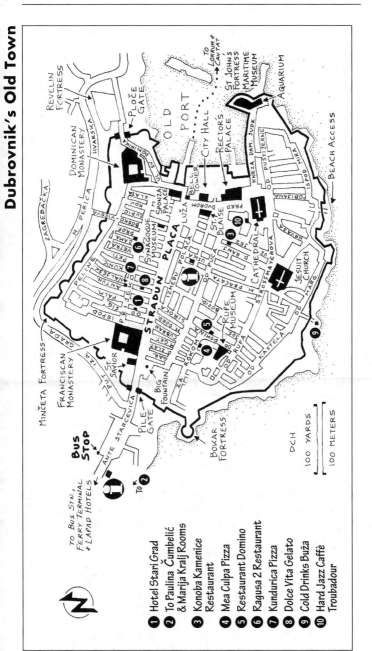

1 Hotel Stari Grad
2 To Paulina Čumbelić & Marija Kralj Rooms
3 Konoba Kamenice Restaurant
4 Mea Culpa Pizza
5 Restaurant Domino
6 Ragusa 2 Restaurant
7 Kundurica Pizza
8 Dolce Vita Gelato
9 Cold Drinks Buža
10 Hard Jazz Caffè Troubadour

and shutterbugs should plan on two hours (15 kn to enter walls, 30-kn audioguide available, July–Aug daily 9:00–20:30, progressively shorter hours off-season until 9:00–15:00 in winter).

▲▲ **Pile Gate (Gradska Vrata Pile)**—The west entrance to the Old Town is the Pile (PEE-leh) Gate. Just outside the gate, you'll find a leafy café terrace, and beyond that, the TI and bus stops to get to Lapad hotels. The huge, fortified peninsula just outside the city walls is the **Fort of St. Lawrence** (Tvrđava Lovrijenac), which is Dubrovnik's oldest fortress and one of the top venues for the Dubrovnik Summer Festival. Usually *Hamlet* is performed here—often starring Goran Višnjić, the Croatian actor who has become an American star on the TV show *ER*.

Inside the gate is a lively little square with lots of interesting landmarks. To the left, you'll see a stairway that leads up to the imposing Minčeta Tower (a good starting point for walking the walls; see above). Next to that is the small **Church of St. Savior** (Crkva Svetog Spasa). This votive church was built as thanks after Dubrovnik made it through a 1520 earthquake. When the massive 1667 quake destroyed the city, this church was one of the only buildings left intact. And during the recent war, the church survived another close call when a shell exploded on the ground right in front of it (you can still see pockmarks from the shrapnel).

The big round structure in the middle of the square is **Onofrio's Big Fountain** (Velika Onofrijea Fontana—named for its architect). In the Middle Ages, Dubrovnik had a complicated aqueduct system that brought water from the mountains 7.5 miles away. The water ended up here, at the town's biggest fountain and main source of water, before continuing on through the city. This plentiful supply of water, large reserves of salt (one of the most important sources of Dubrovnik's wealth), and a massive granary (*rupe,* see below) made little, independent Dubrovnik very siege-resistant.

The big building on the left just beyond the small St. Savior church is the...

▲▲ **Franciscan Monastery Museum (Franjevački Samostan-Muzej)**—This is the most enjoyable of Dubrovnik's many peaceful monasteries. In the Middle Ages, when Dubrovnik wrestled with overpopulation, many young people were encouraged to become monks and nuns, and monasteries flourished.

Enter through the gap between the small church and the big monastery. Just inside the door, notice a turn-of-the-century pharmacy—which still serves residents. (You'll see the original medieval pharmacy in a few minutes.)

Explore the relaxing **cloister.** Examine the capitals at the tops of the 60 Romanesque-Gothic double pillars—each one is different. Notice that some of the portals inside the courtyard are made with a much lighter-colored stone. These had to be repaired after being damaged by bombs in the recent war (the work was done by a French sculptor who also did restoration work on Paris' Notre-Dame).

Continue into the little medieval **pharmacy.** Part of the Franciscans' mission was to contribute to the good health of the citizens, so they opened this pharmacy in 1317. The monastery has had a pharmacy in continual operation ever since. On display are jars, pots, and other medieval pharmacists' tools. The sick would come to get their medicine, by using the little window (on left side), which limited contact with the pharmacist and therefore reduced the risk of passing on disease. Around the room you'll also find some relics, old manuscripts, and an interesting detailed painting of 15th-century Dubrovnik (monastery/pharmacy entry-6 kn, daily 9:00–18:00, less off-season, Placa 2).

▲▲ **Stradun Promenade (a.k.a. Placa)**—Dubrovnik's main pedestrian drag—officially called Placa, but better known as Stradun—is alive with locals and tourists alike. This is the heartbeat of the city, an Old World shopping mall by day and sprawling cocktail party after dark, where everybody seems to be doing the traditional *korzo*, or evening stroll— flirting, ice-cream licking, flaunting, and gawking. A coffee and some of Europe's best people-watching in a prime Stradun café is one of travel's great $2 bargains.

When Dubrovnik was just getting its start in the seventh century, this street was a canal. Romans fleeing from the invading Slavs lived on the island of Ragusa, and the Slavs settled on the shore. In the 11th century, the canal was filled in, the towns merged, and a unique Slavic-Roman culture and language blossomed.

▲▲▲ **Luža Square**—Dubrovnik's central square, just inside Ploče Gate at the east end of the Stradun, is a people magnet.

The centerpiece of the square is **Orlando's Column** (Orlandov Stup). Many other towns have columns like this, though most of them are in northern Germany. Dubrovnik erected the column in 1417, soon after it had shifted allegiances from the oppressive Venetians to the Hungarians. By putting a northern European symbol in the middle of their most important square, Dubrovnik decisively distanced itself from Venice.

Any time an important decision was made by the Republic, the town crier would come to Orlando's column and announce the news. The step he stood on would determine the magnitude of his message— the higher up, the more important the news (the very top of the column was only for special occasions). It was also used as the pillory, where people were publicly punished for their wrongdoings. Look closely to find the thin line on the step in front of Orlando: Exactly as long as the statue's forearm, this mark was Dubrovnik's standard measurement for an "elbow" (no kidding). Now stand in front of Orlando—with his lazy Mona Lisa gaze—and do the following spin-tour to get oriented.

Just to the right of where Orlando is looking is **Sponza Palace** (Sponza-Povijesni Arhiv). This building, from 1522, is the finest surviving example of Dubrovnik's golden age in the 15th to 16th centuries; it's a combination of Renaissance (ground-floor arches) and Venetian Gothic (upstairs windows). Houses up and down the main promenade used to look like this...but after the 1667 earthquake, they were replaced with boring Baroque. This used to be the customs office *(dogana)*, but now it's an exhaustive archive of the city's history. Inside are temporary exhibits and, in the back left corner, a moving memorial with photos of dozens of people from Dubrovnik who were killed in the last war.

To the right of Sponza Palace is the town's **Bell Tower** (Gradski Zvonik). The original dated from 1444, but it was rebuilt when it started to slide in the 1920s. The big octopus clock tells only the hour. Below that, the circle shows the phase of the moon (the greener, the fuller the moon). At the bottom, the old-fashioned digital readout tells the hour (in Roman numerals) and the minutes (in 5-min increments). At the top of each hour (and again 3 minutes later), the time is clanged out on the bell up top by two bronze bell ringers: Maro and Baro. (If all of this reminds you of the very similar clock on St. Mark's Square in Venice, locals are quick to point out that this clock predates that one by several decades.) The clock still has to be wound every two days. Notice the little black hole between the moon phase and the "digital" readout: The clock winder opens this window to get some light. During the recent war, the clock winder's house was destroyed—with the keys inside. For days, the clock bell didn't run. But then, miraculously, the keys were discovered lying in the street. The excited Dubrovnik citizens came together in this square and cheered as the clock was wound and the bell chimed, signaling to the Serbs surrounding the city that they hadn't won yet.

The big building to the right of the Bell Tower is the **City Hall** (Vijećnica). Next to it is **Onofrio's Little Fountain** (Mala Onofrijea Fontana)—the little brother of the one at the other end of the Stradun (see above)—and the **Town Café** (Gradska Kavana), historically Dubrovnik's favorite spot for gossiping and people-watching. Just down this street is the Rector's Palace, and then the Cathedral (for more on each, see below).

Behind Orlando is **St. Blaise's Church** (Crkva Sv. Vlaha), dedicated to the patron saint of Dubrovnik. You'll see statues and paintings of St. Blaise all over town, always holding a model of the city in his left hand. According to legend, a millennium ago, St. Blaise came to a local priest in a dream and warned him that the up-and-coming Venetians would soon attack the city. The priest alerted the authorities, who prepared for war. Of course, the prediction came true. St.

Blaise has been a Dubrovnik symbol—and locals have been resentful of Venice—ever since.

▲ **Rector's Palace (Knežev Dvor)**—In the Middle Ages, the Republic of Dubrovnik was ruled by a rector *(knez),* elected by the nobility. To prevent any one person from getting too popular (and becoming a dictator), the rector's term was limited to one month. Most rectors were in their 50s—near the end of the average lifespan, and less likely to shake things up. During his term, a rector lived upstairs in this palace. Because the rector was expected to focus all of his attention on matters of state, he wasn't allowed to see his family, or even leave the palace.

The exterior is decorated in the Gothic-Renaissance mix that was so common in Dubrovnik before the 1667 earthquake. The Baroque interior houses some old jail cells (downstairs), and the rector's not-too-interesting apartments and a gallery of paintings (upstairs). In the courtyard is the only secular statue created during the centuries-long Republic. Dubrovnik republicans, mindful of the dangers of hero-worship, didn't believe that any one citizen should be singled out. They made only one exception—for Miho Pracat (a.k.a. Michaeli Prazatto), a rich citizen who willed a fleet of ships to the city. But notice that Pracat's statue is displayed in here, behind closed doors—not out in public (15 kn, June–Sept daily 9:00–18:00, less off-season, Pred Dvorom 3).

▲▲ **Cathedral (Katedrala)**—Dubrovnik's original 12th-century cathedral was funded largely by the English king, Richard the Lionhearted. On his way back from the third crusade, Richard was shipwrecked near here. He swore he'd build a church on the spot where he landed—which happened to be on the island of Lokrum, just offshore. At Dubrovnik's request, Richard agreed to build his token of thanks inside the city instead. It was the finest Romanesque church on the Adriatic...before it was destroyed by the 1667 earthquake. This version is 18th-century Roman Baroque.

Inside you'll find an original Titian, a stark contemporary altar, and a quirky **treasury** *(riznica)* packed with 138 relics (treasury entry-5 kn, Mon–Sat 9:00–17:30, Sun 11:00–17:30). Notice that there are three locks on the treasury door—the stuff in here was so important, three different VIPs had to agree before it could be opened (rector, bishop, and local aristocrat). On the table near the door are several of St. Blaise's body parts (pieces of his arm, skull, and leg), all in fancy silver reliquaries. At the back of the room, look for the crucifix with a piece of the "true cross." On a dig in Jerusalem, St. Helen discovered what she believed to be the cross that Jesus was crucified on. It was brought to Constantinople, and the Byzantine czars gave pieces of it to Balkan kings. The folding altar underneath the cross was taken with Dubrovnik ambassadors when they made their annual trip to pay off the Turks. On the right side of the room, the silver casket supposedly holds the actual swaddling clothes of the baby Jesus. Dubrovnik bishops secretly passed these clothes down from generation to generation...until a nun got wind of it, and told the whole town. Pieces of the cloth were cut off to miraculously heal the sick, especially new mothers recovering from a difficult birth. No matter how often it was cut, the cloth always went back to its original form. But then someone tried to use it on the wife of a Bosnian king—since she was Muslim, it couldn't help her, and it never worked again. Whether or not it's true, this legend tells you a lot about the prickly relationships between faiths here in the Balkans.

▲ **Dominican Monastery Museum (Dominikanski Samostan-Muzej)**— You'll find many of Dubrovnik's art treasures—altarpieces and manuscripts—gathered around a peaceful cloister just north of Ploče Gate. Don't miss the triptych by Nikola Božidarović with St. Blaise holding a detailed model of 16th-century Dubrovnik; you'll see this image all over town. As you tour the museum, keep a lookout for other St. Blaises (10 kn, 70-kn English-language book good for art buffs only, June–Sept daily 9:00–18:00, off-season until 17:00).

▲ **Old Port (Stara Luka)**—The old picturesque port faces away from Dubrovnik's historically biggest threat, the Venetians, carefully nestled inside St. John's Fort (on the right as you face the sea). The long seaside building across the bay on the left was the medieval quarantine house. In those days, anyone coming to town had to live in the quarantine house for 40 days before entering town.

From this port, you can catch boats to two nearby destinations. **Lokrum,** the island just offshore, has a monastery-turned-Hapsburg-palace, a small botanical garden, old military fort, hiking trails, café, some rocky beaches, and a little lake called the Dead Sea (Mrtvo More), which is suitable for swimming (25 kn round-trip, 5 kn for map, hrly 9:00–18:00, 2/hr in summer, none in winter). **Cavtat** is a historic seaside village about 12 miles down the coast from Dubrovnik (60 kn round-trip).

▲ **Synagogue Museum (Sinagoga-Muzej)**—When Jews were forced out of Spain in 1492, many of them passed through Dubrovnik en route to Turkey. They found a flourishing and relatively tolerant city, so many stayed. Žudioska ulica (literally "Jewish Street"), just inside Ploče Gate, became the ghetto. Today, the same street is still home to the oldest Sephardic synagogue in Europe. The top floor houses the synagogue itself, and below that is a museum with various Torahs and other artifacts—including the orders *(Naredba)* that Jews in Nazi-era Yugoslavia wear armbands. Of Croatia's 24,000 Jews, only 4,000 survived the Holocaust (10 kn, Mon–Fri 9:00–13:00, closed Sat–Sun).

Rupe **Granary and Ethnographic Museum (Etnografski Muzej Rupe)**—This huge 16th-century building, uphill towards the sea from the middle of Stradun, was Dubrovnik's biggest granary. *Rupe* means "holes"—and it's worth the price of entry just to look down into these cavernous underground grain stores, designed to maintain the perfect temperature to preserve the seeds (17 degrees Celsius, about 63 degrees

Fahrenheit). When the grain had to be dried, it was moved upstairs—which today houses a surprisingly well-presented Ethnographic Museum, with tools, jewelry, clothing, and other artifacts from Dubrovnik's colorful history (5 kn, borrow English-language info sheet, June–Oct daily 9:00–18:00, Nov–May Mon–Sat 9:00–14:00, closed Sun).

Maritime Museum (Pomorski Muzej)—By the 15th century, when Venice's nautical dominance was on the wane, Dubrovnik emerged as a maritime power and as the Mediterranean's most important shipbuilding center. The "argosy" boat (from the word "Ragusa," an early name for Dubrovnik) built here was the Cadillac of ships, frequently mentioned by Shakespeare. This small museum traces the history of Dubrovnik's most important industry with contracts, tools, and models. Though the history is interesting, only boat fanatics will find the museum worth a visit (15 kn, English-language booklet-5 kn, June–Aug daily 9:00–19:00, Sept–Oct daily 9:00–17:00, Nov–May daily 9:00–14:00, downstairs in St. John's Fort due south of Old Port).

Aquarium (Akvarij)—Dubrovnik's aquarium features specimens of local marine life. It's small and not too interesting, offering mostly a chance to get in out of the hot sun and to see the inside of one of the city wall's cavernous forts. Say hello to the huge, greedy grouper that beg for food near the entrance—creepy (15 kn, mid-June–Aug daily 8:00–21:00, April–mid-June and Sept–Oct daily 9:00–19:00, Nov–March daily 9:00–13:00, upstairs in St. John's Fort due south of Old Port).

Take a Dip—If the weather's good and you've had enough of museums, spend a sunny afternoon at the beach. There are no sandy beaches on the mainland near Dubrovnik, but there are lots of suitable pebbly options. Your hotel can direct you to the nearest one (or has its own—often concrete). The two best public beaches are Banje (just outside Ploče Gate east of the Old Town) and the beach in the middle of the Bay of Lapad (near Hotel Kompas).

SLEEPING

Old Town

$$$ The new **Hotel Stari Grad** is Dubrovnik's best splurge. The eight rooms are nothing special, but the location is ideal—a block off the main drag in the Old Town (Sb-€91, Db-€130, extra bed-€39, same prices year-round, air-con, Od Sigurate 4, tel. 020/321-373, fax 020/321-256, www.hotelstarigrad.com, hotelstarigrad@yahoo.com).

$ *Sobes* (**Private Rooms**): You'll find a pair of handy *sobes* just outside the Old Town walls. To reach them, leave the Pile Gate TI to the right, then go down the first flight of stairs on your right. Follow the lanes as they twist around, and you'll wind up at Od Tabakarije, a wide street above a small cove. Two people rent rooms here: English-speaking **Paulina Čumbelić** at #2 (S-160 kn, D-240 kn, T-300 kn; July–Aug: S-

SLEEP CODE

(€1 = about $1.10, 1 kn = about 14 cents, country code: 385, area code: 020)

Sleep Code: **S** = Single, **D** = Double/Twin, **T** = Triple, **Q** = Quad, **b** = bathroom, **s** = shower only, **no CC** = Credit Cards not accepted. Unless otherwise noted, English is spoken, credit cards are accepted, breakfast is included, and the modest tourist tax (7 kn/€1 per person, per night, lower off-season) is not. All Dubrovnik hotels provide free guest parking. Because they get so many European visitors, many hotels quote prices in euros, then make the conversion to kunas when you arrive.

To help you sort easily through these listings, I've divided the rooms into three categories based on the price for a standard double room with bath:

$$$ **Higher Priced**—Most rooms €90 (700 kn) or more.

  $$ **Moderately Priced**—Most rooms between €45–90 (350–700 kn).

   $ **Lower Priced**—Most rooms €45 (350 kn) or less.

The frustrating accommodations scene is Dubrovnik's biggest downside. There are only two hotels inside the Old Town walls—and one of them charges more than €450 a night (Pucić Palace,

190 kn, D-280 kn, T-400 kn, no CC, closed in winter, tel. 020/421-327), and sweet, friendly **Marija Kralj** at #20, who speaks only Croatian (100 kn per person, July–Aug 150 kn per person, no CC, tel. 020/425-483).

Near Boninovo Bay

The next three places cluster around Boninovo Bay, a 15-minute walk from the Old Town (straight up Dr. Ante Starčevića). This is as close as you'll get without paying big bucks. To reach them by bus from Pile Gate, take #1a, #3, #4, #5, #6, #8, or #9. From the Boninovo bus stop, go down Pera Čingrije (the road running parallel to cliff overlooking sea).

$$$ **Hotel Bellevue,** backed up against the cliff rising up from Boninovo Bay, has such a striking location that you may forget you're not in the Old Town. The 50 rooms have class, and the pebbly beach below beckons. The cheaper annex rooms are tired but comfortable and a good value (main building rooms all have sea views and balconies: Sb-580 kn, Db-730 kn, air-con "superior" rooms 20 percent more; cheaper

www.thepucicpalace.com). Any hotel within a 10-minute walk of the Old Town will run you at least €130 (1,030 kn). These inflated prices drive most visitors to the Lapad Peninsula, a 15-minute bus ride west of the Old Town. Though it lacks Old World ambience, Lapad is not without its charm—most hotels cluster around beautiful coves that would be a fine place to vacation, even if the Dubrovnik Old Town weren't around the bend.

One way to combat the high prices and inconvenient locations of Dubrovnik's hotels is to stay in a *sobe* (room in a private home, see "Accommodations in Dalmatia," next page). There are hundreds of *sobes* in greater Dubrovnik, including a handful in the Old Town. Figure about €40 (315 kn) for a double and €32 (250 kn) for a single in peak season (20–30 percent more for stays of less than 3 nights). I've listed a couple of *sobes* handy to the center; for more, visit a local travel agency (Atlas is one of many; see "Helpful Hints," above).

No matter where you stay, prices are much higher in July and August. Reserve ahead in these peak times, especially during the Dubrovnik Summer Festival (July 10–Aug 25). I've listed the shoulder-season prices (June and September), and noted how much of an increase you can expect for July and August. Off-season prices are much lower.

annex rooms: seaview Sb-400–440 kn, non-view Sb-360 kn, seaview Db-540–650 kn, non-view Db-480 kn, non-view rooms come with lots of street noise; all prices 25 percent higher July–Sept, lower Nov–April, elevator, half-board-€12, Pera Čingrije 7, tel. 020/413-095, fax 020/414-058, www.hotel-bellevue.hr, hotel-bellevue@du.hinet.hr).

$$ Hotel Lero is across a busy street from the cliff above the bay. Its 160 reasonably-priced rooms feel new and come with small sea views and access to the Hotel Bellevue's beach (Sb-€60, Db-€80, prices go up 15 percent mid-July–mid-Sept, prices lower off-season, air-con, elevator, Internet access, half-board-€5, Iva Vojnovića 14, tel. 020/332-122, fax 020/332-123, www.hotel-lero.hr, hotel-lero@du.tel.hr).

$ Dubrovnik's fine **Youth Hostel** has 82 beds in 19 rooms (bed in 4- to 6-bed dorm: 95 kn July–Aug, 85 kn June and Sept, 75 kn May and Oct, 65 kn Nov–April, 14 kn more for non-members, includes sheets, breakfast-5 kn, no CC, ulica bana Jelačića 15-17, tel. 020/423-241, tel. & fax 020/412-592, www.hfhs.hr, dubrovnik@hfhs.hr). From Boninovo bus stop, go down Pera Čingrije towards Hotel Bellevue, but

ACCOMMODATIONS IN DALMATIA

Even though they were communists, the Yugoslavs were savvy businessmen. To maximize beach-tourism occupancy in the 1960s and 1970s, they razed charming Old World buildings to make way for new, big resort hotels. Now, throughout Dalmatia, it's virtually impossible to find mid-sized, characteristic pensions; your choices are basically these hulking complexes or a room in a private home...and little in between.

Today the resort hotels, no longer new, usually have faded communist-era furnishings, "beach" access (often on a concrete pad), a travel-agency desk selling tours in the lobby, and a sea-view apéritif bar. The rooms are usually musty, with a moldy-college-dorm ambience. And they're expensive—you'd pay less for the same room in the center of a Western European capital. These hotels are just fine with the busloads of German, Austrian, British, and Slovene tourists who head south for the European answer to Cancún or Acapulco.

But if that doesn't appeal to you, consider a room in a private home *(sobe)*. *Sobes,* usually run by empty nesters, offer travelers a characteristic and money-saving alternative for a quarter of the price of a hotel. Guests are welcome to use the kitchen and cozy dining room, and settle in their own private bedroom (bathroom often down the

take the first right uphill onto ulica bana Jelačića and look for signs up to the hostel on your left.

Lapad Bay

These hotels cluster around Lapad Bay, a 15-minute bus ride from the Old Town (from the bus stop in front of Pile Gate, take #5 to Pošta Lapad). There are about a dozen different hotels within walking distance around the bay, but the following places are the best values.

$$$ Hotel Kompas is a nice big-hotel option on Lapad Bay, right across the street from the beach with 117 plush, modern rooms (standard Sb-480 kn, seaview Sb-585 kn, standard Db-640 kn, seaview Db-780 kn, Db prices 40 percent higher and Sb prices nearly double late-June–Sept, non-smoking rooms, air-con, elevator, Internet access, Šetalište Kralja Zvonimira 56, tel. 020/352-777, fax 020/435-877, www .hotel-kompas.hr, hotel-kompas@du.hinet.hr).

$$–$$$ Hoteli Maestral is a chain of five hotels on the east side of Lapad Bay. They're a lesser value than hotels Kompas and Zagreb, but they have plenty of rooms—some of them cheaper than others—that work in a pinch (figure low-end prices of Db-200–300 kn, high-end hall). You'll give up some privacy and the comforts of a big hotel, but you'll have a better chance of connecting with the locals.

Registered *sobes* have been rated by the government using a system—sometimes arbitrary—that assigns stars based on amenities. There are generally three tiers: deluxe room with private bathroom and included breakfast; standard room with bathroom and no breakfast; and rock-bottom room with a bathroom down the hall and no breakfast.

At any boat dock or bus station in Dalmatia, you'll encounter pushy locals trying to get you to stay in their *sobe*. Many of these *sobes* have not been classified by the government, but they can sometimes turn out to be a good deal. If you trust the sales pitch, and the location seems convenient, give it a look.

I've listed a few *sobes* in this chapter, but to get a wider range of options, wander the streets looking for *sobe* signs. You can also enlist the help of a travel agency, but you'll pay 10–30 percent extra. (To search from home, see www.adriatica.net.) The prices fluctuate with the seasons—just like those of the big hotels—and stays of less than three nights almost always come with a 20–30 percent surcharge.

prices of Db-450–600 kn, 20 percent more in Aug, tel. 020/433-600, fax 020/416-545, www.hotelimaestral.com, hoteli-maestral@du.tel.hr).

$$ Hotel Zagreb is a rarity among Dubrovnik hotels—small and quaint, in an elegant old villa surrounded by a lush garden. The 25 rooms are basic but comfortable (Sb-255 kn, Db-410 kn, prices 30 percent higher July–Aug, prices lower off-season, Šetalište Kralja Zvonimira 27, reception tel. 020/436-146). Hotel Zagreb is technically an annex of **Hotel Sumratin,** just down the street, which has slightly lower prices for 44 not-nearly-as-nice rooms in a less charming setting (Sb-240 kn, Db-380 kn, prices 30 percent higher July–Aug, prices lower off-season, elevator, Šetalište Kralja Zvonimira 31, reception tel. 020/436-333). To reserve at either hotel: tel. 020/436-500, fax 020/436-006, htp-sumratin@du.hinet.hr.

EATING

Dubrovnik's Old Town is packed with tasty eateries serving fresh seafood and pasta dishes. In the mass-tourism tradition, most visitors choose to take the half-board option at their hotel. This can be a good value, but you'll generally find better food (often for better prices) on your own.

Locals unanimously agree that the no-frills **Konoba Kamenice** is tops—with inexpensive, fresh, and delicious seafood dishes on a charming market square as central as can be in the Old Town (most main dishes 35–45 kn, daily 7:00–24:00, can be crowded so you'll often have to wait, Gundulićeva poljana 8, tel. 020/421-499).

Restaurant Domino has pricier cuisine and a more upscale atmosphere (fish dishes for 100 kn, steaks for 85–100 kn, daily 11:00–24:00, Od Domina 6, tel. 020/432-832).

For cheap and tasty pizza, try **Mea Culpa** (pizzas 25–40 kn, daily 8:00–24:00, just off the main drag at Za Rokom 3, tel. 020/323-430).

The street called **Prijeko,** a block towards the mainland from the Stradun promenade, is Dubrovnik's restaurant row. It's lined with outdoor, tourist-oriented eateries—each one with a huckster out front trying to lure in diners. This is hardly a local scene, but a stroll along here is fun, the atmosphere is lively, the sales pitches are entertainingly desperate, and the food is good. The place with the most diners, best reputation, and least aggressive sales pitch is **Ragusa 2** (most main dishes 60–90 kn, cozy tables outside, elegant white-tablecloth ambience inside, daily 9:00–24:00, tel. 020/321-203). **Kundurica,** also on Prijeko, has good, inexpensive pizzas (30–40 kn, daily 11:00–22:00).

If you're staying on the Lapad Peninsula, and don't want to venture into the Old Town for dinner, consider strolling down the tree-shaded **Šetalište Kralja Zvonimira** promenade, lined with touristy but acceptable cafés and restaurants.

There's lots of great gelato in Dubrovnik; one of the best places is **Dolce Vita** (daily 9:00–24:00, a half-block off Stradun at Nalješkovićeva 1a, tel. 020/321-666).

The most scenic spot for a drink is **Cold Drinks "Buža,"** perched on a cliff above the sea, clinging like a barnacle to the outside of the city walls. This is a peaceful, shaded getaway from the bustle of the Old Town (summer daily 9:00–24:00, closed mid-Nov–Jan, find doorway in city wall marked *Cold Drinks* just up from cathedral, behind St. Ignatius' Church).

Hard Jazz Caffè Troubadour is cool, owned by a former member of the Dubrovnik Troubadours, Croatia's answer to the Beatles (drinks and light sandwiches, daily 9:00–24:00, live jazz nightly from 21:00, next to cathedral at Bunićeva poljana 2, tel. 020/323-476).

TRANSPORTATION CONNECTIONS

By Jadrolinija ferry: The big boat leaves Dubrovnik in the morning (usually around 8:00 or 9:00) and goes to **Korčula** (3–4 hrs), **Split** (9–10 hrs), and other coastal destinations (including Stari Grad on Hvar Island and the big northern port city of Rijeka). The boat generally cruises four times each week June–Sept, twice weekly Feb–May. For schedules, see Jadrolinija's user-friendly Web site, www.jadrolinija.hr.

By bus to: Split (almost hrly, 5 hrs), **Korčula** (1/day, 4 hrs), **Zagreb** (4/day, 11 hrs).

By plane: To quickly connect this remote destination with the rest of your trip, consider a cheap flight (see "Getting around the Dalmatian Coast," above.)

Split

Dubrovnik is the darling of the Dalmatian Coast, but Split is Croatia's second city (after Zagreb), bustling with a quarter of a million people. If you've been hopping along the coast, landing in urban Split feels like a return to civilization. While most Dalmatian coastal towns seem made for tourists, Split is real and vibrant, teeming with Croatians living life to the fullest. Though Split throbs to a modern, young beat, its history goes way back—all the way to the Roman Empire. Along with all the trappings of a modern city, Split has some of the best Roman ruins this side of Italy.

In the fourth century, the Roman Emperor Diocletian wanted to move back home to his native Dalmatia to retire, so he built a huge palace here. Eventually, the palace was abandoned. Then locals, fleeing 7th-century Slavic invaders, moved in and made themselves at home, and a medieval town sprouted from the rubble of the old palace. In the 15th century, the Venetians took over the Dalmatian Coast, adding on to the city and building several small palaces. But even as Split grew, the nucleus remained the ruins of Diocletian's Palace. To this day, 2,000 people live or work inside the former palace walls. A maze of narrow alleys is home to fashionable boutiques and galleries, wonderfully atmospheric cafés, and Roman artifacts around every corner.

SPLIT LANDMARKS

English	Croatian	Pronounced
Old Town	**Stari Grad**	STAH-ree grahd
City Harbor	**Gradska Luka**	GRAHD-skah LOO-kah
Harborfront promenade	**Riva**	REE-vah
Peristyle (old Roman square)	**Peristil**	PEH-ree-steel
Adriatic Sea	**Jadran**	YAH-drahn

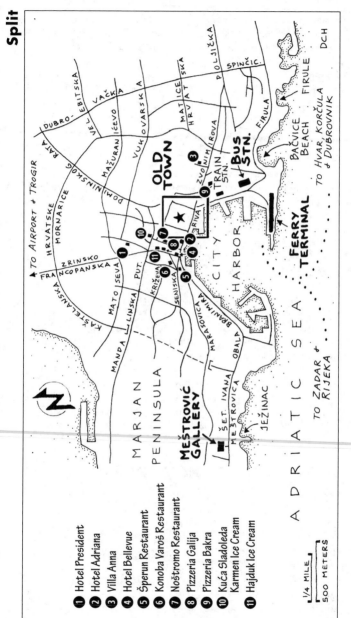

Split

1 Hotel President
2 Hotel Adriana
3 Villa Anna
4 Hotel Bellevue
5 Šperun Restaurant
6 Konoba Varoš Restaurant
7 Noštromo Restaurant
8 Pizzeria Galija
9 Pizzeria Bakra
10 Kuća Sladoleda Karmen Ice Cream
11 Hajduk Ice Cream

1/4 MILE
500 METERS

Planning Your Time

Many visitors to Dalmatia only change boats in Split, but the city is the perfect real-life contrast to the tackiness of Dalmatian beach resorts—it deserves a full day. Begin by strolling the remains of Diocletian's Palace, then have lunch or a coffee break along the Riva promenade. After lunch, browse the shops or visit a couple of Split's museums (the Meštrović Gallery is tops, but a 20-min walk from town). Promenading along the Riva with the natives is *the* evening activity.

ORIENTATION

(area code: 021)

Split sprawls, but almost everything of interest to travelers is around the City Harbor (Gradska Luka). At the top of this port is the Old Town (Stari Grad). Between the Old Town and the sea is Riva, the waterfront pedestrian promenade lined with cafés and shaded by palm trees. The main ferry terminal (Trajektni Terminal) juts out into the harbor from the east side of the port. Between the ferry terminal and the Old Town are the long-distance bus station (Autobusni Kolodvor) and forlorn little train station (Željeznička Stanica). West of the Old Town, poking into the Adriatic, is the lush and hilly Marjan peninsula.

Split's Old Town is made up of two square-shaped sections. The east half was once Diocletian's Palace, and the west half is the medieval town that sprang up next door. The shell of Diocletian's ruined palace provides a checkerboard street plan, with a gate at each end. At the center of the former palace is the Peristyle square (Peristil), where you'll find the TI, cathedral, and highest concentration of Roman ruins.

Tourist Information

Split's **TI** is on the Peristyle square, in the very center of Diocletian's Palace (Mon–Sat 8:00–20:00, Sun 8:00–13:00, tel. 021/345-606). Pick up the free town map and *Welcome to Split* magazine. The TI also sells books, maps, and the Splitcard (see below).

The helpful **Turistički Biro** travel agency, between the two halves of the Old Town on the Riva, books *sobes* and hotels, sells guidebooks and maps, rents scooters and cars, and sells tickets for excursions (mid-July–mid-Aug Mon–Fri 8:00–21:00, Sat 8:00–20:00, Sun 8:00–12:00; off-season Mon–Fri 8:00–20:00, Sat 8:00–14:00, closed Sun, Riva 12, tel. & fax 021/347-100, turist-biro-split@st.hinet.hr).

The **Splitcard** allows you free entry into some museums and offers discounts on several other museums, hotels, restaurants, car rental, and other services (€5/40 kn for 72 hrs, or free if you stay in Split more than 3 days, sold at TI, travel agencies, and hotels). Museums here are cheap (most around 10 kn), so this is a good value only if you use it on more substantial things (like car rental or hotel discounts).

Arrival in Split

By Boat: Split's ferry terminal (Trajektni Terminal) is a 10-minute walk from the center around the east side of the City Port. After leaving the boat, wade through the *sobe* hucksters to the main terminal building, where you'll find ATMs, WCs, a grocery store, and offices for all of the main ferry companies, including Jadrolinija (open long hours daily). You can see the Old Town and Riva from the boat dock; just walk around the port towards the big bell tower.

By Bus or Train: Split's long-distance bus station (Autobusni Kolodvor) and little train station (Željeznička Stanica) are along the east side of the City Port between the ferry terminal and the Old Town. To reach the center, exit to the right and walk along the waterfront towards the big bell tower.

By Plane: Split's airport (Zračna Luka Kaštela) is across the big bay (Kaštelanski Zaljev) 15 miles northwest of the center, near the town of Trogir. A Croatia Airlines bus leaves Split 90 minutes before each flight from the small Air Terminal near the southeast corner of Diocletian's Palace, and meets each arriving flight at the airport (30 kn, 40 min). Figure 300 kn for a taxi to the center. Airport info: tel. 021/203-506.

Getting around Split

Most of what you'll want to see is within walking distance, but some sights (such as the Meštrović Gallery) and hotels are a bit farther out.

By Bus: Local buses, run by Promet, cost 8 kn per ride (or 7 kn if you buy ticket from a kiosk; ask for a *putna karta*). Validate your ticket as you board the bus.

Suburban buses to towns near Split (like Salona or Trogir) leave from two different stations: Some use the Air Terminal at the southeast corner of Diocletian's Palace, but most use the Suburban Bus Station (Prigradski Autobusni Kolodvor, a 15-min walk due north of the Old Town on Domovinskog rata).

By Taxi: Taxis start at 15 kn, then cost around 8 kn per kilometer. Figure 50–60 kn for most rides within the city (for example, from the ferry terminal to most hotels). To call for a taxi, try Radio Taxi (tel. 021/970).

SIGHTS

Diocletian's Palace (Dioklecijanova Palača)

Diocletian grew up just inland from Split, in the town of Salona (Solin in Croatian)—which was then the capital of Dalmatia. He worked his way up the Roman hierarchy and became emperor (A.D. 284–305). Despite all of his achievements, Diocletian is best remembered for two questionable legacies: dividing the huge empire among four emperors

Diocletian's Palace

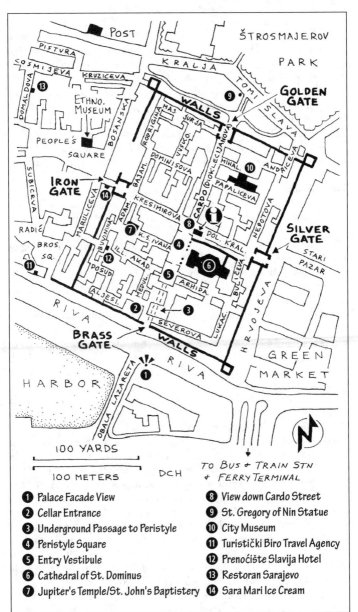

1. Palace Facade View
2. Cellar Entrance
3. Underground Passage to Peristyle
4. Peristyle Square
5. Entry Vestibule
6. Cathedral of St. Dominus
7. Jupiter's Temple/St. John's Baptistery
8. View down Cardo Street
9. St. Gregory of Nin Statue
10. City Museum
11. Turistički Biro Travel Agency
12. Prenoćište Slavija Hotel
13. Restoran Sarajevo
14. Sara Mari Ice Cream

(arguably leading to its decline), and torturing and executing Christians—many of them right here on the Adriatic.

As Diocletian grew older, he decided to come back to his homeland for retirement (since he was in poor health, the medicinal sulfur spring here was another plus). His massive palace took 11 years to build, and huge sections of it still exist, modified by medieval and modern developers alike. Today, it's the only ▲▲▲ sight in town.

Fragments of the palace are poorly marked, and there's not yet any good guidebook or audioguide for tracking down the remains. (This makes Split a good place to take a walking tour or hire a local guide—figure 450 kn/2 hrs; ask TI for details.) But the following self-guided tour explains the basics. To begin, stand in front of the Palace (at the east end of the Riva, at the corner with the yellow information pillar) to get oriented.

Palace Facade—The "front" of today's Split—facing the harbor—was actually the back door of Diocletian's Palace. The water level was much higher, and this back door could be reached only by boat—sort of an emergency exit.

Visually trace the outline of the Palace. On the corner to the right, you'll see a big rectangular guard tower (one of an original 16). To the left, the tower is gone and the corner is harder to pick out (look for the beginning of the newer-looking buildings). The massive palace was more than 600 feet long on each side.

Halfway up the facade, notice the row of 42 arched window frames (today mostly filled in). This seaside half of the palace was where Diocletian and his family lived; imagine him strolling back and forth along this row of windows, enjoying the views of his Adriatic homeland. The inland half of the palace was his servants' quarters and a barracks for bodyguards and soldiers.

Now go through the poorly-marked, low-profile door in the middle of the palace (known as the "Brass Gate"; look for the *i* sign pointing to the TI). Just inside the door is the entrance to...

Diocletian's Cellars (Podrum)—Since the palace was built on land that sloped down to the sea, these chambers were built to level out the main floor. The "cellars" weren't used for storage; they were filled with water from three different sources: a freshwater spring, a sulfur spring, and the ocean. Later, medieval residents dumped their sewage and garbage here, too. Rediscovered only in the last century, the cellars are essential for archaeologists' understanding of the floor plan above. Today, they're used as a gallery for souvenir stands. But before you go shopping, explore the cellars at this end (8 kn, June–Aug daily 9:00–20:00, May daily 10:00–17:00, Sept–mid-Oct daily 10:00–18:00, April and late Oct daily 10:00–14:00, Nov–March Mon–Sat 10:00–14:00, closed Sun).

Begin at the cellars on the left (west) side of the palace. Today, this huge vaulted hall is used for everything from flower and book shows to fashion catwalks. Wander the labyrinth of cellars, and look for the head-less black granite **sphinx.** Diocletian spent much of his time in Egypt, and he brought 13 of these sphinxes here. All but one had their heads and paws cut off, because the superstitious Romans thought this would prevent the cats from hurting their Emperor.

The cellars on the other side of the entry hallway can also be explored, with a marble table used by the Romans (who ate lying down) and some remnants of a Greek palace that was here 600 years before Diocletian's. When you're finished, head back to the main gallery, where you can shop your way down the passage and up the stairs into the...

Peristyle (Peristil)—This square was the centerpiece of Diocletian's Palace. As you walk up the stairs, the entry vestibule into the residence is above your head, Diocletian's mau-soleum is to your right, the street to Jupiter's Temple is on your left, the little chapel straight ahead houses the TI, and beyond it is the narrow street to the former main entrance to the palace, the Golden Gate.

Go to the middle of the square and take it all in. The red granite pillars—which you'll see all over Diocletian's Palace—are from Egypt (notice that the café in the square is called Luxor, where Diocletian spent many of his pre-retirement years). The black sphinx is the only one of Diocletian's collection of 13 that is still intact.

Climb the stairs (above where you came in) into the domed, open-ceiling **entry vestibule.** Impressed? That's the idea. This was the grand entry to Diocletian's living quarters, meant to wow visitors. Emperors were believed to be gods, and Diocletian called himself Jovius—the son of Jupiter, the most powerful of all gods. Four times a year—at the change of the seasons—Diocletian would stand at the entry to this vestibule and overlook the Peristyle. His subjects would lie on the ground in worship, praising his name.

Now go back into the square and climb the steps to the...

Cathedral of St. Dominus (Katedrala Sv. Duje)—The original octag-onal structure was Diocletian's elaborate mausoleum. But after the fall of Rome, it was converted into the town's cathedral. Construction on the bell tower began in the 13th century and took 300 years to com-plete. Before you go inside, notice the sarcophagi ringing the cathedral. In the late Middle Ages, it was believed that being buried closer to a cathedral improved your chances of getting to heaven. This is prime post-mortem real estate.

Step inside. The small multicolored marble pillars around the top of the pulpit were scavenged from Diocletian's mausoleum. These are all that remains of Diocletian's remains...he was a pretty unpopular guy, so what happened to the rest of him is anyone's guess.

Diocletian brutally persecuted his Christian subjects, sometimes in the crypt of this very building. To the left of the main altar is the altar of St. Anastasius—lying on a millstone, which is tied to his neck. On Diocletian's orders, this Christian martyr was drowned in Adriatic. Anastasius was a contemporary of St. Dominus, the namesake for this cathedral, who was an early Christian from Salona also martyred by Diocletian. Posthumous poetic justice: Now Christian saints are entombed in Diocletian's mausoleum...and Diocletian is nowhere to be found (5 kn, daily 7:00–12:00 & 17:00–19:00, Kraj Sv. Duje 5, tel. 021/345-602).

Before you leave the cathedral, ask the guy at the door for the key to...
Jupiter's Temple/St. John's Baptistery—Diocletian believed himself to be Jovius (that's Jupiter Junior). On exiting the mausoleum of Jovius, worshippers would look straight ahead to his dad's temple. (Back then, of course, all of these medieval buildings weren't cluttering up the view.) Make your way through the narrow alley, past another headless, pawless sphinx, to explore the small temple.

The temple has long since been converted into a baptistery—with a big 12th-century baptismal font and a statue of St. John by the great Croatian sculptor Ivan Meštrović (EE-vahn MESH-troh-veech; see page 372; included in cathedral entry, same hours as cathedral, must get key from cathedral clerk).

Head back to the Peristyle and stand in front of the TI with your back to the entry vestibule. The little street just above the TI connects the east and west gates. If you've had enough Roman history, head right (east) to go through the "Silver Gate" and find Split's bustling open-air Green Market. Or, to the left (west), you'll wind up at the "Iron Gate" and People's Square (see "More Sights in Split," next page), and beyond that, the fresh-and-smelly fish market. But if you want to see one last bit of Roman history, continue straight ahead up the...
Cardo—This street—literally "Hot Street"—was the most important in Diocletian's Palace, connecting the main entry with the heart of the complex. As you walk, you'll pass an alley to the City Museum on your right (see "More Sights in Split," next page). Before long, you'll pass through the...
Golden Gate (Zlatna Vrata)—This great gate was the main entry of Diocletian's Palace. Its name came from the golden statues of Diocletian and other Roman VIPs that adorned it. Straight ahead from here is Salona (Solin), which was a bustling city of 60,000 (and Diocletian's hometown) before there was a Split. The big statue by Ivan Meštrović is **St. Gregory of Nin**, a 10th-century Croatian priest who convinced the Vatican to allow Mass to be said in Croatian rather than Latin. People rub his toe for good luck.

More Sights in Split

▲▲ The Riva (Obala Hrvatskog Narodnog Preporoda)—The official name for this seaside pedestrian drag is the "Croatian National Revival Embankment," but locals just call it "Riva" (Italian for "harbor"). This is the town's promenade—an integral part of Mediterranean culture. After a quick dinner, Split residents collect their families and friends for a stroll on the Riva. This offers some of the best people-watching in Eastern Europe; make a point of being here for an hour or two after dinner (even if you have to make a special trip into town from your hotel). At the west end of the Riva, the parade of workaday Croatia continues up Marmontova.

▲ Peoples' Square (Narodni trg)—The lively square at the center of the Old Town is called by locals simply *Pjaca*—pronounced the same as the Italian *piazza*. As you enjoy the bustle, look around to get a quick lesson in Dalmatian history. First, face the former wall of Diocletian's Palace (under the clock tower). This was the western, or so-called "Iron Gate" of the palace. When Diocletian lived in his palace, a Roman village sprouted here. By the 14th century, the medieval town had developed, making this the main square of Split. To the left, the white building jutting out into the square is the Ethnographic Museum (see below). This used to be the City Hall, but all that remains of the original Gothic building is the loggia. Directly to your left as you face the museum is the Nakić House, built in Viennese Secession style when Dalmatia was part of the Hapsburg Empire ruled by Vienna, from Napoleon's downfall through World War I. If you leave the square on the right side of this building, you'll soon reach Split's fish market (Ribarnica).

Ethnographic Museum (Etnografski Muzej)—Those interested in the colorful art and dress of Dalmatian villages will want to visit this museum (10 kn, Mon–Fri 10:00–15:00, Sat 10:00–13:00, closed Sun, Narodni Trg 1, tel. 021/344-164).

City Museum (Muzej Grada)—This small museum, housed in the 15th-century Papalić Palace, displays fragments of Split's Roman and medieval past—including another beheaded sphinx (10 kn, mid-May–mid-Sept Tue–Fri 9:00–12:00 & 18:00–21:00, Sat–Sun 10:00–13:00, closed Mon, July–Aug Tue–Fri 9:00–21:00, Sat–Sun 10:00–13:00, closed Mon, off-season Tue–Fri 9:00–16:00, Sat–Sun 10:00–13:00, closed Mon, Papalićeva 1, tel. 021/344-917).

Radić Brothers Square (Trg Braće Radića)—A Venetian citadel watches over this square, just off the Riva between the two halves of the Old Town. After Split became part of the Venetian Republic, there was a serious danger of naval attack by the Turks, so towers like this were built all along the coast. But this imposing tower had a second purpose—to encourage citizens of Split to forget about any plans of rebellion.

In the middle of the square is a sculpture by Ivan Meštrović of the poet Marko Marulić, considered to be the father of the Croatian language. Behind him is the Baroque Milesi Palace (Palača Milesi), which sometimes hosts special exhibitions.

Split's Outskirts and Beyond

▲▲ **Meštrović Gallery (Galerija Meštrović)**—This museum is dedicated to sculptor Ivan Meštrović (1883–1962), the most important and famous of all Croatian artists. Split's best art museum is housed in a palace designed by the sculptor himself; if you have time, it's worth the 20-minute walk from the Old Town.

Meštrović grew up in a family of poor, nomadic farm workers just inland from Split. At an early age, his drawings and wooden carvings showed promise, and a rich family took him in and made sure he was properly trained. He eventually went off to school in Vienna, where he fell in with the Secession movement and found fame and fortune. Later in life—like Diocletian before him—Meštrović returned to Split and built a huge seaside mansion (today's Meštrović Gallery). During World War II, Meštrović moved abroad to escape the Nazi puppet government and lectured at Notre Dame (in Indiana, not France) and Syracuse (in New York, not Italy).

You'll see Meštrović's works all over Split and throughout Croatia. Most are cast bronze, depicting biblical, mythological, political, and everyday themes. Whether whimsical or emotional, Meštrović's expressive, elongated faces connect with the viewer. In this collection, don't miss *Job*, howling with an agony verging on insanity—carved by the artist in exile, as his country was turned upside-down by World War II. A moving contrast is the quietly poignant *Roman Pietà*, with mournful faces at painful angles pondering the death of Christ (15 kn, Tue–Sat 9:00–13:00 & 17:00–20:00, Sun 9:00–14:00, closed Mon, off-season Tue–Sat 10:00–16:00, Sun 10:00–14:00, closed Mon, Šetalište Ivana Meštrovića 46, tel. 021/358-450).

If you enjoy the gallery, continue five minutes down Šetalište Ivana Meštrovića to **Kaštelet Chapel,** a 16th-century fortified palace Meštrović bought to display his wooden carvings of Jesus' life. The centerpiece is a powerful wooden crucifix (same ticket and hours as gallery).

Marjan—This long, hilly peninsula extends west from the center of Split. This is where Split goes to relax, with out-of-the-way beaches and lots of hiking trails (great views and a zoo on top).

Hit the Beach—Since it's more of a big city than a resort, Split's beaches aren't as scenic (and the water not as clear) as towns farther south. The beach that's most popular—and crowded—is Bačvice, in a sandy cove just east of the main ferry terminal. You'll find less crowded beaches just to the east of Bačvice. Locals like to hike around Marjan, the peninsular city park (see above), ringed with several sunbathing beaches.

Trip to Trogir—Just 12 miles northwest of Split is Trogir, a tiny art-and-medieval-architecture-packed town surrounded by water. It has a bustling market, wonderfully carved old cathedral, and medieval ambience that can only really be appreciated from an outdoor café with a honey-drenched piece of baklava and a Turkish coffee. Get details at the Split TI.

Other Excursions—Consider one of many half-day and full-day excursions: a tour of Split and Trogir (180 kn, half day, 1/week), whitewater rafting on the nearby Cetina River (360 kn, full day, 2/week), the island of Brač (350 kn, full day, 1/week), the island of Hvar (330 kn, full day, 1/week), Brač and Hvar together (450 kn, full day, 1/week), Plitvice Lakes National Park (460 kn, full day, 1/week; see Inland Croatia chapter), or even Dubrovnik (320 kn, full day, 1/week). Get information and tickets at the Turistički Biro on the Riva (see "Tourist Information," above).

SLEEPING

$$$ New, slick **Hotel President** offers 40 plush business-class rooms with all the comforts, overlooking a dreary parking lot a 10-minute walk north of the Old Town (Sb-€80, Db-€120, apartment-€190, mandatory "guest insurance"-10 kn/day, non-smoking rooms, air-con, elevator, garage-€10/day, parking lot-€3.50/day, Starčevićeva 1, tel. 021/305-222, fax 021/305-225, www.hotelpresident.hr, hotel.president@st.hinet.hr).

$$$ Hotel Adriana has seven new rooms in an ideal location, right above the bustling Riva. Choose between harborview front rooms or quieter back rooms. Though the rooms are quite nice, they're an afterthought to the busy restaurant (Sb-556 kn, Db-756 kn, apartment-856–1,000 kn, 10 percent less with cash off-season, prices include tax, elevator, air-con, Riva 8, tel. 021/340-000, fax 021/340-008, www.hotel-adriana.hr, info@hotel-adriana.hr).

$$ Delightful **Villa Anna** may just be the best value on the Dalmatian Coast, with five modern, comfortable rooms in a smart little newly-renovated house just a five-minute walk from the Old Town (Sb-490 kn, Db-590 kn, Tb-690 kn, air-con, street parking, a block up from busy Kralja Zvonimira at Vrh Lučac 16, tel. 021/482-715, fax 021/482-721).

$$ Crumbling **Hotel Bellevue** used to be the grande dame of Split. It's still wonderfully located, at the west end of the Riva, but its 50 rooms are outmoded and extremely tired, as is the staff. Still, it's a decent price for the location (Sb-440 kn, Db-610 kn, Tb-810 kn, apartment-960 kn, breakfast-40 kn, 10 percent cheaper mid-Oct–mid-June, Bana Josipa Jelačića 2, tel. 021/347-499, fax 021/362-383).

$$ Prenoćište Slavija is the only hotel inside Diocletian's Palace. In

SLEEP CODE

(€1 = about $1.10, 1 kn = about 14 cents, country code: 385, area code: 021)

English is spoken at each place. Unless otherwise noted, credit cards are accepted, breakfast is included, and the modest tourist tax (5 kn—less than €1—per person, per night, lower off-season) is not.

To help you sort easily through these listings, I've divided the rooms into three categories based on the price for a standard double room with bath:

$$$ **Higher Priced**—Most rooms €90 (700 kn) or more.
$$ **Moderately Priced**—Most rooms between €70–90 (500–700 kn).
$ **Lower Priced**—Most rooms €70 (500 kn) or less.

Since Split is a big city with more options, the accommodations situation isn't quite as dismal here as in other Dalmatian destinations. There are actually a few good values hiding between the expensive new business-class hotels and the rotting old communist-style places (many of which are slated for reconstruction—or a visit from the wrecking ball).

To locate hotels, see map on page 364.

2003, it was a budget paradise, but rooms will be renovated—and more expensive—in 2004 (Buvinova 2, tel. 021/347-053, fax 021/344-062).

$ _Sobes_ (Private Rooms): Though there are no _sobes_ inside Split's Old Town, there are plenty within a 10-minute walk. **Turistički Biro** can help you find the best fit (figure S-€23, Sb-€25, D-€30, Db-€34, a few euros more July–Aug, 30 percent more for stays of less than 4 nights, office open mid-July–mid-Aug Mon–Fri 8:00–21:00, Sat 8:00–20:00, Sun 8:00–12:00; off-season Mon–Fri 8:00–20:00, Sat 8:00–14:00, closed Sun, Riva 12, tel. & fax 021/347-100, turist-biro -split@st.hinet.hr).

EATING

Split has some wonderful restaurants, but few are in the Old Town, which is home mostly to cafés and fast food joints.

Two excellent Dalmatian-style eateries are just a block off of the west end of the Riva (a few minutes from the Old Town, and well worth the short walk). The small **Šperun** has delicious food and friendly management with a genuine love for Dalmatian cuisine (most main dishes 25–50 kn, plus seafood splurges, daily 9:00–23:00, Šperun 3, tel. 021/346-999). **Konoba Varoš** is also good, but pricier and a bit impersonal (most main dishes 35–70 kn, daily 9:00–24:00, Ban Mladenova 7, tel. 021/396-138).

If you must eat inside the Old Town, consider smoky, local-feeling **Noštromo**—overlooking the fish market, you can bet the seafood's fresh (meat and pasta dishes-50–80 kn, plus seafood splurges, daily 6:00–24:00, Kraj Sv. Marije 10). Also in the Old Town, **Restoran Sarajevo** serves good Balkan meat dishes (grilled meats-50–80 kn, Italian dishes-25–35 kn, not the best for seafood, daily 7:00–24:00, Domaldova 6, tel. 021/347-454).

For wood-fired pizza, locals like two places at opposite ends of town: **Pizzeria Galija** (west end, 35–45 kn, Mon–Sat 9:00–23:00, Sun 12:00–23:00, Tončićeva 12, tel. 021/347-932) and **Pizzeria Bakra** (east end, 25–40 kn, daily 9:00–23:00, Radovanova 2, tel. 021/488-488).

Split has several spots for Italian-gelato-style ice cream *(sladoled).* Convenient and tasty is **Sara Mari,** just inside the west gate of Diocletian's Palace (steps from People's Square). But locals swarm a few blocks northwest of the Old Town to **Kuća Sladoleda Karmen** (daily 8:00–24:00, Slastičarna 2) and **Hajduk** (daily 8:00–24:00, Matošićeva 4).

TRANSPORTATION CONNECTIONS

By Jadrolinija ferry: The boat generally leaves Split at 6:30 in the morning (sometimes 7:00) and heads south, stopping at **Korčula** (3.5–6 hrs, generally around 5 hrs), **Dubrovnik** (7–10.5 hrs, generally around 8 hrs), and sometimes other coastal destinations (4/week June, 3/week July–Sept, 2/week Feb–May). Regional ferries also connect Split to **Korčula Island** via the town of Vela Luka—a long bus trip across the island from Korčula town (see "Transportation Connections—Korčula," page 384). Split's **Jadrolinija office** is in the main ferry terminal (see "Arrival in Split," above), with several smaller branch offices between there and the Old Town (tel. 021/338-333). For details on boats to Italy, see "Getting around the Dalmatian Coast," page 341.

By bus to: Zagreb (at least hrly, 6.5–8 hrs depending on route, 115–135 kn), **Dubrovnik** (12/day—about every 2 hrs, including several very early—4.5 hrs, 100 kn), **Korčula** (one night bus leaves 24:45 and arrives 6:00, 100 kn), **Zadar** (at least hrly, 3 hrs, 70 kn). Zagreb-bound buses also stop at **Plitvice** (confirm with driver and ask him to stop; 4–6 hrs, 70–80 kn). Bus info: toll tel. 060-327-327.

By train to: Zagreb (3/day, 7.25–9 hrs, including 2 night trains), **Budapest** (1 direct night train/day, 17 hrs; or transfer in Zagreb). Train info: toll tel. 060-333-444.

Korčula

To get a break from the Dalmatian Coast's two bustling cities, consider a sleepy island getaway in Korčula (KOHR-choo-lah). In Korčula's medieval quarter—poking out into the sea on a picture-perfect peninsula—tiny lanes branch off the humble main drag like ribs on a fishbone. This street plan is designed to catch both the breeze and the shade.

Korčula was founded by ancient Greeks, became part of the Roman Empire, and was eventually the southern outpost of the Venetian Republic. Four centuries of Venetian rule left Korčula with a quirky Gothic-Renaissance mix and a strong siesta tradition. Though the Venetians also claim him, Korčula insists that the great explorer Marco Polo was born here in 1254. The town's other claims to fame include shipbuilding and the traditional *Moreška* sword dance. This laid-back island village is an ideal place to take a vacation from your busy vacation.

Planning Your Time

Korčula offers little to do besides taking it easy. Wander the medieval Old Town, explore the handful of tiny museums, kick back at a café or restaurant, or bask on the beach. If you're here on a Thursday, be sure to catch the performance of the *Moreška* dance (also Mon July–Aug). One day is more than enough for Korčula—but because of sometimes-sparse ferry schedules, you may end up stranded here for longer. With the extra time, consider a one-day package excursion to Mljet or even to Dubrovnik.

Korčula has a couple of fun annual festivals. The "Return to the Age of Marco Polo" festival is the last week of May, with lots of exhibitions, concerts, dances, and a parade with a costumed Marco Polo returning to his native Korčula after his long visit to China. For 10 days at the beginning of September, Korčula remembers the great 1298 naval battle that took place just offshore, when the Genoese captured Marco Polo. The festivities culminate in a 14-ship reenactment, complete with smoke and sound effects.

ORIENTATION

(area code: 020)

The long, skinny island of Korčula runs alongside the even longer, skinnier Pelješac Peninsula. The main town and best destination on the island—just across a narrow strait from Pelješac—is also called Korčula.

Korčula's compact, highly fortified Old Town (Stari Grad) is on a little peninsula jutting out into the Adriatic. Most tourist facilities—

Korčula

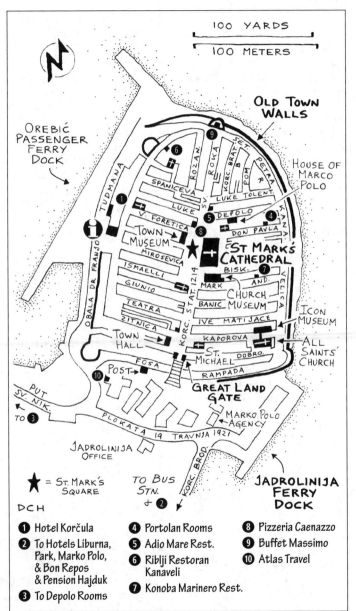

100 YARDS

100 METERS

OREBIĆ PASSENGER FERRY DOCK

OLD TOWN WALLS

HOUSE OF MARCO POLO

TUDMANA

SPANICEVA

ROZAN.

ROKA

KORC. BRAT.

SGT. POM.

SV. PETRA

LUKE TOLENT.

V. LUKE

V. FORETICA

DEPOLO

DON PAVLA

TOWN MUSEUM

MIROSEVICA

ISMAELLI

GIUNIO

TEATRA

ZITNICA

STAT. 1214

KORC.

MARK

BANIC

IVE MATIJACE

ST. MARK'S CATHEDRAL

BISK.

AND.

CHURCH MUSEUM

VELICA

KAZA

KAPOROVA

ICON MUSEUM

ALL SAINTS' CHURCH

OBALA DR FRANJO

TOWN HALL

FOSA

POST

DOBRO.

ST. MICHAEL

RAMPADA

GREAT LAND GATE

PUT SV. NIK.

TO ❸

PLOKATA 19 TRAVNJA 1921

MARKO POLO AGENCY

JADROLINIJA OFFICE

TO BUS STN.

❷

KORC. BROD.

JADROLINIJA FERRY DOCK

★ = ST. MARK'S SQUARE

DCH

❶ Hotel Korčula
❷ To Hotels Liburna, Park, Marko Polo, & Bon Repos & Pension Hajduk
❸ To Depolo Rooms

❹ Portolan Rooms
❺ Adio Mare Rest.
❻ Riblji Restoran Kanaveli
❼ Konoba Marinero Rest.

❽ Pizzeria Caenazzo
❾ Buffet Massimo
❿ Atlas Travel

ATMs, travel agencies, Jadrolinija ferry office, Internet cafés—are where the Old Town peninsula meets the mainland.

Korčula's we-try-harder **TI** is on the west side of the Old Town waterfront next to Hotel Korčula (mid-June–Sept Mon–Sat 8:00–15:00 & 16:00–22:00, less on Sun afternoons, Oct–mid-June Mon–Sat 8:00–15:00, closed Sun, tel. 020/715-701, www.korcula.net). Pick up the free *Korčula* magazine with maps, pictures, hotel listings, and other town information.

Arrival in Korčula

By Boat: Jadrolinija ferries usually arrive on the east side of town. As you exit the boat, the fortified Old Town is on your right. To reach the hotels on the far side of Shell Bay (Liburna, Park, Marko Polo), exit left and walk around the bay (about a 10-min walk). To get to the Old Town, Hotel Korčula, and recommended *sobes,* go straight ahead from the boat landing. In two minutes, you'll come to a big staircase (the Old Town's main entrance gate). On the square in front of these steps, you'll find an ATM, the Atlas travel agency (room booking), and the Jadrolinija office.

Sometimes the Jadrolinija ferry arrives on the west side of town, by Hotel Korčula (also used by Orebić passenger ferry). To reach the center, walk with the Old Town on your left-hand side and turn left around the big round tower. In two minutes, you'll reach the staircase described above.

A few boats (car ferries from Orebić and Drvenik) come to the Dominče dock two peninsulas east of Korčula (near Hotel Bon Repos). Hourly buses connect this dock with Korčula.

By Bus: The bus station is at the southeast corner of Korčula's Shell Bay. If you leave the station with the bay on your left, you'll get to hotels Liburna, Park, and Marko Polo. If you leave with the bay on your right, you'll get to the Old Town, Hotel Korčula, the recommended *sobes,* and the main ferry terminal (see "By Boat," above).

SIGHTS

Korčula's few sights are surprisingly interesting. Aside from the *Moreška* dance, I've listed them roughly in order from the Great Land Gate (the Old Town's main entry) to the tip of the Old Town peninsula.

▲▲*Moreška* **Dance**—Lazy Korčula snaps to life when locals perform a medieval folk dance called the *Moreška* (moh-REHSH-kah). The plot helps

Korčulans remember their hard-fought past: A bad king takes the good king's bride, the dancing forces of good and evil battle, and there's always a happy ending (50 kn, June–mid-Oct every Thu at 21:00, July–Aug also Mon at 21:00, in Gradska Vijećnica theater next to Great Land Gate, in movie theater if bad weather; buy tickets from local travel agency, at your hotel, or at the door).

▲ **Great Land Gate (Veliki Revelin)**— This impressive staircase leads up to the main entrance to the Old Town. Like all of the town's towers, it's adorned with the Venetian winged lion and the coats-of-arms of the doge of Venice (left) and the rector of Korčula (right; the offset coat of arms below was the rector who renovated the gate later). You can climb up the tower to visit a small museum on the *Moreška* dance and enjoy some superb town views.

Just inside the gate is **Franjo Tuđman Square**—recently (in 2001) renamed for the controversial first president of an independent Croatia (see page 336). During the war, Tuđman was considered a hero. In later years, he grew power-hungry and held secret negotiations with the merciless Serbian leader, Slobodan Milošević. But members of his party are still in power and hold important local offices throughout the country, sometimes still adorning a square or street with his name. (The more cynical locals think these names will be changed again before too long.)

On the left inside the gate is the 16th-century **Town Hall and Rector's Palace.** The seal of Korčula symbolizes the town's importance as the southernmost bastion of the Venetian Republic: St. Mark standing below three defensive towers. The little church on the other side of the square is dedicated to **St. Michael** (Crkva Sv. Mihovila). Throughout Croatia, you'll often find churches to St. Michael just inside the town gates, as he is believed to offer saintly protection from enemies. Notice that a passageway connects the church to the building across the street—home to the Brotherhood of St. Michael, one of Korčula's many religious fraternal organizations (see "Icon Museum," below). Now continue up the...

▲ **Street of the Korčulan Statute of 1214 (Ulica Korčulanskog Statuta 1214)**—This street is Korčula's backbone...literally (the street plan is designed as a fish skeleton). While most medieval towns slowly evolved with twisty, mazelike lanes, Korčula was carefully planned. The streets to the west (left) of this one are straight, to allow the refreshing west winds *(maestral)* into town. To the east (right), they're curved (notice you can't see the sea)—to keep out the bad-vibe southeast winds.

The street's complicated name honors a 1214 statute, the oldest known written law in Central Europe, with regulations about everyday life and instructions on maintaining the walls, protecting nature, keeping animals, building a house, and much more.

If you continue a few steps up the street, you'll reach **St. Mark's Square** (Trg Sv. Marka). From here, you're a few steps from the next four sights.

▲▲ **St. Mark's Cathedral (Katedrala Sv. Marka)**—Korčula became a bishopric in the 14th century. In the 19th century—36 bishops later—the Hapsburgs decided to centralize ecclesiastical power in their empire, and removed Korčula's bishop. The town still has this beautiful "cathedral"—but no bishop.

You'll see another Venetian statue of St. Mark (flanked by Adam and Eve) as you duck inside. Above the main altar is an original Tintoretto painting (recently restored in Zagreb). Notice the reliquary under the altar. The Venetians made Mark the patron saint of Korčula, but the townspeople always wanted something that was their own. By the 18th century—after Venetian influence had faded—the town had no relics, so the bishop requested some from the pope. He sent them the relics of St. Theodore, whom Korčulans have taken on as their true patron. (That's who's in the box.)

The chapel to the far left was built later than the rest of the church, when the plague swept across Europe. It's dedicated to St. Rok, who helps heal the sick (which is why he's pointing to a leg wound). Even today, Korčulans remain very religious. When someone falls ill, the bells ring in a special way, and the townspeople flock to the cathedral to pray.

As you leave, notice the weapons on the back wall, used in some of the important battles that have taken place near strategically-situated Korčula.

▲ **Church Museum (Opatska Riznica)**—This small museum has an unusual, fascinating collection. Try to find the following: a ceremonial necklace from Mother Teresa (which she gave to a friend from Korčula), some old 12th-century hymnals, two tiny drawings by Leonardo da Vinci, a coin collection including a 2,400-year-old Greek coin minted here in Korčula, some Croatian modern paintings, and two framed reliquaries with dozens of miniscule relics (10 kn, 40-kn English-language guidebook, June–Aug daily 8:00–21:00, May and Sept–Oct daily 10:00–13:00, closed Nov–April).

▲ **Town Museum (Gradski Muzej)**—Housed in an old mansion, the museum does a fine job of bringing together Korčula's eclectic claims to fame. It's arranged like a traditional Dalmatian home: shop on the ground floor, living quarters in the middle floors, kitchen on top. Notice that many of the interior walls are not finished (including just inside the entry). Archaeologists are continually doing actual "digs" into these walls to learn how medieval houses here were built.

On the ground floor is an exhibit on stonemasonry, displaying some first-century Roman jugs. Upstairs is a display on Korčula's important and long-standing shipbuilding industry, including models of two modern steel ships built here (the town still builds ship parts today). There's also a furnished living room and, in the attic, a kitchen. This was a smart place for the kitchen—if it caught fire, it was less likely to destroy the whole building. Notice the little WC in the corner. A network of pipes took kitchen and other waste through town and out to sea (10 kn, 40-kn English-language book, mid-June–Aug daily 8:00–21:00, May–mid-June and Sept–Oct daily 10:00–13:00, closed Nov–April).

▲ **Marco Polo's House (Kuća Marka Pola)**—Korčula's favorite son is the great 13th-century explorer Marco Polo. Though Polo is associated more with Italy, sailed under the auspices of the Venetian Republic, and technically was a Venetian (since the Republic controlled this region), Korčulans proudly claim him as their own. Marco Polo was the first Westerner to sail to China, bringing back amazing stories and goods like silk that Europeans had never seen before. After his trip, Marco Polo fought in an important naval battle against the Genoese right near Korčula. He was captured, taken to Genoa, and imprisoned. He told his story to a cellmate, who wrote it down, published it, and made the explorer a world-class and much-in-demand celebrity. To this day, kids in swimming pools around the world try to find him with their eyes closed.

Today Korčula is the proud home to "Marco Polo's House"—actually a more recent building on the site of what may or may not have been his family's property—with a modest exhibit about the explorer's life. The house is in poor repair and has been closed recently for renovation, but should be open to visitors in 2004 (just north of cathedral on—where else?—ulica Depolo).

▲ **Icon Museum (Zbirka Ikona)**—Korčula is known for its many brotherhoods—centuries-old fraternal organizations that have sprung up around churches. The Brotherhood of All Saints has been meeting every Sunday after Mass since the 14th century, and they run a small but interesting museum of icons. These golden religious images were brought back from Greece in the 17th century by Korčulans who had been fighting the Turks on a Venetian warship (8 kn, May–Oct, Mon–Sat 10:00–13:00 & 18:00–20:00, closed Nov–April, on Kaprova ulica at the Old Town's southeast tip).

Brotherhoods' meeting halls are often connected to their church by a second-story walkway. Use this one to step in to the Venetian-style **All Saints' Church** (Crkva Svih Svetih). Under the loft in the back of the church, notice the models of boats and tools—donated by Korčula's shipbuilders. Look closely at the painting to the right of the altar. See the guys in the white robes kneeling under Jesus? That's the Brotherhood, who commissioned this painting.

▲ **Old Town Walls**—For several centuries, Korčula held an important strategic position: This was the southernmost border of the Venetian

Republic (Dubrovnik started at the Pelješac Peninsula, just across the sea). The original town walls around Korčula date from at least the 13th century, but the fortifications were extended (and new towers built) over several centuries to defend against various foes of Venice—mostly Turks and pirates.

The most recent tower dates from the 16th century, when the Turks attacked Korčula. The rector and other VIPs fled to the mainland, but a brave priest remained on the island and came up with a plan. All of the women of Korčula dressed up as men, and then everybody in town peeked over the wall—making the Turks think they were up against a huge army. The priest prayed for help, and a strong north wind *(bora)* blew. Not wanting to take their chances with the many defenders and the weather, the Turks sailed away, and Korčula was saved.

By the late 19th century, Korčula was an unimportant Hapsburg beach town, and the walls had no strategic value. The town decided to quarry the top half of its old walls to build new homes (and to improve air circulation inside the city). Today's walls are half as high as they used to be, but fortunately, the town restored many of the towers. Each one has a winged lion—a symbol of Venice—and the seal of the rector of Korčula when the tower was built.

Excursions—Local travel agencies offer day-long excursions to nearby destinations. The most popular options are Dubrovnik (320 kn, 3/week) and the National Park on Mljet Island (190 kn, 2/week). You can buy tickets at any local travel agency (try Atlas or Marko Polo).

SLEEPING

$$ Moderately-Priced Hotels

All five of Korčula's hotels are owned by HTP Korčula. If you don't want to stay in a *sobe*, these are the only game in town. You can reserve rooms at any of them through the main office (tel. 020/726-336, fax 020/711-746, www.korcula.net, htp-korcula@du.tel.hr; at all hotels, credit cards are accepted and there is no air-con and no non-smoking rooms; you'll pay 10 percent more for a seaview room, more July–Aug, and less off-season).

The handiest is **Hotel Korčula,** centrally located in the Old Town. It has a fine seaside terrace restaurant and friendly staff, even if the 20 rooms are outmoded and overpriced (Sb-€58, Db-€90, July–Aug: Sb-€73, Db-€102, less off-season, reception tel. 020/711-078).

Three more hotels cluster around the far side of Shell Bay. All are poorly maintained and overpriced, and share a nice beach. **Hotel Liburna** has 83 rooms—some of them accessible by elevator—and the same prices as Hotel Korčula (reception tel. 020/726-006). **Hotel Park** has 153 rooms, some of them lightly renovated (old rooms: Sb-315 kn, Db-480 kn, July–Aug: Sb-395 kn, Db-560; newer rooms: Sb-365 kn,

SLEEP CODE

(€1 = about $1.10, 1 kn = about 14 cents, country code: 385, area code: 020)
English is spoken at each place. Unless otherwise noted, breakfast is included and the modest tourist tax (7 kn/€1 per person, per night, lower off-season) is not.

Korčula's accommodations options are very limited. There are five hotels in town—all decaying, overpriced resort-style hotels, and all owned by the same company (which is, in turn, government-run). The lack of competition keeps prices high and quality low—and makes *sobes* a particularly good alternative. I've listed two of the best private rooms, but you can also contact one of Korčula's travel agencies to help you find more (you'll pay an additional 20 percent). Try **Atlas Travel** (daily in summer 7:00–20:30, off-season Mon–Sat 8:00–12:00, closed Sun, Trg 19. Travnja, tel. 020/711-060, fax 020/715-580, www.adriatica.net).

Db-560 kn, July–Aug: Sb-460 kn, Db-750 kn, reception tel. 020/726-100). **Hotel Marko Polo** has 109 rooms and an elevator (Sb-365 kn, Db-560 kn, July–Aug: Sb-460 kn, Db-750 kn, reception tel. 020/726-100). The fifth hotel, **Hotel Bon Repos**—another 15 minutes by foot from the Old Town—is, in every sense, the last resort.

$ Lower-Priced *Sobe*

Friendly, English-speaking **Rezi and Antonio Depolo**—probably distant relatives of Marco—rent four wonderful rooms on a bay five minutes by foot from the Old Town. These rooms are better by far than the big hotels, go for a quarter of the price, and are the only air-conditioned rooms I saw in town (Db-€21, July–Aug: Db-€27, 30 percent more for 1- or 2-night stays, room with kitchen-€5 more, prices include tax, basic breakfast-€3.50, big breakfast-€7, no CC, no number on Sv. Nikola, walk along waterfront from Old Town with bay on your right, look for *sobe* sign at the yellow house set back from the street, just before the 2 monasteries, tel. 020/711-621, tereza.depolo@du.hinet.hr).

Anka Portolan, with helpful English-speaking relatives, rents some fine, older-feeling rooms perfectly located in the Old Town (Db-150–200 kn, big 5-person apartment-300 kn, July–Aug: Db-200–300 kn, apartment-400 kn, no extra charge for 1- or 2-night stays if you book direct, no breakfast, no CC, ulica Don Pavla 7, tel. 020/711-711, vitomir.stankovic@du.hinet.hr).

Pension Hajduk rents 25 basic but good rooms a 20-minute walk from the Old Town. It's far from town and the water, but it's cheap, and the friendly Zec family restaurant is a lively local hangout. The rooms are scattered around several buildings connected by a sprawling vegetable garden, which provides fresh produce for guests and for the restaurant's recipes (Sb-120 kn, Db-180 kn, July–Aug: Sb-120 kn, Db-200 kn, breakfast-27 kn extra, no CC, just off Dubrovačka cesta, tel. & fax 020/711-267). To reach Pension Hajduk from the Old Town, walk along Shell Bay, pass the Park and Marko Polo hotels, continue ahead with the inlet on your left, and bear left and uphill at the end of the inlet. When you reach the big road at the top of the hill, look right for the signs.

EATING

Korčula has plenty of tasty seafood restaurants. Try these suggestions, or follow your nose through the Old Town.

Adio Mare offers fine seafood and pleasant, cave-like Old World atmosphere near Marco Polo's House (daily 18:00–24:00, also 12:00–14:00 in peak season, tel. 020/711-253).

You'll find good seafood in a fancier setting at **Riblji Restoran Kanavelić,** near the far end of the Old Town peninsula (non-seafood dishes 20–45 kn, plus seafood splurges, daily 18:00–24:00, tel. 020/711-800).

Konoba Marinero has nicely nautical decor on a peaceful alley just two blocks from the main street in the Old Town (most dishes 35–60 kn, daily 18:00–24:00, from 11:00 in peak season, Marka Andrijića 13, tel. 020/711-170).

For good pizza on St. Mark's Square, try **Pizzeria "Caenazzo"** (daily 9:00–24:00).

The best setting for drinks is at **Buffet "Massimo,"** in a city-wall tower at the tip of the Old Town peninsula. The main dining room is just inside the top of the tower, but if you're just having drinks, climb the ladder and sit up top with wonderful views (pizzas 30–45 kn, otherwise just drinks, daily 17:00–2:00, tel. 020/715-073).

TRANSPORTATION CONNECTIONS

Korčula is reasonably well-connected to the rest of the Dalmatian Coast by boat—though service becomes sparse in the off-season, and it's smart to carefully study boat schedules when planning your itinerary. There are plans in the near future for a more frequent high-speed hydrofoil connecting Korčula town with Split; ask a local TI for details.

By boat: Most travelers get to Korčula by **Jadrolinija** ferry (docks right at Old Town). You can take it to **Split** (4/week June–Sept, 2/week Feb–May, stop at Stari Grad on Hvar Island en route) or **Dubrovnik**

(4/week June, 3/week July–Sept, 2/week Feb–May). You'll find the Jadrolinija office where the Old Town meets the mainland (mid-June–Sept Mon–Fri 8:00–20:00, Sat–Sun 8:00–14:00, Oct–mid-June Mon–Fri 8:00–14:00, Sat–Sun 8:00–13:00, tel. 020/715-410, www.jadrolinija.hr).

There's another way to **Split,** but it requires a very early bus from Korčula to the port at **Vela Luka,** an hour away at the other end of the island. Every day, a local Jadrolinija ferry and a faster hydrofoil leave from the Vela Luka dock and go to Hvar, then on to Split (ferry: Mon–Sat 6:30, Sun 9:30, 1.5 hrs to Hvar, 3 hrs to Split; hydrofoil: Mon–Sat 5:30, Sun 8:00, 30 min to Hvar, 1.5 hrs to Split; bus for Mon–Sat boats leaves Korčula 4:10, bus for Sun boats leaves Korčula 7:45). Confirm these schedules at the Korčula TI or Jadrolinija office before you get up early to make the trip.

By bus to: Dubrovnik (1/day, 3.5 hrs), **Zagreb** (1/day, 9–12 hrs depending on route), **Split** (1/day, 5 hrs, same bus goes to Zagreb), **Vela Luka** (at far end of island, Mon–Fri 7/day, Sat 6/day, Sun 4/day, first bus at 4:10 gets you to the early-morning ferries).

INLAND CROATIA

Zagreb and Plitvice Lakes National Park

Croatia is known for its idyllic coastline, but there are also worthwhile stops in the interior. The underrated capital, Zagreb, with good museums, interesting streets, and a thriving café culture, is worth exploring. Just to the south are the Plitvice Lakes—Croatia's first and most important national park, and one of Europe's best back-to-nature experiences.

Zagreb

While Zagreb doesn't have the world-class sights of Budapest or the stay-a-while charm of Ljubljana, the city offers historic neighborhoods, off-beat museums, and an illuminating contrast to Croatia's coast. As a tourist destination, Zagreb pales in comparison to the sparkling coastal towns. But you can't get a complete picture of modern Croatia without a visit here—away from the touristy resorts, in the lively and livable city that is home to one out of every five Croatians (population around 1 million).

Zagreb began as two walled medieval cities, Gradec and Kaptol, separated by a river. As Croatia fell under the control of various foreign powers—Budapest, Vienna, Berlin, and Belgrade—the two hill towns that would become Zagreb gradually took on more religious and civic importance. Kaptol became a bishopric in 1094, and it's still home to Croatia's most important church. In the 16th century, the *Ban* (Croatia's governor) and the *Sabor* (parliament) called Gradec home. The two towns officially merged in 1850, and soon after, the railroad connecting Budapest with the Adriatic port city of Rijeka was built through the city. Zagreb prospered.

After centuries of being the de-facto religious, cultural, and political capital of Croatia, Zagreb officially became a European capital when the country declared its independence in 1991. In the ensuing war with Serbia, Zagreb was hardly damaged—Serbian bombs hit only a few

Zagreb

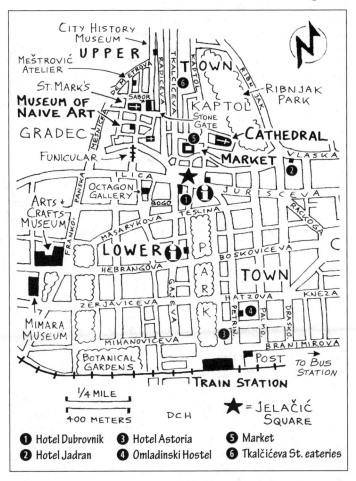

CITY HISTORY MUSEUM →
UPPER TOWN
MEŠTROVIĆ ATELIER
ST. MARK'S
MUSEUM OF NAIVE ART
GRADEC
FUNICULAR
RADIĆEVA
DEMETROVA
TKALČIĆEVA
SABOR
❻
KAPTOL
RIBNJAK PARK
STONE GATE
KAPTOL
❺
CATHEDRAL
MARKET
VLAŠKA
❷
MEŠNIČKA
ILICA
OCTAGON GALLERY
BOGO
❶
ℹ
JURIŠIĆEVA
RAČKOGA
ARTS + CRAFTS MUSEUM
PANSKA
FRANKO-
TESLINA
MASARYKOVA
LOWER ℹ P A R K TOWN
HEBRANGOVA
BOŠKOVIĆEVA
GAJEVA
ZERJAVIĆEVA
HATZOVA
KNEZA
K
PETRIN.
❹
PALMO.
DRAŠKO.
MIMARA MUSEUM
MIHANOVIĆEVA
❸
BRANIMIROVA
BOTANICAL GARDENS
POST
TO BUS STATION
TRAIN STATION

¼ MILE
400 METERS
DCH
★ = JELAČIĆ SQUARE

❶ Hotel Dubrovnik   ❸ Hotel Astoria   ❺ Market
❷ Hotel Jadran   ❹ Omladinski Hostel ❻ Tkalčićeva St. eateries

strategic targets (the bloodiest fighting was to the east and south of here).

Today, less than a decade later, Zagreb has long since repaired the minimal damage, and the capital feels safe, modern, accessible, and forward-looking.

Planning Your Time

Most American visitors just pass through Zagreb, but the city is worth a look. Check your bag at the station and zip into the center for a quick visit—or consider spending the night.

You can get a decent sense of the Croatian capital in just a few short hours. With whatever time you have, make a beeline for Jelačić Square to visit the TI and get oriented. If you're here in the mid-day, get to the market before it closes up at 14:00. If you're in town earlier (or too late for the market), take the funicular up to Gradec, visit the Museum of Native Art, and stroll St. Mark's Square before heading down through the Stone Chapel to the lively Tkalčićeva scene (good for a drink or meal), through the market, and on to Kaptol and the cathedral. With more time, visit some of Zagreb's museums or stroll the "Green Horseshoe." Note that virtually all Zagreb museums are closed on Monday.

ORIENTATION

(area code: 01)

Zagreb, just 30 minutes from the Slovene border, stretches from the foothills of Medvednica ("Bear Mountain") to the Sava River. In the middle of the sprawl, you'll find the modern **Lower Town** (Donji Grad, centered on **Jelačić Square**) and the historic **Upper Town** (Gornji Grad—comprising the original hill towns of **Gradec** and **Kaptol**). To the south is a U-shaped belt of parks, squares, and museums that make up "Lenuci's Green Horseshoe." The east side of the U is a series of three parks, with the train station at the bottom (south) and Jelačić Square at the top (north).

Zagrebians have devised a brilliant scheme for confusing tourists: Street names can be depicted several different ways. For example, the street that is signed as ulica Kralja Držislava ("King Držislav Street") is often called by locals simply Držislavova ("Držislav's"). So if you're looking for a street, don't search for an exact match—be willing to settle for something that just has a lot of the same letters.

Tourist Information: Zagreb has two **TIs**—the handier one is at Jelačić Square (Mon–Fri 8:30–20:00, Sat 9:00–17:00, Sun 10:00–14:00, sometimes longer hours in summer, Trg bana Jelačića 11, tel. 01/481-4051, www.zagreb-touristinfo.hr), and the other is just a few blocks south, along the west side of Zrinjevac Park (Mon, Wed, and Fri 9:00–17:00, Tue and Thu 9:00–18:00, closed Sat–Sun, trg Nikole Šubića Zrinskoga 14, tel. 01/492-1645). Zagreb's TIs are helpful, with piles of well-produced tourist brochures that desperately try to convince visitors to do more than just pass through. Pick up the one-page city map (with handy transit map and regional map on back), the *Zagreb Info A–Z* booklet (including accommodations listings), and the great "City Walks" brochure—with a couple of easy, self-guided walking tours (all free).

The **Zagreb Card** gives you free transportation and discounts on Zagreb sights for 72 hours (60 kn, sold at TI). This doesn't make sense for folks who are day-tripping here, but is a good deal for longer stays. If

ZAGREB LANDMARKS

English	Croatian	Pronounced
Jelačić Square	Trg bana Jelačića	turg BAH-nah YEH-lah-chee-chah
Gradec (original civic hill town)	Gradec	GRAH-dehts
Kaptol (original religious hill town)	Kaptol	KAHP-tohl
Café street between Gradec and Kaptol	Tkalčićeva	tuh-kahl-chee-CHAY-vah
Train station	Glavni Kolodvor	GLAHV-nee KOH-lohd-vor
Bus station	Autobusni Kolodvor	OW-toh-boos-nee KOH-lohd-vor

taking a city tour (see below), you should definitely buy the card—it'll automatically pay for itself.

To get oriented, consider the fun **city tours,** led by local guides dressed up as important historical Zagrebians (140 kn, 3 hrs, part bus and part walking, Wed and Fri at 16:00, Sat–Sun at 10:00, call TI one day ahead to reserve and request English guide, tel. 01/481-4051). If you're taking the tour, notice that you might as well buy the Zagreb Card for a 50 percent discount (you save 70 kn on the tour, the Zagreb Card costs only 60 kn—so you're 10 kn ahead from the start).

Arrival in Zagreb

By Train: Zagreb's train station (Glavni Kolodvor) is conveniently located a few blocks south of Jelačić Square on the "Green Horseshoe." Good signage will direct you to the arrival hall, information desk, ticket windows, ATMs, WCs, and kiosks. The left-luggage office is at the left end of the station, with your back to the tracks (open 24 hrs, 10 kn/day). To reach the center, go straight out the front door. You'll run into a taxi stand, and then the tracks for tram #6 (direction Črnomerec zips you to Jelačić Square; direction Sopot takes you to the bus station). If you walk straight ahead through the long, lush park, you'll wind up at the bottom of Jelačić Square in 10 minutes.

By Bus: The user-friendly bus station (Autobusni Kolodvor) is southeast of the center. The station has all the essentials—ATMs, post office, mini-grocery store, left-luggage counter, and even a chapel. Upstairs, you'll find ticket windows and access to the buses (follow signs to *perone;* wave ticket in front of turnstile to open gate). Tram #6 (in direction Črnomerec) takes you to the train station, then on to Jelačić Square.

By Plane: Zagreb's airport is about 10 miles south of the center. The Croatia Air bus connects the airport to Zagreb's bus station (20 kn, every 30 min, 30-min trip). Figure 180 kn for a taxi from the airport to the center.

Getting around Zagreb

The main mode of public transportation is the **tram,** operated by ZET (Zagreb Electrical Transport, tel. 01/365-1555, www.zet.hr). A single ticket (good for 90 min in one direction, including transfers) costs 8 kn if you buy it from the driver (6.50 kn at kiosk, ask for *ZET karta*). A day ticket *(dnevna karta)* costs 18 kn. The handiest tram for tourists is #6, connecting Jelačić Square with the train and bus stations.

Taxis start at around 15 kn, then run about 7 kn per kilometer (more expensive at night; as always, there are corrupt cabbies—ask for an estimate up front, or call Radio Taxi, tel. 01/970).

SIGHTS

The following sights are listed in the order of a handy one-way circular orientation route, starting at Jelačić Square.

▲▲**Jelačić Square (Trg bana Jelačića)**—Zagreb's main square bustles with life. It's lined with cafés, shops, trams, Baroque buildings, and the TI. When Zagreb consisted of the two hill towns of Gradec and Kaptol, this Donji Grad ("lower town") held the townspeople's farm fields. Today it features a prominent equestrian statue of national hero **Josip Jelačić** (YEH-lah-cheech, 1801–1859), a 19th-century governor who extended citizens' rights and did much to unite the Croats within the Hapsburg Empire. In Jelačić's time, the Hungarians were exerting a lot of

control over Croatia, even trying to make Hungarian the official language. Meanwhile, Budapesters revolted against Hapsburg rule in 1848. Jelačić knew that if the Hungarians got their way—more independence from Vienna—they'd next threaten Croatian culture. Jelačić chose the lesser of two evils, and fought alongside the Hapsburgs to put down the Hungarian uprising. In the Yugoslav era, Jelačić was considered dangerously nationalistic, and this statue was taken down. But when Croatia broke away in 1991, Croatian patriotism was in the air, and Jelačić returned. Though Jelačić originally faced his Hungarian foes to the north, today he's staring down the Serbs to the south.

Get oriented. If you face Jelačić's statue, a long block to your left is a funicular that takes you up to one of Zagreb's original villages, Gradec. To the right, look for the TI. If you leave the square ahead and to the right, you'll reach the other original village, Kaptol, and the cathedral. If you leave the square ahead and to left, then bear right, you'll come to the market (Dolac); bear left, and you'll reach Tkalčićeva, the café street.

▲▲▲Gradec—Eventually absorbed by Zagreb, the city of Gradec (GRAH-dehts) was granted status as a free royal state by the 1242 Golden Bull—meaning that the town answered only and directly to the Holy Roman Emperor (not that pesky nobility bureaucracy). In later years, Gradec became the seat of Croatia's government—including its *Sabor*, or parliament, and *Ban*, or governor.

To reach Gradec from Jelačić Square, go a long block down the busy Ilica. On the way, duck inside the big shopping gallery on the left (at #5, called the Octagon). If you go down the first passage, you'll come to a beautiful stained-glass ceiling and a tie store called **Croata.** This is a reminder that the French may have "invented" the tie, but they were inspired by Croatian soldiers who wore jaunty scarves into battle when they went to fight in the Thirty Years' War. They even named the new accessory *cravate*—after "Croat."

Continue up Ilica and turn right on Tomićeva, where you'll see a small **funicular** (ZET Uspinjača) crawling up the hill. Dating from the late 19th century, this funicular is looked upon fondly by Zagrebians—both as a bit of nostalgia and as a way to avoid some steps. You can walk up if you want, but the ride is more fun and takes only 55 seconds (3 kn, leaves every 10 min daily 6:00–20:00).

From the top of the funicular, you'll enjoy a fine panorama over Zagreb. The tall tower you face as you exit is one of Gradec's original watchtowers, the **Burglars' Tower** (Kula Lotršćak). After the Tartars ransacked Central Europe in the early 13th century, King Béla IV decreed that towns be fortified—so Gradec built a wall and guard towers (just like Kraków and Buda did). Look for the little cannon in the top-floor window. Every day at noon, this cannon fires a shot, supposedly to commemorate a 15th-century victory over the besieging Turks. (Zagrebians hold on to other traditions, too—the lamps on this hill are still gas-powered, lit by a city employee every evening.)

Head up the street next to the tower. Little remains of medieval Gradec. When the Turks overran Europe, they never managed to take Zagreb—but the threat was enough to scare the nobility into the countryside. When the Turks left, the nobles came back, and replaced the medieval buildings here with Baroque mansions. At the first square, to the right, you'll see the Jesuit **Church of Saint Catherine.** It's not much to look at from outside, but the interior is intricately decorated. The same applies to all of the mansions on Gradec. This simple-outside, ornate-inside style is known as "Zagreb Baroque."

As you continue up the street, you'll see the excellent **Croatian Museum of Native Art** (Hrvatski Muzej Naivne Umjetnosti) on the left. This remarkable museum, rated ▲▲, collects paintings and sculptures by untrained peasant artists. These stirring images—including several by the movement's star, Ivan Generalić—are well worth a look (10 kn, Tue–Fri 10:00–18:00, Sat–Sun 10:00–13:00, ulica Sv. Ćirila i Metoda 3, tel. 01/485-1911, www.hmnu.org).

At the end of the block, you'll come to the low-key **St. Mark's Square** (Markov trg), centered on the **Church of St. Mark.** The original church here was from the 12th century, but only a few fragments remain. The colorful tile roof, from 1880, depicts two coats of arms. On the left, the red-and-white checkerboard symbolizes north-central Croatia, the three lions' heads stand for the Dalmatian Coast, and the marten (*kuna,* like the money) running between the two rivers (Sava and Drava) represent Slavonia—Croatia's northern, inland panhandle. On the right is the seal of Zagreb: a walled city with wide-open doors (welcoming in visitors...like you).

As you face the church, to the right is the *Sabor,* or parliament. From the 12th century, Croatian noblemen would gather to make important decisions regarding their territories. This gradually evolved into today's modern parliament (original building around the corner). Across the square (to your left as you face the church) is the **Ban's Palace** (Banski Dvori), today the offices for the president and prime minister. This was one of the few buildings in central Zagreb destroyed in the recent war. In October of 1991, the Serbs shelled it from afar, knowing that Croatian President Franjo Tuđman was inside, but Tuđman survived.

Walk from Gradec to Kaptol—For an interesting stroll from St. Mark's Square to the cathedral, head down the street (Kamenita ulica) to the right of the parliament building. Near the end of the street, you'll see the oldest pharmacy in town (c. 1350, on the right) before coming to Gradec's oldest surviving gate, the **Stone Gate** (Kamenita Vrata). Inside is a moving chapel. The focal point is a painting of Mary that miraculously survived a major fire in 1731. When this medieval gate was reconstructed in the Baroque style, they decided to turn it into a makeshift chapel. The candles represent Zagrebians' prayers, and the stone plaques on the wall give thanks *(Hvala)* for prayers that were answered. Mary was made the official patron saint of Zagreb in 1990.

As you leave the Stone Gate and come to Radićeva, turn right. Take the next left, onto the street called Krvavi Most—literally "Blood Bridge." At the end of Krvavi Most, you'll come to **Tkalčićeva.** This lively café-and-restaurant street used to be a river—the natural boundary between Gradec and Kaptol. The two towns did not always get along, and sometimes fought against each other. Blood was spilled, and the bridge that once stood here between them became known as Blood

Bridge. By the late 19th century, the towns had united, and the river began to stink—so they covered it over with this street.

As you cross Tkalčićeva, you enter the old town of Kaptol. You'll come to the **market** (Dolac), packed with colorful stalls selling produce of all kinds (usually open daily 7:00–14:00). Underneath you is an underground, indoor part of the market, where farmers sell farm-fresh eggs and dairy products (same hours as outdoor market, entrance down below in the direction of Jelačić Square).

On the other side of the market, visit the...

▲▲**Cathedral (Katedrala)**—In 1094, when a diocese was established at Kaptol, this quickly became an important center of high-ranking church officials, and it's still Croatia's most important church. (The country is 90 percent Catholic...though the percentage was lower before the conflict with the Orthodox Serbs.) In the mid-13th century, the original cathedral was destroyed by invading Tartars, who actually used it as a stable. It was rebuilt, only to be destroyed again by an earthquake in 1880. The current version is neo-Gothic, surrounded by Renaissance towers—built to protect the church from the Turks, and part of a larger archbishop's palace. The full name is the Cathedral of the Assumption of the Blessed Virgin Mary and the Saintly Kings Stephen and Ladislav (whew!)—but most locals just call it "the cathedral."

Step inside (free, Mon–Sat 10:00–17:00, Sun 13:00–17:00). Look closely at the silver relief on the first altar: a scene of the Holy Family doing chores around the house (Mary sewing, Joseph and Jesus building a fence...and angels helping out). In the back left corner, find the tombstone of Alojzije Stepinac. He was the Archbishop of Zagreb in World War II, during which time he shortsightedly supported the Nazis—thinking, like many Croatians, that this was the ticket to greater independence from Serbia. When Tito came to power, he put Stepinac on trial and sent him to jail for five years. But Stepinac never lost his faith, and remains to many the most important inspirational figure of Croatian Catholicism.

As you leave the church, look to the back of the left apse. This strange script is the Glagolitic alphabet *(glagoljca)*, invented by Byzantine missionaries Cyril and Methodius in the ninth century to translate the Bible into Slavic languages. Though these missionaries worked mostly in Moravia (today's eastern Czech Republic), their alphabet caught on only here, in Croatia. (Glagolitic was later adapted in Bulgaria to become the Cyrillic alphabet—still used in Serbia, Russia, and other parts east.) In 1991, when Croatia became its own country and nationalism surged, the country flirted with the idea of making this the official alphabet (to differentiate Croatian from the very similar Serbian, and to revive old Croat tradition).

Other Zagreb Museums—Zagreb has lots of forgettable museums, but a few are worth checking out. The **Mimara Museum** (Muzej Mimara) houses the eclectic collection of a wealthy Dalmatian, ranging from ancient artifacts to paintings by Peter Paul Rubens, Rembrandt, Pierre-Auguste Renoir, and Edouard Manet (25 kn, Tue–Sat 10:00–17:00, Thu until 19:00, Sun 10:00–14:00, closed Mon, Rooseveltov trg 5, tel. 01/482-8100).

The **Ivan Meštrović Atelier** features works by the 20th-century Croatian sculptor—see page 372 for more information on this prolific, thoughtful artist (10 kn, Tue–Fri 9:00–14:00, Sat 10:00–18:00, closed Sun–Mon, behind St. Mark's Square at Mletačka 8, tel. 01/485-1123).

The **Arts and Crafts Museum** (Muzej za Umjetnost i Obrt) has an excellent decorative arts collection—mostly furniture, ceramics, and clothes—from the Gothic age to the present (20 kn, Tue–Fri 10:00–18:00, Sat–Sun 10:00–13:00, closed Mon, trg Maršala Tita 10, tel. 01/482-6922).

And the **Zagreb City History Museum** (Muzej Grada Zagreba) covers just that (20 kn, Tue–Fri 10:00–18:00, Sat–Sun 10:00–13:00, closed Mon, at north end of Gradec at Opatička 20, tel. 01/485-1364).

SLEEPING

$$$ Plush **Hotel Dubrovnik** has an ideal location (at the bottom of Jelačić Square) and 268 fine business-class rooms (Sb-€91–105, Db-€125–145, Tb-€180, suite-€185, prices soft, non-smoking floors, elevator, Gajeva 1, tel. 01/487-3555, fax 01/481-8665, www.tel.hr/hotel-dubrovnik, hotel-dubrovnik@hotel-dubrovnik.tel.hr).

SLEEP CODE

(€1 = about $1.10, $1 = about 7 kuna, country code: 385, area code: 01)

Sleep Code: **S** = Single, **D** = Double/Twin, **T** = Triple, **Q** = Quad, **b** = bathroom, **s** = shower only, **no CC** = Credit Cards not accepted. English is spoken at each place. Unless otherwise noted, credit cards are accepted, breakfast is included, and the modest tourist tax (7 kn per person, per night) is not.

To help you sort easily through these listings, I've divided the rooms into three categories based on the price for a standard double room with bath:

$$$ **Higher Priced**—Most rooms 700 kn (€90) or more.
$$ **Moderately Priced**—Most rooms between 400–700 kn (€55–90).
$ **Lower Priced**—Most rooms 400 kn (€55)or less.

$$ **Hotel Jadran** has 48 good rooms near the cathedral, a few blocks east of Jelačić Square (Sb-460 kn, Db-600 kn, extra bed-170 kn, some street noise—ask for quiet room, elevator, Vlaška 50, tel. 01/455-3777, fax 01/461-2151, www.hup-zagreb.hr, jadran@hup-zagreb.hr).

$$ **Hotel Astoria** has 60 drab, old, socialist-era rooms near the train station (Sb-330 kn, Db-500 kn, Tb-600 kn, prices include tax, elevator, Petrinjska ulica 71, tel. 01/484-1222, fax 01/484-1212, hotel-astoria@zg.tel.hr).

$ **Omladinski Hostel Zagreb** is due to wrap up a much-needed renovation in early 2004. These are the cheapest beds in the center, handy to the train station (new prices should be around €15 per dorm bed, S-€25, Sb-€35, D-€30, Db-€40, more for non-members, no CC, elevator, Petrinjska ulica 77, tel. 01/484-1261, fax 01/484-1269, www.hfhs.hr).

EATING

You'll find lots of good and handy cafés and restaurants along **Tkalčićeva,** behind Jelačić Square. For something quicker and even more local, grab a bite at the **market.**

TRANSPORTATION CONNECTIONS

By train to: Rijeka (3/day, 4 hrs), **Split** (3–4/day, 7.5–9 hrs, including direct night trains), **Zadar** (1/day, 9-hr night train with transfer in Knin), **Ljubljana** (8/day, 2.5 hrs), **Vienna** (2/day, 6.5 hrs), **Budapest** (2/day, 5–7 hrs).

By bus to: Plitvice Lakes National Park (at least hrly, 2–2.5 hrs), **Split** (2/hr until 18:00, then hrly, 6–9 hrs), **Dubrovnik** (2 in the early morning, then 4–6 overnight, 11–12.5 hrs), **Korčula** (1/night, 14 hrs). Bus info: www.akz.hr.

Plitvice Lakes National Park
(Nacionalni Park Plitvička Jezera)

Plitvice (PLEET-veet-seh) is one of Europe's most spectacular natural wonders. Imagine Niagara Falls diced and sprinkled over a heavily forested Grand Canyon. There's nothing like this lush valley of 16 terraced lakes, laced together by waterfalls and miles of pleasant plank walks. Countless cascades and strangely clear and colorful water make this park a misty natural wonderland. Years ago, after eight or nine visits, I thought I really knew Europe. Then I discovered Plitvice and realized you can never exhaust Europe's surprises.

Planning Your Time

Plitvice deserves at least a few good hours.
Since it takes some time to get to the park, the
most sensible plan is to spend the night in one
of the park's hotels (comfortable, convenient,
and inexpensive). If you're coming from the
north (e.g., Ljubljana), head to Zagreb in the
morning, spend a few hours seeing the
Croatian capital, then take the bus to Plitvice
in the early evening to spend the night at the
park. Get up early and hit the trails; by early
afternoon, you'll be ready to move on (perhaps
by bus to the coast). Two nights and a full day
at Plitvice is probably overkill for all but the
most avid hikers.

ORIENTATION

(area code: 053)

Plitvice's 16 lakes are divided into the Upper Lakes *(gornja jezera)* and
the Lower Lakes *(donja jezera)*. The park officially has two entrances
(ulaz), each with ticket windows and snack and gift shops. Entrance 1 is
at the bottom of the Lower Lakes, across the busy D1 road from the
park's best restaurant, Lička Kuća (see "Eating," page 403). Entrance 2 is
about 1.5 miles south, at the cluster of Plitvice's three hotels (Jezero,
Plitvice, and Bellevue; see "Sleeping," page 402). There is no town at
Plitvice. The nearest village, Mukinje, is mostly a residential community for park workers (boring for tourists).

Cost and Hours: The price to enter the park varies by season
(July–Aug €12, May–June and Sept–Oct €10, Nov–April €6; ticket
good for entire stay). The hours are also changeable, but generally the
park is open from 7:00 in summer, 8:00 in spring and fall, and 9:00 in
winter; it closes at dusk. Night owls should note that the park never
"closes"; these hours are for the ticket booths and the boat and shuttle
bus system. You can just stroll right into the park at any time of day,
provided that you aren't using the boat or bus (tickets checked only at
boat). To avoid tour groups and field trips, visit early or late in the day.

Tourist Information: A handy map of the trails is on the back of
your ticket, and big maps are posted all over the park. The big 20-kn
map is a good investment; the 60-kn English-language guidebook is
poorly translated and not very helpful (both sold at entrances, hotels,
and shops throughout the park). The park has a good Web site: www
.np-plitvice.com.

Plitvice Lakes National Park

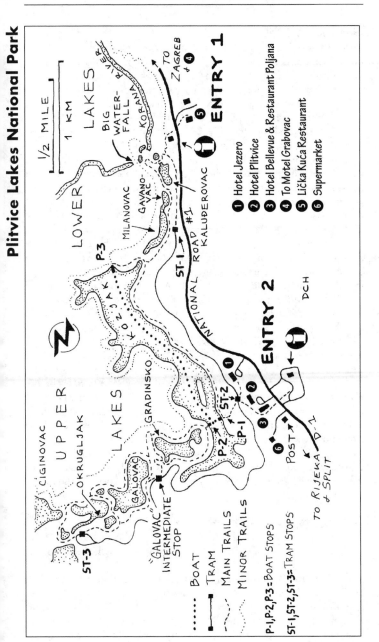

1/2 MILE
1 KM

LOWER LAKES

BIG WATER-FALL

KORANA RIVER

TO ZAGREB
4

ENTRY 1

GAVANOVAC

MILANOVAC

KALUĐEROVAC

P-3

ST-1

NATIONAL ROAD #1

KOZJAK

ENTRY 2

DCH

1

2

ST-2

GRADINSKO

P-1

P-2

3

6

POST

TO RIJEKA & SPLIT

D-1

UPPER LAKES

CIGINOVAC

OKRUGLJAK

GALOVAC

"GALOVAC INTERMEDIATE STOP"

ST-3

❶ Hotel Jezero
❷ Hotel Plitvice
❸ Hotel Bellevue & Restaurant Poljana
❹ To Motel Grabovac
❺ Lička Kuća Restaurant
❻ Supermarket

•••••• BOAT
▬▬ TRAM
— — MAIN TRAILS
· · · · MINOR TRAILS

P-1,P-2,P-3 = BOAT STOPS
ST-1,ST-2,ST-3 = TRAM STOPS

Getting to Plitvice

Plitvice Lakes National Park, a few miles from the Bosnian border, is nearly two hours by car south of Zagreb on National Road #1 (a.k.a. D1). This is the main route connecting Zagreb with the coast, so it can be quite crowded, especially on summer weekends. (A new freeway is being built several miles south of here to make the trip faster; the first phase—from Zagreb to Split—is due to be finished mid-2005.)

By **car**, head south from Zagreb on D1 and get off at the Karlovac exit. Drive south through town and continue on D1, which takes you right to the park (a little over an hour from Karlovac).

Buses leave at least once hourly from Zagreb's main bus station in the direction of Plitvice (various companies; go to ticket window and ask for next departure, 45–65 kn, trip takes 2–2.5 hrs). Most are headed to the coast, and do not routinely stop at the park; when you board, tell the driver where you're going (he may even stop at your specific hotel, or, for the worst-case scenario, he'll drop you at the official Plitvice bus stop, which is a 15-min walk beyond the hotels). If you're going late in the day, beware: There's often a gap in the bus schedule between 17:00 and 20:00—possibly leaving you with more time in Zagreb than you intended. Confirm the schedule online (www.akz.hr) or at the Plitvice office in Zagreb (trg Kralja Komislava 19, tel. 01/461-3586).

By car or bus, you'll see some interesting terrain between Zagreb and Plitvice. As you leave Karlovac, you'll pass through the village of **Turanj,** part of the war zone just a decade ago. It's safe to assume that the destroyed, derelict houses belonged to Serbs who have not come back to reclaim and repair them. Farther along, about 25 miles before Plitvice, you'll pass through the striking village of **Slunj,** picturesquely perched on travertine formations (like Plitvice's) and surrounded by sparkling streams and waterfalls. If you're in a car, this is worth a photo stop. This town, too, looks very different than it did before the war—when it was 30 percent Serb. As in countless other villages in the Croatian interior, the Orthodox church has been destroyed...and locals still seethe when they describe how occupying Serbs "defiled" the town's delicate beauty.

Getting around Plitvice

Of course, Plitvice is designed for hikers. But the park has a few ways (included in the cost of entry) to help speed you through the less interesting bits.

By Shuttle Bus: Buses connect the hotels at Entrance 2 (stop ST2, below Hotel Jezero) with the top of the Upper Lakes (stop ST3) and roughly the bottom of the Lower Lakes (stop ST1, a 10-min walk from Entrance 1). There is an intermediate stop (called "Galovac," for the lake it's closest to), between the hotels and the top of the Upper Lakes, that is marked on maps as only for tour groups, but they'll let off (or pick up) individual travelers if you ask nicely. This stop helps you avoid the less-interesting top half of the Upper Lakes.

In peak season, the bus starts running early and continues until late afternoon (time depends on demand; bus runs from March until the first snow—often Dec).

Note that no local buses can take you along the major road (D1) that connects the entrances, so the only way to get between them without a car is by shuttle bus or by foot.

By Boat: Low-impact electric boats ply the waters of the biggest lake, Kozjak, with three stops: below Hotel Jezero (stop P1), the bottom of the Upper Lakes (P2), and at the far end of Kozjak at the top of the Lower Lakes (P3). From Hotel Jezero to the Upper Lakes is a quick five-minute ride; the boat goes back and forth continuously. From the Upper Lakes to the Lower Lakes takes closer to 20 minutes, and the boat goes about twice per hour (often at the top and bottom of every hour). Unless the lake freezes (about every 5 years), the boat runs in the off-season, too—though frequency drops to hourly, and it stops running earlier.

HIKES AND SIGHTS

Plitvice is a refreshing playground of 16 terraced lakes, separated by natural limestone dams and connected by countless waterfalls. Over time, the water has simultaneously carved out and, with the help of mineral deposits, built up this fluid landscape.

Plitvice became Croatia's first national park in 1949. Thirty years later, it was added to UNESCO's World Heritage list. On Easter Sunday in 1991, the first shots of Croatia's war with Yugoslavia were fired right here—in fact, the war's first casualty was a park policeman, Josip Jović. The Serbs occupied Plitvice until 1995, and many of the Croatians you'll meet here were evacuated and lived near the coastline as refugees. Today the war is a fading memory, and the park is again a popular tourist destination, with 700,000 visitors each year. But Americans are still needlessly wary about coming here; in 2003, only 1.5 percent of the park's visitors came from the United States.

Put on your best walking shoes—Plitvice's system of trails and boardwalks makes it possible for visitors to get up close to the park's beauty. (In some places, the paths literally lead right up the middle of a waterfall.) The official park map and signage recommend a variety of hikes: The red and yellow circles go from the Upper Lakes to the Lower Lakes, and the blue and green circles go from Lower to Upper. But

THE SCIENCE OF PLITVICE

Nearly everyone is impressed by Plitvice, and eventually asks the same question: How did it happen?

Plitvice's magic ingredient is calcium carbonate ($CaCO_3$), which interacts with the plants, algae, and moss in a unique way to create the park's beauty. Remarkably clear water flows into the park from nearby mountains. Minerals coat the vegetation on the bottom of the lakes, reflecting the sunlight to create a striking blue-green coloration. Eventually, this coating becomes thicker, travertine limestone barriers are formed, and waterfalls gradually emerge. The ongoing process means that Plitvice's landscape is always changing.

Wildlife found in the park includes deer, wolves, wildcats, wild boar, and more than 160 species of birds (from eagles to herons to owls). The lakes (and local menus) are full of trout. Perhaps most importantly, Plitvice is home to the brown bear—now extremely endangered in Europe. You'll see bears, the park's mascot, plastered all over tourist literature (and a scary representative in the lobby of Hotel Jezero).

there's no need to adhere strictly to these hikes; invest in the big 20-kn map and make your own route.

I like hiking uphill, from Lower to Upper, which offers slightly better head-on views of the best scenery. (Even though this route has a gradual uphill slope, remember that if you go the other way—downhill—there's a steep climb back up at the end.) Below, I've described a one-way hiking route (going uphill), divided between Upper and Lower. Walking briskly and with a few photo stops, figure an hour for the Lower Lakes, an hour for the Upper Lakes, and a half hour to connect them by boat.

Start at the...

Lower Lakes (Donja Jezera)—The lower half of Plitvice's lakes are accessible from Entrance 1. If you start here, the route marked with the green circle/yellow square leads you along the boardwalks to Kozjak, the big lake that connects the Lower and the Upper Lakes (see below).

From the entrance, you'll descend down a steep path with lots of switchbacks, as well as thrilling views over the canyon of the Lower Lakes. As you reach water level and begin to follow the boardwalks, you'll have great up-close views of the travertine formations that make up Plitvice's many waterfalls. See any trout? If you're tempted to throw in a line, don't. Fishing is strictly forbidden.

Near the beginning of the Lower Lakes trails, you'll have the option to visit the **Big Waterfall** (Veliki Slap). It's worth the 10-minute detour loop to see the biggest of Plitvice's waterfalls, where the Plitvica River plunges 250 feet over a cliff into the valley below. Depending on recent rainfall, the force of the Big Waterfall varies from a light mist to a thundering deluge.

After seeing the Big Waterfall, continue on the boardwalks. On the left, you'll see a smaller trail branch off towards **Šupljara Cave.** You can actually climb through this slippery cave all the way up to the trail overlooking the Lower Lakes. This unassuming cavern is a surprisingly big draw. In the 1960s, several German and Italian Spaghetti Westerns were filmed at Plitvice and in other parts of Croatia (which, to European eyes, has terrain similar to the American West). The most famous, *Der Schatz im Silbersee (The Treasure in Silver Lake)*, was filmed here at Plitvice, and the treasure was hidden in this cave. The movie is still a favorite in Germany—complete with *Deutsch*-speaking "Native Americans"—and popular theme tours bring German tourists to movie locations here in Croatia.

After the cave, you'll stick to the east side of the lakes, then cross over one more time to the west, where you'll cut though a comparatively dull forest. You'll emerge at a pit-stop-perfect clearing with WCs, picnic tables, a souvenir shop, and a self-service restaurant. This is where you can catch the shuttle boat across Lake Kozjak to the bottom of the Upper Lakes (see "Getting around Plitvice," above). While you're waiting for the next boat (usually every 30 min), visit the friendly old ladies in the kiosks selling wheels of cheese and different kinds of strudel (10 kn per piece).

Lake Kozjak (Jezero Kozjak)—This is the park's biggest lake, connecting the Lower and Upper Lakes. The 20-minute boat ride between Plitvice's two halves offers a great chance for a breather. You can hike between the lakes along the west side of Kozjak, but the scenery's not nearly as good as the rest of the park.

Upper Lakes (Gornja Jezera)—Focus your attention on the lower half of the Upper Lakes. From the boat dock, you'll hike up to Gradinsko Lake. The section between here and Galovac Lake is the most striking in the whole park. Enjoy the stroll, take your time, and be thankful you remembered to bring extra film.

Soon after Galovac Lake, you'll see signs pointing up to a bus stop. Most visitors will want to opt for this stop (technically for tours only, but they'll stop for individuals) to return to Entrance 2. From here on up, the scenery is less stunning, the waterfalls are fewer and farther between, and the crowds thin out. If you do continue up to the top of the Upper Lakes, you can catch the shuttle bus (stop ST3, with a WC and food stalls) back to the entrance.

SLEEPING

$$$ **Hotel Jezero** is big and modern, with all the comfort—and charm—of a Holiday Inn. It's well-located, right at the park entrance, and offers hundreds of rooms that feel new-ish but generally have at least one thing that's broken. Parkside rooms have big glass doors and balconies (July–Aug: Sb-€72, Db-€98; May–June and Sept–Oct: Sb-€64, Db-€88; Nov–April: Sb-€51, Db-€68, elevator, reception tel. 053/751-400).

$$ **Hotel Plitvice,** a little less plush than Jezero, offers mod, wide-open public spaces on two floors with no elevators (reception tel. 053/751-100). For rooms, choose from economy (fine, older-feeling; July–Aug: Sb-€50, Db-€68; May–June and Sept–Oct: Sb-€44, Db-€60; Nov–April: Sb-€38, Db-€50), standard (just a teeny bit bigger; July–Aug: Sb-€55, Db-€74; May–June and Sept–Oct: Sb-€49, Db-€66; Nov–April: Sb-€41, Db-€54), or superior (bigger still, with a sitting area; July–Aug: Sb-€61, Db-€82; May–June and Sept–Oct: Sb-€55, Db-€74; Nov–April: Sb-€45, Db-€60).

$ Bare-bones **Hotel Bellevue** is old-feeling and simple (no TVs or elevator), but the price is right and the rooms are sleepable (July–Aug:

SLEEP CODE

(€1 = about $1.10, country code: 385, area code: 053)
English is spoken, credit cards are accepted, and breakfast is included at each place. The tourist tax (7 kn per person, per day) is not included in these prices.

To help you sort easily through these listings, I've divided the rooms into three categories based on the price for a standard double room with bath:

$$$ **Higher Priced**—Most rooms €85 or more.
$$ **Moderately Priced**—Most rooms between €65–85.
$ **Lower Priced**—Most rooms €65 or less.

The most convenient way to sleep at Plitvice is to use the park's lodges, all a good value. To get these prices in 2004, reserve ahead and ask for the Rick Steves rate. Book any of these hotels through the same office (reservation tel. 053/751-015, fax 053/751-013, www.np-plitvice.com, reservations@np-plitvice.com; reception numbers are listed below per hotel in case you need to be reached, or to reach a guest, at a particular hotel).

Sb-€47, Db-€64; May–June and Sept–Oct: Sb-€43, Db-€58; Nov–April: Sb-€35, Db-€46, reception tel. 053/751-700).

$ **Motel Grabovac,** with 31 comfortable rooms, is 7.5 miles north of Plitvice on the road to Zagreb. It's basic and dark, and its restaurant feels like a truck stop (Adriatic-bound buses take a pit stop here en route from Zagreb). Stay here only if you have a car and want to go cheap (July–Aug: Sb-€41, Db-€56; May–June and Sept–Oct: Sb-€38, Db-€52; Nov–April: Sb-€29, Db-€38, reception tel. 053/751-999).

EATING

The park runs all of the restaurants at Plitvice. These places are handy, and the food is tasty and affordable. If you're staying at the hotels, you have the option of paying for **half-board** with your room (lunch or dinner, €11 each May–Oct, €8 each Nov–April). This is designed to be used with the restaurants inside Hotels Jezero and Plitvice, but you can also use the voucher at other park eateries (you'll pay the difference if the bill is more). The half-board option is a fine value and worth doing if you're here for dinner, but don't lock yourself in for lunch—you'll want more flexibility as you explore Plitvice (excellent picnic spots and decent food stands abound inside the park).

Hotel Jezero and **Hotel Plitvice** both have big restaurants with good food and friendly, professional service (half-board for dinner, described above, is a good deal; or order à la carte: fish 50–60 kn, meat dishes 80–100 kn; both daily until 23:00).

Lička Kuća, across the pedestrian overpass from Entrance 1, has a wonderfully dark and smoky atmosphere around a huge open-air wood-fired grill (grilled trout-50 kn, more elaborate dishes up to 100 kn, daily 11:00–24:00, tel. 053/751-024).

Restaurant Poljana, behind Hotel Bellevue, has the same boring park-lodge atmosphere in both of its sections: cheap self-service cafeteria (25–40 kn) and sit-down restaurant with open wood-fired grill (same items and prices as the better-atmosphere Lička Kuća, above; both parts open daily but closed in winter, tel. 053/751-092).

For **picnic** fixings, there's a small supermarket across road D1 from Entrance 2.

TRANSPORTATION CONNECTIONS

To get to the park, see "Getting to Plitvice," above. Moving on from Plitvice is trickier. Buses pass by the park about hourly in each direction—northbound (to **Zagreb,** 2–2.5 hrs) and southbound (to coastal destinations like **Split,** 4–7 hrs, and **Dubrovnik,** 9–10 hrs).

There is no bus station—just a low-profile bus stop shelter: Go out to the main road from either Hotel Jezero or Hotel Plitvice, then turn right; the bus stops are just after the pedestrian overpass. The one on the hotel side of the road is for buses headed for the coast; the stop on the opposite side is for Zagreb. But here's the catch: Many buses that pass through Plitvice don't stop (either because they're full, or because they don't have anyone to drop off there). You can stand at the bus stop and try to flag one down, but it's safer to get help from the park's hotel staff. They can help you figure out which bus suits your schedule, then they'll call ahead to be sure the bus stops for you. If you don't want to make the 15-minute walk out to the bus stop, someone at the hotel can usually drive you out (often for a modest fee).

GATEWAYS TO EASTERN EUROPE

Vienna, Berlin, and Dresden

In this guidebook designed to help you explore the "best of Eastern Europe," I've included three gateway cities—Vienna, Berlin, and Dresden—that are actually part of Western Europe, but serve as logical springboards into the East.

Berlin, the capital of a newly united Germany, was also the capital of East Germany before 1989. For a generation it was cut off from the West, accessible only by a thin ground and air corridor to the rest of Germany and Western Europe. Today it is a thriving cultural and economic power-house, as well as a prime gateway to Poland and the Czech Republic.

Dresden is most famous today for its utter destruction by Allied bombing in World War II. Having been buried behind the Iron Curtain for a generation, it's generally not even considered when Americans plan a German vacation. But it's a cultural capital with a fascinating history and world-class museums, and it makes for an easy stop between Berlin and Prague. Along with Berlin, Dresden is the most important destination in what used to be the communist German Democratic Republic.

Vienna is one of the grandest cities of Europe, very reasonably called the "eastern Paris." It was built to rule the vast multinational

KEY GERMAN PHRASES

German is the predominant language in this book's gateway cities. German—like English, Dutch, Swedish, and Norwegian—is a Germanic language, making it easier on most American ears than Slavic languages (like Czech and Polish) or the mysterious Hungarian tongue.

While many people in Eastern Europe speak at least some English, those who don't are likely to know German (especially in Croatia, a favorite vacation destination for Germans and Austrians).

English	German	Pronounced*
Hello	**Guten Tag**	GOO-tehn tahg
Do you speak English?	**Sprechen Sie Englisch?**	SHPREHKH-ehn zee ENG-lish
Yes / No	**Ja / Nein**	yah / nīn

English	German	Pronounced*
Please / You're welcome / Can I help you?	Bitte	BIT-teh
Thank you	Danke	DAHNG-keh
I'm sorry	Es tut mir leid	ehs toot meer līt
Excuse me (to pass or to get attention)	Entschuldigung	ehnt-SHOOL-dig-oong
Good	Gut	goot
Goodbye	Auf Wiedersehen	owf VEE-der-zayn
one / two	eins / zwei	īns / tsvī
three / four	drei / vier	drī / feer
five / six	fünf / sechs	fewnf / zehks
seven / eight	sieben / acht	ZEE-behn / ahkht
nine / ten	neun / zehn	noyn / tsayn
hundred	hundert	HOON-dert
thousand	tausend	TOW-sehnd
How much?	Wie viel?	vee feel
local currency	euro (€)	OY-roh
Where is...?	Wo ist...?	voh ist
...the toilet	...die Toilette	dee toy-LEH-teh
men	Herren	HEHR-ehn
women	Damen	DAH-mehn
water / coffee	Wasser / Kaffee	VAH-ser / kah-FAY
beer / wine	Bier / Wein	beer / vīn
Cheers!	Prost!	prohst
the bill	die Rechnung	dee REHKH-noong

* When using the phonetics, pronounce ī as the long i sound in "light."

Hapsburg Empire, which included almost all of the destinations in this book...but it started and lost World War I, and consequently, its holdings. Today Vienna is the capital of Austria—small, landlocked, and relatively insignificant. But in its heyday, the Hapsburg Empire (later called the Austro-Hungarian Empire) was Europe's superpower. And most of its citizens were Slavic rather than German. The influence of Vienna is strong on Prague, Budapest, and Slovenia. Historically and culturally, it makes sense to splice Vienna into any eastern adventure. And logistically, Vienna is a natural gateway to Slovenia, Budapest, and Prague.

VIENNA

(Wien)

Vienna is a head without a body. For 640 years the capital of the once-grand Hapsburg empire, she started and lost World War I, and with it her far-flung holdings. Today, you'll find an elegant capital of 1.6 million people (20 percent of Austria's population) ruling a small, relatively insignificant country. Culturally, historically, and from a sightseeing point of view, this city is the sum of its illustrious past. The city of Freud, Brahms, Maria Theresa's many children, a gaggle of Strausses, and a dynasty of Holy Roman Emperors ranks right up there with Paris, London, and Rome.

Vienna has always been the easternmost city of the West. In Roman times, it was Vindobona, on the Danube facing the Germanic barbarians. In medieval times, Vienna was Europe's bastion against the Ottoman Turks (a horde of 200,000 was repelled in 1683). Though the ancient walls held out the Turks, World War II bombs destroyed nearly a quarter of the city's buildings. In modern times, Vienna took a big bite out of the USSR's Warsaw Pact buffer zone.

The truly Viennese person is not Austrian, but a second-generation Hapsburg cocktail, with grandparents from the distant corners of the old empire—Poland, Serbia, Hungary, Romania, the Czech Republic, Slovakia, and Italy. Vienna is the melting-pot capital of a now-collapsed empire that, in its heyday, consisted of 60 million people—only 8 million of whom were Austrian.

In 1900, Vienna's 2.2 million inhabitants made it the world's fifth-largest city (after New York, London, Paris, and Berlin). But the average Viennese mother today has 1.3 children, and the population is down to 1.6 million. (Dogs are the preferred "child.")

Some ad agency has convinced Vienna to make Elisabeth, wife of Emperor Franz Josef, with her narcissism and difficulties with royal life, the darling of the local tourist scene. You'll see "Sissy" all over town. But stay focused on the Hapsburgs who mattered.

Vienna Overview

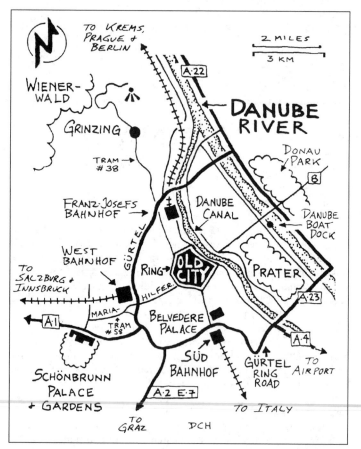

Of the Hapsburgs who ruled Austria from 1273 to 1918, Maria Theresa (ruled 1740–1780) and Franz Josef (ruled 1848–1916) are the most famous. People are quick to remember Maria Theresa as the mother of 16 children (10 survived). This was actually no big deal back then (one of her daughters had 18 kids, and a son fathered 16). Maria Theresa's reign followed the Austrian defeat of the Turks, when Europe recognized Austria as a great power. She was a strong and effective queen. (Her rival, the Prussian emperor, said, "When at last the Hapsburgs get a great man, it's a woman.")

Maria Theresa was a great social reformer. During her reign, she avoided wars and expanded her empire by skillfully marrying her children into the right families. After daughter Marie Antoinette's marriage into the French Bourbon family (to Louis XVI), for instance, a country that had been an enemy became an ally. (Unfortunately for Marie, she arrived in time for the Revolution, and she lost her head.)

A great reformer and in tune with her era, Maria Theresa employed Robin Hood policies to help Austria glide through the age of revolution without turmoil. She taxed the Church and the nobility, provided six years of obligatory education to all children, and granted free health care to all in her realm. She also welcomed the boy genius Mozart into her court.

As far back as the 12th century, Vienna was a mecca for musicians—both sacred and secular (troubadours). The Hapsburg emperors of the 17th and 18th centuries were not only generous supporters of music but fine musicians and composers themselves. (Maria Theresa played a mean double bass.) Composers like Haydn, Mozart, Beethoven, Schubert, Brahms, and Mahler gravitated to this music-friendly environment. They taught each other, jammed together, and spent a lot of time in Hapsburg palaces. Beethoven was a famous figure, walking—lost in musical thought—through Vienna's woods.

After the defeat of Napoleon and the Congress of Vienna in 1815 (which shaped 19th-century Europe), Vienna enjoyed its violin-filled belle époque, which shaped our romantic image of the city—fine wine, chocolates, cafés, and waltzes. "Waltz King" Johann Strauss and his brothers kept Vienna's 300 ballrooms spinning.

This musical tradition continues into modern times, leaving some prestigious Viennese institutions for today's tourists to enjoy: the Opera, the Boys' Choir, and the great Baroque halls and churches, all busy with classical and waltz concerts.

ORIENTATION

(area code: 01)

Vienna—Wien in German (veen)—sits between the Vienna Woods (Wienerwald) and the Danube (Donau). To the southeast is industrial sprawl. The Alps, which arc across Europe from Marseille, end at Vienna's wooded hills. These provide a popular playground for walking and new-wine–drinking. This greenery's momentum carries on into the city. More than half of Vienna is parkland, filled with ponds, gardens, trees, and statue-maker memories of Austria's glory days.

Think of the city map as a target. The bull's-eye is the cathedral, the first circle is the Ring, and the second is the Gürtel. The old town—snuggling around towering St. Stephan's Cathedral south of the Danube—is bound tightly by the Ringstrasse. The Ring, marking what was the city wall, circles the first district (or *Bezirk*). The Gürtel, a broader ring road, contains the rest of downtown (*Bezirkes* 2–9).

Addresses start with the *Bezirk,* followed by street and building number. Any address higher than the ninth *Bezirk* is beyond the Gürtel, far from the center. The middle two digits of Vienna's postal codes show the *Bezirk.* The address "7, Lindengasse 4" is in the seventh district, #4 on Linden Street. Its postal code would be 1070. Nearly all your sightseeing will be done in the core first district or along the Ringstrasse. As a tourist, concern yourself only with this compact old center. When you do, sprawling Vienna suddenly becomes manageable.

Planning Your Time

For a big city, Vienna is pleasant and laid-back. Packed with sights, it's worth two days and two nights on the speediest trip. It seems like Vienna was designed to help people just meander through a day. To be grand-tour efficient, you could sleep in and sleep out on the train (Berlin, Kraków, Warsaw, Venice, Rome, the Swiss Alps, Paris, and the Rhine are each handy night trains away). Budapest is just down the Danube, three hours by train. I'd spend two days this way:

Day 1: 9:00-Circle the Ring by tram, following the self-guided tour (see "Do-It-Yourself Tram Orientation Tour," page 414), 10:00-Drop by TI for any planning and ticket needs, then see the sights in Vienna's old center (described below): Monument against War and Fascism, Kaisergruft crypt, Kärntner Strasse, St. Stephan's Cathedral, and Graben, 12:00-Finger sandwiches for lunch at Buffet Trzesniewski, 13:00-Tour the Hofburg and treasury, 16:00-Time to hit one more museum or shop, or browse and people-watch, 19:30-Choose classical music (concert or opera), House of Music museum, or *Heurige* wine garden.

Day 2: 9:00-Schönbrunn Palace (drivers: This is conveniently on the way out of town toward Salzburg; horse-lovers: You'll need to rearrange—or rush the palace—to see the Lipizzaner stallions' morning practice), 12:00-Lunch at Rosenberger Markt, 13:00-Tour the Opera, 14:00-Kunsthistorisches Museum, 16:00-Your choice of the many sights left to see in Vienna, Evening-See Day 1 evening options.

Tourist Information

Vienna has one real tourist office, a block behind the Opera House at Albertinaplatz (daily 9:00–19:00, tel. 01/24555, www.info.wien.at). Confirm your sightseeing plans and pick up the free and essential city map with a list of museums and hours (also available at most hotels), the monthly program of concerts (called *Wien-Programm*), and the youth guide *(Ten Good Reasons for Vienna).* The TI also books rooms (for a €2.90 fee). While hotel and ticket booking agencies answer questions and give out maps and brochures at the train stations and airport, I'd rely on the TI if possible.

Consider the TI's handy €3.60 *Vienna from A to Z* booklet. Every important building sports a numbered flag banner that keys into this guidebook. A to Z numbers are keyed into the TI's city map. When lost, find one of the "famous-building flags" and match its number to your map. If you're at a famous building, check the map to see what other key numbers are nearby, then check the A to Z book description to see if you want to go in. This system is especially helpful for those just wandering aimlessly among Vienna's historic charms.

The much-promoted €17 Vienna Card might save the busy sight-seer a few euros. It gives you a 72-hour transit pass (worth €12) and discounts of 10–50 percent at the city's museums.

Arrival in Vienna

By Train at the West Station (Westbahnhof): Train travelers arriving from Munich, Salzburg, and sometimes Budapest land at the Westbahnhof. The *Reisebüro am Bahnhof* books hotels (for a €4 fee), has maps, answers questions, and has a train info desk (daily 7:30–21:00). To get to the city center (and most likely, your hotel), catch the U-3 metro (buy your ticket or transit pass—described below—from a *Tabak* shop in the station or from a machine—good on all city transit). U-3 signs lead down to the metro tracks. If your hotel is along Mariahilfer Strasse, your stop is on this line (direction Simmering; see "Sleeping," page 443). If you're sleeping in the center or just sightseeing, ride five stops to Stephansplatz, escalate in the exit direction Stephansplatz, and you'll hit the cathedral. The TI is a five-minute stroll down the busy Kärntner Strasse pedestrian street.

The Westbahnhof has a grocery store (daily 5:30–23:00), ATMs, Internet access, change offices, and storage facilities. Airport buses and taxis wait in front of the station.

By Train at the South Station (Südbahnhof): Those arriving from Prague, Poland, Slovenia, Croatia, and sometimes Budapest land here. The Südbahnhof has all the services, left luggage, and a TI (daily 9:00–19:00). To reach Vienna's center, follow the S *(Schnellbahn)* signs to the right and down the stairs, and take any train in the direction Floridsdorf; transfer in two stops (at Landsstrasse/Wien Mitte) to the U-3 line, direction Ottakring, which goes directly to Stephansplatz and Mariahilfer Strasse hotels. Also, tram D goes to the Ring, and bus #13A goes to Mariahilfer Strasse.

By Train at Franz Josefs Station: If you're coming from Krems (in the Danube Valley), you'll arrive at Vienna's Franz Josefs station. From here, take tram D into town. Better yet, get off at Spittelau (the stop before Josefs) and use its handy U-Bahn station.

By Plane: Vienna's airport (12 miles from town, tel. 01/7007-22233 for info and to connect with various airlines, www.viennaairport.com) is connected by S-Bahn to the very central Wien-Mitte station (€3, 2/hr, 24 min). Beginning in 2004, an even speedier new train connects the airport to Wien-Mitte (€8, 16 min). With these new, faster options now available, the express airport bus (€6, 3/hr, 20 min) will likely be phased out. Taxis into town cost about €35 (including €10 airport surcharge). Hotels arrange for fixed-rate car service to the airport (€30, 30-min ride).

Getting around Vienna

By Bus, Tram, and Metro: Take full advantage of Vienna's simple, cheap, and super-efficient transit system. Buses, trams, and the metro all use the same tickets. Buy your tickets from *Tabak* shops, station machines, or *Vorverkauf* offices in the station. You have lots of choices:

• single tickets (€1.50, €2 if bought on tram, good for 1 journey with necessary transfers)
• 24-hour pass (€5)
• 72-hour pass (€12)
• 7-day pass (€12.50, pass always starts on Mon)
• *Acht Tage Karte:* eight all-day trips for €24 (can be shared, for example, 4 people for 2 days each). With a per-person cost of €3/day (compared to €5/day for a 24-hour pass) this can be a real saver for groups. Kids under 15 travel free on Sundays and holidays.

Take a moment to study the eye-friendly city-center map on metro station walls to internalize how the metro and tram system can help you (metro routes are designated by the end-of-the-line stop). I use the tram mostly to zip along the Ring (tram #1 or #2) and take the metro to out-lying sights or hotels. The free tourist map has essentially all the lines marked, making the too-big €1.50 transit map unnecessary. Numbered lines (such as #38) are trams, numbers followed by an *A* (such as #38A) are buses. Lines that begin with *U* (e.g., U-3) are subways, or *U-Bahnen.* And blue lines are the speedier S-Bahns *(Schnellbahnen).*

Stamp a time on your ticket as you enter the system or tram (stamp it only the first time for a multiple-use pass). Cheaters pay a stiff €44 fine if caught—and then they make you buy a ticket. Rookies miss stops because they fail to open the door. Push buttons, pull latches—do whatever it takes. Study the excellent wall-mounted street map before you exit the metro. Choosing the right exit—signposted from the moment you step off the train—saves lots of walking (for information call 01/790-9105).

By Taxi: Vienna's comfortable, civilized, and easy-to-flag-down taxis start at €2. You'll pay about €8 to go from the Opera to the West Train Station (Westbahnhof). Consider the luxury of having your own car and driver. Johann (John) Lichtl is a kind, honest, English-speaking cabbie who can take up to four passengers in his car (€25/1 hr, €20/hr for 2 or more hours, mobile 0676/670-6750).

By Bike: Handy as you'll find the city's transit system, you may want to rent a bike (list of rental places at the TI). If the tram's not your style, you can circle the Ring on a convenient bike path.

By Buggy: Rich romantics get around by traditional horse and buggy. You'll see the horse buggies, called *Fiakers,* clip-clopping tourists on tours lasting 20 minutes (€40—old town), 40 minutes (€65—old town and the Ring), or one hour (€95—all of the above, but more thorough). You can share the ride and cost with up to five people. Because it's a kind of guided tour, before settling on a carriage, talk to a few drivers and pick one who's fun and speaks English.

Helpful Hints

Banking: ATMs are everywhere. Banks are open weekdays roughly from 8:00 to 15:00 and until 17:30 on Thursday. After-hours, you can change money at train stations, the airport, post offices, or the American Express office (Mon–Fri 9:00–17:30, Sat 9:00–12:00, closed Sun, Kärntner Strasse 21-23, tel. 01/5154-0456).

Post Offices: Choose from the main post office (Postgasse in center, open 24 hrs daily, handy metered phones), West Train Station (daily 6:00–23:00), South Train Station (daily 7:00–22:00), or near the Opera (Mon–Fri 7:00–19:00, closed Sat–Sun, Krugerstrasse 13).

English Bookstores: Consider the **British Bookshop** (Mon–Fri 9:30–18:30, Sat 9:30–17:00, closed Sun, at corner of Weihburggasse and Seilerstätte, tel. 01/512-1945; same hours at branch at Mariahilferstrasse 4, tel. 01/522-6730) or **Shakespeare & Co.** (Mon–Sat 9:00–19:00, closed Sun, north of Höher Markt square, Sterngasse 2, tel. 01/535-5053).

Internet Access: The TI has a list of Internet cafés. BigNet is the dominant outfit (about €3/hr, cheaper if you buy snack or drink, www.bignet.at), with lots of stations at Kärntner Strasse 61 (daily 10:00–24:00), Mariahilfer Strasse 27 (daily 8:00–2:00), and Hoher Markt 8–9 (daily 10:00–24:00). Surfland Internet Café is near the Opera (€1.40 to start, then €0.08/min, daily 10:00–23:00, Krugerstrasse 10, tel. 01/512-7701).

TOURS

Walks—The *Walks in Vienna* brochure at the TI describes Vienna's guided walks. The basic 90-minute Vienna First Glance introductory walk is given daily throughout the summer (€11, 14:00 from TI, in English and German, tel. 01/894-5363, www.wienguide.at).

Local Guides—The tourist board Web site (www.info.wien.at) has a long list of local guides with specialties and contact information. Lisa Zeiler is a good English-speaking guide (2-hr walks for €120—if she's booked, she can set you up with another guide, tel. 01/402-3688, lisa.zeiler@gmx.at).

Bus Tours—The Yellow Cab Sightseeing company offers a one-hour, €12, quickie double-decker bus tour with a tape-recorded narration, departing at the top of each hour (10:00–17:00) from in front of the Opera (corner of Operngasse). Vienna Sightseeing offers hop-on, hop-off tours covering the 13 predictable sightseeing stops. Given Vienna's excellent public transportation and this outfit's meager one-bus-per-hour frequency, I'd take this not to hop on and off, but only to get the narrated orientation drive through town (recorded narration in 8 languages, €20 for 24-hr ticket, or €12 if you stay on for the 60-minute circular ride). Their basic Vienna city sights tour includes a visit to the Schönbrunn Palace and a bus tour around town (€33, 3/day April–Nov, 2/day Dec–March, 3.5 hrs; to book this or get info on other tours, call 01/7124-6830).

Do-It-Yourself Tram Orientation Tour

In the 1860s, Emperor Franz Josef had the city's ingrown medieval wall torn down and replaced with a grand boulevard 190 feet wide. The road, arcing nearly three miles around the city's core, predates all the buildings that line it—so what you'll see is neoclassical, neo-Gothic, and neo-Renaissance. One of Europe's great streets, it's lined with many of the city's top sights. Trams #1 and #2 and a great bike path circle the whole route—and so should you.

This self-service tram tour, rated ▲▲, gives you a fun orientation and a ridiculously quick glimpse of the major sights as you glide by (€1.50, 30-min circular tour). Tram #1 goes clockwise; tram #2, counterclockwise. Most sights are on the outside, so use tram #2 (sit on the right, ideally in the front seat of the front car; or—for maximum view and minimum air—sit in the bubble-front seat of the second car). Start immediately across the street from the Opera House.

You can jump on and off as you go (trams come every 5 min). Read ahead and pay attention—these sights can fly by. Let's go:

☞ Immediately on the left: The city's main pedestrian drag, Kärntner Strasse, leads to the zigzag roof of **St. Stephan's Cathedral.** This tram tour makes a 360-degree circle around the cathedral, staying about this same distance from it.

☞ At first bend (before first stop): Look right toward the tall fountain and the guy on a horse. Schwartzenberg Platz shows off its **equestrian statue** of Prince Charles Schwartzenberg, who fought Napoleon. Behind that is the Russian monument (behind the fountain), which was built in 1945 as a forced thanks to the Soviets for liberating Austria from the Nazis. Formerly a sore point, now it's just ignored.

☞ Going down Schubertring, you reach the huge **Stadtpark** (city park) on the right, which honors many great Viennese musicians and composers with statues. At the beginning of the park, the gold-and-cream concert hall behind the trees is the **Kursalon,** opened in 1867 by the Strauss brothers, who directed many waltzes here. The touristy Strauss concerts are held here (see "Summer Music Scene," page 439).

☞ Immediately after next stop, look right: In the same park, the gilded statue of Waltz King **Johann Strauss** holds a violin as he did when he conducted his orchestra, whipping his fans into a two-stepping frenzy.

Vienna

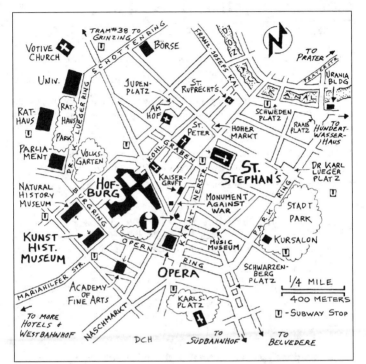

☞ At next stop at end of park: On the left, a green statue of Dr. Karl Lueger honors the popular man who was mayor of Vienna until 1910.

☞ At next bend: On the right, the quaint white building with military helmets decorating the windows was the Austrian ministry of war—back when that was a big operation. Field Marshal Radetzky, a military big shot in the 19th century under Franz Josef, still sits on his high horse. He's pointing toward the post office, the only Art Nouveau building facing the Ring. Locals call the architecture along the Ring "**historicism**" because it's all neo-this and neo-that—generally fitting the purpose of the particular building (for example, farther along the Ring, we'll see a neo-Gothic city hall—recalling when medieval burghers ran the city government in Gothic days, a neoclassical parliament building—celebrating ancient Greek notions of democracy, and a neo-Renaissance opera house—venerating the high culture filling it).

☞ At next corner: The white-domed building over your right shoulder as you turn is the Urania, Franz Josef's 1910 **observatory.** Lean forward and look behind it for a peek at the huge red cars of the giant 100-year-

VIENNA AT A GLANCE

▲▲▲**Opera** Dazzling, world-famous opera house. **Hours:** Visit by 35-min tour only, daily in English, July–Aug at 11:00, 13:00, 14:00, 15:00, and often at 10:00 and 16:00; Sept–June fewer tours, afternoon only, confirm tour times by calling.

▲▲▲**Hofburg Treasury** The Hapsburgs' collection of jewels, crowns, and other valuables—the best on the Continent. **Hours:** Wed–Mon 10:00–18:00, closed Tue.

▲▲▲**Schönbrunn Palace** Spectacular summer residence of the Hapsburgs, similar in grandeur to Versailles. **Hours:** April–Oct daily 8:30–17:00, July–Aug until 18:00, Nov–March daily 8:30–16:30, reservations recommended.

▲▲▲**Kunsthistorisches Museum** World-class exhibit of the Hapsburgs' art collection, including Raphael, Titian, Caravaggio, Bosch, and Brueghel. **Hours:** Tue–Sun 10:00–18:00, Thu until 21:00, closed Mon.

▲▲**St. Stephan's Cathedral** Beautiful, enormous Gothic cathedral in the center of Vienna. **Hours:** Church doors open Mon–Sat 6:00–22:00, Sun 7:00–22:00, officially only open for tourists Mon-Sat 8:30-11:30 & 13:00-16:30, Sun 13:00-16:30.

▲▲**Stephansplatz, Graben, and Kohlmarkt** Atmospheric pedestrian squares and streets around the cathedral. **Hours:** Always open.

▲▲**Hofburg Imperial Apartments** Lavish main residence of the Hapsburgs. **Hours:** Daily 9:00–17:00.

▲▲**Hofburg New Palace Museums** Uncrowded collection of armor, musical instruments, and ancient Greek statues, in the elegant halls of a Hapsburg palace. **Hours:** Wed–Mon 10:00–18:00, closed Tue.

▲▲**Kaisergruft** Crypt for the Hapsburg royalty. **Hours:** Daily 9:30–16:00.

▲▲**KunstHausWien** Modern art museum dedicated to zany local artist/environmentalist Hundertwasser. **Hours:** Daily 10:00–19:00.

▲▲**Haus der Musik** Modern musuem with interactive exhibits on Vienna's favorite pastime. **Hours:** Daily 10:00–22:00.

▲**Monument against War and Fascism** Powerful four-part statue remembering victims of the Nazis. **Hours:** Always open.

▲**Albertina Museum** Newly opened Hapsburg residence with ho-hum apartments and world-class permanent and temporary exhibits. **Hours:** Daily 10:00–18:00, Wed until 21:00.

▲**Kärntner Strasse** Vienna's lively main pedestrian drag, connecting the Opera with the cathedral. **Hours:** Always open.

▲**Lipizzaner Museum** Displays dedicated to the regal Lipizzaner Stallions; horse-lovers should check out their practice sessions. **Hours:** Museum open daily 9:00–18:00, stallions practice across the street roughly Feb–June and Sept–Oct, Tue–Sat 10:00–12:00 when the horses are in town, call to confirm.

▲**Augustinian Church** Hapsburg marriage church, now hosting an 11:00 Sunday Mass with wonderful music. **Hours:** Open daily.

▲**Imperial Furniture Collection** Eclectic collection of Hapsburg furniture. **Hours:** Tue–Sun 10:00–18:00, closed Mon.

▲**Academy of Fine Arts** Small but exciting collection with works by Bosch, Botticelli, Rubens, Guardi, and Van Dyck. **Hours:** Tue–Sun 10:00–16:00, closed Mon.

▲**Belvedere Palace** Elegant palace of Prince Eugene of Savoy, with a collection of 19th- and 20th-century Austrian art (including Klimt). **Hours:** Tue–Sun 10:00–18:00, closed Mon.

▲**Dorotheum** Vienna's highbrow auction house. **Hours:** Mon–Fri 10:00–18:00, Sat 9:00–17:00, closed Sun.

old Ferris wheel in Vienna's Prater Park (fun for families, described in "Top People-Watching and Strolling Sights," page 438).

☛ Now you're rolling along the **Danube Canal.** This "Baby Danube" is one of the many small arms of the river that once made up the Danube at this location. The rest have been gathered together in a mightier modern-day Danube, farther away. This neighborhood was thoroughly bombed in World War II. The buildings across the canal are typical of postwar architecture (1960s). This was the site of the original Roman town, Vindobona. In three long blocks, on the left (opposite the BP station, be ready—it passes fast), you'll see the ivy-covered walls and round Romanesque arches of St. Ruprechts, the oldest church in Vienna (built in the 11th century on a bit of Roman ruins). Remember, medieval Vienna was defined by that long-gone wall which you're tracing on this tour. Relax for a few stops until the corner.

☛ Leaving the canal, turning left up Schottenring, at first stop: On the left, the orange-and-white, neo-Renaissance temple of money, the **Börse,** is Vienna's stock exchange.

☛ Next stop, at corner: The huge, frilly, neo-Gothic church on the right is a "votive church," built as a thanks to God when an 1853 assassination attempt on Emperor Franz Josef failed. Ahead on the right (in front of tram stop) is the Vienna University building (established in 1365, it has no real campus as the buildings are scattered around town). It faces (on the left, behind a gilded angel) a chunk of the old city wall.

☛ At next stop on right: The neo-Gothic city hall, flying the flag of Europe, towers over **Rathaus Platz,** a festive site in summer with a huge screen showing outdoor movies, operas, and concerts. Immediately across the street (on left) is the **Hofburg Theater,** Austria's national theater.

☛ At next stop on right: The neo-Greek temple of democracy houses the **Austrian Parliament.** The lady with the golden helmet is Athena, goddess of wisdom. Across the street (on left) is the royal park called the "Volksgarten."

☛ After the next stop on the right is the **Natural History Museum,** the first of Vienna's huge twin museums. It faces the **Kunsthistorisches Museum,** containing the city's greatest collection of paintings. The **MuseumsQuartier** behind them completes the ensemble with a collection of mostly modern-art museums. A hefty statue of Empress Maria Theresa sits between the museums, facing the grand gate to the **Hofburg,** the emperor's palace (on left). Of the five arches, only the center one was used by the emperor. (Your tour is essentially finished. If you want to jump out here, you're at many of Vienna's top sights.)

☛ Fifty yards after the next stop, on the left through a gate in the black iron fence, is the statue of Mozart. It's one of many charms in the **Burggarten,** which until 1880 was the private garden of the emperor. Vienna had more than its share of intellectual and creative geniuses. A hundred yards farther (on left, just out of the park), the German philosopher Goethe sits in a big, thought-provoking chair playing trivia with Schiller (across the street on your right). Behind the statue of Schiller is the Academy of Fine Arts.

☛ Hey, there's the **Opera** again. Jump off the tram and see the rest of the city.

SIGHTS

Vienna's Old Center

▲▲▲**Opera (Staatsoper)**—The Opera, facing the Ring and near the TI, is a central point for any visitor. While the critical reception of the building 130 years ago led the architect to commit suicide, and though it's been rebuilt since the WWII bombings, it's still a dazzling place (€4.50, by guided 35-min tour only, daily in English, July–Aug at 11:00, 13:00, 14:00, 15:00, and often at 10:00 and 16:00; Sept–June fewer tours, afternoon only). Tours are often canceled for rehearsals and shows, so check the posted schedule or call 01/514-442-613.

The Vienna State Opera—with musicians provided by the Vienna Philharmonic Orchestra in the pit—is one of the world's top opera houses. There are 300 performances a year, except in July and August, when the singers rest their voices. Since there are different operas nearly nightly, you'll see big trucks out back and constant action backstage—all the sets need to be switched each day. Even though the expensive seats normally sell out long in advance, the opera is perpetually in the red and subsidized by the state.

Tickets for seats: For ticket information, call 01/513-1513 (phone answered daily 10:00–21:00, www.culturall.com or www.wiener -staatsoper.at). If seats aren't sold out, last-minute tickets (for pricey seats—up to €100) are sold for €30 from 9:00 to 14:00 only the day before the show.

Standing room: Unless Pavarotti is in town, it's easy to get one of 567 *Stehplätze* (standing-room spots, €2 at the top or €3.50 downstairs). While the front doors open 60 minutes early, a side door (on the Operngasse side, the door under the portico nearest the fountain) is open 80 minutes before curtain time, giving those in the know an early grab at standing-room tickets. Just walk in straight, then head right until you see the ticket booth marked *Stehplätze* (tel. 01/5144-42419). If fewer than 567 people are in line, there's no need to line up early. You can even buy standing-room tickets after the show has started—in case you want only a little taste of opera (see "Rick's crude tip," below). Dress is casual (but do your best) at the standing-room bar. Locals save their spot along the rail by tying a scarf to it.

Rick's crude tip: For me, three hours is a lot of opera. But just to see and hear the Opera House in action for half an hour is a treat. You can buy a standing-room spot and just drop in for part of the show.

Ushers don't mind letting tourists with standing-room tickets in for a short look. Ending time is posted in the lobby—you could stop by for just the finale. If you go at the start or finish, you'll see Vienna dressed up. With all the time you save, consider stopping by...

Sacher Café, home of every chocoholic's fantasy, the Sacher torte, faces the rear of the Opera. While locals complain that the cakes have gone downhill, a coffee and slice of cake here is €8 well invested. For maximum elegance, sit inside (daily 8:00–23:30, Philharmoniker Strasse 4, tel. 01/51456). The adjacent Café Mozart is better for a meal.

The U-Bahn station in front of the Opera is actually a huge underground shopping mall with fast food, newsstands, lots of pickpockets, and even an Opera Toilet Vienna experience (€0.50, *mit Musik*).

▲**Monument against War and Fascism**—A powerful four-part statue stands behind the Opera House on Albertinaplatz. The split white monument, *The Gates of Violence,* remembers victims of the 1938–1945 Nazi rule of Austria. A montage of wartime images—clubs and gas masks, a dying woman birthing a future soldier, slave laborers—sits on a pedestal of granite cut from the infamous quarry at Mauthausen, a nearby concentration camp. The hunched-over figure on the ground behind is a Jew forced to wash anti-Nazi graffiti off a street with a toothbrush. The statue with its head buried in the stone reminds Austrians of the consequences of not keeping their government on track. Behind that, the 1945 declaration of Austria's second republic is cut into the stone. This monument stands on the spot where several hundred people were buried alive while hiding in the cellar of a building demolished in a WWII bombing attack.

Austria was pulled into World War II by Germany, which annexed the country in 1938, saying Austrians were wannabe Germans, anyway. But Austrians are not Germans—never were, never will be. They're quick to tell you that while Austria was founded in 976, Germany wasn't born until 1870. For seven years during World War II (1938–1945), there was no Austria. In 1955, after 10 years of joint occupation by the victorious Allies, Austria regained total independence.

Across the square from the TI, you'll see what looks like a big terrace overlooking the street. This was actually part of Vienna's original defensive rampart. Next to it is the...

▲**Albertina Museum**—For years, this building—the oldest of the Hapsburgs' Vienna residences—was closed for reconstruction. Now it has re-opened its doors so that commoners like you and me can wander its regal halls and enjoy some world-class artwork.

The Albertina consists of various components. First, you can stroll through the Hapsburg state rooms (French classicism—lots of white marble—but pretty ho-hum stuff compared to the apartments in the Hofburg up the street). Second, the Albertina routinely borrows world-famous artwork for special exhibitions; in 2004, you'll see Paul Klee (Feb–April), Rembrandt (April–June), and Piet Mondrian (mid-Oct

2004 through Feb 2005). Finally, the Albertina also has its own spectacular collection of works by Michelangelo, Rubens, Rembrandt, and Raphael, plus a huge sampling of precise drawings by Albrecht Dürer. They're still experimenting with how to exhibit these masterpieces—so ask if your favorite artist is on display (state rooms only-€4, more for other exhibitions, audioguide also available for both permanent and temporary exhibits, daily 10:00–18:00, Wed until 21:00, overlooking Albertinaplatz across from TI and Opera House, tel. 01/534-830).

▲▲Kaisergruft (Remains of the Hapsburgs)—The crypt for the Hapsburg royalty, a block down the street from the Monument against War and Fascism, is covered in detail under "More Hofburg Sights," page 430.

▲Kärntner Strasse—This grand, mall-like street (traffic-free since 1974) is the people-watching delight of this in-love-with-life city. It points south in the direction of the southern Austrian state of Kärnten (for which it's named). Starting from the Opera, you'll find lots of action—shops, street music, the city casino (at #41), American Express (#21–23), and then, finally, the cathedral.

▲▲St. Stephan's Cathedral—Stephansdom is the Gothic needle around which Vienna spins. It has survived Vienna's many wars and symbolizes the city's freedom (church doors open Mon–Sat 6:00–22:00, Sun 7:00–22:00, officially only open for tourists Mon–Sat 8:30–11:30 & 13:00–16:30, Sun 13:00–16:30, otherwise closed for services; during services, you can enter back of church and get to north tower elevator, but unless you're attending Mass, you cannot enter main nave; entertaining English tours daily April–Oct at 15:45, €4, information board inside entry has tour schedules).

This is the third church to stand on this spot. (In fact, an older Romanesque chapel—the Virgilkapelle—is on display in the adjacent metro station.) The last bit of the 13th-century Romanesque church, the portal, round windows of the towers, and fascinating carvings in the tympanum, can be seen on the west end (above the entrance). The church survived the bombs of World War II, but, in the last days of the war, fires from the street fighting between Russian and Nazi troops leapt to the rooftop; the original timbered Gothic rooftop burned, and the cathedral's huge bell crashed to the ground. With a financial outpouring of civic pride, the roof of this symbol of Austria was rebuilt in its original splendor by 1952. The ceramic tiles are purely decorative (locals who contributed to the postwar reconstruction each "own" one for their donation).

Inside, find the Gothic sandstone **pulpit** in the middle of the nave (on left). A spiral stairway winds up to the lectern, surrounded and supported by the four Latin Church fathers: Saints Ambrose, Jerome, Gregory, and Augustine. The railing leading up swarms with symbolism: lizards (animals of light), battle toads (animals of darkness), and the "Dog of the Lord" standing at the top to be sure none of those toads pollutes the sermon. Below the toads, wheels with three parts (the Trinity) roll up, while wheels with four parts (standing for the four seasons, symbolizing mortal life) roll down. This work, by Anton Pilgram, has all the elements of flamboyant Gothic in miniature. But this was around 1500, and the Renaissance was going strong in Italy. While Gothic persisted in the North, the Renaissance spirit had already arrived. Pilgram included what's thought to be a rare self-portrait bust in his work (the guy with sculptor's tools, looking out a window under the stairs). Gothic art was done for the glory of God. Artists were anonymous. In the more humanist Renaissance, man was allowed to shine— and artists became famous.

You can ascend both towers, the north (via crowded elevator inside on the left) and the south (outside right transept, by spiral staircase). The north shows you a big **bell** (the 21-ton Pummerin, cast from the cannon captured from the Turks in 1683, supposedly the second biggest bell in the world that rings by swinging) but a mediocre view (€4, daily 8:30–17:30, July–Aug until 18:00, Nov–March until 17:00). The 450-foot-high **south tower,** called St. Stephan's Tower, offers a great view— 343 tightly wound steps up the spiral staircase (€3, daily 9:00–17:30, this hike burns about 1 Sacher torte of calories). From the top, use your *Vienna from A to Z* to locate the famous sights.

The forlorn **Cathedral Museum** (Dom Museum, outside left transept past horses) gives a close-up look at piles of religious paintings, statues, and a treasury (€5, Tue–Sat 10:00–17:00, closed Sun–Mon, Stephansplatz 6, tel. 01/515-523-560).

▲▲**Stephansplatz, Graben, and Kohlmarkt**—The atmosphere of the church square, Stephansplatz, is colorful and lively. At nearby Graben Street (which was once a *Graben,* or ditch—originally the moat for the Roman military camp), top-notch street entertainers dance around an exotic **plague monument** (at Bräuner Strasse). In medieval times, people did not understand the causes of plagues and figured they were a punishment from God. It was common for survivors to thank God with a monument like this one from the 1600s. Find Emperor Leopold, who ruled during the plague and made this statue in gratitude. (Hint: The typical inbreeding of royal families left him with a gaping underbite.) Below Leopold, Faith (with the help of a disgusting little cupid) tosses old naked women—symbolizing the plague—into the abyss.

Just before the plague monument is Dorotheergasse, leading to the Dorotheum auction house (see "More Sights in Vienna," page 434). Just beyond the monument, you'll pass a fine set of public WCs before dead-ending at the recommended restaurant Julius Meinl am Graben (see "Eating," page 450). Turning left on **Kohlmarkt,** you enter Vienna's most elegant shopping street (except for "American Catalog Shopping," at #5, second floor) with the emperor's palace at the end. Strolling Kohlmarkt, daydream about the edible window displays at **Demel** (#14). These delectable displays change about weekly, reflecting current happenings in Vienna. Drool through the interior (coffee and cake–€7.50). Shops like this boast "K. u. K."—good enough for the *König und Kaiser* (king and emperor—same guy). Just beyond Demel and across the street, at #1152, you can pop into a charming little Baroque carriage courtyard, with the surviving original carriage garages.

Kohlmarkt ends at Michaelerplatz, with a scant bit of Roman Vienna exposed at its center. On the left are the fancy Laden Plankl shop, with traditional formal wear, and the stables of the Spanish Riding School. Study the grand entry facade to the Hofburg Palace—it's neo-Baroque from around 1900. The four heroic giants are Hercules wrestling with his great challenges (much like the Hapsburgs, I'm sure). Opposite the facade, notice the modern Loos House, which was built at about the same time. It was nicknamed the "house without eyebrows" for the simplicity of its windows. This anti–Art Nouveau statement was actually shocking at the time. To quell some of the outrage, the architect added flower boxes. Enter the Hofburg Palace by walking through the gate, under the dome, and into the first square (In der Burg).

Vienna's Hofburg Palace

▲▲**Hofburg**—The complex, confusing, and imposing Imperial Palace, with 640 years of architecture, demands your attention. This first Hapsburg residence grew with the family empire from the 13th century until 1913, when the last "new wing" opened. The winter residence of the Hapsburg rulers until 1918, it's still the home of the Spanish Riding School, the Vienna Boys' Choir, the Austrian president's office, 5,000 government workers, and several important museums.

Rather than lose yourself in its myriad halls and courtyards, focus on three sections: the Imperial Apartments, Treasury, and Neue Burg (New Palace).

Hofburg orientation from In der Burg Square: The statue is of Emperor Franz II, grandson of Maria Theresa, grandfather of Franz Josef, and father-in-law of Napoleon. Behind him is a tower with three kinds of clocks (the yellow disk shows the stage of the moon tonight). On the right, a door leads to the Imperial Apartments. Franz faces the

Vienna's Hofburg Palace

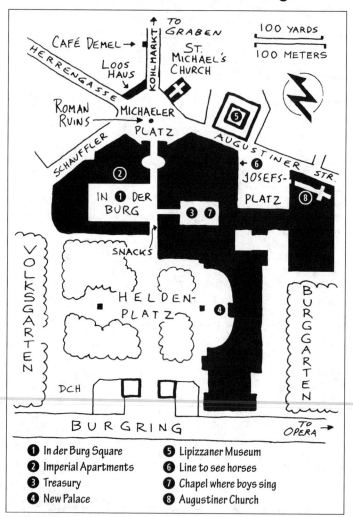

❶ In der Burg Square	❺ Lipizzaner Museum
❷ Imperial Apartments	❻ Line to see horses
❸ Treasury	❼ Chapel where boys sing
❹ New Palace	❽ Augustiner Church

oldest part of the palace. The colorful gate, which used to have a draw-bridge, leads to the 13th-century Swiss Court (named for the Swiss mercenary guards once stationed here), the Schatzkammer (treasury), and the Hofburgkapelle (palace chapel, where the Boys' Choir sings the Mass). For the Heroes' Square and the New Palace, continue opposite the way you entered In der Burg, passing through the left-most tunnel (with a tiny but handy sandwich bar—Hofburg Stüberl, Mon–Fri 7:00–18:00, Sat 9:00–15:00, Sun 10:00–15:00—your best bet if you need a bite or drink before touring the Imperial Apartments).

▲▲**Imperial Apartments (Kaiserappartements)**—These lavish, Versailles-type, "wish-I-were-God" royal rooms are the downtown version of the grander Schönbrunn Palace. If you're rushed and have time for only one palace, do this (€7.50, daily 9:00–17:00, last entry 16:30, from courtyard through St. Michael's Gate, just off Michaelerplatz, tel. 01/533-7570). Palace visits are a one-way romp through 20 rooms. You'll find some helpful English information within, and, with that and the following description, you won't need the €6.90 Hofburg guidebook. The €3.20 audioguide is only worthwhile for a Hapsburg history buff. Tickets include the royal silver and porcelain collection *(Silberkammer)* near the turnstile. If touring the silver and porcelain, do it first to save walking.

Get your ticket, study the big model of the palace complex, and (just after the turnstile) notice the family tree tracing the Hapsburgs from 1273 to their messy WWI demise. The first two rooms give an overview (in English) of Empress Elisabeth's fancy world—her luxury homes and fairy-tale existence. Throughout the tour, banners describe royal life.

Amble through the first several furnished rooms to the...

Waiting room for the audience room: A map and mannequins from the many corners of the Hapsburg realm illustrate the multi-ethnicity of the empire. Every citizen had the right to meet privately with the emperor. Three huge paintings entertained guests while they waited. They were propaganda, showing crowds of commoners enthusiastic about their Hapsburg royalty. On the right: An 1809 scene of the emperor returning to Vienna, celebrating news that Napoleon had begun his retreat. Left: The return of the emperor from the 1814 Peace of Paris, the treaty that ended the Napoleonic wars. (The 1815 Congress of Vienna that followed was the greatest assembly of diplomats in European history. Its goal: to establish peace through a "balance of power" among nations. While rulers ignored nationalism in favor of continued dynastic rule, this worked for about 100 years, until a colossal war—World War I—wiped out Europe's royal families.) Center: Less important, the emperor makes his first public appearance to adoring crowds after recovering from a life-threatening illness (1826). The chandelier—considered the best in the palace—is Baroque, made of Bohemian crystal.

Audience room: Suddenly, you were face-to-face with the emp. The portrait on the easel shows Franz Josef in 1915, when he was over 80 years old. Famously energetic, he lived a spartan life dedicated to duty. He'd stand at the high table here to meet with commoners, who came to show gratitude or make a request. (Standing kept things moving.) On the table, you can read a partial list of 56 appointments he had on January 3, 1910 (family name and topic of meeting).

EMPEROR FRANZ JOSEF

Franz Josef I—who ruled for 68 years (1848–1916)—was the embodiment of the Hapsburg Empire as it finished its six-century-long ride. Born in 1830, Franz Josef had a stern upbringing that instilled in him a powerful sense of duty and—like so many men of power—a love of things military. His uncle, Ferdinand I, was a dimwit, and, as the revolutions of 1848 were rattling royal families throughout Europe, the Hapsburgs replaced him, putting 18-year old Franz Josef on the throne. FJ was very conservative. But worse, he figured he was a talented military tactician, leading Austria into disastrous battles against Italy (which was fighting for its unification and independence) in the 1860s. His army endured severe, avoidable casualties. It was clear: FJ was a disaster as a general. Wearing his uniform to the end, he never saw what a dinosaur his monarchy was becoming, and never thought it strange that the majority of his subjects didn't even speak German. He had no interest in democracy and pointedly never set foot in Austria's parliament building. But, like his contemporary Queen Victoria, he was the embodiment of his empire—old-fashioned but sacrosanct. His passion for low-grade paperwork earned him the nickname "Joe bureaucrat." Mired in these petty details, he missed the big picture. He helped start a world war that ultimately ended the age of monarchs. The year 1918 marked the end of Europe's big royal families: Hohenzollerns (Prussia), Romanovs (Russia), and Hapsburgs (Austria).

Conference room: The emperor presided here over the equivalent of cabinet meetings. Remember, after 1867, he ruled the Austro-Hungarian Empire, so Hungarians sat at these meetings. The paintings on the wall show the military defeat of a popular Hungarian uprising...subtle.

Emperor Franz Josef's study: The desk was originally between the windows. Franz Josef could look up from his work and see his lovely, long-haired empress Elisabeth's reflection in the mirror. Notice the trompe l'oeil paintings above each door, giving the believable illusion of marble relief.

The walls between the rooms are wide enough to hide servants' corridors (the door to his valet's room is in the back left corner). The emperor lived with a personal staff of 14: three valets, four lackeys, two doormen, two manservants, and three chambermaids.

Emperor's bedroom: This features his famous spartan iron bed and portable washstand (necessary until 1880, when the palace got running water). A small painted porcelain portrait of the newlywed royal couple sits on the dresser. Franz Josef lived here after his estrangement from Sissy. An etching shows the empress—an avid hunter—riding sidesaddle while jumping a hedge. The big ornate stove in the corner was fed from behind. Through the 19th century, this was a standard form of heating.

Great salon: See the paintings of the emperor and empress in grand gala ballroom outfits from 1865.

Small salon: This is dedicated to the memory of the assassinated Emperor Maximilian of Mexico (bearded portrait, Franz Josef's brother, killed in 1867). This was also a smoking room—necessary in the early 19th century, when smoking was newly fashionable (but only for men—never in the presence of women).

Empress' bedroom and drawing room: This was Sissy's, refurbished neo-rococo in 1854. She lived here—the bed was rolled in and out daily—until her death in 1898.

Sissy's dressing/exercise room: Servants worked two hours a day on Sissy 's famous hair here. She'd exercise on the wooden structure. While she had a tough time with people, she did fine with animals. Her favorite circus horses, Flick and Flock, prance on the wall.

Sissy's bathroom: Detour into the behind-the-scenes palace. In the narrow passageway, you'll walk by Sissy's hand-painted porcelain WC (on the right). In the main bathroom, you'll see her huge copper tub (with the original wall coverings behind it). Sissy was the first Hapsburg to have running water in her bathroom. From here, you can wander (over the first linoleum ever used in Vienna—from around 1880) through the servants' quarters, with tropical scenes painted by Bergl in 1766. As you leave these rooms and re-enter the imperial world, look back to the room on the left.

Empress' great salon: The room is painted with Mediterranean escapes, the 19th-century equivalent of travel posters. The statue is of Elisa, Napoleon's oldest sister (by the neoclassical master, Canova). In the next room, at the end of the hall, admire the empress' hard-earned thin waist (20 inches at age 16, 21 inches at age 50...after giving birth to 4 children). Turn the corner and pass through the anterooms of Alexander's apartments.

Red salon: The Gobelin wall hangings were a 1776 gift from Marie Antoinette and Louis XVI in Paris to their Viennese counterparts.

Dining room: It's dinnertime, and Franz Josef has called his extended family together. The settings are modest...just silver. Gold was saved for formal state dinners. Next to each name card was a menu with the chef responsible for each dish. (Talk about pressure.) While the Hofburg had tableware for 4,000, feeding 3,000 was a typical day. The cellar was stocked with 60,000 bottles of wine. The kitchen was huge—

SISSY

Empress Elisabeth, Emperor Franz Josef's mysterious, narcissistic, and beautiful wife, is in vogue. She was mostly silent, worked out frantically to maintain her Barbie Doll figure, and spent hours each day tending to her ankle-length hair. Sissy's main goals in life seem to have been preserving her reputation as a beautiful empress and maintaining her fairy-tale hair. In spite of severe dieting and fanatic exercise, age took its toll. After turning 30, she allowed no more portraits to be painted and was generally seen in public with a delicate fan covering her face (and bad teeth). Complex and influential, she was adored by Franz Josef, whom she respected. Her personal mission and political cause was promoting Hungary's bid for nationalism. Her personal tragedy was the death of her son Rudolf, the crown prince, by suicide. Disliking Vienna and the confines of the court, she traveled more and more frequently. Over the years, the restless Sissy and her hardworking husband became estranged. In 1898, while visiting Geneva, Switzerland, she was murdered by an Italian anarchist. Sissy has been compared to Princess Diana because of her beauty, bittersweet life, and tragic death.

50 birds could be roasted on the hand-driven spits at once.

After a few more rooms and the shop, you're back on the street. Two quick lefts take you back to the palace square (In der Burg), where you can pass through the black, red, and gold gate and to the treasury. ▲▲▲Treasury (Weltliche und Geistliche Schatzkammer)—This Secular and Religious Treasure Room contains the best jewels on the Continent. Slip through the vault doors and reflect on the glitter of 21 rooms filled with scepters, swords, crowns, orbs, weighty robes, double-headed eagles, gowns, gem-studded bangles, and an eight-foot-tall, 500-year-old unicorn horn (or maybe the tusk of a narwhal)—which was considered incredibly powerful in the old days, giving its owner the grace of God. These were owned by the Holy Roman Emperor—a divine monarch. The well-produced, included audioguide provides a wealth of information (€7.50, Wed–Mon 10:00–18:00, closed Tue, follow Schatzkammer signs to the Schweizerhof, tel. 01/52524).

Room 2: The personal crown of Rudolf II has survived since 1602—it was considered too well-crafted to cannibalize for other crowns. This crown is a big deal because it's the adopted crown of the Austrian Empire, established in 1806 after Napoleon dissolved the Holy Roman Empire (so named because it tried to be the grand continuation of the Roman Empire). Pressured by Napoleon, the Austrian Francis II—who had been Holy Roman Emperor—became Francis I, Emperor of Austria. Francis I/II (the stern guy on the wall) ruled from 1792 to 1835. Look at the crown. Its design symbolically merges the typical medieval king's crown and a bishop's miter.

Rooms 3 and 4: These contain some of the coronation vestments and regalia needed for the new Austrian emperor.

Room 5: Ponder the Throne Cradle. Napoleon's son was born in 1811 and made king of Rome. The little eagle at the foot is symbolically not yet able to fly, but glory-bound. Glory is symbolized by the star, with dad's big *N* raised high.

Room 11: The collection's highlight is the 10th-century crown of the Holy Roman Emperor. The imperial crown swirls with symbolism "proving" that the emperor was both holy and Roman. The jeweled arch over the top is reminiscent of the parade helmet of ancient Roman emperors whose successors the HRE claimed to be. The cross on top says the HRE ruled as Christ's representative on earth. King Solomon's portrait (on the crown, right of cross) is Old Testament proof that kings can be wise and good. King David (next panel) is similar proof that they can be just. The crown's eight sides represent the celestial city of Jerusalem's eight gates. The jewels on the front panel symbolize the Twelve Apostles.

The nearby 11th-century Imperial Cross preceded the emperor in ceremonies. Encrusted with jewels, it carried a substantial chunk of *the* cross and *the* holy lance (supposedly used to pierce the side of Jesus while on the cross; both items displayed in the same glass case). Look behind the cross to see how it was actually a box that could be clipped open and shut. You can see bits of the "true cross" anywhere, but this is a prime piece—with the actual nail hole.

The other case has jewels from the reign of Karl der Grosse (Charlemagne), the greatest ruler of medieval Europe. Notice Charlemagne modeling the crown (which was made a hundred years after he died) in the tall painting adjacent.

Room 12: The painting shows the coronation of Josef II in 1764. He's wearing the same crown and royal garb you've just seen.

Room 16: Most tourists walk right by perhaps the most exquisite workmanship in the entire treasury, the royal vestments (15th century). Look closely—they are painted with gold and silver threads.

▲**Heroes' Square and the New Palace (Heldenplatz and the Neue Burg)**—This last grand addition to the palace, from just before World War I, was built for Franz Ferdinand but never used. (It was tradition for rulers not to move into their predecessor's quarters.) Its grand facade arches around Heldenplatz, or Heroes' Square. Notice statues of the two great Austrian heroes on horseback: Prince Eugene of Savoy (who beat the Turks that had earlier threatened Vienna) and Archduke Charles (first to beat Napoleon in a battle, breaking Nappy's image of invincibility and heralding the end of the Napoleonic age). The frilly spires of Vienna's neo-Gothic city hall break the horizon, and a line of horse-drawn carriages await their customers.

▲▲**New Palace Museums: Armor, Music, and Ancient Greek Statues**—The Neue Burg—technically part of the Kunsthistorisches Museum across the way—houses three fine museums (same ticket): an armory (with a killer collection of medieval weapons), historical musical instruments, and classical statuary from ancient Ephesus. The included audioguide brings the exhibits to life and lets you actually hear the fascinating old instruments in the collection being played. An added bonus is the chance to wander all alone among those royal Hapsburg halls, stairways, and painted ceilings (€7.50, Wed–Mon 10:00–18:00, closed Tue, almost no tourists, tel. 01/5252-4484).

More Hofburg Sights

These sights are near—and associated with—the palace.

▲**Lipizzaner Museum**—A must for horse-lovers, this tidy museum in the Renaissance Stallburg Palace shows (and tells in English) the 400-year history of the famous riding school. Lipizzaner fans have a warm spot in their hearts for General Patton, who, at the end of World War II—knowing that the Soviets were about to take control of Vienna—ordered a raid on the stable to save the horses and ensure the survival of their fine old bloodlines. Videos show the horses in action on TVs throughout the museum. The "dancing" originated as battle moves: *pirouette* (quick turns) and *courbette* (on hind legs to make a living shield for the knight). The 45-minute movie in the basement theater also has great horse footage (showings alternate between German and English).

A highlight for many is the opportunity to view the stable from a museum window and actually see the famous white horses just sitting there looking common. Don't bother waving...it's a one-way mirror (€5, daily 9:00–18:00, Reitschulgasse 2 between Josefsplatz and Michaelerplatz, tel. 01/533-8658).

Seeing the Lipizzaner Stallions: Seats for performances by Vienna's prestigious Spanish Riding School book up months in advance, but standing room is often available the same day (tickets-€35–105, standing room-€24–28, March–June and Sept–Oct Sun at 11:00, sometimes also Fri at 18:00). Lucky for the masses, training sessions (with music) in a chandeliered Baroque hall are open to the public (€11.50 at the door, roughly Feb–June and Sept–Oct, Tue–Sat 10:00–12:00 when the horses are in town, tel. 01/533-9031, www.srs.at). Tourists line up early at Josefsplatz, gate 2. Save money and avoid the wait by buying the €14.50 combo-ticket that covers both the museum and the training session (and lets you avoid that ticket line). Or, better yet, simply show up late. Tourists line up for hours to get in at 10:00, but almost no one stays for the full two hours—except for the horses. As people leave, new tickets are printed continuously, so you can just waltz in with no wait at all. If you arrive at 10:45, you'll see one group of horses finish and two more perform before they quit at noon.

▲**Augustinian Church**—The Augustinerkirche (on Josefsplatz) is the Gothic and neo-Gothic church where the Hapsburgs latched, then buried, their hearts (weddings took place here and the royal hearts are in the vault). Don't miss the exquisite, tomb-like Canova memorial (neo-classical, 1805) to Maria Theresa's favorite daughter, Maria Christina, with its incredibly sad white-marble procession. The church's 11:00 Sunday Mass is a hit with music-lovers—both a Mass and a concert, often with an orchestra accompanying the choir. To pay, contribute to the offering plate and buy a CD afterwards. (Programs are available at the table by the entry all week.)

▲▲**Kaisergruft, the Remains of the Hapsburgs**—Visiting the imperial remains is not as easy as you might imagine. These original organ donors left their bodies—about 150 in all—in the unassuming Kaisergruft (Capuchin Crypt), their hearts in the Augustinian Church (church open daily, but to see the goods you'll have to talk to a priest; Augustinerstrasse 3), and their entrails in the crypt below St. Stephan's Cathedral. Don't tripe.

Upon entering the Kaisergruft (€4, daily 9:30–16:00, last entry 15:40, behind Opera on Neuer Markt), buy the €0.50 map with a Hapsburg family tree and a chart locating each coffin.

The double coffin of Maria Theresa and her husband is worth a close look for its artwork. Maria Theresa outlived her husband by 15 years—which she spent in mourning. Old and fat, she installed a special lift enabling her to get down into the crypt to be with her dead husband (even though he had been far from faithful). The couple recline—Etruscan style—atop their fancy lead coffin. At each corner are the crowns of the Hapsburgs—the Holy Roman Empire, Hungary, Bohemia, and Jerusalem. Notice the contrast between the rococo splendor of Maria Theresa's tomb and the simple box holding her more modest son, Josef II (at his parents' feet). An enlightened monarch, Josef mothballed the too-extravagant Schönbrunn, secularized the monasteries, established religious tolerance within his realm, and freed the serfs. Josef was a model of practicality (he even invented a reusable coffin)—and very unpopular with other royals.

Franz Josef (1830–1916) is nearby in an appropriately austere military tomb. Flanking Franz Josef are the tombs of his son, Rudolf II, and Empress Elizabeth. Rudolf committed suicide in 1898 and—since the Church wouldn't allow such a burial for someone who took his own life—it took considerable legal hair-splitting to win Rudolf this spot (after examining his brain, it was determined that he was physically retarded and therefore incapable of knowingly killing himself). *Kaiserin* Elisabeth (1837–1898), a.k.a. Sissy, always gets the "Most Flowers" award.

In front of those three is the most recent Hapsburg tomb. Empress Zita was buried in 1989. Her burial procession was probably the last such Old Regime event in European history. The monarchy died hard in Austria.

Rather than chasing down all these body parts, remember that the magnificence of this city is the real remains of the Hapsburgs. Pan up. Watch the clouds glide by the ornate gables of Vienna.

▲**Imperial Furniture Collection (Kaiserliches Hofmobiliendepot)**— Bizarre, sensuous, eccentric, or precious, this is your peek at the Hapsburgs' furniture—from grandma's wheelchair to the emperor's spittoon—all thoughtfully described in English. The Hapsburgs had many palaces, but only the Hofburg was permanently furnished. The rest were furnished on the fly—set up and taken down by a gang of royal roadies called the "Depot of Court Movables" (Hofmobiliendepot). When the monarchy was dissolved in 1918, the state of Austria took possession of the Hofmobiliendepot's inventory—165,000 items. Now this royal storehouse is open to the public in a fine, new, sprawling museum. Don't go here for the Biedermeier or *Jugendstil* furnishings. The older Baroque and rococo pieces are the most impressive and tied most intimately to the royals. Combine a visit to this museum with a stroll down the lively shopping boulevard, Mariahilfer Strasse (€7, Tue–Sun 10:00–18:00, closed Mon, Mariahilfer Strasse 88, tel. 01/5243-3570).

Schönbrunn Palace

Among Europe's palaces, only Schloss Schönbrunn (worth ▲▲▲) rivals Versailles. Located four miles from the center, it was the Hapsburgs' summer residence. It's big (1,441 rooms), but don't worry—only 40 rooms are shown to the public. (The families of 260 civil servants actually rent simple apartments in the rest of the palace.)

While the exterior is Baroque, the interior was finished under Maria Theresa in let-them-eat-cake rococo. The chandeliers are either of hand-carved wood with gold-leaf gilding or of Bohemian crystal. Thick walls hid the servants as they ran around stoking the ceramic stoves from the back, and so on. Most of the public rooms are decorated in neo-Baroque, as they were under Franz Josef (ruled 1848–1916). When WWII bombs rained on the city and the palace grounds, the palace itself took only one direct hit. Thankfully, that bomb, which crashed through three floors—including the sumptuous central ballroom—was a dud.

Reservations and Hours: Schönbrunn suffers from crowds. To avoid the long delays in July and August (mornings are worst), make a reservation by telephone (tel. 01/8111-3239, answered daily 8:00–17:00). You'll get an appointment time and a ticket number. Check in at least 30 minutes early. Upon arrival, go to the group desk, give your number, pick up your ticket, and jump in ahead of the masses. If you show up in peak season without calling first, you deserve the frustration. Wait in line, buy your ticket, and wait until the listed time to enter (which could be tomorrow). Kill time in the gardens or coach museum (palace open April–Oct daily 8:30–17:00, July–Aug until 18:00, Nov–March daily 8:30–16:30). Crowds are worst from 9:30 to 11:30, especially on weekends and in July and August; it's least crowded from 12:00 to 14:00 and after 16:00.

Cost and Tours: The admission price is the price of the tour you select. Choose between two recorded audioguide tours: the Imperial Tour (22 rooms, €8, 35 min, Grand Palace rooms plus apartments of Franz Josef and Elisabeth) or the Grand Tour (40 rooms, €10.50, 50 min, adds apartments of Maria Theresa). The Schönbrunn Pass Classic includes the Grand Tour, Gloriette viewing terrace, maze, court bakery, and privy garden (€18, available April–Oct only; more info: www .schoenbrunn.at). I'd go for the Grand Tour.

Getting to Palace: Take tram #58 from Westbahnhof directly to the palace, or ride U-4 to Schönbrunn and walk 400 yards. The main entrance is in the left side of the palace as you face it.

Coach Museum Wagenburg—The Schönbrunn coach museum is a 19th-century traffic jam of 50 impressive royal carriages and sleighs. Highlights include silly sedan chairs, the death-black hearse carriage (used for Franz Josef in 1916, and most recently for Empress Zita in 1989), and an extravagantly gilded imperial carriage pulled by eight Cinderella horses. This was rarely used other than for the coronation of Holy Roman Emperors, when it was disassembled and taken to Frankfurt for the big event (€4.50, April–Oct daily 9:00–18:00, Nov–March daily 10:00–16:00, last entry 30 min before closing time, closed Mon in winter, 200 yards from palace, walk through right arch as you face palace, tel. 01/877-3244).

Palace Gardens—After strolling through all the Hapsburgs tucked neatly into their crypts, a stroll through the emperor's garden with countless commoners is a celebration of the natural evolution of civilization from autocracy into real democracy. As a civilization, we're doing well.

The sculpted **gardens** (with a palm house, €3.50, May–Sept daily 9:30–18:00, Oct–April daily 9:30–17:00) lead past Europe's oldest **zoo** (*Tiergarten,* built by Maria Theresa's husband for the entertainment and education of the court in 1752; €12, May–Sept daily 9:00–18:30, less off-season, tel. 01/877-9294) up to the **Gloriette,** a purely decorative monument celebrating an obscure Austrian military victory and offering a fine city view (viewing terrace-€2.30, included in €18 Schönbrunn Pass Classic, April–Sept daily 9:00–18:00, July–Aug until 19:00, Oct until 17:00, closed Nov–March). The park itself is free (daily sunrise to dusk, entrance on either side of the palace). A touristy choo-choo train makes the rounds all day, connecting Schönbrunn's many attractions.

More Sights in Vienna

▲▲▲**Kunsthistorisches Museum**—This exciting museum, across the Ring from the Hofburg Palace, showcases the grandeur and opulence of the Hapsburgs' collected artwork. There are European masterpieces galore, all well hung on one glorious floor, plus a fine display of Egyptian, classical, and applied arts.

Starting with the Italian wing of the museum, you get an immediate sense of the richness of this collection—you've walked right into the High Renaissance. Here, you'll see Raphael's graceful *Madonna of the Meadow* and Correggio's voluptuous *Jupiter and Io*. Meander through the Venetian Renaissance rooms to spend time with Titian, and land (with a thud) in the heart of Realism. (Caravaggio's still-shocking *David with the Head of Goliath* shows the artist was distinctly ahead of his time.)

The Baroque rooms offer pudgy winged babies galore—quite a contrast to the simple, direct, and down-to-earth Northern paintings by Dutch and Flemish artists only steps away. Enjoy Hieronymus Bosch's bizarrely crowded work and linger at the paintings by Peter Brueghel, the undisputed master of the slice-of-life village scene. Giuseppe Arcimboldo's *Summer* and *Water* (with faces made of produce and fish, respectively) are always crowd-pleasers. Try the helpful, included audio-guide for the full picture (€9, Tue–Sun 10:00–18:00, Thu until 21:00, closed Mon, tel. 01/525-240).

Sadly, one of the jewels in the museum's crown is now missing. Cellini's *Salt Cellar*, a divine golden salt bowl valued at €50 million, was stolen (to the anguish of the Vienna art world) in 2003 by expert thieves.

▲**Natural History Museum**—In the twin building facing the art museum, you'll find moon rocks, dinosaur stuff, and the fist-sized *Venus of Willendorf*—at 30,000 years old, the world's oldest sex symbol, found in the Danube Valley (€6.50, Wed–Mon 9:00–18:30, Wed until 21:00, closed Tue, tel. 01/521-770).

MuseumsQuartier—This sprawling collection of blocky, modernist museums is housed within the Baroque facade of the former imperial stables. The centerpiece is the **Leopold Museum,** which features modern Austrian art, including the best collection of works by Egon Schiele (1890–1918) and a few works by Kokoschka and Klimt (€9, Wed–Mon 10:00–19:00, Fri 10:00–21:00, closed Tue, behind Kunsthistorisches Museum, U-2 or U-3: Volkstheater/Museumsplatz, Museumsplatz 1–5, tel. 01/525-700).

The new **Museum of Modern Art** (Museum Moderner Kunst Stiftung Ludwig, a.k.a. Mumok), also in the MuseumsQuartier, is Austria's leading modern-art gallery. Its huge, state-of-the-art building displays revolving exhibits showing off art of the last generation—including Klee, Picasso, and Pop (€8, Tue–Sun 10:00–18:00, Thu until 21:00, closed Mon, tel. 01/525-001-440, www.mumok.at). Rounding out the sprawling MuseumsQuartier are an architecture museum,

Transeuropa, Electronic Avenue, children's museum, and the Kunsthalle Wien—an exhibition center for contemporary art. Various combo-tickets are available for those interested in more than just the Leopold Museum (visit www.mqw.at). Walk into the center from the Hofburg side, where the main entrance (with visitor center and info room) leads to a big courtyard with cafés, fountains, and huge lounging sponges surrounded by the quarter's various museums.

▲**Academy of Fine Arts**—This small but exciting collection includes works by Bosch, Botticelli, and Rubens; a Venice series by Guardi; and a self-portrait by 15-year-old Van Dyck (€5, Tue–Sun 10:00–16:00, closed Mon, 3 blocks from Opera at Schillerplatz 3, tel. 01/5881-6225). As you wander the halls of this academy, ponder how history might have been different if Hitler—who applied to study architecture here but was rejected—had been accepted as a student.

▲▲**KunstHausWien: Hundertwasser Museum**—This "make yourself at home" museum is a hit with lovers of modern art. It mixes the work and philosophy of local painter/environmentalist Hundertwasser. Stand

in front of the colorful checkerboard building and consider Hundertwasser's style. He was against "window racism." Neighboring houses allow only one kind of window. But 100H$_2$O's windows are each different—and he encouraged residents to personalize them. He recognized tree tenants as well as human tenants. His buildings are spritzed with a forest and topped with dirt and grassy little parks—close to nature, good for the soul. Floors and sidewalks are irregular—to "stimulate the brain" (although current residents complain it just causes wobbly furniture and sprained ankles). Thus 100H$_2$O waged a one-man fight—during the 1950s and 1960s, when concrete and glass ruled—to save the human soul from the city. (Hundertwasser claimed that "straight lines are godless.") Inside the museum, start with his interesting biography (which ends in 2000). His fun-loving paintings are half *Jugendstil* ("youth style") and half just kids' stuff. Notice the photographs from his 1950s days as part of Vienna's bohemian scene. Throughout the museum, notice the fun philosophical quotes from an artist who believed, "If man is creative, he comes nearer to his creator" (€8 for Hundertwasser Museum, €14 combo-ticket includes special exhibitions, half price on Mon, daily 10:00–19:00, extremely fragrant and colorful garden café, U-3: Landstrasse, Weissgerberstrasse 13, tel. 01/712-0491).

The KunstHausWien provides by far the best look at Hundertwasser. For an actual lived-in apartment complex by the green master, walk five minutes to the one-with-nature **Hundertwasserhaus** (free, at

Löwengasse and Kegelgasse). This complex of 50 apartments, subsidized by the government to provide affordable housing, was built in the 1980s as a breath of architectural fresh air in a city of boring, blocky apartment complexes. While not open to visitors, it's worth visiting for its fun-loving and colorful patchwork exterior and the Hundertwasser festival of shops across the street. Don't miss the view from Kegelgasse to see the "tree tenants" and the internal winter garden residents enjoy.

▲**Belvedere Palace**—This is the elegant palace of Prince Eugene of Savoy—the still-much-appreciated conqueror of the Turks. Eugene, a Frenchman considered too short and too ugly to be in the service of Louis XIV, offered his services to the Hapsburgs. While he was short and ugly indeed, he became the greatest military genius of his age. Today, his palace houses the Austrian gallery of 19th- and 20th-century art. Skip the lower palace and focus on the garden and the upper palace *(Oberes Belvedere)* for a winning view of the city, a fine collection of *Jugendstil* art, and Vienna's best look at the dreamy work of Gustav Klimt (€7.50, Tue–Sun 10:00–18:00, closed Mon, entrance at Prinz Eugen Strasse 27, tel. 01/7955-7134). Your ticket includes the Austrian Baroque and Gothic art in the Lower Palace.

▲▲**Haus der Musik**—Vienna's House of Music has a small first-floor exhibit on the Vienna Philharmonic, and upstairs you'll enjoy fine audiovisual exhibits on each of the famous hometown boys (Haydn, Mozart, Beethoven, Strauss, and Mahler). But the museum is unique for its effective use of interactive touch-screen computers and head-phones to actually explore the physics of sound. You can twist, dissect, and bend sounds to make your own musical language, merging your voice with a duck's quack or a city's traffic roar. Wander through the "sonosphere" and marvel at the amazing acoustics—I could actually hear what I thought only a piano tuner could hear. Pick up a virtual baton to conduct the Vienna Philharmonic Orchestra (each time you screw up, the orchestra stops and ridicules you). A computer will help you compose your own waltz by throwing dice. Really seeing the place takes time. It's open late and makes a good evening activity (€10, daily 10:00–22:00, 2 blocks from Opera at Seilerstatte 30, tel. 01/51648, www.hdm.at).

▲**Vienna's Auction House, the Dorotheum**—For an aristocrat's flea market, drop by Austria's answer to Sotheby's, the Dorotheum. Its five floors of antique furniture and fancy knickknacks have been put up either for immediate sale or auction, often by people who inherited old things they don't have room for (Mon–Fri 10:00–18:00, Sat 9:00–17:00, closed Sun, classy little café on second floor, between Graben and Hofburg at Dorotheergasse 17, tel. 01/515-600). Fliers show schedules for actual auctions, which you are welcome to attend.

Judenplatz Memorial and Museum—Judenplatz marks the location of Vienna's 15th-century Jewish community, one of Europe's largest at the

JUGENDSTIL

Vienna gave birth to its own curvaceous brand of Art Nouveau around the early 1900s: *Jugendstil* ("youth style"). The TI has a brochure laying out Vienna's 20th-century architecture. The best of Vienna's scattered *Jugendstil* sights: the Belvedere Palace collection, the clock on Hoher Markt (which does a musical act at noon), and the gilded, cabbage-domed building at the Ring end of the Naschmarkt (U-1, U-2, or U-4: Karlsplatz, and follow signs to Secession). This gallery (housing a huge Beethoven frieze by Klimt) proclaims the movement's slogan: "To each century its art, and to art its liberty." Klimt, Wagner, and friends (who called themselves the Vienna Secession) first exhibited their "liberty-style" art here in 1897.

time. The square, once filled with a long-gone synagogue, is now dominated by a blocky memorial to the 65,000 Austrian Jews killed by the Nazis. The memorial—a library turned inside out—symbolizes Jews as "people of the book" and causes one to ponder the huge loss of culture, knowledge, and humanity that took place during 1938 to 1945.

The Judenplatz Museum, while sparse, has displays on medieval Jewish life and a well-done video re-creating community scenes from five centuries ago. Wander the scant remains of the medieval synagogue below street level—discovered during the construction of the Holocaust memorial. This was the scene of a medieval massacre. Since Christians weren't allowed to lend money, Jews were Europe's moneylenders. As so often happened in Europe, when Christian locals fell too deeply into debt, they found a convenient excuse to wipe out the local ghetto—and their debts at the same time. In 1421, 200 of Vienna's Jews were burned at the stake. Others who refused a forced conversion committed mass suicide in the synagogue (€3, €7 combo-ticket includes a synagogue and Jewish Museum of the City of Vienna, Sun–Thu 10:00–18:00, Fri 10:00–14:00, closed Sat, Judenplatz 8, tel. 01/535-0431).

Honorable Mention—There's much, much more. The city map lists everything. If you're into butterflies, Esperanto, undertakers, tobacco, clowns, firefighting, Freud, or the homes of dead composers, you'll find them all in Vienna. Several good museums that try very hard but are submerged in the greatness of Vienna include: **Jewish Museum of the City of Vienna** (€5, or €7 combo-ticket includes synagogue and Judenplatz Museum—listed above, Sun–Fri 10:00–18:00, Thu until 20:00, closed Sat, Dorotheergasse 11, tel. 01/535-0431, www.jmw.at), **Historical Museum of the City of Vienna** (Tue–Sun 9:00–18:00, closed

Mon, Karlsplatz), **Folkloric Museum of Austria** (Tue–Sun 10:00–17:00, closed Mon, Laudongasse 15, tel. 01/406-8905), and **Museum of Military History**, one of Europe's best if you like swords and shields (Heeresgeschichtliches Museum, Sat–Thu 9:00–17:00, closed Fri, Arsenal district, Objekt 18, tel. 01/795-610). The vast **Austrian Museum of Applied Arts** (Österreichisches Museum für Angewandte Kunst, or MAK) is Vienna's answer to London's Victoria & Albert collection. The museum shows off the fancies of local aristocratic society, including a fine *Jugendstil* collection (€8, free Sat, open Tue–Sun 10:00–18:00, Tue until 24:00, closed Mon, Stubenring 5, tel. 01/711-360, www.mak.at).

For a walk in the **Vienna Woods,** catch the U-4 metro to Heiligenstadt, then bus #38A to Kahlenberg, for great views and a café overlooking the city. From there, it's a peaceful 45-minute downhill hike to the *Heurigen* of Nussdorf or Grinzing to enjoy some wine (see "Wine Gardens," page 441).

Top People-Watching and Strolling Sights

▲**City Park**—Vienna's Stadtpark is a waltzing world of gardens, memorials to local musicians, ponds, peacocks, music in bandstands, and locals escaping the city. Notice the *Jugendstil* entrance at the Stadtpark metro station. The Kursalon, where Strauss was the violin-toting master of waltzing ceremonies, hosts daily touristy concerts in 3/4 time.

▲**Prater**—Vienna's sprawling amusement park tempts many visitors with its huge 220-foot-tall, famous, and lazy Ferris wheel *(Riesenrad),* roller coaster, bumper cars, lilliputian railroad, and endless eateries. Especially if you're traveling with kids, this is a fun, goofy place to share the evening with thousands of Viennese (daily 9:00–24:00 in summer, but quiet after 22:00, U-1: Praterstern). For a local-style family dinner, eat at Schweizerhaus (good food, great beer) or Wieselburger Bierinsel.

Sunbathing—Like most Europeans, the Austrians worship the sun. Their lavish swimming centers are as much for tanning as swimming. To find the scene, follow the locals to their "Danube Sea" and a 20-mile, skinny, man-made beach along Danube Island. It's traffic-free concrete and grass, packed with in-line skaters and bikers, with rocky river access and a fun park (easy U-Bahn access on U-1 to Donauinsel).

▲**Naschmarkt**—Vienna's ye olde produce market bustles daily near the Opera along Wienzeile Street. It's likeably seedy and surrounded by sausage stands, Turkish *döner kebab* stalls, cafés, and theaters. Each Saturday, it's infested by a huge flea market where, in olden days, locals would come to hire a monkey to pick little critters out of their hair (Mon–Fri 7:00–18:00, Sat 6:00–18:00, closed Sun, closes earlier in winter, U-4: Kettenbruckengasse). For a picnic park, walk a block down Schleifmuhlgasse.

Summer Music Scene

Vienna is Europe's music capital. It's music *con brio* from October through June, reaching a symphonic climax during the Vienna Festival each May and June. Sadly, in July and August, the Boys' Choir, the Opera, and many more music companies are—like you—on vacation. But Vienna hums year-round with live classical music. In the summer, you have these basic choices:

Touristy Mozart and Strauss Concerts—If the music comes to you, it's touristy—designed for flash-in-the-pan Mozart fans. Powdered-wig orchestra performances are given almost nightly in grand traditional settings (€25–50). Pesky wigged-and-powdered Mozarts peddle tickets in the streets with slick sales pitches about the magic of the venue and the

 quality of the musicians. Second-rate orchestras, clad in historic costumes, perform the greatest hits of Mozart and Strauss. While there's not a local person in the audience, the tourists generally enjoy the evening. To sort through all your options, check with the ticket office in the TI (same price as on the street but with all venues to choose from).

Strauss Concerts in the Kursalon—For years, Strauss concerts have been held in the Kursalon, where the Waltz King himself directed wildly popular concerts 100 years ago (€32–49, 4 concerts nightly April–Oct, 1 concert nightly other months, tel. 01/512-5790). Shows are a touristy mix of ballet, waltzes, and a 15-piece orchestra in wigs and old outfits. For the cheap option, enjoy a summer afternoon coffee concert (free if you buy a drink weekends and maybe also weekdays July–Aug 15:00–17:00).

Serious Concerts—These events, including the Opera, are listed in the monthly *Wien-Programm* (available at TI). Tickets run from €36 to €75 (plus a stiff 22 percent booking fee when booked in advance or through a box office like the one at the TI). If you call a concert hall directly, they can advise you on the availability of (cheaper) tickets at the door. Vienna takes care of its starving artists (and tourists) by offering cheap standing-room tickets to top-notch music and opera (1 hour before show time).

Vienna's **Summer of Music Festival** assures that even from June through September, you'll find lots of great concerts, choirs, and symphonies (special *Klang Bogen* brochure at TI; get tickets at Wien Ticket pavilion off Kärntner Strasse next to Opera House or go directly to location of particular event; Summer of Music tel. 01/42717).

Musicals—The Wien Ticket pavilion sells tickets to contemporary American and British musicals (€10–95 with €2.50 standing room) and offers these tickets at half price from 14:00 until 17:00 the day of the show. Or you can reserve (full-price) tickets for the musicals by calling up to one day ahead (call combined office of the 3 big theaters at tel. 01/58885).

Vienna Boys' Choir—The boys sing (heard but not seen, from a high balcony) at Mass in the Imperial Chapel *(Hofburgkapelle)* of the Hofburg (entrance at Schweizerhof, from Josefs Platz go through tunnel) 9:15–10:30 on Sundays, except in July and August. While seats must be reserved two months in advance (€5–29, reserve by fax, e-mail, or mail: fax 011-431-533-992-775 from the U.S., hmk@aon.at, or write Hof-musikkapelle, Hofburg-Schweizerhof, 1010 Wien; tel. for information only—cannot book tickets—01/533-9927), standing room inside is free and open to the first 60 who line up. Rather than line up early, you can simply swing by and stand in the narthex just outside, where you can hear the boys and see the Mass on a TV monitor. Boys' Choir concerts (on stage at the Musikverein) are also given Fridays at 16:00 in May, June, September, and October (€35–48, standing room goes on sale at 15:30 for €15, Karlsplatz 6, U-1, U-2, or U-4: Karlsplatz, tel. 01/5880-4141). They're nice kids, but, for my taste, not worth all the commotion. Remember, many churches have great music during Sunday Mass. Just 200 yards from the Boys' Choir chapel, Augustinian Church has a glorious 11:00 service each Sunday.

CAFÉS

In Vienna, the living room is down the street at the neighborhood coffeehouse. This tradition is just another example of Viennese expertise in good living. Each of Vienna's many long-established (and sometimes even legendary) coffeehouses has its individual character (and characters). They offer newspapers, pastries, sofas, elegance, smoky ambience, and "take all the time you want" charm for the price of a cup of coffee. Order it *melange* (with a little milk) or *schwarzer* (black). Rather than buy the *Herald Tribune* ahead of time, buy a cup of coffee and read it for free, Vienna-style.

These are my favorites: **Café Hawelka,** with a dark, "brooding Trotsky" atmosphere, paintings by struggling artists who couldn't pay for coffee, a saloon-wood flavor, chalkboard menu, smoked velvet couches, an international selection of newspapers, and a phone that rings for regulars (Wed–Mon 8:00–2:00, Sun from 16:00, closed Tue, just off Graben, Dorotheergasse 6); **Café Central,** with *Jugendstil* decor and great *Apfelstrudel* (high prices and stiff staff, Mon–Sat 8:00–22:00, Sun 10:00-18:00, Herrengasse 14, tel. 01/533-376-326); the **Café Sperl,** dating from 1880 with furnishings identical to the day it opened, from the coat tree to the chairs (Mon–Sat 7:00–23:00, Sun 11:00–20:00 except closed Sun July–Aug, just off Naschmarkt near Mariahilfer

Strasse, Gumpendorfer 11, tel. 01/586-4158); and the basic, untouristy **Café Ritter** (daily 7:30–23:30, Mariahilfer Strasse 73, U-3: Neubaugasse, near several recommended hotels, tel. 01/587-8237).

WINE GARDENS

The *Heurige* is a uniquely Viennese institution celebrating the *Heurige,* or new wine. When the Hapsburgs let Vienna's vintners sell their own wine tax-free, several hundred families opened *Heurigen* (wine-garden restaurants clustered around the edge of town), and a tradition was born. Today, they do their best to maintain the old-village atmosphere, serving the homemade new wine (the last vintage, until November 11, when a new vintage year begins) with light meals and strolling musicians. Most *Heurigen* are decorated with enormous antique presses from their vineyards. Wine gardens might be closed on any given day; always call ahead to confirm, if you have your heart set on a particular place. (For a near-*Heurige* experience right downtown, drop by Gigerl Stadtheuriger; see "Eating," page 450.)

At any *Heurige,* fill your plate at a self-serve cold-cut buffet (€6–9 for dinner). Dishes to look out for: *Stelze* (grilled knuckle of pork), *Fleischlaberln* (fried ground meat patties), *Schinkenfleckerln* (pasta with cheese and ham), *Schmalz* (a spread made with pig fat), *Blunzen* (black pudding...sausage made from blood), *Presskopf* (jellied brains and innards), *Liptauer* (spicy cheese spread), *Kornspitz* (whole-meal bread roll), and *Kummelbraten* (crispy roast pork with caraway). Waitresses will then take your wine order (€2.20 per quarter liter, about 8 oz). Many locals claim it takes several years of practice to distinguish between *Heurige* and vinegar.

There are more than 1,700 acres of vineyards within Vienna's city limits, and countless *Heurige* taverns. For a *Heurige* evening, rather than go to a particular place, take a tram to the wine-garden district of your choice and wander around, choosing the place with the best ambience.

Getting to the *Heurigen:* You have three options: trams and buses, a 15-minute taxi ride, or a goofy tourist train.

Trams make a trip to the Vienna Woods quick and affordable. The fastest way is to ride U-4 to its last stop, Heiligenstadt, where trams and buses in front of the station fan out to the various neighborhoods. Ride tram D to its end point for Nussdorf. Ride bus #38A for Grinzing and on to the Kahlenberg viewpoint—#38A's end station (note that tram #38—different from bus #38A—starts at the Ring and finishes at Grinzing). To get to Neustift am Walde, ride U-6 to Nussdorfer Strasse and catch bus #35A. Connect Grinzing and Nussdorf with bus #38A and tram D (transfer at Grinzingerstrasse).

The **Heuriger Express** train is tacky but handy and relaxing, chugging you on a hop-on, hop-off circle from Nussdorf through Grinzing and around the Vienna Woods (€7.30, 50 min, daily April–Oct

12:00–19:00, departs from end station of tram D in Nussdorf at the top of every hr, tel. 01/479-2808).

Here are four good *Heurige* neighborhoods:

Grinzing: Of the many *Heurige* suburbs, Grinzing is the most famous, lively...and touristy. Many people precede their visit to Grinzing by riding bus #38A to its end (up to Kahlenberg for a grand Vienna view) and then ride 20 minutes back into the *Heurige* action. From the Grinzing tram stop, follow Himmelgasse uphill toward the onion-top dome. You'll pass plenty of wine gardens—and tour buses—on your way up. Just past the dome, you'll find the heart of the *Heurige.*

Pfarrplatz: Between Grinzing and Nussdorf, this area features several decent spots, including the famous and touristy **Beethovenhaus** (Mon–Sat 16:00–24:00, Sun 11:00–24:00, bus #38A stop: Fernsprechamt/Heiligenstadt, walk 5 min uphill on Dübling Nestelbachgasse to Pfarrplatz 2, tel. 01/370-3361). Beethoven lived—and composed his Sixth Symphony—here in 1817. He hoped the local spa would cure his worsening deafness. **Weingut and Heuriger Werner Welser,** a block uphill from Beethoven's place, is lots of fun, with music nightly from 19:00 (daily 15:30–24:00, Probusgasse 12, tel. 01/318-9797).

Nussdorf: A less-touristy district—characteristic and popular with locals—Nussdorf has plenty of *Heurige* ambience. Right at the end station of tram D, you'll find three long and skinny places side by side: **Heuriger Kierlinger** (daily 15:30–24:00, Kahlenbergerstrasse 20, tel. 01/370-2264), **Steinschaden** (daily 15:00–24:00, Kahlenbergerstrasse 18, tel. 01/370-1375), and **Schübel-Auer Heuriger** (Tue–Sat 16:00–24:00, closed Sun–Mon, Kahlenbergerstrasse 22, tel. 01/370-2222). Walk through any of these and you pop out on Kahlenbergerstrasse, where a walk uphill takes you to some more eating and drinking fun: **Bamkraxler** (the tree jumper), the only beer garden amid all these vineyards. It's a fun-loving, youthful place with fine keg beer and a regular menu, rather than the *Heurige* cafeteria line (€6–10 meals, veggie options, Tue–Sat 16:00–24:00, Sun 11:00–24:00, closed Mon, Kahlenbergerstrasse 17, tel. 01/318-8800).

Neustift am Walde: This neighborhood has lots of *Heurigen,* plenty of charm, and the fewest tourists of all (U-6: Nussdorferstrasse, then bus #35A stop: Neustift am Walde). A line of big, venerable places invite you through welcoming arches that lead up terraced backyards filled with rough tables until you hit the actual vineyards. Pop into **Weingut Wolff** (Wed–Sun 16:00–24:00, closed Mon–Tue, Rathstrasse 50, tel. 01/440-3727) and **Fuhrgassl Huber Weingut** (daily 14:00–24:00, live music Tue–Sat 19:00–24:00, Neustift am Walde 68, tel. 01/440-1405) and take your choice. If you want to really be rural—surrounded by vineyards—hike 10 minutes from there to **Weinhof Zimmermann** (Mon–Fri 15:00–23:00, Sat–Sun 12:00–23:00, Mitterwurzergasse 20, tel. 01/440-1207). Find Mitterwurzergasse—the lane behind the two places listed above—and hike to the right. Look for the sign taking you uphill into a farm. There you'll see 50 rough picnic tables between the farmhouse and the vines.

NIGHTLIFE

If old music and new wine aren't your thing, Vienna has plenty of alternatives. For an up-to-date rundown on fun after dark, get the TI's free *Ten Good Reasons for Vienna* booklet. An area known as the "Bermuda Dreieck" (Triangle), north of the cathedral between Rotenturmstrasse and Judengasse, is the hot local nightspot, with lots of classy pubs, or *Beisl* (such as Krah Krah, Salzamt, Slammer, and Bermuda Bräu), and music spots. On balmy summer evenings, the liveliest scene is at Danube Island (especially during the Summer Stage festival). If you just want a good movie, the English Cinema Haydn plays three different English-language movies nightly (Mariahilfer Strasse 57, tel. 01/587-2262).

SLEEPING

Within the Ring, in the Old City Center

You'll pay extra to sleep in the atmospheric old center, but if you can afford it, staying here gives you the best classy Vienna experience.

$$$ **Pension Pertschy** circles an old courtyard and is bigger and more hotelesque than the others listed here. Its 50 rooms are huge, but well-worn and a bit musty. Those on the courtyard are quietest (Sb-€77, Db-€112–162 depending on size, cheaper off-season, extra bed-€30, non-smoking rooms, elevator, U-1 or U-3: Stephensplatz, Hapsburgergasse 5, tel. 01/534-490, fax 01/534-4949, www.pertschy.com, pertschy @pertschy.com).

$$$ **Pension Neuer Markt** is a four-star place that feels family-run, with 37 quiet, comfy, old-feeling rooms in a perfectly central locale (Ss-€81, Sb-€95, Ds-€88, Db-€112, prices can vary with season and room size, extra bed-€20, elevator, Seilergasse 9, tel. 01/512-2316, fax 01/513-9105, www.hotelpension.at/neuermarkt, neuermarkt@hotelpension.at).

$$$ **Pension Aviano** is another peaceful four-star place, with 17 comfortable rooms on the fourth floor above lots of old center action (Sb-€82, Db-€122–142 depending on size, 15 percent cheaper Nov–March, extra bed-€30, elevator, non-smoking rooms, between Neuer Markt and Kärntner Strasse at Marco d'Avianogasse 1, tel. 01/512-8330, fax 01/5128-3306, aviano@pertschy.com).

$$$ **Hotel Schweizerhof** is a classy 55-room place with big rooms, three-star comforts, and a more formal ambience. It's centrally located midway between St. Stephan's Cathedral and the Danube canal, with all its rooms at least four floors above any street noise (Sb-€84–88, Db-€109–131, Tb-€131–146, low prices are for July–Aug and slow times, with cash and

Hotels and Restaurants in Central Vienna

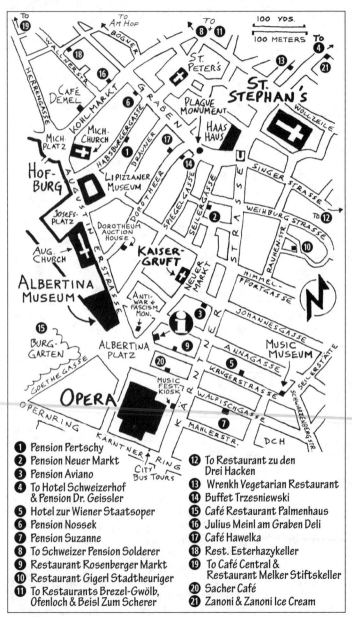

1 Pension Pertschy
2 Pension Neuer Markt
3 Pension Aviano
4 To Hotel Schweizerhof & Pension Dr. Geissler
5 Hotel zur Wiener Staatsoper
6 Pension Nossek
7 Pension Suzanne
8 To Schweizer Pension Solderer
9 Restaurant Rosenberger Markt
10 Restaurant Gigerl Stadtheuriger
11 To Restaurants Brezel-Gwölb, Ofenloch & Beisl Zum Scherer

12 To Restaurant zu den Drei Hacken
13 Wrenkh Vegetarian Restaurant
14 Buffet Trzesniewski
15 Café Restaurant Palmenhaus
16 Julius Meinl am Graben Deli
17 Café Hawelka
18 Rest. Esterhazykeller
19 To Café Central & Restaurant Melker Stiftskeller
20 Sacher Café
21 Zanoni & Zanoni Ice Cream

SLEEP CODE

(€1 = about $1.10, country code: 43, area code: 01)
Sleep Code: **S** = Single, **D** = Double/Twin, **T** = Triple, **Q** = Quad, **b** = bathroom, **s** = shower only, **no CC** = Credit Cards not accepted. English is spoken at each place. Unless otherwise noted, credit cards are accepted and breakfast is included.

To help you sort easily through these listings, I've divided the rooms into three categories, based on the price for a standard double room with bath:

    $$$ **Higher Priced**—Most rooms €110 or more.
    $$ **Moderately Priced**—Most rooms between €75–110.
    $ **Lower Priced**—Most rooms €75 or less.

Book accommodations by phone a few days in advance. Most places will hold a room without a deposit if you promise to arrive before 17:00. My recommendations stretch mainly from the center, and along the likeable Mariahilfer Strasse, to the Westbahnhof (West Station). Even places with elevators often have a few stairs to climb, too.

this book get your best price and then claim a 10 percent discount, elevator, Bauernmarkt 22, U-1 or U-3: Stephansplatz, tel. 01/533-1931, fax 01/533-0214, www.schweizerhof.at, office@schweizerhof.at).

$$$ Hotel zur Wiener Staatsoper (the Schweizerhof's sister hotel) is quiet and rich. Its 22 tight rooms come with high ceilings, chandeliers, and fancy carpets on parquet floors—ideal for people whose hotel tastes are a cut above mine. The singles are tiny, with beds too short for anyone over six feet tall (Sb-€76–88, Db-€109–131, Tb-€131–146, extra bed-€22, prices depend on season, July–Aug and Dec–March are cheaper, elevator, U-1, U-2, or U-4: Karlsplatz, a block from Opera at Krugerstrasse 11, tel. 01/513-1274, fax 01/513-127-415, www .zurwienerstaatsoper.at, office@zurwienerstaatsoper.at).

$$ At Pension Nossek, an elevator takes you above any street noise into Frau Bernad's and Frau Gundolf's world, where the children seem to be placed among the lace and flowers by an interior designer. Right on the wonderful Graben, this is a particularly good value (26 rooms, S-€46–54, Ss-€58, Sb-€66–88, Db-€105, €25 extra for sprawling suites, extra bed-€35, no CC, elevator, U-1 or U-3: Stephansplatz, Graben 17, tel. 01/5337-0410, fax 01/535-3646, www.pension-nossek.at, reservation@pension-nossek.at).

$$ Pension Suzanne, as Baroque and doily as you'll find in this price range, is wonderfully located a few yards from the Opera. It's small, but run with the class of a bigger hotel; the 26 rooms are packed with properly Viennese antique furnishings. Streetside rooms come with some noise (Sb-€72, Db-€90–111 depending on size, extra bed-€30, spacious apartment for up to 6 also available, discounts in winter, elevator, a block from Opera, U-1, U-2, or U-4: Karlsplatz, follow signs for the Opera exit, Walfischgasse 4, tel. 01/513-2507, fax 01/513-2500, www.pension-suzanne.at, info@pension-suzanne.at).

$$ Schweizer Pension Solderer, family-owned for three generations, is run by Anita. She runs an extremely tight ship (lots of rules), but offers 11 homey rooms, parquet floors, and lots of tourist info (S-€35–42, Ss-€51–55, Sb-€58–62, D-€55–62, Ds-€65–75, Db-€80–85, Tb-€95–105, Qb-€120–125, prices depend on season and room size, no CC, non-smoking, elevator, laundry-€11/load, U-2 and U-4: Schottenring, Heinrichsgasse 2, tel. 01/533-8156, fax 01/535-6469, www.schweizerpension.com, schweizer.pension@chello.at).

$$ Pension Dr. Geissler has 23 comfortable rooms on the eighth floor of a modern building about 10 blocks northeast of St. Stephan's, near the canal (S-€43, Ss-€63, Sb-€72, D-€60, Ds-€72, Db-€90, 20 percent less in winter, elevator, U-1 and U-4: Schwedenplatz, Postgasse 14, tel. 01/533-2803, fax 01/533-2635, www.hotelpension.at/dr-geissler, dr.geissler@hotelpension.at).

Hotels and Pensions along Mariahilfer Strasse

Lively Mariahilfer Strasse connects the West Station and the city center. The U-3 metro line, starting at the Westbahnhof, goes down Mariahilfer Strasse to the cathedral. This very Viennese street is a tourist-friendly and vibrant area filled with local shops and cafés. Most hotels are within a few steps of a metro stop, just one or two stops from the West Train Station (direction from the station: Simmering).

$$$ NH Hoteles, a Spanish chain, runs two stern, passionless business hotels a few blocks apart on Mariahilfer Strasse. Both rent ideal-for-families suites, each with a living room, two TVs, bathroom, desk, and kitchenette (rack rate: Db suite-€170, going rate usually closer to €105, plus €13 per person for optional breakfast, cheaper Sat–Sun, apartments for 2–3 adults, kids under 12 free, non-smoking rooms, elevator). The 78-room **NH Atterseehaus** is at Mariahilfer Strasse 78 (U-3: Zieglergasse, tel. 01/5245-6000, fax 01/524-560-015, nhatterseehaus @nh-hotels.com), and the **NH Wien** has 106 rooms at Mariahilfer Strasse 32 (U-3: Neubaugasse, tel. 01/521-720, fax 01/521-7215, nhwien@nh-hotels.com). The Web site for both is www.nh-hotels.com.

$$ Pension Corvinus is bright, modern, and warmly run by a Hungarian family: Miklos, Judit, and Zoltan. Its eight comfortable rooms are spacious with small yacht-type bathrooms (Sb-€58, Db-€91,

Tb-€105, extra bed-€26, non-smoking rooms, portable air-con-€10, elevator, free Internet access, parking garage-€11/day, on the third floor at Mariahilfer Strasse 57–59, tel. 01/587-7239, fax 01/587-723-920, www.corvinus.at, hotel@corvinus.at). If heading for the Corvinus, don't be pirated by the people in the Haydn Hotel (below).

$$ Pension Mariahilf is a four-star place offering a clean, aristocratic air in an affordable and cozy pension package. Its 12 rooms are spacious but outmoded, with an Art Deco flair. You'll find the latest American magazines and even free Mozart balls at the reception desk (Sb-€59–66, Db-€95–102, Tb-€124, lower prices are for longer stays, elevator, U-3: Neubaugasse, Mariahilfer Strasse 49, tel. 01/586-1781, fax 01/586-178-122, penma@atnet.at, warmly run by Frau and Herr Ender).

$$ Haydn Hotel, in the same building the Pension Corvinus (listed above), is a big, fancy, dark place with 40 spacious rooms that have seen better days (Sb-€58–70, Db-€72–100, suites and family apartments, extra bed-€30, portable air-con-€12, elevator, free Internet access, Mariahilfer Strasse 57–59, tel. 01/587-4414, fax 01/586-1950, www.haydn-hotel.at, info@haydn-hotel.at).

$$ Hotel Admiral is a huge, quiet, family-run hotel with 80 large, comfortable rooms. Alexandra works hard to keep her guests happy, though others on the staff are less friendly (Sb-€66, Db-€91, extra bed-€23, prices promised through 2004 with this book, cheaper in winter, breakfast-€5 per person, free parking, U-2 or U-3: Volkstheater, a block off Mariahilfer Strasse at Karl Schweighofer Gasse 7, tel. 01/521-410, fax 01/521-4116, www.admiral.co.at, hoteladmiralwien@aon.at).

$ Pension Hargita rents 24 generally small, bright, and tidy rooms (mostly twins) with Hungarian decor. This spick-and-span, well-run, well-located place is an excellent value (S-€31, Ss-€35, Sb-€50, D-€45, Ds-€52, Db-€60, Ts-€63, Tb-€71, Qb-€87, breakfast-€3 per person, credit card adds 3 percent to cost and not for 1-night stays, U-3: Zieglergasse, corner of Mariahilfer Strasse and Andreasgasse, Andreasgasse 1, tel. 01/526-1928, fax 01/526-0492, www.hargita.at, pension @hargita.at, classy Amalia SE).

$ Pension Lindenhof rents 19 worn but clean rooms and is filled with plants (S-€29, Sb-€36, D-€49, Db-€65, no CC, elevator, U-3: Neubaugasse, Lindengasse 4, tel. 01/523-0498, fax 01/523-7362, pensionlindenhof@yahoo.com, Gebrael family, Zara and Keram SE).

$ K&T Boardinghouse rents four big, comfortable rooms facing the bustling Mariahilfer Strasse above a sex shop (S-€40, D-€50, Db-€60, Tb-€80, Qb-€100, 2-night minimum, no breakfast, no CC, non-smoking, free Internet access, 3 flights up, no elevator, Mariahilfer Strasse 72, tel. 01/523-2989, fax 01/522-0345, www.kaled.at, kaled @chello.at, Tina SE).

Two women rent rooms out of their dark and homey apartments in the same building at Lindengasse 39 (classic old elevator). Each has high

Vienna: Hotels and Restaurants
Outside the Ring

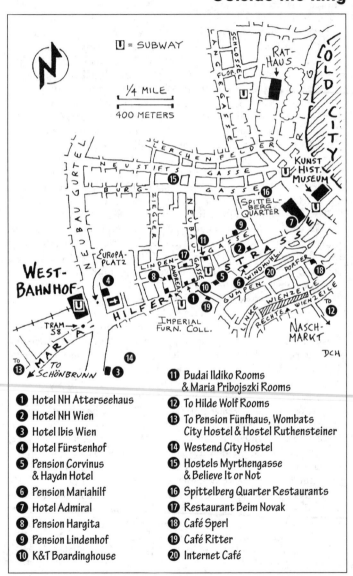

DCH

1 Hotel NH Atterseehaus
2 Hotel NH Wien
3 Hotel Ibis Wien
4 Hotel Fürstenhof
5 Pension Corvinus
   & Haydn Hotel
6 Pension Mariahilf
7 Hotel Admiral
8 Pension Hargita
9 Pension Lindenhof
10 K&T Boardinghouse

11 Budai Ildiko Rooms
    & Maria Pribojszki Rooms
12 To Hilde Wolf Rooms
13 To Pension Fünfhaus, Wombats
    City Hostel & Hostel Ruthensteiner
14 Westend City Hostel
15 Hostels Myrthengasse
    & Believe It or Not
16 Spittelberg Quarter Restaurants
17 Restaurant Beim Novak
18 Café Sperl
19 Café Ritter
20 Internet Café

ceilings and Old World furnishings, with two cavernous rooms sleeping two to four and a skinny twin room, all sharing one bathroom. These places are great if you're on a tight budget and wish you had a grandmother to visit in Vienna: $ **Budai Ildiko** lives on the mezzanine level and speaks English (S-€29, D-€44, T-€64, Q-€82, no breakfast but free coffee, no CC, laundry, apt. #5, tel. 01/523-1058, tel. & fax 01/526-2595, budai@hotmail.com). $ **Maria Pribojszki** lives on the first floor (D-€48, D for 2 nights-€44, T-€69, Q-€88, breakfast-€4 per person, no CC, no clothes-washing in room, smoky place, apt. #7, tel. 01/523-9006, b&b@aon.at).

$ **Hilde Wolf,** with the help of her grandson, Patrick, shares her homey apartment with travelers. Her four huge but stuffy rooms are like old libraries (S-€33, D-€48, T-€70, Q-€90, breakfast-€4, no CC, U-2: Karlsplatz, 3 blocks below Naschmarkt at Schleifmühlgasse 7, tel. 01/586-5103, fax 01/689-3505, www.schoolpool.at/bb, santa.claus@aon.at).

Near the Westbahnhof Train Station

$$ **Hotel Ibis Wien,** a modern high-rise hotel with American charm, is ideal for anyone tired of quaint old Europe. Its 340 cookie-cutter rooms are bright, comfortable, and modern and have all the conveniences (Sb-€64, Db-€79, Tb-€94, prices €5 more per room May–June, Aug, and Sept–Oct, breakfast-€9 per person extra, non-smoking rooms, elevator, parking garage-€10/day, exit Westbahnhof to the right and walk 400 yards, Mariahilfer Gürtel 22-24, tel. 01/59998, fax 01/597-9090, h0796@accor-hotels.com).

$$ **Hotel Fürstenhof,** right across from the station, charges top euro for its 58 spacious but borderline-musty rooms. This venerable hotel has an Old World maroon-velvet feel (S-€44, Sb-€67–92, D-€62, Db-€108, Tb-€114, Qb-€120, elevator, Internet access-€6/hr, Europaplatz 4, tel. 01/523-3267, fax 01/523-326-726, www.hotel-fuerstenhof.com, reception@hotel-fuerstenhof.com).

$ **Pension Fünfhaus** is big, clean, stark, and quiet—almost institutional. Although the neighborhood is run-down and comes with a few ladies loitering late at night, this 47-room place is a good value (S-€30, Sb-€38, D-€44, Db-€51, T-€66, Tb-€72, apartments for 4 people-€90, prices promised through 2004 with this book, no CC, closed mid-Nov–Feb, Sperrgasse 12, tel. 01/892-3545 or 01/892-0286, fax 01/892-0460, Frau Susi Tersch). Half the rooms are in the fine main building and half are in the annex, which has good rooms but is near the train tracks and a bit scary on the street at night. From the station, ride tram #52 or #58 two stops down Mariahilfer Strasse to Kranzgasse stop, then backtrack two blocks to Sperrgasse.

Cheap Dorms and Hostels near Mariahilfer Strasse

$ **Believe It or Not** is a tiny, basic place with two coed rooms for up to 10 travelers and the cheapest beds in town. Hardworking and friendly Gosha warns that this place is appropriate only for the young at heart. It's locked up from 10:00 to 12:30, has kitchen facilities, and has no curfew (bed–€13.50, €10 Nov–Easter, no CC, Myrthengasse 10, ring apt. #14, tel. 01/526-4658, www.believe-it-or-not-vienna.at, believe_it _or_not_vienna@hotmail.com, SE).

$ **Jugendherberge Myrthengasse** is a well-run youth hostel (260 beds–€16–18 each in 3- to 6-bed rooms, includes sheets and breakfast, non-members pay €3.50 extra, some private rooms for couples and families, Myrthengasse 7, tel. 01/523-6316, fax 01/523-5849, hostel@chello.at).

$ **Westend City Hostel,** just a block from the West Station and Mariahilfer Strasse, is new, with 180 beds in 4- to 12-bed dorms (€16–18 per bed including sheets, breakfast, and a locker, no CC, laundry, Internet access–€4.40/hr, Fügergasse 3, tel. 01/597-6729, fax 01/597-672-927, www.westendhostel.at, westendcityhostel@aon.at, SE).

$ Other hostels with €14 beds near Mariahilfer Strasse are **Wombats City Hostel** (Grangasse 6, tel. 01/897-2336, wombats@chello.at) and **Hostel Ruthensteiner** (also has doubles for €20 per person, Robert-Hamerling-Gasse 24, tel. 01/893-4202, info@hostelruthensteiner.com).

EATING

The Viennese appreciate the fine points of life, and right up there with waltzing is eating. The city has many atmospheric restaurants. As you ponder the Slavic and Eastern European specialties on menus, remember that Vienna's diverse empire may be gone, but its flavor lingers.

While cuisines are routinely named for countries, Vienna claims to be the only *city* with a cuisine of its own: Vienna soups come with fillings (semolina dumpling, liver dumpling, or pancake slices). *Gulasch* is a beef ragout of Hungarian origin (spiced with onion and paprika). Of course, Viennese schnitzel (Wiener schnitzel) is a breaded and fried veal cutlet. Another meat specialty is boiled beef *(Tafelspitz).* While you're sure to have *Apfelstrudel,* try the sweet cheese strudel, too (*Topfenstrudel,* wafer-thin strudel pastry filled with sweet cheese and raisins).

On nearly every corner, you can find a colorful *Beisl* (Viennese tavern) filled with poetry teachers and their students, couples loving without touching, housewives on their way home from cello lessons, and waiters who enjoy serving hearty food and good drink at an affordable price. Ask at your hotel for a good *Beisl.*

Wherever you're eating, some vocabulary will help. Try the *grüner Veltliner* (dry white wine), *Traubenmost* (a heavenly grape juice—alcohol-free but on the verge of wine), *Most* (the same thing but lightly alcoholic), and *Sturm* (stronger than *Most,* autumn only). The local red wine (called *Portugieser*) is pretty good. Since the Austrian wine is often sweet, remember the word *trocken* (dry). You can order your wine by the *Viertel* (quarter liter, 8 oz) or *Achtel* (eighth liter, 4 oz). Beer comes in a *Krügel* (half liter, 17 oz) or *Seidel* (0.3 liter, 10 oz).

Near St. Stephan's Cathedral

All of these places are within a five-minute walk of the cathedral.

Gigerl Stadtheuriger offers a near-*Heurige* experience (à la Grinzing, see "Wine Gardens," page 441), often with accordion or live music—without leaving the city center. Just point to what looks good. Food is sold by the weight; 200 grams is about a quarter of a pound (cheese and cold meats cost about €2.50–5 per 100 grams, salads are about €2 per 100 grams; price sheet is posted on the wall to right of buffet line, 10 *dag* equals 100 grams). They also have menu entrées, along with spinach strudel, quiche, *Apfelstrudel,* and, of course, casks of new and local wines. Meals run €7–11 (daily 15:00–24:00, indoor/outdoor seating, behind cathedral, a block off Kärntner Strasse, a few cobbles off Rauhensteingasse on Blumenstock, tel. 01/513-4431).

Am Hof square (U-3: Herrengasse) is surrounded by a maze of atmospheric medieval lanes; the following places are all within a block of the square. **Restaurant Ofenloch** serves good, old-fashioned Viennese cuisine with friendly service, both indoors and out. This 300-year-old eatery, with great traditional ambience, is central, but not over-run with tourists (main dishes €15–22, Tue–Sat 11:30–24:00, Mon 18:00–24:00, closed Sun, Kurrentgasse 8, tel. 01/533-8844). **Brezel-Gwölb,** a wonderfully atmospheric wine cellar with outdoor dining on a quiet square, serves delicious light meals, fine *Krautsuppe,* and old-fashioned local dishes. It's ideal for a romantic late-night glass of wine (daily 11:30–1:00, leave Am Hof on Drahtgasse, then take first left to Ledererhof 9, tel. 01/533-8811). Around the corner, **Beisl "Zum Scherer"** is just as untouristy, with indoor or outdoor seating, a soothing woody atmosphere, intriguing decor, and local specialties (Mon–Sat 11:00–24:00, closed Sun, Judenplatz 7, tel. 01/533-5164). Just below Am Hof, the ancient and popular **Esterhazykeller** has traditional fare deep underground or outside on a delightful square (Mon–Fri 11:00–23:00, Sat–Sun 16:00–23:00, self-service buffet in lowest cellar or from menu, Haarhof 1, tel. 01/533-2614).

These wine cellars are fun and touristy but typical, in the old center, with reasonable prices and plenty of smoke: **Melker Stiftskeller,** less touristy, is a *Stadtheurige* in a deep and rustic cellar with hearty, inexpensive meals and new wine (Tue–Sat 17:00–24:00, closed Sun–Mon, between Am Hof and Schottentor metro stop at Schottengasse 3, tel. 01/533-5530). **Zu den Drei Hacken** is famous for its local specialties

(Mon–Sat 11:00–23:00, closed Sun, indoor/outdoor seating, Singer-strasse 28, tel. 01/512-5895).

Wrenkh Vegetarian Restaurant and Bar is popular for its high veg-etarian cuisine. Chef Wrenkh offers daily lunch menus (€8–10) and dinner plates (€8–13) in a bright, mod bar or in a dark, smoke-free, fancier restaurant (daily 11:30–24:00, Bauernmarkt 10, tel. 01/533-1526).

Buffet Trzesniewski is an institution—justly famous for its elegant and cheap finger sandwiches and small beers (€0.70 each). Three dif-ferent sandwiches and a *kleines Bier (Pfiff)* make a fun, light lunch. Point to whichever delights look tasty and pay for them and a drink. Take your drink tokens to the lady on the right. Sit on the bench and scoot over to a tiny table when a spot opens up (Mon–Fri 8:30–19:30, Sat 9:00–17:00, closed Sun, 50 yards off Graben, nearly across from brooding Café Hawelka, Dorotheergasse 2, tel. 01/512-3291). This is a good oppor-tunity to try the fancy grape juices—*Most* or *Traubenmost* (see page 450).

Julius Meinl am Graben has been famous since 1862 as a top-end delicatessen with all the gourmet fancies (including a highly rated restau-rant upstairs, shop open Mon–Fri 8:00–19:30, Sat 8:30–17:00, closed Sun, restaurant Mon–Sat until 24:00, closed Sun, Am Graben 19, tel. 01/532-3334).

Akakiko Sushi: If you're just schnitzeled out, this small chain of Japanese restaurants with an easy sushi menu may suit you. The bento box meals are tasty. Three locations are very convenient (all open daily 10:00–24:00): Singerstrasse 4 (a block off Kärntner Strasse near the cathedral), Heidenschuss 3 (near other recommended eateries just off Am Hof), and Mariahilfer Strasse 42–48 (fifth floor of Kaufhaus Gerngross, near many recommended hotels).

Ice Cream! For a gelato treat or fancy dessert with a mob of happy Viennese, stop by the thriving **Zanoni & Zanoni** (daily 7:00–24:00, 2 blocks up Rotenturmstrasse from cathedral at Lugeck 7, tel. 01/512-7979).

Near the Opera

Café Restaurant Palmenhaus, overlooking the palace garden *(Burggarten)*, tucked away in a green and peaceful corner two blocks behind the Opera in the Hofburg's backyard, is a world apart. If you want to eat modern Austrian cuisine with palm trees rather than tourists, this is it. And at the edge of a huge park, it's great for families (€11 lunches, €15 dinners, daily 10:00–2:00, serious vegetarian dishes, fish, and an extensive wine list, indoors in greenhouse or outdoors, at Burggarten, tel. 01/533-1033). While nobody goes to the Palmenhaus for good prices, the **Palmenhaus BBQ**—a cool parkside outdoor pub just below that uses the same kitchen—is a wonderful value with more casual service (summer Wed–Sat from 20:00, closed Sun–Tue, open in good weather only, informal with €8 BBQ and meals posted on chalkboard).

Rosenberger Markt Restaurant is my favorite for a fast, light, and central lunch. Just a block toward the cathedral from the Opera, this place—while not cheap—is brilliant. Friendly and efficient, with special theme rooms for dining, it offers a fresh, smoke-free, and healthy cornucopia of food and drink (daily 10:30–23:00, lots of fruits, veggies, fresh-squeezed juices, addictive banana milk, ride the glass elevator downstairs, Maysedergasse 2, tel. 01/512-3458). You can stack a small salad or veggie plate into a tower of gobble for €2.50.

Spittelberg Quarter

A charming cobbled grid of traffic-free lanes and Biedermeier apartments has become a favorite place for Viennese wanting a little dining charm between the MuseumsQuartier and Mariahilfer Strasse (handy to many recommended hotels; take Stiftgasse from Mariahilfer Strasse, or wander over here after you close down the Kunsthistorisches or Leopold Museum). Tables tumble down sidewalks and into breezy courtyards filled with appreciative locals enjoying dinner or a relaxing drink. Stroll Spittelberggasse, Schrankgasse, and Gutenberggasse and pick your favorite place. Check out the courtyard inside Spittelberggasse 3, and don't miss the vine-strewn wine garden inside Schrankgasse 1. I ate well and cheaply at **Plutzer Bräu** (daily 11:00–2:00, good daily specials and beer from the keg, Schrankgasse 4, tel. 01/526-1215). For traditional Viennese cuisine with tablecloths, consider the classier **Witwe Bolte** (Mon–Fri 11:30–15:00 & 17:30–23:30, Sat–Sun 11:30–23:20, Gutenberggasse 13, tel. 01/523-1450).

Near Mariahilfer Strasse

Mariahilfer Strasse is filled with reasonable cafés serving all types of cuisine. **Restaurant Beim Novak** serves good local cuisine away from the modern rush (Mon–Fri 11:30–15:00 & 18:00–22:00, open Sat for dinner Sept–March, closed Sun, a block down Andreasgasse from Mariahilfer Strasse at Richtergasse 12, tel. 01/523-3244).

Naschmarkt is Vienna's best Old World market, with plenty of fresh produce, cheap local-style eateries, cafés, and *döner kebab* and sausage stands (Mon–Fri 7:00–18:00, Sat 6:00–18:00, closed Sun, closes earlier in winter, U-4: Kettenbrückengasse).

TRANSPORTATION CONNECTIONS

Vienna has two main train stations: the Westbahnhof (West Train Station), serving Munich, Salzburg, Melk, and Budapest; and the Südbahnhof (South Train Station), serving Italy, Budapest, Prague, Poland, Slovenia, and Croatia. A third station, Franz Josefs, serves Krems and the Danube Valley (but Melk is served by the Westbahnhof). Metro line U-3 connects the Westbahnhof with the center, tram D takes you from the Südbahnhof and the Franz Josefs station to downtown, and tram #18 connects West and South stations. Train info: tel. 051717 (wait through long German recording for operator).

By train to: Melk (hrly, 75 min, sometimes change in St. Pölten), **Krems** (hrly, 1 hr), **Salzburg** (hrly, 3 hrs), **Innsbruck** (every 2 hrs, 5.5 hrs), **Budapest** (6/day, 3 hrs), **Prague** (4/day, 4.5 hrs), **Český Krumlov** (5/day, 6–7 hrs, up to 3 changes), **Munich** (hrly, 5.25 hrs, change in Salzburg, a few direct trains), **Berlin** (2/day, 10 hrs, longer on night train), **Zürich** (3/day, 9 hrs), **Ljubljana** (7/day, 6–7 hrs, convenient early-morning direct train, others change in Villach or Maribor), **Zagreb** (8/day, 6.5–10.5 hrs, 3 direct, others with up to 3 changes including Villach and Ljubljana), **Kraków** (4/day, 6.5–9 hrs, 2 direct including a night train), **Warsaw** (4/day, 7.5–10 hrs, 2 direct including a night train), **Rome** (1/day, 13.5 hrs), **Venice** (3/day, 7.5 hrs, longer on night train), **Frankfurt** (4/day, 7.5 hrs), **Amsterdam** (1/day, 14.5 hrs).

To Eastern Europe: Vienna is the springboard for a quick trip to Prague and Budapest—three hours by train from Budapest (€37 one-way, €47 round-trip if you stay 4 days or less, free with Eurail) and four hours from Prague (€41 one-way, €82 round-trip, €53 round-trip with Eurail). Americans don't need a visa to enter the Czech Republic, but Canadians do; neither nationality needs a visa for Hungary. Purchase tickets at most travel agencies. Eurail passholders bound for Prague must pay to ride the rails in the Czech Republic; for details, see "Transportation Connections" in the Berlin chapter.

By boat: In the summer, Hungarian-based Mahart runs daily high-speed hydrofoils down the Danube to Budapest. The boat leaves Vienna April and Sept–Oct at 9:00 and arrives in Budapest at 14:30 (it's slower upstream, from Budapest to Vienna: 9:00–15:20); May through August, the boat leaves Vienna at 8:00 and arrives in Budapest at 13:30 (Budapest to Vienna: 8:00–14:20). In August, a second boat does the same trip, leaving Vienna at 13:00 and arriving Budapest at 18:30 (Budapest to Vienna: 13:00–19:20). The trip costs €75 one-way. On any of these boats, you can also stop in the Slovak capital, Bratislava. To confirm times and prices, and to buy tickets, contact Mahart (Vienna tel. 01/729-2161, Budapest tel. 1/484-4000, www.mahartpassnave.hu).

BERLIN

No tour of Germany is complete without a look at its historic and reunited capital, a construction zone called Berlin. Stand over ripped-up tracks and under a canopy of cranes and watch the rebirth of a European capital. Enjoy the thrill of walking over what was the Wall and through Brandenburg Gate.

Berlin has had a tumultuous recent history. After the city was devastated in World War II, it was divided by the Allied powers: The American, British, and French sectors became West Berlin, and the Russian sector, East Berlin. The division was set in stone when the East built the Berlin Wall in 1961. The Berlin Wall lasted 28 years. In 1990, less than a year after the Wall fell, the two Germanys officially became one. When the dust settled, Berliners from both sides of the once-divided city faced the monumental challenge of reunification.

The last decade has taken Berlin through a frenzy of rebuilding. And while there's still plenty of work to be done, a new Berlin is emerging. Berliners joke they don't need to go anywhere because the city's always changing. Spin a postcard rack to see what's new. A five-year-old guidebook on Berlin covers a different city.

Reunification has had its negative side, and locals are fond of saying "the Wall survives in the minds of some people." Some "Ossies" (impolite slang for Easterners) miss their security. Some "Wessies" miss their easy ride (military deferrals, subsidized rent, and tax breaks). For free spirits, walled-in West Berlin was a citadel of freedom within the East.

The city government has been eager to charge forward with little nostalgia for anything that was Eastern. Big corporations and the national government have moved in, and the dreary swath of land that was the Wall has been transformed. City planners are boldly taking Berlin's reunification and the return of the national government as a good opportunity to make Berlin a great capital once again.

ORIENTATION

(area code: 030)

Berlin is huge, with nearly four million people. But the tourist's Berlin can be broken into four digestible chunks:

1. The area around Bahnhof Zoo and the grand Kurfürstendamm Boulevard, nicknamed "Ku'damm" (transportation, tours, information, hotel, shopping hub).

2. Former downtown East Berlin: Brandenburg Gate, Unter den Linden boulevard, Museum Island (Pergamon), the area around Oranienburger Strasse, and Alexanderplatz.

3. The new city center: Kulturforum museums, Potsdamer Platz, the Jewish Museum, and Wall-related sights.

4. Charlottenburg Palace and museums, on the outskirts of the city.

Planning Your Time

Because of the city's location, try to enter and/or leave by either night train or plane. I'd give Berlin two days and spend them this way:

Day 1: 10:00–Take a guided walking tour (offered by Original Berlin Walks, see "Tours," page 460). After lunch, take my Do-It-Yourself Orientation Tour (described on page 461), stopping midway to scale the new dome of the Reichstag building, then finishing with a

Berlin Sightseeing Modules

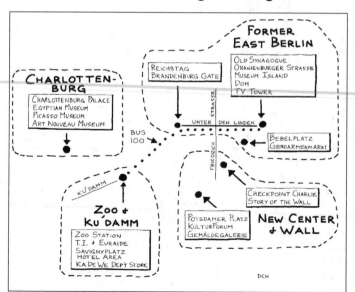

walk through eastern Berlin. End your day at the Pergamon Museum.

Day 2: Spend the morning lost in the painted art of the Gemälde-galerie. After lunch, hike or taxi via Potsdamer Platz to the Topography of Terror exhibit and along the surviving Zimmerstrasse stretch of Wall to the Museum of the Wall at Checkpoint Charlie. With extra time, consider visiting the Jewish Museum.

If you are maximizing your sightseeing, you could squeeze a hop-off, hop-on bus tour into Day 1 and start Day 2 with a visit to the Egyptian and Picasso museums at Charlottenburg. Remember that the Museum of the Wall is open late and most museums are closed on Monday.

Tourist Information

Berlin's TIs are run by a for-profit agency working for the city's big hotels, which colors the information they provide. The main TI is five minutes from the Bahnhof Zoo, in the Europa Center (with Mercedes symbol on top, enter outside to left at Budapester Strasse 45, April–Oct Mon–Sat 8:30–20:30, Sun 10:00–18:30, Nov–March Mon–Sat 10:00–19:00, Sun 10:00–18:00; call toll tel. 0190/016-316 €1/min; tel. from U.S.: 011-49-700/8623-7546, www.berlin-tourism.de). Smaller TIs are in the Brandenburg Gate (daily April–Oct 9:30–19:00, Nov–March 10:00–18:00) and at the bottom of the TV Tower at Alexanderplatz (April–Oct daily 9:00–20:00, Nov–March daily 10:00–18:00).

The TIs sell a good city map (€0.50—get it), the *Berlin Programm* (a €1.60 comprehensive German-language monthly that lists upcoming events and museum hours, www.berlin-programm.de), the Museumspass (a.k.a. *Schaulust*, €10, 3-day pass to several museums, including many of the biggies, see "Helpful Hints," page 459), and the German-English bimonthly *Berlin Calendar* magazine (€1.20, with timely features on Berlin and a partial calendar of events). The TIs also offer a €3 room-finding service (but only to hotels that give them kickbacks—many don't). Most hotels have free city maps.

EurAide's information office, in the Bahnhof Zoo, provides a great service. They have answers to all your questions about Berlin or train travel around Europe. It's staffed by Americans (so communication is simple), and they have a knack for predicting your needs, then publishing free fliers to serve them (Mon–Fri 8:30–12:00 & 13:00–16:30, Sat 8:30–12:00, closed Sun, closed Sat–Sun Oct–March, closed Jan, located in the train station *Reisezentrum*, great opportunity to get future *couchette* reservations nailed down ahead of time, Prague Excursion passes available—see "Transportation Connections" on page 500, www.euraide.de). EurAide also sells all public transit tickets, including the one-day bus/metro pass (€6.10), the Welcome Card (see "Getting around Berlin," next page), and city maps—making a trip to the TI probably unnecessary. To get the most out of EurAide, organize your questions and needs before your visit.

Arrival in Berlin

By Train at Bahnhof Zoo: Berlin's central station is called Bahnhof Zoologischer Garten (because it's near Berlin's famous zoo), or "Zoo" for short (rhymes with "toe"). Coming from Western Europe, you'll probably land at Zoo. It's small, well organized, and handy (lockers and baggage check available in back of station).

Upon arrival by train, orient yourself like this: Inside the station, follow signs to Hardenbergplatz. Step into this busy square filled with city buses, taxis, the transit office, and derelicts. The Original Berlin Walks start from the curb immediately outside the station at the top of the taxi stand (see "Tours," page 460). Between you and the McDonald's across the street is the stop for bus #100 (departing to the right for the Do-It-Yourself Orientation Tour). Turn right and tiptoe through the riffraff to the eight-lane highway, Hardenbergstrasse. Walk to the median strip and stand with your back to the tracks. Ahead you'll see the black, bombed-out hulk of the Kaiser Wilhelm Memorial Church and the Europa Center (Mercedes symbol spinning on roof), which houses the main TI. Just ahead on the left, amid the traffic, is the BVG transport information kiosk (buy a €6.10 day pass covering the subway and buses, and pick up a free subway map). If you're facing the church, my recommended hotels are behind you to your right.

If you arrive at Berlin's other train stations (trains from most of Eastern Europe arrive at Ostbahnhof), no problem: Ride another train (fastest option) or the S-Bahn or U-Bahn (runs every few min) to Bahnhof Zoo and pretend you arrived here.

By Plane: See "Transportation Connections," page 500.

Getting around Berlin

Berlin's sights spread far and wide. Right from the start, commit yourself to the fine public transit system.

By Subway and Bus: The U-Bahn (*Untergrund-Bahn,* Berlin's subway), S-Bahn (*Schnell-Bahn,* or fast train, mostly above ground and with fewer stops), *Strassenbahn* (streetcars), and all buses are consolidated into one "BVG" system that uses the same tickets. Here are your options:

• Basic ticket *(Einzel Fahrschein)* for two hours of travel on buses or subways (€2.10; *Erwachsener* means adult—anyone 14 or older).

• A day pass *(Tageskarte)* covering zones A and B—the city proper—€6.10, good until 3:00 the morning after. To get out to Potsdam, you need a ticket covering zone C (€6.30). (For longer stays, a 7-day *Tageskarte* is also available—€22, or €28 including zone C; or buy two WelcomeCards, see below.)

• A cheap short-ride ticket *(Kurzstrecke Erwachsener)* for a single short ride of six bus stops or three subway stations, with one transfer (€1.20).

• The Berlin/Potsdam **WelcomeCard** gives you three days of transportation in zones A, B, and C, and those same three days of minor discounts on lots of minor and a few major museums (including Checkpoint Charlie), sightseeing tours (including the recommended Berlin Walks), and music and theater events (€19, valid for an adult and up to 3 kids younger than 14). The WelcomeCard is a good deal for a three-day trip (since three one-day transit cards alone cost only €0.70 less than the WelcomeCard) and worth considering for a two-day trip.

Buy your tickets or cards from machines at U- or S-Bahn stations or at the BVG pavilion in front of Bahnhof Zoo (English instructions). To use the machine, first select the type of ticket you want, then load in the coins or paper. Punch your ticket in a red or yellow clock machine to validate it (or risk a €40 fine). The double-decker buses are a joy (can buy ticket on bus), and the subway is a snap. The S-Bahn (but not U-Bahn) is free with a validated Eurailpass (but it uses a Flexipass day).

Sections of the U- or S-Bahn sometimes close temporarily for repairs. In this situation, a bus route replaces the train (*Ersatzverkehr,* or "replacement transportation").

By Taxi: Taxis are easy to flag down, and taxi stands are common. A typical ride within town costs €5–8, and a cross-town trip (for example, Zoo to Alexanderplatz) will cost you around €14. A local law designed to help people get safely and affordably home from their subway station late at night is handy for tourists any time of day: A short ride of no more than two kilometers (1.25 miles) is a flat €3. (Ask for "*Kurzstrecke, drei euro, bitte.*") To get this cheap price, you must hail a cabbie on the street rather than go to a taxi stand (from a stand, it's a minimum €5 charge). Cabbies aren't crazy about the law, so insist on the price and be sure to keep the ride short.

By Bike: Be careful: In Berlin, motorists don't brake for bikers (and bikers don't brake for pedestrians). Fortunately, some roads and sidewalks have special red-painted bike lanes. Just don't ride on the regular sidewalk—it's *nicht erlaubt* (not allowed—that's *verboten* to you and me).

In western Berlin, you can rent good bikes at the **Bahnhof Zoo** left-luggage counter (in back of station, next to lockers; they come with lock, airpump, and mounted basket, €10/day, €23/3 days, €35/7 days, daily 6:15–21:00, passport required, €50 cash deposit); in the east, go to **Fahrradstation** at Hackesche Höfe (€15/day, Mon–Fri 8:00–20:00, Sat–Sun 10:00–16:00, Rosenthaler Strasse 40, tel. 030/2045-4500).

Helpful Hints

Monday Activities: Most museums are closed on Monday. Save Monday for Berlin Wall sights, the Reichstag building, the Do-It-Yourself Orientation Tour (see below), walking/bus tours, the Jewish Museum, churches, the zoo, or shopping along Kurfürstendamm (Ku'damm) Boulevard or at the Kaufhaus des Westens

(KaDeWe) department store. (When Monday is a holiday—as it is several times a year—museums are open then and closed Tuesday.)

Museums: All **state museums,** including the Pergamon Museum and Gemäldegalerie (plus others as noted in "Sights," page 475), are free on the first Sunday of each month. There are two different types of discount passes for Berlin's state museums (www.smpk.de, different from the mostly private museums and sights covered by the WelcomeCard—"Getting around Berlin," above). The state museums are covered by a **one-day ticket** (*Tageskarte*, €6, not valid for special exhibitions, purchase at participating museums, not sold at TI). Entry at most of these museums costs €6, so admission to one essentially includes all of the others on the same day. For longer stays, consider the three-day *"Schaulust"* **Museumspass,** which covers most of the state museums as well as several others (including the Jewish Museum). Only €4 more than the day ticket, it's valid for three times as long and is an excellent value if you'll be doing more than two days of museum-hopping (€10, not valid for special exhibitions, purchase at TI or at participating museums). Note that if a museum is closed on one of the days of your Museumspass, you have access to that museum on the fourth day to make up for lost time.

Addresses: Many Berlin streets are numbered with odd and even numbers on the same side of the street, often with no connection to the other side (for example, Ku'damm #212 can be across the street from #14). To save steps, check the white street signs on curb corners; many list the street numbers covered on that side of the block.

Travel Agency: Last Minute Flugbörse can help you find a flight in a hurry (next to TI in Europa Center, tel. 030/2655-1050, www .lastminuteflugboerse.de).

Internet Access: You'll find cheap, fast Internet access at easyInternetcafé (daily 24 hrs, Ku'damm 224, 10-min walk from Bahnhof Zoo and near recommended hotels, buy ticket at self-service machines, instructions in English).

Laundry: Schnell und Sauber Waschcenter is a handy launderette near my recommended hotels (daily 6:00–23:00, €5–9 wash and dry, Leibnizstrasse 72, four blocks west of Savignyplatz, near intersection with Kantstrasse).

TOURS

▲▲▲**City Walking Tours**—The Original Berlin Walks offers a variety of worthwhile tours led by enthusiastic guides who are native English speakers. The company, run by Englishman Nick Gay, offers a three-hour **Discover Berlin** introductory walk daily year-round at 10:00 and also at 14:30 from April through October for €12 (€9 if you're under 26 or with WelcomeCard). Just show up at the taxi rank in front of Bahnhof Zoo (or 20 min later in eastern Berlin, at the Kilkenny Irish Pub entrance inside Hackescher Markt S-Bahn station). Their high-quality, high-energy guides also offer other tours: **Infamous Third Reich Sites** (€10, €7.50 with WelcomeCard, at 10:00 May–Sept Wed, Fri, and Sat–Sun; March–April and Oct Sat–Sun only), **Jewish Life in Berlin** (€10, €7.50 with WelcomeCard, Mon at 10:00 May–Sept), and **Potsdam** (€15, €11.20 with WelcomeCard, see "Sights—Near Berlin," page 489). Many of the Third Reich and Jewish history sights are difficult to pin down without these excellent walks. Also consider their six-hour trip to the **Sachsenhausen** Concentration Camp, intended "to challenge precon-ceptions," according to Nick (€15, €11.20 with WelcomeCard, at 10:15 May–Sept Tue, Thu, and Sat–Sun; March–April and Oct Tue and Sat; requires transit day ticket with zone C—or buy from guide, call office for tour specifics). Confirm tour schedules at EurAide or by phone with Nick or his wife and partner, Serena (private tours also available, tel. 030/301-9194, www.berlinwalks.com, berlinwalks@snafu.de).

For a more exhaustive (or, for some, exhausting) walking tour of Berlin, consider **Brewer's Berlin Tours,** run by Terry, a former British embassy worker in East Berlin, and his well-trained staff. These daily tours—especially the in-depth Total version—are legendary for their length, and best for those with a long attention span and a serious inter-est in Berlin (€10 for either tour, all-day Total Berlin starts at 10:00 and can last 5–8 hrs, 4-hr Classic Berlin starts at 12:00, both meet at taxi stand in front of Friedrichstrasse S-Bahn station, look for red sign, also does Potsdam tours twice weekly, mobile 0179/739-5389, www.brewersberlin.com).

▲**City Bus Tours**—For bus tours, you have two choices:

1. Full-blown, three-hour bus tours. Contact Severin & Kühn (€22, daily 10:00 and 14:00, live guides in 2 languages, from Ku'damm 216, tel. 030/880-4190) or take BVG buses from Ku'damm 18 (€20, 2.5 hrs, leave every 30–60 min daily 10:00–17:00, tel. 030/885-9880).

2. Hop-on, hop-off circle tours. Several companies make a circuit of the city (City-Circle Sightseeing is good, offered by Severin & Kühn). The TI has all the brochures. The tour offers unlimited hop-on, hop-off privileges for its 14-stop route with a good English narration (€18, 10:00–18:00, last bus leaves from Ku-damn at 16:00, 2–4/hr, 2-hr loop, taped commentary). Just hop on where you like and pay the driver. On a sunny day when some double-decker buses go topless, these are a pho-tographer's delight, cruising slowly by just about every top sight in town.

Do-It-Yourself Orientation Tour

Here's an easy ▲▲▲ introduction to Berlin. Half the tour is by bus, the other half is on foot. Berlin's bus #100 (direction Mollstrasse and Prenzlauer Allee) is a sightseer's dream, stopping at Bahnhof Zoo,

BERLIN AT A GLANCE

▲▲▲**Reichstag** Germany's historic Parliament building, topped with a striking dome you can ascend. **Hours:** Daily 8:00–24:00, last entry 22:00.

▲▲▲**Museum of the Wall at Checkpoint Charlie** Moving museum near the former site of the famous border checkpoint between the American and Soviet sectors, with stories of brave escapes during the Cold War and the gleeful days when the wall fell. **Hours:** Daily 9:00–22:00.

▲▲▲**Gemäldegalerie** Germany's top collection of 13th- through 18th-century European paintings, featuring Dürer, Van Eyck, Rubens, Titian, Raphael, Caravaggio, and more. **Hours:** Tue–Sun 10:00–18:00, Thu until 22:00, closed Mon.

▲▲**Brandenburg Gate** One of Berlin's most famous landmarks, a multi-arched gateway, at the former border of East and West. **Hours:** Always open.

▲▲**Unter den Linden** Leafy boulevard through the heart of former East Berlin, lined with some of the city's top sights. **Hours:** Always open.

▲▲**Pergamon Museum** The only essential museum on Museum Island (just off Unter den Linden), featuring the fantastic second-century B.C. Greek Pergamon Altar. **Hours:** Tue–Sun 10:00–18:00, Thu until 22:00, closed Mon.

▲▲**Berlin Wall** Mostly gone, but parts of the wall are still visible, including the East Side Gallery and a chunk near the Topography of Terror (former SS and Gestapo headquarters). **Hours:** Always open.

▲▲**Jewish Museum Berlin** User-friendly museum celebrating Jewish culture, in a highly conceptual building. **Hours:** Daily 10:00–20:00, Mon until 22:00.

▲▲**Gendarmenmarkt** Inviting square bounded by twin churches, a chocolate shop, and the concert hall. **Hours:** Always open.

▲▲**New Synagogue** Largest prewar synagogue in Berlin, destroyed by Nazis, with a facade that has since been rebuilt. **Hours:** Sun–Thu 10:00–18:00, Fri 10:00–14:00, closed Sat, May–Aug Sun–Mon until 20:00 and Fri until 17:00.

▲▲▲**Egyptian Museum** Proud home of the exquisite 3,000-year-old bust of Queen Nefertiti. **Hours:** Tue–Sun 10:00–18:00, closed Mon.

▲**Kaiser Wilhelm Memorial Church** Evocative destroyed church in the heart of the former West Berlin, with a modern annex. **Hours:** Church open Mon–Sat 10:00–16:00, closed Sun, annex open daily 9:00–19:00.

▲**Kurfürstendamm** West Berlin's main boulevard (nicknamed Ku'damm), packed with tourists and upscale shops. **Hours:** Always open.

▲**Käthe Kollwitz Museum** Features the black-and-white art of the local artist who conveyed the suffering of Berlin's stormiest century. **Hours:** Wed–Mon 11:00–18:00, closed Tue.

▲**Kaufhaus des Westens (KaDeWe)** The "department store of the West"—the biggest on the Continent—is where East Berliners flocked when the wall came down. **Hours:** Mon–Fri 9:30–20:00, Sat 9:00–16:00, closed Sun.

▲**Potsdamer Platz** The Times Square of old Berlin, long a postwar wasteland, now rebuilt with huge glass skyscrapers (can ascend 300-foot-tall Kollhoff tower), an underground train station, and—covered with a huge canopy—the Sony Center mall with eateries. **Hours:** Always open.

▲**Music Instruments Museum** Impressive collection of historic instruments. **Hours:** Tue–Fri 9:00–17:00, Sat–Sun 10:00–17:00, closed Mon.

▲**Charlottenburg Palace** Skippable Baroque Hohenzollern palace on the edge of town, across street from Egyptian Museum. **Hours:** Tue–Sun 10:00–17:00, closed Mon.

▲**Berggruen Collection** Notable works by Picasso, Matisse, van Gogh, Cézanne, and Paul Klee. **Hours:** Tue–Fri 10:00–18:00, Sat–Sun 11:00–18:00, closed Mon.

▲**Bröhan Museum** Collection of Art Nouveau and Art Deco furnishings. **Hours:** Tue–Sun 10:00–18:00, closed Mon.

Tiergarten Berlin's "Central Park," stretching two miles from Bahnhof Zoo to Brandenburg Gate, with the Siegessäule (Victory Column) in the
(continued on next page)

center. **Hours:** Park always open, column climbable April–Sept Mon–Thu 9:30–18:30, Fri–Sun 9:30–19:00, Oct–March daily 9:30–17:30, closes in the rain.

Bebelplatz Square on Unter den Linden bounded by great buildings and an interesting book-burning memorial. **Hours:** Always open.

Neue Wache Touching memorial to the victims of fascism. **Hours:** Always open.

Berlin Cathedral Towering church over popular Lustgarten park on Museum Island. **Hours:** Mon–Sat 9:00–20:00, Sun 11:30–18:00, summer Thu until 22:00.

Fernsehturm A 1,200-foot-tall TV tower with observation deck, in eastern Berlin. **Hours:** March–Oct daily 9:00–1:00, Nov–Feb daily 10:00–24:00.

Europa Center/Hotel Palace, Siegessäule, Reichstag, Brandenburg Gate, Unter den Linden, Pergamon Museum, and ending at Alexanderplatz. If you have the €18 and two hours for a hop-on, hop-off bus tour (described above), take that instead. But this short €2.10 bus ride is a fine city introduction. Buses leave from Hardenbergplatz in front of the Bahnhof Zoo (and nearly next door to the Europa Center TI, in front of Hotel Palace). Buses come every 10 minutes, and single tickets are good for two hours—so take advantage of hop-on-and-off privileges. Climb aboard, stamp your ticket (giving it a time), and grab a seat on top. You could ride the bus all the way, but I'd get out at the Reichstag and walk to Alexanderplatz.

Part 1: By Bus #100 from Bahnhof Zoo to the Reichstag

(This is about a 10-min ride. Note: The upcoming stop will light up on the reader board inside the bus.)

☛ On your left and then straight ahead, before descending into the tunnel, you'll see the bombed-out hulk of the **Kaiser Wilhelm Memorial Church,** with its postwar sister church (described below) and the **Europa Center.** This is the west-end shopping district, a bustling people zone with big department stores nearby. When the Wall came down, East Berliners flocked to this area's department stores (especially KaDeWe, described below). Soon after, the biggest, swankiest new stores were built in the East. Now the West is trying to win

Berlin

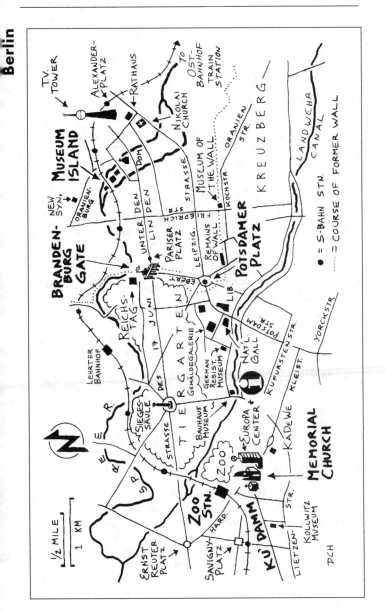

those shoppers back by building even bigger and better shopping centers around Europaplatz. Across from the Zoo station, the under-construction Zoofenster tower will be taller than all the buildings you see here.

Emerging from the tunnel, on your immediate right you'll see the Berlin tourist information office.

☛ At the stop in front of Hotel Palace: on the left, the elephant gates mark the entrance to the **Berlin Zoo** and its aquarium (described below).

☛ Driving down Kurfürstenstrasse, you'll pass several Asian restaurants—a reminder that, for most, the best food in Berlin is not German. Turning left, with the huge Tiergarten in the distance ahead, you'll cross a canal and see the famous **Bauhaus Archive** (an off-white, blocky building) on the right. The Bauhaus movement ushered in a new age of modern architecture that emphasized function over beauty, giving rise to the blocky steel-and-glass skyscrapers in big cities around the world. On the left is Berlin's new embassy row. The big turquoise wall marks the communal home of all five Nordic embassies.

☛ The bus enters a 400-acre park called the **Tiergarten,** packed with cycle paths, joggers, and nude sunbathers. The Victory Column (Siegessäule, with the gilded angel, described below) towers above this vast city park that was once a royal hunting grounds, now nicknamed the "green lungs of Berlin."

☛ On the left, a block after leaving the Siegessäule: The 18th-century, late-rococo **Bellevue Palace** is the German White House. Formerly a Nazi VIP guest house, it's now the residence of the federal president (whose power is mostly ceremonial). If the flag's out, he's in.

☛ Driving along the Spree River: This park area was a residential district before World War II. Now, on the left-hand side, it's filled with the buildings of the **new national government.** The huge brick "brown snake" complex was built to house government workers—but it didn't sell—so now its apartments are available to anyone. A Henry Moore sculpture entitled *Butterfly* floats in front of the slope-roofed House of World Cultures (Berliners have nicknamed this building "the pregnant oyster"). The modern tower (next on left) is a carillon with 68 bells (1987).

☛ While you could continue on bus #100, it's better on foot from here. Leap out at the Platz der Republik. Through the trees on the left you'll see Germany's new and sprawling chancellery. Started during the more imperial rule of Helmut Kohl, it's now considered overly grand. The big park is the Platz der Republik, where the Siegessäule stood until Hitler moved it. The gardens were recently dug up to build underground train tracks to serve Berlin's new main train station (the Lehrter Bahnhof, across the field). Watch your step—excavators found a 250-pound undetonated American bomb.

☛ Just down the street stands the **Reichstag.** As you approach the old building with the new dome, look for the row of slate slabs imbedded in the ground (looks like a fancy slate bicycle rack). This is a memorial to the 96 politicians who were murdered and persecuted because their politics didn't agree with Chancellor Hitler's. Each slab is marked with a name and the party that politician belonged to—mostly KPD (Communists) and SPD (Socialists).

Throughout Berlin, you'll see posters advertising a play called *Ich bin's nicht, Adolf Hitler es gewesen* (It wasn't me, Adolf Hitler did it). The photo is of a model by Hitler's architect Albert Speer of what Berlin was to look like when the Nazis controlled the planet. Hitler planned to rename his capital city "Germania Metropolis." The enormous dome is the Great Hall of the People. Below it and to the right is the tiny Reichstag. Imagine this huge 950-foot-high dome dwarfing everything in Berlin (in the field to your left as you face the Reichstag).

Now visit the Reichstag (open late, no lines in evening) and continue the walk below.

▲▲▲Reichstag Building—The Parliament building—the heart of German democracy—has a short but complicated and emotional history. When it was inaugurated in the 1890s, the last emperor, Kaiser Wilhelm, disdainfully called it the "house for chatting." It was from here that the German Republic was proclaimed in 1918. In 1933, this symbol of democracy nearly burned down. While the Nazis blamed a Communist plot, some believe that Hitler himself planned the fire, using it as a handy excuse to frame the Communists and grab power. As World War II drew to a close, Stalin ordered his troops to take the Reichstag from the Nazis by May 1 (the workers' holiday). More than 1,500 Nazis made their last stand here—extending World War II by two days. On April 30, 1945, it fell to the Allies. It was hardly used from 1933 to 1999. For its 101st birthday, in 1995, the Bulgarian-American artist Christo wrapped it in silvery-gold cloth. It was then wrapped again in scaffolding, rebuilt by British architect Lord Norman Foster, and turned into the new parliamentary home of the Bundestag (Germany's lower house). To many Germans, the proud resurrection of the Reichstag—which no longer has a hint of Hitler—symbolizes the end of a terrible chapter in German history.

The **glass cupola** rises 155 feet above the ground, and a double staircase winds 755 feet to the top for a grand view. Inside the dome, a cone of 360 mirrors reflects natural light into the legislative chamber below. Lit from inside at night, this gives Berlin a memorable nightlight. The environmentally friendly cone also helps with air circulation, drawing hot air out of the legislative chamber and pulling in cool air from below.

Hours: Free, daily 8:00–24:00, last entry 22:00, most crowded 10:00–16:00 (wait in line to go up—good street musicians, metal detectors, no big luggage allowed, some hour-long English tours when parliament is not sitting, tel. 030/2273-2152, www.bundestag.de).

Line-Beating Tip: Those with table reservations at the Dachgarten rooftop restaurant don't wait in the long lines. Go straight to the front and tell them you have a reservation. Reserve in advance by phone or e-mail (Dachgarten, €15–26 entrées with a view, daily 9:00–16:30 & 18:30–24:00, tel. 030/2262-9933, kaeferreservierung.berlin@feinkost-kaefer.de).

Self-Guided Tour: As you approach the building, look above the door, surrounded by stone patches from WWII bomb damage, to see the motto and promise: *Dem Deutschen Volke* (to the German people). The open and airy lobby towers 100 feet high with 65-foot-tall colors of the German flag. Glass doors show the **central legislative chamber.** The message: There will be no secrets in government. Look inside. The seats are "Reichstag blue," a lilac-blue color designed by the architect to brighten the otherwise gray interior. The German eagle (a.k.a. the "fat hen") spreads his wings behind the podium. Notice the doors marked "Yes," "No," and "Abstain"...the Bundestag's traditional "sheep jump" way of counting votes (for critical and close votes, all 669 members leave and vote by walking through the door of their choice).

Ride the elevator to the base of the glass **dome.** Take time to study the photos and read the circle of captions—an excellent exhibit telling the Reichstag story. Then study the surrounding architecture: a broken collage of old on new, like Germany's history. Notice the dome's giant and unobtrusive sunscreen that moves as necessary with the sun. Peer down through the skylight to look over the shoulders of the elected representatives at work. For Germans, the best view is down—keeping a close eye on their government.

Start at the ramp nearest the elevator and wind up to the top of the **double ramp.** Take a 360-degree survey of the city as you hike: First, the big park is the **Tiergarten,** the "green lungs" of Berlin. Beyond that is the **Teufelsberg,** or Devil's Hill (built of rubble from the bombed city in the late 1940s and famous during the Cold War as a powerful ear of the West—notice the telecommunications tower on top). Given the violent and tragic history of Berlin, a city blown apart by bombs and covered over by bulldozers, locals say, "You have to be suspicious when you see the nice green park." Find the **Seigessäule,** the Victory Column (moved by Hitler in the 1930s from in front of the Reichstag to its present position in the Tiergarten). Next, scenes of the new Berlin spiral into your view— **Potsdamer Platz,** marked by the conical glass tower that houses Sony's European headquarters. The yellow building to the right is the Berlin Philharmonic Concert Hall. Continue circling left, and find the green chariot atop the **Brandenburg Gate.** A monument to the Gypsy Holocaust will be built between the Reichstag and Brandenburg Gate.

(Gypsies, as disdained by the Nazis as the Jews, lost the same percentage of their population to Hitler.) Another Holocaust memorial will be built just south of Brandenburg Gate. Next, you'll see **former East Berlin** and the city's next huge construction zone, with a forest of 300-foot-tall skyscrapers in the works. Notice the TV tower (with the Pope's Revenge—explained below), the Berlin Cathedral's massive dome, the red tower of the city hall, the golden dome of the New Synagogue, and the Reichstag's **roof garden restaurant** (see above). Follow the train tracks in the distance to the left toward a huge construction zone marking the future central Berlin train station, Lehrter Bahnhof. Just in front of it, alone in a field, is the Swiss Embassy. This used to be surrounded by buildings, but now it's the only one left. Complete your spin tour with the blocky **Chancellery,** nicknamed by locals "the washing machine." It may look like a pharaoh's tomb, but it's the office and home of Germany's most powerful person, the chancellor and his team.

Let's continue our walk and cross what was the Berlin Wall. Leaving the Reichstag, turn left around the building. You'll see the Brandenburg Gate ahead on your right.

Part 2: Walking Tour from Brandenburg Gate up Unter den Linden to Alexanderplatz

Allow a comfortable hour for this walk through eastern Berlin, including time for dawdling (but not including museum stops).

▲▲**Brandenburg Gate**—The historic Brandenburg Gate (1791, the last survivor of 14 gates in Berlin's old city wall—this one led to the city of Brandenburg), crowned by a majestic four-horse chariot with the Goddess of Peace at the reins, was the symbol of Prussian Berlin...and later the symbol of a divided Berlin. Napoleon took the statue to the Louvre in Paris in 1806. When the Prussians got it back, she was renamed the Goddess of Victory. The gate sat unused, part of a sad circle dance called the Wall, for more than 25 years. Now postcards all over town show the ecstatic day—November 9, 1989—when the world enjoyed the sight of happy Berliners jamming the gate like flowers on a parade float. Pause a minute and think about struggles for freedom—past and present. (There's actually a "quiet room" built into the gate for this purpose, daily 11:00–18:00.)

Around the gate, look at the information boards with pictures of how much this area changed throughout the 20th century. The latest chapter: The shiny white gate was completely restored in 2002 (financed mostly by Deutsche Telekom). The TI within the gate is open daily April–Oct 9:30–19:00, Nov–March 10:00–18:00.

Unter den Linden

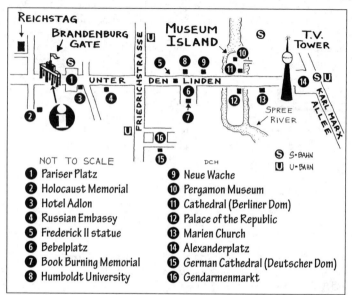

NOT TO SCALE

1. Pariser Platz
2. Holocaust Memorial
3. Hotel Adlon
4. Russian Embassy
5. Frederick II statue
6. Bebelplatz
7. Book Burning Memorial
8. Humboldt University
9. Neue Wache
10. Pergamon Museum
11. Cathedral (Berliner Dom)
12. Palace of the Republic
13. Marien Church
14. Alexanderplatz
15. German Cathedral (Deutscher Dom)
16. Gendarmenmarkt

Ⓢ S-BAHN
Ⓤ U-BAHN

▲**Pariser Platz**—From in front of Brandenburg Gate, face Pariser Platz (toward the east). Unter den Linden leads to the TV tower in the distance (the end of this walk). The space used to be filled with important government buildings—all bombed to smithereens. Today, Pariser Platz is unrecognizable as the deserted no-man's-land it became under the communist regime. Sparkling new banks, embassies (the French Embassy rebuilt where it was before World War II), and a swanky hotel have filled in the void.

Crossing through the gate, look to your right to a construction site—formerly the "death strip." The **U.S. Embassy** once stood here, and a new one will stand in the same spot (due to be completed in 2006). This new embassy has been controversial; for safety's sake, Uncle Sam wanted it away from other buildings, but the Germans preferred it in its original location. A compromise was reached, building the embassy by the gate—but rerouting several major roads to reduce the security risk. The new **Holocaust memorial,** consisting of more than 2,500 gravestone-like pillars, will be completed in 2004 and will stand behind the new embassy.

The **DZ Bank building** (next to the old-new site of the U.S. Embassy) is by Frank Gehry, the unconventional American architect famous for Bilbao's golden Guggenheim, Prague's Dancing House, and Seattle's EMP. Gehry fans might be surprised at the DZ Bank building's low profile. Structures on Pariser Platz are expected to be bland so as not to draw attention away from the Brandenburg Gate. (The glassy facade of the Academy of Arts, next to Gehry's building, is controversial for that very reason.) For your fix of the good old Gehry, step into the lobby and check out its undulating interior.

Brandenburg Gate, the center of old Berlin, sits on a major boulevard, running east–west through Berlin. The western segment, called Strasse des 17. Juni, stretches for four miles from the Siegessäule (past the flea market—see page 479) to the Olympic Stadium. For our walk, we'll follow this city axis in the opposite direction, east, up what is known as Unter den Linden—into the core of old imperial Berlin and past what was once the palace of the Hohenzollern family who ruled Prussia and then Germany. The palace—the reason for just about all you'll see—is a phantom sight, long gone (though some Berliners hope to rebuild it).

▲▲Unter den Linden—This is the heart of former East Berlin. In Berlin's good old days, Unter den Linden was one of Europe's grand boulevards. In the 15th century, this carriageway led from the palace to the hunting grounds (today's big Tiergarten). In the 17th century, Hohenzollern princes and princesses moved in and built their palaces here so they could be near the Prussian emperor.

Named centuries ago for its thousand linden trees, this was the most elegant street of Prussian Berlin before Hitler's time and the main drag of East Berlin after his reign. Hitler replaced the venerable trees—many 250 years old—with Nazi flags. Popular discontent actually drove him to replant linden trees. Today, Unter den Linden is no longer a depressing Cold War cul-de-sac, and its pre-Hitler strolling café ambience is returning.

As you walk toward the giant TV tower, the big building you see jutting out into the street on your right is the **Hotel Adlon.** It hosted such notables as Charlie Chaplin, Albert Einstein, and Greta Garbo. (This was where Garbo said, "I want to be alone," during the filming of *Grand Hotel.*) Destroyed in World War II, the grand Adlon was rebuilt in 1996. See how far you can get inside.

The Unter den Linden S-Bahn station ahead of you is one of Berlin's former **ghost subway stations.** During the Cold War, most underground train tunnels were simply blocked at the border. But a few Western lines looped through the East. To make a little hard Western cash, the Eastern government rented the use of these tracks to the West, but the stations (which happened to be in East Berlin) were strictly off-limits. For 28 years, the stations were unused, as Western trains slowly passed through, seeing only eerie DDR (East German) guards and lots of cobwebs. Literally within days of the fall of the Wall, these stations were reopened, and today they are a time-warp (with dreary old green tiles and original signage). Go down into the station, walk along the track, and exit on the other side, following signs to *Russische Botschaft*...the Russian Embassy.

The **Russian Embassy** was the first big postwar building project in East Berlin. It's built in the powerful, simplified, neoclassical style Stalin liked. While not as important now as it was a few years ago, it's immense as ever. It flies the Russian white, red, and blue. Find the hammer-and-sickle motif decorating the window frames. Continuing past the Aeroflot Airline offices, look across the street to the right to see the back of the **Komische Oper** (comic opera; program and view of ornate interior posted in window). While the exterior is ugly, the fine old theater interior, amazingly missed by WWII bombs, survives. The shop ahead on your right is an amusing mix of antiques, local guide-books, knickknacks, and East Berlin nostalgia souvenirs.

The West lost no time in consuming the East; consequently, some are feeling a wave of nostalgia—*Ost*-algia—for the old days of East Berlin. In recent local elections, nearly half of East Berlin's voters—and 6 per-cent of West Berliners—voted for the old Communist Party. One symbol of that era has been given a reprieve. As you continue to Friedrichstrasse, look at the DDR–style pedestrian lights, and you'll realize that someone had a sense of humor back then. The perky red and green men—*Ampelmännchen*—were under threat of replacement by the far less jaunty Western signs. Fortunately, the DDR signals will be kept after all.

At **Friedrichstrasse,** look right. Before the war, the Unter den Linden/Friedrichstrasse intersection was the heart of Berlin. In the 1920s, Berlin was famous for its anything-goes love of life. This was the cabaret drag, a springboard to stardom for young and vampy entertain-ers like Marlene Dietrich. (Born in 1901, Dietrich starred in the first German "talkie" and then headed straight to Hollywood.) Today, this boulevard, lined with super department stores (such as Galeries Lafayette, with its cool marble and glass waste-of-space interior, Mon–Fri 9:30–20:00, Sat 9:00–16:00, closed Sun; belly up to its amaz-ing ground floor viewpoint) and big-time hotels (such as the Hilton and Four Seasons), has slowly begun to replace Ku'damm as the grand com-merce and café boulevard of Berlin—though the West is retaliating with some new stores of its own. Across from Galeries Lafayette is American Express (handy for any train ticket needs, Mon–Fri 9:00–19:00, Sat 10:00–13:00, closed Sun, travel agency tel. 030/201-7400, to replace traveler's checks, call 0800/185-3100).

If you continued down Friedrichstrasse, you'd wind up at the Checkpoint Charlie Museum in about 10 minutes (see "Sights—Eastern Berlin," page 482). But for now, continue along Unter den Linden. You'll notice big, colorful water pipes around here, and throughout Berlin. As long as the city remains a big construction zone, it will be laced with these drainage pipes—key to any building project. Berlin's high water table means any new basement comes with lots of pumping out.

Continue down Unter den Linden a few more blocks, past the large equestrian statue of **Frederick II** ("the Great"), and turn right into the square (Bebelplatz). Stand on the glass window in the center. (Construction of an underground parking lot might prevent you from reaching the glass plate.)

Frederick the Great—who ruled from 1740 to 1786—established Prussia as a military power. This square was the center of the "new Rome" Frederick envisioned. Much of Frederick's palace actually survived World War II but was torn down by the communists since it symbolized the imperialist past. Now some Berliners want to rebuild the palace, from scratch, exactly as it once was. Other Berliners insist that what's done is done.

Bebelplatz is bounded by great buildings. The German State Opera was bombed in 1941, rebuilt to bolster morale and to celebrate its centennial in 1943, and bombed again in 1945. The former state library is where Lenin studied much of his exile away (climb to the second floor of the library to see a stained glass window depicting his life's work with almost biblical reverence; there's a good café with light food, Tim's Canadian Deli, downstairs). The round Catholic St. Hedwig's Church—nicknamed the "upside-down teacup"—was built to placate the subjects of Catholic lands Frederick added to his empire. (Step inside to see the cheesy DDR government renovation.)

Humboldt University, across Unter den Linden, was one of Europe's greatest. Marx and Lenin (not the brothers or the sisters) studied here as did Grimm (both brothers) and more than two dozen Nobel Prize winners. Einstein—who was Jewish—taught here until taking a spot at Princeton in 1932 (smart guy).

Look down through the glass you're standing on: The room of empty bookshelves is a memorial to the notorious Nazi **book burning.** It was on this square in 1933 that staff and students from the university threw 20,000 newly forbidden books (like Einstein's) into a huge bonfire on the orders of the Nazi propaganda minister Joseph Goebbels.

Continue down Unter den Linden. The next square on your right holds the Opernpalais' restaurants (see "Eating," page 498). On the university side of Unter den Linden, the Greek temple–like building is the **Neue Wache** (the emperor's New Guardhouse, from 1816). When the Wall fell, this memorial to the victims of fascism was transformed into a new national memorial. Look inside where a replica of the Käthe Kollwitz statue, *Mother with Her Dead Son,* is surrounded by thought-provoking silence. This marks the tombs of Germany's unknown soldier and the unknown concentration camp victim. The inscription in front reads, "To the victims of war and tyranny." Read the entire statement in English (on wall, right of entrance).

After the Neue Wache, the next building you'll see is the **German History Museum** (Deutsches Historisches Museum im Zeughaus, Thu–Tue 10:00–18:00, Thu until 20:00, closed Wed, tel. 030/203-040, www.dhm.de), but I find its new I. M. Pei–designed annex with a spiraling glass staircase more interesting (to find it, go down the street—Hinter dem Giesshaus—to the left of the museum).

Just before the bridge, wander left along the canal through a tiny but colorful arts-and-crafts market (weekends only, a larger flea market is just outside the Pergamon Museum; see page 479). Canal tour boats leave from here.

Go back out to the main road and cross the bridge to **Museum Island,** home of Germany's first museums and today famous for its Pergamon Museum (see "Sights—Eastern Berlin," page 482). Eventually, all of the museums on this island will be connected by underground tunnels and consolidate the art collections of East and West Berlin—creating a massive complex intended to rival the Louvre. Today, the museum complex starts with an imposing red neoclassical facade on the left (a musty museum of antiquities; Pergamon is behind it). For 300 years, the square (Lustgarten) has flip-flopped between military parade ground and people-friendly park—depending upon the political tenor of the time. In 1999, it was made into a park again (read history posted in corner opposite church).

The towering church is the 100-year-old **Berlin Cathedral** (Berliner Dom, €4, €5 includes access to dome gallery, Mon–Sat 9:00–20:00, Sun 11:30–18:00, on summer Thu church—but not dome gallery—open until 22:00, www.berliner-dom.de; May–Sept organ concerts offered most Wed,–Fri at 15:00, free with regular admission, for other concerts visit ticket office on Lustgarten side, Mon–Fri 10:00–17:30, closed Sat–Sun, tel. 030/2026-9136). Inside, the great reformers (Luther, Calvin, and company) stand around the brilliantly restored dome like stern saints guarding their theology. Frederick I rests in an ornate tomb (right transept, near entrance to dome). The 270-step climb to the outdoor dome gallery is tough, but offers pleasant, breezy views of the city at the finish line (last entry 30 min before closing, dome closes in bad weather and at 17:00 in winter). The crypt downstairs is not worth a look.

Across the street is the decrepit **Palace of the Republic** (with the copper-tinted windows). A symbol of the communist days, it was East Berlin's parliament building and futuristic entertainment complex. Although it officially has a date with the wrecking ball, many Easterners want it saved, and its future is still uncertain.

Before crossing the next bridge (and leaving Museum Island), look right. The pointy twin spires of the 13th-century Nikolai Church mark the center of medieval Berlin. This Nikolai-Viertel (district) was restored by the DDR and was trendy in the last years of socialism. Today, it's dull and, with limited time, not worth a visit. As you cross the bridge, look left in the distance to see the gilded **New Synagogue,** rebuilt after WWII bombing (described below). Across the river to the left of the bridge is the construction site of a new shopping center with a huge aquarium in the center. The elevator will go right through the middle of an undersea world.

Walk toward **Marien Church** (from 1270, interesting but very faded old *Dance of Death* mural inside door) at the base of the TV tower. The big, red-brick building past the trees on the right is the **city hall,** built after the revolution of 1848 and arguably the first democratic building in the city. In the park are grandfatherly statues of Marx and Engels (nicknamed by locals "the old pensioners"). Surrounding them are stainless steel monoliths depicting the struggles of the workers of the world.

The 1,200-foot-tall **Fernsehturm (TV Tower)** offers a fine view from halfway up (€6.50, March–Oct daily 9:00–1:00, Nov–Feb daily 10:00–24:00, tel. 030/242-3333). The tower offers a handy city orientation and an interesting view of the flat, red-roofed sprawl of Berlin—including a peek inside the city's many courtyards *(Höfe)*. Consider a kitschy trip to the observation deck for the view and lunch in its revolving restaurant (reservations smart for dinner, same phone number). Built (with Swedish know-how) in 1969, the tower was meant to show the power of the atheistic state at a time when DDR leaders were having the crosses removed from church domes and spires. But when the sun shined on their tower, the greatest spire in East Berlin, a huge cross, reflected on the mirrored ball. Cynics called it "The Pope's Revenge." East Berliners dubbed the tower "The Big Asparagus." They joked that if it fell over, they'd have an elevator to the West.

Farther east, pass under the train tracks into **Alexanderplatz.** This area—especially the Kaufhof—was the commercial pride and joy of East Berlin. Today, it's still a landmark, with a major U- and S-Bahn station.

For a ride through workaday eastern Berlin, with its Lego-hell apartments (dreary even with their new face-lifts), hop back on bus #100 from here. It loops five minutes to the end of the line and then, after a couple minutes' break, heads on back. (This bus retraces your route, finishing at Bahnhof Zoo.) Consider extending this foray into eastern Berlin to Karl Marx Allee (see "Sights—Eastern Berlin," page 482).

SIGHTS

Western Berlin

Western travelers still think of Berlin's "West End" as the heart of the city. While it's no longer that, the West End still has the best infrastructure to support your visit and works well as a home base. Here are a few sights within an easy walk of your hotel and the Zoo station.

▲**Kurfürstendamm**—West Berlin's main drag, Kurfürstendamm boulevard (nicknamed "Ku'damm"), starts at Kaiser Wilhelm Memorial Church and does a commercial cancan for two miles. In the 1850s, when Berlin became a wealthy and important capital, her new rich chose Kurfürstendamm as their street. Bismarck made it Berlin's Champs-

Western Berlin

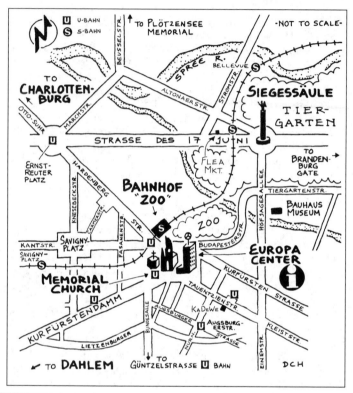

Elysées. In the 1920s, it became a chic and fashionable drag of cafés and boutiques. During the Third Reich, as home to an international community of diplomats and journalists, it enjoyed more freedom than the rest of Berlin. Throughout the Cold War, economic subsidies from the West made sure that capitalism thrived on Ku'damm. And today, while much of the old charm has been hamburgerized, Ku'damm is still a fine place to feel the pulse of the city and enjoy the elegant shops (around Fasanenstrasse), department stores, and people-watching.

▲**Kaiser Wilhelm Memorial Church (Gedächtniskirche)**—The church was originally a memorial to the first emperor of Germany, who died in 1888. Its bombed-out ruins have been left standing as a memorial to the destruction of Berlin in World War II. Under a fine mosaic ceiling, a small exhibit features interesting photos about the bombing and before-and-after models of the church (free, Mon–Sat 10:00–16:00, closed Sun, www.gedaechtniskirche.com).

After the war, some Berliners wanted to tear the church down and build it anew. Instead, it was decided to keep the ruin as a memorial, and stage a competition to design a modern add-on section. The winning selection—the short, modern building (1961) next to the church—offers a world of 11,000 little blue windows (free, daily 9:00–19:00). The blue glass was given to the church by the French as a reconciliation gift. For more information on both churches, pick up the English booklet (€2.60). The lively square between the churches and the Europa Center (a shiny high-rise shopping center built as a showcase of Western capitalism during the Cold War) usually attracts street musicians.

▲**Käthe Kollwitz Museum**—This local artist (1867–1945), who experienced much of Berlin's stormiest century, conveys some powerful and mostly sad feelings about motherhood, war, and suffering through the black-and-white faces of her art (€5, €1 pamphlet has English explanations of a few major works, Wed–Mon 11:00–18:00, closed Tue, a block off Ku'damm at Fasanenstrasse 24, tel. 030/882-5210, www.kaethe-kollwitz.de).

▲**Kaufhaus des Westens (KaDeWe)**—The "department store of the West," with a staff of 2,100 to help you sort through its vast selection of 380,000 items, claims to be the biggest department store on the Continent. You can get everything from a haircut and train ticket (basement) to souvenirs (third floor). The theater and concert box office on the sixth floor charges an 18 percent booking fee, but they know all your options (cash only). The sixth floor is also a world of gourmet taste treats. The biggest selection of deli and exotic food in Germany offers plenty of classy opportunities to sit down and eat. Ride the glass elevator to the seventh floor's glass-domed Winter Garden self-service cafeteria—fun but pricey (Mon–Fri 9:30–20:00, Sat 9:00–16:00, closed Sun, tel. 030/21210, U-Bahn Wittenbergplatz). The Wittenbergplatz U-Bahn station (in front of KaDeWe) is a unique opportunity to see an old-time station. Enjoy its interior.

Berlin Zoo—More than 1,400 different kinds of animals call Berlin's famous zoo home—or so the zookeepers like to think. Germans enjoy seeing the pandas at play (straight in from the entrance). I enjoy seeing the Germans at play (€9 for zoo or world-class aquarium, €14 for both, children half price, daily 9:00–18:30, Nov–Feb until 17:00, aquarium closes at 18:00, feeding times—*Fütterungszeiten*—posted on map just inside entrance, enter near Europa Center in front of Hotel Palace or opposite Bahnhof Zoo on Hardenbergplatz, Budapester Strasse 32, tel. 030/254-010).

Erotic Art Museum—This offers three floors of graphic (mostly 18th-century) Oriental art, a tiny theater showing erotic silent movies from the early 1900s, and a special exhibit on the queen of German pornography, the late Beate Uhse. This amazing woman, a former test pilot for the Third Reich and groundbreaking purveyor of condoms and sex ed in the 1950s, was the female Hugh Hefner of Germany and CEO of a huge chain of porn shops. If you're traveling far and are sightseeing selectively, the sex museums in Amsterdam or Copenhagen are much better. This one, though well described in English, is little more than prints and posters (€5, daily 9:00–24:00, last entry 23:00, hard-to-beat gift shop, at corner of Kantstrasse and Joachimstalerstrasse, a block from Bahnhof Zoo, tel. 030/886-0666). If you just want to see sex, you'll see much more for half the price in a private video booth next door.

Central Berlin

Hitler and the Third Reich—While many come to Berlin to see Hitler sights, these are essentially invisible. The German Resistance Museum (described below) is in German only and difficult for the tourist to appreciate. The Topography of Terror (SS and Gestapo headquarters) is a fascinating exhibit but—again—only in German, and all that remains of the building is its foundation. (Both museums have helpful audioguides in English.) Hitler's bunker is completely gone (near Potsdamer Platz). Your best bet for "Hitler sites" is to take the Infamous Third Reich Sites walking tour offered by Berlin Walks (see "Tours," page 460). EurAide has a good flier listing and explaining sites related to the Third Reich.

Tiergarten/Siegessäule—Berlin's "Central Park" stretches two miles from Bahnhof Zoo to Brandenburg Gate. Its centerpiece, the Siegessäule (Victory Column), was built to commemorate the Prussian defeat of France in 1870. The pointy-helmeted Germans rubbed it in, decorating the tower with French cannons and paying for it all with francs received as war reparations. The three lower rings commemorate Bismarck's victories. I imagine the statues of Moltke and other German military greats—which lurk in the trees nearby—goose-stepping around the floodlit angel at night. Originally standing at the Reichstag, the immense tower was actually moved to this position by Hitler in 1938 to complement his anticipated victory parades. At the first level, notice how WWII bullets chipped the fine marble columns. Climbing its 285 steps earns you a breathtaking Berlin-wide view and a close-up look at the gilded angel made famous in the U2 video (€2.20, April–Sept Mon–Thu 9:30–18:30, Fri–Sun 9:30–19:00, Oct–March daily 9:30–17:30, closes in the rain, WCs for paying guests only, no elevator, bus #100, 030/8639-8560). From the tower, the grand Strasse des 17. Juni (named for a workers' uprising against the DDR government in the 1950s) leads east to the Brandenburg Gate.

Flea Market—A colorful flea market with great antiques, more than 200 stalls, collector-savvy merchants, and fun German fast-food stands thrives weekends beyond Siegessäule on Strasse des 17. Juni (S-Bahn Tiergarten).

German Resistance Memorial (Gedenkstätte Deutscher Widerstand)— This memorial and museum tells the story of the German resistance to Hitler. The Benderblock was a military headquarters where an ill-fated attempt to assassinate Hitler was plotted (the actual attempt occurred in Rastenburg, eastern Prussia). Stauffenberg and his co-conspirators were shot here in the courtyard. While explanations are in German only, the spirit that haunts the place is multi-lingual (free, Mon–Fri 9:00–18:00, Thu until 20:00, Sat–Sun 10:00–18:00, free and good English audioguide with passport, €3 printed English translation, no crowds, near Kulturforum just south of Tiergarten at Stauffenbergstrasse 13, enter in courtyard, door on left, main exhibit is on third floor, bus #129, tel. 030/2699-5000).

▲**Potsdamer Platz**—The Times Square of Berlin, and possibly the busiest square in Europe before World War II, Potsdamer Platz was cut in two by the Wall and left a deserted no-man's-land for 40 years. This immense commercial/residential/entertainment center (with the European corporate headquarters of Sony and others), sitting on a futuristic transportation hub, was a vision begun in 1991 when it was announced that Berlin would resume its position as capital of Germany. Sony, Daimler-Chrysler, and other huge corporations have turned it once again into a center of Berlin. While most of the complex just feels big (the arcade is like any huge, modern, American mall), the entrance to the complex and Sony Center Platz are worth a visit.

For an overview of the new construction, and a scenic route to Sony Center Platz, go to the east end of Potsdamer Strasse, facing the skyscrapers (the opposite end from Kulturforum, at main intersection of Potsdamer Strasse/Leipziger Strasse and Ebert Strasse/Stressemanstrasse, U-Bahn: Potsdamer Platz). Find the green hexagonal clock tower with the traffic lights on top. This is a replica of the first automatic **traffic light** in Europe, which once stood at the six-street intersection of Potsdamer Platz. On either side of Potsdamer Strasse, you'll see huge cubical entrances to the brand-new underground Potsdamer Platz train station (due to open in 2005). Near these entrances, notice the **glass cylinders** sticking out of the ground. The mirrors on the tops of the tubes move with the sun to collect the light and send it underground. Now go in one of the train station entrances and follow signs to "Sony Center." (While you're down there, look for the other ends of the big glass tubes.)

You'll come up the escalator into **Sony Center** under a grand canopy. At night, multicolored floodlights play on the underside of this

tent. Office workers and tourists eat here by the fountain, enjoying the parade of people. The modern Bavarian Lindenbrau beer hall—the Sony boss wanted a *Bräuhall*—serves good traditional food (big salads, 3-foot-long taster boards of 8 different beers, daily 11:00–24:00, tel. 030/2575-1280). The adjacent Josty Bar is built around a surviving bit of a venerable hotel that was a meeting place for Berlin's rich and famous before the bombs (daily 9:00–1:00, tel. 030/2575-9702). You can browse the futuristic Sony Style Store, visit the Filmhaus (a museum with an exhibit on Marlene Dietrich), and do some surfing at Web Free TV (on the street).

Across Potsdamer Strasse, you can ride what's billed as "the fastest elevator in Europe" to skyscraping rooftop **views.** You'll travel at nearly 30 feet per second to the top of the 300-foot-tall Kollhoff tower (€3.50, Tue–Sun 11:00–20:00, closed Mon, in red brick building at Potsdamer Platz 1, tel. 030/2529-4372, www.panoramapunkt.de).

Kulturforum, in Central Berlin

Just west of Potsdamer Platz, with several top museums and Berlin's concert hall, is the city's cultural heart (admission to all sights covered by €6 day card or 3-day *Schaulust* Museumspass, free on first Sun of month). Of its sprawling museums, only the Gemäldegalerie is a must. The tourist info telephone number for all Kulturforum museums is 030/266-2951. To reach the Kulturforum, take the S- or U-Bahn to Potsdamer Platz, then walk along Potsdamer Platz and Potsdamer Strasse. From the Zoo station, you can also take bus #200 to Philharmonie. Across Potsdamer Strasse from the Kulturforum is the huge National Library (free English periodicals).

▲▲▲**Gemäldegalerie**—Germany's top collection of 13th- through 18th-century European paintings (more than 1,400 canvases) is beautifully displayed in a building that is a work of art in itself. Follow the excellent free audioguide. The North Wing starts with German paintings of the 13th to 16th centuries, including eight by Dürer. Then come the Dutch and Flemish—Jan Van Eyck, Brueghel, Rubens, Van Dyck, Hals, and Vermeer. The wing finishes with German, English, and French 18th-century art, such as Gainsborough and Watteau. An octagonal hall at the end features a fine stash of Rembrandts. The South Wing is saved for the Italians—Giotto, Botticelli, Titian, Raphael, and Caravaggio (€6, Tue–Sun 10:00–18:00, Thu until 22:00, closed Mon, clever little loaner stools, great salad bar in cafeteria upstairs, Matthäikirchplatz 4).

New National Gallery (Neue Nationalgalerie)—This features 20th-century art, with ever-changing special exhibits (€6, Tue–Fri 10:00–18:00,

Eastern Berlin

WHAT WAS THE WALL 1961–1989

NEW SYNAGOGUE

ORANIENBURGER

T.V. TOWER

LEHRTER

FRIEDRICH STRASSE

PERGAMON MUSEUM

HACK. MARKT.

ALEX-ANDER-PLATZ

TIER-

REICHS-TAG

BRANDEN-BURG GATE

GER. HIST. MUSEUM

MUSEUM ISLAND

CHANCEL-LORY

BUS 100 TO ZOO

NEUE WACHE

MARIEN CHURCH

Dom

STR. DES 17 JUNI

UNTER DEN LINDEN

MARX-ENGELS PLATZ

RATHAUS STR.

RATHAUS

TO SIEGESSÄULE

BUS 100 TO ALEX. PLATZ

PALACE OF REP.

MÜHL. BR.

NIKOLAI CHURCH OLD TOWN

TO OST-BAHN-HOF

GARTEN

POTSDAMER PLATZ

GENDARMEN MARKT

LEIPZIGER STR.

TIERGARTENSTRASSE

GEMÄLDE-GALERIE

FORMER LUFTWAFFE

FRIEDRICHSTRASSE

SPREE

NAT'L GALL.

EB. STR.

PHIL-HARMONIE

"FORMER CHECKPOINT CHARLIE"

"EAST"

POTSDAM.

TOPOG. OF TERROR

"WEST"

CITY LIBRARY

PORTION OF WALL STILL STANDING

BUS 129

MUSEUM OF THE WALL

KOCHSTRASSE

ORANIEN STR.

SCHÖNEBERGSTRASSE

KOCH-STRASSE

LINDENSTR.

BUS 129 TO KU'DAMM

ANHALTER BAHNHOF (RUINS)

JEWISH MUSEUM

KREUZBERG

Ⓢ S-BAHN
Ⓤ U-BAHN
NOT ALL STATIONS ARE SHOWN

DCH

NOTE: MAP NOT TO SCALE BRAND. GATE TO T.V. TOWER IS A 15-MIN. WALK

Thu until 22:00, Sat–Sun 11:00–18:00, closed Mon, café downstairs).
Museum of Arts and Crafts (Kunstgewerbemuseum)—Wander through a thousand years of applied arts—porcelain, fine *Jugendstil* (Art Nouveau) furniture, Art Deco, and reliquaries. There are no crowds and no English descriptions (€3, Tue–Fri 10:00–18:00, Sat–Sun 11:00–18:00, closed Mon).
▲**Musical Instruments Museum**—This impressive hall is filled with 600 exhibits from the 16th century to modern times. Wander among old keyboard instruments and funny-looking tubas. There's no English, aside from a €0.10 info sheet, but it's fascinating if you're into pianos (€3, Tue–Fri 9:00–17:00, Sat–Sun 10:00–17:00, closed Mon,

the low-profile white building east of the big, yellow Philharmonic Concert Hall, tel. 030/254-810).

Poke into the lobby of Berlin's Philharmonic Concert Hall and see if there are tickets available during your stay (ticket office open Mon–Fri 15:00–18:00, Sat–Sun 11:00–14:00, must purchase tickets in person, box office tel. 030/2548-8132).

Eastern Berlin

▲▲**Pergamon Museum**—Of the museums on Museumsinsel (Museum Island), just off Unter den Linden, only the Pergamon is essential. Its highlight is the fantastic Pergamon Altar. From a second-century B.C. Greek temple, it shows the Greeks under Zeus and Athena beating the giants in a dramatic pig pile of mythological mayhem. Check out the action spilling onto the stairs. The Babylonian Ishtar Gate (glazed blue tiles from sixth century B.C.) and many ancient Greek and Mesopotamian treasures are also impressive (€6, covered by Museumspass, Tue–Sun 10:00–18:00, Thu until 22:00, closed Mon, free on first Sun of month, courtyard café, behind Museum Island's red stone museum of antiquities, Am Kupfergraben, tel. for all sights on Museum Island: 030/2090-5577 or 030/209-050). The excellent audioguide (free with admission) covers the museum's highlights. Don't mind the scaffolding. Renovation projects (due to last until 2008) may cause small sections of the museum to close temporarily in 2004, but the museum will remain open.

Old National Gallery—Also on Museum Island, this gallery shows 19th-century German Romantic art: man against nature, Greek ruins dwarfed in enchanted forests, medieval churches, and powerful mountains (€6, covered by Museumspass, Tue–Sun 10:00–18:00, Thu until 22:00, closed Mon, free on first Sun of month, tel. 030/2090-5801).

▲▲**The Berlin Wall**—The 100-mile "Anti-Fascist Protective Rampart," as it was called by the East German government, was erected almost overnight in 1961 to stop the outward flow of people (3 million leaked out between 1949 and 1961). The 13-foot-high Wall *(Mauer)* had a 16-foot tank ditch, a no-man's-land that was 30 to 160 feet wide, and 300 sentry towers. During its 28 years, there were 1,693 cases when border guards fired, 3,221 arrests, and 5,043 documented successful escapes (565 of these were East German guards). The carnival atmosphere of those first years after the Wall fell is gone, but hawkers still sell "authentic" pieces of the Wall, DDR (East German) flags, and military paraphernalia to gawking tourists. Pick up the free brochure *Berlin: The Wall,* available at EurAide or the TI, which traces the history of the Wall and helps you find the remaining chunks and other Wall-related sights in Berlin. You can also rent a *Here We Go* audioguide about the Wall, which starts at Checkpoint Charlie, guides you along Zimmerstrasse to Potsdamer Platz, and then brings you back via Leipziger Strasse and Mauerstrasse (€5, 80 min).

▲▲▲Museum of the Wall at Checkpoint Charlie (Mauermuseum Haus am Checkpoint Charlie)—While the famous border checkpoint between the American and Soviet sectors is long gone, its memory is preserved by one of Europe's most interesting museums: The House at Checkpoint Charlie. During the Cold War, it stood defiantly—spitting distance from the border guards—showing off all the clever escapes over, under, and through the Wall.

Today, while the drama is over and hunks of the Wall stand like victory scalps at its door, the museum still tells a gripping history of the Wall, recounts the many ingenious escape attempts (early years with a cruder wall saw more escapes), and includes plenty of video and film coverage of those heady days when people-power tore down the Wall (€7.50, assemble 10 tourists and get in for €4.50 each, €3 audioguide, discount with WelcomeCard but not covered by Museumspass, cash only, daily 9:00–22:00, U-6 to Kochstrasse or—better from Zoo—line 2 to Stadtmitte, Friedrichstrasse 43–45, tel. 030/253-7250, www.mauermuseum.de). If you're pressed for time, this is a good after-dinner sight.

Americans—the Cold War victors—have the biggest appetite for Wall-related sights. Where the gate once stood, notice the thought-provoking post with larger-than-life posters of a young American soldier facing east and a young Russian soldier facing west. Around you are reconstructions of the old checkpoint. It's not named for a person, but for Number Three—as in Alpha (at the East–West German border, a hundred miles west of here), Bravo (as you enter Berlin proper), and Charlie (the most famous because it was the only place where foreigners could pass). A few yards away (on Zimmerstrasse), a glass panel describes the former checkpoint. From there, a double row of cobbles in Zimmerstrasse marks where the Wall once stood (these innocuous cobbles run throughout the city, tracing the former Wall's path). Follow it one very long block to Wilhelmstrasse and a surviving stretch of Wall.

When it fell, the Wall was literally carried away by the euphoria. What did manage to survive has been nearly devoured by a decade of persistent "Wall peckers." The park behind the Zimmerstrasse/Wilhelmstrasse bit of Wall marks the site of the command center of Hitler's Gestapo and SS (explained by English plaques throughout). It's been left undeveloped as a memorial to the tyranny once headquartered here. In the park is...

The Topography of Terror—Because of the horrible things planned here, rubble of the Gestapo and SS buildings will always be left as rubble. The SS, Hitler's personal bodyguards, grew to become a state-within-a-state, with its talons in every corner of German society. Along an excavated foundation of the building, an exhibit tells the story of National Socialism and its victims in Berlin (free, info booth open May–Sept daily 10:00–20:00, Oct–April daily 10:00–18:00 or until dark, free English audioguide with your passport as a deposit, tel. 030/2548-6703).

Across the street (facing the Wall) is the German Finance Ministry (Bundesministerium der Finanzen). Formerly the headquarters of the Nazi air force, this is the only major Hitler-era government building that survived the war's bombs. The communists used it to house their—no joke—Ministry of Ministries. Walk up Wilhelmstrasse (to the north) to see an entry gate (on your left) that looks much like it did when Germany occupied nearly all of Europe. On the north side of the building (farther up Wilhelmstrasse, at corner with Leipziger Strasse) is a wonderful example of communist art. The mural (from the 1950s) is classic Social Realism, showing the entire society—industrial laborers, farmworkers, women, and children—all happily singing the same patriotic song. This was the communist ideal. For the reality, look at the ground in the courtyard in front of the mural to see an enlarged photograph from a 1953 uprising here against the communists—quite a contrast.

▲▲Jewish Museum Berlin—This new museum is one of Europe's best Jewish sights. The highly conceptual building is a sight in itself, and the museum inside—an overview of the rich culture and history of Europe's Jewish community—is excellent. The Holocaust is appropriately remembered, but it doesn't overwhelm this celebration of Jewish life.

Designed by the American architect Daniel Libeskind, the zinc-walled building's zigzag shape is pierced by voids symbolic of the irreplaceable cultural loss caused by the Holocaust. Enter the museum through the 18th-century Baroque building next door, then go through an underground tunnel to reach the main exhibit. While underground, you can follow the Axis of Exile to a disorienting slanted garden with 49 pillars, or to the Axis of Holocaust, an eerily empty tower shut off from the outside world.

When you emerge from underground, climb the stairs to the engaging, thought-provoking, and accessible museum. There are many interactive exhibits (spell your name in Hebrew) and pieces of artwork (the *Fallen Leaves* sculpture in the building's largest void is especially powerful), and it's all very kid-friendly (peel the giant garlic and climb through a pomegranate tree). English explanations interpret both the exhibits and the design of the very symbolic building. The museum is in a nondescript residential neighborhood a 10-minute walk from the Checkpoint Charlie museum, but it's well worth the trip (€5, covered by Museumspass, discount with WelcomeCard, daily 10:00–20:00, Mon until 22:00, closed on Jewish holidays, tight security includes bag check and metal detectors, U-Bahn line 1, 6, or 15 to Hallesches Tor, take exit marked Jüdisches Museum, exit straight ahead, then turn right on Franz-Klühs-Strasse, museum is 5 min ahead on your left at Lindenstrasse 9, tel. 030/2599-3300, www.jmberlin.de). The museum has a good café/restaurant (lunch 12:00–16:00, daily special-€9, snacks at other times, tel. 030/2593-9760).

East Side Gallery—The biggest remaining stretch of the Wall is now "the world's longest outdoor art gallery." It stretches for nearly a mile and is covered with murals painted by artists from around the world. The murals are routinely whitewashed, so new ones can be painted. This length of the Wall makes a poignant walk. For a quick look, just go to Ostbahnhof station and look around (exit towards river and turn left on Mühlenstrasse; the freshest and most colorful art is at this end). The gallery only survives until a land ownership dispute can be solved, when it will likely be developed like the rest of the city. (Given the recent history, imagine the complexity of finding rightful owners of all this suddenly very-valuable land.) If you walk the entire length, you'll find a small Wall souvenir shop at the end (they'll stamp your passport with the former East German stamp) and a bridge crossing the river to a subway station at Schlesisches Tor (in Kreuzberg).

Kreuzberg—This district—once abutting the dreary Wall and inhabited mostly by poor Turkish guest laborers and their families—is still run-down, with graffiti-riddled buildings and plenty of student and Turkish street life. It offers a gritty look at melting-pot Berlin in a city where original Berliners are as rare as old buildings. Berlin is the fourth-largest Turkish city in the world, and Kreuzberg is its "downtown." But to call it a "little Istanbul" insults the big one. You'll see *döner kebab* stands, shops decorated with spray paint, and mothers wearing scarves. For a dose of Kreuzberg without getting your fingers dirty, joyride on bus #129 (catch it near Jewish Museum). For a colorful stroll, take U-Bahn to Kottbusser Tor and wander—ideally on Tuesday and Friday between 12:00 and 18:00, when the Turkish Market sprawls along the bank of the Maybachufer Canal.

▲▲**Gendarmenmarkt**—This delightful and historic square is bounded by twin churches, a tasty chocolate shop, and the concert hall (designed by Schinkel, the man who put the neoclassical stamp on Berlin and Dresden) for the Berlin symphony. In summer, it hosts a few outdoor cafés, *Biergartens,* and sometimes concerts. The name of the square—part French and part German—reminds us that in the 17th century, a fifth of all Berliners were French émigrés, Protestant Huguenots fleeing Catholic France. Back then, tolerant Berlin was a magnet for the persecuted. The émigrés vitalized the city with new ideas and know-how.

The Deutscher Dom (German Cathedral, described below) has a history exhibit worthwhile for history buffs. The Franzosischer Dom (French Cathedral) offers a humble museum on the Huguenots (€1.50,

Tue–Sun 12:00–17:00, closed Mon) and a chance to climb 254 steps to the top for a grand city view (€1.50, daily 9:00–19:00).

Fassbender & Rausch, on the corner near the Deutscher Dom, is Europe's biggest **chocolate store.** After 150 years of chocolate-making, this family-owned business proudly displays its sweet delights—250 different kinds—on a 55-foot-long buffet. Truffles are sold for about €0.50 each. The shop's evangelical Herr Ostwald (a.k.a. Benny) would love you to try his best-seller: tiramisu (Mon–Fri 10:00–20:00, Sat 10:00–16:00, closed Sun, corner of Mohrenstrasse at Charlottenstrasse 60, tel. 030/2045-8440).

German Cathedral—The Deutscher Dom houses the thought-provoking "Milestones, Setbacks, Sidetracks" (Wege, Irrwege, Umwege) exhibit, which traces the history of the German parliamentary system. The exhibit is well done and more interesting than it sounds. There are no English descriptions, but you can follow a fine and free 90-minute-long audioguide (passport required for deposit; to start, follow the blue arrows downstairs) or buy the detailed €10 guidebook (free, June–Aug Tue–Sun 10:00–19:00, Tue until 22:00, closed Mon, Sept–May Tue–Sun 10:00–18:00, Tue until 22:00, closed Mon, on Gendarmenmarkt just off Friedrichstrasse, tel. 030/2273-0431).

▲▲**New Synagogue**—A shiny gilded dome marks the New Synagogue, now a museum and cultural center on Oranienburger Strasse. Only the dome and facade have been restored, and a window overlooks a vacant field marking what used to be the synagogue. The largest and finest synagogue in Berlin before World War II, it was desecrated by Nazis on Crystal Night in 1938, bombed in 1943, and partially rebuilt in 1990. Inside, past tight security, there's a small but moving exhibit on the Berlin Jewish community through the centuries with some good English descriptions (ground floor and first floor). On its facade, the *Vergesst es nie* message—added by East Berlin Jews in 1966—means "Never forget." East Berlin had only a few hundred Jews, but now that the city is united, the Jewish community numbers about 12,000 (€3, Sun–Thu 10:00–18:00, Fri 10:00–14:00, closed Sat, May–Aug Sun–Mon until 20:00 and Fri until 17:00, last entry 30 min before closing, U-Bahn Oranienburger Tor, Oranienburger Strasse 28/30, tel. 030/8802-8300, www.cjudaicum.de).

Oren, a popular near-kosher café, is next to the synagogue (see "Eating—Eastern Berlin," page 500). If you're heading for the Pergamon Museum next, take a shortcut by turning left after leaving the synagogue, then right on Monbijoustrasse. Cross the canal and turn left to the museum.

A block from the synagogue, walk 50 yards down Grosse Hamburger Strasse to a little park. This street was known for 200 years as the "street of tolerance" because the Jewish community donated land to Protestants so that they could build a church. Hitler turned it into the "street of death" *(Todes Strasse)*, bulldozing 12,000 graves of the city's oldest Jewish cemetery and turning a Jewish old-folks home into a deportation center. Note the two memorials—one erected by the former East Berlin government and one built later by the city's unified government. Somewhere nearby, a plainclothes police officer keeps watch over this park.

▲**Oranienburger Strasse**—Berlin is developing so fast, it's impossible to predict what will be "in" next year. The area around Oranienburger Strasse is definitely trendy (but is being challenged by hip Friedrichshain, farther east).

While the area immediately around the synagogue is dull, 100 yards away things get colorful. The streets behind Grosse Hamburger Strasse flicker with atmospheric cafés, *Kneipen* (pubs), and art galleries.

At night, techno-prostitutes line Oranienburger Strasse. Prostitution is legal here, but there's a big debate about taxation. Since they don't get unemployment insurance, why should they pay taxes?

A block in front of the Hackescher Markt S-Bahn station is **Hackesche Höfe**—with eight courtyards bunny-hopping through a wonderfully restored 1907 *Jugendstil* building. It's full of trendy restaurants, theaters, and cinema (playing movies in their original languages). This is a fine example of how to make huge city blocks livable—Berlin's apartments are organized around courtyard after courtyard off the main roads.

Karl Marx Allee—The buildings along Karl Marx Allee in East Berlin (just beyond Alexanderplatz) were completely leveled by the Soviets in 1945. When Stalin decided this main drag should be a showcase street, he had it rebuilt with lavish Soviet aid and named it Stalin Allee. Today, this street, done in the bold "Stalin Gothic" style so common in Moscow back in the 1950s, has been restored (and named after Karl Marx), providing a rare look at Berlin's communist days. Cruise down Karl Marx Allee by taxi or ride the U-Bahn to Strausberger Platz and walk to Schillingstrasse. There are some fine Social Realist reliefs on the buildings, and the lampposts incorporate the wings of a phoenix (rising from the ashes) in their design.

Natural History Museum (Museum für Naturkunde)—This place is worth a visit just to see the largest dinosaur skeleton ever assembled. While you're there, meet "Bobby" the stuffed ape (€3.50, Tue–Fri 9:30–17:00, Sat–Sun 10:00–18:00, closed Mon, last entry 30 min before closing, U-Bahn line 6 to Zinnowitzer Strasse, Invalidenstrasse 43, tel. 030/2093-8591).

Around Charlottenburg Palace

The Charlottenburg district—with a cluster of fine museums across the street from a grand palace—makes a good side-trip from downtown.

Charlottenburg Palace Area

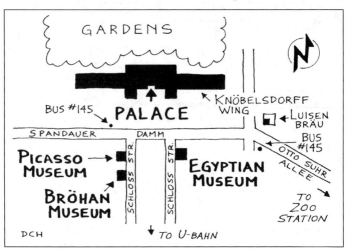

Ride U-2 to Sophie-Charlotte Platz and walk 10 minutes up the tree-lined boulevard Schlossstrasse (following signs to *Schloss*), or—much faster—catch bus #145 (direction Spandau) direct from Bahnhof Zoo.

For a Charlottenburg lunch, the **Luisen Bräu** is a comfortable brewpub restaurant with a copper and woody atmosphere, good local "microbeers" (*dunkles* are dark, *helles* light), and traditional German grub (€5–8 meals, daily 9:00–24:00, fun for groups, across from palace at Luisenplatz 1, tel. 030/341-9388).

▲**Charlottenburg Palace (Schloss)**—If you've seen the great palaces of Europe, this Baroque Hohenzollern palace comes in at about number 10 (behind Potsdam, too). It's even more disappointing since the main rooms can be toured only with a German guide (€8 includes 50-min tour, €2 to see just upper floors without tour, €7 to see palace grounds excluding tour areas, last tour 1 hr before closing, cash only, Tue–Sun 10:00–17:00, closed Mon, tel. 030/320-911).

The **Knöbelsdorff Wing** features a few royal apartments. Go upstairs and take a substantial hike through restored-since-the-war, gold-crusted white rooms (€5 depending on special exhibitions, free English audioguide, Tue–Fri 10:00–18:00, Sat–Sun 11:00–18:00, closed Mon, last entry 30 min before closing, when facing the palace walk toward the right wing, tel. 030/3209-1202).

▲▲**Egyptian Museum**—Across the street from the palace, the Egyptian Museum offers one of the great thrills in art appreciation—gazing into the still-young and beautiful face of 3,000-year-old Queen Nefertiti, the wife of King Akhenaton (€6, covered by Museumspass,

Tue–Sun 10:00–18:00, closed Mon, free on first Sun of month, free English audioguide, Schlossstrasse 70, tel. 030/343-5730).

This bust of Queen Nefertiti, from 1340 B.C., is perhaps the most famous piece of Egyptian art in Europe. Discovered in 1912, it shows the Marilyn Monroe of the early 20th century, with all the right beauty marks: long neck, symmetrical face, and just the right makeup (she's called "Berlin's most beautiful woman"). The bust never left its studio, but served as a master model for all other portraits of the queen. (That's probably why the left eye was never inlaid.) Buried for over 3,000 years, she was found by a German team who, by agreement with the Egyptian government, got to take home any workshop models they found. Although this bust is not representative of Egyptian art, it has become a symbol for Egyptian art by popular acclaim. Don't overlook the rest of the impressive museum, wonderfully lit and displayed, but with little English aside from the audioguide.

The Egyptian section of the 19th-century Royal Prussian Museum was originally in the Neues Museum on Museum Island. After World War II, the collection was divided between East and West. Plans are in the works to reunite the collection in its original Museum Island building, the Bodesmuseum, which is currently under renovation (due to be completed in 2010).

▲Berggruen Collection: Picasso and His Time—This tidy little museum is a pleasant surprise. Climb three floors through a fun and substantial collection of Picasso. Along the way, you'll see plenty of notable work by Matisse, van Gogh, and Cézanne. Enjoy a great chance to meet Paul Klee (€6, covered by Museumspass, Tue–Fri 10:00–18:00, Sat–Sun 11:00–18:00, closed Mon, free the first Sun of month, Schlossstrasse 1, tel. 030/3269-580).

▲Bröhan Museum—Wander through a dozen beautifully furnished Art Nouveau *(Jugendstil)* and Art Deco living rooms, a curvy organic world of lamps, glass, silver, and posters. English descriptions are posted on the wall of each room on the main floor. While you're there, look for the fine collection of Impressionist paintings by Karl Hagemeister (€4–6 depending on special exhibits, covered by Museumspass excluding special exhibits, Tue–Sun 10:00–18:00, closed Mon, Schlossstrasse 1A, tel. 030/3269-0600, www.broehan-museum.de).

Near Berlin

▲Sanssouci Palace, New Palace, and Park, Potsdam—With a lush park strewn with the extravagant whimsies of Frederick the Great, the sleepy town of Potsdam has long been Berlin's holiday retreat. Frederick's super-rococo Sanssouci Palace is one of Germany's most dazzling. His equally extravagant New Palace (Neues Palais), built to disprove rumors that Prussia was running out of money after the costly Seven Years' War, is on the other side of the park (it's a 30-min walk between palaces).

Greater Berlin

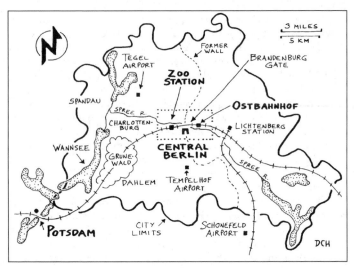

Your best bet for seeing Sanssouci Palace is to take the Potsdam TI's walking tour (see below). Otherwise, to make sense of all the ticket and tour options for the two palaces, stop by the palaces' TI (TI is across the street from windmill near Sanssouci entrance, helpful English-speaking staff, tel. 0331/969-4202).

Sanssouci Palace: Even though *sans souci* means "without a care," it can be a challenge for an English speaker to have an enjoyable visit. The palaces of Vienna, Munich, and even Würzburg offer equal sightseeing thrills with far fewer headaches. While the grounds are impressive, the interior of Sanssouci Palace can be visited only by a one-hour tour in German (with a borrowed English text), and these tours get booked up quickly. The only English option is the Potsdam TI's tour (see next page).

If you take a German tour of Sanssouci, you must be at the palace in person to get your ticket and the appointment time for your tour. In the summer, if you arrive by 9:00, you'll get right in. If you arrive after 10:00, plan on a wait. If you arrive after 12:00, you may not get in at all (€8, April–Oct Tue–Sun 9:00–17:00, closed Mon, Nov–March Tue–Sun 9:00–16:00, closed Mon, tel. 0331/969-4190).

New Palace: Use the English texts to tour Frederick's New Palace (€5, plus €1 for optional live tour in German, May–Oct Sat–Thu 9:00–17:00, closed Fri, Nov–April Sat–Thu 9:00–16:00, closed Fri). If you also want to see the king's apartments, you must take a required 45-minute tour in German (€5, offered May–Oct daily at 11:00 and 14:00). Off-season (Nov–April), the king's apartments are closed, and you can visit the rest of the New Palace only on a German tour (€5); it can take up to an hour for enough people to gather.

Walking Tours: The Potsdam TI's handy walking tour includes Sanssouci Palace, offering the only way to get into the palace with an English-speaking guide (€25 covers walking tour, palace, and park, 11:00 daily except Mon, 3.5 hrs, departs from Film Museum across from TI, reserve by phone, in summer reserve at least 2 days in advance, tel. 0331/275-5850, Potsdam TI hours: April–Oct Mon–Fri 9:00–19:00, Sat–Sun 10:00–16:00, less off-season, 5-min walk from Potsdam S-Bahn station, walk straight out of station and take first right onto An der Orangerie, Friedrich-Ebert Strasse 5, tel. 0331/275-5850).

A "Discover Potsdam" walking tour (which doesn't include Sanssouci Palace) is offered by "The Original Berlin Walks" and led by a native English-speaking guide. The tour leaves from Berlin at 9:40 on Saturdays May through October (€15, or €11.20 if under age 26 or with WelcomeCard, meet at taxi stand at Zoo Station, public transportation not included but can buy ticket from guide, no booking necessary, tel. 030/301-9194). The guide takes you to Cecilienhof Palace (site of postwar Potsdam conference attended by Churchill, Stalin, and Truman), through pleasant green landscapes to the historic heart of Potsdam for lunch, and to Sanssouci Park.

What to Avoid: Potsdam's much-promoted Wannsee boat rides are torturously dull.

Getting to Potsdam: Potsdam is easy to reach from Berlin (17 min on direct Regional Express/RE trains from Bahnhof Zoo every 30 min, or 30 min direct on S-Bahn #7 from Bahnhof Zoo to Potsdam station; both covered by transit pass with zones A, B, and C). If you're taking the Potsdam TI's tour, walk to the TI from the Potsdam S-Bahn stop (see "Walking Tours," above, for directions). If not taking the TI tour, catch bus #695 from the Potsdam station to the palaces (3/hr, 20 min). Use the same bus #695 to shuttle between the sights in the park. For a more scenic approach, take tram #96 or #X98 from the Potsdam station to Luisenplatz, then walk 15 minutes through the park and enjoy a classic view of Sanssouci Palace.

Other Day Trips—EurAide has researched and printed a *Get Me Outta Here* flier describing good day trips to small towns and another flier on the nearby Sachsenhausen concentration camp (which many think is as interesting as Dachau; a Sachsenhausen day trip is also offered by The Original Berlin Walks, see "City Walking Tours," page 460).

NIGHTLIFE

For the young and determined sophisticate, *Zitty* and *Tip* are the top guides to alternative culture (in German, sold at kiosks). Also pick up the free schedules *Flyer* and *030* in bars and clubs. *Berlin Programm* lists a nonstop parade of concerts, plays, exhibits, and cultural events (in German, www.berlin-programm.de); the *Ex-Berliner* has less information but is entirely in English (both sold at kiosks and TIs).

Oranienburger Strasse's trendy scene (see "Sights—Eastern Berlin," page 482) is already being eclipsed by the action at Friedrichshain and Kollwitzplatz farther east. Tourists stroll the Ku'damm after dark.

Visit KaDeWe's ticket office for your music and theater options (sixth floor, 18 percent fee but access to all tickets). Ask about "competitive improvisation" and variety shows.

For jazz (blues and boogie, too) near recommended Savignyplatz hotels, consider **A Trane Jazz Club** (daily, 21:00–2:00, Bleibtreustrasse 1, tel. 030/313-2550) and **Quasimodo Live** (Kantstrasse 12a, under Delphi Cinema, tel. 030/312-8086). For quality blues and New Orleans–style jazz, stop by **Ewige Lampe** (from 21:00, Niebuhrstrasse 11a).

Bar Jeder Vernunft offers modern-day cabaret a short walk from the recommended hotels. This variety show under a classic old tent perched atop a modern parking lot is a hit with German speakers, but can still be worthwhile for non–German speakers (as some of the music shows are in a sort of "Dinglish"). Even some Americans perform here periodically. Tickets are generally around €15, and shows change regularly (shows start at 20:30, closed Sun, seating can be a bit cramped, Schaperstrasse 24, tel. 030/883-1582).

To spend an evening enjoying Europe's largest revue theater, consider **Revue Berlin** at the Friedrichstadt Palast. The show basically depicts the history of Berlin, and is choreographed in a funny and musical way that's popular with the Lawrence Welk–type German crowd. It's even entertaining for your entire English-speaking family (€13–51, Tue–Sat 20:00, also Sat–Sun at 16:00, U-Bahn Oranienburger Tor, tel. 030/284-8830, www.friedrichstadtpalast.de).

SLEEPING

Near Savignyplatz and Bahnhof Zoo

These hotels and pensions are a 5- to 15-minute walk from Bahnhof Zoo (or take S-Bahn to Savignyplatz). Hotels on Kantstrasse have street noise. Ask for a quieter room in back. The area has an artsy charm going back to the cabaret days in the 1920s, when it was the center of Berlin's gay scene. Of the accommodations listed in this area, Pension Peters offers the best value for budget travelers.

$$$ Pension Savoy rents 16 comfortable and colorfully decorated rooms with all the amenities. You'll love the cheery old pastel breakfast room and the friendly staff (who speak just enough English). Most rooms overlook a quiet courtyard (Ss-€62, Sb-€73, Db-€102–109, extra person-€34–46, elevator, Meinekestrasse 4, tel. 030/881-3700, fax 030/882-3746, www.hotel-pension-savoy.de).

SLEEP CODE

(€1 = about $1.10, country code: 49, area code: 030)

Sleep Code: **S** = Single, **D** = Double/Twin, **T** = Triple, **Q** = Quad, **b** = bathroom, **s** = shower only, **no CC** = Credit Cards not accepted, **SE** = Speaks English, **NSE** = No English. Unless otherwise noted, credit cards are accepted, English is spoken, and breakfast is included.

To help you sort easily through these listings, I've divided the rooms into three categories, based on the price for a standard double room with bath:

$$$ **Higher Priced**—Most rooms €100 or more.
$$ **Moderately Priced**—Most rooms between €80–100.
$ **Lower Priced**—Most rooms €80 or less.

I have concentrated my hotel recommendations around Savignyplatz. While Bahnhof Zoo and Ku'damm are no longer the center of Berlin, the trains, TI, and walking tours are all still handy to Zoo. And the streets around the tree-lined Savignyplatz (a 10-min walk behind the station) have a neighborhood charm. While towering new hotels are being built in the new center, simple, small, and friendly good-value places abound only here. My listings are generally located a couple of flights up in big, run-down buildings. Inside, they are clean, quiet, and spacious enough so that their well-worn character is actually charming. Rooms in back are on quiet courtyards.

The city is packed and hotel prices go up on holidays, including Green Week in mid-January, Easter weekend, the first weekend in May, Ascension weekend in May, the Love Parade (a huge techno-Woodstock, second weekend in July), Germany's national holiday (Oct 2–4), Christmas, and New Year's.

During slow times, the best values are actually business-class rooms on the push list booked through the TI. But as the world learns what a great place Berlin is to visit, a rising tide of tourists will cause these deals to fade away.

$$$ Hotel Astoria is a friendly, three-star, business-class hotel with 32 comfortably furnished rooms and affordable summer and weekend rates (high season Db-€117–128; prices drop to Sb-€86–97, Db-€94–118 during low season of July–Aug, Nov–Feb, or any 2 weekend nights or if slow; breakfast-€10 extra, rooms with showers are cheaper

Berlin's Savignyplatz Neighborhood

1 Pension Savoy	**8** Hotel Carmer 16
2 Hotel Astoria	**9** Hotel Imperator
3 Hecker's Hotel	**10** Pension Peters
4 Hotel Askanischerhof	**11** Pension Alexis
5 Hotel Atlanta	**12** Hotel Crystal Garni
6 Hotel-Pension Funk	**13** Jugendgastehaus am Zoo Hostel
7 Hotel Bogota	**14** To Hotels Austriana, Insel Rügen, Bella & Curtis; To Weyers Café Rest.

- **15** Dicke Wirtin Pub
- **16** Restaurant Die Zwölf Apostel
- **17** Ristorante San Marino
- **18** Restaurant Zillemarkt
- **19** Restaurant Tomasa
- **20** A Trane Jazz Club
- **21** Käthe Kollwitz Museum
- **22** To Launderette

than rooms with baths, non-smoking floors, elevator, free Internet access, parking-€13/day, around corner from Bahnhof Zoo at Fasanen-strasse 2, tel. 030/312-4067, fax 030/312-5027, www.hotelastoria.de, info@hotelastoria.de).

$$$ **Hecker's Hotel** is an ultramodern, four-star business hotel with 69 rooms and all the sterile Euro-comforts (Sb-€125, Db-€150, breakfast-€15, weekends breakfast included, all rooms-€200 during conferences, non-smoking rooms, elevator, parking-€9/day, between Savignyplatz and Ku'damm at Grolmanstrasse 35, tel. 030/88900, fax 030/889-0260, www.heckers-hotel.com).

$$$ **Hotel Atlanta** has 30 newly renovated rooms in an older building with big leather couches, half a block south of Ku'damm. It's next to Gucci, on an elegant shopping street (Ss-€40–70, Sb-€60–99, Db-

€80–120, Tb-€100-140, Qb-€120–160, non-smoking rooms, Fasanenstrasse 74, tel. 030/881-8049, fax 030/881-9872, www.hotelatlanta .de, hatlanta68266759@aol.com).

$$$ **Hotel Askanischerhof** is the oldest *Zimmer* in Berlin, posh as can be with 16 sprawling antique-furnished rooms. Photos on the walls brag of famous movie-star guests. Frau Glinicke offers Old World service and classic Berlin atmosphere (Sb-€95–110, Db-€117–145, extra bed-€25, free parking, non-smoking rooms, elevator, Ku'damm 53, tel. 030/881-8033, fax 030/881-7206, www.askanischer-hof.de, info @askanischer-hof.de).

$$$ **Hotel Carmer 16,** with 30 bright, airy rooms, feels like a big, professional hotel with all the comfy extras but with a cold reception staff (Sb-€76–93, Db-€93–122, extra person-€35, some rooms have balconies, elevator and a few stairs, beauty parlor and mini-spa upstairs, Carmerstrasse 16, tel. 030/3110-0500, fax 030/3110-0510, carmer16@t-online.de).

$$ **Hotel-Pension Funk,** the former home of a 1920s silent-movie star, is delightfully quirky. Kind manager Herr Michael Pfundt offers 14 elegant old rooms with rich Art Nouveau furnishings (S-€34–57, Ss-€41–72, Sb-€52–82, D-€52–82, Ds-€72–93, Db-€82–113, extra person-€23, prices guaranteed through 2004 with this book, cash preferred, Fasanenstrasse 69, a long block south of Ku'damm, tel. 030/882-7193, fax 030/883-3329, www.hotel-pensionfunk.de, berlin@hotel-pensionfunk.de).

$$ **Hotel Bogota** has 125 unique rooms and several large lounges in a sprawling, drab old maze of a building that once housed the Nazi Chamber of Culture. (After the war, German theater stars were "denazified" here before they could go back to work.) Pieces of the owner's modern art collection lurk around every corner. Take a peek at the bizarre collage in the atrium, with mannequins suspended from the ceiling (S-€44, Ss-€55–57, Sb-€66–72, D-€66–69, Ds-€74–77, Db-€94–98, extra bed-€20, children under 12 free, prices guaranteed through 2004 with this book, non-smoking rooms, elevator, bus #109 from Bahnhof Zoo to Schlüterstrasse 45, tel. 030/881-5001, fax 030/883-5887, www.hotelbogota.de, hotel.bogota@t-online.de).

$$ **Hotel-Pension Imperator** fills a sprawling floor of a grand building with 11 big, quiet, and Old World–elegant rooms and a clientele that includes the occasional actor or musician (S-€42, Ss-€58, Sb-€65, D-€78, Ds-€88–93, Db-€98, Ts-€118, no CC, elevator, Meinekestrasse 5, tel. 030/881-4181, fax 030/885-1919).

$ **Pension Peters,** run by a German-Swedish couple, is sunny and central with a cheery breakfast room. Decorated sleek Scandinavian, with every room renovated, it's a winner (S-€36, Ss-€46, Sb-€58, D-€51, Ds-€67, Db-€66–77, extra bed-€8, kids under 12 free, family room, 3 percent extra if you pay with plastic, prices guaranteed through 2004 with this book, Internet access, 10 yards off Savignyplatz at

Kantstrasse 146, tel. 030/3150-3944, fax 030/312-3519, www.pension -peters-berlin.de, penspeters@aol.com, Annika and Christoph SE). The same family also runs a larger hotel just outside of Berlin (see Hotel Pankow under "More Berlin Hotels," next page) and rents apartments (ideal for small groups and longer stays).

$ **Pension Alexis** is a classic old-European four-room pension in a stately 19th-century apartment run by Frau and Herr Schwarzer. The shower and toilet facilities are older and cramped, but this, more than any other Berlin listing, has you feeling at home with a faraway aunt (S-€42, D-€65, T-€97, Q-€128, no CC, big rooms, handheld showers, Carmerstrasse 15, tel. 030/312-5144, enough English spoken).

$ **Hotel Crystal Garni** is professional and offers small, well-worn, comfortable rooms and a *vollkorn* breakfast room (S-€36, Sb-€41, D-€47, Ds-€57, Db-€66–77, elevator, a block past Savignyplatz at Kantstrasse 144, tel. 030/312-9047, fax 030/312-6465, run by John and Dorothy Schwarzrock and Herr Vasco Flascher).

$ **Jugendgastehaus am Zoo** is a bare-bones, cash-only youth hostel that takes no reservations and hardly has a reception desk. It's far less comfortable and only marginally cheaper than simple hotels (85 beds, dorm beds-€18, S-€25, D-€44, includes sheets, no breakfast, no CC, Hardenbergstrasse 9a, tel. 030/312-9410, fax 030/312-5430).

South of Ku'damm

Several small hotels are nearby in a charming, café-studded neighborhood 300 yards south of Ku'damm, near the intersection of Sächsische Strasse and Pariser Strasse (bus #109 from Bahnhof Zoo, direction: Airport Tegel). They are less convenient from the station than most of the Savignyplatz listings above.

$$ **Hotel Austriana,** with 25 modern and bright rooms, is warmly and energetically run by Thomas (S-€33–43, Ss-€41–48, Sb-€49–67, Ds-€62–69, Db-€78–89, Ts-€78–96, Qs-€96–104, prices higher for holidays and conferences, half the rooms have balconies, elevator, Pariser Strasse 39, tel. 030/885-7000, fax 030/8857-0088, www.austriana.de, austriana@t-online.de).

$$ **Insel Rügen Hotel,** in the same building as the Austriana, has 31 rooms and ornate, Eastern decor (S-€28, Ss-€39, D-€51, Ds-€61–66, Db-€77–82, elevator, Pariser Strasse 39, tel. 030/884-3940, fax 030/8843-9437, www.insel-ruegen-hotel.de, ir-hotel@t-online.de).

$$ **Hotel-Pension Bella,** a clean, simple, masculine-feeling place with high ceilings, rents nine big, comfortable rooms but is a lesser value (S-€30–45, Ss/Sb-€45–65, D-€50–65, Ds-€70–85, Db-€80–90, extra person-€10, apartment also available, elevator, bus #249 from Zoo, Ludwigkirchstrasse 10a, tel. 030/881-6704, fax 030/8867-9074, www .pension-bella.de, pension.bella@t-online.de).

$ **Hotel-Pension-Curtis,** in the same building as the Austriana and Insel Rügen (recommended above), has 10 hip, piney, basic rooms (S-€32–37, Ss-40–45, Ds-€60–70, Ts-€75–83, Qs-€90–100, no CC, elevator, Pariser Strasse 39, tel. 030/883-4931, fax 030/885-0438).

More Berlin Hotels
Away from the Center
$ **Hotel Pankow** is a new, fresh, colorful 43-room place run by friendly Annika and Christoph (from the Pension Peters, above). It's a 30-minute commute north of downtown but a good value (S-€29, Sb-€44, D-€39, Db-€59, T-€49, Tb-€69, Q-€55, Qb-€75, family rooms, children under 16 free in room with parents, elevator, Internet access, free parking in lot or €3/day in garage, tram station in front of hotel takes you to the center in 30 min, Pasewalker Strasse 14-15, tel. 030/486-2600, fax 030/4862-6060, www.hotel-pankow-berlin.de, hotelpankow@aol.com).

Near Augsburgerstrasse U-Bahn Stop
$$ Consider **Hotel-Pension Nürnberger Eck** (S-€45, Sb-€60, D-€70, Db-€92, Nürnberger Strasse 24a, tel. 030/235-1780, fax 030/2351-7899) or **Hotel Arco** (Sb-€64–75, Db-€82–92, Geisbergerstrasse 30, tel. 030/235-1480, fax 030/2147-5178, www.arco-hotel.de).

Near Güntzelstrasse U-Bahn Stop
$ Choose between **Pension Güntzel** (Ds-€59, Db-€69–79, single rooms €16 less, Güntzelstrasse 62, tel. 030/857-9020, fax 030/853-1108, www.pension-guentzel.de), **Pension Finck** (S-€39, Ss-€42, D-€45, Ds-€59, €3 extra for 1-night stays, no CC, Güntzelstrasse 54, tel. 030/861-2940, fax 030/873-8223), or **Hotel Pension München** (S-€40, Sb-€55, Db-€75, also Güntzelstrasse 62, tel. 030/857-9120, fax 030/8579-1222, www.hotel-pension-muenchen-in-berlin.de).

In Eastern Berlin
$$$ **Hotel Unter den Linden** is ideal for those nostalgic for the days of Soviet rule, although nowadays at least, the management tries to be efficient and helpful. Formerly one of the best hotels in the DDR, this huge, blocky place, right on Unter den Linden in the heart of what was East Berlin, is reasonably comfortable and reasonably priced. Built in 1966, with prison-like corridors, it has 331 modern, plain, and comfy rooms (Sb-€67–87, Db-€109–123, non-smoking rooms, at intersection of Friedrichstrasse, Unter den Linden 14, tel. 030/238-110, fax 030/2381-1100, www.hotel-unter-den-linden.de, reservation @hotel-unter-den-linden.de).

Hostels in South and Eastern Berlin

Berlin is known among budget travelers for its fun, hip hostels. Here are four good bets (all prices listed per person): **Studentenhotel Meininger 10** (€23 per person, includes sheets and breakfast, no CC, no curfew, elevator, free parking, near city hall on JFK Platz, Meiningerstrasse 10, U-Bahn: Rathaus Schoneberg, tel. 030/7871-7414, fax 030/7871-7412, www.meininger-hostels.de), **Mitte's Backpacker Hostel** (€15 dorm beds, S-€30, D-€23–28, T-€20, Q-€18, sheets-€2.50, no breakfast, could be cleaner, no curfew, Internet access-€6/hr, laundry, bike rental-€15/day, English newspapers, U-Bahn: Zinnowitzerstrasse, Chauseestrasse 102, tel. 030/2839-0965, fax 030/2839-0935, www.backpacker.de, info@backpacker.de), **Circus** (dorm bed-€13–15, S-€28–32, D-€21–24, T-€18–20, Q-€16–18, 2-person apartment with kitchen-€65–75, 4-person apartment-€115-130, breakfast-€4, sheets-€2, no CC, no curfew, Internet access, 2 locations, U-Bahn: Rosa-Luxemburg Platz, Rosa-Luxemburg Strasse 39, or U-Bahn: Rosenthaler Platz, Weinbergsweg 1a, both tel. 030/2839-1433, fax 030/2839-1484, www.circus-berlin.de, info@circus-berlin.de), or **Clubhouse** (dorm bed-€14, bed in 5- to 7-bed room-€17, S-€32, D-€23, T-€20, breakfast-€3, sheets-€2, no CC, Internet access, on second floor, nightclub below, in hip Oranienburger Strasse area, S- or U-Bahn: Friedrichstrasse, Kalkscheunenstrasse 4-5, tel. 030/2809-7979, fax 030/2809-7977, www.clubhouse-berlin.de, info@clubhouse-berlin.de).

EATING

Don't be too determined to eat "Berlin-style." The city is known only for its mildly spicy sausage. Still, there is a world of restaurants in this ever-changing city to choose from. Your best approach may be to choose a neighborhood, rather than a particular restaurant.

For quick and easy meals, colorful pubs—called *Kneipen*—offer light meals and the fizzy local beer, Berliner Weiss. Ask for it *mit Schuss* for a shot of fruity syrup in your suds. If the kraut is getting *Wurst,* try one of the many Turkish, Italian, or Balkan restaurants. Eat cheap at *Imbiss* snack stands, bakeries (sandwiches), and falafel/kebab places. Bahnhof Zoo has several bright and modern fruit-and-sandwich bars and a grocery (daily 6:00–24:00).

Western Berlin
Near Savignyplatz

Several good places are on or within 100 yards of Savignyplatz. Take a walk and survey these: **Dicke Wirtin** is a smoky old pub with traditional old-Berlin *Kneipe* atmosphere, famously cheap *Gulaschsuppe,* and salads (daily 12:00–4:00, just off Savignyplatz at Carmerstrasse 9, tel. 030/312-4952). **Die Zwölf Apostel** restaurant is trendy for leafy candlelit ambience and Italian food. A dressy local crowd packs the place for €10 pizzas and €15 to €30 meals. Late-night partygoers appreciate Apostel's great breakfast (daily, 24 hrs, no CC, outside seating in summer until 10:00, immediately across from Savigny S-Bahn entrance, Bleibtreustrasse 49, tel. 030/312-1433). **Ristorante San Marino,** on the square, is another good Italian place, serving cheaper pasta and pizza (daily 11:00–1:00, Savignyplatz 12, tel. 030/313-6086). **Zillemarkt Restaurant,** which feels like an old-time Berlin beer garden, serves traditional Berlin specialties in the garden or in the rustic candlelit interior (€10 meals, daily 10:00–24:00, near the S-Bahn tracks at Bleibtreustrasse 48a, tel. 030/881-7040).

Tomasa is most popular for its weekend breakfast (reservations smart) but also has a nice dinner atmosphere with a completely German crowd (€15 dinner plates, daily 10:00–24:00, a block off Savignyplatz at Knesebackstrasse 22, tel. 030/312-8310).

Weyers Café Restaurant, serving quality international and German cuisine, is a great value and worth a short walk. It's sharp, with white tablecloths, but not stuffy. On a sunny day, its patio is packed with locals (€10 dinner plates, daily 8:00–2:00, seating indoors or outside on the leafy square, Pariser Strasse 16, reservations smart after 20:00, tel. 030/881-9378).

Ullrich Supermarkt is the neighborhood grocery store (Mon–Fri 9:00–20:00, Sat 9:00–16:00, closed Sun, Kantstrasse 7, under the tracks near Bahnhof Zoo). There's plenty of fast food near Bahnhof Zoo and on Ku'damm.

Near Bahnhof Zoo

Self-Service Cafeterias: The top floor of the famous department store, **KaDeWe,** holds the Winter Garden Buffet view cafeteria, and its sixth-floor deli/food department is a picnicker's nirvana. Its arterials are clogged with more than 1,000 kinds of sausage and 1,500 types of cheese (Mon–Fri 9:30–20:00, Sat 9:00–16:00, closed Sun, U-Bahn: Wittenbergplatz). **Wertheim** department store, a half-block from the Memorial Church, has cheap food counters in the basement and a city view from its fine self-service cafeteria, Le Buffet, located up six banks of escalators (Mon–Fri 9:30–20:00, Sat 9:00–16:00, closed Sun, U-Bahn: Ku'damm). **Marche,** a chain that's popped up in big cities all over Germany, is another inexpensive, self-service cafeteria within a half block of the Kaiser Wilhelm church (Mon–Thu 8:00–22:00, Fri–Sat 8:00–24:00, Sun 10:00–22:00, plenty of salads, fruit, made-to-order omelettes, Ku'damm 14, tel. 030/882-7578).

At Bahnhof Zoo: Terrassen am Zoo is a good restaurant right in the station, offering peaceful decency amidst a whirlwind of travel activity (daily 6:00–22:00, upstairs, next to track 1, tel. 030/315-9140).

Eastern Berlin
Along Unter den Linden

The Opernpalais, preening with fancy prewar elegance, hosts a number of pricey restaurants. Its **Operncafé** has the best desserts and the longest dessert bar in Europe (daily 8:00–24:00, across from university and war memorial at Unter den Linden 5, tel. 030/202-683); sit down and enjoy perhaps the classiest coffee stop in Berlin. The beer and tea garden in front has a cheap food counter (from 10:00, depending on weather). More students and fewer tourists eat in the student facilities at Humboldt University across the street (go through courtyard, enter building through main door, follow signs to cafeteria on right or cheaper, government-subsidized *Mensa* on left, both closed weekends).

Oren Restaurant and Café is a trendy, stylish, near-kosher/vegetarian place next to the New Synagogue. The food is pricey but good, and the ambience is happening (daily 12:00–1:00, Sun open at 10:00, Sat until 3:00, north of Museum Island about 5 blocks away at Oranienburger Strasse 28, tel. 030/282-8228).

Near Pergamon Museum

Try the **Kupfer Keller,** a small basement restaurant, for a short list of traditional German grub, including *Berliner Kartoffelsuppe*—Berlin potato soup (Tue–Sun 11:00–18:00, closed Mon, at corner of Bauhof Strasse and Am Kupfergraben, across from Pergamon).

Deponie3 is a trendy Berlin *Kneipe* usually filled with students from the nearby Humboldt University. Garden seating in the back is nice if you don't mind the noise of the S-Bahn passing directly above you. The interior is a cozy, wooden wonderland of a bar, serving basic sandwiches, salads, and daily specials (sometimes with live music, open Mon–Fri from 9:00, Sat–Sun from 10:00, Georgenstrasse 5, 1 block from Pergamon under S-Bahn tracks, tel. 030/2016-5740).

Near Checkpoint Charlie

Lekkerbek, a busy little bakery and cafeteria, sells inexpensive and tasty salads, soups, pastas, and sandwiches (Mon–Fri 6:00–18:00, Sat 7:00–13:00, closed Sun, a block from Checkpoint Charlie museum at Kochstrasse subway stop, Friedrichstrasse 211, tel. 030/251-7208). For a classier sit-down meal, try **Café Adler,** across the street from the museum (Mon–Sat 10:00–24:00, Sun 10:00–19:00, Friedrichstrasse 20b, tel. 030/251-8965).

TRANSPORTATION CONNECTIONS

Berlin has three train stations (with more on the way). Bahnhof Zoo was the West Berlin train station and still serves Western Europe: Frankfurt, Munich, Hamburg, Paris, and Amsterdam. The Ostbahnhof (former East Berlin's main station) still faces east, serving Prague, Warsaw, Vienna, and Dresden. The Lichtenberg Bahnhof (eastern Berlin's top U- and S-Bahn hub) also handles a few eastbound trains. Expect exceptions. All stations are conveniently connected by subway and even faster by train. Train info: tel. 01805-996-633.

By train to: Frankfurt (14/day, 5 hrs), **Munich** (14/day, 7 hrs, 10 hrs overnight), **Köln** (hrly, 6.5 hrs), **Amsterdam** (4/day, 7 hrs), **Budapest** (2/day, 13 hrs; 1 goes via Czech Republic and Slovakia, so Eurail is not valid), **Copenhagen** (4/day, 8 hrs, change in Hamburg), **London** (4/day, 15 hrs), **Paris** (6/day, 13 hrs, change in Köln, 1 direct night train), **Zürich** (12/day, 10 hrs, 1 direct night train), **Prague** (4/day, 5 hrs, no overnight trains), **Warsaw** (4/day, 8 hrs, 1 night train from Lichtenberg Station; reservations required on all Warsaw-bound trains), **Kraków** (2/day, 10 hrs), **Vienna** (2/day, 12 hrs via Czech Republic; for second-class ticket, Eurailers pay an extra €23 if under age 26 or €31 if age 26 or above; otherwise, take the Berlin–Vienna via Passau train—nightly at 20:00).

Eurailpasses don't cover the Czech Republic. The **Prague Excursion pass** picks up where Eurail leaves off, getting you from any border into Prague and then back out to Eurail country again within seven days (first class-€50, second class-€40, youth second class-€35, buy from EurAide at Berlin's Bahnhof Zoo or Munich's Hauptbahnhof and get reservations—€3—at the same time).

There are **night trains** from Berlin to Amsterdam, Munich, Köln, Brussels, Paris, Vienna, Budapest, Kraków, Warsaw, Stuttgart, Basel, and Zürich, but there are no night trains from Berlin to anywhere in Italy or Spain. A *Liegeplatz,* or berth (€15–21), is a great deal; inquire at EurAide at Bahnhof Zoo for details. Beds cost the same whether you have a first- or second-class ticket or railpass. Trains are often full, so get your bed reserved a few days in advance from any travel agency or major train station in Europe. Note: Since the Paris–Berlin night train goes through Belgium, railpass holders cannot use a Eurail Selectpass to cover this ride unless they've selected Belgium.

Berlin's Three Airports

Allow €20 for a taxi ride to or from any of Berlin's airports. **Tegel Airport** handles most flights from the United States and Western Europe (4 miles from center, catch the faster bus #X9 to Bahnhof Zoo, or bus #109 to Ku'damm and Bahnhof Zoo for €2; bus TXL goes to Alexanderplatz in East Berlin). Flights from the east and on Buzz Airlines usually arrive at **Schönefeld Airport** (12.5 miles from center, short walk to S-Bahn, catch S-9 to Zoo Station). **Templehof Airport**'s future is uncertain (in Berlin, bus #119 to Ku'damm or U-Bahn 6 or 7). The central telephone number for all three airports is 01805-000-186. For British Air, call 01805-266-522, Delta at 01803-337-880, SAS at 01803-234-023, or Lufthansa at 01803-803-803.

DRESDEN

Dresden, the capital of Saxony, surprises visitors with fine Baroque architecture and impressive museums. It's historical, intriguing, and fun. While the city is packed with tourists, 85 percent of them are German. Until Americans rediscover Dresden's Baroque glory, you'll feel like you're in on a secret.

At the peak of its power in the 18th century, the capital of Saxony ruled most of present-day Poland and eastern Germany from the bank of the Elbe River. Dresden native Augustus the Strong was both prince elector of Saxony and king of Poland. He imported artists from all over Europe, peppering his city with stunning Baroque buildings. Dresden's architecture and dedication to the arts—along with the gently rolling hills surrounding the city—earned it the nickname "Florence on the Elbe."

Sadly, Dresden is today best known for its destruction in World War II. American and British pilots firebombed the city on the night of February 13, 1945. More than 50,000 people were killed and 85 percent of the historical center was destroyed. (American Kurt Vonnegut, who was a POW in Dresden during the firebombing, later memorialized the event in his novel *Slaughterhouse-Five*.) Dresden is still rebuilding.

When Germany was divvied up at the end of World War II, Dresden wound up in the Soviet sector. Forty years of communist rule left its outskirts—and even some of its center—a nightmare of blocky, utilitarian Stalinist architecture. But older Dresdeners feel some nostalgia for the Red old days, when "everyone had a job." Today, Saxony's unemployment rate is 19 percent. Even so, Dresden is a young and vibrant city, crawling with happy-go-lucky students who barely remember communism.

Central Dresden

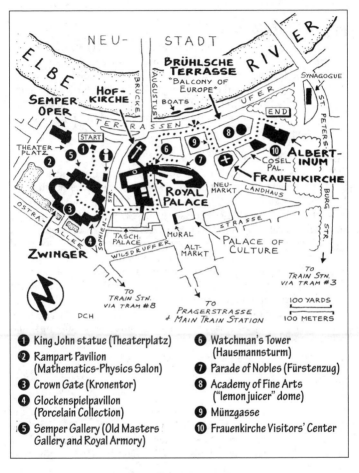

1. King John statue (Theaterplatz)
2. Rampart Pavilion (Mathematics-Physics Salon)
3. Crown Gate (Kronentor)
4. Glockenspielpavillon (Porcelain Collection)
5. Semper Gallery (Old Masters Gallery and Royal Armory)
6. Watchman's Tower (Hausmannsturm)
7. Parade of Nobles (Fürstenzug)
8. Academy of Fine Arts ("lemon juicer" dome)
9. Münzgasse
10. Frauenkirche Visitors' Center

ORIENTATION

(area code: 0351)

Dresden's city center lies at a curve in the Elbe River. The Old Town (Altstadt) is south of the Elbe, and the New Town (Neustadt) is to the north. Dresden is big, with half a million residents, but virtually all of its sights are within easy strolling distance along the south bank of the Elbe in the Old Town. The main train station (Hauptbahnhof) is a 5-minute tram ride or a 15-minute walk south of the historical center, partly along the heavily communist-influenced Prager Strasse. The New Town, to the north of the river, is more residential. It boasts virtually no sights, but can be fun to explore and has some recommended hotels and restaurants.

Planning Your Time

Dresden, conveniently located halfway between Prague and Berlin, is well worth a stop. If you're short on time, Dresden's top sights can be seen in a midday break on your Berlin–Prague train ride (it's about 2.5 hours from both). Catch the early train, throw your bag in a locker in the station (€2), do the self-guided tour (below), and visit some museums before taking an evening train out. If you have more time, Dresden merits an overnight stay.

Tourist Information

Dresden has two TIs: in the heart of the Altstadt in the neoclassical Schinkelwache building at **Theaterplatz** (next to the Zwinger, Mon–Fri 10:00–18:00, Sat–Sun 10:00–16:00) and in a freestanding kiosk at the train-station end of **Prager Strasse** (Mon–Fri 9:30–18:00, Sat 9:30–16:00, closed Sun, general TI tel. 0351/491-920, www.dresden-tourist .de). Both tourist offices book rooms (€3 per person), sell concert and theater tickets, and operate travel agencies. Get the handy, free one-page map of Dresden with a listing of key sights, hours, and prices on the back. Also ask for the free *Kultur Quartier Dresden* brochure, with English information on the city's cultural sights.

The **Dresden City Card** sold at the TIs gives you admission to all of Dresden's top museums, discounts on some lesser museums, and unlimited use of the city's transit system (€18/48 hrs; €29 for 72-hr "Regional" version, including outlying areas). If you are only here for the day, skip it—instead, buy a one-day museum pass, called a *Tageskarte* (€10, covers all state museums, including all listed below; available at participating museums).

Many of Dresden's museums (including all Zwinger museums, the Royal Palace, and Watchman's Tower) are closed on Monday. The Albertinum (including the New Masters Gallery and Green Vault) is closed on Thursday. The Web site for all Dresden museums is www .skd-dresden.de.

Local Guide: Dr. Günther Kirsch, a good guide, authored one of the souvenir picture books you'll see around town (€28/hr, reserve several weeks ahead if possible, tel. 0351/459-1601).

Arrival in Dresden

Dresden has two major train stations. If you're coming for the day and want easiest access to the sights, use the Hauptbahnhof, just south of the Old Town. Exit the station following signs for taxis and trams, cross the tracks to the opposite side, and take tram #8 (departing to your left), which zips you to the historical center (Theaterplatz stop). If you'd rather walk to the Old Town (15 min), you'll get a dose of the communist era as you stroll the Soviet-style Prager Strasse (turn left out of station, go under railway overpass, and take pedestrian walkway over construction zone).

The Neustadt station serves the New Town north of the river, near some recommended hotels. From the Neustadt station, tram #11 runs to Am Zwingerteich, a park in the center right next to the sights. Trains run between the Hauptbahnhof and Neustadt station every 10 minutes (€3, 10-min ride; also connected by slower tram #3).

Getting around Dresden

The city is well connected by slick new trams and buses. Buy tickets at the machines in the backs of trams. One ride costs €1.50 (or €0.90 for a *Kurzstrecke*—short stretch—of fewer than 4 stops). A 24-hour ticket *(Tageskarte)* costs €4. Free use of the public transit is included with the City Card (see above).

DO-IT-YOURSELF DRESDEN
BAROQUE BLITZ TOUR

Dresden's main sights are conveniently clustered along a delightfully strollable promenade next to the Elbe. Though Dresden has a long and colorful history, focus on the three eras that have shaped it the most: Dresden's golden age in the mid-18th century under Augustus the Strong; the city's WWII destruction by firebombs; and the communist regime that took over at the war's end and continued until 1989.

The following walk laces together all of Dresden's top sights. It should take you about an hour, not counting museum stops (which could be substantial). Unless otherwise noted, Dresden's museums are light on English information (no audioguides) but heavy on sightseeing value.

Theaterplatz—Begin at Theaterplatz (convenient drop-off point for tram #8 from Hauptbahnhof). Face the equestrian statue (King John, an unimportant mid-19th-century ruler) in the middle of the square. In front of you, behind the statue, is the Saxon State Opera House—nicknamed the **Semper Oper** after its architect, Gottfried Semper (can be toured with a German-speaking guide, €5, 1 hr, enter on right side, tel. 0351/491-1496). Three opera houses have stood in this spot: the first was destroyed by a fire in 1869, the second by firebombs in 1945. The Semper Oper continues to be a world-class venue, and tickets for the Saxon State Orchestra (the world's oldest) are hard to come by (on sale

Dresden

TO BERLIN

NEUSTADT STATION

❸

BAUTZ-NER STR. ❺ TO PFUND'S DAIRY

THERES.

ALBERTPLATZ

ANTON

HAIN

KÖNIG.

❹

❽ ❾

N E U S T A D T

ALBERT STR.

WIGARDSTR.

HAUPTSTR.

MARIEN-BRÜCKE

PALAIS PLATZ

GR. MEISS.

KÖPCKE STR.

CAROLA BRÜCKE

R I V E R

E L B E

HOF-KIRCHE

AUGUSTUS BRÜCKE

PATH

BOATS

SYNA-GOGUE

SEMPER OPER

BRÜHLSCHE TERRASSE

ALBERT-INUM

THEATER PLATZ

❻

FRAUEN-KIRCHE

TO YENIDZE & SLAUGHTER HOUSE-FIVE

OSTRA-

ℹ

ROYAL PALACE

NEU-MARKT

ZWINGER

WILSD. STR.

ALT-MARKT

❼

RATHAUS

¼ MILE

A L T S T A D T

400 METERS

WAISENHAUS

ALLEE

REITBAHN STR.

PRAGERSTRASSE

ST. PETERSBURGER

❶ = KEY TRAM STOP

❶ Hotel Rest. Kipping

❷ Hotels Bastei, Königstein & Lilienstein

❸ Hotel Bayerischer Hof Dresden

❹ Hotel Martha Hospiz

❺ AHA (Apart Hotel Akzent)

❻ Münzgasse (Hilton Hotel, Rest. Kleppereck & Dampf Schiff Bierhaus)

❼ Restaurant Altmarkt Keller

❽ Wenzel Prager Bierstuben

❾ Ausonia Restaurant

❷

MAIN STATION

❶ LIND.

TO PRAGUE VIA E-55

a year in advance; box office in Schinkelwache TI across the square, Mon–Fri 10:00–18:00, Sat 10:00–13:00, closed Sun, tel. 0351/491-1705, fax 0351/491-1700, www.semperoper.de).

Let's get oriented. Behind you is the Hofkirche, with its distinctive openwork steeple, and behind that is the sprawling Royal Palace (both described below). When facing the Opera House, on your left is the neoclassical Schinkelwache (Guardhouse, houses the TI). The big building behind it and to its right is the Semper Gallery, the east wing of the Zwinger (your next stop). All the buildings you see here—Dresden's Baroque treasures—are replicas. The originals were destroyed by American and British bombs in a single night. For almost 60 years, Dresden has been rebuilding—and there's lots more work to do.

Walk through the passageway into the Zwinger courtyard (to your left as you face the Semper Oper), noticing the Crown Gate on the opposite site lowering majestically into view. Stop in the middle of the courtyard, where we'll survey all four wings.

The Zwinger—This palatial building is a Baroque masterpiece, the pride and joy of the Wettin dynasty. The Wettins ruled Saxony for nearly 900 years—right up until the end of the First World War. At its peak, Saxony had not a king, but an elector. The prince elector of Saxony—one of a handful of nobles who elected the Holy Roman Emperor—was one of Germany's most powerful people. The 18th century was Saxony's golden age. Friedrich Augustus I, prince elector of Saxony, wheeled and dealed—and converted from his Saxon Protestantism to a more Polish-friendly Catholicism—to become King Augustus II of Poland. Legends paint Augustus as a macho, womanizing, powerful, ambitious, properly Baroque man—a real Saxon superstar. A hundred years after his death, historians—or was it the Saxon tourist office?—dubbed him "the Strong." Today tour guides love to impart silly legends about Augustus, who supposedly fathered 365 children and could break a horseshoe in half with his bare hands.

Like most Wettins, Augustus the Strong was unlucky at war, but a clever diplomat and a lover of the arts. We can thank Augustus and the rest of the Wettins—and the nobles who paid them taxes—for Dresden's rich architectural and artistic heritage. Anticipating WWII bombs, Dresdeners preserved their town's art treasures by storing them in underground mines and cellars in the countryside.

The courtyard where the Zwinger now stands was the site of a fortress in the Middle Ages. By Augustus' time, it was used for celebrations of Saxon royalty. Face the west wing (with the Crown Gate on your left). You're looking at the **Rampart Pavilion (Wallpavillon),** the first wing of the palace—an orangery built for Augustus' fruit trees. Stairs lead to a fine Zwinger view from the terrace above. This wing of the Zwinger houses the fun **Mathematics-Physics Salon** (see "Sights—Dresden's Zwinger," page 512). Turn to the left, facing the **Crown Gate**

(Kronentor); its golden crown is topped by four eagles, symbolizing Polish royalty (remember, Augustus was also king of Poland). Turn again to the left to see the **Glockenspielpavillon.** The **glockenspiel** near the top of the gate has 40 bells. Because they are made of Meissen porcelain, they can play half-tones (sharps and flats), giving them a bigger repertoire than metal-bell glockenspiels (bells chime every 15 min and play melodies at 11:15, 14:15, and 17:15). Above the glockenspiel stands Hercules, with the Earth on his back—a fitting symbol for Augustus the Strong. This wing of the Zwinger also houses Augustus the Strong's **Porcelain Collection** (see "Sights—Dresden's Zwinger," page 512). Turn once more to the left (with the Crown Gate behind you) to see the **Semper Gallery.** This Zwinger wing was added to the original courtyard a hundred years later by Gottfried Semper (of opera house fame). It houses Dresden's best museum, the **Old Masters Gallery,** as well as the **Royal Armory**.

Take time to enjoy some of the Zwinger's excellent museums. When you're finished, exit the Zwinger through the Glockenspielpavillon (east gate). Halfway through the corridor, notice the timelines telling the history of the Zwinger in German: to the right, its construction, and to the left, its destruction and reconstruction. Notice the Soviet spin: On May 8, 1945, the Soviet army liberated Dresden from "fascist tyranny" *(faschistischen Tyrannei),* and from 1945 to 1964, the Zwinger was rebuilt with the "power of the workers and peasants" *(Arbeiter- und Bauern-Macht).*

As you exit the corridor, jog to the left, cross the street and the tram tracks, and walk down the perpendicular Taschenberg Strasse with the yellow Taschenberg Palace on your right. Go under the passageway between the Royal Palace and the yellow palace. Ahead of you and to the right, the blocky modern building is the...

Palace of Culture (Kulturpalast)—This theater, built by the communist government in 1969, is still used for concerts today. The faded green tarp near the top covers a mural depicting communist themes: workers; strong women; care for the elderly; teachers and students; and, of course, the red star and the seal of the former East Germany. The tarp went up soon after the communists went out—supposedly because the mural was in disrepair—and it's been up ever since. This is an interesting commentary on the way Dresdeners have adapted to a post-communist world.

Now turn left (with the Palace of Culture behind you). Walk toward the tallest tower ahead on the left (the climbable **Watchman's Tower,** described below). On your left is the east wing of the sprawling...

Royal Palace (Residenzschloss)—The palace is still being repaired from the WWII firebombing; the farther you walk, the more destruction you'll see. Its reconstruction will take many years. When finished, the Royal Palace will house civic offices and the city's massive art collection—only one-third of which is currently in museums.

Just before you reach the tunnel, look for the bombed-out gap in the wall to your left. This was the palace's **Great Courtyard.** Across the courtyard you see the black-and-white decoration on the inside of the western wing. These images, called sgraffito, are scratched into plaster over charcoal. Continue through the tunnel. Halfway through the tunnel on your right-hand side is a door to the Palace Museum and access to the Watchman's Tower for a great view (see "More Sights in Dresden," page 512). When you're finished climbing the tower, exit the tunnel. You have just come through the Georgenbau gate into the **Palace Square.** Ahead of you and to the left is the...

Hofkirche (Cathedral)—Why does Dresden, a stronghold of local-boy Martin Luther's Protestant Reformation, boast such a beautiful Catholic cathedral? When Augustus the Strong died, his son wanted to continue as king of Poland, like his father. The pope wouldn't allow it unless Augustus Junior agreed to build a Catholic church in Dresden. Today, the Hofkirche is the largest church in Saxony—although just 5 percent of Saxons are Catholic. The passageway connecting the church with the palace allowed the royal family to avoid walking in the street with commoners. The cathedral's roof is ringed by sculptures of 78 religious and allegorical figures by Lorenzo Mattelli. Go inside and find the Memorial Chapel (behind you and to the right as you face the main altar), dedicated to those who died in the firebombing and to all victims of violence. The evocative *pietà* altarpiece (1973) is made of Meissen porcelain. The basement houses the royal crypt, including the heart of the still-virile Augustus the Strong—which, according to legend, beats when a pretty woman comes near (free, enter through side door facing palace, Mon–Thu and Sat 8:00–19:00, Fri 13:00–19:00, Sun 7:00–19:00, access to crypt only with free German tour, schedule posted by door, tel. 0351/484-4712, www.kathedrale-dresden.de). The 3,000-pipe organ is played for the public on Wednesdays and Saturdays at 11:30 (April–Dec only).

As you leave the Hofkirche, look back at the palace. To the left, next to the palace's main entrance, you'll see a long, yellow mural called the...

Parade of Nobles (Fürstenzug)—This mural shows the 35 members of Saxon royalty, in chronological order, dating back to the Middle Ages. It was created out of the Saxons' need to commemorate their heritage, particularly after Saxony became a part of Germany in 1870. Painted on 24,000 tiles of Dresden china, the mural is longer than a football field (335 feet) and longer than the Watchman's Tower is tall. At the end of the parade, notice the non-royals: students, painters, and teachers. Behind them, you'll see commoners: a miner, a farmer, and a carpenter. The smug-looking fellow at the very end is the creator of the mural, Wilhelm Walther. Walk about 20 yards along the mural and find Augustus the Strong, atop a white stallion rearing up (labeled with his Polish name,

Augustus II): dynamic, powerful, perfectly Baroque. Although the entire parade passes through plants and flowers, only the lady-killer Augustus' horse tramples a rose.

When you're finished looking at the mural, return to the Palace Square facing the river. Climb the big staircase on your right and walk along the...

Brühlsche Terrasse—This "Balcony of Europe" was once Dresden's defensive rampart—look ahead along the side of the terrace facing the river to see openings for cannons and other weapons. By Baroque times, fortresses were no longer necessary, and this became one of Europe's most charming promenades. Stroll, and enjoy the leafy canopy of linden trees. Past the first fountain and the café, belly up to the railing facing the Elbe River.

Elbe River Overview—Dresden has the world's largest and oldest fleet of historic **paddleboat steamers:** nine riverboats from the 19th century (some of which still have plaques bragging, "10-year warranty"). The hills in the distance are home to Saxon vineyards, producing Germany's northernmost wine. Because only a small amount of the land is suitable for vineyards, Saxon wine is expensive and enjoyed mostly by locals. Below you to the left is the bridge called **Augustusbrücke,** connecting Dresden's Old Town with the New Town. Look under the bridge. The water during the massive flood in August of 2002 filled about two-thirds of the arches.

Look across the bridge to the **New Town.** While 85 percent of Dresden's Old Town was decimated by Allied firebombs, much of the New Town survived. The 18th-century apartment buildings here were restored—giving the area a Baroque look instead of the blocky Soviet style predominant on the Old Town side of the river. At the far end of the Augustusbrücke, look for the golden equestrian statue, a symbol of Dresden—Augustus the Strong, the **Goldene Reiter** (golden rider), facing east to his kingdom of Poland. Behind that, the **Three Kings Church** (Dreikönigskirche) marks a neighborhood with some recommended restaurants (see "Eating," page 515). To the right of Augustusbrücke are some governmental buildings, and upriver to the far right, lots of Soviet-style apartments. The interesting mosque-shaped building in the distance to the far left (marked Yenidze) was originally a tobacco factory designed to advertise Turkish cigarettes, and is now an office building with restaurants and nightclubs.

Continue walking along the Brühlsche Terrasse. Pass the pastel Baroque building on the right—once a gallery, now owned by Hilton and home to restaurants. Ahead on the right, you'll see the glass domes of the **Academy of Fine Arts.** (Locals call the big dome on the right "the lemon juicer.") Just before you get to this building, go down the stairs on your right and head toward the huge scaffolding. You'll walk along **Münzgasse,** which has lots of trendy restaurants with outdoor seating (see "Eating," page 515). This street re-creates the lively café scene of prewar Dresden. When the Frauenkirche (ahead of you) is rebuilt, the streets around it will teem with restaurants and cafés like these. At the end of Münzgasse, you'll see the massive reconstruction project of the...

Frauenkirche (Church of Our Lady)—Augustus the Strong grew jealous of the mighty Catholic domes of Venice and London, and demanded that a proper Lutheran church be built in Dresden. Completed in 1743, this was Germany's biggest Protestant church (310 feet high). Its unique central stone cupola design gave it the nickname "handbell church"—like St. Peter's in Rome. (Pictures of the church can be found around the reconstruction site and on postcard racks around Dresden.) Then, on the night of February 13, 1945, the firebombs came. When the smoke cleared the next morning, the Frauenkirche was still standing. It burned for two days before finally collapsing. After the war, the Frauenkirche was kept in rubble as a peace monument and the site of many memorial vigils.

In 1992, the reconstruction of the church began. The restorers are using as many of the church's original stones as possible, fitting the church together like a giant jigsaw puzzle. One third of the finished church will be original stones, and new pieces are custom-made to fill in the gaps. The project is due to be completed in 2005, a year before the city's 800th anniversary. The reconstruction will cost more than €100 million—90 percent of which has come from donors around the world.

The site is well described by signs (most in English). Look closely at the church facade: You can see where the original, dark stones meet the new, brighter pieces. Around the church to the right is the small square of Neumarkt; here you'll see rows of scaffolding where chunks of the church—old and new—are sorted and cataloged. For more information, visit the nearby **Frauenkirche Visitors Center,** which features models and photographs of how the Frauenkirche once looked—and how it will look again in 2005 (Mon–Fri 10:00–18:00, Sat–Sun until 17:00, grayish-green building beyond yellow palace at Georg-Treu-Platz 3, follow signs for Treffpunkt Frauenkirche, tel. 0351/486-7757 or 0351/656-0660).

When you're finished exploring the Frauenkirche or munching along Münzgasse, you could end your Dresden walk with a visit to the nearby **Albertinum,** which houses the rest of Dresden's top museums (19th- and 20th-century art and breathtaking treasury items, see "More Sights—Dresden," next page; to reach Albertinum, go up stairs at end of courtyard across from Frauenkirche Visitors' Center, then turn right).

SIGHTS

Dresden's Zwinger

All museums in the Zwinger have the same hours: Tue–Sun 10:00–18:00, closed Mon (tel. 0351/491-4678 or 0351/491-4622).

▲▲▲**Old Masters Gallery (Gemäldegalerie Alte Meister)**— Dresden's best museum features works by Raphael, Titian, Rembrandt, Rubens, Vermeer, and more. Find the cityscapes of Dresden, painted during its golden age by Canaletto. These paintings of mid-18th-century Dresden feature the Hofkirche (still under construction) and the newly completed Frauenkirche. (Upstairs, you'll find paintings of Venice by his more famous uncle, also called "Canaletto.") Other highlights include Vermeer's pensive *Girl at a Window Reading a Letter,* the extensive Rubens collection, and Rembrandt's jaunty self-portrait—with Saskia on his lap and a glass of ale held aloft. But you'll kick yourself if you miss Raphael's masterful *Sistine Madonna.* The portrait features Madonna and Child, Saints Sixtus and Barbara, and wispy angel faces in the clouds. But more recently, the stars of this painting are the pair of whimsical angels in the foreground. These lovable tykes—of T-shirt and poster fame— connect the heavenly world of the painting with you and me (€6, includes Royal Armory entry, included in day ticket, no English explanations so consider the good €10.20 English guidebook, Tue–Sun 10:00–18:00, in Zwinger's Semper Gallery, tel. 0351/491-4678 or 0351/491-4622).

Royal Armory (Rüstkammer)—Packed with swords and suits of armor, the armory is especially fun for its tiny children's armor and the jousting exhibit in the back (€3 alone, or free with entry to Old Masters Gallery, included in day ticket, Tue–Sun 10:00–18:00, in Zwinger across passage from Old Masters Gallery).

Mathematics-Physics Salon (Mathematisch-Physikalischer Salon)— This fun collection features globes, lenses, and clocks from the 16th to 19th centuries (€3, included in day ticket, Tue–Sun 10:00–18:00, in Zwinger).

Porcelain Collection (Porzellansammlung)—Augustus the Strong was obsessed with fancy china; he liked to say he had "porcelain sickness." Here you can enjoy some of his symptoms (€5, included in day ticket, Tue–Sun 10:00–18:00, in Zwinger).

More Sights in Dresden

▲▲**Albertinum**—This historic building houses several of Dresden's best collections. **The Sculpture Collection** (Skulpturensammlung) is on the ground floor, but the best parts are upstairs: The **Green Vault** (Grünes Gewölbe), a treasure-trove of Saxon royalty, features extravagant ivory, silver, and gold knickknacks. Examine the incredibly elaborate diorama of the Delhi Court birthday celebration of a mogul (a thinly veiled stand-in for Augustus the Strong). The adjacent **Coin Cabinet** (Münzkabinett) is also interesting. The **New Masters Gallery**

(Gemäldegalerie Neue Meister) features works by 19th- and 20th-century greats such as Renoir, Rodin, van Gogh, Degas, and Klimt. My favorites include Otto Dix's moving triptych *War* (painted between the two World Wars), Gustav Klimt's *Buchenwald,* and Rodin's *Thinker* at the top of the main stairwell (€6, included in day ticket, Fri–Wed 10:00–18:00, closed Thu, at far end of Brühlsche Terrasse, tel. 0351/491-4714 or 0351/491-4622).

▲Dresden Royal Palace Exhibition and Watchman's Tower (Dresdner Schlossausstellung und Hausmannsturm)—While the museum—detailing the history and reconstruction of the palace—is skippable, the Watchman's Tower is well worth the 160 steps for a panoramic view of Dresden. On the way up, you'll see exhibits (in German but with interesting photos and blueprints) about the tower's construction and reconstruction (€2.50 for tower and museum, included in day ticket, Tue–Sun 10:00–18:00, closed Mon, tower closed but museum open Nov–March, entrance inside Royal Palace's Georgenbau gate next to Parade of Nobles mural, tel. 0351/491-4678 or 0351/491-4622).

Prager Strasse—This pedestrian mall—connecting the train station and the historic center—was built by the communists after the war. This street reflects Soviet ideals: big, blocky, functional buildings without extraneous ornamentation. As you stroll down Prager Strasse, imagine these buildings without any of the color or advertising. (Stores "advertised" with simple signs reading Milk, Bread, or simply Products.) In October 1989, special trains carrying Eastern Europeans came through Dresden, heading from the West German embassy in Prague to sanctuary in Western Europe. This street was jammed with people hoping to get on those trains. (The Wall fell a few weeks later.) Today, the street is filled with corporate logos, shoppers with lots of choices, and scruffy, loitering teenagers.

SLEEPING

In the Old Town (Altstadt)

$$$ Hilton Dresden has 340 luxurious rooms in heart of the Altstadt, one block from the river, some with views of the Frauenkirche. Complete with porters, fitness club, pool, and several restaurants, it's everything you would expect from a four-star chain hotel (Sb-€155–190, Db-€170–205, breakfast-€18, An der Frauenkirche 5, tel. 0351/864-2777, fax. 0351/864-2889, www.dresden.hilton.com, rm_dresden@hilton.com).

$$ Hotel Kipping is tidy, located right by the Hauptbahnhof, and professionally run by the friendly and proper Kipping brothers (Ranier and Peter). The building was one of few in this area to survive the firebombing—in fact, several people took shelter here during the attack (Sb-€70–95, Db-€85–115, suite for 1-€115–130, for 2-€130–145,

SLEEP CODE

(€1 = about $1.10, country code: 49, area code: 0351)

Sleep Code: **S** = Single, **D** = Double/Twin, **T** = Triple, **Q** = Quad, **b** = bathroom, **s** = shower only, **no CC** = Credit Cards not accepted, **SE** = Speaks English, **NSE** = No English. Unless otherwise noted, credit cards are accepted, English is spoken, and breakfast is included.

To help you sort easily through these listings, I've divided the rooms into three categories, based on the price for a standard double room with bath:

   $$$ **Higher Priced**—Most rooms €120 or more.
    $$ **Moderately Priced**—Most rooms between €80–120.
     $ **Lower Priced**—Most rooms €80 or less.

Dresden is packed with big, conference-style hotels; characteristic, family-run places are harder to come by. Most buildings in the old center were destroyed by the firebombing and replaced by big, blocky buildings—the communists weren't fans of quaint. The TI has a room-booking service (€3 per person).

child's bed–€20, prices guaranteed through 2004 with this book, elevator, free parking, Winckelmannstrasse 6, tram #8 whisks you to the center, tel. 0351/478-500, fax 0351/478-5099, www.hotel-kipping.de, reception@hotel-kipping.de).

$ Hotels Bastei, Königstein, and Lilienstein are cookie-cutter members of the Ibis chain, goose-stepping single-file up Prager Strasse (listed in order from the station to the center). Each is practically identical, with 360 rooms (newly renovated Bastei is a couple euros more in high season). Though utterly lacking in charm, they are an excellent value at a convenient location between the Hauptbahnhof and the Old Town (Sb–€56–66, Db–€68–84, apartment–€95, breakfast–€9 extra per person, air-con, elevator, Internet access–€6/hr, parking–€6.50/day, can't miss them on Prager Strasse; Bastei reservation tel. 0351/4856-6661, fax 0351/4856-5555, hotel-bastei@ibis-dresden.de; Königstein reservation tel. 0351/4856-6662, fax 0351/4856-6666, hotel-koenigstein@ibis-dresden.de; Lilienstein reservation tel. 0351/4856-6663, fax 0351/4856-7777, hotel-lilienstein @ibis-dresden.de; Web site for all three: www.ibis-hotel.de). Skip their overpriced, below-average hotel restaurants. Instead, eat in the Old Town—or, closer, at Hotel Kipping (see "Eating," next page).

In the New Town (Neustadt)

These hotels are in tidy residential neighborhoods north of the Elbe, best reached via the Neustadt train station. All three hotels are connected to the center by tram #11.

$$$ Hotel Bayerischer Hof Dresden, across from the Neustadt train station, offers 50 rooms and classy, grand public spaces (Sb-€90–100, Db-€120–135, junior suite-€130–145, suite-€140–170, elevator, non-smoking rooms, free parking, Antonstrasse 33–35, yellow building across from station, tel. 0351/829-370, fax 0351/801-4860, www.bayerischer-hof-dresden.de, info@bayerischer-hof-dresden.de).

$$ Hotel Martha Hospiz, near the recommended restaurants on Königstrasse, is a bright, cheery, 50-room place. The two old buildings that make up the hotel have been smartly renovated and connected in back with a glassed-in winter garden and an outdoor breakfast terrace on a charming garden. It's a 10-minute walk to the historical center and a five-minute walk to the Neustadt station (S-€54, Sb-€72–84, Db-€102–118, extra bed-€26, elevator, leaving Neustadt station, turn right on Hainstrasse, left on Theresenstrasse, and then right on Nieritzstrasse to #11, tel. 0351/81760, fax 0351/817-6222, www.vch.de/marthahospiz.dresden, marthahospiz.dresden@t-online.de).

$ AHA (Apart Hotel Akzent), run by friendly and accommodating Albrecht (SE), has a homey and welcoming ambience. This place rents 29 simple but neat apartments with kitchens; all except the top floor have balconies. It's a bit farther from the center—10 minutes by foot east of Albertplatz, a 20-minute walk or a quick ride on tram #11 from the center—but its friendliness, coziness, and good value make it a winner (Sb-€60–65, Db-€70–90, twin Db-€90–100, elevator, Bautzner Strasse 53, tel. 0351/800-850, fax 0351/8008-5114, www.ahahotel.de, info@ahahotel.de).

EATING

Dresden's ancient beer halls were destroyed in the firebombing and were not replaced by the communists. As Dresden comes back to life after 40 years of communist repression, every restaurant seems bright, shiny, and modern.

In the Old Town

Closest to the city's key sights, you'll find several tasty, affordable restaurants with outdoor seating along **Münzgasse,** the street that connects the Brühlsche Terrasse and the Frauenkirche. **Restaurant Kleppereck** serves hearty German food and some Saxon specialties (entrées €10–15, Mon–Fri 11:00–24:00, Sat–Sun 11:00-22:00, Münzgasse 10, tel. 0351/496-5123). Across the street, **Dampf Schiff Bierhaus** serves similar fare with equal helpings of trendy, traditional, and nautical (daily 11:00–24:00, tel. 0351/864-2826).

Altmarkt Keller, a few blocks farther from the river on Altmarkt, is a festive beer cellar that serves Saxon and Bohemian food and has several Czech beers on tap. The lively crowd, cheesy music, and jolly murals add to the fun. The giant mural inside the entryway—representing the friendship between Dresden and Prague—reads, "The sunshine of life is drinking and being happy" (entrées €8–10, daily 11:00–24:00, Altmarkt 4 by the McDonald's, tel. 0351/481-8130).

Restaurant Kipping, in the recommended hotel of the same name, serves international cuisine and Saxon specialties. Their sauerbraten is *wunderbar* (entrées €9–12, Mon–Sat 18:00–22:30, closed Sun, Winckelmannstrasse 6, tel. 0351/478-500).

In the New Town

If you want to venture farther for dinner, consider the New Town, across the Augustusbrücke. Although the main drag of the New Town is glum (lots of communist architecture), just a block away is the charming Baroque Königstrasse, where you'll find these restaurants.

Wenzel Prager Bierstuben is a woodsy bar that spills out into an airy, glassed-in gallery (entrées €8–10, daily 11:00–24:00, Königstrasse 1, tel. 0315/804-2010).

Ausonia, an Italian restaurant run by Luigi Murolo and his family, will give you a break from mustard and kraut (€7–9 pizza or pasta, daily 11:30–23:30, Königstrasse 9, tel. 0351/803-3123).

Erlebnisgastronomie (Experience Gastronomy)

All the rage among Dresdeners (and German tourists in Dresden) is *Erlebnisgastronomie.* Elaborately decorated theme restaurants have sprouted next to the biggest-name sights all over town, with over-the-top theme-park decor and historically costumed waitstaff. These can offer a fun change of pace and aren't the bad value you might suspect. Consider **Pulver Turm** (soldiers in the Powder Tower, An Der Frauenkirche 12a, tel. 0351/262-600), **Sophienkeller** (royal wait staff in the Taschenberg Palace, even has a rotating carousel table with suspended swing-chairs you sit in while you eat, daily 11:00–24:00, Taschenberg 3, tel. 0351/497-260, www.sophienkeller-dresden.de), or **Silber Stolln** (silver mine in the New Town at Hauptstrasse 1a, tel. 0351/808-220).

TRANSPORTATION CONNECTIONS

By train to: Berlin (every 2 hrs, 2.25 hrs), **Prague** (7/day, 3 hrs), **Munich** (every 2 hrs, 7 hrs, transfer in Leipzig, Nürnberg, or Fulda), **Frankfurt** (every 2 hrs, 4.5 hrs). Train info: tel. 01805-996-633.

UNDERSTANDING YUGOSLAVIA

Americans struggle to understand the complicated break-up of Yugoslavia, which was a largely artificial union of the South Slavic peoples. During the Yugoslav era, it was no less confusing—as the old joke went, Yugoslavia had seven distinct peoples in six republics, with five languages, three religions (Orthodox, Catholic, and Muslim), and two alphabets (Roman and Cyrillic), but only one Yugoslav—Tito.

Here's an oversimplified, boiled-down-to-the-basics history to get you started as you begin your own exploration of Slovenia and Croatia, two of the six countries that were briefly called Yugoslavia.

Who's Who

For starters, you have to get a handle on the Balkans—the southeastern European peninsula between the Adriatic and the Black Sea, stretching from Hungary to Greece. The Balkan Peninsula has always been a crossroads of cultures. The Illyrians, Greeks, and Romans had settlements here before the Slavs moved into the region from the north around the seventh century. During the next millennium and a half, the western part of the peninsula—which would become Yugoslavia—became divided by a series of cultural, ethnic, and religious fault lines that separate the Christian West, the Orthodox East, and the Muslim south.

The most important Balkan influences were **Western Christianity** (Roman Catholicism, primarily brought to the region by Charlemagne, and later reinforced by the Austrian Hapsburgs), **Eastern Orthodox Christianity** (from the Byzantine Empire), and **Islam** (from the invading Ottoman Turks).

Two major historical factors made the Balkans what they are today: The first was the **split of the Roman Empire** in the fourth century A.D., dividing the Balkans down the middle into west (Catholic/Roman) and east (Orthodox/Byzantine)—roughly along today's Bosnian-Serbian border. Second was the **invasion of the Islamic Ottoman Turks** in the 14th century. The Turkish victory at the Battle of Kosovo (1389) began five centuries of Islamic influence in Serbia (less in other parts of the region), dividing the Balkans into north (Christian) and south (Islam). These two major events essentially divided the Balkans into quarters.

Over the years, several ethnic identities (defined by religion) emerged: the Christian **Croats** and **Slovenes** (mostly west of the Dinaric Mountains, along the Adriatic coast and north, towards Austria); the Orthodox **Serbs** (mostly east of the Dinaric range); and the Muslim **Bosniaks** (Serbs or Croats who converted to Islam under the Turks, mostly living in the Dinaric Mountains). To complicate matters, the

Yugoslav Succession

region is also home to several non-Slavic groups—such as **Hungarians** (in the northern province of Vojvodina) and **Albanians,** concentrated in the southern province of Kosovo (descended from the Illyrians who lived here long before the Greeks and Romans).

Of course, these geographic divisions are extremely general. The groups overlapped a lot...which is exactly why the breakup of Yugoslavia was so contentious. One of the biggest causes of this ethnic mixing came in the 16th century. The Ottoman Empire was threatening to overrun Europe, and the Austrian Hapsburgs wanted a buffer zone—a "human shield." The Hapsburgs encouraged Serbs who were fleeing from Turkish invasions to settle along the frontier (along today's Croatian-

Bosnian border—known as Vojna Krajina, or "military frontier"). The Serbs stayed long after the Turks had left, establishing homes in predominantly Croat communities.

After the Turkish threat in Central Europe subsided in the late 17th century, some of the Balkans (basically today's Slovenia and Croatia) became part of the Austrian Hapsburg Empire. The Turks stayed longer in the south and east (today's Bosnia-Herzegovina and Serbia)—making the cultures in these regions more different still. Serbia finally gained its independence from the Ottomans in the mid-19th century, but it wasn't too long before World War I started...after a disgruntled Serbian nationalist killed the Austrian archduke.

South Slavs Unite

When the Austro-Hungarian Empire fell at the end of World War I, the European map was redrawn for the 20th century. After centuries of being governed by foreign powers, the southern Slavs began to see their shared history as more important than their minor differences. A tiny country of 2 million Slovenes or 4 million Croats couldn't have survived. Rather than be absorbed by a non-Slavic power, the south Slavs decided that there was safety in numbers and banded together as a single state—first called the "Kingdom of the Serbs, Croats, and Slovenes" (1918), later known as Yugoslavia (literally, "Union of the South Slavs"—*yugo* means "south"). "Yugoslav unity" was in the air, but this new union was artificial and ultimately bound to fail (not unlike the partnership between the Czechs and Slovaks, formed at the same time and for the same reasons).

From the very beginning, the Serbs, Croats, and Slovenes struggled for power within the new union. Serbia already had a very strong prewar king, Alexander Karađorđević, who immediately made attempts to give his nation a leading role in the federation. A nationalistic Croatian politician named Stjepan Radić, pushing for a more equitable division of powers, was shot by a Serb during a parliament session in 1928. Karađorđević abolished the parliament and became dictator. Six years later, infuriated Croatian separatists killed him.

Many Croat nationalists sided with the Nazis in World War II as a way to distance themselves from Serbia. The Nazi puppet government in Croatia (called Ustaše) conducted an extermination campaign, murdering hundreds of thousands of Serbs (along with Jews and Gypsies) living in Croatia—the first use of ethnic cleansing in Yugoslavia.

At the end of World War II, the rest of Eastern Europe was "liberated" by the Soviets—but the Yugoslavs regained their independence on their own, as their communist partisan army forced out the Nazis. After the short but rocky Yugoslav union between the World Wars, it seemed that no one could hold the southern Slavs together in a single nation. But there was one man who could, and did: Tito.

Tito

Communist Party president and war hero Josip Broz—who dubbed himself with the simple nickname Tito—emerged as a political leader after World War II. With a Croatian mother, a Slovene father, a Serbian wife, and a home in Belgrade, Tito was a true Yugoslav. For the next three decades, he managed to keep Yugoslavia intact—essentially by the force of his own personality.

Tito's new incarnation of Yugoslavia aimed for a more equitable division of powers. It was made up of six republics, each with its own parliament and president: **Croatia** (mostly Catholic Croats), **Slovenia** (mostly Catholic Slovenes), **Serbia** (mostly Orthodox Serbs, with some Hungarians in the northern province of Vojvodina and Albanians in the southern province of Kosovo), **Bosnia-Herzegovina** (the most diverse—Muslims, Serbs, and Croats), **Macedonia** (split about evenly between Albanians and Macedonians—who are claimed variously by Serbs, Greeks, and Bulgarians), and **Montenegro** (mostly Serb-like Montenegrins). Each republic managed its own affairs...but always under the watchful eye of president-for-life Tito, who said that the borders between the republics should be like "white lines in a marble column."

Tito's Yugoslavia was communist, but it wasn't Soviet communism; you'll find no statues of Lenin or Stalin here. Despite strong pressure from Moscow, Tito refused to ally himself with the Soviets—and therefore received good will (and $2 billion) from the United States. Tito's vision was for a Yugoslavia that worked with both East and West, without being dominated by either. (This "third way" was not appreciated by the Soviet or American governments.) Yugoslavia was the most free of the communist states: While large industry was nationalized, Tito's system allowed for small businesses. This experience with market economy benefited Yugoslavs when Eastern Europe's communist regimes eventually fell. And even during the communist era, Yugoslavia remained a popular tourist destination, keeping its standards more in line with the West than the Soviet states.

Some would say that Tito was no better than Stalin, especially early on, when he staged brutal Soviet-style "show trials" to intimidate potential dissidents, and imprisoned church leaders such as Alojzije Stepinac (see page 393). But today, most former Yugoslavs consider Tito more of a hero than a villain, and usually speak of him with reverence.

Things Fall Apart

With Tito's death in 1980, Yugoslavia's six constituent republics gained more autonomy, with a rotating presidency. But before long, the delicate union Tito had held together began to unravel. In the late 1980s, Serbian President Slobodan Milošević used ethnic-motivated conflicts in the province of Kosovo to grab more centralized power. Other republics (especially Slovenia and Croatia) feared that he would gut their nation to create a "Greater Serbia" instead of a friendly coalition of diverse Yugoslav republics—and Yugoslavia started breaking apart.

The Slovene Secession: Slovenia was the first Yugoslav republic to hold free elections, in the spring of 1990. The voters wanted their own nation. After months of stockpiling weapons, Slovenia closed its borders and declared independence from Yugoslavia on June 25, 1991. Along with being the most ethnically homogeneous of the Yugoslav nations, Slovenia was also the most Western-oriented, most prosperous, and smallest. Belgrade briefly fought the Slovenes, but after 10 days and only 66 deaths, Yugoslavia decided to let Slovenia have its independence.

The Croatian Conflict: As Slovenia geared up for independence, Croatia decided it would follow suit. But in the months leading up to Croatia's secession, the 600,000 Serbs living in Croatia—especially those in the city of Knin—saw the writing on the wall and began to rise up. Inspired by Slobodan Milošević's rhetoric, Croatian Serbs began the so-called "tree trunk revolution"—blocking important tourist roads with logs and other barriers. Tensions escalated, and the first shots of the conflict were fired on Easter Sunday of 1991 at Plitvice Lakes National Park, between Croatian policemen and Serb irregulars from Knin.

By the time Croatia declared its independence (on the same day as Slovenia), it was already embroiled in the beginnings of a bloody war. The new nation of Croatia did not address the status of its more than half-million Serb residents. So Croatian Serbs, nervous about their rights and backed by the Serbian-dominated Yugoslav Army, in turn declared independence from Croatia. The Yugoslav Army swept in, supposedly to keep the peace between Serbs and Croats—but it soon became obvious that they were there to support the Serbs. The ill-prepared Croatian resistance was made up mostly of policemen and a few soldiers who defected from the Yugoslav Army, and they were quickly overwhelmed. The Serbs gained control over a large swathe of inland Croatia, mostly around the Bosnian border (including Plitvice) and in Croatia's inland panhandle (the region of Slavonia). They called this territory, about a quarter of the country, the **Republic of Serbian Krajina** (*krajina* means "border"). This new "country" (hardly recognized by any other nations) minted their own money and had their own army, much to the consternation of Croatia—which was now worried about the safety of Croats living in Krajina.

As the Serbs advanced, hundreds of thousands of Croats fled to the coast and lived as refugees in resort hotels. (Many of these hotels—such as the prominent Marjan in Split—are still being refurbished.) The Serbs began a campaign of **ethnic cleansing,** systematically removing Croatians from their territory—often by murdering them. The bloodiest siege was at the town of **Vukovar,** which the Yugoslav army surrounded and shelled relentlessly for three months. At the end of the siege, thousands of Croat soldiers and civilians mysteriously disappeared. Many of these people were later discovered in mass graves; hundreds are still missing, and bodies are still continually being found. In a surprise move, Serbs also attacked the tourist capital of **Dubrovnik** (see page 349). By early 1992, both Croatia and the Republic of Serbian Krajina had established their borders, and a tense ceasefire fell over the region.

The standoff lasted until 1995, when the now well-equipped Croatian Army retook the Serbian-occupied areas in a series of two offensives—**"Lightning"** *(Blijesak)*, in the northern part of the country (Slavonia), and **"Storm"** *(Oluja)*, further south. Some Croats retaliated for earlier ethnic cleansing by doing much of the same to Serbs— torturing them, killing them, and dynamiting their homes. Croatia quickly established the borders that exist today, and the Erdut Agreement brought peace to the region—but most of the 600,000 Serbs who once lived in Croatia/Krajina fled to Serbia or were killed. Today only a few thousand Serbs remain in Croatia. While Serbs have long since been legally invited back to their ancestral Croatian homes, few have returned—afraid of the "welcome" they might receive from the Croat neighbors who killed their relatives or blew up their houses just a few years ago.

The War in Bosnia-Herzegovina: The situation was even more complicated in Bosnia-Herzegovina (which I'll refer to as "Bosnia" for simplicity). Bosnia declared its independence from Yugoslavia four months after Croatia and Slovenia did. But Bosnia was always at the crossroads of Balkan culture, and therefore even more diverse than Croatia—with large Serb and Croat populations, as well as Muslim Bosniaks and Albanian Kosovars. In the spring of 1992, Serbs within Bosnia (with the support of Serbia) began a campaign of ethnic cleansing against the Bosniaks and Croats. Before long, the Croats did the same against the Serbs. The three groups fought a brutal war for the next three years, until the 1995 Dayton Peace Accords carefully divided Bosnia among the different ethnicities. Today Bosnia continues to work on its tenuous peace, rebuild its devastated country, and bring its infrastructure up to its neighbors' standards.

Kosovo: The ongoing Yugoslav crisis finally reached its peak in the Serbian province of Kosovo. After years of poor treatment by the Serbs, Kosovars rebelled in 1998. The Yugoslav Army moved in, and in March of 1999, they began a campaign of ethnic cleansing. Thousands of Kosovars were murdered, and hundreds of thousands fled into Albania and Macedonia. NATO planes bombed Serb positions for two months, forcing the Serb army to leave Kosovo in the summer of 1999.

The Fall of Milošević: After years of bloody conflicts, Serbian public opinion had clearly swung against their president. The transition began gradually in early 2000, spearheaded by Otpor and other nonviolent, grassroots, student-based opposition movements. These organizations used clever PR strategies to gain support and convince Serbians that real change was possible. As anti-Milošević sentiments gained momentum, opposing political parties banded together and got behind one candidate, Vojislav Koštunica. Public support for Koštunica mounted, and when the arrogant Milošević called an early election in September of 2000, the Serbian strongman was soundly defeated. Though Milošević tried to claim that the election results were invalid, determined Serbs streamed into their capital, marched on their parliament, and—like the Czechoslovaks a decade before—peacefully took back their nation.

Today's "Yugoslavia": The nation of "Yugoslavia" no longer exists, having been officially renamed "Serbia and Montenegro"—the only two republics that remain in the union of South Slavs. Though the Montenegrins wanted independence, Serbia made concessions to keep the nations loosely united. While they share an army, each country has its own government and currency (Montenegro officially uses the euro, even though it's not in the EU).

Finding their Way: The Former Yugoslav Republics

Today, Slovenia and Croatia are as stable as Western Europe, Bosnia-Herzegovina is slowly putting itself back together, and Slobodan Milošević is on trial for war crimes in The Hague.

But these South Slav neighbors—once countrymen—still don't get along. Croatians still smolder when they talk about the Serbs. In Dubrovnik, travel agencies reluctantly admit that a day trip to Montenegro is the most popular excursion, but are quick to mention that they personally have no interest in visiting this Serb stronghold. Silly border disputes belie lingering grudges. For example, in an ongoing feud, Croatia insists Slovenia should not be allowed to operate its only port, Koper. According to a technicality of international law, Slovenia's tiny 29-mile-long coastline shouldn't have a port because it's between peninsulas belonging to other nations (Italy and Croatia)—but until now, everyone looked the other way. Of course, shutting down Koper would conveniently force more business to nearby Croatian ports.

Though the hard feelings are fading, they're still strong in some parts—especially those that were most war-torn. When Serbs or Croats encounter other Yugoslavs in their travels, they immediately evaluate each other's accent to determine: Are they one of us, or one of them?

Americans visiting the former Yugoslav republics have a responsibility to keep an open mind. Just because the United States supported Croatia in the war and Slobodan Milošević is a barbaric villain doesn't mean the Serbs were the only bad guys. In the streets and the trenches, it was never that clear-cut. Just ask the more than half-million Serbs who lived for generations in today's Croatia, but were brutally forced from their homes. Ethnic cleansing took place on both sides.

The good news is that things are finally on the mend in the Balkans. Slovenes and Croats welcome foreign visitors with an enthusiastic hospitality that this region was known for long before Yugoslavia existed.

APPENDIX

Let's Talk Telephones

To make international calls, you need to break the codes: the international access codes and country codes (see below). For more information on making local, long-distance, and international calls, please see "Telephones, Mail, and E-Mail," on page 27 of the Introduction.

International Access Codes

When making an international call, first dial the international access code (011 if you're calling from the U.S.A. or Canada; 00 if you're calling from Europe). All European countries use "00" as their international access code.

Country Codes

After you've dialed the international access code, dial the code of the country you're calling.

Austria—43	Ireland—353
Belgium—32	Italy—39
Britain—44	Morocco—212
Canada—1	Netherlands—31
Croatia—385	Norway—47
Czech Rep.—420	Poland—48
Denmark—45	Portugal—351
Estonia—372	Slovakia—421
Finland—358	Slovenia—386
France—33	Spain—34
Germany—49	Sweden—46
Gibraltar—350	Switzerland—41
Greece—30	Turkey—90
Hungary—36	United States—1

European Calling Chart

Just smile and dial, using this key:
AC = Area Code, LN = Local Number.

European Country	Calling long distance within ...	Calling from the U.S.A./ Canada to ...	Calling from a European country to ...
Austria	AC + LN	011 + 43 + AC (without the initial zero) + LN	00 + 43 + AC (without the initial zero) + LN
Belgium	LN	011 + 32 + LN (without initial zero)	00 + 32 + LN (without initial zero)
Britain	AC + LN	011 + 44 + AC (without initial zero) + LN	00 + 44 + AC (without initial zero) + LN
Croatia	AC + LN	011 + 385 + AC (without initial zero) + LN	00 + 385 + AC (without initial zero) + LN
Czech Republic	LN	011 + 420 + LN	00 + 420 + LN
Denmark	LN	011 + 45 + LN	00 + 45 + LN
Finland	AC + LN	011 + 358 + AC (without initial zero) + LN	00 + 358 + AC (without initial zero) + LN
France	LN	011 + 33 + LN (without initial zero)	00 + 33 + LN (without initial zero)
Germany	AC + LN	011 + 49 + AC (without initial zero) + LN	00 + 49 + AC (without initial zero) + LN
Greece	LN	011 + 30 + LN	00 + 30 + LN
Hungary	06 + AC + LN	011 + 36 + AC + LN	00 + 36 + AC + LN

European Country	Calling long distance within ...	Calling from the U.S.A./ Canada to ...	Calling from a European country to ...
Ireland	AC + LN	011 + 353 + AC (without initial zero) + LN	00 + 353 + AC (without initial zero) + LN
Italy	LN	011 + 39 + LN	00 + 39 + LN
Netherlands	AC + LN	011 + 31 + AC (without initial zero) + LN	00 + 31 + AC (without initial zero) + LN
Norway	LN	011 + 47 + LN	00 + 47 + LN
Poland	AC + LN	011 + 48 + AC (without initial zero) + LN	00 + 48 + AC (without initial zero) + LN
Portugal	LN	011 + 351 + LN	00 + 351 + LN
Slovenia	AC + LN	011 + 386 + AC (without initial zero) + LN	00 + 386 + AC (without initial zero) + LN
Spain	LN	011 + 34 + LN	00 + 34 + LN
Sweden	AC + LN	011 + 46 + AC (without initial zero) + LN	00 + 46 + AC (without initial zero) + LN
Switzerland	LN	011 + 41 + LN (without initial zero)	00 + 41 + LN (without initial zero)
Turkey	AC (if no initial zero is included, add one) + LN	011 + 90 + AC (without initial zero) + LN	00 + 90 + AC (without initial zero) + LN

- The instructions above apply whether you're calling a fixed phone or cell phone.

- The international access codes (the first numbers you dial when making an international call) are 011 if you're calling from the U.S.A./Canada, or 00 if you're calling from anywhere in Europe.

- To call the U.S.A. or Canada from Europe, dial 00, then 1 (the country code for the U.S.A. and Canada), then the area code and number. In short, 00 + 1 + AC + LN = Hi, Mom!

U.S. Embassies and Consulates

Austria: U.S. Embassy, Marriott Building 4th floor, Gartenbaupromenade 2, Vienna, tel. 01/313-390, www.usembassy.at

Croatia: U.S. Embassy, 2 Thomas Jefferson Street, Zagreb, tel. 01/661-2200, consular services tel. 661-2300, www.usembassy.hr

Czech Republic: U.S. Embassy, Trziste 15, Prague, tel. 257-530-663, www.usembassy.cz

Germany: U.S. Embassy, Clayallee 170, Berlin, tel. 030/832-9233, www.usembassy.de

Hungary: U.S. Embassy, Szabadság tér 12, H-1054 Budapest, tel. 1/475-4400, after hours tel. 1/475-4703 or 1/475-4924, www.usembassy.hu

Poland: U.S. Embassy, aleje Ujazdowskie 29/31, Warsaw, tel. 022/504-2000; U.S. Consulate, ulica Stolarska 9, Kraków, tel. 012/424-5100, fax 012/424-5103, www.usinfo.pl

Slovenia: U.S. Embassy, Prešernova 31, Ljubljana, tel. 01/200-5500, fax 01/200-5555, www.usembassy.si

National Holidays

These national holidays (when many sights are closed) are observed in Eastern Europe. Note this isn't a complete list; holidays strike without warning.

Jan 1: New Year's Day (all countries)
Jan 6: Epiphany (Croatia)
Feb 20: Slovene Cultural Day (Slovenia)
March 15: Revolution Day (Hungary)
April 11: Easter Sunday (all countries)
April 12: Easter Monday (all countries)
April 27: Resistance Day (Slovenia)
May 1: Labor Day (all countries)
May 2: Constitution Day (Poland)
May 31: Whitmonday (Hungary)
June 10: Corpus Christi Day (Poland, Croatia)
June 22: Croatian Uprising Day (Croatia)
June 25: National Day (Slovenia), Croatian State Day (Croatia)
Aug 5: Patriotic Gratitude Day (Croatia)
Aug 15: Assumption of Mary (Poland, Slovenia, Croatia)
Aug 20: National Day (Hungary)
Oct 23: Republic Day (Hungary)
Nov 1: All Saints' Day (Poland, Slovenia, Croatia)
Nov 11: Independence Day (Poland)
Dec 25: Christmas Day (all countries)
Dec 26: Boxing Day (Hungary), Independence Day (Slovenia), St. Stephen's Day (Croatia)

2004

JANUARY

S	M	T	W	T	F	S
				1	2	3
4	5	6	7	8	9	10
11	12	13	14	15	16	17
18	19	20	21	22	23	24
25	26	27	28	29	30	31

FEBRUARY

S	M	T	W	T	F	S
1	2	3	4	5	6	7
8	9	10	11	12	13	14
15	16	17	18	19	20	21
22	23	24	25	26	27	28
29						

MARCH

S	M	T	W	T	F	S
	1	2	3	4	5	6
7	8	9	10	11	12	13
14	15	16	17	18	19	20
21	22	23	24	25	26	27
28	29	30	31			

APRIL

S	M	T	W	T	F	S
				1	2	3
4	5	6	7	8	9	10
11	12	13	14	15	16	17
18	19	20	21	22	23	24
25	26	27	28	29	30	

MAY

S	M	T	W	T	F	S
						1
2	3	4	5	6	7	8
9	10	11	12	13	14	15
16	17	18	19	20	21	22
23/30	24/31	25	26	27	28	29

JUNE

S	M	T	W	T	F	S
		1	2	3	4	5
6	7	8	9	10	11	12
13	14	15	16	17	18	19
20	21	22	23	24	25	26
27	28	29	30			

JULY

S	M	T	W	T	F	S
				1	2	3
4	5	6	7	8	9	10
11	12	13	14	15	16	17
18	19	20	21	22	23	24
25	26	27	28	29	30	31

AUGUST

S	M	T	W	T	F	S
1	2	3	4	5	6	7
8	9	10	11	12	13	14
15	16	17	18	19	20	21
22	23	24	25	26	27	28
29	30	31				

SEPTEMBER

S	M	T	W	T	F	S
			1	2	3	4
5	6	7	8	9	10	11
12	13	14	15	16	17	18
19	20	21	22	23	24	25
26	27	28	29	30		

OCTOBER

S	M	T	W	T	F	S
					1	2
3	4	5	6	7	8	9
10	11	12	13	14	15	16
17	18	19	20	21	22	23
24/31	25	26	27	28	29	30

NOVEMBER

S	M	T	W	T	F	S
	1	2	3	4	5	6
7	8	9	10	11	12	13
14	15	16	17	18	19	20
21	22	23	24	25	26	27
28	29	30				

DECEMBER

S	M	T	W	T	F	S
			1	2	3	4
5	6	7	8	9	10	11
12	13	14	15	16	17	18
19	20	21	22	23	24	25
26	27	28	29	30	31	

Numbers and Stumblers

• Europeans write a few of their numbers differently than we do: 1 = $\mathcal{1}$, 4 = $\mathcal{4}$, 7 = $\mathcal{7}$. Learn the difference or miss your train.

• Europeans write dates as day/month/year (Christmas is 25/12/04).

• Commas are decimal points, and decimals are commas. A dollar and a half is 1,50. There are 5.280 feet in a mile.

• When counting with fingers, start with your thumb. If you hold up your first finger to request one item, you'll probably get two.

• What we Americans call the second floor of a building is the first floor in Europe.

• Europeans keep the left "lane" open for passing on escalators and moving sidewalks. Keep to the right.

Climate

Here is a list of average temperatures (first line—average daily low; second line—average daily high; third line—days of rain). This can be helpful in planning your itinerary, but I have never found European weather to be particularly predictable, and these charts ignore humidity.

J	F	M	A	M	J	J	A	S	O	N	D

AUSTRIA • Vienna

J	F	M	A	M	J	J	A	S	O	N	D
25°	28°	30°	42°	50°	56°	60°	59°	53°	44°	37°	30°
34°	38°	47°	58°	67°	73°	76°	75°	68°	56°	45°	37°
15	14	13	13	13	14	13	13	10	13	14	15

CROATIA • Dubrovnik

J	F	M	A	M	J	J	A	S	O	N	D
42°	43°	57°	52°	58°	65°	69°	69°	64°	57°	51°	46°
53°	55°	58°	63°	70°	78°	83°	82°	77°	69°	62°	56°
13	13	11	10	10	6	4	3	7	11	16	15

CZECH REPUBLIC • Prague

J	F	M	A	M	J	J	A	S	O	N	D
23°	24°	30°	38°	46°	52°	55°	55°	49°	41°	33°	27°
31°	34°	44°	54°	64°	70°	73°	72°	65°	53°	42°	34°
13	11	10	11	13	12	13	12	10	13	12	13

GERMANY • Berlin

J	F	M	A	M	J	J	A	S	O	N	D
23°	23°	30°	38°	45°	51°	55°	54°	48°	40°	33°	26°
35°	38°	48°	56°	64°	70°	74°	73°	67°	56°	44°	36°
17	15	12	13	12	13	14	14	12	14	16	15

HUNGARY • Budapest

J	F	M	A	M	J	J	A	S	O	N	D
25°	28°	35°	44°	52°	58°	62°	60°	53°	44°	38°	30°
34°	39°	50°	62°	71°	78°	82°	81°	74°	61°	47°	39°
13	12	11	11	13	13	10	9	7	10	14	13

POLAND • Kraków

J	F	M	A	M	J	J	A	S	O	N	D
22°	22°	30°	38°	48°	54°	58°	56°	49°	42°	33°	28°
32°	34°	45°	55°	67°	72°	76°	73°	66°	56°	44°	37°
16	15	12	15	12	15	16	15	12	14	15	16

SLOVENIA • Ljubljana

J	F	M	A	M	J	J	A	S	O	N	D
25°	25°	32°	40°	48°	54°	57°	57°	51°	43°	36°	30°
36°	41°	50°	60°	68°	75°	80°	78°	71°	59°	47°	39°
13	11	11	13	16	16	12	12	10	14	15	15

Temperature Conversion

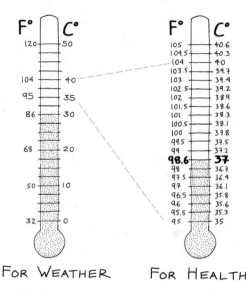

For Weather   For Health

Metric Conversion (approximate)

1 inch = 25 millimeters | 32 degrees F = 0 degrees C
1 foot = 0.3 meter | 82 degrees F = about 28 degrees C
1 yard = 0.9 meter | 1 ounce = 28 grams
1 mile = 1.6 kilometers | 1 kilogram = 2.2 pounds
1 centimeter = 0.4 inch | 1 quart = 0.95 liter
1 meter = 39.4 inches | 1 square yard = 0.8 square meter
1 kilometer = 0.62 mile | 1 acre = 0.4 hectare

Faxing Your Hotel Reservation

Use this handy form for your fax or find it online at
www.ricksteves.com/reservation. Photocopy and fax away.

One-Page Fax

To: _____ @ _____
              hotel   fax

From: _____ @ _____
              name   fax

Today's date: ____ / _____ / ____
                   day   month   year

Dear Hotel _____,

Please make this reservation for me:

Name: _____

Total # of people: _____   # of rooms: _____   # of nights: _____

Arriving: ____ / _____ / ____   My time of arrival (24-hr clock): _____
              day   month   year   (I will telephone if I will be late)

Departing: ____ / _____ / ____
               day   month   year

Room(s): Single___ Double___ Twin___ Triple___ Quad___

With: Toilet___ Shower___ Bath___ Sink only___

Special needs: View___ Quiet___ Cheapest___ Ground Floor___

Credit card: Visa___ MasterCard___ American Express___

Card #: _____

Expiration date: _____

Name on card: _____

You may charge me for the first night as a deposit. Please fax, e-mail, or mail
me confirmation of my reservation, along with the type of room
reserved, the price, and whether the price includes breakfast. Please also
inform me of your cancellation policy. Thank you.

_____
Signature

_____
Name

_____
Address

_____
City   State   Zip Code   Country

_____
E-mail Address

Road Scholar Feedback for
BEST OF EASTERN EUROPE 2004

*We're all in the same travelers' school of hard knocks. Your feedback
helps us improve this guidebook for future travelers. Please fill this out (or
use the online version at www.ricksteves.com/feedback), attach
more info or any tips/favorite discoveries if you like, and send it to us.
As thanks for your help, we'll send you our quarterly travel newsletter free
for one year. Thanks! —Rick*

**Of the recommended accommodations/restaurants used,
which was:**

Best _____

       Why? _____

Worst _____

       Why? _____

**Of the sights/experiences/destinations recommended by
this book, which was:**

Most overrated _____

       Why? _____

Most underrated _____

       Why? _____

Best ways to improve this book:

_____

_____

I'd like a free newsletter subscription:

_____ Yes   _____ No   _____ Already on list

_____

Name

_____

Address

_____

City, State, Zip

_____

E-mail Address

Please send to: ETBD, Box 2009, Edmonds, WA 98020

INDEX

ABOUT THE AUTHORS
RICK STEVES

RICK STEVES is on a mission: to help make European travel accessible and meaningful for Americans. Rick has spent 100 days every year since 1973 exploring Europe. He's researched and written 24 travel guidebooks. He writes and hosts the public television series Rick Steves Europe, now in its seventh season. With the help of his hard-working staff of 60 at Europe through the Back Door, Rick organizes and leads tours of Europe and offers an information-packed Web site (www.ricksteves.com). Rick, his wife (and favorite travel partner) Anne, and their two teenage children, Andy and Jackie, call Edmonds, just north of Seattle, home.

CAMERON HEWITT

CAMERON HEWITT grew up listening to the Polish nursery rhymes of his grandfather, Jan Pavel Dąbrowski. Twenty years later, he took a trip to Eastern Europe—and he was hooked. Today, Cameron guides Eastern Europe tours for Rick Steves. When he's not on the road, Cameron is a guidebook editor (and in-house Eastern Europe Czar) at Rick Steves' Europe Through the Back Door. He lives in Seattle with his sweetie Shawna.

The authors would like to acknowledge our friends and colleagues for their invaluable insights. Thanks to Ian Watson, Dave Hoerlein, Rick Garman, and Trevor Holmes; *Děkuji* to Honza Vihan (Czech Republic); *Dziękuję* to Katarzyna Derlicka (Poland); *Köszönöm* to Boreczky Elemér (Hungary); *Hvala* to Marijan Krišković, Tina Hiti, and Sašo Golub (Slovenia and Croatia); and *D'akujeme* to Susana Minich (Slovakia).

Free, fresh travel tips, all year long.

Visit **www.ricksteves.com**
to get Rick's free
64-page newsletter... and more!

Rick Steves

COUNTRY GUIDES 2004

Best of Europe
Best of Eastern Europe
France
Germany, Austria & Switzerland
Great Britain
Ireland
Italy
Scandinavia
Spain & Portugal

CITY GUIDES 2004

Amsterdam, Bruges & Brussels
Florence & Tuscany
London
Paris
Provence & The French Riviera
Rome
Venice

MORE EUROPE FROM RICK STEVES

Europe 101
Europe Through the Back Door 2004
Mona Winks
Postcards from Europe

More Savvy. More Surprising. More Fun.